Lecture Notes in Computer Science

Lecture Notes in Artificial Intelligence 14232

Founding Editor

Jörg Siekmann

The series Lecture Notes in Artificial Intelligence (LNAI) was established in 1988 as a topical subseries of LNCS devoted to artificial intelligence.

The series publishes state-of-the-art research results at a high level. As with the LNCS mother series, the mission of the series is to serve the international R & D community by providing an invaluable service, mainly focused on the publication of conference and workshop proceedings and postproceedings.

Maosong Sun · Bing Qin · Xipeng Qiu ·
Jiang Jing · Xianpei Han · Gaoqi Rao · Yubo Chen
Editors

Chinese Computational Linguistics

22nd China National Conference, CCL 2023
Harbin, China, August 3–5, 2023
Proceedings

Springer

Editors
Maosong Sun
Department of Computer Science
and Technology
Tsinghua University
Beijing, China

Xipeng Qiu
Fudan University
Shanghai, China

Xianpei Han
Chinese Academy of Sciences
Institute of Software
Beijing, China

Yubo Chen
Chinese Academy of Sciences
Institute of Automation
Beijing, China

Bing Qin
Harbin Institute of Technology
Harbin, China

Jiang Jing
School of Computing and Information
Singapore Management University
Singapore, Singapore

Gaoqi Rao
Beijing Language and Culture University
Beijing, China

ISSN 0302-9743 ISSN 1611-3349 (electronic)
Lecture Notes in Artificial Intelligence
ISBN 978-981-99-6206-8 ISBN 978-981-99-6207-5 (eBook)
https://doi.org/10.1007/978-981-99-6207-5

LNCS Sublibrary: SL7 – Artificial Intelligence

This Springer imprint is published by the registered company Springer Nature Singapore Pte Ltd.
The registered company address is: 152 Beach Road, #21-01/04 Gateway East, Singapore 189721, Singapore

Preface

Welcome to the proceedings of the 22nd China National Conference on Computational Linguistics (22nd CCL). The conference and symposium were hosted and co-organized by Harbin Institute of Technology, China.

CCL is an annual conference (bi-annual before 2013) that started in 1991. It is the flagship conference of the Chinese Information Processing Society of China (CIPS), which is the largest NLP academic and industrial community in China. CCL is a premier nation-wide forum for disseminating new scholarly and technological work in computational linguistics, with a major emphasis on computer processing of the languages in China. The Program Committee selected 82 papers (54 Chinese papers and 28 English papers) out of 278 submissions for publication. For each of the submission, 3 reviewers were assigned in double-blind. More reviewers joined when severe controversy appeared, aiding the domain chair to give the final decision. The final acceptance rate of CCL 2023 was 29.5%. The 28 English papers in this proceedings volume cover the following topics:

- Fundamental Theory and Methods of Computational Linguistics (1)
- Information Retrieval, Dialogue and Question Answering (4)
- Text Generation, Dialogue and Summarization (3)
- Knowledge Graph and Information Extraction (7)
- Machine Translation and Multilingual Information Processing (1)
- Language Resource and Evaluation (3)
- Social Computing and Sentiment Analysis (3)
- Pre-trained Language Models (3)
- NLP Applications (3)

The final program for the 22nd CCL was the result of intense work by many dedicated colleagues. We want to thank, first of all, the authors who submitted their papers, contributing to the creation of the high-quality program. We are deeply indebted to all the Program Committee members for providing high-quality and insightful reviews under a tight schedule, and extremely grateful to the sponsors of the conference. Finally, we extend a special word of thanks to all the colleagues of the Organizing Committee and secretariat for their hard work in organizing the conference, and to Springer for their assistance in publishing the proceedings.

We thank the staff and faculties of CIPS for helping to make the conference successful, and we hope all the participants enjoyed the CCL conference in Harbin.

July 2023

Maosong Sun
Bing Qin
Xipeng Qiu
Jing Jiang
Xianpei Han

Organization

Program Committee

Conference Chairs

Maosong Sun	Tsinghua University, China
Ting Liu	Harbin Institute of Technology, China

Program Chairs

Xipeng Qiu	Fudan University, China
Jing Jiang	Singapore Management University, Singapore
Xianpei Han	Institute of Software, CAS, China

Area Co-chairs

Information Retrieval, Text Classification and Question Answering

Xianling Mao	Beijing Institute of Technology, China
Yunshan Ma	National University of Singapore, Singapore

Text Generation, Dialogue and Summarization

Gao Yang	Beijing Institute of Technology, China
Piji Li	Nanjing University of Aeronautics and Astronautics, China
Lingpeng Kong	University of Hong Kong, China

Machine Translation and Multilingual Information Processing

Yun Chen	Shanghai University of Finance and Economics, China
Jiatao Gu	Meta, USA

Minority Language Information Processing

Xuebo Liu	Harbin Institute of Technology (Shenzhen), China
Hui Huang	University of Macau, China

Knowledge Graph and Information Extraction

Jintao Tang	National University of Defense Technology, China
Ningyu Zhang	Zhejiang University, China
Yixin Cao	Singapore Management University, Singapore

Social Computing and Sentiment Analysis

Ruifeng Xu	Harbin Institute of Technology, China
Lin Gui	Warwick University, UK

NLP Applications

Wei Wei	Huazhong University of Science and Technology, China
Jie Yang	Zhejiang University, China
Wenpeng Yin	Temple University, USA

Fundamental Theory and Methods of Computational Linguistics

Kehai Chen	Harbin Institute of Technology (Shenzhen), China
HongChen Wu	Peking University, China

Language Resource and Evaluation

Yidong Chen	Xiamen University, China
Chunyu Jie	City University of Hong Kong, China

Pre-trained Language Models

Hao Zhou	Tsinghua University, China
Yankai Lin	Renmin University of China, China
Pengfei Liu	Shanghai Jiao Tong University, China

Local Arrangement Chairs

Bing Qin	Harbin Institute of Technology, China
Xiaocheng Feng	Harbin Institute of Technology, China

Evaluation Chairs

Hongfei Lin	Dalian University of Technology, China
Zhenghua Li	Soochow University, China
Bin Li	Nanjing Normal University, China

Publication Chairs

Gaoqi Rao	Beijing Language and Culture University, China
Yubo Chen	Institute of Automation, CAS, China

Chair of Frontier Forum

JiaJun Zhang	Institute of Automation, CAS, China

Workshop Chairs

Yang Feng	Institute of Computing Technology, CAS, China
Peng Li	Tsinghua University, China

Sponsorship Chairs

Ruifeng Xu	Harbin Institute of Technology, China
Kang Liu	Institute of Automation, CAS, China

Publicity Chair

Zhongyu Wei	Fudan University, China

Website Chair

Baotian Hu	Harbin Institute of Technology, China

System Demonstration Chairs

Sendong Zhao	Harbin Institute of Technology, China
Hao Zhou	Tsinghua University, China

Student Seminar Chairs

Yankai Lin	Renmin University of China, China
Tianxiang Sun	Fudan University, China

Finance Chair

Yuxing Wang	Tsinghua University, China

Reviewers

Aihetamujiang Aihemaiti	Xinjiang Technical Institute of Physics and Chemistry, CAS, China
Bin Li	Nanjing Normal University, China
Bin Liang	Harbin Institute of Technology, China
Bo Chen	Institute of Software, CAS, China
Bo Wang	Tianjin University, China
Bowei Zou	JD Research, China
Changyi Xiao	University of Science and Technology of China
Chen Chen	Nankai University, China
Chen Henry Wu	China Medical University, China
Chen Jia	Westlake University, China
Chen Sung Lin	National Cheng-Kung University, China
Chenggang Mi	Xi'an International Studies University, China
Chen Xu	Northeastern University, China
Chengzhi Zhang	Nanjing Normal University, China
Chi Chen	Tsinghua University, China
Chi Hu	Northeastern University, China
Dakun Zhang	SYSTRAN, France
Dawei Lu	Renmin University of China, China
Dequan Zheng	Harbin University of Commerce
Derek F. Wong	University of Macau, China
Fan Yuan	Nanjing University of Aeronautics and Astronautics, China
Fangqi Zhu	Harbin Institute of Technology (Shenzhen), China
Gaole He	Delft University of Technology, The Netherlands
Gaoqi Rao	Beijing Language and Culture University, China
Gongbo Tang	Beijing Language and Culture University, China
Guangyou Zhou	Central China Normal University, China
Guoxiu He	East China Normal University, China
Hai Hu	Shanghai Jiao Tong University, China
Halidanmu Abudukelimu	Xinjiang University of Finance & Economics, China
Hanqing Wang	Shanghai University of Finance and Economics, China
Hao Fei	National University of Singapore, Singapore
Hao Zhou	Byte Dance AI Lab, China
Helen Jin	University of Pennsylvania, USA
Heng Chen	Guangdong University of Foreign Studies, China
Hexuan Deng	Harbin Institute of Technology, China
Hongchao Liu	Shandong University, China

Maoxi Li	Jiangxi Normal University, China
MeiLing Liu	Northeast Forestry University, China
Meiqi Chen	Peking University, China
Mengxia Yu	University of Notre Dame, USA
Mucheng Ren	Beijing Institute of Technology, China
Muyun Yang	Harbin Institute of Technology, China
Ningyu Zhang	Zhejiang University, China
Nuo Qun	Tibet University, China
Pan Haowen	University of Science and Technology of China, China
Peide Zhu	Technische Universiteit Delft, The Netherlands
Peijie Huang	South China Agricultural University, China
Peiju Liu	Fudan University, China
Pengfei Cao	Institute of Automation, CAS, China
Pengyuan Liu	Beijing Language and Culture University, China
Pengzhi Gao	Baidu, China
Piji Li	Nanjing University of Aeronautics and Astronautics, China
Qi Huang	Xiangnan University, China
Qi Su	Beijing University, China
Qi Zeng	University of Illinois at Urbana-Champaign, USA
Qian Li	Beihang University, China
Qiang Yang	Hong Kong University of Science and Technology, China
Qianlong Wang	Harbin Institute of Technology (Weihai), China
Qianqian Dong	Byte Dance AI Lab, China
Qinan Hu	Institute of Linguistics, CASS, China
Qingkai Zeng	University of Notre Dame, USA
Renfen Hu	Beijing Normal University, China
Rile Hu	Beijing Yuzhi Yunfan Technology Co., Ltd., China
Rong Ye	Byte Dance Co., Ltd., China
Rui Dong	Xinjiang Technical Institute of Physics and Chemistry, CAS, China
Rui Wang	Harbin Institute of Technology (Shenzhen), China
Rui Xia	Nanjing University of Science and Technology, China
Shaoru Guo	Institute of Automation, CAS, China
Shengxiang Gao	Kunming University of Science and Technology, China
Shi Feng	Northeastern University, China
Shili Ge	Guangdong University of Foreign Studies, China
Shiwei Chen	Peng Cheng Laboratory, China

Shizhu He	Institute of Automation, CAS, China
Shuaichen Chang	Ohio State University, USA
Shudong Liu	University of Macau, China
Shujian Huang	Nanjing University, China
Shuo Wang	Tsinghua University, China
Shuyang Jiang	Peking University, China
Silei Xu	Stanford University, USA
Sisi Huang	Huaqiao University, China
Tao He	Harbin Institute of Technology, China
Tieyun Qian	Wuhan University, China
Wei Huang	Beijing Language and Culture University, China
Wei Tang	University of Science and Technology of China, China
Wei Zou	University of CAS, China
Weidong Zhan	Beijing University, China
Weiguang Qu	Nanjing Normal University, China
Weihong Zhong	Harbin Institute of Technology, China
Weijie Yu	Renmin University of China, China
Weizhe Yuan	New York University, USA
Wen Zhang	Zhejiang University, China
Wenhao Zhu	Nanjing University, China
Wenkai Yang	Peking University, China
Wenliang Chen	Soochow University, China
Wenpeng Lu	Qilu University of Technology, China
Xia Li	Guangdong University of Foreign Studies, China
Xiabing Zhou	Soochow University, China
Xiachong Feng	Harbin Institute of Technology, China
Xiang Ao	Institute of Computing Technology, CAS, China
Xiang Li	Xiaomi Inc., China
Xiang Zhao	National University of Defense Technology, China
Xiangyu Duan	Soochow University, China
Xiaocheng Feng	Harbin Institute of Technology, China
Xiaodan Hu	University of Illinois at Urbana-Champaign, USA
Xiaofei Zhu	Chongqing University of Technology, China
Xiaojing Bai	Tsinghua University, China
Xiaojun Zhang	Xi'an Jiaotong-Liverpool University, China
Xiaopeng Bai	East China Normal University, China
Xiaotong Jiang	Soochow University, China
Xinchi Chen	Amazon, USA
Xinglin Lyu	Soochow University, China
Xinyu Wang	ShanghaiTech University, China

Xinyu Zuo	Tencent Inc., China
Xiuying Chen	King Abdullah University of Science & Technology, Saudi Arabia
Xuri Tang	Huazhong University of Science and Technology, China
Yachao Li	Zhengzhou University, China
Yanan Cao	Institute of Information Engineering, CAS, China
Yang Liu	Tsinghua University, China
Yang Sun	Harbin Institute of Technology, China
Yanjiao Li	Shandong University, China
Yankai Lin	Renmin University of China, China
Yanming Sun	University of Macau, China
Yao Meng	Lenovo Inc., China
Yaqin Wang	Guangdong University of Foreign Studies, China
Yequan Wang	Tsinghua University, China
Yichong Huang	Harbin Institute of Technology, China
Yidong Chen	Xiamen University, China
Yong Chen	Beijing University of Posts and Telecommunications, China
Yougang Lyu	Shandong University, China
Yu Bai	Beijing Institute of Technology, China
Yu Lu	Institute of Automation, CAS, China
Yuanchao Liu	Harbin Institute of Technology, China
Yuanxing Liu	Harbin Institute of Technology, China
Yuanzhe Zhang	Institute of Automation, CAS, China
Yubo Chen	Institute of Automation, CAS, China
Yubo Ma	Nanyang Technological University, Singapore
Yufeng Chen	Beijing Jiaotong University, China
Yun Chen	Shanghai University of Finance and Economics, China
Yunshan Ma	National University of Singapore, Singapore
Yuru Jiang	Beijing Information Science & Technology University, China
Yuxuan Gu	Harbin Institute of Technology, China
Zhangyin Feng	Harbin Institute of Technology, China
Zhaohui Li	Pennsylvania State University, USA
Zhen Wu	Nanjing University, China
Zhichang Zhang	Northwest Normal University, China
Zhichao Xu	University of Utah, USA
Zhiqi Huang	University of Massachusetts, USA
Zhiqiang Pan	National University of Defense Technology, China

Zhiwei He	Shanghai Jiao Tong University, China
Zhixing Tan	Tsinghua University, China
Zhiyang Teng	Nanyang Technological University, Singapore
Zhongqing Wang	Soochow University, China
Zhoujun Cheng	Shanghai Jiao Tong University, China
Zhu Junguo	Harbin Institute of Technology, China
Zhufeng Pan	Tsinghua University, China
Zixiang Ding	Nanjing University of Science and Technology, China

Organizers

Chinese Information Processing Society of China

Tsinghua University

Harbin Institute of Technology, China

Publishers

Lecture Notes in Artificial Intelligence, Springer

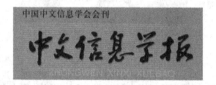

Journal of Chinese Information Processing

Journal of Tsinghua University
(Science and Technology)

Sponsoring Institutions

Platinum

Gold

Silver

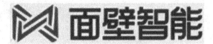

Contents

Knowledge Graph and Information Extraction

Machine Translation and Multilingual Information Processing

Language Resource and Evaluation

Fundamental Theory and Methods of Computational Linguistics

The Contextualized Representation of Collocation

Daohuan Liu and Xuri Tang(✉)

Huazhong University of Science and Technology, Wuhan, China
{liudh,xrtang}@hust.edu.cn

Abstract. Collocate list and collocation network are two widely used representation methods of collocations, but they have significant weaknesses in representing contextual information. To solve this problem, we propose a new representation method, namely the contextualized representation of collocate (CRC), which highlights the importance of the position of the collocates and pins a collocate as the interaction of two dimensions: association strength and co-occurrence position. With a full image of all the collocates surrounding the node word, CRC carries the contextual information and makes the representation more informative and intuitive. Through three case studies, i.e., synonym distinction, image analysis, and efficiency in lexical use, we demonstrate the advantages of CRC in practical applications. CRC is also a new quantitative tool to measure lexical usage pattern similarities for corpus-based research. It can provide a new representation framework for language researchers and learners.

Keywords: Collocation · Representation Methods · Visualization

1 Introduction

Collocation is an important concept in the fields of linguistics and computational linguistics [1–3], which can be widely used in language teaching, discourse analysis and other fields. Currently, there are two widely used representation methods of collocation, namely collocate list and collocation network. However, they are both flawed.

Collocate list takes the list of collocate words as the main form and generally provides the correlation strength, co-occurrence frequency, etc. between the node word and the collocate word[1]. Sometimes a collocate list may also include information such as the total frequency of collocates, the frequency of appearing on the left and right sides, etc. Table 1 shows the collocation list of the node word *importance* in a small news corpus.

[1] We follow the names by [3], and call the focal word in the collocation a "node word" (Node), and call the word appearing in the other position in the collocation a "collocate word" (Collocate).

M. Sun et al. (Eds.): CCL 2023, LNAI 14232, pp. 3–16, 2023.
https://doi.org/10.1007/978-981-99-6207-5_1

Table 1. Sample Collocate List of *importance* as a node. Pointwise Mutual Information is adopted to measure the association strength between two words (`measure = PMI`); Only collocates with 2 or more co-occurrences are considered (`min_freq = 2`); Only collocates with an association strength greater than 7.5 are displayed (`thresh = 7.5`)

Collocate	PMI	Co-occur Frequency
attach	11.216	29
underscore	9.223	2
emphasize	8.821	4
stress	8.811	19
aware	8.528	3
awareness	8.386	2
great	7.555	28

The expression capability is very limited through collocate lists, as they could neither present the interaction between collocates nor be visually friendly to readers. However, connectivity is an important feature of collocation knowledge [4]. In order to improve these weaknesses, [5] implemented the representation method of collocation graph and network[2] (see Fig. 1). In a collocation graph, the collocates are scattered around and connected to the central word (node). The closer a collocate is linked to the node, the stronger it is associated with it. Compared to collocate list, collocation graph improves the visualization and enables the interaction of multiple collocations through node connection and graph extension. [6] also demonstrates the possible applications of collocation networks with cases including discourse analysis, language learning, and conceptual metaphor research.

However, these two traditional representation methods both have many critical flaws. The fundamental problem is that they neglect the natural language as a kind of sequence data. Collocate list regards collocation as a simple juxtaposition of tokens, and collocation graph regards each word as a free discrete data point in the space. Nevertheless, the context information is not only related to the semantics of the collocates surrounding a node but also related to the order and the position of the words.

First of all, they only tell the semantic relations but ignore the syntactic relations between nodes and collocates. The semantic association between nodes and collocates is direct and clear. [1] defines collocation as a container for semantic associations between the two words; and the meaning of a word comes not only from itself, but also from other words that co-occur with it. The association scores shown in both collocate list and collocation graph are an evaluation of co-occurrence, in other sense, a reflection of the semantic relationship. Nevertheless, [8] addresses that the syntactic association between the node and the collocate

[2] A collocation network is a connected network of multiple collocation graphs. The two terms "collocation network" and "collocation graph" are used interchangeably in this paper, referring to the same representation method.

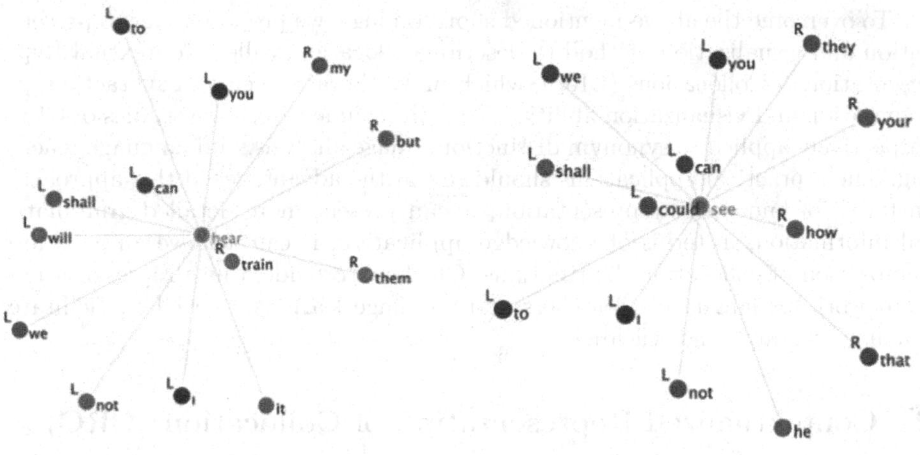

Fig. 1. Sample Collocation Graphs of *hear* and *see* for image comparison, based on the corpora of World War I poems [7]

is also an essential part, acknowledging collocation as a complex of syntactic and semantic knowledge. He also sorts out the key role of syntactic relations in semantic theories and their applications through related studies [9,10]. The syntactic nature of collocations is mainly reflected in the fact that collocations have direction and span. For instance, the two semantically related words *student* and *diligent* generally do not appear as "student diligent" in actual language use, which is syntactically incorrect in most cases; while "diligent student" or "student is diligent" is much more common and intuitively correct application. This shows that the collocation knowledge is actually an overall model that is restricted both by semantic relations and grammatical relations.

Secondly, they fail to reflect the relative position (relative distance) between nodes and collocates. [11] pointed out that the two components in a collocation tend to have fixed positions, i.e., one word always appears on the left or right side of the other word. For example, among the collocates in Table 1, *attach* mostly appears on the left side of the node *importance*. In the case that the positions of these two words are reversed, the syntactic relationship between the two words should also change. According to the data samples in the corpus, *importance* mostly acts as the object in *attach-importance* collocations, while *importance* often serves as the subject in *importance-attach* collocations.

Finally, these two representations cannot reflect the freedom of choice of collocates, which would restrict the usage of collocation in practice. This is not conducive to group collocates and find patterns with respect to semantic or syntactic relations. For example, if we want to find other predicates to substitute *attach* for the node *importance*, it is hard to tell from a raw collocate list or collocation graph. In order to satisfy this requirement, an extra screening operation such as Part-of-Speech (POS) tagging or syntactic analysis is required.

To overcome the above-mentioned shortcomings, we propose a new representation and visualization method to describe collocation, called Contextual Representation of Collocations (CRC), which makes improvements in syntactic representation and visualization abilities. We will include three case studies of CRC respectively applied to synonym distinction, image analysis, and language teaching. These practical applications should reveal the advantages of this approach. In terms of knowledge representation, it can present more detailed grammatical information; in terms of knowledge application, it can achieve an accurate comparison of collocation distributions. CRC can provide a new representation framework for language researchers and language learners, as well as facilitate language research and teaching.

2 Contextualized Representation of Collocation (CRC)

While retaining the dimension of association strength, CRC promotes the relative position of collocates to another major feature dimension, so that each collocate can present those two important attributes at the same time. Therefore, the essence of the CRC is a two-dimensional scatter plot.

Figure 2 is an instance of CRC, which is based on the same data source as Table 1. The code string in the caption means that the figure is generated using PMI as the association measure, min_freqency of collocates is 2, and the strength threshold for display is 0.6. The key features of this visualization will be explained in detail.

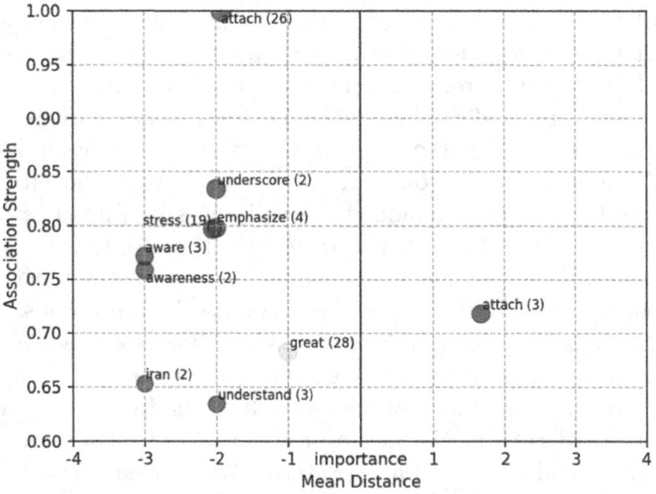

Fig. 2. CRC of node *importance* (`measure=PMI`, `min_freq=2`, `thresh=0.6`)

2.1 Conflated Linear Representation

Compared with the network structure of collocation graph, CRC follows the linear characteristics of natural language and uses conflated linear representation in expressing the relations of all the collocate-node pairs. In Fig. 2, collocation relations are described as parallel horizontal lines, and compressed in a certain space range. This parallel and linear presentation helps to visually compare the commonalities and differences of different collocations, which is the basis of all the other advantages of CRC. In our implementation, we arrange the longitudinal spatial distribution of all collocate-node pairs according to their association score[3]. For the convenience of drawing and reading, the scores are normalized to [0,1]. The closer to 1, the higher the collocation strength.

2.2 Positional Information

In Fig. 2, the horizontal dimension represents grammatical relations in terms of direction and distance. In this instance, the distance of each collocate is the average of the distances of all the collocate-node pair occurrences. `Distance=0` is the position of the node word (*importance*).

Foregrounding positional information is the core contribution of CRC, as well as the key feature that distinguishes CRC from the other two representation methods. It is easy to understand that if the positional information is removed from Fig. 2, all the collocate points will appear on the same vertical line, hence, it will degenerate into a simple visualization of the collocate list. Instead, if the Cartesian coordinate system is transformed into a polar coordinate system, it then becomes a collocation graph with fixed node positions.

Positional information reflects the order of words, and the order of words further reflects the syntactic relationship. This can benefit CRC users with plenty of straightforward linguistic knowledge. Taking Fig. 2 as an example, we could observe at least the following facts:

- The word *attach* tends to appear on the left of *importance* (`frequency=26`, `strength=1.00`) rather than on the right (`frequency=3`, `strength=0.72`), which might imply the *attach-importance* collocation is more likely to be used in active voice instead of passive voice.
- The word *importance* has a strong right-leaning tendency [12], which means it expects to be modified by a modifier prior to it.
- Collocates like *attach*, *underscore*, *emphasize*, *stress*, and *understand* might all play similar grammatical roles in the relationship with the node *importance*, because they all appear in the -2 position.
- People tend not to say "attach importance" but to use "attach great importance", which can be reckoned from their positions (*attach* = –2, *great* = –1,

[3] We use various measuring algorithms to calculate association scores and pick the intuitively best one from all the results. The adopted measuring method for each case is described in the captions of the figures.

importance = 0). This shows that CRC could also be used to recognize continuous word clusters and phrase patterns, making CRC more prospective in the application of analyzing and teaching. And it is capturing common contexts that the node is often used in. And this is also the reason why this representation of collocation is termed "contextualized".

2.3 Visualization Strategy

In addition to its advantage in context modelling of the node, as a representation method, CRC could be easily visualized with many visualization strategies. It can combine many spatial methods and visual symbols to expand the expression and presentation of collocation knowledge. As mentioned before, in addition to implementing the CRC in the plane Cartesian coordinate system, it can also be realized in the polar coordinate system; the size, color, and grayscale (transparency) of the data points in the figure can all be useful tools to group or describe collocates.

In general, compared with existing collocation representation methods, i.e., collocate list and collocate network, CRC can intuitively present richer context information and provide convenience for researchers who use collocation analysis. In the following sections, we will apply CRC in three case studies of recent years to demonstrate the superiority of the new representation method.

3 Case Study 1: CRC in Synonym Distinction

Many researchers utilize collocation analysis to distinguish synonyms. Liu has studied the usage differences of many synonym sets in English with the COCA corpus using a behavioral profile approach [13,14]. He also analyzed the learners' misuse of three synonym groups by comparing the use of these words in a second-language learner corpus [15]. [16] compared the usage patterns and semantic differences of the two synonyms, *absolutely* and *utterly*, with the help of collocation lists and the Key-Word-In-Context (KWIC) function provided by the COCA corpus. Their conclusions are largely based on random sampling and qualitative analysis. Obviously, the above research methods take a large manual workload in observation and statistics. The use of CRC can not only carry out descriptive conclusions easily and clearly but also provide quantitative measures to differentiate synonyms. In this case study, we use CRC to restudy the differences among the synonyms *Actually*, *Really*, *Truly*, and *Genuinely*, and try to verify some findings reported by [14]. We choose a smaller corpus, BROWN, instead of COCA as the data source of this case study for its availability. The frequencies of each adverb in the BROWN corpus are shown in Table 2. It can be found that these four adverbs have a similar frequency proportion although the total data amount of BROWN is much smaller than COCA. Since *Genuinely* is not found in BROWN, we only study the other three adverbs.

We retrieve the free collocates of *actually*, *really*, and *truly* from the corpus and generate three CRC instances (Fig. 3). According to the frequency ratio of

Table 2. Frequencies of the four adverbs respectively in COCA and BROWN

Corpus	#actually	#really	#truly	#genuinely
COCA	105,039	263,087	20,504	3,065
BROWN	166	275	57	0

these three words, we set the thresholds of association strength to 0.3, 0.5 and 0.1 respectively for better visualization effects.

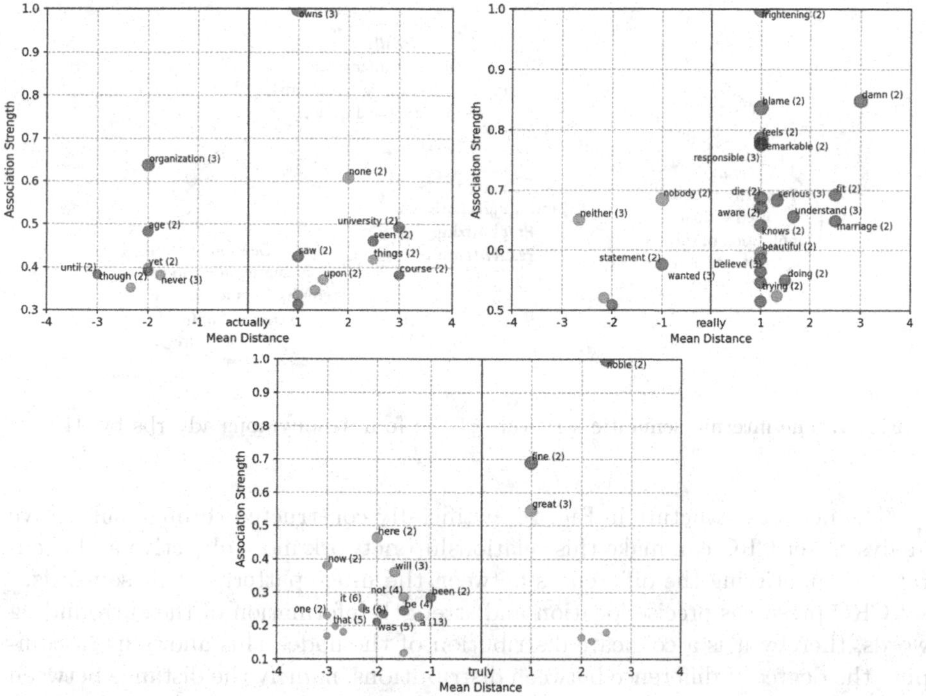

Fig. 3. CRCs of node *actually*, *really* and *truly* (`measure=PMI`, `min_freq=2`, `thresh` differs to accommodate to the number of data points for a better visualization)

The usage pattern of *really* is significantly different from the other two words. There are much more highly associated collocates to the right of *really* (especially at `position=1`) than *actually* and *truly*, suggesting that *really* is more often used as verb and adjective modifiers. As for *actually*, it is hard to find its clear usage pattern from the distribution of collocates on both sides. However, when compared to *truly*, it could be observed that *actually* is surrounded by more content words and has many adversative words on the left side (e.g. *never*, *yet*, *though*, *until*), indicating that it may be used more as a disjunct. The CRC visualization of *truly* presents few meaningful collocates, but we can also reckon that *truly* is prone to occur as an adjective modifier from the limited samples. Moreover, from its potential context (*will/be* + *truly* + *fine/great*, etc.) we can infer that it is prone to be used for attitude emphasis and enhancement.

The above inferences are entirely based on CRC figures and are basically consistent with the main findings of [14] (see Fig. 4) who adopted rigorous and systematic statistical methods (Hierarchical configural frequency analysis, HCFA). This demonstrates that CRC is a fast and handy tool in certain lexical studies. Of course, it would also be encouraged that researchers use other corpus approaches such as concordance and HCFA as auxiliary verification methods.

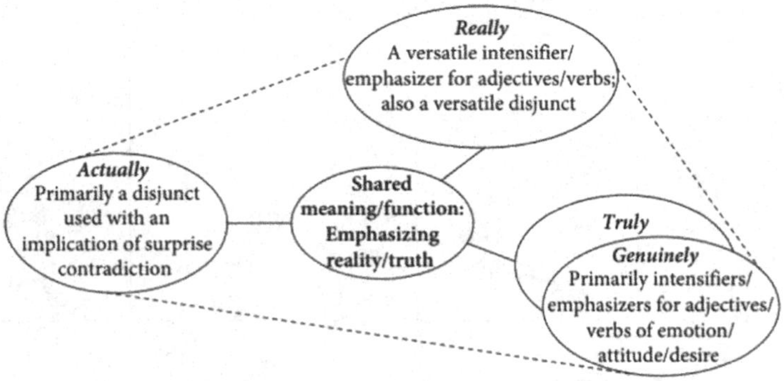

Fig. 4. The internal semantic structure of the four synonymous adverbs by [14]

The network structure in Fig. 4 is artificially constructed through subjective analysis. Yet CRC can make this relationship network more objective and accurate by quantifying the differences between the usage patterns of these words.

CRC preserves precise location and strength information of the surrounding words, thereby it is a collocate distribution of the node. This allows us to compute the degree of difference between distributions, namely the distance between CRCs. The smaller the distance is, the more similar the usage patterns of the two words. To compute the distance between two distributions, we are free to apply any suitable distance algorithm. Here we use a simple processing flow:

(1) For a common collocation word, calculate the Euclidean distance between the coordinates of the word on the two graphs.
(2) For unique collocations, they are not included in the distance calculation.
(3) Finally, average the Euclidean distance between all points to obtain the comprehensive distance.

Using the above algorithm, we obtained three distances (Fig. 5, the number of valid collocation words actually involved in the calculation is indicated in brackets). Our results show slight divergence from Fig. 4, as Liu and Espino considers *really* more similar to *truly* but CRC distance indicates that *really* is closer to *actually* (D(*really*, *actually*) = 0.1641) rather than *truly* (D(*really*, *truly*) = 0.1853). This difference might be due to BROWN's insufficient amount of data. It is also interesting to see CRC applied to COCA and verify if the semantic structure in Fig. 4 is accurate.

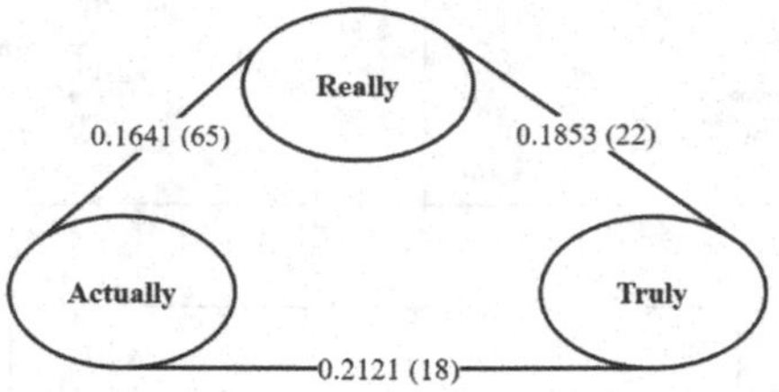

Fig. 5. The collocation distribution distance of *actually*, *really*, and *truly* in the BROWN corpus. The number of valid collocation words actually involved in the calculation is indicated in brackets (`measure=PMI`, `min_freq=2`)

4 Case Study 2: CRC in Image Analysis

As an analytical tool, collocation is also widely used in other fields besides linguistic research. In the area of journalism and information communication, collocations are also used in assistance to discourse analysis, image analysis, and sentiment analysis [17]. For example, [18] inspected the verb collocates on the right side of *we* in the interpreting corpus of press conferences, so as to analyze the image construction strategy of the government. In the field of digital humanities, collocation could also facilitate the style analysis of writing and author [7,19,20], as well as the image analysis of characters in the literary works. We select an image analysis task in a literary work and use CRC as an analyzing tool for research and discussion.

We pick the classic fiction "Lord of the Flies" [21] as our research subject, because the characters in this novel have distinctive characteristics and the language is simple and straightforward. Its characters and images have been heatedly discussed through book reviews and literary interpretations [22,23], yet CRC may reveal the character-building methods from a corpus perspective. We select three main characters: Ralph, Jack and Simon as research objectives. Their right-side verb collocates are retrieved and described through CRC (Fig. 6). Before extracting collocations, the text is lower-cased and POS tagged. Different thresholds of association strength are applied in order to show a similar amount of collocates.

By comparing the three CRC figures, it can be found that when describing different characters, different verbs are used to shape the image of the characters. From the sentiment of verbs used to describe the character, we can infer the author's tendency in the image-building of each character.

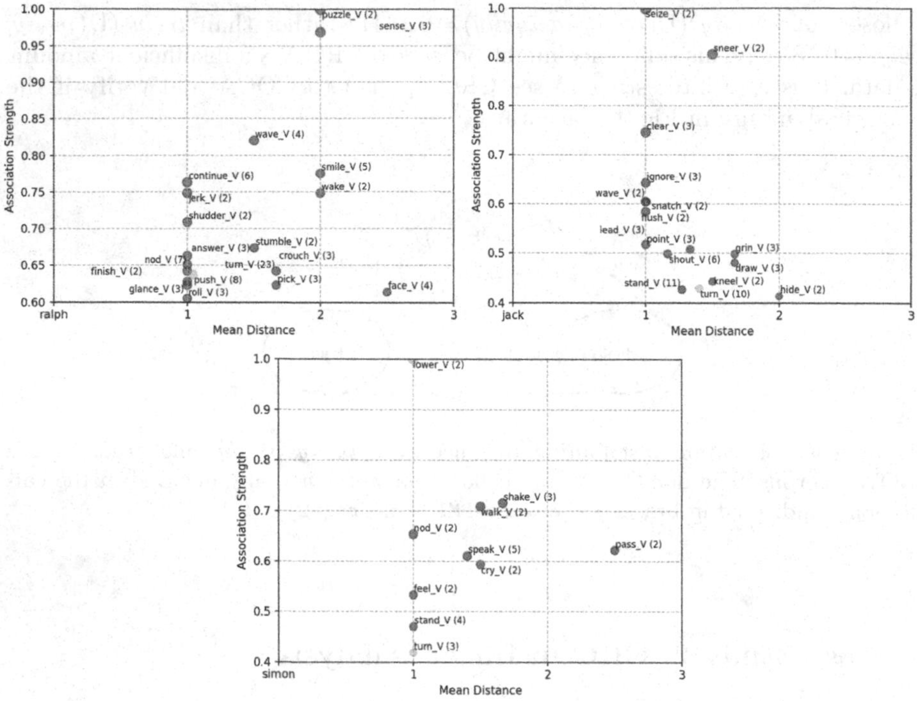

Fig. 6. CRCs of node *ralph*, *jack* and *simon* (`measure=PMI`, `min_freq=2`, `thresh` differs to accommodate to the number of data points for a better visualization)

Ralph is the main positive leader in the fiction, representing civilization and democracy before and after World War II. Ralph's CRC shows many clues in favor of that description. Verbs such as *puzzle*, *sense*, and *shudder* place Ralph on the opposite side of chaos and violence; others like *answer* and *nod* depict Ralph actively affirming and responding to others' opinions. These behaviors together shape Ralph as a "democratic man, the symbol of consent" [23]. Jack is the representative of brutality and power. His unique behaviors include *seize*, *snatch*, *clear*, and *ignore*, which show Jack's tendency to command and enforce, in consistent with the evaluation by [23]: "Jack then, is authoritarian man ... like Hitler and Mussolini". Simon is regarded as "the Christ-figure, the voice of revelation" [23]. From his unique behaviors *lower*, *walk*, *speak*, *feel*, etc., readers envisage a sanctified image with calm, humility, detachment, and transcendence.

Apart from unique behaviors, similar behaviors are also described with verbs with different semantic polarities. For example, the author uses *smile* for Ralph but *sneer* and *grin* for Jack to express laugh; this further consolidates the contrasting images of the two characters.

5 Case Study 3: CRC and Efficiency in Lexical Use

Collocations could also play a role in second language acquisition and language teaching. The mastery of collocation is considered to be the decisive factor for the naturalness of a language learner's expression [24]. One of the cases of collocation network illustrated by [6] is the analysis and evaluation of different-level second language learners' expression. The selected corpus is Trinity Lancaster Corpus (TLC) of spoken L2 English [25], a transcribed corpus of English interview responses. Brezina divided the corpus into three sub-groups according to the speakers' language proficiency levels: Pre-intermediate (B1), Intermediate (B2) and Advanced and Proficiency (C1/C2). The most common collocates of the three verbs *make*, *take* and *do* used by students at these levels are shown with collocation graphs. Brezina observed a rise in the richness of collocates as the proficiency level lifts for *make*, but found no such "clear relationship between increasing proficiency and a higher number of collocates" on *take* and *do* [6, p.73]. This implies that the increase in collocate richness is not the decisive factor in measuring one's language proficiency.

When talking about the language learner's communicative language competencies, a competitive language learner should not only "has a good command of a very broad lexical repertoire" (vocabulary range) but also masters "idiomatic expressions and colloquialisms" and use words "correct and appropriate" (vocabulary control) [26, pp.112, 114]. In other words, the collocation network alone cannot reveal the relationship between the group's collocation performance and their language competency, because collocation network cannot tell the above aspects, i.e., the naturalness and accuracy of the collocations.

While CRC with its quantitative ability (as used in Sect. 3) is a solution to the above problem. To examine whether the speakers' language competency truly matches their labeled level, we select the native speaker sub-group (NS) as a reference corpus, and respectively compute the CRC distances between NS with B1, B2, and C1/C2, so as to evaluate the usage patterns between different levels. Intuitively, we may expect the gap becomes smaller from B1 to C1/C2, because native speakers usually produce the most natural expressions.

The CRC distances of B1-NS, B2-NS and C1/C2-NS are shown in Table 3, including those of *take* and *do*. It can be seen that the speakers' usage pattern of *make* is approaching that of native speakers from B1 to C1/C2. However, statistics on the other two verbs do not present a similar trend; *do* even displays a totally opposite attitude, showing an increasing discrepancy from native speakers as "language level" rises. A possible explanation might be the insufficient data samples. For instance, only 30 common collocates are used to calculate the CRC distance between C1/C2 and NS, most of which are trivial words with low association strength such as *not*, *what*, and *want*.

Nevertheless, the findings are basically in line with that of Brezina [6] but in a more comprehensive and more precise manner. Besides, the distances on word pairs disclose the most misused collocates of the node, which might be helpful in language evaluation and grammar correction. To be specific, CRC could tell which collocates are most distantly distributed in the usage pattern of language

Table 3. The collocation distribution distance of *make*, *take* and *do* in the three bands and NS corpus. The number of valid collocation words actually involved in the calculation is indicated in brackets (`measure=Log-Likelihood`, `min_freq=2`)

Distance	B1-NS	B2-NS	C1/C2-NS
make	0.19 (48)	0.1453 (101)	0.1223 (93)
take	0.2349 (32)	0.1743 (49)	0.2077 (45)
do	0.0915 (116)	0.1371 (66)	0.1436 (30)

learners and of native speakers, so as to improve the learners' worst-acquired collocation knowledge.

6 Conclusions and Future Work

This paper re-examines two widely used representation methods of collocation, i.e., collocate list and collocation network. In view of their weakness in expressing contextual information, we propose a new representation method, namely the contextualized representation of collocation (CRC). CRC adopts conflated linear representation and highlights the importance of the position of the collocates. It pins a collocate as the interaction of two dimensions, i.e., association strength and co-occurrence position. With a full image of all the collocates surrounding the node word, CRC carries the contextual information and makes the representation much more informative and intuitive. We did three case studies to demonstrate the advantages of CRC in practical applications, covering synonym distinction, image analysis, and efficiency in lexical use. Besides, CRC provides a new quantitative tool to measure lexical usage pattern similarities for corpus-based research.

We believe that the potential power of CRC is far beyond the cases we have discussed. As an auxiliary corpus tool, it may also be used directly in teaching activities. The importance of corpus tools in language teaching is investigated by [27], who used some of the searching functions provided by COCA, mainly the collocation tool, to improve students' phrasal integrity. Their survey shows that most students are happy to use corpus tools to test their language intuition, though the aids are less effective for students with poor performance. CRC can be used as a good visualized presentation tool for phrase, collocation and idiom studying, and should intuitively be more friendly to "weaker students" because it is much more easy-reading and more informative compared with collocate list and collocation network. Apart from teaching, CRC may also be extended or adapted to fit more needs and scenarios. For example, CRC is also suitable for visualizing constructions [28] and collostructions [29] because it follows the sequential nature of the language.

In summary, we hope that CRC can provide a new representation framework for language researchers and learners, and will lead them to address the importance of contextual information in research and learning. More applications of CRC in teaching and research are worthy of further empirical study in the future.

References

1. Firth, J.R.: Modes of meaning. In: Papers in Linguistics, pp. 1934–1951. Oxford University Press, Oxford (1957)
2. Halliday, M.A.K., Hasan, R.: Cohesion in English. Longman Group Ltd., London (1976)
3. Sinclair, J.: Corpus, Concordance, Collocation. Oxford University Press, Oxford (1991)
4. Phillips, M.: Aspects of Text Structure: An Investigation of the Lexical Organisation of Text. North-Holland, Amsterdam (1985)
5. Brezina, V., McEnery, T., Wattam, S.: Collocations in context: a new perspective on collocation networks. Int. J. Corpus Linguist. **20**(2), 139–173 (2015)
6. Brezina, V.: Collocation graphs and networks: selected applications. In: Cantos-Gómez, P., Almela-Sánchez, M. (eds.) Lexical Collocation Analysis. QMHSS, pp. 59–83. Springer, Cham (2018). https://doi.org/10.1007/978-3-319-92582-0_4
7. Taner, C., Hakan, C.: A warring style: a corpus stylistic analysis of the first world war poetry, digital scholarship in the humanities, fqab047 (2021). https://doi.org/10.1093/llc/fqab047
8. Tang, X.: Collocation and Predicate Semantics Computation. Wuhan University Press, Wuhan (2018)
9. Katz, J.J., Fodor, J.A.: The structure of a semantic theory. Language **39**(2), 170–210 (1963). https://doi.org/10.2307/411200
10. Petruck, M.R.: Frame semantics. In: Handbook of Pragmatics, vol. 2 (1996)
11. Qu, W.: Research on Automatic Word Disambiguation of Modern Chinese. Science Press, Beijing (2008)
12. Wang, D., Zhang, D., Tu, X., Zheng, X., Tong, Z.: Collocation extraction based on relative conditional entropy. J. Beijing Univ. Posts Telecommun. **30**(6), 40 (2007)
13. Liu, D.: Is it a chief, main, major, primary, or principal concern?: a corpus-based behavioral profile study of the near-synonyms. Int. J. Corpus Linguist. **15**(1), 56–87 (2010)
14. Liu, D., Espino, M.: Actually, genuinely, really, and truly: a corpus-based behavioral profile study of near-synonymous adverbs. Int. J. Corpus Linguist. **17**(2), 198–228 (2012)
15. Liu, D.: A corpus study of Chinese EFL learners' use of circumstance, demand, and significant: an in-depth analysis of L2 vocabulary use and its implications. J. Second Lang. Stud. **1**(2), 309–332 (2018)
16. Xiong, Y.H., Liu, D.F.: A corpus-based analysis of english near-synonymous adverbs: absolutely, utterly. J. Literat. Art Stud. **12**(4), 359–365 (2022)
17. Koteyko, N., Jaspal, R., Nerlich, B.: Climate change and "climategate' in online reader comments: a mixed methods study. Geograph. J. **179**(1), 74–86 (2013)
18. Pan, F., Hei, Y.: Government image-building in Chinese-English press interpretation: a case study of the collocation of personal pronoun "we". Foreign Lang. Teach. **5**, 8 (2017)
19. Vickers, B.: Identifying Shakespeare's additions to the Spanish tragedy (1602): a new (er) approach. Shakespeare **8**(1), 13–43 (2012)

20. Wijitsopon, R.: A corpus-based study of the style in Jane Austen's novels. Manusya: J. Humanit. **16**(1), 41–64 (2013)
21. Golding, W.: Lord of the flies. Faber & Faber (1954)
22. Oldsey, B., Weintraub, S.: Lord of the flies: Beezlebub revisited. Coll. English **25**(2), 90–99 (1963). https://doi.org/10.2307/373397
23. Spitz, D.: Power and authority: an interpretation of golding's "Lord of the Flies". Antioch Rev. **30**(1), 21–33 (1970). https://doi.org/10.2307/4637248
24. Oktavianti, I.N., Sarage, J.: Collocates of 'great' and 'good' in the corpus of contemporary American English and Indonesian EFL textbooks. Stud. English Lang. Educ. **8**(2), 457–478 (2021)
25. Gablasova, D., Brezina, V., Mcenery, T., Boyd, E.: Epistemic stance in spoken L2 English: the effect of task and speaker style. Appl. Linguist. **38**(5), 613–637 (2017)
26. Council of Europe. Council for Cultural Co-operation. Education Committee. Modern Languages Division. Common European framework of reference for languages: Learning, teaching, assessment. Cambridge University Press (2001)
27. Boldarine, A.C., Rosa, R.G.: Prepping a prep course: a corpus linguistics approach. BELT-Braz. English Lang. Teach. J. **9**(2), 379–394 (2018)
28. Fillmore, C.J.: The mechanisms of "construction grammar". In: Annual Meeting of the Berkeley Linguistics Society, vol. 14, pp. 35–55 (1988)
29. Stefanowitsch, A., Gries, S.T.: Collostructions: investigating the interaction of words and constructions. Int. J. Corpus Linguist. **8**(2), 209–243 (2003)

Information Retrieval, Dialogue and Question Answering

Ask to Understand: Question Generation for Multi-hop Question Answering

Jiawei Li[1], Mucheng Ren[1], Yang Gao[1,2(✉)], and Yizhe Yang[1]

[1] School of Computer Science and Technology, Beijing Institute of Technology, Beijing, China
{jwli,renm,gyang,yizheyang}@bit.edu.cn

[2] Beijing Engineering Research Center of High Volume Language Information Processing and Cloud Computing Applications, Beijing, China

Abstract. Multi-hop Question Answering (QA) requires the machine to answer complex questions by finding scattering clues and reasoning from multiple documents. Graph Network (GN) and Question Decomposition (QD) are two common approaches at present. The former uses the "black-box" reasoning process to capture the potential relationship between entities and sentences, thus achieving good performance. At the same time, the latter provides a clear reasoning logical route by decomposing multi-hop questions into simple single-hop sub-questions. In this paper, we propose a novel method to complete multi-hop QA from the perspective of Question Generation (QG). Specifically, we carefully design an end-to-end QG module on the basis of a classical QA module, which could help the model understand the context by asking inherently logical sub-questions, thus inheriting interpretability from the QD-based method and showing superior performance. Experiments on the HotpotQA dataset demonstrate that the effectiveness of our proposed QG module, human evaluation further clarifies its interpretability quantitatively, and thorough analysis shows that the QG module could generate better sub-questions than QD methods in terms of fluency, consistency, and diversity.

1 Introduction

Unlike single-hop QA [19,26,30] where the answers could usually be derived from a single paragraph or sentence, multi-hop QA [34,39] is a challenging task that requires soliciting hidden information from scattered documents on different granularity levels and reasoning over it in an explainable way.

The HotpotQA [39] was published to leverage the research attentions on reasoning processing and explainable predictions. Figure 1 shows an example from HotpotQA, where the question requires first finding the name of the company (*Tata Consultancy Services*), and then the address of the company (*Mumbai*). While, a popular stream of Graph Network-based (GN) approaches [4,7,11,32] was proposed due to the structures of scattered evidence could be captured by the graphs and reflected in the representing vectors. However, the reasoning process

M. Sun et al. (Eds.): CCL 2023, LNAI 14232, pp. 19–36, 2023.
https://doi.org/10.1007/978-981-99-6207-5_2

of the GN-based method is entirely different from human thoughts. Specifically, GN tries to figure out the underlying relations between the key entities or sentences from the context. However, the process is a "black-box"; we do not know which nodes in the network are involved in reasoning for the final answer, thus showing relatively poor interpretability.

Inspired by that human solves such questions by following a transparent and explainable logical route, another popular stream of Question Decomposition-based (QD) approaches became favored in recent years [12,17,21,22]. The method mimics human reasoning to decompose complex questions into simpler, single-hop sub-questions; thus, the interpretability is greatly improved by exposing intermediate evidence generated by each sub-question. Nevertheless, the general performance is usually much worse than GN-based ones due to error accumulation that arose by aggregating answers from each single-hop reasoning process. Furthermore, the sub-questions are generated mainly by extracting text spans from the original question to fill the template. Hence the sub-questions are challenging to guarantee in terms of quality, such as fluency, diversity, and consistency with the original question intention, especially when the original questions are linguistically complex.

In this work, we believe that asking the question is an effective way to elicit intrinsic information in the text and is an inherent step towards understanding it [23]. Thus, we propose resolving these difficulties by introducing an additional QG task to teach the model to ask questions. Specifically, we carefully design and add one end-to-end QG module based on the classical GN-based module. Unlike the traditional QD-based methods that only rely on information brought by the question, our proposed QG module could generate fluent and inherently logical sub-questions based on the understanding of the original context and the question simultaneously.

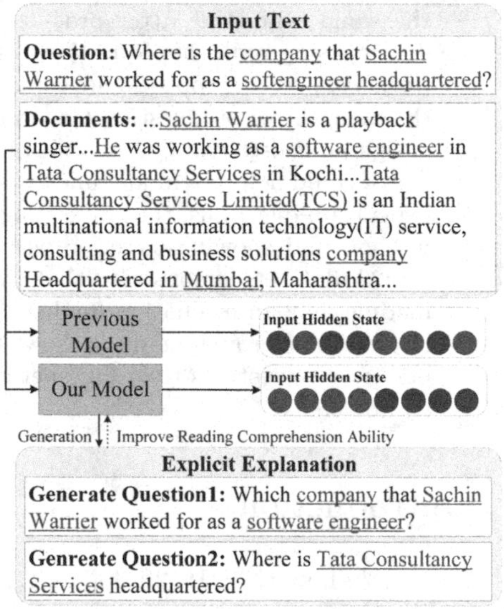

Fig. 1. An example from HotpotQA dataset. Text in blue is the first-hop information and text in red is the second-hop information. The mixed encoding of the first-hop information (•) and the second-hop information (•) will confuse models with weaker reading comprehension. (Color figure online)

Our method enjoys three advantages: First, it achieves better performance. Our approach preserves the GN module, which could collect information scattered throughout the documents and allows the model to understand the context in depth by asking questions. Moreover, the end-to-end training avoids the error accumulation issue; Second, it brings better interpretability because explainable evidence for its decision making could be provided in the form of sub-questions; Thirdly, the proposed QG module has better generalization capability. Theoretically, it can be plugged and played on most traditional QA models.

Experimental results on the HotpotQA dataset demonstrate the effectiveness of our proposed approach. It surpasses the GN-based model and QD-based model by a large margin. Furthermore, robust performance on the noisy version of HotpotQA proves that the QG module could alleviate the shortcut issue, and visualization on sentence-level attention indicates a clear improvement in natural language understanding capability. Moreover, a human evaluation is innovatively introduced to quantify improvements in interpretability. Finally, exploration on generated sub-questions clarifies diversity, fluency, and consistency.

2 Related Work

Multi-hop QA. In multi-hop QA, the evidence for reasoning answers is scattered across multiple sentences. Initially, researchers still adopted the ideas of single-hop QA to solve multi-hop QA [5,41]. Then the graph neural network that builds graphs based on entities was introduced to multi-hop QA tasks and achieved astonishing performance [4,7,32]. While, some researchers paid much attention to the interpretability of the coreference reasoning chains [12,17,21,22]. By providing decomposed single-hop sub-questions, the QD-based method makes the model decisions explainable.

Interpretability Analysis in NLP. An increasing body of work has been devoted to interpreting neural network models in NLP in recent years. These efforts could be roughly divided into structural analyses, behavioral studies, and interactive visualization [2].

Firstly, the typical way of structural analysis is to design probe classifiers to analyze model characteristics, such as syntactic structural features [9] and semantic features [36]. Secondly, the main idea of behavioral studies is that design experiments that allow researchers to make inferences about computed representations based on the model's behavior, such as proposing various challenge sets that aim to cover specific, diverse phenomena, like systematicity exhaustivity [13,27]. Thirdly, for interactive visualization, neuron activation [8], attention mechanisms [14] and saliency measures [15] are three main standard visualization methods.

Question Generation. QG is the task of generating a series of questions related to the given contextual information. Previous works on QG focus on rule-based approaches. [10] used a template-based approach to complete sentence extraction and QG in an unsupervised manner. [6] developed Syn-QG using a rule-based approach. The system consists of serialized rule modules that transform input documents into QA pairs and use reverse translation counting, resulting in highly fluent and relevant results. One of the essential applications of QG is to construct pseudo-datasets for QA tasks, thereby assisting in improving their performance [1,20,40].

Our work is most related to [23], which produces a set of questions asking about all possible semantic roles to bring the benefits of QA-based representations to traditional SRL and information extraction tasks. However, we innovatively leverage QG into complicated multi-hop QA tasks and enrich representations by asking questions at each reasoning step.

3 Methods

Multi-hop QA is challenging because it requires a model to aggregate scattered evidence across multiple documents to predict the correct answer. Probably, the final answer is obtained conditioned on the first sub-question is correctly answered. Inspired by humans who always decompose complex questions into single-hop questions, our task is to automatically produce naturally-phrased sub-questions asking about every reasoning step given the original question and a passage. Following the reasoning processing, the generated sub-questions further explain why the answer is predicted. For instance, in Fig. 1, the answer "*Mumbai*" is predicted to answer *Question2* which is conditioned on *Question1*'s answer. More importantly, we believe that the better questions the model asks, the better it understands the reading passage and boosts the performance of the QA model in return.

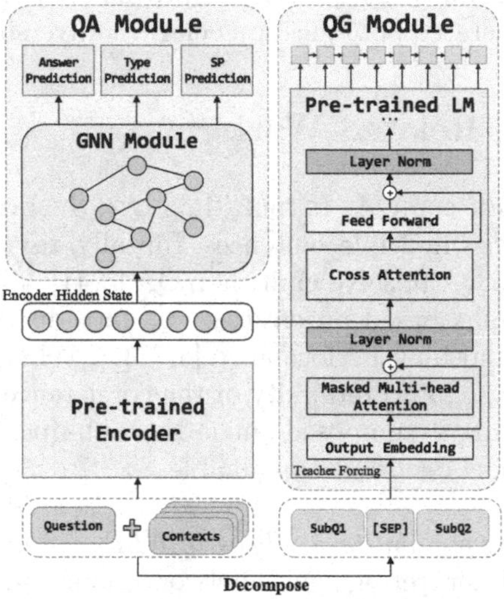

Fig. 2. Overall model architecture.

Figure 2 illustrates the overall framework of our proposed model. It consists of two modules: QA module (Sect. 3.1) and QG module (Sect. 3.2). The QA module could help model to solve multi-hop QA in a traditional way, and the QG module allows the model to solve the question in an interpretable manner by asking questions. These two modules share the same encoder and are trained end-to-end with multi-task strategy.

3.1 Question Answering Module

Encoder. A key point of the GN-based approach to solving QA problems is the initial encoding of entity nodes. Prior studies have shown that pre-trained models are beneficial for increasing the comprehension of the model [24,38], which enables better encoding of the input text. In Sect. 3.2 we will mention that encoder will be shared to the QG module to further increase the model's reading comprehension of the input text through the QG task. Here we chose BERT as the encoder considering its strong performance and simplicity.

GNN Encode Module. The representation ability of the model will directly affect the performance of QA. Recent works leverage graphs to represent the relationship between entities or sentences, which have strong representation ability [11,31,37]. We believe that the advantage of graph neural networks is essential for solving multi-hop questions. Thus, we adopt the GN-based model DFGN[1] [37] that has been proven to be effective in HotpotQA.

[37] build graph edges between two entities if they co-exist in one single sentence. After encoding the question Q and context C by the pre-trained encoder, DFGN extracts the entities' representation from the encoder output by their location information. Both mean-pooling and max-pooling are used to represent the entities' embeddings. Then, a graph neural network propagates node information to its neighbors. A soft mask mechanism is used to calculate the relevance score between each entity and the question in this process. The soft mask score is used as the weight value of each entity to indicate its importance in the graph neural network computation. At each step, the query embedding should be updated by the entities embedding of the current step by a bi-attention network [28]. The entities embeddings in the t-th reasoning step:

$$\mathbf{E}^t = \mathrm{GAT}([m_1^{t-1}e_1^{t-1}, m_2^{t-1}e_2^{t-1}, ..., m_n^{t-1}e_n^{t-1}]), \tag{1}$$

where e_i^{t-1} is the i-th entity's embedding at the $(t-1)$-th step and e_i^0 is the i-th entity's embedding produced both mean-pooling and max-pooling results from encoder output according to its position. m_i^{t-1} is the relevance score, which is also called soft mask score in previous, between i-th entity and the question at the $(t-1)$-th step calculated by an attention network. GAT is graph attention networks proposed by [33].

In each reasoning step, every entity node gains some information from its neighbors. An LSTM layer is then used to produce the context representation:

$$\mathbf{C}^t = \mathrm{LSTM}([\mathbf{C}^{t-1}; \mathbf{M}\mathbf{E}^{t\top}]), \tag{2}$$

where M is the adjacency matrix which records the location information of the entities.

The updated context representations are used for different sub-tasks: (i) answer type prediction; (ii) answer start position and answer end position; (iii) extract support facts prediction. All three tasks are jointly performed through multitasking learning.

$$\mathcal{L}_{qa} = \lambda_1\mathcal{L}_{start} + \lambda_2\mathcal{L}_{end} + \lambda_3\mathcal{L}_{type} + \lambda_4\mathcal{L}_{para}, \tag{3}$$

where λ_1, λ_2, λ_3, λ_4 are hyper-parameters[2].

[1] QA module is not the main focus of this work, and DFGN is one of the representative off-the-shelf QA models. In fact, any QA model could be adopted to replace it.

[2] In our experiments, we set $\lambda_1 = \lambda_2 = \lambda_3 = 1$, $\lambda_4 = 5$.

3.2 Question Generation Module

Question Generation Training Dataset. A key challenge of training the QG module is that it is challenging to obtain the annotated sub-questions dataset. To achieve this, we take the following steps to generate sub-question dataset automatically:

First of all, according to the annotations provided by the HotpotQA dataset, the questions in the training set could be classified into the following two types: **Bridge** (70%) and **Comparison** (30%), where the former one requires finding evidence from first hop reasoning then use it to find second-hop evidence, while the latter requires comparing the property of two different entities mentioned in the question.

Then we leverage the methods proposed by [21] to process these two types respectively. Specifically, we adopt an off-the-shelf span predictor `Pointer` to map the question into several points, which could be for segmenting the question into various text spans.

Finally, we generated sub-questions by considering the type of questions and index points provided by `Pointer`. Concretely, for **Bridge** questions like *Kristine Moore Gebbie is a professor at a university founded in what year?*, `Pointer` could divided the question into two parts: *Kristin Moore Gebbie be a professor at a university* and *founded in what year?*. Then some question words are inserted into the first part as the first-hop evidence like *Kristin Moore Gebbie be a professor at which university*, denoted as S^A. Afterward, an off-the-shelf single QA model is used to find the answer for the first sub-question, and the answer would be used to form the second sub-question like *Flinders University founded in what year?*, denoted as S^B. On the other hand, for **Comparison** questions like *Do The Importance of Being Icelandic and The Five Obstructions belong to different film genres?*. `Pointer` would divide it into three parts: first entity(*The Importance of Being Icelandic*), second entity (*The Five Obstructions*), and target property (*film genre*). Then two sub-questions could be further generated by inserting question words to these parts like S^A :*Do The Importance of Being Icelandic belong to which film genres?* and S^B : *Do The Five Obstructions belong to which film genres?*

Pre-trained Language Model (LM) as Generator. After automatically creating the sub-question dataset, the next step is to train the QG module from scratch. Specifically, the structure of whole QG module is designed as seq2seq, where it shares the encoder with QA module and adopts GPT-2 [25] as the decoder. During training stage, the input of decoder is formed as: $[\text{bos}, y_1^A, y_2^A, ..., y_n^A, [\text{SEP}], y_1^B, y_2^B, ..., y_n^B, \text{eos}]$, where [SEP] is the separator token, **bos** is the start token and **eos** is the end token. y_i^A and y_i^B are the i-th token in constructed sub-questions S^A and S^B respectively.

Then the training objective of the QG module is to maximize the conditional probability of the target sub-questions sequence as follows:

$$\mathcal{L}_{qg} = \sum_{i=1}^{n} \log\mathcal{P}(y_t|y_{<t}, h), \tag{4}$$

where h is encoder hidden state. Finally, QG module and QA module are trained together in end-to-end multi-task manner, and the overall loss is defined as:

$$\mathcal{L}_{\text{multitask}} = \mathcal{L}_{qa} + \mathcal{L}_{qg}. \quad (5)$$

4 Experiments

4.1 Dataset

We evaluate our approach on HotpotQA [39] under the distraction setting, a popular multi-hop QA dataset taking the explanation ability of models into accounts. Expressly, for each question, two gold paragraphs with ground-truth answers and supporting facts are provided, along with 8 'distractor' paragraphs that were collected via bi-gram TF-IDF retriever (i.e., 10 paragraphs in total). Furthermore, HotpotQA contains two types of subtasks: a) Answer prediction; and b) Supporting facts prediction; both subtasks adopt the same evaluation metrics: Exact Match (EM) and Partial Match (F1).

4.2 Implementation Details

We implement the model via HuggingFace library [35]. In detail, DFGN is selected as a QA module by following the details provided by [37]. While, for the QG module, the pre-trained decoder language model is initialized with GPT2 [25]. The number of shared encoder layers is set as 12, the number of decoder layers is 6, the maximum sequence length is 512. We train the model on four TITAN RTX GPUs for 30 epochs at a batch size of 8, where each epoch tasks for around 2 h. We select Adam [18] as our optimizer with a learning rate of 5e-5 and a warm-up ratio of 10%. In general, we determine the hyperparameters by comparing the final EM and F1 scores.

4.3 Comparison Models

Baseline Model. A neural paragraph-level QA model introduced in [39] and original proposed by [3].

DFGN. The classic GN-based model [37], which is trained in an end-to-end fashion for multi-hop QA task. We select this as the primary QA module in our approach, and reproduce the DFGN model by using the BERT-base pre-trained model under the hyperparameter settings released by [39].

DecompRC. The classic QD-based model that decomposes each question into several sub-questions [21]. We reproduce the DecompRC model by following the same QD instruction illustrated in [21].

Table 1. Performance comparison on the development set of HotpotQA in the distractor setting. * indicates the results implemented by us.

Model	Answer		Sup Fact		Joint	
	EM	F1	EM	F1	EM	F1
Baseline Model	44.44	58.28	21.95	66.66	11.56	40.86
DecompRC	55.20	69.63	–	–	–	–
DFGN* (Bridge)	53.38	69.14	47.72	**84.44**	29.79	58.67
DFGN* (Comparison)	**63.75**	69.48	70.68	89.98	46.74	63.56
DFGN* (Total)	55.46	69.21	52.33	82.12	33.19	59.66
DFGN (Total)	55.66	69.34	53.10	82.24	33.68	59.86
Ours (Bridge)	**56.24**	**71.67**	**51.06**	81.16	**33.61**	**61.75**
Ours (Comparison)	63.08	**69.59**	**73.03**	**90.36**	**49.23**	**64.45**
Ours (Total)	**57.79**	**71.36**	**55.77**	**83.33**	**36.99**	**62.52**

5 Analysis

Table 1 shows the performance of various models on the development set of HotpotQA. In general, our method attains substantial improvement across all tasks when compared to either the GN-based method or the QD-based approach. This demonstrates that the integration of the QG task can effectively augment the model's textual understanding capabilities. Additionally, our method exhibits consistent enhancement in performance for both types of questions. Notably, the performance on bridge-type questions, which necessitate linear reasoning chains, experiences a marked improvement, underscoring the efficacy of posing questions at each reasoning stage. In subsequent sections, we will further explore the functionality, interpretability, and quality of the sub-questions generated by the QG module, providing a comprehensive analysis of our proposed method's strengths and potential applications.

5.1 Does it Alleviate Shortcut Problem by Adding Question Generation Module?

In order to validate the capacity of the QG module to concentrate on uncovering the authentic reasoning process, as opposed to exploiting shortcuts for predicting answers, we further undertake QA tasks using baselines and our model on Adversarial MultiHopQA. This dataset was initially introduced by [16] and is designed to challenge the model's comprehension capabilities. Specifically, multiple noisy facts, constructed by substituting entities within the reasoning chain, are incorporated into the original HotpotQA dataset with the intent to confound the model. For instance, in the example provided in Fig. 3, the noisy facts are formulated by replacing key entities present in Support Fact2. These noisy facts retain the same sentence structure as the support facts but convey disparate meanings, thereby compelling the model to thoroughly comprehend the context. This additional layer of complexity serves to rigorously test our proposed QG module, ensuring it remains focused on elucidating the genuine reasoning process.

Table 2 shows the performance between the DFGN model and our model on the Adversarial-MultiHopQA dataset. In general, DFGN experiences a significant decline in performance, indicating that the existing QA model has poor robustness and is vulnerable to adversarial attacks. This further indicates that the model solves questions by mostly remembering patterns. On the other hand, by adding a QG module, the performance degradation of our method is significantly reduced. We think this is mainly because asking questions is an important strategy for guiding the model to understand the text.

Table 2. Performance of DFGN model and ours on HotpotQA dataset and its noisy version Adversarial-MultiHopQA (marked with *).

Model	Answer	
	EM	F1
DFGN	55.66	69.34
DFGN*	48.08(−13.62%)	61.28(−11.62%)
Ours	57.79	71.36
Ours*	52.34**(-9.43%)**	65.12**(−8.74%)**

We further prove this point through a case study shown in Fig. 3. To answer the original question, the correct reasoning chain is *2014 S S/S → WINNER → YG Entertainment*. However, when there exists an overlap in the context between facts (i.e. *South Korean boy group*), the current main-stream method, which strengthens representation by solely capturing internal relationships over entities or documents, usually regards the incorrect entity (i.e. *YG Arthur* or *YG Republic)* as a key node of reasoning chain, where so-called shortcut issue. It does not understand the reasoning process but remembers certain context patterns. However, our method mitigates such issues by reinforcing representations by asking a question at each reasoning step. As such, it could remain robust despite these disturbances.

5.2 Does Generated Sub-question Provide Better Interpretability?

Past works have proved that interpretability can be improved by exposing evidence from decomposed sub-questions. However, few quantitative analyses have been carried out on interpretability due to its subjective nature. In this paper, we use human evaluation to quantify the improvement of interpretability brought by our QG module.

Specifically, we design human evaluation by following steps: First, we assemble 16 well-educated volunteers and divide them into two groups, A and B; Second, we randomly sample 8 Bridge type questions from the dev set and manually write out the correct two-hop reasoning chain for solving each question. Afterward, we replace the entity that appeared in each correct reasoning chain with other confusing entities selected from context to generate three more wrong reasoning chains (i.e., each question has 4 reasoning chains.). Then shuffle them and combine them with the original question to form a four-way multi-choice QA; Third, for each group, we ask them to figure out the correct reasoning chain

Question: 2014 S/S is the debut album of a South Korean boy group that was formed by who? **Support Fact1:** 2014 S/S is the debut album of South Korean group WINNER. **Support Fact2:** Winner, often stylized as WINNER, is a South Korean boy group formed in 2013 by YG Entertainment and debuted in 2014. **reasoning chain:** 2014 S/S WINNER YG Entertainment
Noisy Fact1: Juarez, often stylized as Juarez, is a South Korean boy group formed in 2013 by YG Arthur and debuted in 2014. **Noisy Fact2:** Epic, often stylized as Epic, is a South Korean boy group formed in 2013 by YG Republic and debuted in 2014. **Noisy Fact3:** ... **No reasoning chain with Support Fact1!**
Right Answer: YG Entertainment (from ours) **Disturbances:** YG Arthur; YG Republic (from baselines)

Fig. 3. An example of the noisy dataset. The red text indicates a reasoning path with complete reasoning logic. The blue text indicates some other entities which have a similar structure with the red texts, but they can be inferred from the logical relationships. (Color figure online)

and record the time elapsed for finishing all questions. To be noticed, besides original questions and reasoning chains, we provide different additional information for each group to facilitate them, all supporting facts for Group A, and all sub-questions generated by our QG for Group B. For more details, please refer to Appendix.

Table 3 presents the results of the two groups. Remarkably, Group B has higher accuracy and takes less time. Therefore, we could argue that sub-questions generated by our QG contain more concise and precise explanations for problem-solving and further proves that the QG module can indeed improve interpretability.

Table 3. Average results for accuracy and time elapsed of human evaluation.

Group	Accuracy	Time(s)
A (Support Facts)	65.63%	981
B (Sub-questions)	**85.94%**	**543**

5.3 Does Asking Questions Enhance the Natural Language Understanding Capability?

In this work, we believe that the ability to exhaustively generate a set of logical questions according to a complex scenario allows for a comprehensive, interpretable, and flexible way of excavating the information hidden in natural language text, thereby enhancing the natural language understanding ability.

The self-attention mechanism in the pre-trained model is crucial for the model to understand the input information. Generally, the more critical a sentence is in its context, the greater attention weights it deserves. Thus, to verify whether the QG module could edify the model to carry out deep understanding intrinsically, we compare the sentence-level attention weight of our model with and without the QG module. In particular, we account for the number of increases in attention weight of support facts after adding the QG module. As shown in the last row of Table 4, the attention weight of around 80% of support facts is increased, which proves that the model is more prone to focus on meaningful information with the aid of the QG task.

Furthermore, Fig. 4 visualizes the changes in attention weights over supporting facts between DFGN and our method. In this case, sentences $S_{1,5,6,7}$ are considered as supporting facts. DFGN fails to predict all supporting facts and focuses on the wrong ones while our method works properly.

Table 4. Comparison between sub-questions generated by QG and template on diversity, LM score and Attention weights.

Indicators	Methods	Win	Tie	Loss
Diversity	QG vs. QD	**57.64%**	26.70%	15.66%
LM Score	QG vs. QD	**60.22%**	–	39.78%
Attention weight	QG vs. w/o QG	**79.51%**	–	20.49%

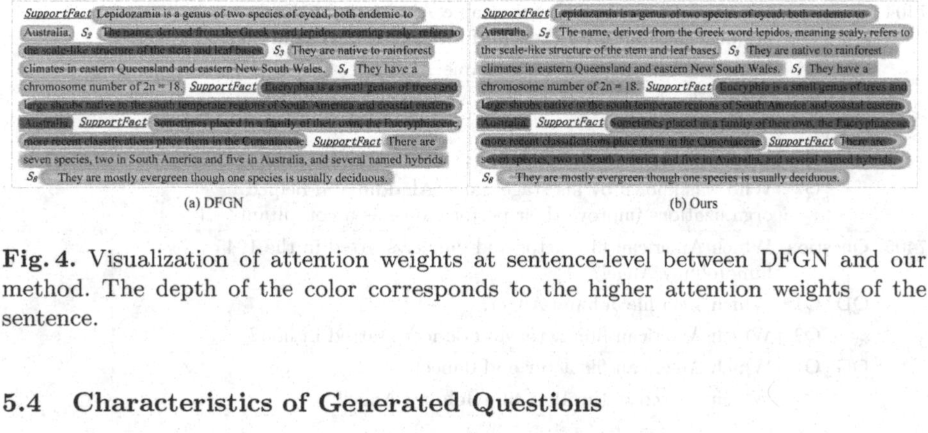

Fig. 4. Visualization of attention weights at sentence-level between DFGN and our method. The depth of the color corresponds to the higher attention weights of the sentence.

5.4 Characteristics of Generated Questions

QG can indeed promote an in-depth understanding of the model, but *what are the characteristics of the generated questions that contribute to this?* Specifically, what are the distinctive features of the sub-questions we generate using the QG module compared to the previous QD-based methods, which generate sub-questions using templates. Through case and statistical analysis, we find that the sub-questions generated by the QG module exhibit the following characteristics:

Consistency. As mentioned in Sect. 3.2, prior QD-based methods necessitate the implementation of a span predictor to dissect questions into constituent text spans. During the segmentation process, errors are predisposed to accumulate, rendering the generated sub-questions susceptible to inconsistencies with the original question. This issue becomes increasingly prevalent when the original

Table 5. Results on linguistic **fluency** and **diversity** of sub-questions generated by QG compared to those generated by template. ✓ indicate the method performs better, ÃŮ indicate performs worse, and - indicate performs competitively.

ID			Question/Sub-question	Fluency	Diversity
1	Question		In 1991 Euromarche was bought by a chain that operated how any hypermarkets at the end of 2016?		
	QD	Q1	Which chain that operated how any hypermarkets?	×	×
		Q2	In 1991 Euromarche was bought by Euromarche at the end of 2016?		
	QG	Q1	In 1991 Euromarche was bought by which chain?	✓	✓
		Q2	Carrefour's oprated how many hypermarkets at the end of 2016?		
2	Question		Do The Importance of Being Icelandic and The Five Obstructions belong to different film genres?		
	QD	Q1	Do the Importance of Being Icelandic and The Five Obstructions belong to different film genres?	×	×
		Q2	Do the importance of?		
	QG	Q1	Does the Importance of Being Icelandic and The Five Obstructions belong to which film genres?	✓	✓
		Q2	Does The Five Obstructions belong to which film genres?		
......					
7404	Question		Who was known by his stage name Aladin and helped organizations improve their performance as a consultant?		
	QD	Q1	Who was known by his stage name Aladin?	✓	×
		Q2	Who helped organizations improve their performance as a consultant?		
	QG	Q1	His stage name Aladdin?	×	✓
		Q2	Who was known by his stage name Aladdin and helped organizations improve their performance as a consultant?		
7405	Question		Which American film actor and dancer starred in the 1945 film Johnny Angel?		
	QD	Q1	Which 1945 file Johnny Angel?	×	-
		Q2	Which American film actor and dancer starred in noir?		
	QG	Q1	Which American file actor and dancer?	✓	-
		Q2	Which starred in the 1945 film Johnny Angel?		

question exhibits linguistic complexity. As illustrated by the second example in Table 5, the pair of sub-questions generated by template-based approaches erroneously deconstruct the original question, culminating in a question intention that deviates significantly from the original intent. Consequently, such sub-questions characterized by incongruent intent can mislead the model. In contrast, our proposed QG module is designed to facilitate a comprehensive understanding of the original question, utilizing abundant contextual information to generate logically ordered sub-questions. Ultimately, this approach ensures that the intentions of the combined sub-questions remain consistent with the original question, mitigating the risk of misinterpretation by the model.

Fluency. The fluidity and grammatical integrity of a sentence play a crucial role in accurately conveying meaning, particularly in the case of questions. When a question is plagued by grammatical inaccuracies or incoherence, it becomes challenging for individuals or computational models to comprehend, potentially leading to misinterpretation of the intended inquiry. This issue is widespread and inescapable in numerous datasets, primarily due to the manual construction of questions, as exemplified by the first instance in Table 5. In the original question, a typographical error (*how many* → *how any*) causes a shift in the intended meaning. Nonetheless, it remains feasible to discern the correct response from the additional information offered by the original question and general knowledge. Regrettably, the sub-question produced by the QD-based technique incorporates the typographical error, and the model fails to ascertain the accurate intention due to the limited information available within the sub-question. Moreover, syntactic errors are prone to accrue since determining the boundaries and attributes of text spans proves to be a challenging task, leading to subpar readability.

Contrastingly, our QG module is capable of leveraging contextual information and the embedded knowledge within the language model to rectify typographical errors. Simultaneously, it can employ the capabilities of the pre-trained language model to generate coherent sentences, thus alleviating the impact of syntactic errors. To assess fluency, we utilize the Language Model Score (LMS)[3] as a metric. As demonstrated in Table 4, over 60% of the questions generated by QG modules exhibit higher scores compared to those produced by the QD method.

Diversity. [29] highlight that the diversity of generated questions can directly impact QA performance. However, sub-questions produced by QD methods tend to be monotonous and laborious due to constraints on vocabulary and templates. In contrast, our proposed QG module can gently mitigate these challenges and enhance question diversity. Relying on the pretrained LM, the QG module is capable of incorporating contextually appropriate words into sub-questions, adapting to various situations. This is exemplified by the inclusion of *Carrefour* in the first example provided in Table 5, which results in more diverse and rational sub-questions. In our analysis, we consider the number of words in sub-questions that did not appear in the original question as a measure of diversity. As demonstrated in Table 4, approximately 57% of sub-questions generated by our method exhibit greater diversity, underlining the advantages of our proposed QG module.

6 Conclusion

In this paper, drawing inspiration from human cognitive behavior, we posit that the act of asking questions serves as a crucial indicator for determining whether a model genuinely comprehends the input text. Consequently, we introduce a QG module designed to tackle multi-hop QA tasks in an interpretable manner. Building upon traditional QA modules, the incorporation of the QG module effectively

[3] https://github.com/simonepri/lm-scorer.

enhances natural language understanding capabilities, delivering superior and robust performance through the process of asking questions. Furthermore, we conduct a quantitative analysis of interpretability, as provided by sub-questions, utilizing human evaluation and elucidating interpretability through attention visualization. Ultimately, we substantiate that the sub-questions derived from the QG method surpass those obtained via the QD method in terms of linguistic fluency, consistency, and diversity, underscoring the benefits of our proposed approach.

7 Limitations

Although our research presents numerous advantages, certain limitations persist. The lack of comparison with extant SOTA methods and validation on alternative datasets constitute two principal shortcomings. Despite these issues, we maintain our advocacy for the "ask to understand" concept, positing that the integration of a QG task can bolster a model's interpretability and comprehension capabilities.

Primarily, the rationale behind our decision not to utilize top SOTA models as baselines is that these approaches often entail the application of meticulously designed, task-specific, and labor-intensive GNN to the encoder segment. Conversely, we posit that our method operates in a plug-and-play manner; validating its efficacy on two rudimentary baselines suggests that it may also be applicable to other models. Consequently, outperforming SOTA methods in terms of performance is not the central contribution of this paper.Additionally, question decomposition serves as a vital component of our work, and we employ DecompRC to parse multi-hop questions into single-hop queries. Since DecompRC is tailored specifically for HotpotQA, adapting it to other multi-hop QA datasets may not yield the anticipated results; thus, we solely verify our methods on HotpotQA.

Finally, grounded in our core concept of "asking to understand," the applicability and reliability of the QA model in industrial contexts are significantly enhanced. Our model delivers answers accompanied by comprehensive multi-hop questions, enabling agents to evaluate the accuracy of the response. Furthermore, our model aids agents in "understanding by asking," delineating the steps involved in obtaining the answer and facilitating a more profound comprehension of the information's origin.

A Appedix: Human Evaluation Instruction

Specifically, we design human evaluation by following steps:

1. We assemble 16 well-educated volunteers and randomly divide them into two groups, A and B. Each group contains 8 volunteers and evenly gender.
2. We randomly sample 8 Bridge type[4] questions from the dev set, and manually write out the correct two-hop reasoning chain for solving each question.

[4] Because Bride type questions always has deterministic linear reasoning chains.

3. We replace the entity that appeared in each correct reasoning chain with other confusing entities selected from context to generate three more wrong reasoning chains (i.e., each question has 4 reasoning chains.), then shuffle them and combine them with the original question to form a four-way multi-choice QA.
4. For group A, except the original question, final answer and four reasoning chains, we also provide supporting facts. Then volunteers are asked to find the correct reasoning chain.
5. For group B, except the original question, final answer and four reasoning chains, we also provide the sub-questions generated by our QG module. Then volunteers are asked to find the correct reasoning chain.
6. We count the accuracy and time elapsed for solving problem.

Beyond that, some details are worth noting:

- The volunteers participated in the human evaluation test are all well-educated graduate students with skilled English.
- We use the online questionnaire platform to design the electronic questionnaire.
- The questionnaire system can automatically score according to the pre-set reference answers, and count the time spent on answering the questions.
- The timer starts when the volunteer clicks “accept" button on the questionnaire, and ends when the volunteer clicks “submit" button.
- Volunteers are required to answer the questionnaire without any interruption, ensuring that all time spent is for answering questions.
- Before starting filling the questionnaire, we provide a sample example as instruction to teach the volunteers how to find the answer.

The interface of human evaluation for each group could be found in Fig. 5 and Fig. 6.

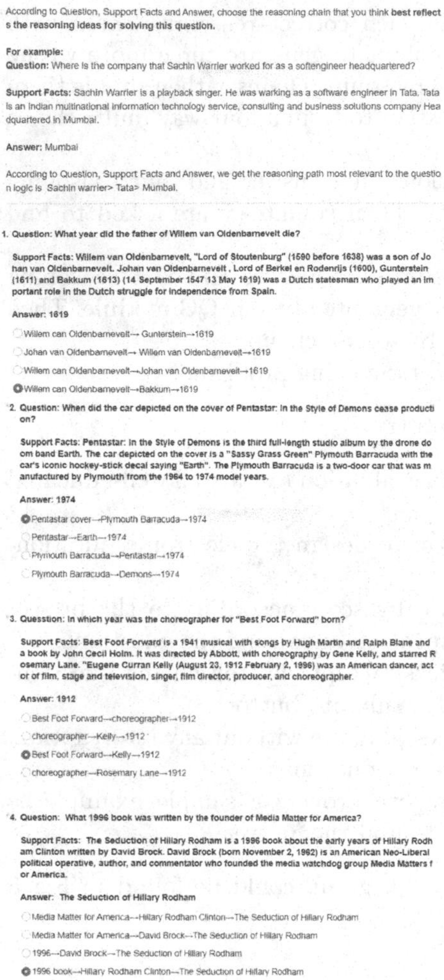

Fig. 5. Interface for human evaluation of choosing reasoning chain based on support facts.

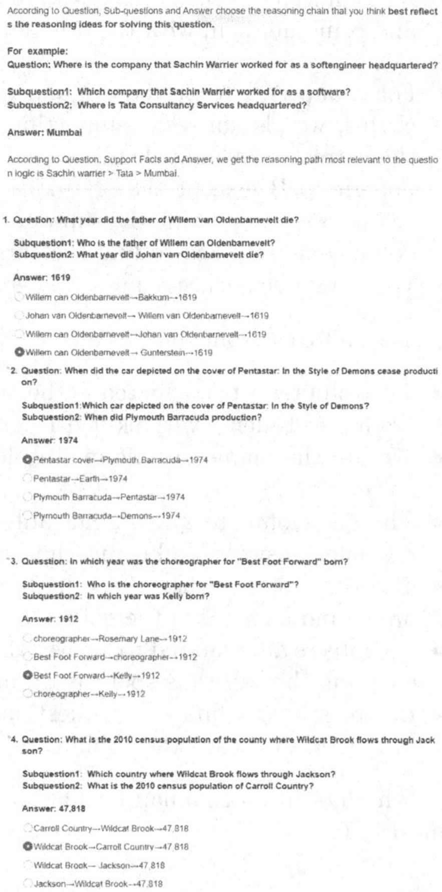

Fig. 6. Interface for human evaluation of choosing reasoning chain based on sub-questions.s

References

1. Alberti, C., Andor, D., Pitler, E., Devlin, J., Collins, M.: Synthetic qa corpora generation with roundtrip consistency. arXiv preprint arXiv:1906.05416 (2019)
2. Belinkov, Y., Glass, J.: Analysis methods in neural language processing: a survey. Trans. Assoc. Comput. Linguist. **7**, 49–72 (2019)
3. Clark, C., Gardner, M.: Simple and effective multi-paragraph reading comprehension. In: Proceedings of the 56th ACL, vol. 1: Long Papers, pp. 845–855 (2018)
4. De Cao, N., Aziz, W., Titov, I.: Question answering by reasoning across documents with graph convolutional networks. In: ACL, pp. 2306–2317 (2019)

5. Dhingra, B., Jin, Q., Yang, Z., Cohen, W., Salakhutdinov, R.: Neural models for reasoning over multiple mentions using coreference. In: Proceedings of the 2018 Conference of the North American Chapter of the Association for Computational Linguistics: Human Language Technologies, vol. 2 (Short Papers), pp. 42–48 (2018)
6. Dhole, K.D., Manning, C.D.: Syn-qg: syntactic and shallow semantic rules for question generation (2021)
7. Ding, M., Zhou, C., Chen, Q., Yang, H., Tang, J.: Cognitive graph for multi-hop reading comprehension at scale. In: ACL, pp. 2694–2703 (2019)
8. Durrani, N., Sajjad, H., Dalvi, F., Belinkov, Y.: Analyzing individual neurons in pre-trained language models. arXiv preprint arXiv:2010.02695 (2020)
9. Elazar, Y., Ravfogel, S., Jacovi, A., Goldberg, Y.: Amnesic probing: behavioral explanation with amnesic counterfactuals. Trans. Assoc. Comput. Linguist. **9**, 160–175 (2021)
10. Fabbri, A.R., Ng, P., Wang, Z., Nallapati, R., Xiang, B.: Template-based question generation from retrieved sentences for improved unsupervised question answering (2020)
11. Fang, Y., Sun, S., Gan, Z., Pillai, R., Wang, S., Liu, J.: Hierarchical graph network for multi-hop question answering (2020)
12. Fu, R., Wang, H., Zhang, X., Zhou, J., Yan, Y.: Decomposing complex questions makes multi-hop qa easier and more interpretable. In: EMNLP, pp. 169–180 (2021)
13. Gardner, M., et al.: Evaluating models' local decision boundaries via contrast sets. arXiv preprint arXiv:2004.02709 (2020)
14. Hao, Y., Dong, L., Wei, F., Xu, K.: Self-attention attribution: interpreting information interactions inside transformer. arXiv preprint arXiv:2004.11207 (2020)
15. Janizek, J.D., Sturmfels, P., Lee, S.I.: Explaining explanations: axiomatic feature interactions for deep networks. J. Mach. Learn. Res. **22**(104), 1–54 (2021)
16. Jiang, Y., Bansal, M.: Avoiding reasoning shortcuts: adversarial evaluation, training, and model development for multi-hop qa. In: ACL (2019)
17. Jiang, Y., Bansal, M.: Self-assembling modular networks for interpretable multi-hop reasoning. In: EMNLP-IJCNLP, pp. 4474–4484 (2019)
18. Kingma, D.P., Ba, J.: Adam: a method for stochastic optimization (2017)
19. Lai, G., Xie, Q., Liu, H., Yang, Y., Hovy, E.: RACE: large-scale ReAding comprehension dataset from examinations. In: ACL, pp. 785–794 (2017)
20. Lee, D.B., Lee, S., Jeong, W.T., Kim, D., Hwang, S.J.: Generating diverse and consistent qa pairs from contexts with information-maximizing hierarchical conditional vaes. arXiv preprint arXiv:2005.13837 (2020)
21. Min, S., Zhong, V., Zettlemoyer, L., Hajishirzi, H.: Multi-hop reading comprehension through question decomposition and rescoring. In: ACL (2019)
22. Nishida, K., et al.: Multi-task learning for multi-hop qa with evidence extraction (2019)
23. Pyatkin, V., Roit, P., Michael, J., Goldberg, Y., Tsarfaty, R., Dagan, I.: Asking it all: generating contextualized questions for any semantic role. In: Proceedings of the 2021 Conference on EMNLP, pp. 1429–1441 (2021)
24. Qiu, X., Sun, T., Xu, Y., Shao, Y., Dai, N., Huang, X.: Pre-trained models for natural language processing: a survey. Sci. China Technol. Sci. **63**, 1872–1897 (2020)
25. Radford, A., Wu, J., Child, R., Luan, D., Amodei, D., Sutskever, I., et al.: Language models are unsupervised multitask learners. OpenAI blog **1**(8), 9 (2019)
26. Rajpurkar, P., Zhang, J., Lopyrev, K., Liang, P.: SQuAD: 100,000+ questions for machine comprehension of text. In: EMNLP, pp. 2383–2392 (2016)

27. Ravichander, A., Dalmia, S., Ryskina, M., Metze, F., Hovy, E., Black, A.W.: Noiseqa: challenge set evaluation for user-centric question answering. arXiv preprint arXiv:2102.08345 (2021)
28. Seo, M., Kembhavi, A., Farhadi, A., Hajishirzi, H.: Bidirectional attention flow for machine comprehension (2018)
29. Sultan, M.A., Chandel, S., Fernandez Astudillo, R., Castelli, V.: On the importance of diversity in question generation for QA. In: ACL (2020)
30. Trischler, A., et al.: NewsQA: a machine comprehension dataset. In: Proceedings of the 2nd Workshop on Representation Learning for NLP, pp. 191–200 (2017)
31. Tu, M., Huang, K., Wang, G., Huang, J., He, X., Zhou, B.: Interpretable multi-hop reading comprehension over multiple documents (2020)
32. Tu, M., Wang, G., Huang, J., Tang, Y., He, X., Zhou, B.: Multi-hop reading comprehension across multiple documents by reasoning over heterogeneous graphs. In: ACL, pp. 2704–2713 (2019)
33. Veličković, P., Cucurull, G., Casanova, A., Romero, A., Lio, P., Bengio, Y.: Graph attention networks. arXiv preprint arXiv:1710.10903 (2017)
34. Welbl, J., Stenetorp, P., Riedel, S.: Constructing datasets for multi-hop reading comprehension across documents. TACL **6**, 287–302 (2018)
35. Wolf, T., et al.: Huggingface's transformers: state-of-the-art natural language processing (2020)
36. Wu, Z., Peng, H., Smith, N.A.: Infusing finetuning with semantic dependencies. Trans. Assoc. Comput. Linguist. **9**, 226–242 (2021)
37. Xiao, Y., et al.: Dynamically fused graph network for multi-hop reasoning (2019)
38. Yang, A., et al.: Enhancing pre-trained language representations with rich knowledge for machine reading comprehension. In: Proceedings of the 57th Annual Meeting of the Association for Computational Linguistics, pp. 2346–2357. Association for Computational Linguistics, Florence (2019). https://doi.org/10.18653/v1/P19-1226. https://aclanthology.org/P19-1226
39. Yang, Z., et al.: Hotpotqa: a dataset for diverse, explainable multi-hop question answering. In: EMNLP, pp. 2369–2380 (2018)
40. Zhang, S., Bansal, M.: Addressing semantic drift in question generation for semi-supervised question answering. arXiv preprint arXiv:1909.06356 (2019)
41. Zhong, V., Xiong, C., Keskar, N.S., Socher, R.: Coarse-grain fine-grain coattention network for multi-evidence question answering. arXiv preprint arXiv:1901.00603 (2019)

Learning on Structured Documents for Conditional Question Answering

Zihan Wang[1,2], Hongjin Qian[1,2], and Zhicheng Dou[1,2(✉)]

[1] Gaoling School of Artificial Intelligence, Renmin University of China, Beijing, China
{wangzihan0527,ian}@ruc.edu.cn

[2] Engineering Research Center of Next-Generation Intelligent Search and Recommendation, MOE, Beijing, China
dou@ruc.edu.cn

Abstract. Conditional question answering (CQA) is an important task in natural language processing that involves answering questions that depend on specific conditions. CQA is crucial for domains that require the provision of personalized advice or making context-dependent analyses, such as legal consulting and medical diagnosis. However, existing CQA models struggle with generating multiple conditional answers due to two main challenges: (1) the lack of supervised training data with diverse conditions and corresponding answers, and (2) the difficulty to output in a complex format that involves multiple conditions and answers. To address the challenge of limited supervision, we propose LSD (Learning on Structured Documents), a self-supervised learning method on structured documents for CQA. LSD involves a conditional question generation method and a contrastive learning objective. The model is trained with LSD on massive unlabeled structured documents and is fine-tuned on labeled CQA dataset afterwards. To overcome the limitation of outputting answers with complex formats in CQA, we propose a pipeline that enables the generation of multiple answers and conditions. Experimental results on the ConditionalQA dataset demonstrate that LSD outperforms previous CQA models in terms of accuracy both in providing answers and conditions.

1 Introduction

Recently, question answering (QA) has gained increasing interest in the field of Natural Language Processing. Various types of question answering tasks, such as knowledge-based QA (Cui et al. 2017), open domain QA (Kwiatkowski et al., 2019), and multi-hop QA (Yang et al. 2018), have been extensively studied. Among them, conditional question answering (CQA) (Sun et al. 2022a) is becoming increasingly important in various contexts, such as medical diagnosis, legal consultation, financial analysis, and more. Unlike the traditional question answering problem that only accepts a question and returns an answer, CQA involves understanding a complex and lengthy document, finding all possible answers under different **conditions**, and determining under what **condition** the answer is applicable. Figure 1 shows an example for CQA, where the answer could be different when the questioner is under different conditions. The CQA

M. Sun et al. (Eds.): CCL 2023, LNAI 14232, pp. 37–57, 2023.
https://doi.org/10.1007/978-981-99-6207-5_3

Question:

Scenario: My partner earn less than £50,000. I also earn less than £50,000 but receiving a dividend. My pay and dividend when added together will be more than £50,000.
Question: Will I be eligible to apply for child benefit ?

Answer:

Answer: Yes
Conditions: you're responsible for bringing up a child who is: a) under 16, b) under 20 if they stay in approved education ...
Answer: No
Conditions: you earn £60,000

Document:

Section 1: How it works
You get Child Benefit if you're responsible for bringing up a child who is:
a) under 16,
b) under 20 if they stay in approved education or training.
Section 2: What you'll get
· You can get Child Benefit if your (or your partner's) individual income is over £50,000, but you may be taxed on the benefit.
· If your partner's income is also over £50,000 but yours is higher, you're responsible for paying the tax charge.
· Once you earn £60,000 you lose all of your benefit through tax.
Section 3: Eligibility
...

Fig. 1. An example for CQA. The right side is a snapshot of a document discussing the policy of claiming Child Benefits. The green text span is the condition that has been satisfied. The yellow and blue text spans are the conditions for "Yes" and "No" respectively. (Color figure online)

task includes providing potential answers "yes" and "no" and their corresponding conditions based on the given question and scenario.

Previous studies on CQA can be broadly categorized into two groups: extractive and generative methods. Extractive methods (Ainslie et al. 2020) (Sun et al. 2021) extract the most relevant span from a document as answers and conditions. In contrast, generative methods (Izacard and Grave 2021) (Sun et al. 2022b) use a generative model to generate answers along with their corresponding conditions directly. However, current CQA models face two common challenges. Firstly, the supervised data for CQA is limited and expensive to obtain. Unlike traditional QA datasets, CQA requires specific annotations that include scenarios, answers, and conditions, making the data collection process more extensive and time-consuming. Secondly, current CQA models are unable to provide multiple conditional answers in a coherent and controlled format. Extractive methods for CQA are mostly only able to provide a single answer or condition for a question, limiting their ability to produce multiple conditional answers. Conversely, generative methods may generate inconsistent and incoherent answers and conditions due to their inherent randomness, especially when generating multiple conditional answers. These challenges underscore the need for improved approaches to effectively handle the generation of multiple conditional answers in CQA.

In order to solve the problem of limited supervision, we propose a self-supervised learning method called LSD (Learning on Structured Documents). LSD consists of two main components: conditional question generation and contrastive learning. For conditional question generation, our intuition is that if a more precise context that contains sufficient information to answer a conditional question can be passed to the QA model, then the conditional answers given through this context will have high accuracy and can be used for subsequent training. To achieve this goal, we propose a selective extraction process that extracts parts of a structured document that are likely to be able to answer a conditional question. For a certain selected part of the document, we use a state generator to generate a conditional question and user scenario, and use a label generator to generate highly believed answers. For contrastive learning, we use four methods of document perturbation to perturb the structure of the document, including node reordering, repetition, masking, and deletion. These methods will change the content of the document but have little impact on its semantics. We design a contrastive learning objective that encourages the model to give similar representations of document corresponding sentences before and after perturbation, enabling the model to learn effective semantic representations from complex documents and helping with conditional question answering.

To solve the problem of complex output formats, we propose a pipeline that can generate multiple answers and their corresponding conditions. Our pipeline extracts answer spans from sentences, generating query vectors for each answer and key vectors for each candidate condition. Afterward, we calculate the query-key matching score for each answer and condition, and choose the best matches as the final output. Unlike existing methods, our pipeline utilizes the structure of documents to generate questions and conditions, and can generate controllable multiple conditional answers.

To verify the effectiveness of our method, we conduct experiments on the conditionalQA dataset (Sun et al. 2022a). The experimental results showed that our method outperformed all baseline models in terms of answer and condition accuracy, indicating that our method can provide accurate answers and corresponding conditions to effectively answer conditional questions.

In summary, our contributions are three-fold:

(1) We propose LSD, a self-supervised learning method for structured documents based on question generation and contrastive learning, which effectively solves the problem of insufficient supervision for conditional question answering;
(2) We propose a pipeline that generates a query and key vectors for candidate answers and conditions and matching similarity for them, which can provide controllable conditional answers;
(3) The experimental results indicate that our method can answer conditional questions more effectively compared to previous conditional question answering methods.

2 Related Work

2.1 Conditional Question Answering

Conditional question answering (CQA) has been studied using extractive and generative methods. Extractive methods, such as ETC (Ainslie et al. 2020) and DocHopper (Sun et al. 2021), use two separate models to extract answers and conditions. ETC pipeline uses two separate encoders to extract answers from supporting documents and identify conditions. DocHopper, on the other hand, iteratively attends to different sentences to predict evidences, answers and conditions step-by-step. Generative methods such as FiD (Izacard and Grave 2021) use a single generative model to generate answers with conditions. FiD splits documents into sentences, encodes the sentences separately, and jointly decodes all encoded representations to generate answers with conditions. TReasoner (Sun et al. 2022b) is a discriminative-generative model that first checks whether each sentence could be a condition and then generates the answer with the context. However, these models suffer from several limitations, including a lack of sufficient supervised data, which can lead to overfitting and poor reasoning capabilities. Furthermore, pipeline designs have a limited ability to generate multiple hybrid-type answers and conditions. Therefore, improving the performance of CQA through a suitable pipeline is crucial, and our work aims to address these challenges.

2.2 Self-Supervised Learning

Self-supervised learning methods have gained significant traction in recent years, as they allow models to learn powerful representations without relying on large amounts of labeled data. Various language models, such as GPT-3 (Brown et al. 2020), BERT (Devlin et al. 2019), RoBERTa (Liu et al. 2019), BART (Lewis et al. 2020), have leveraged unsupervised pre-training to achieve remarkable results on extensive natural language tasks. There have also been multilingual approaches like XLM (Conneau et al. 2020), unsupervised machine translation (Lample et al. 2018), question generation techniques such as QA-based multiple-choice question generation (Le Berre et al. 2022), Web-pretraining (Guo et al. 2022), and deep reinforcement learning (Chen et al. 2019). On the other hand, contrastive learning has emerged as a powerful method for representation learning, with models like SimCSE (Gao et al. 2021), ELECTRA (Clark et al. 2020), DPR-QA (Karpukhin et al. 2020) and XMOCO (Yang et al. 2021) achieving state-of-the-art results across various natural language understanding and generation tasks by learning to distinguish between semantically similar and dissimilar inputs.

3 Preliminaries: Structured Documents

Structured documents contain complex and rich structural information, which is beneficial for learning conditional question answering. In this work, our model is trained on HTML documents, a widely used type of structured document. HTML documents are easily accessible and often contain rich semantic information, including tables, lists, and more. The underlying structure of an HTML document is represented by the Document Object Model (DOM) tree, wherein the entire document constitutes the root node, and individual elements are organized as child nodes within the hierarchy.

A diagram of a DOM tree is shown in Fig. 2. Since HTML does not always demonstrate a clear hierarchy among elements, we adopt a tag precedence order to convert HTML documents into trees, thus making the relationships between elements explicit. We order commonly used tags as: ⟨title⟩ - ⟨h⟩ - ⟨p⟩ - ⟨li⟩/⟨tr⟩. Each node's parent is the closest preceding higher-level node. For example, the ⟨h1⟩ tag is a section title and is the parent of ⟨h2⟩ subsection titles. The ⟨h2⟩ tag is a subheading and is the parent of ⟨p⟩ text elements. We omit tags that do not contain important information, such as ⟨b⟩ (bold),⟨i⟩ (italic), and ⟨a⟩ (hyperlink) tags. With our approach, each sentence within the HTML document can be clearly represented as a node in the document tree.

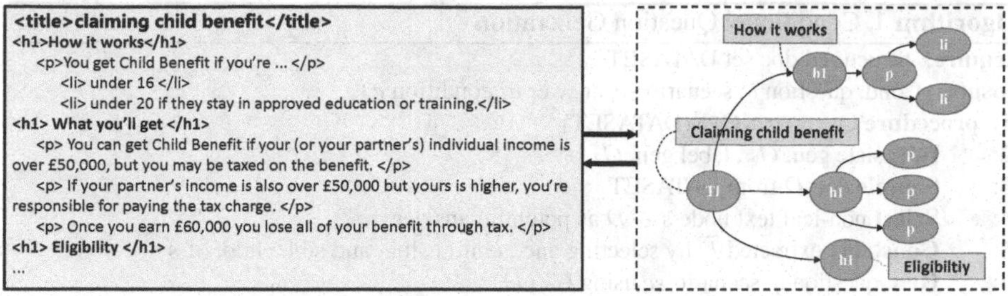

Fig. 2. An example of the schematic diagram of a DOM tree. HTML tags can be used to create a hierarchy of sentences in a document, with some tags considered more senior than others. The nearest former superior tag of a node is its parent node.

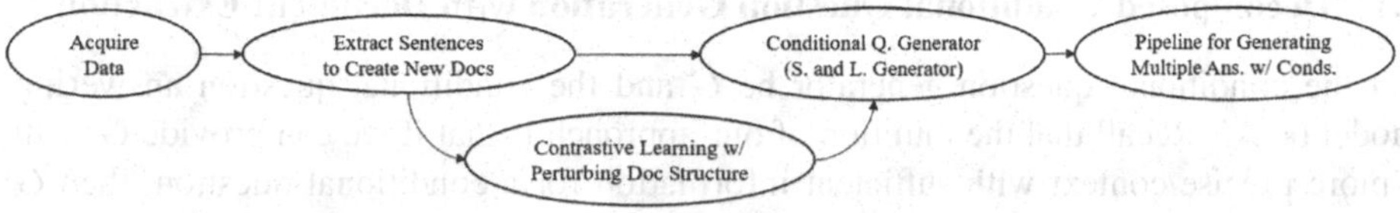

Fig. 3. An overall illustration of our approach.

To compile a corpus of structured documents for the CQA task, we consider the following criteria:

- Logical Structure: Documents should possess clear logical structures, including specific conditions and provisions, to facilitate conditional reasoning in the CQA task
- Standardized Format: Documents should adhere to a standardized HTML format with minimal noise, such as advertisements.
- Data Quality: The corpus should comprise formal, authoritative, and reviewed documents to ensure data reliability and accuracy.

Based on these criteria, we propose to train our model to learn on **national government websites**, which are known for their formal and authoritative nature. We conduct web scraping to gather documents, filtering for policy documents, laws and regulations, and administrative guidelines, as they tend to exhibit clear logical structures and contain specific conditions relevant to the CQA task. For additional details regarding the construction of the corpus, which is referred to as DATASET, please refer to Appendix A.

4 Our Approach

In this section, we will introduce our proposed method LSD, which includes a conditional question generation module and a contrastive learning method for self-supervised learning on structured documents. After that, we will illustrate our pipeline that generates multiple conditional answers by calculating the matching score of answers and candidate conditions with query and key vectors. The overall process of our method is shown in Fig. 3.

Algorithm 1. Conditional Question Generation

Require: Structured doc set DATASET
Ensure: Cond. question q, scenario sc, answer a, condition c
procedure QUESTIONGEN(DATASET)
  Init: state gen. G_S, label gen. G_L
  Sample doc D from DATASET
  Select non-leaf text node $s \in D$ as potential answer
  Construct extracted $\overline{D}$ by selecting anc., child., sibl., and sibl. child. of s
  Gen. question q, scenario sc using $G_S(\overline{D})$
  Gen. cond. answers $A = (a_i, c_i)$ using $G_L(q, sc, \overline{D})$
end procedure

4.1 Decomposed Conditional Question Generation with Document Extraction

Let the conditional question generator be G and the conditional question answering model be M. Recall that the intuition of our approach is that if we can provide G with a more precise context with sufficient information for a conditional question, then G can answer the question correctly, and the obtained question-answer data can be used to train M. To achieve this, we adopt a two-step method: selective extraction and question generation. A specific overview of conditional question generation is in Algorithm 1.

Table 1. Statistics of the ConditionalQA train dataset for guiding selective extraction.

	answers	conditions
leaf node	86.93%	92.53%
text node	92.49%	98.33%

(a) Features of answers and condition nodes: whether they are leaf nodes or text nodes.

	a-a pairs	c-c pairs	a-c pairs
sibling-sibling	66.55%	53.67%	–
parent-child	–	–	39.59%

(b) Features of answer and condition pairs: answer pairs (a-a), condition pairs (c-c), and answer-condition pairs (a-c).

4.1.1 Selective Extraction

Selective extraction aims for precise context to generate conditional questions. The main requirement for the selected context is to contain sufficient information to answer a conditional question. To guide our extraction strategy, we analyzed the ConditionalQA dataset, which also leverages structural documents for the CQA task. (Table 1). We analyzed the occurrence and correlations between answers and conditions, and observed several features: (1) answers and conditions are mainly located in leaf text nodes, such as ⟨p⟩ and ⟨li⟩ nodes; (2) answers are usually siblings; (3) conditions for extractive answers may be their child nodes; (4) sibling nodes with the same parent node can serve as parallel answers.

Guided by these insights, our extraction method involves the following steps. Firstly, we randomly select a non-leaf text node as a potential answer, because conditional answers are most likely to be such nodes. Then, we then extract its ancestors, children, siblings, and their children from the document tree, because: (1) ancestor nodes provide the macro context of higher-level topics; (2) child nodes offer potential conditions;

Table 2. Basic operations for Contrastive Learning.

Operation	Description	Advantages
Node masking	Mask node with [MASK] of same length	Focus on structure & context
Node deletion	Delete non-root node & descendants	Learn node dependencies & importance
Node cloning	Clone node & descendants as another child	Identify semantically similar elements
Node shuffling	Shuffle child nodes within parent	Understand impact of node order

(3) siblings, along with their children, provide parallel answers. Afterward, we obtain an extracted document that enables generating conditional questions aligned with the original text and answerable with accuracy.

4.1.2 Question Generation

The question generation approach are decomposed into two tasks: state generation and label generation. The first task is to generate question q and scenario sc given the extracted structured document $\overline{D}$, and the second task is to generate highly accurate conditional answers $A = \{(a_1, c_1), (a_2, c_2), \ldots\}$, where a_i is an answer and c_i denotes the corresponding conditions. We leverage a state generator G_S, a sequence-to-sequence (Sutskever et al. 2014) generative model to provide diverse content, and a conditional answer extraction model G_L, an extractive model to provide accurate answers. More information on the network structure and training process of G can be found in Appendix C.

In general, by leveraging structured documents for precise document extraction and supervised generator training, we ensure that we can identify the locations of potential answers and conditions within structured documents, thereby achieving the generation of high-quality conditional questions and ensuring the correct answering of questions for subsequent training.

4.2 Purturbation-Based Document Contrastive Learning

Our contrastive learning approach on structured documents involves the following steps: document perturbation, positive sample generation, and contrastive loss computation. At the training stage, the computed loss is added to the total training loss for optimization.

4.3 Document Perturbation

To perturb the original document D and obtain a perturbed document $\hat{D}$, we introduce a set of basic operations T that can be applied to the document structure. These operations, detailed in Table 2, include node masking, node deletion, node cloning, and node shuffling. Assume the original document D has a title s_0 and m nodes $(n_1, n_2, ..., n_m)$. Starting with the original document D_0, we apply k random operations from the set T to generate the perturbed document $\hat{D} = D_k$. Each operation T_i is applied as $T_i(D_j) = D_{j+1}$ for any T_i selected from T.

4.3.1 Positive Pair Generation

We get positive pairs from D and $\hat{D}$ for loss calculation. For the ith node n'_i in the perturbed document $\hat{D}$, there is a corresponding source node n_{k_i} in the original document D. We form positive pairs using tags t'_i and t_{k_i} that serves as global tokens of the nodes, which effectively convey node type and semantics despite structural changes during document perturbation.

4.3.2 Contrastive Loss Computation

We use the InfoNCE loss $\mathcal{L}_{CL}(D, \hat{D})$ for contrastive learning, defined as:

$$\mathcal{L}_{CL}(D, \hat{D}) = \sum_{i=1}^{m'} \frac{e^{\text{sim}(t'_i, t_{k_i})}}{e^{\text{sim}(t'_i, t_{k_i})} + \sum_{t^-_{k_i}} e^{\text{sim}(t'_i, t^-_{k_i})}}, \tag{1}$$

where m' is the total number of nodes in $\hat{D}$, t'_i and t_{k_i} represents a positive pair, and $t^-_{k_i}$ represents tags of any nodes other than n_{k_i} in D. sim computes the similarity between tags using the dot product of their hidden states from a neural document encoder, detailed in Sect. 4.3. The loss encourages high similarity between each t'_i and t_{k_i} while minimizing similarity with negative tags $t^-_{k_i}$.

In general, our contrastive learning approach enables self-supervised training by perturbing structured documents to construct contrastive pairs. By reinforcing node correspondence in structured documents, the method supports conditional question answering models in accurately capturing semantic connections between conditions and answers in complex contexts.

4.4 Pipeline for Answering Conditional Questions

Our proposed pipeline, illustrated in Fig. 4, comprises three steps: (1) document encoding, (2) multiple answer extraction, (3) condition determination. An auxiliary task Evidence Node Finding is added when necessary (Appendix D).

4.4.1 Document Encoding

In the document encoding process, we first construct the input sequence, which consists of special tokens "[yes]" and "[no]" document content, question, and scenario. The special tokens are used to represent affirmative/negative answers. We represent the input sequence as follows:

$$\begin{aligned}\text{Input} &= \text{“[yes][no]document : ”} + D \\ &\quad + \text{“question : ”} + q + \text{“Scenario : ”} + sc,\end{aligned}$$

where [yes] and [no] are special tokens for yes/no answers. It is passed to E returning hidden states:

$$\begin{aligned}\text{Output} &= \text{Transformer(Input)} \\ &= h_{[\text{yes}]}, h_{[\text{no}]}, ...h_{t_i}, h_{a_{ij}}, ...,\end{aligned}$$

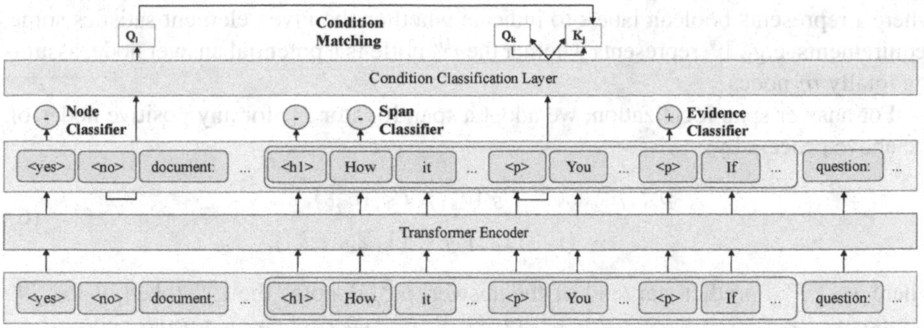

Fig. 4. Our pipeline to answer conditional questions.

where $h_{[\text{yes}]}, h_{[\text{no}]}$ are hidden states of special tokens, h_{t_i} represents hidden state of the tag of the ith node in the document, and $h_{a_{ij}}$ represents hidden state of the ith node's j^{th} token. These hidden states are used by the multi-layer perceptron (MLP) classifiers P_S, P_N, P_V to calculate probabilities for answer extraction and condition determination.

4.4.2 Multiple Answer Extraction

To simplify the answer extraction process, we assume that a node has no more than one answer, and we retain only one answer if multiple exist. Since it's rare that a node has multiple answers, this process simplifies extraction by identifying potential answer nodes and determining the answer's start and end positions within the node.

We use two classifiers: a node classifier P_N to identify answer-containing nodes (or yes/no tokens) and an answer span classifier P_S to locate the answer's position within selected nodes.

For node classification, we set:

$$\begin{aligned} p^N_{\text{yes/no}} &= P_N(h_{[\text{yes}]/[\text{no}]}), \\ p^N_i &= P_N(h_{t_i}), \end{aligned} \tag{2}$$

where p represents probabilities given by these classifiers. From the above, we can obtain yes/no answers and sentences containing extractive answers from node classification results. At training, We set a Binary Cross Entropy (BCE) loss for node classification:

$$\mathcal{L}_{\text{bool}} = \frac{\text{BCE}(p^N_{\text{yes}}, \mathbb{I}^N_{\text{yes}}) + \text{BCE}(p^N_{\text{no}}, \mathbb{I}^N_{\text{no}})}{2}, \tag{3}$$

$$\mathcal{L}_{\text{extractive}} = \frac{1}{m}\sum_{i=1}^{m} \text{BCE}(p^N_i, \mathbb{I}^N_i), \tag{4}$$

$$\mathcal{L}_{\text{N}} = \mathcal{L}_{\text{bool}} + \mathcal{L}_{\text{extractive}}, \tag{5}$$

where $\mathbb{I}$ represents boolean labels to indicate whether the given element satisfies some requirements, e.g., $\mathbb{I}_i^N$ represents whether the ith node is a potential answer node, assuming totally m nodes.

For answer span localization, we adopt a span locator P_S for any positive nodes of the above process by:

$$\begin{aligned} p_{j1}^{S_i}, p_{j2}^{S_i}, ... &= P_{S_i}(a_{j1}^A), P_{S_i}(a_{j2}^A), ..., \\ &(i \in (1,2), j \in (1,2,...,k)), \end{aligned} \tag{6}$$

where P_{S_1}, P_{S_2} predict start/end of the answer, a_{ju}^A denotes the uth token of the jth predicted node n_j^A to have an answer, and $p_{ju}^{S_i}$ are the predicted probabilities. At training, we adopt a span loss:

$$\mathcal{L}_\text{S} = \frac{1}{2k_r} \sum_{i=1}^{2} \sum_{j=1}^{k_r} \sum_{u=1}^{l_{n_j^A}} \frac{1}{l_{n_j^A}} \text{BCE}(p_{ju}^{S_i}, \mathbb{I}_{ju}^{S_i}), \tag{7}$$

where k_r represents the real count of answers and $l_{n_j^A}$ represents the number of tokens of n_j^A.

4.4.3 Condition Determination

To align with the document structure, we define that a potential condition must be a node in the document. Therefore, the condition determination process is to predict the probability of a node being the condition of an answer. To model this, we assign query vectors to answers, and key vectors to nodes:

$$\begin{aligned} h_i^Q &= W^Q \,\text{ReLU}(W^H h_i), \\ h_j^K &= W^K \,\text{ReLU}(W^H h_j), \end{aligned} \tag{8}$$

where h_i, h_j denotes the hidden state of ith answer and j^{th} sentence. W^H, W^Q, W^K are transformation matrices, h_i^Q, h_j^K denotes the query vector of ith answer and the key vector of jth sentence.

Then, we calculate on conditions:

$$p_{ij}^C = \text{sigmoid}(h_i^Q \cdot h_j^K), \tag{9}$$

where p_{ij}^C denotes the probability of jth node to be the condition of the ith answer. We adopt the following loss for training:

$$\mathcal{L}_\text{C} = \frac{1}{k_r m} \sum_{i=1}^{k_r} \sum_{j=1}^{m} \text{BCE}(p_{ij}^C, \mathbb{I}_{ij}^C). \tag{10}$$

From the above process, we can fuse the representations of answers and conditions to model the condition determination process. Therefore, our pipeline has resolved the conditional question answering task. At training, we linearly mix up all losses mentioned:

$$\mathcal{L}_\text{train} = \mathcal{L}_\text{N} + \mathcal{L}_\text{S} + \mathcal{L}_\text{C} + \mathcal{L}_\text{CL}. \tag{11}$$

5 Experiments

5.1 Datasets and Evaluation Metrics

To construct a dataset of structured documents, we scrape web pages from English websites. Our data collection process is detailed in Appendix A. To evaluate LSD's effectiveness on CQA, we conduct experiments on ConditionalQA (Sun et al. 2022a) dataset. It consists of extractive questions, yes/no questions, and not-answerable questions. The task is to find all answers with corresponding conditions on a structured document based on the given questions and scenarios.

Evaluation.

To evaluate model performance, we adopt the metrics of EM/F1 and EM/F1 with conditions, which are introduced in the ConditionalQA (Sun et al., 2022a) dataset. EM/F1 are conventional metrics, and EM/F1 with conditions jointly measures the correctness of the answer and the predicted conditions. For not answerable questions, EM and F1 are 1.0 if and only if no answer is predicted.

5.2 Results

We compared the LSD model with all of the baseline models for CQA. To evaluate the model's performance in both answering questions and providing conditions, we present results for the entire ConditionalQA dataset and its subset of conditional questions.

Table 3. The results of our experiments on the ConditionalQA dataset. "EM/F1" shows the standard EM/F1 metrics based on the answer span only. "w/ conds" shows the conditional EM/F1 metrics introduced in (Sun et al. 2022a). The results for the baseline models are taken from (Sun et al. 2022a) (Sun et al. 2022b)

	Yes/No		Extractive		Conditional		Overall	
	EM/F1	w/conds	EM/F1	w/conds	EM/F1	w/conds	EM/F1	w/conds
ETC-pipeline	63.1/63.1	47.5/47.5	8.9/17.3	6.9/14.6	39.4/41.8	2.5/3.4	35.6/39.8	26.9/30.8
DocHopper	64.9/64.9	49.1/49.1	17.8/26.7	15.5/23.6	42.0/46.4	3.1/3.8	40.6/45.2	31.9/36.0
FiD	64.2/64.2	48.0/48.0	25.2/37.8	22.5/33.4	45.2/49.7	4.7/5.8	44.4/50.8	35.0/40.6
TReasoner	**73.2/73.2**	**54.7/54.7**	34.4/48.6	30.3/43.1	51.6/56.0	12.5/14.4	57.2/63.5	**46.1/51.9**
LSD (ours)	71.6/71.6	51.6/51.6	**39.9/56.4**	**31.6/43.8**	**57.3/61.8**	**21.4/25.1**	**58.7/66.2**	45.0/50.5

5.2.1 Main Result

Table 3 shows the results on the entire conditionalQA dataset. The result indicates that:

(1) LSD outperforms all baselines in EM/F1 and conditional EM/F1 for extractive and conditional questions, demonstrating the effectiveness of our conditional question generation and contrastive learning.

Table 4. Experimental results on the subset of questions in ConditionalQA (dev) with conditional answers. Results of the baseline models are obtained from (Sun et al. 2022a) (Sun et al. 2022b). The first two models "do not provide any conditions when they achieved the best performance on the overall dataset".

	Answer (w/conds)	Conditions (P/R/F1)
ETC-pipeline	/	/
DocHopper	/	/
FiD	3.2/4.6	98.3/2.6/2.7
FiD (cond)	6.8/7.4	12.8/63.0/21.3
TReasoner	10.6/12.2	34.4/40.4/37.8
LSD (ours)	**21.4/25.1**	**69.3/39.4/50.2**

(2) LSD performs not as well as TReasoner in Yes/No questions. We speculate that its attributed to LSD inclination to provide conditional answers due to training with our question generation system (Appendix B), which is penalized by the evaluation metric in (Sun et al. 2022a).
(3) In "w/ conds" overall results, LSD performs less well than TReasoner, potentially due to TReasoner's specialized multi-hop reasoning for condition determination, which may warrant further enhancement in LSD.

5.2.2 Conditional Accuracy

To further evaluate our model's ability to provide conditions for answers, we additionally report results on the subset of conditional questions in Table 4. We evaluate the results using the "w/ conds" metric, as well as precision, recall, and F1 of retrieved conditions for conditional answers. The result shows that our method significantly outperforms the current model in providing conditions.

6 Analysis

In this section, we conduct an ablation study to investigate the impact of our document modeling designs and contrastive learning. We further analyze the question generation process by evaluating the quality of generated questions and the accuracy of generated labels.

6.1 Ablation Study

We conduct an ablation study on the dataset to investigate the impact of conditional question generation and contrastive learning. Results on the dev set of ConditionalQA in Table 5 show that both conditional question generation and contrastive learning are of importance, as removing either of them causes a significant performance drop in the final results.

Table 5. Ablation study of our model on the dev set of ConditionalQA.

	Yes/No		Extractive		Conditional		Overall	
	EM/F1	w/conds	EM/F1	w/conds	EM/F1	w/conds	EM/F1	w/conds
LSD (ours)	**71.6/71.6**	**51.6 / 51.6**	**39.9 / 56.4**	**31.6/43.8**	**57.3/61.8**	**21.4/25.1**	**58.7 / 66.2**	**45.0/50.5**
w/o CL	69.6/69.6	49.9/49.9	38.0/55.7	29.8/43.2	54.6/59.1	19.4/23.2	56.9/64.8	43.3/49.4
w/o QG	67.9/67.9	47.1/47.1	37.2/54.9	29.0/42.5	54.0/58.6	17.8/21.6	55.7/63.7	41.6/47.6

Table 6. Evaluation on our question generation method.

	ROUGE (%)	BLEU (%)
question	42.07	38.19
scenario	39.57	41.65

(a) Evaluation on state generator's output quality.

	Yes/No	Extractive	Conditional	Overall
EM/F1 (%)	79.6/79.6	51.2/67.2	69.9/73.8	67.8/75.0
w/conds (%)	50.8/50.8	38.9/51.3	33.4/35.5	47.9/53.4

(b) Evaluation on accuracy of generated labels.

6.2 State Generator's Output Quality

We use BLEU and ROUGE-L to measure the state generator's generated questions and scenarios' similarity to questions and scenarios from the evaluation dataset for question generation, QG-dev (detailed in Appendix C). The results are shown in Table 6a. Some examples are shown in Appendix E.

6.3 Label Generator's Output Accuracy

We evaluate our label generator's capability in providing accurate answers for questions given the extracted documents from QG-dev, shown in Table 6b. The result shows that the label generator can provide accurate answers given a selected context from the document.

7 Conclusion and Limitations

In this paper, we present Learning on Structured Documents (LSD), a self-supervised learning method for conditional question answering. LSD uses a conditional question generation method to leverage massive structured documents while improving conciseness, and applies contrastive learning to learn effective semantic representations from complex documents. We further propose a pipeline that could generate multiple answers and conditions to better handle the CQA task. We verify the effectiveness of the proposed method on the ConditionalQA dataset. For future work, we plan to investigate how to better generate conditional questions and improve our model's performance in providing correct answers.

Despite the effectiveness of LSD in utilizing the structure of massive unsupervised data, there are still some potential points for improvement. One issue is that the state generator is only trained on answerable questions, leading to a distribution bias that there might be unanswerable questions. In addition, our pipeline can still not handle the position where a sentence has more than one answer, which limits our model's performance for broader scenarios. We will resolve these issues in future work.

Acknowledgements. This work was supported by National Natural Science Foundation of China No. 62272467, Beijing Outstanding Young Scientist Program No. BJJWZYJH012019100020098, and Public Computing Cloud, Renmin University of China. The work was partially done at Beijing Key Laboratory of Big Data Management and Analysis Methods.

Appendix

A DATASET Curation Details

Table 7. Statistics of our scraped dataset. We present document count, average document length measured by word (Avg. w) and sentences (Avg. s), average sentence length (Avg w/s) and tag distribution (h:p:li/tr).

	UK	US	CA	Overall
count	17,881	577	12,115	30,573
Avg. w	709	179	2,538	1423
Avg. s	54	26	128	83
Avg. w/s	12.9	6.9	19.8	17.0
Tag dist.	14:45:41	38:40:22	10:40:50	12:41:57

DATASET contains a total of 30,573 documents, approximately 362MB in size (1×10^8 tokens). The statistics of our scraped dataset are shown in Table 7. The data curation process are detailed below.

A.1 Data Acquisition

To build DATASET, we scrape web pages from government websites: https://www.gov.uk, https://www.ca.gov, and https://www.usa.gov, as they have professional English material and have a massive number of well-structured documents, such as policies, regulations, and proposals.

A.2 Data Filtering

Page Category Filtering. We use automated web scraping to categorize pages on the selected government websites based on URL. We retaine only pages related to policy documents, regulatory provisions, administrative guidelines, etc.

Content Validity Check. We further examined the retained pages to exclude invalid, redundant, or duplicate documents.

A.3 Data Cleaning

Tag Normalization. We use automated cleaning and standardization tools to fix irregular HTML tags and attributes in documents, close unclosed tags, and standardize attribute values.

Irrelevant Content Removal. We remove nodes without text, advertisements, hyperlinks, images, videos, and other irrelevant information, retaining textual content for better model understanding of document structure and content.

Node Filtering. We filtere nodes containing document content, i.e., $< h1 >$ to $< h6 >$ (headings), $< p >$ (paragraphs), $< li >$ (list items), $< tr >$ (table rows), etc.

DOM Tree Construction. We use an HTML parser to parse the filtered nodes and construct the Document Object Model (DOM) tree following the method proposed in Sect. 3.

A.4 Dataset Splitting

We split the processed dataset into training and validation sets for model training and performance evaluation with a ratio of 4:1.

B Question Generation Details

Table 8. Statistics of our generated dataset and ConditionalQA dataset in comparison. We present the percentage of every type of questions, average answer count, condition count, condition count, context length and document length (by word) if applicable.

Our Dataset	Yes/No	Extractive	Conditional
Percentage	52.4	47.5	45.1
Avg. answer	1.36	1.46	1.86
Avg. condition	0.89	1.04	2.14
Avg. context	292	350	413
Avg. document	1,467	1,260	1,525
ConditionalQA	Yes/No	Extractive	Conditional
Percentage	51.1	44.6	23.4
Avg. document		1358	

We present the statistics to show our question generation module's behavior on the scraped augmentation corpus. We randomly generate 1,000 samples with the QG module and present results in Table 8.

C Implementation Details

C.1 Network Structure and Setup

For the conditional question generator G: we adopt BART[1] (Lewis et al. 2020), a seq-to-seq transformer for state generator G_S; for label generator G_L, we adopt the same setting of M, as detailed below.

For conditional question answering model M: We adopt Longformer[2] (Beltagy et al. 2020), a Transformer designed for long complex context, for the neural document encoder E; for MLP classifiers P_N, P_S, P_V, we set num_layers=2 and dim_hidden_states=768; for transformation matrices, we set $\dim(W_H) = (3072, 768)$ and $\dim(W^Q) = \mathrm{Dim}(W^K) = (768, 3072)$.

To setup Longformer, we set the HTML tags as its global tokens. For extremely long documents beyond length limit, we chunk them into pieces with overlap and aggregate predicted answers from these pieces.

C.2 Training Conditional Question Generator

To train conditional question generator G, we use 80% data of the ConditionalQA train set, named QG-train, and the rest for evaluation, named QG-dev. We take the descendants and ancestors of all given evidence sentences from the document for extraction. We train G on QG-train for 10 epochs, adopting the Adam (Kingma and Ba 2015) optimizer, setting learning rate to 3e-5 and batch size to 32.

C.3 Training Conditional Question Answerer

Training conditional question answering model M consists of two stages. In the self-supervised stage, we train M on our scraped dataset for 20 epochs, with a newly generated question and answer data for every epoch. We use the LAMB (You et al. 2020) optimizer for this stage, with the learning rate set to 1e-4 and the batch size set to 256. In the supervised stage, we adopt the Adam (Kingma and Ba 2015) optimizer, setting the learning rate to 3e-5 and batch size to 32, and trained on ConditionalQA train set for 50 epochs. For both stages of training, we adopt a warm-up episode of 10% proportion with linear learning rate decay. For document chunking, We set the maximum of document length to 2000 to fit into the GPU memory, with an overlap of 100 tokens. For contrastive learning, we adopt k=5.

D Auxiliary Task: Evidence Node Finding

To improve model reasoning for yes/no questions, we introduce an auxiliary task to identify evidence nodes supporting the answer. The task is jointly trained with others and is active when datasets provide evidence information. We use an evidence classifier P_V for this task and define:

[1] https://huggingface.co/facebook/bart-large.

[2] https://huggingface.co/allenai/longformer-large-4096.

$$p_i^V = P_V(\mathrm{h}_{\mathrm{t}_\mathrm{i}}), \tag{12}$$

$$\mathcal{L}_\mathrm{E} = \frac{1}{m}\sum_{i=1}^{m} \mathrm{BCE}(p_i^V, \mathbb{I}_i^V), \tag{13}$$

When the evidence node finding task is activated, the training loss turns to:

$$\mathcal{L}_\mathrm{train} = \mathcal{L}_\mathrm{N} + \mathcal{L}_\mathrm{S} + \mathcal{L}_\mathrm{C} + \mathcal{L}_\mathrm{CL} + \mathcal{L}_\mathrm{E}. \tag{14}$$

E Case Studies for Question Generation

In this section, we provide 3 generated questions and the model-generated questions and conditional answers.

Example 1

Context:

⟨title⟩Funding Opportunities⟨/title⟩
⟨h1⟩Funding Opportunities⟨/h1⟩
⟨h2⟩Current Opportunities⟨/h2⟩
⟨p⟩Winter Collaborative Networks⟨/p⟩
⟨li⟩GC Key access⟨/li⟩
⟨li⟩SecureKey Concierge (Banking Credential) access⟨/li⟩
⟨li⟩Personal Access Code (PAC) problems or EI Access Code (AC) problems⟨/li⟩
⟨li⟩Social Insurance Number (SIN) validation problems⟨/li⟩
⟨li⟩Other login error not in this list⟨/li⟩

Generated Contents:

Question:

What type of access is required for the Winter Collaborative Networks funding opportunity?

Scenario:

I am interested in applying for the Winter Collaborative Networks funding opportunity, but I am unsure of what type of access is required.

Answers and Conditions:

[GC Key access, None],
[SecureKey Concierge (Banking Credential) access, None],
[Personal Access Code (PAC) problems or EI Access Code (AC) problems, None],
[Social Insurance Number (SIN) validation problems, None],
[Other login error not in this list, None]

Example 2, 3

Context:

⟨title⟩Claim Capital Allownces⟨/title⟩
⟨h1⟩What you can claim on⟨/h1⟩

⟨p⟩You can claim capital allowances on items that you keep to use in your business - these are known as ‘plant and machinery’.⟨/p⟩

⟨p⟩In most cases you can deduct the full cost of these items from your profits before tax using annual investment allowance (AIA).⟨/p⟩

⟨p⟩If youâĂŹre a sole trader or partnership and have an income of £150,000 or less a year, you may be able to use a simpler system called cash basis instead.⟨/p⟩

⟨h2⟩What does not count as plant and machinery⟨/h2⟩

⟨p⟩You cannot claim plant and machinery allowances on:⟨/p⟩

⟨li⟩things you lease (unless you have a hire purchase contract or long funding lease) - you must own them⟨/li⟩

⟨li⟩items used only for business entertainment, for example a yacht or karaoke machine⟨/li⟩

⟨li⟩land⟨/li⟩

⟨li⟩structures, for example bridges, roads, docks⟨/li⟩

⟨li⟩buildings, including doors, gates, shutters, mains water and gas systems⟨/li⟩

⟨p⟩You may be able to claim structures and buildings allowance on structures and buildings.⟨/p⟩

⟨h2⟩What counts as plant and machinery⟨/h2⟩

⟨p⟩Plant and machinery includes:⟨/p⟩

⟨li⟩items that you keep to use in your business, including cars⟨/li⟩

⟨li⟩costs of demolishing plant and machinery⟨/li⟩

⟨li⟩parts of a building considered integral, known as ‘integral features’⟨/li⟩

⟨li⟩some fixtures, for example, fitted kitchens or bathroom suites⟨/li⟩

⟨li⟩alterations to a building to install plant and machinery - this does not include repairs⟨/li⟩

⟨p⟩Claim repairs as business expenses if youâĂŹre a sole trader or partnership - deduct from your profits as a business cost if youâĂŹre a limited company.⟨/p⟩

⟨h3⟩Integral features⟨/h3⟩

⟨p⟩Integral features are:⟨/p⟩

⟨li⟩lifts, escalators and moving walkways⟨/li⟩

⟨li⟩space and water heating systems⟨/li⟩

⟨li⟩air-conditioning and air cooling systems⟨/li⟩

⟨li⟩hot and cold water systems (but not toilet and kitchen facilities)⟨/li⟩

⟨li⟩electrical systems, including lighting systems⟨/li⟩

⟨li⟩external solar shading⟨/li⟩

⟨h3⟩Fixtures⟨/h3⟩

⟨p⟩You can claim for fixtures, for example:⟨/p⟩

⟨li⟩fitted kitchens⟨/li⟩

⟨li⟩bathroom suites⟨/li⟩

⟨li⟩fire alarm and CCTV systems⟨/li⟩

⟨p⟩You can claim if you rent or own the building, but only the person who bought the item can claim.⟨/p⟩

⟨p⟩When you buy a building from a previous business owner you can only claim for integral features and fixtures that they claimed for.⟨/p⟩

⟨p⟩You must agree on the value of the fixtures with the seller. If you do not you cannot claim for them. Agreeing the value also means the person selling the assets can account correctly for them.⟨/p⟩
⟨h2⟩If you let residential property⟨/h2⟩
⟨p⟩You can only claim for items to be used in a residential property if either:⟨/p⟩
⟨li⟩you run a furnished holiday lettings business⟨/li⟩
⟨li⟩the item is to be used in the common parts of a residential building, for example, a table in the hallway of a block of flats⟨/li⟩
⟨h2⟩Care workers⟨/h2⟩
⟨p⟩There are special rules if you run a care business.⟨/p⟩

Generated Contents:
Question:
Can I claim capital allowances on a yacht used for entertaining clients?

Scenario:
I am a business owner and I want to purchase a yacht to entertain clients. I want to know if they can claim capital allowances on it.

Answers and Conditions:
[No, None]

Question:
Can I claim capital allowances on the commercial building I purchased for my business?

Scenario:
I am a business owner and I recently purchased a commercial building to use as a location for my business.

Answers and Conditions:
[No, [⟨p⟩You cannot claim plant and machinery allowances on:⟨/p⟩, ⟨li⟩buildings, including doors, gates, shutters, mains water, and gas systems⟨/li⟩]]
[Yes, ⟨p⟩You may be able to claim structures and buildings allowance on structures and buildings.⟨/p⟩]

References

Ainslie, J., et al.: ETC: encoding long and structured inputs in transformers. In: Webber, B., Cohn, T., He, Y., Liu, Y. (eds.) Proceedings of the 2020 Conference on Empirical Methods in Natural Language Processing, EMNLP 2020, Online, 16–20 November 2020, pp. 268–284. Association for Computational Linguistics (2020)

Beltagy, I., Peters, M.E., Cohan, A.: Longformer: The long-document transformer (2020). CoRR, abs/2004.05150

Brown, T.B., et al.: Language models are few-shot learners. In: Larochelle, H., Ranzato, M.A., Hadsell, R., Balcan, M.F., Lin, H.T. (eds.) Advances in Neural Information Processing Systems 33: Annual Conference on Neural Information Processing Systems 2020, NeurIPS 2020, 6–12 December 2020, virtual (2020)
Chen, Y., Wu, L., Zaki, M.J.: Natural question generation with reinforcement learning based graph-to-sequence model (2019). CoRR, abs/1910.08832
Clark, K., Luong, M.T., Le, Q.V., Manning, C.D.: ELECTRA: pre-training text encoders as discriminators rather than generators. In: ICLR (2020)
Conneau, A., et al.: Unsupervised cross-lingual representation learning at scale. In: Jurafsky, D., Chai, J., Schluter, N., Tetreault, J.R. (eds.) Proceedings of the 58th Annual Meeting of the Association for Computational Linguistics, ACL 2020, Online, 5–10 July 2020, pp. 8440–8451. Association for Computational Linguistics (2020)
Cui, W., Xiao, Y., Wang, H., Song, Y., Hwang, S., Wang, W.: KBQA: learning question answering over QA corpora and knowledge bases. Proc. VLDB Endow. **10**(5), 565–576 (2017)
Devlin, J., Chang, M.W., Lee, K., Toutanova, K.: BERT: pre-training of deep bidirectional transformers for language understanding. In: Burstein, J., Doran, C., Solorio, T. (eds.) Proceedings of the 2019 Conference of the North American Chapter of the Association for Computational Linguistics: Human Language Technologies, NAACL-HLT 2019, Minneapolis, MN, USA, 2–7 June 2019, vol. 1 (Long and Short Papers), pp. 4171–4186. Association for Computational Linguistics (2019)
Gao, T., Yao, X., Chen, D.: Simcse: simple contrastive learning of sentence embeddings. In: Moens, M.F., Huang, X., Specia, L., Yih, S.W. (eds.) Proceedings of the 2021 Conference on Empirical Methods in Natural Language Processing, EMNLP 2021, Virtual Event/Punta Cana, Dominican Republic, 7–11 November 2021, pp. 6894–6910. Association for Computational Linguistics (2021)
Guo, Y., et al.: Webformer: pre-training with web pages for information retrieval. In: Proceedings of the 45th International ACM SIGIR Conference on Research and Development in Information Retrieval, SIGIR 2022, New York, NY, USA, pp. 1502–1512. Association for Computing Machinery (2022)
Izacard, G., Grave, E.: Leveraging passage retrieval with generative models for open domain question answering. In: Merlo, P., Tiedemann, J., Tsarfaty, R. (eds.) Proceedings of the 16th Conference of the European Chapter of the Association for Computational Linguistics: Main Volume, EACL 2021, Online, 19–23 April 2021, pp. 874–880. Association for Computational Linguistics (2021)
Karpukhin, V., et al.: Dense passage retrieval for open-domain question answering. In: Webber, B., Cohn, T., He, Y., Liu, Y. (eds.) Proceedings of the 2020 Conference on Empirical Methods in Natural Language Processing, EMNLP 2020, Online, 16–20 November 2020, pp. 6769–6781. Association for Computational Linguistics (2020)
Kingma, D.P., Ba, J.: Adam: a method for stochastic optimization. In: Bengio, Y., LeCun, Y. (eds.) 3rd International Conference on Learning Representations, ICLR 2015, San Diego, CA, USA, 7–9 May 2015, Conference Track Proceedings (2015)
Kwiatkowski, T., et al.: Natural questions: a benchmark for question answering research. Trans. Assoc. Comput. Linguist. **7**, 452–466 (2019)
Lample, G., Conneau, A., Denoyer, L., Ranzato, M.: Unsupervised machine translation using monolingual corpora only. In: 6th International Conference on Learning Representations, ICLR 2018, Vancouver, BC, Canada, 30 April–3 May 2018, Conference Track Proceedings. OpenReview.net (2018)
Le Berre, G., Cerisara, C., Langlais, P., Lapalme, G.: Unsupervised multiple-choice question generation for out-of-domain Q&A fine-tuning. In: Proceedings of the 60th Annual Meeting of the Association for Computational Linguistics, Dublin, Ireland, May 2022, vol. 2: Short Papers, pp. 732–738. Association for Computational Linguistics (2022)

Lewis, M., et al.: BART: denoising sequence-to-sequence pre-training for natural language generation, translation, and comprehension. In: Jurafsky, D., Chai, J., Schluter, N., Tetreault, J.R. (eds.) Proceedings of the 58th Annual Meeting of the Association for Computational Linguistics, ACL 2020, Online, 5–10 July 2020, pp. 7871–7880. Association for Computational Linguistics (2020)

Liu, Y., et al.: Roberta: a robustly optimized bert pretraining approach (2019). CoRR, abs/1907.11692

Sun, H., Cohen, W.W., Salakhutdinov, R.: End-to-end multihop retrieval for compositional question answering over long documents (2021). CoRR, abs/2106.00200

Sun, H., Cohen, W.W., Salakhutdinov, R.: Conditionalqa: a complex reading comprehension dataset with conditional answers. In: Muresan, S., Nakov, P., Villavicencio, A. (eds.) Proceedings of the 60th Annual Meeting of the Association for Computational Linguistics, ACL 2022, Dublin, Ireland, 22–27 May 2022, vol. 1: Long Papers, pp. 3627–3637. Association for Computational Linguistics (2022a)

Sun, H., Cohen, W.W., Salakhutdinov, R.: Reasoning over logically interacted conditions for question answering (2022b). CoRR, abs/2205.12898

Sutskever, I., Vinyals, O., Le, Q.V.: Sequence to sequence learning with neural networks. In: Ghahramani, Z., Welling, M., Cortes, C., Lawrence, N.D., Weinberger, K.Q. (eds.) Advances in Neural Information Processing Systems 27: Annual Conference on Neural Information Processing Systems 2014, Montreal, Quebec, Canada, 8–13 December 2014, pp. 3104–3112 (2014)

Yang, Z., et al.: Hotpotqa: a dataset for diverse, explainable multi-hop question answering. In: Riloff, E., Chiang, D., Hockenmaier, J., Tsujii, J. (eds.) Proceedings of the 2018 Conference on Empirical Methods in Natural Language Processing, Brussels, Belgium, 31 October–4 November 2018, pp. 2369–2380. Association for Computational Linguistics (2018)

Yang, N., Wei, F., Jiao, B., Jiang, D., Yang, L.: xMoCo: cross momentum contrastive learning for open-domain question answering. In: Proceedings of the 59th Annual Meeting of the Association for Computational Linguistics and the 11th International Joint Conference on Natural Language Processing, Online, August, vol. 1: Long Papers), pp. 6120–6129. Association for Computational Linguistics (2021)

You, Y., et al.: Large batch optimization for deep learning: training BERT in 76 minutes. In: 8th International Conference on Learning Representations, ICLR 2020, Addis Ababa, Ethiopia, 26–30 April 2020. OpenReview.net (2020)

Overcoming Language Priors with Counterfactual Inference for Visual Question Answering

Zhibo Ren, Huizhen Wang(✉), Muhua Zhu, Yichao Wang, Tong Xiao, and Jingbo Zhu

NLP Lab, School of Computer Science and Engineering, Northeastern University, Shenyang, China
rzb1998@qq.com, wanghuizhen@mail.neu.edu.cn

Abstract. Recent years have seen a lot of efforts in attacking the issue of language priors in the field of Visual Question Answering (VQA). Among the extensive efforts, causal inference is regarded as a promising direction to mitigate language bias by weakening the direct causal effect of questions on answers. In this paper, we follow the same direction and attack the issue of language priors by incorporating counterfactual data. Moreover, we propose a two-stage training strategy which is deemed to make better use of counterfactual data. Experiments on the widely used benchmark VQA-CP v2 demonstrate the effectiveness of the proposed approach, which improves the baseline by 21.21% and outperforms most of the previous systems.

Keywords: Visual Question Answering · Language Priors · Counterfactual Inference

1 Introduction

As an AI-complete task to answer questions about visual content, Visual Question Answering (VQA) has seen surging interest in recent years. The task is thought to be extremely challenging since a VQA system requires the capability of visual and language understanding and the capability of multi-modal reasoning. Recent researches in this field have paid increasing attention to the issue of language priors, aka language bias [2]. The issue of language priors is caused by spurious correlation between the question pattern and the answer. See the example in Fig. 1, "yellow" is the most likely answer to the question "what color are the bananas" in the training data. So a simple solution to answering the question is to give the answer "yellow" with no reference to visual content. Such a short cut can achieve an accuracy of 54.5% for the question.

To overcome language priors in VQA, previous works generally resort to data augmentation. In this direction, visual and textual explanations can be used as the data for augmentation [10,20]. Besides, counterfactual training samples are

M. Sun et al. (Eds.): CCL 2023, LNAI 14232, pp. 58–71, 2023.
https://doi.org/10.1007/978-981-99-6207-5_4

also regarded as a valuable source for the purpose [8,12,17,28]. In the direction of causal effect for VQA, more recent work is counterfactual VQA that focuses on the inference instead of training phase [18], though, we still think of counterfactual data augmentation as an efficient and effective way to solve the issue of language priors. So in this paper we first design novel causal graphs specifically for the task of VQA, and then use the causal graphs to guide the generation of counterfactual data. Finally, to make better use of counterfactual data, we propose a two-stage training strategy. We evaluate the proposed approach on the widely used benchmark VQA-CP v2. Extensive experiments demonstrate the effectiveness of the approach, which improves over the baseline by 21.21% and outperforms most of previous systems. Moreover, to evaluate the generalization ability of the approach, we also experiment with VQA v2 and find that our approach achieves the best performance on the dataset.

The contributions of the paper are as follows.

- For the task of counterfactual VQA, we design a novel causal graph and methods to construct counterfactual data.
- Our approach achieves significant improvements over the baseline and is one of the best-performing systems on the benchmarks.

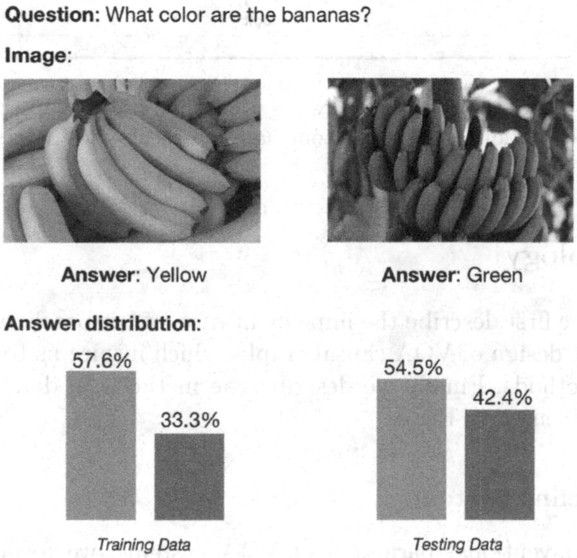

Fig. 1. An example from VQA v2 which is used to illustrate 1) the task of visual question answering, and 2) the issue of language priors. (Color figure online)

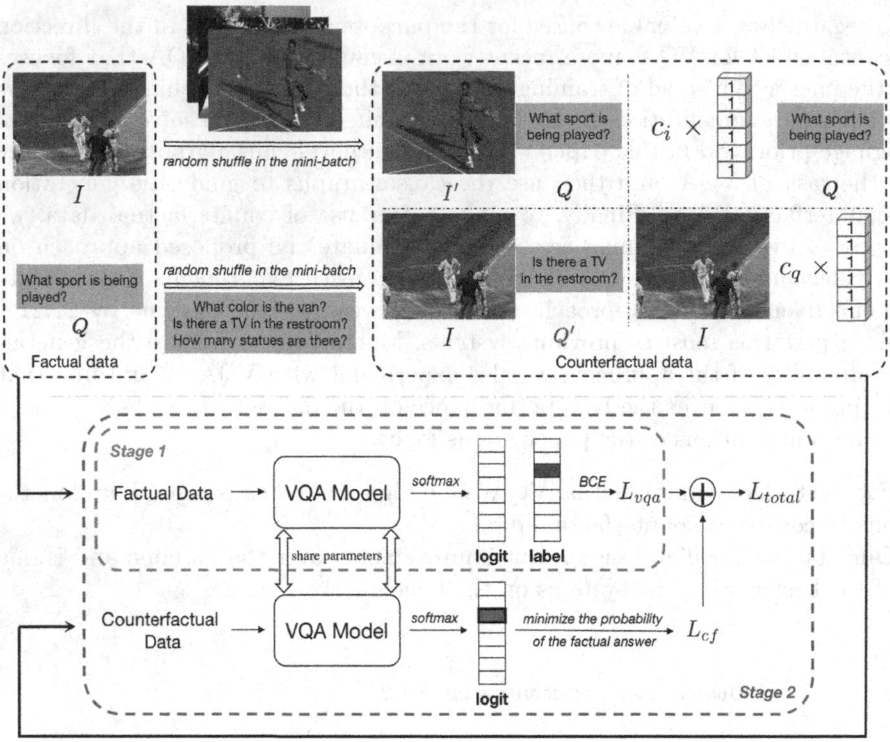

Fig. 2. Illustration of our approach, where the upper half presents the process of counterfactual data generation and the bottom half represents the process of two-stage training.

2 Methodology

In this section, we first describe the implementation of our baseline system. Then we introduce the design of VQA causal graphs which inspire us to come up with the proposed methods. Finally we describe the methods in detail. The system framework is presented in Fig. 2.

2.1 The Baseline System

Following the conventional paradigm of VQA systems, we formalize the task as a multi-class classification problem. In general, a VQA dataset consists of N instances which are tuples of an image, a textual question, and the corresponding answer, denoted as $D = \{I_i, Q_i, A_i\}_{i=1}^{N}$. VQA models take an image-question pair (I, Q) as input, and predict an answer A by following

$$A^* = \arg\max_{A \in \mathcal{A}} P(A|I_i, Q_i), \tag{1}$$

where $P(A|I_i, Q_i)$ can be any model-based functions that map (I, Q) to produce a distribution over the answer space $\mathcal{A}$. Conventional VQA systems are generally composed of three components:

- **Feature Extraction**, which extracts the features of images and question as visual representation and text representation, respectively.
- **Multimodal Feature Fusion**, which fuses image and text features into the same vector space.
- **Answer Prediction**, which produces the answer prediction through a classifier.

We follow [4] to implement our baseline system. The baseline system pays special attention to feature extraction by integrating a combined bottom-up and top-down attention mechanism to enable attention calculation at the fine-grained level of objects. Within the approach, the bottom-up attention proposes image regions while the top-down mechanism determines feature weightings.

2.2 Causal Graph for VQA

To better understand the casual graphs we propose for the VQA task, we need to revisit the procedure of VQA data annotation. Specifically, when curating a dataset, annotators are required to produce a question regarding visual content of a presented image and give a correct answer. Therefore, we can construct a casual graph to exhibit the relationship between three variables: the image I, the question Q, and the answer A. Figure 3(a) illustrates the casual graph, where I indirectly and directly affects A through $I \rightarrow Q \rightarrow A$ and $I \rightarrow A$, respectively. In the chain of $I \rightarrow Q \rightarrow A$, the question Q acts as a mediator to influence A. If we control the mediator Q, the causal association between I and A in the chain $I \rightarrow Q \rightarrow A$ will be blocked, that is, when the association between I and A is not well learned through $I \rightarrow A$ (the middle and right graph in Fig. 3(a)), the model will give the answer based on the question only but ignore the content of the image. This phenomenon corresponds exactly to the language prior problem in VQA. Therefore, we propose to introduce counterfactual data to weaken the effect that comes from the chain $I \rightarrow Q \rightarrow A$, which is shown in Fig. 3(b).

2.3 Automatic Generation of Counterfactual Data

We propose two methods to construct counterfactual data, corresponding to multimodal counterfactual data and unimodal counterfactual data, respectively.

Multimodal Counterfactual Data. First of all, we realize that the issue of language priors is caused by the chain $I \rightarrow Q \rightarrow A$, so we need to mitigate the influence of this branch on the selection of the answer. Inspired by [28], for each pair(I_i, Q_i) in factual data, we construct counterfactual data (I'_i, Q_i) by shuffling image I_i in the same mini-batch, such that the image and the question in counterfactual data are mismatched. The causal graph of counterfactual image data is shown in Fig. 4(a). Following the same idea, we also propose to construct

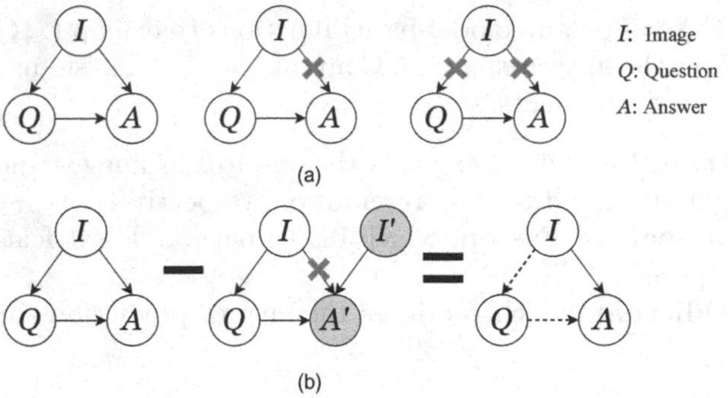

Fig. 3. (a) Casual graph for VQA. (b) Overcome language priors with counterfactual data.

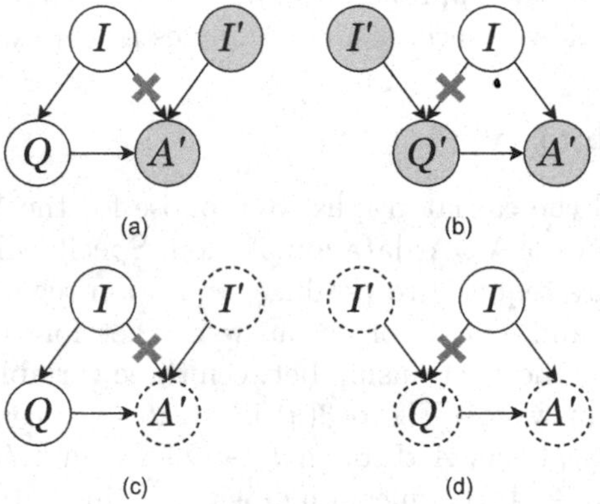

Fig. 4. Causal graph demonstrating the methods for generating counterfactual data.

counterfactual question data by shuffling questions in the same mini-batch. The corresponding causal graph is illustrated in Fig. 4(b). Subsequent experiments show that incorporation of multimodal counterfactual question data is also beneficial to the performance, which demonstrates the presence of vision bias in the VQA task, a phenomenon not often mentioned before.

It is worth noting that we do not resort to any extra human annotations during the construction of the multimodal counterfactual data, but simply make use of the factual data itself. The underlying idea is quite different from the methods proposed in previous works for the construction of counterfactual data [8,12,17].

Unimodal Counterfactual Data. We further consider to construct unimodal counterfactual data. We hope the model to accept information from only one modality as input. Concretely, we construct unimodal counterfactual data by passing only images$(I_i, \emptyset)$ or questions$(\emptyset, Q_i)$ into the model, which the causal graph is illustrated in Fig. 4(c)(d). However, the model cannot handle the case where the input is empty during implementation, so we choose to use a learnable

Table 1. Comparison with the state-of-the-art methods on the VQA-CP v2 test set and VQA v2 validation set. The evaluation metric is accuracy, and the backbone of all models is UpDn. Overall best scores are **bold** and the second best of scores are underlined.

Systems	VQA-CP v2 test(%)				VQA v2 val(%)			
	All	Y/N	Num	Other	All	Y/N	Num	Other
UpDn	39.74	42.27	11.93	46.05	63.48	81.18	42.14	<u>55.66</u>
GVQA	31.3	57.99	13.68	22.14	48.24	72.03	31.17	34.65
SAN	24.96	38.35	11.14	21.74	52.41	70.06	39.28	47.84
Systems without counterfactual inference								
DLR	48.87	70.99	18.72	45.57	57.96	76.82	39.33	48.54
VGQE	48.75	–	–	–	<u>64.04</u>	–	–	–
AdvReg	41.17	65.49	15.48	35.48	62.75	79.84	42.35	55.16
RUBi	44.23	67.05	17.48	39.61	–	–	–	–
LMH	52.01	72.58	31.12	46.97	56.35	65.06	37.63	54.69
CVL	42.12	45.72	12.45	48.34	–	–	–	–
Unshuffling	42.39	47.72	14.43	47.24	61.08	78.32	42.16	52.81
RandImg	55.37	83.89	41.6	44.2	57.24	76.53	33.87	48.57
SSL	57.59	86.53	29.87	<u>50.03</u>	<u>63.73</u>	–	–	–
Systems with counterfactual inference								
CSS	58.95	84.37	49.42	48.21	59.91	73.25	39.77	55.11
CSS+CL	59.18	86.99	<u>49.89</u>	47.16	57.29	67.29	38.40	54.71
CF-VQA	53.55	**91.15**	13.03	44.97	63.54	**82.51**	<u>43.96</u>	54.30
MUTANT	**61.72**	<u>88.90</u>	49.68	**50.78**	62.56	82.07	42.52	53.28
This Paper	<u>60.95</u>	87.95	**50.41**	49.70	**64.11**	<u>82.23</u>	**44.09**	**56.75**

parameter c multiplied by a matrix whose elements are all ones and the shape is same as image representation or text representation as the null modal information. Finally, the unimodal counterfactual data can be represented as (I_i, c_q) and (c_i, Q_i).

2.4 Two-Stage Training Strategy

In the real world, we can only give the right answer when we see the right factual image-question pair. Conversely, we often cannot give the correct answer when we see a counterfactual image-question pair. But usually in this case the correct answer will change and the previously correct answer will often become the wrong answer, which is the only thing we know for sure. We hope to solve language prior problems by using counterfactual image data in the manner shown in Fig. 3(b). Specifically, when the VQA model takes the counterfactual image data as input, we construct the loss function by minimizing the probability of the ground truth answer:

$$\begin{aligned} P(A'|I_i', Q_i) &= softmax(F(I_i', Q_i)) \\ L_{mm\_cf\_i} &= P(A'|I_i', Q_i)[k] \end{aligned} \tag{2}$$

where k denotes the index of the ground truth in the answer set A. For the counterfactual question data, the corresponding loss function is similar to Eq. (2): , which can be defined as:

$$\begin{aligned} P(A'|I_i, Q_i') &= softmax(F(I_i, Q_i')) \\ L_{mm\_cf\_q} &= P(A'|I_i, Q_i')[k] \end{aligned} \tag{3}$$

Finally, the loss of the multimodal counterfactual data is defined as:

$$L_{mm\_cf} = \lambda_i^{mm} L_{mm\_cf\_i} + \lambda_q^{mm} L_{mm\_cf\_q}, \tag{4}$$

where λ_i and λ_q are hyperparameters.

Similar to multimodal counterfactual data, the unimodal counterfactual loss function can be defined as:

$$\begin{aligned} P(A'|c_i, Q_i) &= softmax(F(c_i, Q_i)) \\ L_{um\_cf\_i} &= P(A'|c_i, Q_i)[k] \end{aligned} \tag{5}$$

$$\begin{aligned} P(A'|I_i, c_q) &= softmax(F(I_i, c_q)) \\ L_{um\_cf\_q} &= P(A'|I_i, c_q)[k] \end{aligned} \tag{6}$$

The total loss of unimodal counterfactual data is defined as:

$$L_{um\_cf} = \lambda_i^{um} L_{um\_cf\_i} + \lambda_q^{um} L_{um\_cf\_q} \tag{7}$$

Simply combining counterfactual and factual data together as training data may render these two types of data interfere with each other. For this reason, we adopt a two-stage training strategy, which utilize factual data and the normal VQA loss function for training in the first stage and utilize counterfactual data and counterfactual loss functions in the second stage. are introduced on top of the first stage to alleviate the problem of the language priors of the VQA model:

$$L_{total} = L_{vqa} + \lambda^{mm} L_{mm\_cf} + \lambda^{um} L_{um\_cf} \tag{8}$$

3 Experiments

3.1 Datasets and Comparative Systems

Datasets. We conducted extensive experiments on the most widely used benchmark VQA-CP v2 [2] adopting the standard evaluation metric. Because the dataset of VQA v2 [13] has the language prior problem, [2] reorganized the data splitting of VQA v2 to construct VQA-CP v2 where answers have different distributions in the training and validation set. Thus, VQA-CP v2 is an appropriate benchmark for evaluating the generalization ability of VQA models. Briefly, the training set of VQA-CP v2 contains approximately 121k images and 245k questions, and the test set consists of approximately 98k images and 220k questions.

Comparative Systems. System participating in the comparison against our approach can be categorized into two groups: 1) systems without counterfactual inference, including **DLR** [14], **VGQE** [16], **AdvReg** [21], **RUBi** [7], **LMH** [9], **Unshuffling** [23], **RandImg** [24], **SSL** [28], and 2) systems with counterfactual inference, including **CF-VQA** [18], **CSS** [8], **CL** [17], and **MUTANT** [12].

3.2 Implementation Details

As mentioned above, our VQA system builds on the base of UpDn [4]. Following previous researches, we use the Faster-RCNN [22] model previously trained by [4] to extract image features. We extract 36 region features for each image and the dimension of each region feature is set to 2048. Moreover, each question is padded so as to have the same length of 14 tokens, and each token in questions is encoded by the pretrained language model BERT [11] with a dimension of 768. Then word embeddings are fed into GRUs to obtain the question representation with a dimension of 1280. Inspired by SSL [28], we also add a BatchNorm layer before the MLP classifier of UpDn. We train our model for 25 epochs every time. We adopt the Adam optimizer to update model parameters, whose learning rate is set to 0.001 and the learning rate decreases by half every 5 epochs after 10 epochs. The batch size is set to 256. We implement our system using PyTorch, and we train our model with one Nvidia 2080Ti card.

3.3 Main Experimental Results

Table 1 presents the comparison results between our approach and previous systems on both VQA-CP v2. From the results, we can see that our approach significantly improves the baseline UpDn by +21.21% on VQA-CP v2. The improvement demonstrates the effectiveness of our approach on mitigating the issue of language prior. Moreover, our approach outperforms all the comparative systems on VQA-CP v2 except for MUTANT which requires additional human annotations of key objects in images. Moreover, we can see our approach achieves stable performance on VQA v2 with the best performance over all the previous systems. To demonstrate the generality of our approach, we also experiment with VQA v2, and the results show that our approach achieves the best performance among all the participating systems.

3.4 Experiment Analysis

Impact of Counterfactual Data Combination
We proposed several types of counterfactual data, so we conducted a study on the effect of each type of counterfactual data and the effect of their combinations. From the results shown in Table 2, we have the following observations:

- Both counterfactual image data (I_i', Q_i) and counterfactual question data (I_i, Q_i') are able to improve the performance. The use of counterfactual image data achieves significant improvements, while the counterfactual question data achieves relatively limited improvements. This suggests that the main cause of the language prior problem is the superficial correlation between questions and answers, but there are also some vision bias that cannot be ignored.
- Both multimodal counterfactual data and unimodal counterfactual data can improve the model performance, which demonstrates that these data can prompt the generalization ability of model.

Table 2. Impact of different types of counterfactual data, evaluated on VQA-CP v2 test set. MM refers to multimodal counterfactual data and UM refers to unimodal counterfactual data, respectively

	Counterfactual Data				Acc.
	(I_i', Q_i)	(I_i, Q_i')	(c_i, Q_i)	(I_i, c_q)	
	-				41.52
MM	✔	–	–	–	57.59
	–	✔	–	–	41.87
	✔	✔	–	–	**59.05**
UM	–	–	✔	–	41.83
	–	–	–	✔	41.70
	–	–	✔	✔	**41.88**
Total	✔	✔	✔	✔	**60.95**

In summary, the above experimental results verify the validity of the counterfactual data.

Impact of Varying Settings of λ
As we can see from the results in Table 2, different types of counterfactual data have diverse effect on the performance. So we need to evaluate the effect of varying settings of the hyperparameters λ in the loss functions. We divide λ into three groups for comparison and conducted extensive experiments with different λ values. From results in Table 3, we can observe that the model gets the best performance when $\lambda_i^{mm} : \lambda_q^{mm}$ is 1:0.7, $\lambda_i^{um} : \lambda_q^{um}$ is 1:1, and $\lambda^{mm} : \lambda^{um}$ is 1:1.

Impact of Varying Starting Points of the Second Stage Training
In the process of two-stage training, different starting points of the second stage tend to achieve different results. So we conducted an experiment to show the effect of varying starting points. As can be seen in Fig. 5, starting the training on counterfactual data too early or too late will bring negative effect on the performance. Empirically, we find the second stage can start its training at the 12th epoch.

Impact of Different Backbones
We also conducted experiments on another backbones SAN [26] to verify that our approach is model agnostic. From the results in Table 4, we can observe that our approach can achieve significant improvements no matter what backbone is used.

4 Related Work

Visual Question Answering Visual Question Answering aims to answer the question according to the given image, which involves both natural language processing and computer vision techniques. At present, the dominant methods are attention-based models. [4,26,27] use attentions mechanisms to capture the alignment between images and natural language in order to learn the

Table 3. Impact of different ratio between λ. We divide λ into three groups(λ_i^{mm} : λ_q^{mm}), (λ_i^{um} : λ_q^{um}),(λ^{mm} : λ^{um}) according to the counterfactual data used, with the latter group realized on the best results of the previous group's experiment. The evaluation metric is accuracy(%).

λ	Ratio	VQA-CP v2 test(%)
λ_i^{mm}:λ_q^{mm}	1:0.5	58.06
	1:0.7	**59.46**
	1:1	59.32
	1:2	59.15
	1:3	58.76
λ_i^{um}:λ_q^{um}	1:0.5	60.03
	1:0.7	60.29
	1:1	**60.34**
	1:2	59.51
	1:3	58.07
λ^{mm}:λ^{um}	1:0.5	60.17
	1:0.7	60.53
	1:1	**60.95**
	1:2	58.21
	1:3	60.29

Table 4. Performance of different backbones on VQA-CP v2 test set.

Methods	Overall(%)	Gap $\Delta\uparrow$
UpDn	39.74	**+21.21**
UpDn + counterfactual data	**60.95**	
SAN	24.96	**+27.46**
SAN + counterfactual data	**52.42**	

intrinsic interactions between image regions and words. [6] maps two modal features(visual and textual features) into a common feature space and then passes the joint embedding into the classifier to obtain the answer of the question. Another methods including that compositional models that [5] applies neural module network to the VQA task, which is a combination of several modular networks. The neural module network is dynamically generated according to the linguistic structure of the question. [25] introduces external knowledge to help model with answering the questions.

Attacking Language Priors in VQA

Despite the progress made in the field of VQA, recent researches have found that VQA systems tend to exploit superficial correlations between question patterns and answers to achieve state-of-the-art performance [1,15]. To help build a robust VQA system, [2] propose a new benchmark named VQA-CP whose training and testing data have vast distributions. Recent solutions to overcome the language priors can be grouped into two categories as without counterfactual inference [9, 23,28] and with counterfactual inference [3,8,12,17,19].

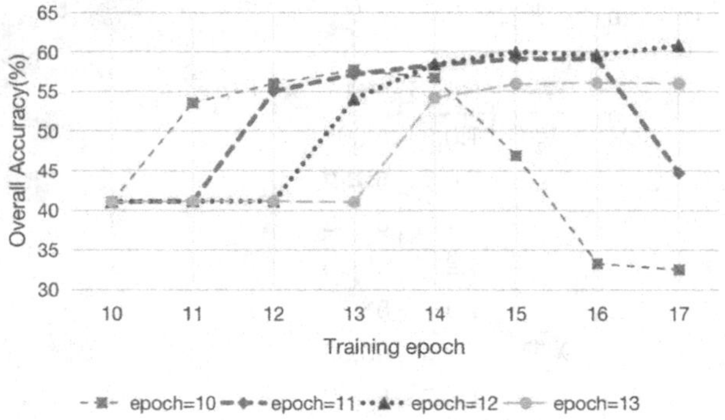

Fig. 5. Impact of different starting points of the second stage training, evaluated on the VQA-CP v2 test set.

For the methods that without counterfactual inference, RUBi [7] proposes to dynamically adjust the weights of samples according to the effect of the bias, LMH [9] ensembles a question-only branch to discriminates which questions can be answered without utilizing image and then penalizes these questions. Unshuffling [23] describes a training procedure to capture the patterns that are stable across environments while discarding spurious ones. SSL [28] proposes a self-supervised framework that generates labeled data to balance the biased data.

For the methods that with counterfactual inference, One solution is to modify model architecture that implement counterfactual inference to reduce the language bias [18]. The other one is to synthesize counterfactual samples to improve the robustness of VQA systems [3,8,12,17,19]. CSS [8] generates the counterfactual samples by masking objects in the image or some keywords in the question.

Based on CSS, CL [17] introduces a contrastive learning mechanism to force the model to learn the relationship between original samples, factual samples and counterfactual samples. MUTANT [12] utilizes the extra object-name annotations to locates critical objects in the image and critical words in the question and then mutates these critical elements to generate counterfactual samples.

5 Conclusion and Future Work

To mitigate the effect of language priors in the VQA task, we proposed a causal inference approach that automatically generates counterfactual data and utilize the data in a two-stage training strategy. We also designed several causal graphs to guide the generation of counterfactual data. Extensive experiments on the benchmark VQA-CP v2 shows that our system achieves significant improvements over the baselines and outperforms most of previous works. Moreover, our system achieves the best performance on VQA v2 which demonstrates the capability of generalization.

The starting point of the second stage training is critical to the performance, in our future work, we would like to determine the starting point in an automatic way. Moreover, it is interesting to evaluate the performance when other networks such as SAN are used as the backbone. We will also study this problem in our future work.

Acknowledgements. This work was supported in part by the National Science Foundation of China (No. 62276056), the National Key R&D Program of China, the China HTRD Center Project (No. 2020AAA0107904), the Natural Science Foundation of Liaoning Province of China (2022-KF-16-01), the Yunnan Provincial Major Science and Technology Special Plan Projects (No. 202103AA080015), the Fundamental Research Funds for the Central Universities (Nos. N2216016, N2216001, and N2216002), and the Program of Introducing Talents of Discipline to Universities, Plan 111 (No. B16009).

References

1. Agrawal, A., Batra, D., Parikh, D.: Analyzing the behavior of visual question answering models. In: Proceedings of EMNLP, pp. 1955–1960 (2016)
2. Agrawal, A., Batra, D., Parikh, D., Kembhavi, A.: Don't just assume; look and answer: overcoming priors for visual question answering. In: Proceedings of CVPR, pp. 4971–4980 (2018)
3. Agrawal, V., Shetty, R., Fritz, M.: Towards causal VQA: revealing and reducing spurious correlations by invariant and covariant semantic editing. In: Proceedings of CVPR, pp. 9690–9698 (2019)
4. Anderson, P., et al.: Bottom-up and top-down attention for image captioning and visual question answering. In: Proceedings of CVPR, pp. 6077–6086 (2018)
5. Andreas, J., Rohrbach, M., Darrell, T., Klein, D.: Neural module networks. In: Proceedings of CVPR, pp. 39–48 (2016)
6. Antol, S., et al.: VQA: visual question answering. In: Proceedings of ICCV, pp. 2425–2433 (2015)

7. Cadène, R., Dancette, C., Ben-younes, H., Cord, M., Parikh, D.: Rubi: reducing unimodal biases for visual question answering. In: Proceedings of NeurIPS, pp. 839–850 (2019)
8. Chen, L., Yan, X., Xiao, J., Zhang, H., Pu, S., Zhuang, Y.: Counterfactual samples synthesizing for robust visual question answering. In: Proceedings of CVPR, pp. 10797–10806 (2020)
9. Clark, C., Yatskar, M., Zettlemoyer, L.: Don't take the easy way out: ensemble based methods for avoiding known dataset biases. In: Proceedings of EMNLP-IJCNLP, pp. 4067–4080 (2019)
10. Das, A., Agrawal, H., Zitnick, L., Parikh, D., Batra, D.: Human attention in visual question answering: do humans and deep networks look at the same regions? Comput. Vis. Image Underst. **163**, 90–100 (2017)
11. Devlin, J., Chang, M., Lee, K., Toutanova, K.: BERT: pre-training of deep bidirectional transformers for language understanding. In: Proceedings of NAACL-HLT, pp. 4171–4186 (2019)
12. Gokhale, T., Banerjee, P., Baral, C., Yang, Y.: MUTANT: a training paradigm for out-of-distribution generalization in visual question answering. In: Proceedings of EMNLP, pp. 878–892 (2020)
13. Goyal, Y., Khot, T., Summers-Stay, D., Batra, D., Parikh, D.: Making the V in VQA matter: elevating the role of image understanding in visual question answering. In: Proceedings of CVPR, pp. 6325–6334 (2017)
14. Jing, C., Wu, Y., Zhang, X., Jia, Y., Wu, Q.: Overcoming language priors in VQA via decomposed linguistic representations. In: Proceedings of AAAI, pp. 11181–11188 (2020)
15. Kafle, K., Kanan, C.: An analysis of visual question answering algorithms. In: Proceedings of CVPR, pp. 1983–1991 (2017)
16. KV, G., Mittal, A.: Reducing language biases in visual question answering with visually-grounded question encoder. In: Vedaldi, A., Bischof, H., Brox, T., Frahm, J.-M. (eds.) ECCV 2020. LNCS, vol. 12358, pp. 18–34. Springer, Cham (2020). https://doi.org/10.1007/978-3-030-58601-0_2
17. Liang, Z., Jiang, W., Hu, H., Zhu, J.: Learning to contrast the counterfactual samples for robust visual question answering. In: Proceedings of EMNLP, pp. 3285–3292 (2020)
18. Niu, Y., Tang, K., Zhang, H., Lu, Z., Hua, X., Wen, J.: Counterfactual VQA: a cause-effect look at language bias. In: Proceedings of CVPR, pp. 12700–12710 (2021)
19. Pan, J., Goyal, Y., Lee, S.: Question-conditional counterfactual image generation for VQA. arXiv, preprint arXiv:1911.06352 (2019)
20. Park, D.H., et al.: Multimodal explanations: justifying decisions and pointing to the evidence. In: Proceedings of CVPR, pp. 8779–8788 (2018)
21. Ramakrishnan, S., Agrawal, A., Lee, S.: Overcoming language priors in visual question answering with adversarial regularization. In: Proceedings of NeurIPS, pp. 1548–1558 (2018)
22. Ren, S., He, K., Girshick, R.B., Sun, J.: Faster R-CNN: towards real-time object detection with region proposal networks. In: Proceedings of NeurIPS, pp. 91–99 (2015)
23. Teney, D., Abbasnejad, E., van den Hengel, A.: Unshuffling data for improved generalization in visual question answering. In: Proceedings of ICCV, pp. 1397–1407 (2021)

24. Teney, D., Abbasnejad, E., Kafle, K., Shrestha, R., Kanan, C., van den Hengel, A.: On the value of out-of-distribution testing: an example of goodhart's law. In: Proceedings of NeurIPS (2020)
25. Wu, Q., Wang, P., Shen, C., Dick, A.R., van den Hengel, A.: Ask me anything: free-form visual question answering based on knowledge from external sources. In: Proceedings of CVPR, pp. 4622–4630 (2016)
26. Yang, Z., He, X., Gao, J., Deng, L., Smola, A.J.: Stacked attention networks for image question answering. In: Proceedings of CVPR, pp. 21–29 (2016)
27. Yu, Z., Yu, J., Cui, Y., Tao, D., Tian, Q.: Deep modular co-attention networks for visual question answering. In: Proceedings of CVPR, pp. 6281–6290 (2019)
28. Zhu, X., Mao, Z., Liu, C., Zhang, P., Wang, B., Zhang, Y.: Overcoming language priors with self-supervised learning for visual question answering. In: Proceedings of IJCAI, pp. 1083–1089 (2020)

Rethinking Label Smoothing on Multi-Hop Question Answering

Zhangyue Yin[1], Yuxin Wang[1], Xiannian Hu[1], Yiguang Wu[1], Hang Yan[1], Xinyu Zhang[2], Zhao Cao[2], Xuanjing Huang[1], and Xipeng Qiu[1(✉)]

[1] School of Computer Science, Fudan University, Shanghai, China
{yinzy21,wangyuxin21,xnhu21}@m.fudan.edu.cn,
{ygwu20,hyan19,xjhuang,xpqiu}@fudan.edu.cn
[2] Huawei Poisson Lab, Hangzhou, China
{zhangxinyu35,caozhao1}@huawei.com

Abstract. Multi-Hop Question Answering (MHQA) is a significant area in question answering, requiring multiple reasoning components, including document retrieval, supporting sentence prediction, and answer span extraction. In this work, we present the first application of label smoothing to the MHQA task, aiming to enhance generalization capabilities in MHQA systems while mitigating overfitting of answer spans and reasoning paths in the training set. We introduce a novel label smoothing technique, F1 Smoothing, which incorporates uncertainty into the learning process and is specifically tailored for Machine Reading Comprehension (MRC) tasks. Moreover, we employ a Linear Decay Label Smoothing Algorithm (LDLA) in conjunction with curriculum learning to progressively reduce uncertainty throughout the training process. Experiment on the HotpotQA dataset confirms the effectiveness of our approach in improving generalization and achieving significant improvements, leading to new state-of-the-art performance on the HotpotQA leaderboard.

Keywords: Multi-Hop Question Answering · Label Smoothing

1 Introduction

Multi-Hop Question Answering (MHQA) is a rapidly evolving research area within question answering that involves answering complex questions by gathering information from multiple sources. This requires a model capable of performing several reasoning steps and handling diverse information structures. In recent years, MHQA has attracted significant interest from researchers due to its potential for addressing real-world problems. The mainstream approach to MHQA typically incorporates several components, including a document retriever, a supporting sentence selector, and a reading comprehension module [11,25,28]. These components collaborate to accurately retrieve and integrate relevant information from multiple sources, ultimately providing a precise answer to the given question.

Y. Wang—Equal contribution.

M. Sun et al. (Eds.): CCL 2023, LNAI 14232, pp. 72–87, 2023.
https://doi.org/10.1007/978-981-99-6207-5_5

Training set:
Gold Doc1: ***Love or Leave***
"Love or Leave" was the Lithuanian entry in the Eurovision Song Contest 2007, performed in English by 4FUN.
Gold Doc2: ***Lithuania in the Eurovision Song Contest***
Lithuania has participated in the Eurovision Song Contest (known in Lithuania as "Eurovizija") 18 times since its debut in 1994, where Ovidijus Vyšniauskas finished last, receiving nul points.
Question: How many times does the song writer of "Love or Leave" have participated in the Eurovision Song Contest?
Answer: 18 times

Validation set:
Gold Doc1: ***Binocular (horse)***
"Love or Leave" was the Lithuanian entry in the Eurovision Song Contest 2007, performed in English by 4FUN.
Gold Doc2: ***Tony McCoy***
Based in Ireland and the UK, McCoy rode a record 4,358 winners, and was Champion Jockey a record 20 consecutive times, every year he was a professional.
Question: The primary jockey of Binocular was Champion Jockey how many consecutive times?
Answer: 20

(a) Different Answer Span

Non-Gold Doc: ***F. W. Woolworth Building (Watertown, New York)***
(1) The Woolworth Building is an historic building in Watertown, New York.
(2) It is a contributing building in the Public Square Historic District.
(3) Plans for the Woolworth Building were begun in 1916 by Frank W. Woolworth, the founder of the Woolworth's chain of department stores.

Gold Doc1: ***Woolworth Building***
(1) The Woolworth Building, at 233 Broadway, Manhattan, New York City, designed by architect Cass Gilbert and constructed between 1910 and 1912, is an early US skyscraper.

Gold Doc2: ***1 New York Plaza***
(1) 1 New York Plaza is an office building in New York City's Financial District, built in 1969 at the intersection of South and Whitehall Streets.
(2) It is the southernmost of all Manhattan skyscrapers.

Question: Which was built first Woolworth Building or 1 New York Plaza?
Answer: Woolworth Building
Evidence Sentences: ["Woolworth Building", 0], ["1 New York Plaza",0]

(b) Multiple Feasible Reasoning Paths

Fig. 1. Causes of errors in answer span and multi-hop reasoning within the HotpotQA dataset. In Figure (a), the answer from the training set contains a quantifier, while the answer from the validation set does not. Figure (b) demonstrates that the correct answer can be inferred using a non-gold document without requiring information from gold doc1.

Despite the remarkable performance of modern MHQA models in multi-hop reasoning, they continue to face challenges with answer span errors and multi-hop reasoning errors. A study by S2G [28] reveals that the primary error source is answer span errors, constituting 74.55%, followed by multi-hop reasoning errors. This issue arises from discrepancies in answer span annotations between the training and validation sets. As illustrated in Fig. 1(a), the training set answer includes the quantifier "times", while the validation set answer does not. Upon examining 200 samples, we found that around 13.7% of answer spans in the HotpotQA validation set deviate from those in the training set.

Concerning multi-hop reasoning, we identified the presence of unannotated, viable multi-hop reasoning paths in the training set. As depicted in Fig. 1(b), the non-gold document contains the necessary information to answer the question, similar to gold doc1, yet is labeled as an irrelevant document. During training, the model can only discard this reasoning path and adhere to the annotated reasoning path. Given that current MHQA approaches primarily use cross-entropy loss for training multiple components, they tend to overfit annotated answer spans and multi-hop reasoning paths in the training set. Consequently, we naturally pose the research question for this paper: *How can we prevent MHQA models from overfitting answer spans and reasoning paths in the training set?*

Label smoothing is an effective method for preventing overfitting, widely utilized in computer vision [24]. In this study, we introduce label smoothing to multi-hop reasoning tasks for the first time to mitigate overfitting. We propose a simple yet efficient MHQA model, denoted as $\mathbf{R}^3$, comprising **R**etrieval, **R**efinement, and **R**eading Comprehension modules. Inspired by the F1 score, a commonly used metric for evaluating

MRC task performance, we develop F1 Smoothing, a novel technique that calculates the significance of each token within the smooth distribution. Moreover, we incorporate curriculum learning [1] and devise the **L**inear **D**ecay **L**abel Smoothing **A**lgorithm (LDLA), which gradually reduces the smoothing weight, allowing the model to focus on more challenging samples during training. Experimental results on the HotpotQA dataset [30] demonstrate that incorporating F1 smoothing and LDLA into the $\mathbf{R}^3$ model significantly enhances performance in document retrieval, supporting sentence prediction, and answer span selection, achieving state-of-the-art results among all published works.

Our main contributions are summarized as follows:

- We introduce label smoothing to multi-hop reasoning tasks and propose a baseline model, $\mathbf{R}^3$, with retrieval, refinement, and reading comprehension modules.
- We present F1 smoothing, a novel label smoothing method tailored for MRC tasks, which alleviates errors caused by answer span discrepancies.
- We propose LDLA, a progressive label smoothing algorithm integrating curriculum learning.
- Our experiments on the HotpotQA dataset demonstrate that label smoothing effectively enhances the MHQA model's performance, with our proposed LDLA and F1 smoothing achieving state-of-the-art results.

2 Related Work

Label Smoothing. Label smoothing is a regularization technique first introduced in computer vision to improve classification accuracy on ImageNet [24]. The basic idea of label smoothing is to soften the distribution of true labels by replacing their one-hot encoding with a smoother version. This approach encourages the model to be less confident in its predictions and consider a broader range of possibilities, reducing overfitting and enhancing generalization [14,16,19]. Label smoothing has been widely adopted across various natural language processing tasks, including speech recognition [2], document retrieval [18], dialogue generation [21], and neural machine translation [5,6,15].

In addition to traditional label smoothing, several alternative techniques have been proposed in recent research. For example, Xu et al. [29] suggested the **T**wo-**S**tage **LA**bel smoothing (TSLA) algorithm, which employs a smoothing distribution in the first stage and the original distribution in the second stage. Experimental results demonstrated that TSLA effectively promotes model convergence and enhances performance. Penha and Hauff [18] introduced label smoothing for retrieval tasks and proposed using BM25 to compute the label smoothing distribution, which outperforms the uniform distribution. Zhao et al. [31] proposed Word Overlapping, which uses maximum likelihood estimation [23] to optimally estimate the model's training distribution.

Multi-Hop Question Answering. Multi-hop reading comprehension (MHRC) is a demanding task in the field of machine reading comprehension (MRC) that closely resembles the human thought process in real-world scenarios. Consequently, it has gained significant attention in the field of natural language understanding in recent years. Several datasets have been developed to foster research in this area, including

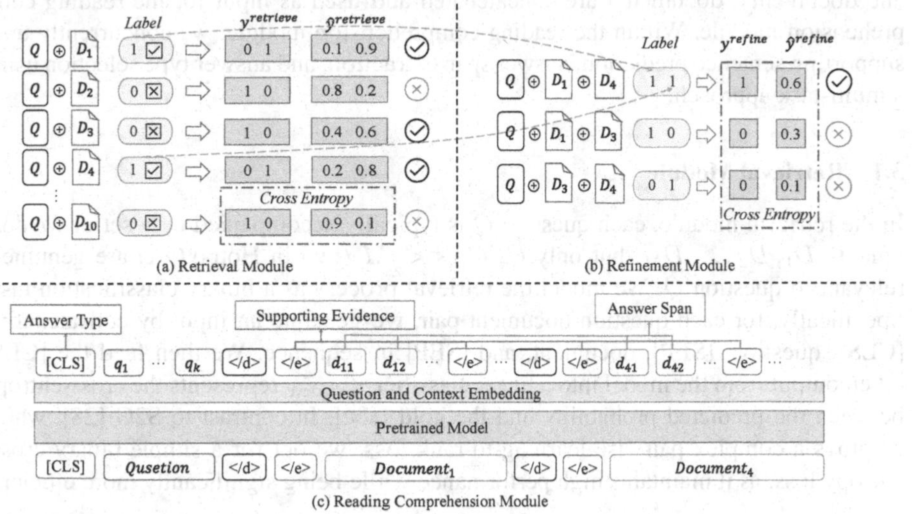

Fig. 2. Overview of our $\mathbf{R}^3$ model, which consists of three main modules: **R**etrieval, **R**efinement, and **R**eading Comprehension.

HotpotQA [30], WikiHop [26], and NarrativeQA [9]. Among these, HotpotQA [30] is particularly representative and challenging, as it requires the model to not only extract the correct answer span from the context but also identify a series of supporting sentences as evidence for MHRC.

Recent advances in MHRC have led to the development of several graph-free models, such as QUARK [7], C2FReader [22], and S2G [28], which have challenged the dominance of previous graph-based approaches like DFGN [20], SAE [25], and HGN [4]. C2FReader [22] suggests that the performance difference between graph attention and self-attention is minimal, while S2G's [28] strong performance demonstrates the potential of graph-free modeling in MHRC. FE2H [11], which uses a two-stage selector and a multi-task reader, currently achieves the best performance on HotpotQA, indicating that pre-trained language models alone may be sufficient for modeling multi-hop reasoning. Motivated by the design of S2G [28] and FE2H [11], we introduce a our model $\mathbf{R}^3$.

3 Framework

Figure 2 depicts the overall architecture of $\mathbf{R}^3$. The retrieval module serves as the first step, where our system selects the most relevant documents, which is essential for filtering out irrelevant information. In this example, document1, document3, and document4 are chosen due to their higher relevance scores, while other documents are filtered out. Once the question and related documents are given, the refinement module further selects documents based on their combined relevance. In this instance, the refinement module opts for document1 and document4. Following this, the question and document1, document4 are concatenated and used as input for the reading comprehension module. Within the reading comprehension module, we concurrently train supporting sentence prediction, answer span extraction, and answer type selection using a multi-task approach.

3.1 Retrieval Module

In the retrieval module, each question Q is typically accompanied by a set of M documents $D_1, D_2 \ldots, D_M$, but only $C, |C| << M$ (two in HotpotQA) are genuinely relevant to question Q. We model the retrieval process as a binary classification task. Specifically, for each question-document pair, we generate an input by concatenating [CLS], question, [SEP], document, and [SEP] in sequence. We then feed the [CLS] token output from the model into a linear classifier. $\mathcal{L}_{\text{retrieve}}$ represents the cross-entropy between the predicted probability and the gold label. In contrast to S2G [28], which employs a complex pairwise learning-to-rank loss, we opt for a simple binary cross-entropy loss, as it maintains high performance while being significantly more efficient.

$$\begin{aligned}\mathcal{L}_{\text{retrieve}} = \mathbb{E}[-\frac{1}{M}\sum_{i=1}^{M}(y_i^{\text{retrieve}} \cdot log(\hat{y}_i^{\text{retrieve}}) \\ +(1 - y_i^{\text{retrieve}}) \cdot log(1 - \hat{y}_i^{\text{retrieve}}))],\end{aligned} \tag{1}$$

where $\hat{y}_i^{\text{retrieve}}$ is the probability predicted by the model and y_i^{retrieve} is the ground-truth label. M is the number of provided documents. $\mathbb{E}$ means the expectation of all samples.

$$y_i^{\text{retrieve}} = \begin{cases} 1 & D_i \text{ is a golden document.} \\ 0 & D_i \text{ is a non-golden document.} \end{cases} \tag{2}$$

3.2 Refinement Module

In the refinement module, we select the top K relevant documents from the previous step and form pairs, resulting in C_K^2 combinations. Emphasizing inter-document interactions crucial for multi-hop reasoning, we concatenate the following sequence: [CLS], question, [SEP], document1, [SEP], document2, [SEP]. Similar to the retrieval module, we extract the [CLS] token output from the model and pass it through a classifier. Pairs containing two gold-standard documents are labeled as 1, while others are labeled as 0. The refinement module thus filters out irrelevant documents, producing a more concise set for further processing.

$$\mathcal{L}_{\text{refine}} = \mathbb{E}[-\sum_{i=1}^{C_K^2} y_i^{\text{refine}} log(\hat{y}_i^{\text{refine}})], \tag{3}$$

where $\hat{y}_i^{\text{refine}}$ is predicted document pair probability and y_i^{refine} is the ground-truth label, C_K^2 is number of all combination.

$$y_i^{\text{refine}} = \begin{cases} 1 & C_i \text{ consists of two gold documents.} \\ 0 & \text{otherwise.} \end{cases} \tag{4}$$

We use a single pretrained language model as the encoder for both the retrieval and refinement module, and the final loss is a weighted sum of $\mathcal{L}_{\text{retrieve}}$ and $\mathcal{L}_{\text{refine}}$. λ_1 and λ_2 are accordingly coefficients of $\mathcal{L}_{\text{retrieve}}$ and $\mathcal{L}_{\text{refine}}$.

$$\mathcal{L}_{\text{total}} = \lambda_1 \mathcal{L}_{\text{retrieve}} + \lambda_2 \mathcal{L}_{\text{refine}}. \tag{5}$$

3.3 Reading Comprehension Module

In the reading comprehension module, we use multi-task learning to simultaneously predict supporting sentences and extract answer span. HotpotQA [30] contains samples labeled as "yes" or "no". The practice of splicing "yes" and "no" tokens at the beginning of the sequence [11] could corrupt the original text's semantic information. To avoid the impact of irrelevant information, we introduce an answer type selection header trained with a cross-entropy loss function.

$$\mathcal{L}_{\text{type}} = \mathbb{E}[-\sum_{i=1}^{3} y_i^{\text{type}} log(\hat{y}_i^{\text{type}})], \tag{6}$$

where $\hat{y}_i^{\text{fine}}$ denotes the predicted probability of answer type generated by our model, and y_i^{fine} represents the ground-truth label. answer type includes "yes", "no" and "span".

$$y_i^{\text{type}} = \begin{cases} 0 & \text{Answer is no.} \\ 1 & \text{Answer is yes.} \\ 2 & \text{Answer is a span.} \end{cases} \tag{7}$$

To extract the span of answers, we use a linear layer on the contextual representation to identify the start and end positions of answers, and adopts cross-entropy as the loss function. The corresponding loss terms are denoted as $\mathcal{L}_{\text{start}}$ and $\mathcal{L}_{\text{end}}$ respectively. Similar to previous work S2G [28] and FE2H [11], we also inject a special placeholder token $< /e>$ and use a linear binary classifier on the output of $< /e >$ to determine whether a sentence is a supporting fact. The classification loss of the supporting facts is denoted as $\mathcal{L}_{\text{sup}}$, and we jointly optimize all of these objectives in our model.

$$\mathcal{L}_{\text{reading}} = \lambda_3 \mathcal{L}_{\text{type}} + \lambda_4 (\mathcal{L}_{\text{start}} + \mathcal{L}_{\text{end}}) + \lambda_5 \mathcal{L}_{\text{sup}}. \tag{8}$$

4 Label Smoothing

Label smoothing is a regularization technique that aims to improve generalization in a classifier by modifying the ground truth labels of the training data. In the one-hot setting, the probability of the correct category $q(y|x)$ for a training sample (x, y) is typically defined as 1, while the probabilities of all other categories $q(\neg y|x)$ are defined as 0. The cross-entropy loss function used in this setting is typically defined as follows:

$$\mathcal{L} = -\sum_{k=1}^{K} q(k|x) \log(p(k|x)), \tag{9}$$

Algorithm 1. Linear Decay Label Smoothing.

Require: training epochs $n > 0$; smoothing weight $\epsilon \in [0, 1]$; decay rate $\tau \in [0, 1]$; uniform distribution u

Initialize: Model parameter $w_0 \in \mathcal{W}$;
Input: Optimization algorithm $\mathcal{A}$
for $i = 0, 1, \dots, n$ **do**
  $\epsilon_i \leftarrow \epsilon - i\tau$
  if $\epsilon_i < 0$ **then**
    $\epsilon_i \leftarrow 0$
  end if
  sample(x_t, y_t)
  $y_t^{LS} \leftarrow (1 - \epsilon_i)y_i + \epsilon u$
  $w_{i+1} \leftarrow \mathcal{A}{-}step(w_i; x_i, y_i^{LS})$
end for

where $p(k|x)$ is the probability of the model's prediction for the k-th class. Specifically, label smoothing mixes $q(k|x)$ with a uniform distribution $u(k)$, independent of the training samples, to produce a new distribution $q'(k|x)$.

$$q'(k|x) = (1 - \epsilon)q(k|x) + \epsilon u(k), \tag{10}$$

where ϵ is the weight controls the importance of $q(k|x)$ and $u(k)$ in the resulting distribution. $u(k)$ is construed as $\frac{1}{K}$ of the uniform distribution, where K is the total number of categories. Next, we introduce two novel label smoothing methods.

4.1 Linear Decay Label Smoothing

Our proposed Linear Decay Label Smoothing Algorithm (LDLA) addresses the abrupt changes in training distribution caused by the two-stage approach of TSLA, which can negatively impact the training process. In contrast to TSLA, LDLA decays the smoothing weight at a constant rate per epoch, promoting a more gradual learning process.

Given a total of n epochs in the training process and a decay size of τ, the smoothing weight ϵ for the i-th epoch can be calculated as follows:

$$\epsilon_i = \begin{cases} \epsilon - i\tau & \epsilon - i\tau \geq 0 \\ 0 & \epsilon - i\tau < 0 \end{cases} \tag{11}$$

Algorithm 1 outlines the specific steps of the LDLA algorithm. LDLA employs the concept of curriculum learning by gradually transitioning the model's learning target from a smoothed distribution to the original distribution throughout the training process. This approach incrementally reduces uncertainty during training, enabling the model to progressively concentrate on more challenging samples and transition from learning with uncertainty to certainty. Consequently, LDLA fosters more robust and effective learning.

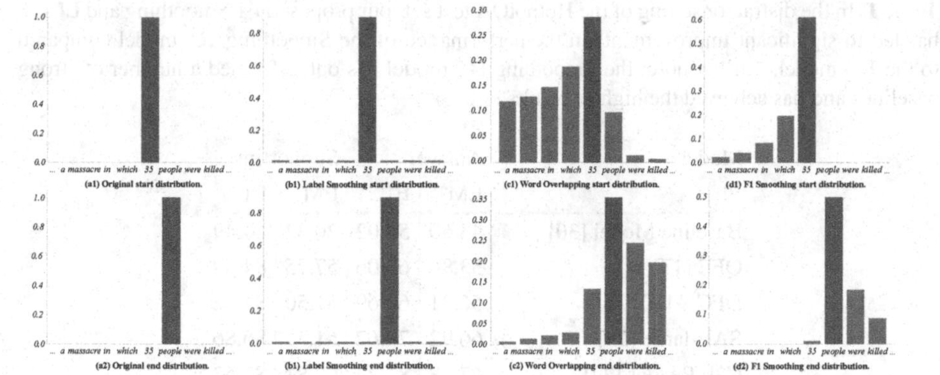

Fig. 3. Visualization of original distribution and different label smoothing distributions, including Label Smoothing, Word Overlapping, and F1 Smoothing. The first row shows the distribution of the start token, and the second row shows the distribution of the end token. The gold start and end tokens are highlighted in red. (Color figure online)

4.2 F1 Smoothing

Unlike traditional classification tasks, MRC requires identifying both the start and end positions of a span. To address the specific nature of this task, a specialized smoothing method is required to achieve optimal results. In this section, we introduce F1 Smoothing, a technique that calculates the significance of a span based on its F1 score.

Consider a sample x that contains a context S and an answer a_{gold}. The total length of the context is denoted by L. We use $q_s(t|x)$ to denote the F1 score between a span of arbitrary length starting at position t in S and the ground truth answer a_{gold}. Similarly, $q_e(t|x)$ denotes the F1 score between a_{gold} and a span of arbitrary length ending at position t in S .

$$q_s(t|x) = \sum_{\xi=t}^{L-1} F1\left((t,\xi), a_{\text{gold}}\right). \tag{12}$$

$$q_e(t|x) = \sum_{\xi=0}^{t} F1\left((\xi,t), a_{\text{gold}}\right). \tag{13}$$

The normalized distributions are noted as $q_s^{'}(t|x)$ and $q_e^{'}(t|x)$, respectively.

$$q_s^{'}(t|x) = \frac{exp(q_s(t|x))}{\sum_{i=0}^{L-1} exp(q_s(i|x))}. \tag{14}$$

$$q_e^{'}(t|x) = \frac{exp(q_e(t|x))}{\sum_{i=0}^{L-1} exp(q_e(i|x))} \tag{15}$$

To decrease the computational complexity of F1 Smoothing, we present a computationally efficient version in Appendix 7. Previous research [31] has investigated various label smoothing methods for MRC, encompassing traditional label smoothing and word

Table 1. In the distractor setting of the HotpotQA test set, our proposed F1 Smoothing and LDLA has led to significant improvements in the performance of the Smoothing $\mathbf{R}^3$ model compared to the $\mathbf{R}^3$ model. Furthermore, the Smoothing $\mathbf{R}^3$ model has outperformed a number of strong baselines and has achieved the highest results.

Model	Answer		Supporting	
	EM	F1	EM	F1
Baseline Model [30]	45.60	59.02	20.32	64.49
QFE [17]	53.86	68.06	57.75	84.49
DFGN [20]	56.31	69.69	51.50	81.62
SAE-large [25]	66.92	79.62	61.53	86.86
C2F Reader [22]	67.98	81.24	60.81	87.63
HGN-large [4]	69.22	82.19	62.76	88.47
FE2H on ELECTRA [11]	69.54	82.69	64.78	88.71
AMGN+ [10]	70.53	83.37	63.57	88.83
S2G+EGA [28]	70.92	83.44	63.86	88.68
FE2H on ALBERT [11]	71.89	**84.44**	64.98	89.14
$\mathbf{R}^3$ (ours)	71.27	83.57	65.25	88.98
Smoothing $\mathbf{R}^3$ (ours)	**72.07**	84.34	**65.44**	**89.55**

overlap smoothing. As illustrated in Fig. 3, F1 Smoothing offers a more accurate distribution of token importance in comparison to Word Overlap Smoothing. This method reduces the probability of irrelevant tokens and prevents the model from being misled during training.

5 Experiment

5.1 Dataset

We evaluate our approach on the distractor setting of HotpotQA [30], a multi-hop question-answer dataset with 90k training samples, 7.4k validation samples, and 7.4k test samples. Each question in this dataset is provided with several candidate documents, two of which are labeled as gold. In addition to this, HotpotQA also provides supporting sentences for each question, encouraging the model to explain the inference path of the multi-hop question-answer. We use the Exact Match (EM) and F1 score (F1) to evaluate the performance of our approach in terms of document retrieval, supporting sentence prediction, and answer extraction.

5.2 Implementation Details

Our model is built using the Pre-trained language models (PLMs) provided by HuggingFace's Transformers library [27].

Table 2. Comparison of our retrieval and refinement module with previous baselines on HotpotQA dev set. Label smoothing can further enhance model performance.

Model	EM	F1
SAE_{large} [25]	91.98	95.76
$S2G_{large}$ [28]	95.77	97.82
$FE2H_{large}$ [11]	96.32	98.02
$\mathbf{R}^3$ (ours)	96.50	98.10
Smoothing $\mathbf{R}^3$	**96.85**	**98.32**

Table 3. Performances of cascade results on the dev set of HotpotQA in the distractor setting.

Model	Answer		Supporting	
	EM	F1	EM	F1
SAE	67.70	80.75	63.30	87.38
S2G	70.80	–	65.70	–
$\mathbf{R}^3$	71.39	83.84	66.32	89.54
Smoothing $\mathbf{R}^3$	**71.89**	**84.65**	**66.75**	**90.08**

Retrieval and Refinement Module We used RoBERTa-large [12] and ELECTRA-large [3] as our PLMs and conducted an ablation study on RoBERTa-large [12]. Training on a single RTX3090 GPU, we set the number of epochs to 8 and the batch size to 16. We employed the AdamW [13] optimizer with a learning rate of 5e-6 and a weight decay of 1e-2.

Reading Comprehension Module. We utilized RoBERTa-large [12] and DeBERTa-v2-xxlarge [8] as our PLMs, performing ablation studies on RoBERTa-large [12]. To train RoBERTa-large, we used an RTX3090 GPU, setting the number of epochs to 16 and the batch size to 16. For the larger DeBERTa-v2-xxlarge model, we employed an A100 GPU, setting the number of epochs to 8 and the batch size to 16. We used the AdamW optimizer [13] with a learning rate of 4e-6 for RoBERTa-large and 2e-6 for DeBERTa-v2-xxlarge, along with a weight decay of 1e-2 for optimization.

5.3 Experimental Results

We utilize ELECTRA-large [3] as the PLM for the retrieval and refinement modules, and DeBERTa-v2-xxlarge for the reading comprehension module. The $\mathbf{R}^3$ model incorporating F1 Smoothing and LDLA methods is referred to as Smoothing $\mathbf{R}^3$. LDLA is employed for document retrieval and supporting sentence prediction, while F1 Smoothing is applied for answer span extraction. As shown in Table 1, Smoothing $\mathbf{R}^3$ achieves improvements of 0.8% and 0.77% in EM and F1 for answers, and 0.19% and 0.57% in EM and F1 for supporting sentences compared to the $\mathbf{R}^3$ model. Among the tested label smoothing techniques, F1 smoothing and LDLA yield the most significant performance improvement.

Table 4. Various label smoothing methods applied to retrieval modules.

Setting	EM	F1
Baseline	95.93±.05	97.91±.09
LS	96.06±.11	97.94±.04
TSLA	96.21±.01	98.05±.05
LDLA	**96.57**±.05	**98.18**±.04

Table 5. Various label smoothing methods applied to supporting sentence prediction.

Setting	EM	F1
Baseline	66.94±.05	90.50±.02
LS	66.88±.02	90.53±.02
TSLA	67.42±.05	90.72±.05
LDLA	**67.63**±.04	**90.85**±.03

We compare the performance of our retrieval and refinement module, which uses ELECTRA-large as a backbone, to three advanced works: SAE [25], S2G [28], and FE2H [11]. These methods also employ sophisticated selectors for retrieving relevant documents. We evaluate the performance of document retrieval using the EM and F1 metrics. Table 2 demonstrates that our $\mathbf{R}^3$ method outperforms these three strong baselines, with Smoothing $\mathbf{R}^3$ further enhancing performance.

In Table 3, we evaluate the performance of the reading comprehension module, which employs DeBERTa-v2-xxlarge [8] as the backbone, on documents retrieved by the retrieval and refinement module. Our $\mathbf{R}^3$ model outperforms strong baselines SAE and S2G, and further improvements are achieved by incorporating F1 Smoothing and LDLA. These results emphasize the potential for enhancing performance through the application of label smoothing techniques.

5.4 Label Smoothing Analysis

In our study of the importance of label smoothing, we used RoBERTa-large [12] as the backbone for our model. To ensure the reliability of our experimental results, we conducted multiple runs with different random number seeds (41, 42, 43, and 44) to ensure stability.

In our experiments, we compared three label smoothing strategies: Label Smoothing (LS), Two-Stage Label smoothing (TSLA), and Linear Decay Label smoothing (LDLA). The initial value of ϵ in our experiments was 0.1, and in the first stage of TSLA, the number of epochs was set to 4. For each epoch in LDLA, ϵ was decreased by 0.01.

Retrieval Module. As shown in Table 4, label smoothing effectively enhances the generalization performance of the retrieval module. LDLA outperforms TSLA with a higher EM (0.36%) and F1 score (0.13%), demonstrating superior generalization capabilities.

Supporting Sentence Prediction We assess the impact of label smoothing on the supporting sentence prediction task. The results presented in Table 5 indicate that TSLA exhibits an increase of 0.48% in EM and 0.22% in F1 compared to the baseline. Additionally, LDLA further enhances the performance by 0.21% in EM and 0.13% in F1 when compared to TSLA.

Table 6. Analysis of different label smoothing methods for Answer Span Extraction.

Methods	EM	F1
Baseline	69.11±.02	82.21±.03
LS	69.30±.02	82.56±.09
TSLA	69.32±.10	82.66±.09
LDLA	69.39±.12	82.69±.03
Word Overlapping	69.60±.09	82.68±.13
F1 Smoothing	**69.93**±.07	**83.05**±.10

Table 7. Error analysis on Answer Span Errors and Multi-hop Reasoning Errors.

Model	Answer Span Errors	Multi-Hop Reasoning Errors
S2G	1612	550
$\mathbf{R}^3$	1556	562
Smoothing $\mathbf{R}^3$	1536 (↓ 1.3%)	545(↓ 3.0%)

Answer Span Extraction. Table 6 highlights the impact of label smoothing methods on answer span extraction in the reading comprehension module. LS, TSLA, and LDLA exhibit slight improvements compared to the baseline. The advanced Word Overlapping technique demonstrates an average improvement of 0.49% in EM and 0.47% in F1, respectively, compared to the baseline. In contrast, our proposed F1 Smoothing technique achieves an average EM improvement of 0.82% and an average F1 score improvement of 0.84%. These results suggest that F1 Smoothing can enhance performance on MRC tasks more effectively than other smoothing techniques.

5.5 Error Analysis

To gain a deeper understanding of how label smoothing effectively enhances model performance, we examined the model's output on the validation set, focusing on answer span errors and multi-hop reasoning errors. First, we define these two types of errors as follows:

- Answer Span Errors: The predicted answer and the annotated answer have a partial overlap after removing stop words, but are not identical.
- Multi-hop Reasoning Errors: Due to reasoning errors, the predicted answer and the annotated answer are entirely different.

By implementing label smoothing, as shown in Table 7, Smoothing $\mathbf{R}^3$ experienced a 1.3% reduction in answer span errors, decreasing from 1556 to 1536, and a 3.0% decrease in multi-hop reasoning errors, dropping from 562 to 545. Smoothing $\mathbf{R}^3$ shows a significant reduction in both types of errors compared to the S2G model. This finding suggests that incorporating label smoothing during training can effectively prevent the model from overfitting the answer span and reasoning paths in the training set, thereby improving the model's generalization capabilities and overall performance.

6 Conclusion

In this study, we first identify the primary challenges hindering the performance of MHQA systems and propose using label smoothing to mitigate overfitting issues during MHQA training. We introduce F1 smoothing, a novel smoothing method inspired by the widely-used F1 score in MRC tasks. Additionally, we present LDLA, a progressive label smoothing algorithm that incorporates the concept of curriculum learning. Comprehensive experiments on the HotpotQA dataset demonstrate that our proposed model, Smoothing $\mathbf{R}^3$, achieves significant performance improvement when using F1 smoothing and LDLA. Our findings indicate that label smoothing is a valuable technique for MHQA, effectively improving the model's generalization while minimizing overfitting to particular patterns in the training set.

Acknowledgement. We would like to express our heartfelt thanks to the students and teachers of Fudan Natural Language Processing Lab. Their thoughtful suggestions, viewpoints, and enlightening discussions have made significant contributions to this work. We also greatly appreciate the strong support from Huawei Poisson Lab for our work, and their invaluable advice. We are sincerely grateful to the anonymous reviewers and the domain chairs, whose constructive feedback played a crucial role in enhancing the quality of our research. This work was supported by the National Key Research and Development Program of China (No.2022CSJGG0801), National Natural Science Foundation of China (No.62022027) and CAAI-Huawei MindSpore Open Fund.

7 Appendix A

In order to alleviate the complexity introduced by multiple for loops in the F1 Smoothing method, we have optimized Eq. (12) and Eq. (13). We use $L_a = e^* - s^* + 1$ and $L_p = e - s + 1$ to denote respectively the length of gold answer and predicted answer.

$$q_s(t|x) = \sum_{\xi=t}^{L-1} \mathrm{F1}\left((t,\xi), a_{\mathrm{gold}}\right). \tag{16}$$

If $t < s^*$, the distribution is

$$q_s(t|x) = \sum_{\xi=s^*}^{e^*} \frac{2(\xi - s^* + 1)}{L_p + L_a} + \sum_{\xi=e^*+1}^{L-1} \frac{2L_a}{L_p + L_a}, \tag{17}$$

else if $s^* \leq t \leq e^*$, we have the following distribution

$$q_s(t|x) = \sum_{\xi=s}^{e^*} \frac{2L_p}{L_p + L_a} + \sum_{\xi=e^*+1}^{L-1} \frac{2(e^* - s + 1)}{L_p + L_a}. \tag{18}$$

In Eq. 17 and 18, $L_p = e - i + 1$.

We can get $q_e(t|x)$ similarly. If $t > e^*$,

$$q_e(t|x) = \sum_{\xi=s^*}^{e^*} \frac{2(e^* - \xi + 1)}{L_p + L_a} + \sum_{\xi=0}^{s^*-1} \frac{2L_a}{L_p + L_a}, \tag{19}$$

else if $s^* \leq t \leq e^*$,

$$q_e(t|x) = \sum_{\xi=s^*}^{e} \frac{2L_p}{L_p + L_a} + \sum_{\xi=0}^{s^*-1} \frac{2(e - s^* + 1)}{L_p + L_a}. \tag{20}$$

In Eqs. 19 and 20, $L_p = i - s + 1$.

References

1. Bengio, Y., Louradour, J., Collobert, R., Weston, J.: Curriculum learning. In: Danyluk, A.P., Bottou, L., Littman, M.L. (eds.) Proceedings of the 26th Annual International Conference on Machine Learning, ICML 2009, Montreal, Quebec, Canada, June 14–18, 2009. ACM International Conference Proceeding Series, vol. 382, pp. 41–48. ACM (2009). https://doi.org/10.1145/1553374.1553380
2. Chorowski, J., Jaitly, N.: Towards better decoding and language model integration in sequence to sequence models. In: INTERSPEECH (2017)
3. Clark, K., Luong, M., Le, Q.V., Manning, C.D.: ELECTRA: pre-training text encoders as discriminators rather than generators. In: 8th International Conference on Learning Representations, ICLR 2020, Addis Ababa, Ethiopia, 26–30 April 2020. OpenReview.net (2020). https://openreview.net/forum?id=r1xMH1BtvB
4. Fang, Y., Sun, S., Gan, Z., Pillai, R., Wang, S., Liu, J.: Hierarchical graph network for multi-hop question answering. In: Proceedings of the 2020 Conference on Empirical Methods in Natural Language Processing (EMNLP), pp. 8823–8838. Association for Computational Linguistics, Online (2020). https://doi.org/10.18653/v1/2020.emnlp-main.710
5. Gao, Y., Wang, W., Herold, C., Yang, Z., Ney, H.: Towards a better understanding of label smoothing in neural machine translation. In: Proceedings of the 1st Conference of the Asia-Pacific Chapter of the Association for Computational Linguistics and the 10th International Joint Conference on Natural Language Processing, pp. 212–223. Association for Computational Linguistics, Suzhou, China (2020). https://aclanthology.org/2020.aacl-main.25
6. Graça, M., Kim, Y., Schamper, J., Khadivi, S., Ney, H.: Generalizing back-translation in neural machine translation. In: Proceedings of the Fourth Conference on Machine Translation (Volume 1: Research Papers), pp. 45–52. Association for Computational Linguistics, Florence, Italy (2019). https://doi.org/10.18653/v1/W19-5205, https://aclanthology.org/W19-5205
7. Groeneveld, D., Khot, T., Mausam, Sabharwal, A.: A simple yet strong pipeline for HotpotQA. In: Proceedings of the 2020 Conference on Empirical Methods in Natural Language Processing (EMNLP), pp. 8839–8845. Association for Computational Linguistics, Online (2020). https://doi.org/10.18653/v1/2020.emnlp-main.711, https://aclanthology.org/2020.emnlp-main.711
8. He, P., Gao, J., Chen, W.: Debertav 3: improving deberta using electra-style pre-training with gradient-disentangled embedding sharing. ArXiv preprint abs/ arXiv: 2111.09543 (2021)
9. Kočiský, T., et al.: The NarrativeQA reading comprehension challenge. Trans. Assoc. Comput. Linguist. **6**, 317–328 (2018)
10. Li, R., Wang, L., Wang, S., Jiang, Z.: Asynchronous multi-grained graph network for interpretable multi-hop reading comprehension. In: IJCA, pp. 3857–3863 (2021)
11. Li, X.Y., Lei, W.J., Yang, Y.B.: From easy to hard: two-stage selector and reader for multi-hop question answering. ArXiv preprint abs/ arXiv: 2205.11729 (2022)
12. Liu, Y., et al.: Roberta: A robustly optimized bert pretraining approach. ArXiv preprint abs/ arXiv: 1907.11692 (2019)

13. Loshchilov, I., Hutter, F.: Decoupled weight decay regularization. arXiv preprint arXiv:1711.05101 (2017)
14. Lukasik, M., Bhojanapalli, S., Menon, A.K., Kumar, S.: Does label smoothing mitigate label noise? In: Proceedings of the 37th International Conference on Machine Learning, ICML 2020, 13–18 July 2020, Virtual Event. Proceedings of Machine Learning Research, vol. 119, pp. 6448–6458. PMLR (2020). https://proceedings.mlr.press/v119/lukasik20a.html
15. Lukasik, M., Jain, H., Menon, A., Kim, S., Bhojanapalli, S., Yu, F., Kumar, S.: Semantic label smoothing for sequence to sequence problems. In: Proceedings of the 2020 Conference on Empirical Methods in Natural Language Processing (EMNLP), pp. 4992–4998. Association for Computational Linguistics, Online (2020). https://doi.org/10.18653/v1/2020.emnlp-main.405
16. Müller, R., Kornblith, S., Hinton, G.E.: When does label smoothing help? In: Wallach, H.M., Larochelle, H., Beygelzimer, A., d'Alché-Buc, F., Fox, E.B., Garnett, R. (eds.) Advances in Neural Information Processing Systems 32: Annual Conference on Neural Information Processing Systems 2019, NeurIPS 2019, 8–14 December 2019, Vancouver, BC, Canada, pp. 4696–4705 (2019). https://proceedings.neurips.cc/paper/2019/hash/f1748d6b0fd9d439f71450117eba2725-Abstract.html
17. Nishida, K., et al.: Answering while summarizing: Multi-task learning for multi-hop QA with evidence extraction. In: Proceedings of the 57th Annual Meeting of the Association for Computational Linguistics. pp. 2335–2345. Association for Computational Linguistics, Florence, Italy (2019). https://doi.org/10.18653/v1/P19-1225, https://aclanthology.org/P19-1225
18. Penha, G., Hauff, C.: Weakly supervised label smoothing. In: Hiemstra, D., Moens, M.-F., Mothe, J., Perego, R., Potthast, M., Sebastiani, F. (eds.) ECIR 2021. LNCS, vol. 12657, pp. 334–341. Springer, Cham (2021). https://doi.org/10.1007/978-3-030-72240-1_33
19. Pereyra, G., Tucker, G., Chorowski, J., Kaiser, Ł., Hinton, G.: Regularizing neural networks by penalizing confident output distributions. arXiv preprint arXiv:1701.06548 (2017)
20. Qiu, L., et al.: Dynamically fused graph network for multi-hop reasoning. In: Proceedings of the 57th Annual Meeting of the Association for Computational Linguistics, pp. 6140–6150. Association for Computational Linguistics, Florence, Italy (2019). https://doi.org/10.18653/v1/P19-1617, https://aclanthology.org/P19-1617
21. Saha, S., Das, S., Srihari, R.: Similarity based label smoothing for dialogue generation. ArXiv preprint abs/ arXiv: 2107.11481 (2021
22. Shao, N., Cui, Y., Liu, T., Wang, S., Hu, G.: Is Graph structure necessary for multi-hop question answering? In: Proceedings of the 2020 Conference on Empirical Methods in Natural Language Processing (EMNLP), pp. 7187–7192. Association for Computational Linguistics, Online (2020). https://doi.org/10.18653/v1/2020.emnlp-main.583, https://aclanthology.org/2020.emnlp-main.583
23. Su, L., Guo, J., Fan, Y., Lan, Y., Cheng, X.: Label distribution augmented maximum likelihood estimation for reading comprehension. In: Caverlee, J., Hu, X.B., Lalmas, M., Wang, W. (eds.) WSDM 2020: The Thirteenth ACM International Conference on Web Search and Data Mining, Houston, TX, USA, 3–7 February 2020, pp. 564–572. ACM (2020). https://doi.org/10.1145/3336191.3371835
24. Szegedy, C., Vanhoucke, V., Ioffe, S., Shlens, J., Wojna, Z.: Rethinking the inception architecture for computer vision. In: 2016 IEEE Conference on Computer Vision and Pattern Recognition, CVPR 2016, Las Vegas, NV, USA, 27–30 June, 2016, pp. 2818–2826. IEEE Computer Society (2016). https://doi.org/10.1109/CVPR.2016.308
25. Tu, M., Huang, K., Wang, G., Huang, J., He, X., Zhou, B.: Select, answer and explain: interpretable multi-hop reading comprehension over multiple documents (2020)
26. Welbl, J., Stenetorp, P., Riedel, S.: Constructing datasets for multi-hop reading comprehension across documents. Trans. Asso. Comput. Linguist. **6**, 287–302 (2018)

27. Wolf, T., et al.: Transformers: State-of-the-art natural language processing. In: Proceedings of the 2020 Conference on Empirical Methods in Natural Language Processing: System Demonstrations, pp. 38–45. Association for Computational Linguistics, Online (2020). https://doi.org/10.18653/v1/2020.emnlp-demos.6, https://aclanthology.org/2020.emnlp-demos.6
28. Wu, B., Zhang, Z., Zhao, H.: Graph-free multi-hop reading comprehension: a select-to-guide strategy. ArXiv preprint abs/ arXiv: 2107.11823 (2021)
29. Xu, Y., Xu, Y., Qian, Q., Li, H., Jin, R.: Towards understanding label smoothing. ArXiv preprint abs/ arXiv: 2006.11653 (2020)
30. Yang, Z., Qi, P., Zhang, S., Bengio, Y., Cohen, W., Salakhutdinov, R., Manning, C.D.: HotpotQA: A dataset for diverse, explainable multi-hop question answering. In: Proceedings of the 2018 Conference on Empirical Methods in Natural Language Processing, pp. 2369–2380. Association for Computational Linguistics, Brussels, Belgium (2018). https://doi.org/10.18653/v1/D18-1259, https://aclanthology.org/D18-1259
31. Zhao, Z., Wu, S., Yang, M., Chen, K., Zhao, T.: Robust machine reading comprehension by learning soft labels. In: Proceedings of the 28th International Conference on Computational Linguistics, pp. 2754–2759. International Committee on Computational Linguistics, Barcelona, Spain (Online) (2020). https://doi.org/10.18653/v1/2020.coling-main.248, https://aclanthology.org/2020.coling-main.248

Text Generation, Dialogue and Summarization

Unsupervised Style Transfer in News Headlines via Discrete Style Space

Qianhui Liu, Yang Gao(✉), and Yizhe Yang

School of Computer Science and Technology, Beijing Institute of Technology, Beijing, China
{3120201048,gyang,yizheyang}@bit.edu.cn

Abstract. The goal of headline style transfer in this paper is to make a headline more attractive while maintaining its meaning. The absence of parallel training data is one of the main problems in this field. In this work, we design a **d**iscrete style space for unsupervised **h**eadline **s**tyle **t**ransfer, short for **D-HST**. This model decomposes the style-dependent text generation into content-feature extraction and style modelling. Then, generation decoder receives input from content, style, and their mixing components. In particular, it is considered that textual style signal is more abstract than the text itself. Therefore, we propose to model the style representation space as a discrete space, and each discrete point corresponds to a particular category of the styles that can be elicited by syntactic structure. Finally, we provide a new style-transfer dataset, named as **TechST**, which focuses on transferring news headline into those that are more eye-catching in technical social media. In the experiments, we develop two automatic evaluation metrics — style transfer rate (STR) and style-content trade-off (SCT) — along with a few traditional criteria to assess the overall effectiveness of the style transfer. In addition, the human evaluation is thoroughly conducted in terms of assessing the generation quality and creatively mimicking a scenario in which a user clicks on appealing headlines to determine the click-through rate. Our results indicate the D-HST achieves state-of-the-art results in these comprehensive evaluations.

1 Introduction

A style makes sense under pragmatic use and becomes a protocol to regularize the manner of communication [Jin et al. 2022; Khalid and Srinivasan 2020]. So, the task of text style transfer is to paraphrase the source text in a desired style-relevant application [Toshevska and Gievska 2021]. In practical use, the style is data-driven and task-oriented in different area [Jin et al. 2022].

The absence of parallel training data for a certain style is one of the difficult problems. Continuous latent space mapping is a typical method for unsupervised style transfer to address the issue. Guo et al. (2021; Liu et al. 2020) model the latent space to a Gaussian distribution. Points in latent space are moved to the target representation with some style guidance. Nangi et al. (2021; John et al. 2018; Romanov et al. 2018) disentangle the continuous latent representation purely according to its content, and replace

M. Sun et al. (Eds.): CCL 2023, LNAI 14232, pp. 91–105, 2023.
https://doi.org/10.1007/978-981-99-6207-5_6

the source attribute to the target one. However, there are two problems of the continuous space approach. Firstly, the style is highly abstract so that it is unstable and too sparse to accurately represent the style in the continuous space. Second, the continuous vector-based representation is difficult to manipulate and cannot be examined at a finer level. To control the style transfer and enhance its explainability, several kinds of discrete signals are used to represent the style. For instance, Reid and Zhong (2021; Tran et al. 2020; Li et al. 2018) employ Mask-Retrieve-Generate strategy to decompose style attributes by word-level editing actions. But, these methods express styles in a highly discrete way which fail to capture the relationships between words or sentences.

To more effectively describe the style in a highly abstract and discrete manner while also capturing the semantic relations in the texts, we propose a latent and **d**iscrete style space for **h**eadline **s**tyle **t**ransfer, abbreviated as **D-HST**. This model decomposes style-dependent text generation into content-feature extraction and style modeling. Therefore, we design a dual-encoder and a shared single-decoder framework to accomplish the overall generation. Due to the lack of parallel training data, we have to synthesize adequate training pairs to accommodate the content extraction and the style modeling. Given a target stylistic headline, we first automatically generate a content-similar input as well as style-consistent input for feeding the dual encoders. As the textual style signal is expected to be rather abstract and limited compared to the text itself, we propose to model the style representation space as a discrete space, with each discrete point denoting a particular category of the styles that can be elicited by syntactic structure.

Also, we provide a new style-transfer dataset derived from the real scenarios, named as **TechST**, which transfers news headlines into the ones that are more attractive to readers. Although several datasets are currently available for this purpose [Jin et al. 2020], but the appealing styles—such as humor and romance—are taken from fictional works of literature, which we believe makes them unsuitable for usage as an *attractive* style for headlines. In the experiments, we design two automatic evaluation metrics, including style transfer rate (STR) and style-content trade-off (SCT) - along with a few traditional criteria to assess the overall of the style transfer. Additionally, the quality of the generation is thoroughly evaluated, and the click-through rate is calculated by creatively simulating a scenario in which a user clicks on attractive headlines. Our findings show that the D-HST performs at the cutting edge in these thorough assessments. In conclusion, our article mainly has the following contributions.

- We propose an unsupervised style transfer method with discrete style space, which is capable of disentangling content and style.
- We propose new metrics in automatic evaluation and human evaluation, and achieves state-of-the-art results in these comprehensive evaluations.
- We provide a novel dataset derived from actual events to convert news headlines into catchy social media headlines.

2 Related Work

Attractive Headline Generation. It is crucial to generate eye-catching headlines for an article. Gan et al. (2017) proposes to generate attractive captions for images and videos with different styles. Jin et al. (2020) introduces a parameter sharing scheme to generate eye-catchy headlines with three different styles, humorous, romantic, and clickbait. Li et al. (2021) proposes a disentanglement-based model to generate attractive headlines for Chinese news. We build upon this task by rewriting source headlines to attractive ones.

Text Style Transfer. There are mainly three kinds of methods used in TST task. 1) **Modeling in the Latent space** Mueller et al. (2017; Liu et al. 2020) use continuous space revision to search for target space. Shen et al. (2017; Sun and Zhu Jian) learn a mapper function in source and target space. John et al. (2018; Romanov et al. 2018; Hu et al. 2017) explicitly disentangle content and style in latent space. However, the style is highly abstract so that it is unstable and too sparse to accurately represent the style in the continuous space. 2) **ProtoType Editing** It is a word replacement method. Li et al. (2018; Tran et al. 2020) propose three-stage methods to replace stylist words with retrieved words in the target corpus. Reid and Zhong (2021) uses Levenshtein editing to search target stylist words. These methods work well on Content-Preferences dataset, like sentiment, debias. 3) **Control Code Index** Keskar et al. (2019; Dai et al. 2019) use a control sign embedding to controls the attribute of generated text. Yi et al. (2021) controls style using a style encoder. These methods don't learn style in a fine-grained way and the style space is a block-box. We combine the first and third methods, using a control code to control style and modeling a style space with appropriate distribution.

To model the discrete style in an unsupervised fashion, we propose to inherit the third and fourth methods. Specifically, we construct pseudo data to enrich the content-based parallel data and style-based para. Further, different from the previously styled latent space, we model it as a discrete one based on the claim that style is highly abstract and more sparse compared to content. We will describe this in detail in the next section.

3 Methodology

We are given samples $Y = \{y_1, y_2, \dots y_m\}$ from the style dataset S. The objective of our task is to transfer a headline sentence to a new headline equipped with the style of the target data S, while maintaining its originally semantic content.

3.1 Model Overview

Our proposed **D-HST** model consists of a duel-encoder and a single shared decoder in an unsupervised setting. It begins by constructing a pseudo-parallel dataset which comprises of two pairs of inputs-and-outputs. One of the inputs is X^Y_{cont}, which is generated by using a pre-trained paraphrasing model and has input that is content-similar to output Y. The other input is X^Y_{style}, which is collected in style dataset S and uses inputs of sentences with the same style as output Y based on the defined style (Sect. 3.2).

The model structure is described in Sect. 3.3. One of the inputs is **content input** X^Y_{cont} encoded by a content encoder, then fed into a content pooling to extract its sentence-level feature, denoted as $Z^Y_{cont} = pool_{cont}(enc_{cont}(X^Y_{cont}))$. Similarly, the other input is **style input** X^Y_{style} encoded by a style encoder, then fed into a style pooling to get style representation Z^Y_{style}. The hypothesis is that the pooling serves as a bottleneck which can disentangle the representation of content and style with help of proper loss function (Sect. 3.4). The overall model architecture is shown in Fig. 1.

3.2 Pseudo Parallel Data Construction

Content Input. Prior work has demonstrated that paraphrasing techniques can translate source sentences into standard written sentences while maintaining their substance [Mitamura and Nyberg (2001)]. In our approach, we assume that a special style (such as attractiveness, informality in the experiment) of a sentence can be removed after paraphrasing. We use a pretrained paraphrasing model[1] to remove stylist attribute, and construct the content inputs X_{cont}^{Y}.

As the paraphrasing model often produces multiple outcomes, in the experiment, we select top 5 generations as a candidate set for the content input. Then, we calculate bertscore to estimate the similarity between the generated candidates and the output Y. Only candidates with similarity between 0.75 to 0.95 are kept to preserve as much content information as possible and prevent significantly overlapping generation.

Style Input. We suppose that a certain syntactic structure can reflect the style. For example, attractive headlines often employ interrogative questions; informal conversations frequently use ellipsis; and impolite language often employ imperative sentences. To collect more parallel headlines to train the style-based modules, we construct the style input X_{style}^{Y} that shares the same syntactic structure yet different content with target Y, from the data in style dataset S. In order to filter out the content information in the style input, we use a set of sentences C_{style}^{Y} that share the same syntactic structure for X_{style}^{Y}, then average these sentences with a learnable parameter.

Specifically, we use a chunk parser FlairNLP[2] to get the syntactic structure of these headlines. We first get the chunk label for each word using the chunk parser. Then, we merge the spans having the same label. Based on the assumption that words such as "who", "whether" and "how" are function words that guide special sentence patterns, we set a separate label QP to mark the leading words of interrogative sentences. We get some distinct syntactic structures, each of which has some corresponding headlines. We assume that if one syntactic structure occurs in less than 10 headlines, it is not representative. Then, we filter the syntactic structure and its corresponding sentences if its syntactic structure occurs in less than 10 headlines. Table 1 shows examples of processed syntactic structures and their corresponding sentences.

---

1 https://huggingface.co/tuner007/pegasus_paraphrase.

2 https://github.com/flairNLP/flair.

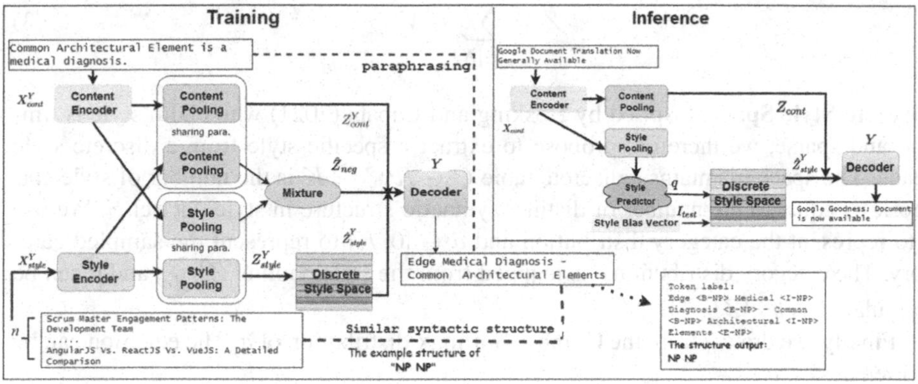

Fig. 1. The framework of the D-HST model. The training phase and inference phase are depicted in the figure.

Table 1. Examples of syntactic structures and their corresponding headline sentences. These examples indicate that some sentences can express the same style representation by syntactic structure.

Syntactic Structure	QP VP NP	CD NP VP
Sentences	How to Become a DevOps Engineer How to Scale Your SaaS Business How to Do API Testing	3 Tech Debt Metrics Every Engineer Should Know 7 Top Kubernetes Health Metrics You Must Monitor 10 Software Testing Interview Questions You Haven't Heard Before

3.3 Model Architecture

The duel-encoder and the shared decoder are both based on standard Transformer model [Vaswani et al. (2017)]. The content inputs and style inputs are both encoded by their separate encoders, that are content encoder and style encoder, respectively. Each token is fed to the encoder and obtains embeddings $\{e_1, e_2, ..., e_{|X|}\} = enc(X)$, where $|X|$ is the length of the input sentence, $e_t \in R^H$, H is the dimension of transformer.

Feature Extractor. To facilitate the disentanglement between the content semantics and the stylistic attributes, we elicit their distinct features by pooling the multi-dimensional representation in accordance with the method used in Liu and Lapata (2019). Specifically, a multi-head pooling is adopted to extract features. We employed attention a_t, where t represents a token, to calculate its importance score for the whole sentence. The equation is:

$$\alpha_t = \frac{\exp a_t}{\sum_{t \in |X|} \exp a_i} \tag{1}$$

$$a_t = k_t e_t \tag{2}$$

where $k_t \in R^H$ is a learnable parameter. The value of each token V_t is also computed using a linear projection of e_t. Finally, we take a weighted average to get the pooling output Z.

$$Z = \sum_{t \in |X|} \alpha_t V_t \tag{3}$$

Discrete Style Space. Inspired by Hosking and Lapata (2021) who claim style is limited and sparse, we therefore propose to extract a specific style from a discrete style space. The space maintains a discrete table $C \in R^{K \times D}$, K is the number of style categories[3], equal to the number of distinct syntactic structure in style dataset S. We use q to represent the category distribution and $\tilde{q} \in [0, K]$ to represent the sampled category. The category distribution q is mapped from the style pooling Z^Y_{style}, and it can be formulated as $p(q|Z^Y_{style})$.

Finally, we draw $\tilde{q}$ from the Gumbel-Softmax distribution of q. The equation can be written as:

$$\tilde{q} \sim \text{Gumbel-Softmax}(q) \tag{4}$$

The style representation, $\hat{Z}^y_{style} = C(\tilde{q})$, maps from the discrete code $\tilde{q}$. $\hat{Z}^Y_{style}$ ought to be as near as the input Z^Y_{style}. So we get a loss term:

$$\mathcal{L}_q = \| \ Z^Y_{style} - sg(C(\tilde{q})) \ \|_2 \tag{5}$$

Because the gradient could be broken at stop gradient sg, the loss is not derivable. We employ a reparameterization trick [Kingma and Welling (2013)] to update parameters and exponential moving average Roy et al. (2018) strategy to update the discrete table.

Style Bias. We assume that each sentence has its own style score. For example "You Can't Reset Your Fingerprint" is more obviously attractive than "AI-Assisted Coding with Tabnine" in terms of its expressing style, although they are both in style dataset. Therefore, we manually rank each sentence in the style dataset S based on external knowledge I_{test}. Details of the external knowledge are shown in Sect. 5.

We believe that syntactic structure can be used to define the style category and that sentences with the same structure may score similarly in terms of style. Each style is expected to be encoded into a specific category, and categories with higher style scores are more likely to be selected in inference. $I \in R^K$ is a one-hot vector and serves as a pre-labeled supervisory signal, representing the correspondence between styles and categories. For example, $I_m \in R^K$ encodes the style category to which the sentence m belongs. In training phase, we expect each style is encoded into a specific category, so we let the output of the category distribution q fit supervisory signal I. The equation can be written as:

$$\mathcal{L}_r = \| \ I - \text{softmax}(q) \ \|_2 \tag{6}$$

In inference phase, for all sentences, we use the fixed discrete style bias distribution $I_{test} \in R^K$ to increase the probability of choosing a high-scoring style. And we set the probability for each category in I_{test} to be the normalized style score.

[3] $K = 324$ in our TechST dataset.

Mixture Module. We also design a mixture module to serve as negative knowledge to guide decoder to leave away from the content of X^{Y}_{style} and the style of X^{Y}_{cont}. We use a small full connect network with the concatenation of $Z_{cs} = pool_{cont}(enc_{style}(X^{Y}_{style}))$ and $Z_{sc} = pool_{style}(enc_{cont}(X^{Y}_{cont}))$ as input, written as $Z_{neg} = MLP(Z_{cs}, Z_{sc})$

Finally, the overall hidden representation Z can be written as $Z = Z^{Y}_{cont} + \hat{Z}^{Y}_{style} + Z_{neg}$. And the target distribution $p(Y|Z) = dec(Z)$.

3.4 Model Training

We first describe the training process that makes the model to capture its local independence information separately.

We set triples $((X^{Y}_{cont}, X^{Y}_{style}), Y)$ as input and output, respectively. To produce strong style signals, we use a set of style sentences C^{Y}_{style} in the same style as Y. The selection strategy has been described in Sect. 3.2 and the style representation is weighted with a learnable parameter κ, such as $Z^{Y}_{style} = \sum_{c_i \in C^{Y}_{style}} pool_{style}(enc_{style}(c_i))\kappa_{ci}$. Then, $\hat{Z}^{Y}_{style}$ is sampled from the style space. It is trained to generate target Y with the overall hidden representation Z, which is the sum of content encoding Z^{Y}_{cont}, style encoding $\hat{Z}^{Y}_{style}$ and negative knowledge encoding Z_{neg}. The factorised reconstruction loss term can be written as:

$$\mathcal{L}_Y = \sum_t \log p(w_t|w_1, w_2 ... w_{t-1}; Z) \tag{7}$$

The final objective function is:

$$\mathcal{L} = \mathcal{L}_Y + \delta\mathcal{L}_q + \epsilon\mathcal{L}_r \tag{8}$$

3.5 Inference

Since we don't have any style input X^{Y}_{style} for inference, only X_{cont} in source dataset is available and transferred to the defined target style. As such, the well-trained style encoder and mixture module can not be directly adopted in the inference. To fill this gap, we further train a style predictor module to alternatively select a sample to represent the most stylistic category for the following decoder. This predictor is formulated as $p(q|X^{Y}_{cont}) = MLP(pool_{style}(enc_{cont}(X^{Y}_{cont})))$. The additional predictor is trained to predict the well-trained style category distribution q through X^{Y}_{cont}. q is mapped from Z^{Y}_{style} and represents as $p(q|Z^{Y}_{style})$. So we distill the distribution $p(q|X^{Y}_{cont})$ to the well-trained distribution $p(q|Z^{Y}_{style})$. The loss term is:

$$\mathcal{L}_{KL} = -KL(sm(p(q|X^{Y}_{cont}))||sm(p(q|Z^{Y}_{style}))) \tag{9}$$

where sm is short for softmax function. In inference phase, we sample $\tilde{q} \sim ((1 - \gamma)\text{sm}(q) + \gamma I_{test})$ 3 times and generate 3 candidate outputs. Finally, we select the one with highest content preservation with the input, calculated by bertscore.

4 Tasks and Datasets

For the headline style transfer task, we focus on attractive news headline transfer on technology topics. Technology news headlines are always formal. For example, "Google Document Translation Now Generally Available." is a common style for an event headline. On the contrary, technology blog headlines in social media tend to be special and catch readers' eyes. In this paper, we define this kind of headline as "**Attractive**" style. To highlight the characteristics of style, the previous example can be transferred as "Google Goodness: Document Now Available". The goal of this task is to transfer the formal news headlines to more attractive blog headlines in technology domain.

Datasets. Our attractive technology dataset **TechST** was crawled from Dzone[4], including stylistic technology blog headlines and users' pageviews. This data was used to train the style transfer model. We also crawled technology news headlines from InfoQ[5] as non-stylistic headlines for testing. The task is to transfer the headlines in InfoQ to a new style that is modelled with the Dzone dataset. Both of them were crawled from the beginning to November 2011. We filtered out the blog headlines with pageviews less than 500 and the ones more than 22 words as we believe shorter headlines are attractive. Finally, we get 60,000 samples for training and 2,000 samples for testing.

We also use a cornerstone dataset Grammarly's Yahoo Answers Formality Corpus (GYAFC) [Rao and Tetreault (2018)] for formality transfer. It contains 53,000 paired formal and informal sentences in two domains. To meet our requirement of unsupervised style transfer setting, the task is to transfer the formal sentences to informal ones. Only informal sentences in the Family and Relationships categories were used for training and validation.

5 Experiments and Results

External Knowledge. As mentioned in Sect. 3.3, external knowledge is used to estimate the style strength. To some extents, users' pageviews reflect attractiveness of the style. We first parsed all the syntactic structures of sentences in the style dataset. Then, we calculate average-pageviews for each syntactic structure. The more average-pageviews the structure receives, the higher style score it has. We acknowledge that style isn't the only factor that affects pageviews, content also contributes to it. For example, headlines with syntactic structure like "NP VP" are common, but some headlines with such structure may have high pageviews. To eliminate the impact of content, we add a pageview variance term. Specifically, if sentences with same syntactic structure show little pageview variance, it is speculated that pageviews are determined by the syntactic structure. On the contrary, if the variance is significant, it suggests that other elements, such as content, are influencing pageviews. As such, the style score must be penalized. Finally, we define our style score as:

[4] https://dzone.com/.
[5] https://www.infoq.com/.

$$I^i_{test} = \frac{mean(a)^{\omega}}{var(a)^{\nu}} \tag{10}$$

I^i_{test} represent the style score of category i, a is the collection of the sentences having style i. ω and ν are hyperparameters.

For GYAFC dataset, no such corresponding information is provided, so we set all syntactic structures the same style score.

Experiment Setup. We use 6-layers transformers to train our model. Each transformer has 8 attention heads and 768 dimensional hidden state. Dropout with 0.1 was added to each layer in the transformer. Encoder and decoder initialized from BART base. Hyperparameters δ and ϵ in loss function are set to 0.5. In external knowledge building, we set $\omega = 2$, $\mu = 0.05$.

We trained our model on a 3090 GPU for 20 epochs taking about 5 h with gradient accumulation every 2 steps. We chose the best checkpoint for the testing through a validation process.

Baselines. We compared the proposed model against the following three strong baseline approaches in text style transfer: **BART+R** [Lai et al. (2021)] is trained by fine-tune BART model with an extra BLEU reward and style classification reward. This model uses parallel dataset. In order to meet our requirement of unsupervised style transfer setting, we used pseudo-parallel data X^Y_{cont} and Y as input and target in the following experiment. **StyIns** [Yi et al. (2021)] leverages the generative flow technique to extract stylistic properties from multiple instances to form a latent style space, and style representations are then sampled from this space. **TSST** [Yi et al. (2021)] proposes a retrieval-based context-aware style representation that uses an extra retriever module to alleviate the domain inconsistency in content and style.

5.1 Automatic Metrics

To quantitatively evaluate the effectiveness of style transfer task which calls for both the transfer of styles as well as the preservation of content semantics, we newly designed two metrics of Style Transfer Rate (STR) and Style-Content Trade-off (SCT), respectively.

Content Preservation (CP). It is calculated by the similarity between the input and the transferred output leveraged by standard metric Bertscore [Zhang et al.(2019)].

Style Transfer Rate. The traditional style transfer methods [Lai et al. (2021)] use a well-trained style classifier to testify if a sentence has been successfully transferred into a targeted style. But, this method is more suitable for polar word replacement, such as sentiment transfer in review generation. For the cases of eye-catching or written formality transfer, we propose a rule-based yet easy-to-use transfer metric, named as STR. We calculate the STR according to the percentage of syntactic structures changed between the generated output and its input as follows:

$$STR = \frac{\sum_{i \in C_{test}} \text{structure}(X^i_{cont}) \neq \text{structure}(O^i)}{|C_{test}|} \tag{11}$$

Table 2. The automatic evaluation results on our model and all baselines on both TechST and GYAFC datasets.

Dataset	Model	CP	STR	SCT	PPL
TechST	StyIns	0.773	0.377	0.253	48.39
	BART+R	**0.962**	0.394	0.280	92.48
	TSST	0.874	0.488	0.313	104.68
	D-HST	0.665	**0.846**	**0.372**	**15.48**
GYAFC	StyIns	0.811	0.666	0.366	26.51
	BART+R	**0.896**	0.663	0.381	12.61
	TSST	0.829	0.625	0.356	23.19
	D-HST	0.641	**0.944**	**0.382**	**10.11**

Table 3. Human evaluation.

Models	Interestedness	Fluency
D-HST	1.711	1.763
StyIns	1.05	1.413
BART+R	1.219	1.906
TSST	1.181	1.463

where $|C_{test}|$ is the number of testing data, X^i_{cont} and O^i represent content input and generated output, respectively.

Style-Content Trade-Off. In order to integrate the STR and CP into a single measure, we take their harmonic means as follows:

$$SCT = \frac{2}{\frac{1}{\text{STR}} + \frac{1}{\text{CP}}} \tag{12}$$

Language Fluency. We fine-tuned the GPT-2 model (Radford et al., 2019) on our stylistic dataset S and use it to measure the perplexity (PPL) on the generated outputs.

5.2 Overall Performance

We compared the performance of our model against with the baselines in Table 2. D-HST performs the best across all the metrics except for the CP metric. From the results we can find that, firstly, our model achieves very obvious advantage in STR metric (nearly 50% margin) indicate the thorough and outstanding performance on style transfer; Secondly, our D-HST identifies the most harmonious balance point between content preservation and style transfer revealed by the SCT metric; Thirdly, our language model GPT-2 was fine-tuned in stylistic data, therefore, the PPL metric favors fluent sentences adhere more closely to the given style format. Although the BART+R model receives best fluency in human evaluation (Table 3), it mostly fails in our automatic fluency metric. When evaluating the content preservation, we discourage the CP metric from being

Table 4. Example outputs generated by different models. Red parts represent stylistic attributes D-HST captures.

	Example #1	Example #2	Example #3
Input	IBM to Acquire Red Hat for $34 Billion	Microsoft Releases Azure Open AI Service Including Access to Powerful GPT-3 Models	EF Core Database Providers
StyIns	IBM to Acquire Red Hat for $34 Billion	AWS and Cloudflare Add Bot Management Features to Their Firewalls	A Core Database Providers
BART+R	IBM to Acquire Red Hat for $ 34 Billion	Microsoft Releases Azure Open AI Service with Powerful GPT-3 Models	EF Core Database Providers
TSST	IBM to Acquire Red Hat for $ 34 Billion	Microsoft Releases Azure Open AI Service Including Access to Powerful QR Models	Using Core Database Providers
D-HST	Why IBM Acquires Red Hat for $34M	Microsoft Azure: Accessing Open-Source Microsoft Machine Models	Going Into Core Database Providers

Table 5. Examples of generated headlines given specific style category.

	Example #1	Example #2
Input	The New Microsoft Edge - Microsoft Build 2020	Qwik, a Resumable Javascript Framework
Category	Category2: VP NP	
	Introducing Microsoft's New Microsoft Edge	Using a Resumable JavaScript Framework
	Category95: QP VP NP	
	How to Build Microsoft's New Microsoft Edge	How to Develop a Resumable Javascript Framework

as high as possible since the extremely high similarity (like close to 1) implies the exactly same words are used in sentences. However, what is required is a change in style that involves a particular number of words. Therefore, we argue that CP is acceptable around 0.64-0.66[6], which can preserve the source content while transferring the style.

6 We randomly sample 60 headlines from the baseline model and our model evenly, and ask the annotators to select the ones that transfer style and preserve content, and the bertscore of the selected headlines mostly falls between 0.63-071.

To gain further insight on the performance of the style transfer, we sampled real examples from our model and baselines on TechST dataset, as shown in Table 4. StyIns and BART+R nearly copy the content of input; TSST has difficulty in generating fluent sentences. D-HST can transfer the style on the premise of basically preserving the content.

5.3 Human Evaluation

To assess the quality of text generated using D-HST from human perspective, we designed two human evaluations based on the performance in TechST dataset. First, we randomly sampled 20 groups headlines generated from baselines and D-HST, respectively. 10 postgraduates annotators were asked to score the candidates according to the following attributes from 0 to 2. *Fluency*: how fluent and readable the headline is? *Interestedness*: is the generated headline interesting? The final score of each model is calculated by averaging all judged scores. The results in Table 3 show that headlines generated by our proposed D-HST model receives most popularity compared to other models, indicated by the *Interestedness* metric. Additionally, both BART+R and D-HST generate fluent headlines.

The second human evaluation was designed to compute the click-through rate based on users' real click behavior. It is the most straightforward method of testifying **attractiveness**. When giving many headlines to real readers, we will examine which model receives the most clicks in this evaluation. Specifically, we selected 11 postgraduate annotators, each of whom was given a list of news headlines. The annotators were asked to click on those headlines that are most attractive to them. To make the selection as fair as possible, we carefully design to let the headlines generated by each model distribute evenly across the list, and the headline order was randomly shuffled to eliminate the effect of position on the probability of being clicked. Finally, each list contained 36 headlines (Each model generates 9 headlines, D-HST and three baselines models compared in this experiment) and the annotators were asked to click on 5 most attractive ones. As shown in Fig. 2, the largest rate (reaches 58%) obtained by the D-HST mainly conform to the previously quantitative results. We can conclude that D-HST generates the most appealing and acceptably fluent headlines.

5.4 Discrete Style Space and Controllability

To investigate whether style information is encoded in categories of discrete style space, we inspect to select two kinds of structures to control the generated headlines' styles in the inference stage. The outcomes are shown in Table 5. As it clearly demonstrates, category 2 and category 95 contain two distinct syntactic structures which are "VP NP" and "QP VP NP", respectively. Based on them, given the same input, our D-HST model is capable of generating different attractive headlines match the chosen structures. The results again indicate that the stylistic features are well disentangled and it is easy to control the style of generated results.

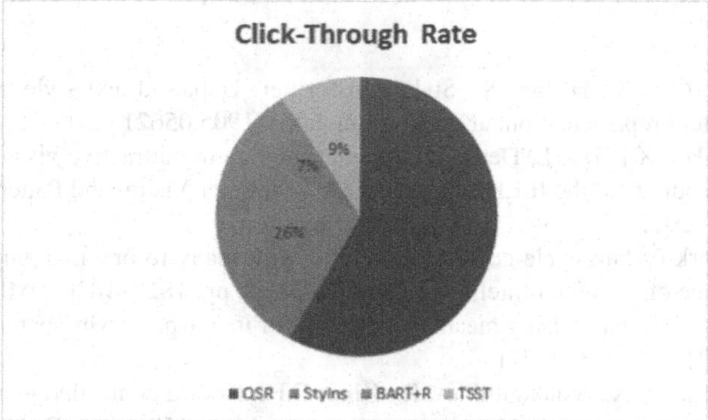

Fig. 2. Human evaluation of click-through rate.

Table 6. Evaluation of the style bias strength γ

Dataset	Strength	CP	STR	SCT	PPL
TechST	$\gamma = 0$	0.669	0.817	0.368	14.97
	$\gamma = 0.1$	0.668	0.824	0.369	15.17
	$\gamma = 0.3$	0.665	0.844	0.372	15.48
	$\gamma = 0.5$	0.661	0.857	0.373	15.81

5.5 Style Bias Strength

As mentioned in Sect. 3.5, external knowledge I_{test} is inserted as the style bias in the inference. The style category $K = 324$ in TechST dataset. To investigate how the style bias strength γ affects the final generation, we chose different values on γ and evaluate the performance in a series of automatic metrics, presented in Table 6. Through the experiment, we find that adding a style bias is effective for style transfer, and the scores of STR and SCT increase. The generation quality of the model has no significant fluctuation as the style strength increase, indicating that the model has strong generalization and is insensitive to the parameter.

6 Conclusion

This paper presents an unsupervised model for headline style transfer. It consists of content, style and their mixing components, which are together fed to decoder for headline generation. In particular, we propose to extract the style features in a discrete style space, and each discrete point corresponds to a particular category of the styles. Our system is comprehensively evaluated by both quantitative and qualitative metrics, and it produces cutting-edge outcomes in two typical datasets. Our work can be applied in the scenarios of formality machine translation, politeness transfer in intelligent customer service, spoken language transfer in live broadcast delivery. It can also be followed by the task of paraphrase and data augmentation.

References

Dai, N., Liang, J., Qiu, X., Huang, X.: Style transformer: Unpaired text style transfer without disentangled latent representation. arXiv preprint arXiv:1905.05621 (2019)

Gan, C., Gan, Z., He, X., Gao, J., Deng, L.: Stylenet: generating attractive visual captions with styles. In: Proceedings of the IEEE Conference on Computer Vision and Pattern Recognition, pp. 3137–3146 (2017)

Guo, Q., et al.: Fork or fail: cycle-consistent training with many-to-one mappings. In: International Conference on Artificial Intelligence and Statistics, pp. 1828–1836. PMLR (2021)

Hosking, T., Lapata, M.: Factorising meaning and form for intent-preserving paraphrasing. arXiv preprint arXiv:2105.15053 (2021)

Hu, Z., Yang, Z., Liang, X., Salakhutdinov, R., Xing, E.P.: Toward controlled generation of text. In: International Conference on Machine Learning, pp. 1587–1596. PMLR (2017)

Jin, D., Jin, Z., Zhou, J.T., Orii, L., Szolovits, P.: Hooks in the headline: Learning to generate headlines with controlled styles. arXiv preprint arXiv:2004.01980 (2020)

Jin, D., Jin, Z., Zhiting, H., Vechtomova, O., Mihalcea, R.: Deep learning for text style transfer: A survey. Comput. Linguist. **48**(1), 155–205 (2022)

John, V., Mou, L., Bahuleyan, H., Vechtomova, O.: Disentangled representation learning for non-parallel text style transfer. arXiv preprint arXiv:1808.04339 (2018)

Keskar, N.S., McCann, B., Varshney, L.R., Xiong, C., Socher, R.: Ctrl: A conditional transformer language model for controllable generation. arXiv preprint arXiv:1909.05858 (2019)

Khalid, O., Srinivasan, P.: Style matters! investigating linguistic style in online communities. In: Proceedings of the International AAAI Conference on Web and Social Media, vol. 14, pp. 360–369 (2020)

Kingma, D.P., Welling, M.: Auto-encoding variational bayes. arXiv preprint arXiv:1312.6114 (2013)

Lai, H., Toral, A., Nissim, M.: Thank you bart! rewarding pre-trained models improves formality style transfer. arXiv preprint arXiv:2105.06947 (2021)

Li, J., Jia, R., He, H., Liang, P.: Delete, retrieve, generate: a simple approach to sentiment and style transfer. arXiv preprint arXiv:1804.06437 (2018)

Li, M., Chen, X., Yang, M., Gao, S., Zhao, D., Yan, R.: The style-content duality of attractiveness: Learning to write eye-catching headlines via disentanglement. In Proceedings of the AAAI Conference on Artificial Intelligence, vol. 35, pp. 13252–13260 (2021)

Liu, Y., Lapata, M.: Hierarchical transformers for multi-document summarization. arXiv preprint arXiv:1905.13164 (2019)

Liu, D., Jie, F., Zhang, Y., Pal, C., Lv, J.: Revision in continuous space: Unsupervised text style transfer without adversarial learning. In Proceedings of the AAAI Conference on Artificial Intelligence, vol. 34, pp. 8376–8383 (2020)

Mitamura, T., Nyberg, E.: Automatic rewriting for controlled language translation. In: The Sixth Natural Language Processing Pacific Rim Symposium (NLPRS 2001) Post-Conference Workshop, Automatic Paraphrasing: Theories and Applications (2001)

Mueller, J., Gifford, D., Jaakkola, T.: . Sequence to better sequence: continuous revision of combinatorial structures. In: International Conference on Machine Learning, pp. 2536–2544. PMLR (2017)

Nangi, S.R., Chhaya, N., Khosla, S., Kaushik, N., Nyati, H.: Counterfactuals to control latent disentangled text representations for style transfer. In: Proceedings of the 59th Annual Meeting of the Association for Computational Linguistics and the 11th International Joint Conference on Natural Language Processing, vol. 2: Short Papers, pp. 40–48 (2021)

Rao, S., Tetreault, J.: Dear sir or madam, may i introduce the gyafc dataset: Corpus, benchmarks and metrics for formality style transfer. arXiv preprint arXiv:1803.06535 (2018)

Reid, M., Zhong, V.: Lewis: Levenshtein editing for unsupervised text style transfer. arXiv preprint arXiv:2105.08206 (2021)
Romanov, A., Rumshisky, A., Rogers, A., Donahue, D.: Adversarial decomposition of text representation. arXiv preprint arXiv:1808.09042 (2018)
Roy, A., Vaswani, A., Neelakantan, A., Parmar, N.: Theory and experiments on vector quantized autoencoders. arXiv preprint arXiv:1805.11063 (2018)
Shen, T., Lei, T., Barzilay, R., Jaakkola, T.: Style transfer from non-parallel text by cross-alignment. In: Advances in Neural Information Processing Systems 30 (2017)
Sun, S., Zhu, J.: Plug-and-play textual style transfer
Toshevska, M., Gievska, S.: A review of text style transfer using deep learning. IEEE Trans. Artifi. Intell. (2021)
Tran, M., Zhang, Y., Soleymani, M.: Towards a friendly online community: An unsupervised style transfer framework for profanity redaction. arXiv preprint arXiv:2011.00403 (2020)
Vaswani, A.: Attention is all you need. In: Advances in Neural Information Processing Systems 30 (2017)
Yi, X., Liu, Z., Li, W., Sun, M.: Text style transfer via learning style instance supported latent space. In: Proceedings of the Twenty-Ninth International Conference on International Joint Conferences on Artificial Intelligence, pp. 3801–3807 (2021)
Zhang, T., Kishore, V., Wu, F., Weinberger, K.Q., Artzi, Y.: Bertscore: Evaluating text generation with bert. arXiv preprint arXiv:1904.09675 (2019)

Lexical Complexity Controlled Sentence Generation for Language Learning

Jinran Nie[1], Liner Yang[1(✉)], Yun Chen[2], Cunliang Kong[1], Junhui Zhu[1], and Erhong Yang[1]

[1] Beijing Language and Culture University, Beijing, China
yangliner@blcu.edu.cn
[2] Shanghai University of Finance and Economics, Shanghai, China

Abstract. Language teachers spend a lot of time developing good examples for language learners. For this reason, we define a new task for language learning, lexical complexity controlled sentence generation, which requires precise control over the lexical complexity in the keywords to examples generation and better fluency and semantic consistency. The challenge of this task is to generate fluent sentences only using words of given complexity levels. We propose a simple but effective approach for this task based on complexity embedding while controlling sentence length and syntactic complexity at the decoding stage. Compared with potential solutions, our approach fuses the representations of the word complexity levels into the model to get better control of lexical complexity. And we demonstrate the feasibility of the approach for both training models from scratch and fine-tuning the pre-trained models. To facilitate the research, we develop two datasets in English and Chinese respectively, on which extensive experiments are conducted. Experimental results show that our approach provides more precise control over lexical complexity, as well as better fluency and diversity.

Keywords: Lexical Complexity · Language Learning · Complexity Embedding

1 Introduction

In the fields of language teaching and acquisition, language instructors and textbook compilers need to make teaching materials with example sentences, either synthetically designed or from authentic resources [5,27]. In most cases, they are required to create appropriate example sentences that only use the words at particular complexity for language learners passing through different learning levels [20,30], which is very time-consuming and exhausting. Automatically generating good examples can support educators and language learners in obtaining, analyzing, and selecting proper example sentences. Besides, it can also assist in the development of graded reading materials [1,3,39].

For language learners, good examples are not only required to be fluent and diverse but also match the level of the learners, especially the level of vocabulary. Therefore, it is necessary to effectively control the lexical complexity in good examples generation, which is a task of controllable text generation.

M. Sun et al. (Eds.): CCL 2023, LNAI 14232, pp. 106–126, 2023.
https://doi.org/10.1007/978-981-99-6207-5_7

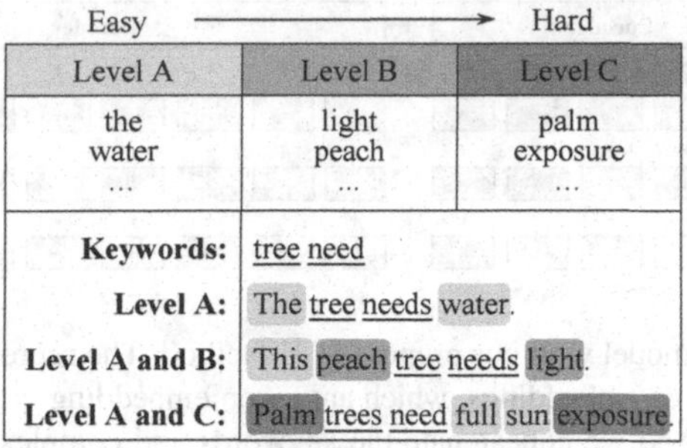
Easy
Hard
Level A
Level B
Level C
the
water
...
light
peach
...
palm
exposure
...
Keywords: tree need
Level A: The tree needs water.
Level A and B: This peach tree needs light.
Level A and C: Palm trees need full sun exposure.

Fig. 1. An example for lexical complexity controlled sentence generation. There are three complexity levels (A, B, and C) from easy to hard. Given the keywords "tree" and "need", we will generate "The tree needs water." if required to use all words from level A and generate "This peach tree needs light." if required to use words from both level A and B as both "peach" and "light" are in level B.

Controllable text generation (CTG), a significant area of natural language generation, contains a series of tasks that aim to generate text according to the given controlled requirements [34,52]. CTG systems usually focus on controlling text attributions such as sentiment [15,40,53], topic [8,17,46] or keywords [12,13,55], generating poems or couplets with specific formats [7,43,44], and even predicting descriptions from structured data [38,45,56]. However, few works have been devoted to strict control over the lexical complexity for text generation. Although lexical simplification has been paid attention to the text simplification task through substitution [19], it cannot strictly control the lexical complexity levels of the generated sentence.

To this end, we propose a new task of lexical complexity controlled sentence generation, which requires that keywords and complexity levels be given to generate a sentence including the keywords and consisting of the words in the given complexity levels. For example, as shown in Fig. 1, we assume that there are three complexity levels (A, B, and C) from easy to hard. Given the keywords, we can generate sentences consisted with words of different complexity according to the given levels.

It is challenging to generate fluent sentences for given keywords while using the words only at specific complexity levels. This can be regarded as an extension and a particular case of lexical CTG task [13,28,55]. Differently, it combines two aspects of constraints during generation: keywords constraint the semantics, and lexical complexity levels constraint the surface form. It is difficult for the model to select suitable words from a specific subspace satisfying the above two constraints in each generation process. We formulate this problem in Sect. 2.1.

Some previous works can be customized as solutions to this problem, which are divided into three branches: controlled decoding, prompting, and reranking. The first method forces to change the probability distribution during the decoding phase to ensure that only words of the specified levels are used in the generation [8,33]. But the hard constraint may lead to poor quality generation quality. The second one considers lexical complexity through prompting [4,24,36] in the input of the model, which introduce coarse grained information of training and inference. The method of reranking is to

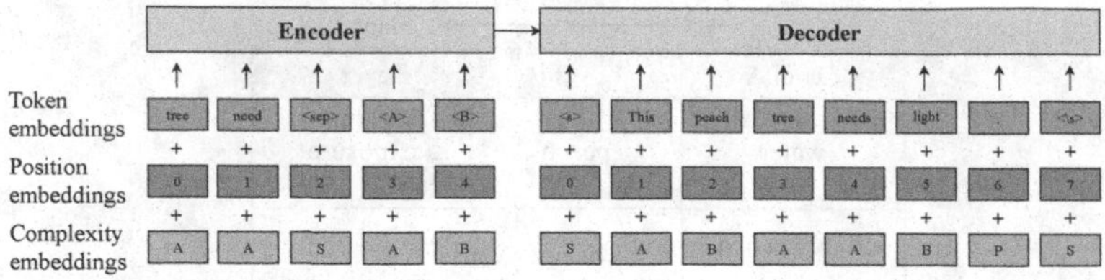

Fig. 2. Encoder-Decoder model with our proposed CE method. The representation of each input token is a summary of three embeddings, which are token embedding, position embedding, and complexity embedding. And we concatenate the keywords and complexity level tokens as the input sequence of the encoder. Note that the special tokens correspond to the complexity level of "S", and the punctuation correspond to "P".

select the sentence that best meets the lexical complexity requirements from the candidates [31,37], which executes after decoding and does not consider lexical complexity in the training time.

The complexity constraint requires models to aware of lexical complexity and respond to complexity control signals. Therefore, we use two mechanisms as enhancements to the transformer-based models. *For the complexity awareness*, we propose the Complexity Embedding (**CE**) method, which represents the complexity levels with trainable embeddings. We incorporate the CEs into both training and prediction processes by fusing the CEs and word embeddings as token representations, which is simple but effective. *For responding to complexity control signals*, we concatenate special tokens corresponding to specific complexity levels with the keywords as the input sequence. To combine the awareness and response, we use CEs to represent these special tokens. The experiments show that our proposed method is effective for both training from scratch and fine-tuning the pre-trained language models. And compared to the baseline methods, our method achieves significant improvement in the restriction of lexical complexity levels and generation quality. Our main contributions include:

- We propose a new task of lexical complexity controlled sentence generation and two datasets in English and Chinese for this task. To evaluate the satisfaction of the lexical complexity constraint, we develop four metrics.
- We propose a new method for this task based on complexity embedding.
- The experimental results show that the complexity embedding method we proposed significantly outperforms the baseline methods which are implemented for this task.

2 Method

2.1 Problem Definition

Lexical Complexity Controlled Sentence Generation aims at keywords to sentence generation with desired complexity levels. First, we give the keywords set $K = \{k_1, k_2, ..., k_m\}$ and the complexity levels $L = \{l_1, l_2, ..., l_n\}$ which correspond to a subset $D = \{W_1 \cup W_2 \cup ... \cup W_n\}$ of the whole vocabulary V and W_i is the word set of complexity level l_i. The control elements in this task include three parts:

First, we define a predicate $F(K, Y)$ to be a boolean function indicating the occurrence of keyword k_i in a generated sequence $Y = y_1, y_2, ..., y_t$, and t is the sequence length.

$$C_1 = F(K, Y) \tag{1}$$
$$F(K, Y) \equiv \forall\, i, k_i \in Y \tag{2}$$

where C_1 is the keywords constraint which means the keywords are required to be included in the generated sentence.

Second, we define a predicate $G(Y, D)$ to be a boolean function indicating the occurrence of a word y_i which is a word of the sentence Y in a word set D.

$$C_2 = G(Y, D) \tag{3}$$
$$G(Y, D) \equiv \forall\, i, y_i \in D \tag{4}$$

where C_2 is the complexity constraint on word which means the words in the generated sentence are required to be the words of the given complexity levels.

Then, we define a predicate $H(Y, W_i)$ to be a boolean function indicating that there exist at least one word in the generated sentence in the W_i.

$$C_3 = H(Y, W_1) \wedge H(Y, W_2) ... \wedge H(Y, W_n) \tag{5}$$
$$H(Y, W_i) \equiv \exists\, j, y_j \in W_i \tag{6}$$

where C_3 is the constraint on the species of complexity level which means the lexical levels of the generated sentence need cover all the given levels.

The task requires to seek optimal sequences in which all constraints are satisfied as much as possible. The formula is as follows:

$$\hat{Y} = \arg\max_{Y \in \mathcal{Y}} \log P_\theta(Y|K, L) \quad \text{where} \quad \sum_{i=1}^{N} C_i = N \tag{7}$$

where N is the number of constraints and $N = 3$.

2.2 Complexity Embedding

As illustrated in Fig. 2, our model is based on the encoder-decoder architecture. To make the model aware of the complexity levels, we fuse the complexity into the task by designing a lexical complexity embedding for each token. To make the model respond to specific complexity levels, we insert special tokens corresponding to complexity levels into the input sequence as controllable elements. This section introduces these two key components as well as the training and inference strategy.

We initialize a learnable matrix $\mathbf{M} \in \mathbb{R}^{U \times dim}$ as representations of complexity levels, where U is the total number of complexity levels, and dim is the dimensions of each embedding. For each token input to the encoder and decoder, we retrieve a predefined hash-table to obtain its complexity level l_i. Then we get the corresponding complexity embedding by $com_i = \mathrm{M}_i$. The final embedding of this token emb_i is as following:

$$emb_i = tok_i + pos_i + com_i \tag{8}$$

where tok_i and pos_i are token and positional embeddings, which are obtained according to Transformer model [47].

For example, as shown in Fig. 2, when two keywords "tree" and "need" along with two complexity levels A and B are required, the sentence "This peach tree needs light." is generated which satisfies both constraints. We use different complexity representations (mapping into a complexity embedding) for words of different complexity levels. And the complexity representations of special tokens and punctuation are also different.

In practice, we apply the BPE (byte pair encoding) [41] algorithm to split words into sub-word tokens to mitigate the OOV (out-of-vocabulary) problem. We mark each sub-word with the same complexity level as the original word. More details about the complexity levels can be found in the Appendix A.

2.3 Controllable Elements

As illustrated in Eq. 4, each word in the sentence Y is constrained to the word set D. To achieve this, we design a set of special tokens $Z = \{z_1, z_2, \ldots, z_n\}$, where each token corresponds to a complexity level in L.

We concatenate the keywords and the special tokens as the input sequence $X = [K; \langle sep \rangle; Z]$. And we refer the special tokens Z as controllable elements, as they control the complexity of the generated sentence. Note that the complexity embedding of z_i is that of the level l_i.

2.4 Training Complexity Embedding

We train the complexity embedding in the Transformer model from scratch or fine-tune the pre-trained model discriminatively as there is no complexity embedding layer in the pre-trained process. If a model is trained from scratch, the parameters of complexity embedding will be trained the same as other parameters in the model. If the complexity embedding is added to a pre-trained model for fine-tuning, we first train the complexity embedding layer by fixing the original parameters of the pre-trained model and then fine-tune the whole model.

During the training process, in fact, both the word embedding and the complexity embedding are in a teach-forcing pattern through the ground truth. At the time of inference, the next word embedding at each step will be predicted by the probability distribution of the vocabulary of the model. Since the complexity level of the next word is unknown at each step of the inference stage, we utilize a look-up table method to map the predicted token id to complexity id. The table is a mapping relation between the token id and its complexity id on the whole vocabulary. At each step, the token id will be predicted by the model. We get its complexity id through its token id and the table. The complexity id and token id will then be given as the input for the next step of inference.

2.5 Length and Syntactic Complexity Control

The length of the generated text is also a factor that language learners may consider, and there is a correlation between text length and syntactic complexity. From a statistical view, text length and syntactic complexity are generally positively correlated. Thus, we design a method to dynamically control text length and syntactic complexity, which is used in the decoding stage. We set three sentence length modes: short, normal, and long, and the sentence length mode also corresponds to the syntactic complexity. We introduce length penalties to beam search in the decoding time in different modes. The formula for calculating the penalty coefficient is as follows:

$$Penalty = N^{pen} \tag{9}$$

where N is the counts of keywords, $pen = -1, 0, 1$ if the mode is short, normal or long respectively. We have observed from statistics that the larger the number of given keywords leads the longer the generated sentences. Therefore, we set the relationship between the length penalty and the number of keywords. In the mode of short or long, if the number of keywords is larger, the greater the penalty required.

3 Datasets and Evaluation Metrics

3.1 Dataset Construction

We present two datasets for lexical complexity controlled sentence generation in English and Chinese. The English raw corpus is collected from the monolingual English News dataset in ACL2019 WMT. The Chinese raw corpus is collected from 500 textbooks for Chinese L2 learners. We adopt the English word complexity levels in the Common European Framework of Reference for Languages (CEFR)[1] which is divided into six complexity levels (A1, A2, B1, B2, C1, and C2). The word complexity levels in Chinese Proficiency Grading Standards for International Chinese Language Education (CPGS)[2] is divided into seven complexity levels (1 to 7). The process for cleaning data is divided into three steps: split the raw data into sentences and choose the proper sentences; obtain the keywords from the sentences; get the lexical complexity levels from the sentences. More details of the two datasets are in the Appendix B.

3.2 Evaluation Metrics

Generated Quality To evaluate the quality of generated text, we employ some automatic evaluate metrics in three aspects. 1) N-gram Similarity with References: we use **BLEU** [32], **METEOR** [21], and **NIST** [9] evaluate the difference between generated texts and reference texts, which are commonly utilized in machine translation and text generation. 2) Diversity: We use 2-gram and 4-gram of **Entropy** [54] and 1-gram and 2-gram of **Distinct** [23] to evaluate lexical diversity. 3) Fluency: Following previous

[1] https://www.englishprofile.org/wordlists/evp.

[2] https://www.chinesetest.cn/index.do

works [13,55], to assess the fluency of generated sentences, we report the perplexity (**PPL**) over the test set using the pre-trained GPT-2 [35] large model.

Satisfaction of Lexically Controlling The control elements of lexical complexity controlled sentence generation have introduced in the Sect. 2.1. Our metrics are corresponding to the three constraints.

– **Keywords Constraint**. For this aspect, we introduce Keywords Constraint (**K-C**) satisfaction metric on word-level, which is computed using the percentage of the keywords contained in the generated sentences. The formular describe is as below:

$$K - C = \frac{1}{N} \sum\nolimits_{i=1}^{N} \text{count}_i^{C_1} / m_i \tag{10}$$

where N is the total number of samples in the test dataset, $\text{count}_i^{C_1}$ is the number of keywords included in the generated sentence of the i-th sample, which satisfy the constraint of C_1, and m_i is the number of the keywords of the input on the i-th sample.

– **Word Complexity Constraint**. The purpose of this metric is to calculate the Accuracy (**ACC**) of the words that meet the lexical complexity levels requirement in the generated sentence. As shown in the following formula:

$$ACC = \frac{1}{N} \sum\nolimits_{i=1}^{N} \text{count}_i^{C_2} / t_i \tag{11}$$

where $\text{count}_i^{C_2}$ is the number of the words that satisfy the constraint C_2 of the i-th sample, and t_i is the length of the generated sentence of the i-th sample.

– **Complexity Levels Constraint**. We propose three metrics to evaluate the satisfaction of the species of the required complexity levels. It is unreasonable that the ACC is still 100% if given two complexity levels but the words of generated sentence only covers one of the levels. Thus we design the metrics of Precision (**P**), Recall (**R**), and **F1** to calculate the satisfaction of complexity level constraint. The formular describes are as follows:

$$P = \frac{1}{N} \sum\nolimits_{i=1}^{N} \text{count}_i^{C_3} / g_i \tag{12}$$

$$R = \frac{1}{N} \sum\nolimits_{i=1}^{N} \text{count}_i^{C_3} / n_i \tag{13}$$

$$F1 = \frac{2}{N} \sum\nolimits_{i=1}^{N} \text{count}_i^{C_3} / (n_i + g_i) \tag{14}$$

where $\text{count}_i^{C_3}$ is the number of the complexity levels satisfy the constraint C_3 of the i-th sample, n_i is the number of the complexity levels given in the source of the i-th sample, and g_i is the number of the complexity levels of the generated sentence of the i-th sample.

Table 1. Generation quality evaluation results on English dataset.

Metrics	BLEU(%)		NIST(%)		METEOR(%)	Entropy(%)		Distinct(%)		PPL
	B-2	B-4	N-2	N-4		E-2	E-4	D-1	D-2	
Training Transformer from scratch										
K2S	16.58	4.57	3.14	3.27	15.23	8.20	10.23	**5.93**	24.76	74.91
Ctrl-decoding	12.12	3.16	2.45	2.61	11.72	7.28	9.22	5.27	20.14	286.50
Prompting	18.19	5.73	3.57	3.64	15.93	8.30	10.36	6.10	25.55	52.10
Reranking	**18.47**	6.27	3.52	3.60	15.99	7.87	9.79	5.93	22.70	47.81
CE (ours)	18.37	**6.66**	**3.64**	**3.69**	**16.06**	**8.43**	**10.47**	5.80	**25.75**	**42.06**
Fine-tuning BART										
K2S	17.40	5.96	3.20	3.26	15.60	8.60	10.52	6.36	28.53	33.11
Ctrl-decoding	14.17	3.55	2.73	2.48	13.15	8.03	9.87	5.96	21.96	223.43
Prompting	19.36	6.88	3.59	3.67	16.09	**8.93**	**10.81**	**7.22**	**33.84**	39.65
Reranking	18.95	6.54	3.54	3.58	16.03	8.72	10.67	6.60	30.09	34.24
CE (ours)	**19.80**	**7.22**	**3.61**	**3.69**	**16.34**	8.50	10.48	6.41	27.56	**28.48**

4 Experiments

Our experiments are based on the two datasets introduced in Sect. 3. Besides the strong baselines of controlled decoding, prompting and reranking mentioned in Sect. 4.2, we generate the sentence by setting the keys as the input directly as the basic baseline (K2S). This baseline does not require complexity levels, which are just learnt from the data. Our evaluations include automatic evaluation and human evaluation. The automatic metrics have been introduced in the Sect. 3.

4.1 Experimental Setup

Our experimental setup contains two aspects:training from scratch and fine-tuning. From scratch training experiments are on the Transformer model [47], which is the most widely used model in text generation. The fine-tuning experiments are on the pre-trained model of BART [22], which has superior generation ability. During inference, we run greedy decoding on all models for a fair comparison. We implement all models with the Fairseq library[3] and the BART pre-trained model is from HuggingFace Transformers library[4] [51]. All models are trained and tested on NVIDIA TITAN Xp GPU.

From Scratch Training Setup. We adopt the typical Transformer [47] as the model trained from scratch. We utilize a learning rate of 3e-4 and set the warming-up schedule

[3] https://github.com/pytorch/fairseq.
[4] https://github.com/huggingface/transformers.

with 4000 steps for training. We train our model for around 100 epochs. The optimization algorithm is Adam [18]. We set the maximum number of input tokens as 8192, which is the same as transformer-based baselines.

Fine-tuning Setup. We initialize our model with BART-base [22], which has comparable parameters to generation baselines. For generation baselines and our models, we use Adam [18] with an initial learning rate of 1e-5 to update parameters for four epochs and choose the checkpoints with the lowest validation loss. We train our model for around 30 epochs. We set the maximum number of input tokens as 2048.

Table 2. Satisfaction of controlling evaluation results on English dataset.

Metrics (%)	K-C	ACC	P	R	F1
Training Transformer from scratch					
K2S	96.93	95.68	89.03	83.27	84.93
Ctrl-decoding	85.56	99.02	97.84	83.51	89.19
Prompting	96.85	98.91	97.35	90.86	93.46
Reranking	97.33	96.80	91.81	87.97	88.98
CE (ours)	**98.00**	**99.10**	**98.09**	**92.84**	**94.96**
Fine-tuning BART					
K2S	97.51	95.26	88.79	84.63	85.58
Ctrl-decoding	89.73	**99.34**	**98.57**	84.19	90.33
Prompting	96.57	97.79	95.77	90.17	92.25
Reranking	98.52	96.10	92.36	88.96	91.87
CE (ours)	**98.68**	99.13	98.54	**93.72**	**95.77**

Table 3. Generation quality evaluation results on Chinese dataset.

Metrics	BLEU(%)		NIST(%)		METEOR(%)	Entropy(%)		Distinct(%)		PPL
	B-2	B-4	N-2	N-4		E-2	E-4	D-1	D-2	
Training Transformer from scratch										
K2S	13.92	4.17	2.73	2.76	15.00	8.83	10.20	8.60	37.70	48.32
Ctrl-decoding	12.84	3.57	2.48	2.50	13.70	8.70	10.30	6.08	34.90	224.59
Prompting	13.90	3.81	2.70	2.73	14.35	8.53	10.05	7.47	33.35	45.61
Reranking	15.46	5.37	**2.98**	**3.02**	15.34	8.84	10.15	9.13	37.88	38.56
CE (ours)	**15.69**	**6.27**	2.91	2.94	**16.04**	**9.28**	**10.58**	**10.68**	**47.71**	**34.53**
Fine-tuning BART										
K2S	14.97	4.39	3.08	3.10	16.56	8.60	10.06	9.91	37.13	**21.76**
Ctrl-decoding	12.54	3.71	2.38	2.55	14.04	8.73	10.25	9.96	37.85	129.86
Prompting	16.81	5.47	3.15	3.17	16.24	8.69	10.13	10.04	38.33	31.75
Reranking	16.53	6.42	**3.29**	**3.36**	16.61	8.81	10.08	10.15	38.96	53.47
CE (ours)	**17.07**	**6.46**	3.18	3.26	**16.73**	**9.34**	**10.27**	**10.55**	**48.76**	26.52

Table 4. Satisfaction of controlling evaluation results on Chinese dataset.

Metrics (%)	K-C	ACC	P	R	F1
Training Transformer from scratch					
K2S	87.36	92.74	85.40	68.40	73.75
Ctrl-decoding	71.83	**99.96**	**99.96**	61.79	74.73
Prompting	85.54	98.88	97.79	80.23	86.88
Reranking	88.22	96.70	93.05	75.74	81.59
CE (ours)	**89.61**	98.87	97.49	**88.80**	**92.17**
Fine-tuning BART					
K2S	92.12	93.73	86.88	68.87	74.37
Ctrl-decoding	82.52	**99.18**	**98.65**	65.26	76.41
Prompting	86.94	98.73	97.98	81.78	88.02
Reranking	90.14	97.21	95.44	76.78	83.95
CE (ours)	**92.58**	99.07	97.91	**89.34**	**92.85**

4.2 Baseline

Controlled Decoding. We consider a strategy of controlled decoding [8] to realize the generated sentence consists of the words belonging to the given complexity levels. Since we know the words of the complexity level to be used in the sentence, we can restrict the words of the subset of the vocabulary to only be used in the decoding stage. The specific method is to set the probability of words outside the subset to zero so that they can meet the requirements of the word complexity level.

Prompting. Prompting is another feasible method for controlled text generation [57]. Inspired by the prefix-tuning [24], which uses continuous vectors as prompts, we add the required complexity levels as the prefix for controlling in the input of the generation model.

Reranking. Inspired by previous works [31,37], we select the sentence that best meets the lexical complexity requirements from the N-best candidates. We take the score that is the sum of ACC score and $F1$ score on the test reference hypothesis from this N-best list and choose the candidate that has the largest score. The detail of the re-ranking method is shown as the Algorithm 1 in Appendix C.

4.3 Experimental Results

The experimental results on English dataset are shown in Table 1 and Table 2. From the evaluation of generation quality in Table 1, it can be seen that the method of complexity

Table 5. Human evaluations for fine-tuning BART model on two datasets.

Metrics (%)	Semantics	Fluency	Diversity
English dataset			
Ctrl-decoding	2.68	2.40	2.92
Prompting	**4.63**	3.25	3.45
Reranking	4.60	3.39	3.40
CE (ours)	4.62	**3.82**	**3.54**
Chinese dataset			
Ctrl-decoding	3.89	2.82	3.27
Prompting	4.23	3.08	3.02
Reranking	4.37	3.29	3.16
CE (ours)	**4.57**	**3.80**	**3.71**

embedding has competitive results in different aspects, especially on fluency. In general, the CE method has better performance in the control of lexical complexity, especially on the metrics of R and F1. The method of controlled decoding has poor performance on PPL because it forces the distribution of the logits to concentrate on the words of given complexity levels in the decoding stage. This hard constraint pattern will impact the fluency of the generated sentences. But its performances on the metrics of ACC and P are better than other methods from Table 2. The methods of prompting and reranking are two competitive baselines. The prompting method has better performance in the control of the word complexity because it has considered the word complexity levels in training. But the reranking method has better generation quality on the whole metrics of Table 1.

The experimental results on Chinese dataset are shown in Table 3 and Table 4. We can draw similar conclusions from these two tables. Our approach performs well in terms of both text generation quality and lexical complexity control. The rerank approach outperforms prompt in all aspects of generation quality, both in terms of similarity to ground truth and in diversity and fluency, and even achieves the best NIST metrics for the Chinese dataset.

4.4 More Analyses and Discussion

The CE method we proposed has an excellent performance in controlling lexical complexity. The reason is that the CE method not only keeps the consistency of training and prediction but also considers the information of the complexity at the token level. Thus, it has more precise control of lexical complexity. And it also has competitive generation quality in the aspect of fluency and similarity with the reference. From the metrics of Entropy and Distinct, its diversity has a little poor performance in terms of the fine-tuning pattern on the English dataset. We think the main reason is that the vocabulary of the English word complexity levels is less than which of the Chinese, so the token level restrictions of complexity embedding will impact the diversity of the sentences. The Chinese dataset, on the other hand, has a much larger coverage of vocabulary with complexity and the dataset comes from the field of second language teaching, so the diversity of our model is better. It is worth noting that our CE method performs best in terms of lexical complexity control, especially the metrics of K-C, R, and F1, compared to the baseline model. This indicates that the CE method has higher coverage on complexity levels due to it takes into account the complexity of each word.

Table 6. The length and depth of syntactic tree of generated sentences in different modes.

Metric/Mode	Short	Normal	Long
Length	15.3	24.6	36.8
Syn-Depth	9.3	11.1	13.5

4.5 Length and Syntactic Complexity Control

We evaluate the length and the depth of the syntactic tree of generated text in the modes of short, normal and long, which can reflect the complexity of the generated text. As shown in the Table 6, the experiment of controlling sentence length and syntactic complexity is on the English dataset. In the long mode, the generated sentences are longer, and the syntactic tree is deeper. In the short mode, the generated sentences are shorter, and the syntactic tree depth is smaller. The length penalty in the decoding stage can effectively control the sentence length while affecting the complexity of the syntax.

4.6 Human Evaluation

We conduct a human evaluation to further compare our model with the three baselines with fine-tuning the BART model on two datasets. For each model, we randomly select 200 generated sentences from the test set for each dataset and invite three annotators to label the sentences, who are postgraduates of the major in linguistics. To evaluate the quality of the sentences, annotators rate the sentences on three dimensions: semantic consistency between the keywords and sentence; the fluency of the sentence; the diversity of the sentence [55]. The score is range from 0 to 5. As shown in Table 5, our method has better performance at the three aspects of human evaluation, especially the fluency and diversity. We give some real cases of two datasets in the Appendix D. From the cases study we can find that the CE method can cover more lexical complexity levels than the baseline methods. This also confirms the reason why the CE method that we proposed has a better performance on R and F1 metrics of the automatic evaluation.

5 Related Work

Lexical constraint text generation is to generate a complete text sequence, given a set of keywords as constraints [55]. Previous works involve enhanced beam search [14,

33] and the stochastic search methods [42,55]. Currently, Seq2Seq-based models such as Transformer and pre-trained models have been increased in generation with lexical constraint [10,25,26,48,49]. But lexically constrained text generation is not able to control the complexity of words used in the generation, which is different from our work.

Text readability assess research has shown that lexical complexity is also a crucial aspect of evaluating the complexity of a text for text readability assess task [6]. In the relevant study of sentence-level readability, it is generally accepted that apart from sentence length, the most predictive indicator is the number of difficult words in the sentence [50]. In our work, we follow the definition and vocabulary of lexical complexity of text readability assess.

Text simplification In text simplification field, lexical substitution, the replacement of complex words with simpler alternatives, is an integral part of sentence simplification and has been the subject of previous work [2,29]. Differently, our work can strictly control the lexical complexity levels of the generated sentence, not only simplify the lexical complexity.

6 Conclusions

To summarize, we introduce a new task of lexical complexity controlled sentence generation, where word complexity must be strictly controlled in generating. To promote the development of this task, we develop two datasets and four metrics for the controlled element. In this paper, we also develop a series of alternate solutions for this task and propose a novel method based on complexity embedding to obtain better control of lexical complexity in a generation. Our results indicate that the complexity embedding method has better performance in controlling the lexical complexity and competitive generation quality.

Acknowledgement. This work was supported by the funds of Research Project of the National Language Commission No. ZDI145-24. We would like to thank all anonymous reviewers for their valuable comments and suggestions on this work.

A Complexity Embedding Id

The English words have six levels. And the Chinese words have seven levels (Diff 1–7). We give the design of the complexity embedding id for this two language in the Table 7. Note that, if a word is out of the complexity level vocabulary, its complexity is "$\langle out \rangle$" which is mapping into id 7 in English corpus and 8 in Chinese corpus. In addition, the special tokens such as "$\langle s \rangle$" "$\langle pad \rangle$" "$\langle \backslash s \rangle$" "$\langle unk \rangle$" are the common meaning in data preprocessing for model training.

B Details of Datasets Construction

B.1 English Dataset

We adopt the English word complexity levels in the Common European Framework of Reference for Languages (CEFR)[5] which is divided into six complexity levels (A1, A2, B1, B2, C1, and C2). First, we need to restrict the words in the corpus to ensure most of the words are in the complexity level vocabulary. Then, we need to extract keywords from the sentences. In this process, we command the number of keywords is related to the length of the sentence, and the number of keywords is between 1 to 5. Finally, we obtain the complexity information of each sentence through the complexity level vocabulary. The English raw corpus is collected from the monolingual English News dataset in ACL2019 WMT. We select those sentences which have 90% words in the complexity level vocabulary of CEFR. After the processes mentioned above, we get 199k samples in the English corpus, and we split the train, validation and test dataset as shown in the Table 8.

Table 7. Complexity Embedding Id.

English		Chinese	
Token	Id	Token	Id
Punctuation	0	Punctuation	0
A1-C2	1–6	Diff 1–7	1–7
$\langle out \rangle$	7	$\langle out \rangle$	8
$\langle sep \rangle$	8	$\langle sep \rangle$	9
$\langle s \rangle$	8	$\langle s \rangle$	9
$\langle pad \rangle$	8	$\langle pad \rangle$	9
$\langle ns \rangle$	8	$\langle ns \rangle$	9
$\langle unk \rangle$	8	$\langle unk \rangle$	9

B.2 Chinese Dataset

The word complexity levels in Chinese Proficiency Grading Standards for International Chinese Language Education (CPGS)[6] is divided into six complexity levels (1 to 7). The Chinese raw corpus is collected from 500 textbooks for Chinese learners. These textbooks contain two types of text: essay and dialogue. We split these texts into sentences and throw away those short sentences. If the raw text is a dialogue, after splitting, we need to remove the speaker's name to guarantee it is a proper sentence. Then, we command the number of keywords is related to the length of the sentence, and the number of keywords is between 1 to 5. After the processes mentioned above, we get 156k samples in the Chinese corpus, as shown in the Table 8.

[5] https://www.englishprofile.org/wordlists/evp.

[6] https://www.chinesetest.cn/index.do

B.3 Analysis of the Datasets

Coverage of Words with Levels. We first analyze the two datasets from the coverage rate of complexity level vocabulary. Due to the requirement of complexity level, the target text is proper to cover most of the vocabulary of complexity level. Both of the two datasets have covered over 93% of the vocabulary of complexity levels.

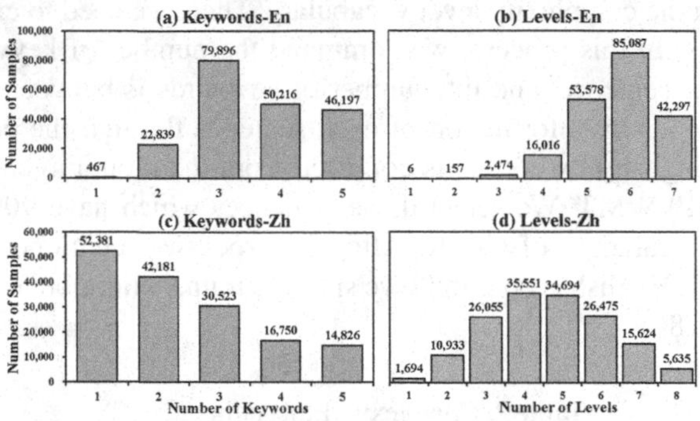

Fig. 3. Distributions of the number of keywords and complexity levels.

Table 8. Statistics of the two datasets.

Dataset	Train	Valid	Test	Total
English	180,000	16,000	3,615	199,615
Chinese	140,000	14,000	2,661	156,661

Distributions of the Number of Keywords and Complexity Levels. One or multiple complexity levels and keywords are given as the input to generate sentences. We give the distribution of the number of keywords and the complexity levels in Fig. 3. From the statistics of (a) and (c) in Fig. 3, the number of keywords in all samples has covered the range of 1 to 5 both in the English and Chinese datasets, but the distributions are quite different. On account of the average sentence length of English news data is longer than the Chinese corpus, the number of keywords in English is larger. From the statistics in (b) and (d) of Fig. 3, the number of complexity levels distribution of the Chinese dataset is close to a standard normal distribution, and the English dataset concentrates on a wider range of complexity levels. This indicates that in the English dataset it tends to use more words of different complexity levels in the same sentence.

C Algorithm of Reranking

The algorithm is the detail of reranking method. We select the sentence that best meets the lexical complexity requirements from the N-best candidates, and $N = 10$. On the test set, We take the sum of ACC score and $F1$ score. The, we choose the candidate that has the largest score.

D Case Study

We choose some cases of the fine-tuning pattern from two datasets. The English cases are in the Table 9, and the Chinese cases are in the Table 10. In both tables, the required keywords as well as appearing in the sentences are shown in blue font, and certain given grades as well as words actually appearing in the sentences for the corresponding grade are shown in red font.

Algorithm 1. Reranking Method

Input: Generated n best candidate sentences $H = (h_0, h_1, h_2, ..., h_{n-1})$ for given keywords and $n = 10$

Output: Sentence having highest score

```
Let score = 0
for each sentence h_j in H do
    ACC = F_acc(h_j)
    F1 = F_f1(h_j)
    score_j = ACC + F1
    if score_j > score then
        score = score_j
        ret = h_j
    end if
end for
return ret
```

E Related Methods

E.1 Controlled Decoding

The gradients of an external discriminator is directly used to the generation of a pre-trained language model toward the target topic [8]. The output probabilities of a language model is modified by using the output of a discriminator that determines whether the future text will contain the desired attribute. Different from the controlled decoding methods, our method considers the constraint of lexical complexity during both training and prediction.

E.2 Prompting

The prompting method has emerged as a new way to perform natural language processing by conditioning on extra information. Brown et al. propose to use a task description and a few examples to adapt the GPT-3 model to downstream tasks, which is referred to as in-context learning [4]. Their prompts are manually designed. Gao et al. present LM-BFF for automatic prompts generation [11]. Liang et al. propose prefix-tuning, which uses continuous vectors as prompts [24]. Compared to the prompting method, our method fuses more fine-grained information on lexical complexity in model training.

E.3 Reranking

The reranking approach has been proved to have excellent performance in machine translation [31] and text generation [37]. The reranking method rescores the n-best candidates through a model or a function and selects the highest scoring candidate as the final prediction [16]. Unlike the reranking method, our method do not need to process the outputs after decoding.

F Limitation

Our proposed task has wide applications in the field of language teaching, and the proposed method has precise control over lexical difficulty. However, the task requires that

Table 9. Generated examples from the English dataset.

Keywords: refuse, accept, country ; **Complexity Levels:** A1, A2, B1, C1	
Ctrl-decoding	I refuse to accept that this is a matter of time for the country, but I do not accept it
Prompting	I refuse to accept that I am the only one who has been elected to the country, but I am not
Reranking	I refuse to accept that this is the best thing I can do for the country," he said
CE (ours)	I refuse to accept that this is a country that is going to be a place where people are going to be unsafe
Keywords: public, maintain, lose ; **Complexity Levels:** A1, A2, B1, B2	
Ctrl-decoding	I do not think the public will maintain the power to lose, but I do not think it will
Prompting	The public will maintain the public's ability to lose, and the public will not lose, and they will not lose
Reranking	I don't want to be in public, but I don't want to maintain my weight and lose
CE (ours)	The public must maintain their faith and not lose , and we will continue to do everything we can to protect them
Keywords: football, Leicester, City, magical ; **Complexity Levels:** A1, A2, B1, B2, C2	
Ctrl-decoding	I think football is a great way to play for the game and to be able to play for the best of the game against the game against the game against the game and the way we play against the game against the game against the game against the game is not the same, but the way we are magical
Prompting	I think football is going to be the best of Leicester City, but I think it's a magical moment for us to have to play with
Reranking	This is a football game for Leicester City, and it's a magical moment for us to be part of the game and be a part of it
CE (ours)	It's a football club that has been around for a long time and to see Leicester City win the title is magical

the lexical complexity is known first. The vocabulary difficulty table is the experience summed up by the predecessors, and it is difficult to apply to all vocabulary. Therefore, we are actively exploring how to make the model automatically understand all vocabulary difficulties so that it can cover a wider vocabulary at generation.

Table 10. Generated examples from the Chinese dataset.

Keywords: 生活； **Complexity Levels:** 1, 2, 3, 7	
Ctrl-decoding	生活中，我最喜欢的就是吃面。
Prompting	生活中的一切都是为了生活。
Reranking	我们的生活很美好，也很快乐。
CE (ours)	没有工作压力的生活多让人羡慕啊！
Keywords: 春天, 姑娘； **Complexity Levels:** 1, 2, 3	
Ctrl-decoding	春天来了，姑娘又来了，他还在那儿等着我呢。
Prompting	春天来了，姑娘又来了，他的眼睛也变得很美丽。
Reranking	春天到了，一个年轻的姑娘爱上了他。
CE (ours)	春天来了，我认识了一位美丽的姑娘，他非常喜欢这个姑娘。
Keywords: 喜欢； **Complexity Levels:** 1, 7	
Ctrl-decoding	我喜欢吃中国菜，我喜欢吃中国菜。
Prompting	我喜欢看中国电影。
Reranking	你喜欢什么样的女孩子呢?
CE (ours)	我最喜欢逗它们玩儿。
Keywords: 别人, 可能, 意思; **Complexity Levels:** 1, 2	
Ctrl-decoding	别人看我懂了，我觉得我有可能去做一个人，意思是要看他。
Prompting	别人可能不会说，如果你觉得自己可能有可能，你可能会觉得自己是个很难的意思。
Reranking	如果别人问你一个问题，你的意思是什么?
CE (ours)	别人可能不知道你的意思，你要做我喜欢的，要我愿意跟别人说。

References

1. Al-Jarf, R.: Efl students' difficulties with lexical and syntactic features of news headlines and news stories. Technium Soc. Sci. J. **17**, 524 (2021)
2. Alonzo, O., Seita, M., Glasser, A., Huenerfauth, M.: Automatic text simplification tools for deaf and hard of hearing adults: benefits of lexical simplification and providing users with autonomy. In: Proceedings of the 2020 CHI Conference on Human Factors in Computing Systems, pp. 1–13 (2020)
3. Amer, M.A.B.: Lexical density and readability of secondary stage English textbooks in Jordan. Int. J. Manage. Modern Educ. **2**(2), 11–20 (2021)

4. Brown, T., et al.: Language models are few-shot learners. Adv. Neural. Inf. Process. Syst. **33**, 1877–1901 (2020)
5. Caro, K., Mendinueta, N.R.: Lexis, lexical competence and lexical knowledge: a review. J. Lang. Teach. Res. **8**(2) (2017)
6. Chakraborty, S., Nayeem, M.T., Ahmad, W.U.: Simple or complex? Learning to predict readability of bengali texts. In: Proceedings of the AAAI Conference on Artificial Intelligence. vol. 35, pp. 12621–12629 (2021)
7. Chen, H., Yi, X., Sun, M., Li, W., Yang, C., Guo, Z.: Sentiment-controllable Chinese poetry generation. In: IJCAI, pp. 4925–4931 (2019)
8. Dathathri, S., et al.: Plug and play language models: A simple approach to controlled text generation. arXiv preprint arXiv:1912.02164 (2019)
9. Doddington, G.: Automatic evaluation of machine translation quality using n-gram co-occurrence statistics. In: Proceedings of the Second International Conference on Human Language Technology Research, pp. 138–145 (2002)
10. Fan, Z., et al.: An enhanced knowledge injection model for commonsense generation. arXiv preprint arXiv:2012.00366 (2020)
11. Gao, T., Fisch, A., Chen, D.: Making pre-trained language models better few-shot learners. arXiv preprint arXiv:2012.15723 (2020)
12. He, X.: Parallel refinements for lexically constrained text generation with bart. arXiv preprint arXiv:2109.12487 (2021)
13. He, X., Li, V.O.: Show me how to revise: Improving lexically constrained sentence generation with xlnet. In: Proceedings of the AAAI Conference on Artificial Intelligence. vol. 35, pp. 12989–12997 (2021)
14. Hu, J.E., et al.: Improved lexically constrained decoding for translation and monolingual rewriting. In: Proceedings of the 2019 Conference of the North American Chapter of the Association for Computational Linguistics: Human Language Technologies, Volume 1 (Long and Short Papers), pp. 839–850 (2019)
15. Hu, Z., Yang, Z., Liang, X., Salakhutdinov, R., Xing, E.P.: Toward controlled generation of text. In: International Conference on Machine Learning, pp. 1587–1596. PMLR (2017)
16. Imamura, K., Sumita, E.: Ensemble and reranking: using multiple models in the nict-2 neural machine translation system at wat2017. In: Proceedings of the 4th Workshop on Asian Translation (WAT2017), pp. 127–134 (2017)
17. Khalifa, M., Elsahar, H., Dymetman, M.: A distributional approach to controlled text generation. arXiv preprint arXiv:2012.11635 (2020)
18. Kingma, D.P., Ba, J.: Adam: a method for stochastic optimization. arXiv preprint arXiv:1412.6980 (2014)
19. Kriz, R., Miltsakaki, E., Apidianaki, M., Callison-Burch, C.: Simplification using paraphrases and context-based lexical substitution. In: Proceedings of the 2018 Conference of the North American Chapter of the Association for Computational Linguistics: Human Language Technologies, Volume 1 (Long Papers), pp. 207–217 (2018)
20. Laufer, B.: Lexical thresholds and alleged threats to validity: a storm in a teacup? Reading Foreign Lang. **33**(2), 238–246 (2021)
21. Lavie, A., Agarwal, A.: Meteor: An automatic metric for MT evaluation with high levels of correlation with human judgments. In: Proceedings of the Second Workshop on Statistical Machine Translation, pp. 228–231 (2007)
22. Lewis, M., et al.: Bart: Denoising sequence-to-sequence pre-training for natural language generation, translation, and comprehension. arXiv preprint arXiv:1910.13461 (2019)
23. Li, J., Galley, M., Brockett, C., Gao, J., Dolan, B.: A diversity-promoting objective function for neural conversation models. arXiv preprint arXiv:1510.03055 (2015)

24. Li, X.L., Liang, P.: Prefix-tuning: optimizing continuous prompts for generation. In: Proceedings of the 59th Annual Meeting of the Association for Computational Linguistics and the 11th International Joint Conference on Natural Language Processing (Volume 1: Long Papers), pp. 4582–4597 (2021)
25. Liu, Y., Wan, Y., He, L., Peng, H., Yu, P.S.: Kg-bart: knowledge graph-augmented bart for generative commonsense reasoning. arXiv preprint arXiv:2009.12677 (2020)
26. Liu, Y., Zhang, L., Han, W., Zhang, Y., Tu, K.: Constrained text generation with global guidance-case study on commongen. arXiv preprint arXiv:2103.07170 (2021)
27. Lu, D., Qiu, X., Cai, Y.: Sentence-level readability assessment for L2 Chinese learning. In: Hong, J.-F., Zhang, Y., Liu, P. (eds.) CLSW 2019. LNCS (LNAI), vol. 11831, pp. 381–392. Springer, Cham (2020). https://doi.org/10.1007/978-3-030-38189-9_40
28. Miao, N., Zhou, H., Mou, L., Yan, R., Li, L.: Cgmh: constrained sentence generation by metropolis-hastings sampling. In: Proceedings of the AAAI Conference on Artificial Intelligence. vol. 33, pp. 6834–6842 (2019)
29. Nishihara, D., Kajiwara, T., Arase, Y.: Controllable text simplification with lexical constraint loss. In: Proceedings of the 57th Annual Meeting of the Association for Computational Linguistics: Student Research Workshop, pp. 260–266 (2019)
30. Nordlund, M., Norberg, C.: Vocabulary in EFL teaching materials for young learners. Int. J. Lang. Stud. **14**(1), 89–116 (2020)
31. Pandramish, V., Sharma, D.M.: Checkpoint reranking: an approach to select better hypothesis for neural machine translation systems. In: Proceedings of the 58th Annual Meeting of the Association for Computational Linguistics: Student Research Workshop, pp. 286–291 (2020)
32. Papineni, K., Roukos, S., Ward, T., Zhu, W.J.: Bleu: a method for automatic evaluation of machine translation. In: Proceedings of the 40th Annual Meeting of the Association for Computational Linguistics, pp. 311–318 (2002)
33. Post, M., Vilar, D.: Fast lexically constrained decoding with dynamic beam allocation for neural machine translation. arXiv preprint arXiv:1804.06609 (2018)
34. Prabhumoye, S., Black, A.W., Salakhutdinov, R.: Exploring controllable text generation techniques. arXiv preprint arXiv:2005.01822 (2020)
35. Radford, A., Wu, J., Child, R., Luan, D., Amodei, D., Sutskever, I., et al.: Language models are unsupervised multitask learners. OpenAI blog **1**(8), 9 (2019)
36. Raffel, C., et al.: Exploring the limits of transfer learning with a unified text-to-text transformer. J. Mach. Learn. Res. **21**(140), 1–67 (2020)
37. Ravaut, M., Joty, S., Chen, N.F.: Summareranker: a multi-task mixture-of-experts re-ranking framework for abstractive summarization. arXiv preprint arXiv:2203.06569 (2022)
38. Ribeiro, L.F., Zhang, Y., Gurevych, I.: Structural adapters in pretrained language models for amr-to-text generation. arXiv preprint arXiv:2103.09120 (2021)
39. Ryu, J., Jeon, M.: An analysis of text difficulty across grades in Korean middle school English textbooks using Coh-Metrix. J. Asia TEFL **17**(3), 921 (2020)
40. Samanta, B., Agarwal, M., Ganguly, N.: Fine-grained sentiment controlled text generation. arXiv preprint arXiv:2006.09891 (2020)
41. Sennrich, R., Haddow, B., Birch, A.: Neural machine translation of rare words with subword units. arXiv preprint arXiv:1508.07909 (2015)
42. Sha, L.: Gradient-guided unsupervised lexically constrained text generation. In: Proceedings of the 2020 Conference on Empirical Methods in Natural Language Processing (EMNLP), pp. 8692–8703 (2020)
43. Shao, Y., Shao, T., Wang, M., Wang, P., Gao, J.: A sentiment and style controllable approach for Chinese poetry generation. In: Proceedings of the 30th ACM International Conference on Information and Knowledge Management, pp. 4784–4788 (2021)

44. Sheng, Z., et al.: Songmass: automatic song writing with pre-training and alignment constraint. In: Proceedings of the AAAI Conference on Artificial Intelligence. vol. 35, pp. 13798–13805 (2021)
45. Su, Y., Vandyke, D., Wang, S., Fang, Y., Collier, N.: Plan-then-generate: controlled data-to-text generation via planning. arXiv preprint arXiv:2108.13740 (2021)
46. Tang, H., Li, M., Jin, B.: A topic augmented text generation model: Joint learning of semantics and structural features. In: Proceedings of the 2019 Conference on Empirical Methods in Natural Language Processing and the 9th International Joint Conference on Natural Language Processing (EMNLP-IJCNLP), pp. 5090–5099 (2019)
47. Vaswani, A., et al.: Attention is all you need. Adv. Neural Inform. Process. Syst. **30**, 5998–6008 (2017)
48. Wang, H., et al.: Retrieval enhanced model for commonsense generation. arXiv preprint arXiv:2105.11174 (2021)
49. Wang, Y., Wood, I., Wan, S., Dras, M., Johnson, M.: Mention flags (mf): constraining transformer-based text generators. In: Proceedings of the 59th Annual Meeting of the Association for Computational Linguistics and the 11th International Joint Conference on Natural Language Processing (Volume 1: Long Papers), pp. 103–113 (2021)
50. Weiss, Z., Meurers, D.: Assessing sentence readability for German language learners with broad linguistic modeling or readability formulas: When do linguistic insights make a difference? In: Proceedings of the 17th Workshop on Innovative Use of NLP for Building Educational Applications (BEA 2022), pp. 141–153 (2022)
51. Wolf, T., et al.: Huggingface's transformers: State-of-the-art natural language processing. arXiv preprint arXiv:1910.03771 (2019)
52. Zhang, H., Song, H., Li, S., Zhou, M., Song, D.: A survey of controllable text generation using transformer-based pre-trained language models. arXiv preprint arXiv:2201.05337 (2022)
53. Zhang, R., Wang, Z., Yin, K., Huang, Z.: Emotional text generation based on cross-domain sentiment transfer. IEEE Access **7**, 100081–100089 (2019)
54. Zhang, Y., et al.: Generating informative and diverse conversational responses via adversarial information maximization. arXiv preprint arXiv:1809.05972 (2018)
55. Zhang, Y., Wang, G., Li, C., Gan, Z., Brockett, C., Dolan, B.: Pointer: constrained progressive text generation via insertion-based generative pre-training. arXiv preprint arXiv:2005.00558 (2020)
56. Zhao, C., Walker, M., Chaturvedi, S.: Bridging the structural gap between encoding and decoding for data-to-text generation. In: Proceedings of the 58th Annual Meeting of the Association for Computational Linguistics, pp. 2481–2491 (2020)
57. Zou, X., Yin, D., Zhong, Q., Yang, H., Yang, Z., Tang, J.: Controllable generation from pre-trained language models via inverse prompting. In: Proceedings of the 27th ACM SIGKDD Conference on Knowledge Discovery & Data Mining, pp. 2450–2460 (2021)

Improving Zero-Shot Cross-Lingual Dialogue State Tracking via Contrastive Learning

Yu Xiang[1], Ting Zhang[2], Hui Di[3], Hui Huang[4], Chunyou Li[1], Kazushige Ouchi[3], Yufeng Chen[1], and Jinan Xu[1](✉)

[1] Beijing Key Lab of Traffic Data Analysis and Mining, Beijing Jiaotong University, Beijing 100044, China
{21120422,21120368,chenyf,jaxu}@bjtu.edu.cn

[2] Global Tone Communication Technology Co., Ltd., Beijing, China
zhangting01@gtcom.com.cn

[3] Toshiba (China) Co., Ltd., Beijing, China
dihui@toshiba.com.cn, kazushige.ouchi@toshiba.co.jp

[4] Harbin Institute of Technology, Harbin, China
22b903058@stu.hit.edu.cn

Abstract. Recent works in dialogue state tracking (DST) focus on a handful of languages, as collecting large-scale manually annotated data in different languages is expensive. Existing models address this issue by code-switched data augmentation or intermediate fine-tuning of multilingual pre-trained models. However, these models can only perform implicit alignment across languages. In this paper, we propose a novel model named Contrastive Learning for Cross-Lingual DST (CLCL-DST) to enhance zero-shot cross-lingual adaptation. Specifically, we use a self-built bilingual dictionary for lexical substitution to construct multilingual views of the same utterance. Then our approach leverages fine-grained contrastive learning to encourage representations of specific slot tokens in different views to be more similar than negative example pairs. By this means, CLCL-DST aligns similar words across languages into a more refined language-invariant space. In addition, CLCL-DST uses a significance-based keyword extraction approach to select task-related words to build the bilingual dictionary for better cross-lingual positive examples. Experiment results on Multilingual WoZ 2.0 and parallel MultiWoZ 2.1 datasets show that our proposed CLCL-DST outperforms existing state-of-the-art methods by a large margin, demonstrating the effectiveness of CLCL-DST.

Keywords: Dialogue state tracking · Cross-lingual transfer learning · Contrastive learning

1 Introduction

Dialogue state tracking is an essential part of task-oriented dialogue systems [34], which aims to extract user goals or intentions throughout a dialogue process and encode them into a compact set of dialogue states, i.e., a set of slot-value pairs. In recent years, DST models have achieved impressive success with adequate training data. However, most

M. Sun et al. (Eds.): CCL 2023, LNAI 14232, pp. 127–141, 2023.
https://doi.org/10.1007/978-981-99-6207-5_8

models are restricted to monolingual scenarios since collecting and annotating task-oriented dialogue data in different languages is time-consuming and costly [1]. It is necessary to investigate how to migrate a high-performance dialogue state tracker to different languages when no annotated target language dialogue data are available.

Previous approaches are generally divided into the following three categories: (1) Data augmentation methods with neural machine translation system [24]. Although translating dialogue corpora using machine translation is straightforward, it has inherent limitation of heavily depending on performance of machine translation. (2) Pre-trained cross-lingual representation [16]. The approach applies a cross-lingual pre-trained model, such as mBERT [4], XLM [3] and XLM-RoBERTa (XLM-R) [2] as one of the components of the DST architecture and then is trained with task data directly. However, the approach does not introduce cross-lingual information during the training process. (3) Code-switched data augmentation [17,18,22]. The method replaces words randomly from the source language to the target language with a bilingual dictionary as a way to achieve data augmentation. Nevertheless, a synonym substitution with some meaningless words may introduce noise that impairs the semantic coherence of the sentence. Besides, the model only use the code-switched corpus as the training data, ignoring the interaction between the original and code-switched sentences. Consequently, these models can not sufficiently learn the semantic representation of the corpus.

To address the above-mentioned issues, we propose a novel model named **C**ontrastive **L**earning for **C**ross-**L**ingual DST (CLCL-DST), which utilizes contrastive learning (CL) for cross-lingual adaptation. CLCL-DST first captures comprehensive cross-lingual information from different perspectives and explores the consistency of multiple views through contrastive learning [11]. Simultaneously, as dialogue state tracking is to predict the state of slots in each turn of the dialogue, we consider it as a token-level task and then employ the same fine-grained CL. Specifically, we obtain the encoded feature representation of each slot in the original sentence and the corresponding code-switched sentence from the multilingual pre-trained model, respectively. We then employ fine-grained CL to align the representations of slot tokens in different views. By introducing CL, Our model is able to distinguish between the code-switched utterance and a set of negative samples, thus encouraging representations of similar words in different languages to align into a language-invariant feature space (Subsect. 3.1).

Furthermore, CLCL-DST introduces a significance-based keyword extraction approach to obtain task-related keywords with high significance scores in different domains. For example, in the price range domain, some words like "cheap", "moderate" and "expensive" are more likely to have higher significance scores than background words, such as "a", "is" and "do". Specifically, Our approach obtains the semantic representation of sentences and corresponding subwords by encoder. Then the approach gets the significance scores of the words by calculating the cosine similarity and get the keywords of the dataset based on the scores. We then replace these keywords with the corresponding words in the target language to generate multilingual code-switched data pairs. These code-switched keywords can be considered as cross-lingual views sharing the same meaning, allowing the shared encoder to learn some direct bundles of meaning in different languages. Thus, our keyword extraction approach facilitates the transfer of cross-lingual information and strengthens the ties across different languages (Subsect. 3.2).

We evaluate our model on two benchmark datasets. For the Multilingual WoZ 2.0 dataset [20] which is single-domain, our model outperforms the existing state-of-the-art model by 4.1% and 4.8% slot accuracy for German (De) and Italian (It) under the zero-shot setting, respectively. For the parallel MultiWoZ 2.1 dataset [8] which is multi-domain, our method outperforms the current state-of-the-art by 22% and 38.7% in joint goal accuracy and slot f1 for Chinese (Zh), respectively. Moreover, further experiments show that introducing fine-grained CL performs better than coarse-grained CL. We also investigate the impact of different keyword extraction approaches on the model to demonstrate the superiority of our extraction approach.

Our main contributions can be summarized as follows:

- To the best of our knowledge, this is the first work on DST that leverages fine-grained contrastive learning to explicitly align representations across languages.
- We propose to utilize a significance-based keyword selection approach to select task-related keywords for code-switching. By constructing cross-lingual views through these keywords makes the model more effective in transferring cross-lingual signals.
- Our CLCL-DST model achieves state-of-the-art results on single-domain cross-lingual DST tasks, and it boasts the unique advantage of performing effective zero-shot transfer under the multi-domain cross-lingual setting, demonstrating the effectiveness of CLCL-DST.

2 Related Work

2.1 Dialogue State Tracking

Methods of dialogue state tracking can be divided into two categories, ontology-based and open-vocabulary DST. The first method selects the possible values for each slot directly from a pre-defined ontology and the task can be seen as a value classification task for each slot [7,14,15,27]. However, in practical applications, it is difficult to define all possible values of slots in advance, and the computational complexity increases significantly with the size of the ontology.

The open-vocabulary approach attempts to solve the above problems by extracting or generating slot values directly from the dialogue history [23]. [29] generates slot values directly for each slot at every dialogue turn. The model uses GRU to encode the dialogue history and decode the value with a copy mechanism. Some recent works [9,33] adopt a more efficient approach by decomposing DST into two tasks: state operation prediction and value generation. SOM-DST [9] firstly predicts state operation on each slot and then generates the value of the slot that needs updating. [32] proposes a framework based on the architecture of SOM-DST, with a single BERT as both the encoder and the decoder.

2.2 Zero-Shot Cross-Lingual Dialogue State Tracking

There is a growing demand for dialogue systems supporting different languages, which requires large-scale training data with high quality. However, these data are only available within a few languages. It remains a challenge to migrate dialogue state tracker from the source language to the target language.

Cross-lingual dialogue state tracking can be divided into two categories: single-domain and multi-domain. In single-domain, XL-NBT [1] first implements cross-lingual learning under the zero-shot setting by pre-training a dialogue state tracker for the source language using a teacher network. MLT [17] adopts a code-mixed data augmentation framework, leveraging attention mechanism to obtain the code-mixed training data for learning the interlingual semantics across different languages. CLCSA [22] further explores the dynamic replacement of words from source language to target language during training. Based on CLCSA architecture, XLIFT-DST [19] improves the performance by intermediate fine-tuning of pre-trained multilingual models using parallel and conversational movie subtitles datasets.

In multi-domain, the primary benchmark is the Parallel MultiWoZ 2.1 dataset [8] originating from the Ninth Dialogue Systems and Technologies Challenge (DSTC-9) [8]. This challenge is designed to build a dialogue state tracker to evaluate a low-resource target language dataset using the learned knowledge of the source language. All the submissions in this challenge use the translated version of the dataset, transforming the problem into a monolingual dialogue state tracking task. XLIFT-DST employs SUMBT [14] as the base architecture and achieves competitive results on the parallel MultiWoZ 2.1 dataset through intermediate fine-tuning. Unlike these works, we leverage code-switched data with CL to further align multiple language representations under the zero-shot setting.

2.3 Contrastive Learning

Contrastive learning aims at pulling close semantically similar examples (positive samples) and pushing apart dissimilar examples (negative samples) in the representation space. SimCSE [6] proposes a simple dropout approach to construct positive samples and achieves state-of-the-art results in semantic textual similarity tasks. Cline [26] constructs semantically negative instances without supervision to improve the robustness of the model against semantically adversarial attacks. GL-CLEF [21] leverages bilingual dictionaries to generate code-switched data as positive samples, and incorporates different grained contrastive learning to achieve cross-lingual transfer. Our model incorporates fine-grained CL to align similar representations between the source and target languages.

3 Methodology

In this section, we set up the notations that run throughout the paper first, before describing our CLCL-DST model which explicitly uses contrastive learning to achieve cross-lingual alignment in dialogue state tracking. Then, we introduce a significance-based code-switching approach on how to select task-related keywords in the utterance and code-switch the input sentence dynamically in detail. The main architecture of our model is illustrated in Fig. 1.

Notation. Suppose the dialogue has T turns. We define the dialogue utterance at turn t as $D_t = R_t \oplus ; \oplus U_t \oplus$ [SEP], where R_t and $U_t (1 \leq t \leq T)$ are the system response and the user utterance respectively. $\oplus$ denotes token concatenation, and the semicolon ; is a separation symbol, while [SEP] marks the end boundary of the dialogue. Besides, we represent the dialogue states as $B = \{B_1, ..., B_T\}$, where $B_t = [\text{SLOT}]^1 \oplus b_t^1 \oplus ... \oplus [\text{SLOT}]^I \oplus b_t^I$ denotes I states combination at the t-th turn. I is the total number of slots. The i-th slot-value pair b_t^i is defined as:

$$b_t^i = S^i \oplus - \oplus V_t^i, \tag{1}$$

where S^i is a slot and V_t^i is the corresponding slot value. $[\text{SLOT}]^i$ and – are separation symbols. The representations at $[\text{SLOT}]^i$ position are used for state operation prediction and contrastive learning. We use the same special token [SLOT] for all $[\text{SLOT}]^i$. The input tokens in CLCL-DST are spliced by previous turn dialogue utterance D_{t-1}, current turn dialogue utterance D_t and previous turn dialogue states B_{t-1} [9]:

$$X_t = [\text{CLS}] \oplus D_{t-1} \oplus D_t \oplus B_{t-1}, \tag{2}$$

where [CLS] is a special token to mark the start of the context. Next, we will elaborate each part in detail.

3.1 Fine-Grained Contrastive Learning Framework

We introduce our fine-grained contrastive learning framework (CLCL-DST) with an encoder-decoder architecture consisting of two modules: state operation prediction and value generation. The encoder, i.e., state operation predictor, uses a multilingual pre-trained model to predict the type of the operations to be performed on each slot. The decoder, i.e., slot value generator, generates values for those selected slots.

Encoder. The encoder of CLCL-DST is based on mBERT architecture. We feed the code-switched sentence $X_{t,cs}$ into the encoder and obtain the output representation $H_{t,cs} \in \mathbb{R}^{|X_t| \times d}$, where $h_{t,cs}^{[\text{CLS}]}, h_{t,cs}^{[\text{SLOT}]^i} \in \mathbb{R}^d$ are the outputs corresponding to [CLS] and $[\text{SLOT}]^i$. $h_{t,cs}^{[\text{SLOT}]^i}$ is passed into a four-way classification layer to calculate the probability $P_{enc,t}^i \in \mathbb{R}^{|\mathcal{O}|}$ of operations in the i-th slot at the t-th turn:

$$P_{enc,t}^i = \text{softmax}\left(W_{enc} h_{t,cs}^{[\text{SLOT}]^i} + b\right), \tag{3}$$

where W_{enc} and b are learnable parameters.

$\mathcal{O}$ = {CARRYOVER, DELETE, DONTCARE, UPDATE} denotes four state operations of each slot [9]. Specifically, CARRYOVER indicates that the slot value remains unchanged; DELETE changes the value to NULL; and DONTCARE means that the slot is not important at this turn and does not need to be tracked [29]. Only when the UPDATE is predicted does the decoder generate a value for the corresponding slot.

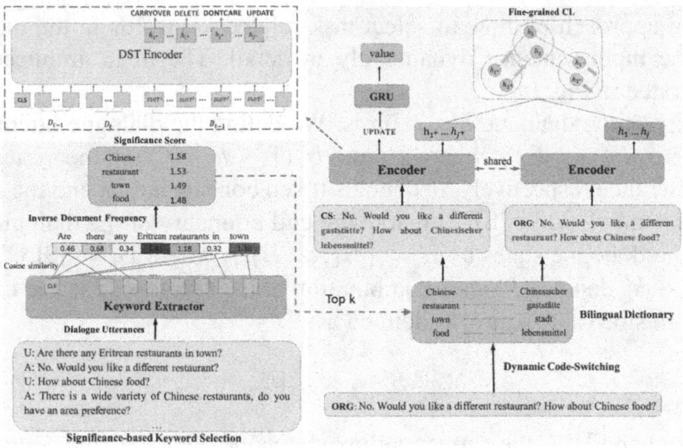

Fig. 1. The overview of the proposed CLCL-DST. The input of our model consists of previous turn dialogue utterances D_{t-1}, current turn dialogue utterances D_t and previous dialogue state B_{t-1}. For simplicity, we only put one turn of dialogue on the picture. The model constructs a bilingual dictionary by obtaining keywords from the significance-based code-switching approach, and then generates code-switched data. The data are fed to the encoder to obtain a feature representation of each slot subsequently. **ORG** denotes the original sentence and **CS** denotes the corresponding code-switched sentence. In the part of **Fine-grained CL**, different color denotes different representation spaces for origin utterance, positive and negative samples. The decoder generates the value for the slot whose state operation is predicted to **UPDATE**.

Our main learning objective is to train the encoder to match predicted state operation with the ground truth operation. So the loss for state operation is formulated as:

$$\mathcal{L}_{enc,t} = -\frac{1}{I}\sum_{i=1}^{I}\left(Y_{enc,t}^{i}\right)^{\top}\log\left(P_{enc,t}^{i}\right), \tag{4}$$

where $Y_{enc,t}^{i} \in \mathbb{R}^{|\mathcal{O}|}$ is the ground truth operation for the j-th slot.

Decoder. We employ GRU as decoder to generate the value of dialogue state for each domain-slot pair whose operation is UPDATE. GRU is initialized with $g_t^{i,0} = W_t$ and $e_t^{i,0} = h_t^{[\text{SLOT}]^i}$. The probability distribution of the vocabulary is calculated as:

$$P_{dec,t}^{i,k} = \text{softmax}\left(\text{GRU}\left(g_t^{i,k-1}, e_t^{i,k}\right) \times E\right) \in \mathbb{R}^{|V|}, \tag{5}$$

where k is decoding step, $E \in \mathbb{R}^{|V|\times d}$ is the word embedding space shared with the encoder, and $|V|$ is the size of multilingual vocabulary. The overall loss for generating slot value is the average of the negative log-likelihood loss:

$$\mathcal{L}_{dec,t} = -\frac{1}{|\mathbb{U}_t|}\sum_{i\in\mathbb{U}_t}\left[\frac{1}{K_t^i}\sum_{k=1}^{K_t^i}\left(Y^{i,k}\right)^{\top}\log\left(P_{dec,t}^{i,k}\right)\right], \tag{6}$$

where $|\mathbb{U}_t|$ is the number of slots which require value generation, K_t^i indicates the number of ground truth value to be generated for the i-th slot. $Y^{i,k} \in \mathbb{R}^{|V|}$ represents the one-hot vector of the ground truth token generated for the i-th slot at the k-th decoding step.

Fine-Grained Contrastive Learning. In order to better capture the common features between the source language and the target language, our model utilizes fine-grained CL to pull closer the representation of similar sentences across different languages. The key to CL is to find high-quality positive and negative pairs corresponding to the original utterance. The positive sample should be semantically consistent with the original utterance and provides cross-lingual view as well. In our scenario, we choose code-switched input $X_{t,cs}$ as the positive sample of X_t, while other inputs in the same batch are treated as negative samples.

As state operation of each slot is a token-level task, we utilize a fine-grained CL loss to facilitate token alignment. To achieve fine-grained cross-lingual transfer, our method selects the output representation $h_t^{[\mathrm{SLOT}]^i}$ of the special token $[\mathrm{SLOT}]^i$ for contrastive learning, as these I tokens are able to convey the semantics of the slots in the query. The i-th slot token loss is defined as:

$$\mathcal{L}_{cl,t}^i = -\frac{1}{I}\sum_{j=1}^{I} \log \frac{cos\left(h_t^i, h_t^{j^+}\right)}{cos\left(h_t^i, h_t^{j^+}\right) + \sum_{k=0,k\neq j}^{\mathrm{I}-1} cos\left(h_t^i, h_t^{k^-}\right)}, \tag{7}$$

where h_t^i is the abbreviation of $h_t^{[\mathrm{SLOT}]^i}$, $h_t^{j^+}$ and $h_t^{k^-}$ are positive and negative samples of $h_t^{[\mathrm{SLOT}]^i}$ respectively. The total loss $\mathcal{L}_{cl,t}$ is calculated by adding up all tokens CL loss.

The overall objective in CLCL-DST at dialogue turn t is the sum of individual losses above:

$$\mathcal{L}_t = \mathcal{L}_{enc,t} + \mathcal{L}_{cl,t} + \mathcal{L}_{dec,t}. \tag{8}$$

3.2 Significance-Based Code-Switching

The importance of different words in a dialogue utterance varies. For example, in the price range domain, “cheap" and “expensive" are more likely to be keywords, while in the area domain, keyword set might include orientation terms such as “center", “north" and “east". Assuming that a dataset contains v words constituting a vocabulary $\mathcal{V}$, we construct a subset of keywords $\mathcal{K} \subseteq \mathcal{V}$ for code-switching. Subsequently, the encoder of CLCL-DST serves to extract keywords in the training data.

Given the input token $X_t = (w_t^1, w_t^2, ..., w_t^n)$ at the t-th turn, n denotes the number of words. We feed X_t into encoder, and obtain the representation $h_t^{[\mathrm{CLS}]} \in \mathbb{R}^d$ of the special token [CLS]. Then the sentence embedding vector W_t is calculated as:

$$W_t = \tanh(W_{pool} h_t^{[\mathrm{CLS}]} + b), \tag{9}$$

where W_{pool} and b are learnable parameters. Then the cosine similarity between each token $w_t \in X_t$ and the sentence embedding vector W_t is computed as:

$$Sim(w_t) = \cos(w_t, W_t). \tag{10}$$

$Sim(w_t)$ reflects the degree of associations between w_t and sentence embedding W_t. A higher value of the significance score $Sim(w_t)$ indicates a higher probability of w_t to be a keyword. For words that are tokenized into subwords, we average the significance scores of each subword to obtain the word score.

Equation 10 calculates the significance score of words in a sentence. To get the keyword set $\mathcal{K}$ in training set, we add all significance scores for token w in training set and multiply them by the inverse document frequency (IDF) [31] of w:

$$S(w) = \log \frac{N}{|\{x \in X : w \in x\}|} \cdot \sum_{x \in X : w \in x} Sim(w), \tag{11}$$

where N denotes the number of the input in the training dataset, $|\{x \in X : w \in x\}|$ indicates the number of the input containing w. The IDF term can reduce the weight of words which appear frequently in the dataset, assigning meaningless words (e.g., "for" and "an") with a lower score.

We select top-k words according to the significance scores to get a keyword set K, and use the bilingual dictionary MUSE [12] to construct the code-switched dictionary $Dic = ((s_1, t_1), ...(s_k, t_k))$, where s and t refer to the source and target language words respectively. k is the number of keywords. In addition, we translate the whole words in ontology and add them to Dic due to their important role in the sentence.

Inspired by [22], we randomly replace some words in source language sentence with corresponding target words with a fixed probability if they appear in Dic. Since words from the source language may have multiple translations in Dic, we randomly select one of them for substitution. Notably, the input token X in our model includes dialogue utterance D and dialogue states B, we just replace source words in D as B shares the same slots across languages. Finally, we can get the code-switched input tokens $X_{t,cs}$ from X_t as:

$$X_{t,cs} = [\text{CLS}] \oplus D_{t-1,cs} \oplus D_{t,cs} \oplus B_{t-1}, \tag{12}$$

4 Experiments

4.1 Datasets

We evaluate our model on two datasets as follows:

- **Multilingual WoZ 2.0 dataset** [20]: A restaurant domain dialogue dataset expanded from WoZ 2.0 [28], which contains three languages (English, German, Italian) and 1200 dialogues for each language. The corpus consists of three goal-tracking slot types: food, price range and area. The task is to learn a dialogue state tracker only in English and evaluate it on the German and Italian datasets, respectively.

- **Parallel MultiWoZ dataset** [8]: A seven domains dialogue dataset expanded from MultiWoZ 2.1 [5]. Parallel MultiWoZ contains two languages (English, Chinese) and 10K dialogues. The Chinese corpus is obtained through Google Translate and manually corrected by experts.

4.2 Compared Methods

We compare our approach with the following methods:

- **XL-NBT** [1] utilizes bilingual corpus and bilingual dictionaries to transfer the teacher's knowledge of the source language to a student tracker in the target languages.
- **MLT** [17] constructs code-switched data through the attention layer for training.
- **CLCSA** [22] dynamically constructs multilingual code-switched data by randomly replacing words, so as to better fine-tune mBERT and achieve outstanding results in multiple languages.
- **SUMBT** [14] uses a non-parametric distance measure to score each candidate slot-value pair. We replace BERT with mBERT on the cross-lingual setup.
- **SOM-DST** [9] employs BERT as the encoder and uses a copy-based RNN to decode upon BERT outputs.
- **DST-as-PROMPTING** [13] introduces an approach that uses schema-driven prompting to provide history encoding and then utilizes T5 to generate slot values directly. Here, we use the multilingual version of T5 - mT5 [30].
- **XLIFT-DST** [19] leverages task-related parallel data to enhance transfer learning by intermediate fine-tuning of pre-trained multilingual models. For parallel MultiWoZ, XLIFT-DST uses the architecture of SUMBT, while uses the state tracker in CLCSA for Multilingual WoZ 2.0.

4.3 Implementation Details

Our method leverages the pre-trained mBERT-base[1] implemented by HuggingFace as the encoder, with 12 Transformer blocks and 12 self-attention heads. One layer GRU is used as the decoder. The encoder shares the same hidden size s with the decoder, which is 768. Adam optimizer [10] is applied to optimize all parameters with a warmup strategy for the 10% of the total training steps. The peak learning rate is set to 4e-5 for encoder and 1e-4 for decoder, respectively. Besides, we use greedy decoding for generating slot values.

For Multilingual WoZ dataset, the batch size is set to 64 and the maximum sequence length to 200. For parallel MultiWoZ dataset, the batch size and the maximum sequence length are 16 and 350 respectively. We replace the word for each dialogue with a fixed probability of 0.6. The training is performed for 100 epochs as default, and we choose the best checkpoint on the validation set to test our model.

[1] https://huggingface.co/bert-base-multilingual-uncased.

4.4 Evaluation Metrics

Table 1. Slot accuracy and joint goal accuracy on Multilingual WoZ 2.0 dataset under zero-shot setting when trained with English task data. Please see text for more details. **Bold** indicates the best score in that column. CLCL-DST denotes our approach.

Model	German		Italian	
	slot acc.	joint acc.	slot acc.	joint acc.
XL-NBT [1]	55.0	30.8	72.0	41.2
MLT [17]	69.5	32.2	69.5	31.4
Transformer based				
mBERT	57.6	15.0	54.6	12.6
CLCSA [22]	83.0	63.2	82.2	61.3
XLIFT-DST [19]	85.2	**65.8**	84.3	66.9
CLCL-DST (ours)	**89.3**	63.2	**89.1**	**67.0**

The metrics in dialogue state tracking are turn-level which include Slot Accuracy, Joint Goal Accuracy and Slot F1. Slot Accuracy is the proportion of the correct slots predicted in all utterances. Joint Goal Accuracy is the proportion of dialogue turns where all slot values predicted at a turn exactly match the ground truth values, while Slot F1 is the Macro-average of F1 score computed over the slot values at each turn.

4.5 Main Results

Results for the Multilingual WoZ dataset are illustrated in Table 1. We can see that CLCL-DST outperforms the state-of-the-art model (XLIFT-DST) by 4.1% and 4.8% in slot accuracy for De and It respectively. This demonstrates that our model is able to explicitly bring similar representations of different languages closer together through contrastive learning than augmenting transfer learning process with intermediate fine-tuning of pre-trained multilingual models.

To further study the effectiveness of our model under the zero-shot setting, We also test CLCL-DST on parallel MultiWoZ in Table 2. As there are only a few baselines available for this dataset, we re-implement some monolingual models such as SUMBT, SOM-DST, DST-as-PROMPTING into multilingual scenarios. We find that our model has 22% and 38.7% improvement over XLIFT-DST in joint goal accuracy and slot f1 for target language Zh under the zero-shot setting. It is worth noting that the joint goal accuracy of all these baseline models is relatively low. The possible reason is that these models do not learn considerable cross-lingual representations in the multi-domain cases, making it difficult to migrate for complex slots. Specifically, In the SOM-DST model, its decoder utilizes the soft-gated copy mechanism [25] in addition to GRU, which introduces additional noise from the source language and is not applicable to multilingual settings. In DST-as-PROMPTING, the model only leverages mT5

Table 2. Joint goal accuracy and slot F1 on parallel MultiWoZ dataset under zero-shot learning setting when trained with English task data and tested on Zh language. '†' denotes results from [19]. '‡' denotes our re-implemented results for the models based on corresponding multilingual pretrained models.

Model	joint acc.	slot f1.
SUMBT [14] †	1.9	14.8
SOM-DST [9] ‡	1.7	10.6
DST-as-PROMPTING [13] ‡	2.5	17.6
XLIFT-DST †	5.1	40.7
CLCL-DST (ours)	**27.1**	**79.4**
In-language training †	15.8	70.2
Translate-Train †	11.1	54.2
Translate-Test †	26.5	77.0

to generate slot values directly without learning deeply cross-lingual interaction information. Besides, we also refer to the results of translation-based methods from [19] in Table 2. Our model still outperforms all of them. These results further indicate that our proposed CLCL-DST leveraging code-switched data with contrastive learning boosts the performance of dialogue state tracker.

5 Ablation Studies

We conduct ablation experiments to explore the effect of fine-grained contrastive learning and the significance-based keyword extraction approach on the overall performance for the Multilingual WoZ 2.0 dataset.

5.1 The Effect of Fine-Grained Contrastive Learning

In addition to fine-grained CL, we also introduce coarse-grained CL for aligning similar sentences across different languages. To be specific, we align the sentence embedding W_t from Eq. 9 with its corresponding code-switched positive representations W_t^+. The objective for coarse-grained CL is written as follows:

$$\mathcal{L}_{sl,t} = -\log \frac{\cos\left(W_t, W_t^+\right)}{\cos\left(W_t, W_t^+\right) + \sum_{k=0,k\neq j}^{\mathrm{I}-1} \cos\left(W_t, W_t^{k-}\right)}, \tag{13}$$

where $W_t^{k^-}$ is the negative sample for W_t at the t-th turn.

As results shown in Table 3, we can conclude that different granularities of contrastive learning are effective for our model, especially fine-grained CL since it can bring more improvement to CLCL-DST. Using fine-grained CL improves 1.4% and 5.5% in slot accuracy and joint goal accuracy for De, and 9.3% and 26% for It, respectively, compared to coarse-grained CL. Since the goal of dialogue state tracking is to

Table 3. Slot accuracy and joint goal accuracy) for different grained contrastive learning under zero-shot setting. "CL" denotes the abbreviation of contrastive learning.

Method	German		Italian	
	slot acc.	joint acc.	slot acc.	joint acc.
w/o CL	82.5	52.0	86.8	60.0
Coarse-grained CL	87.9	57.7	79.8	41.0
Fine-grained CL	**89.3**	**63.2**	**89.1**	**67.0**

predict the state of slots in each turn of the dialogue, it can be considered as a token-level task, so fine-grained CL is better suited for this task compared to coarse-grained CL. Also, our approach selects specific tokens representing slots instead of all tokens in the dialogue for contrastive learning, which can reduce the noise caused by other semantically irrelevant tokens.

5.2 The Effect of Significance-Based Code-Switching

In this section we further explore the impact of keyword extraction algorithm on CLCL-DST. Table 4 shows the performance of different keyword extraction strategies. We try other four approaches to obtain the mapping dictionaries and compare them with the significance-based code-switching approach: (1) choosing words based on their frequency in our training set and converting them to target languages by MUSE; (2) using the whole ontology, which contains 90 words approximately; (3) combining the dictionaries obtained from (1) and (2) to form a new dictionary; (4) extracting keywords using only TF-IDF algorithm.

Table 4. Slot accuracy and joint goal accuracy on Multilingual WoZ 2.0 dataset for different keywords extraction approaches under zero-shot setting. The Method column represents the strategy for extracting keywords. "Onto" is the abbreviation of ontology. "+" denotes the merging of dictionaries obtained by the two methods.

Method	German		Italian	
	slot acc.	joint acc.	slot acc.	joint acc.
MUSE	86.4	59.4	84.0	54.5
Onto	86.2	56.0	81.8	46.8
MUSE+Onto	88.0	57.8	88.4	66.3
TF-IDF+Onto	86.5	55.3	87.9	66.0
Significance-based	87.9	60.4	**89.1**	63.5
Significance-based+Onto	**89.3**	**63.2**	**89.1**	**67.0**

Compared with only considering the frequency of words in the corpus, our significance-based code-switching approach can also make use of the numerous linguistic information carried in the multilingual pretrained model, so that the selected words

Table 5. Slot accuracy and joint goal accuracy on Multilingual WoZ 2.0 dataset for different number of keywords under zero-shot setting.

Number of keywords	German		Italian	
	slot acc.	joint acc.	slot acc.	joint acc.
200	86.5	60.4	85.1	61.5
500	88.2	62.3	86.8	64.4
1000	**89.3**	63.2	**89.1**	**67.0**
2000	88.6	**63.3**	86.9	66.3
5000	88.9	62.9	87.4	66.5

are more representative of the utterance. This approach enables the selected words to better express the main idea of the text. At the same time, words in ontology such as place names, food names, etc. are originally special words in the dataset, which occupy an important position in the text. Adding these words to our dictionary can further improve the performance of the model.

Table 5 shows the influence of different number of keywords on our model. We can see that the model has the best or second-best performance when k is 1000. As k continues to increase, the additional keywords are less indicative, so they even have a negative impact on model performance.

6 Conclusion

In this paper, we propose a novel zero-shot adaptation method CLCL-DST for cross-lingual dialogue state tracking. Our approach leverages fine-grained contrastive learning to explicitly align representations across languages. Besides, we introduce the significance-based code-switching approach to replace task-relevant words with target language for generating code-switched sentences on downstream tasks. Our method obtains new state-of-the-art results on Multilingual WoZ dataset and parallel MultiWoZ dataset, which demonstrates its effectiveness. In the future, we would investigate better training objectives for cross-lingual DST task, especially on multi-domain area, to further boost the dialogue system on multi-lingual scenarios. We would also explore better positive and negative samples when applying contrastive learning on DST task.

Acknowledgement. The research work descried in this paper has been supported by the National Key R&D Program of China (2020AAA0108005), the National Nature Science Foundation of China (No. 61976015, 61976016, 61876198 and 61370130) and Toshiba (China) Co., Ltd. The authors would like to thank the anonymous reviewers for their valuable comments and suggestions to improve this paper.

References

1. Chen, W., et al.: XL-NBT: a cross-lingual neural belief tracking framework. In: Proceedings of the 2018 Conference on Empirical Methods in Natural Language Processing, pp. 414–424 (2018)

2. Conneau, A., et al.: Unsupervised cross-lingual representation learning at scale. In: Proceedings of the 58th Annual Meeting of the Association for Computational Linguistics, pp. 8440–8451 (2020)
3. Conneau, A., Lample, G.: Cross-lingual language model pretraining. In: Advances in Neural Information Processing Systems, vol. 32 (2019)
4. Devlin, J., Chang, M.W., Lee, K., Toutanova, K.: BERT: pre-training of deep bidirectional transformers for language understanding. In: Proceedings of the 2019 Conference of the North American Chapter of the Association for Computational Linguistics: Human Language Technologies, Volume 1 (Long and Short Papers), pp. 4171–4186 (2019)
5. Eric, M., et al.: MultiWOZ 2.1: a consolidated multi-domain dialogue dataset with state corrections and state tracking baselines. In: Proceedings of the Twelfth Language Resources and Evaluation Conference, pp. 422–428 (2020)
6. Gao, T., Yao, X., Chen, D.: SimCSE: simple contrastive learning of sentence embeddings. In: 2021 Conference on Empirical Methods in Natural Language Processing, EMNLP 2021, pp. 6894–6910. Association for Computational Linguistics (ACL) (2021)
7. Goel, R., Paul, S., Hakkani-Tür, D.: HyST: a hybrid approach for flexible and accurate dialogue state tracking. Proc. Interspeech **2019**, 1458–1462 (2019)
8. Gunasekara, C.: Overview of the ninth dialog system technology challenge: DSTC9. In: DSTC9 Workshop at AAAI 2021 (2021)
9. Kim, S., Yang, S., Kim, G., Lee, S.W.: Efficient dialogue state tracking by selectively overwriting memory. In: Proceedings of the 58th Annual Meeting of the Association for Computational Linguistics, pp. 567–582 (2020)
10. Kingma, D.P., Ba, J.: Adam: a method for stochastic optimization. arXiv preprint arXiv:1412.6980 (2014)
11. Lai, S., Huang, H., Jing, D., Chen, Y., Xu, J., Liu, J.: Saliency-based multi-view mixed language training for zero-shot cross-lingual classification. In: Findings of the Association for Computational Linguistics: EMNLP 2021, pp. 599–610 (2021)
12. Lample, G., Conneau, A., Ranzato, M., Denoyer, L., Jégou, H.: Word translation without parallel data. In: International Conference on Learning Representations (2018)
13. Lee, C.H., Cheng, H., Ostendorf, M.: Dialogue state tracking with a language model using schema-driven prompting. In: Proceedings of the 2021 Conference on Empirical Methods in Natural Language Processing, pp. 4937–4949 (2021)
14. Lee, H., Lee, J., Kim, T.Y.: SUMBT: slot-utterance matching for universal and scalable belief tracking. In: Proceedings of the 57th Annual Meeting of the Association for Computational Linguistics, pp. 5478–5483 (2019)
15. Lin, W., Tseng, B.H., Byrne, B.: Knowledge-aware graph-enhanced GPT-2 for dialogue state tracking. In: Proceedings of the 2021 Conference on Empirical Methods in Natural Language Processing, pp. 7871–7881 (2021)
16. Lin, Y.T., Chen, Y.N.: An empirical study of cross-lingual transferability in generative dialogue state tracker. arXiv preprint arXiv:2101.11360 (2021)
17. Liu, Z., Winata, G.I., Lin, Z., Xu, P., Fung, P.: Attention-informed mixed-language training for zero-shot cross-lingual task-oriented dialogue systems. In: Proceedings of the AAAI Conference on Artificial Intelligence, vol. 34, pp. 8433–8440 (2020)
18. Liu, Z., Winata, G.I., Xu, P., Lin, Z., Fung, P.: Cross-lingual spoken language understanding with regularized representation alignment. In: Proceedings of the 2020 Conference on Empirical Methods in Natural Language Processing (EMNLP), pp. 7241–7251 (2020)
19. Moghe, N., Steedman, M., Birch, A.: Cross-lingual intermediate fine-tuning improves dialogue state tracking. In: Proceedings of the 2021 Conference on Empirical Methods in Natural Language Processing, pp. 1137–1150 (2021)
20. Mrkšić, N., et al.: Semantic specialization of distributional word vector spaces using monolingual and cross-lingual constraints. Trans. Assoc. Comput. Linguist. **5**, 309–324 (2017)

21. Qin, L., et al.: GL-CleF: a global-local contrastive learning framework for cross-lingual spoken language understanding. In: Proceedings of the 60th Annual Meeting of the Association for Computational Linguistics (Volume 1: Long Papers), pp. 2677–2686 (2022)
22. Qin, L., Ni, M., Zhang, Y., Che, W.: CoSDA-ML: multi-lingual code-switching data augmentation for zero-shot cross-lingual NLP. In: Proceedings of the Twenty-Ninth International Conference on International Joint Conferences on Artificial Intelligence, pp. 3853–3860 (2021)
23. Ren, L., Ni, J., McAuley, J.: Scalable and accurate dialogue state tracking via hierarchical sequence generation. In: Proceedings of the 2019 Conference on Empirical Methods in Natural Language Processing and the 9th International Joint Conference on Natural Language Processing (EMNLP-IJCNLP), pp. 1876–1885 (2019)
24. Schuster, S., Gupta, S., Shah, R., Lewis, M.: Cross-lingual transfer learning for multilingual task oriented dialog. In: Proceedings of the 2019 Conference of the North American Chapter of the Association for Computational Linguistics: Human Language Technologies, Volume 1 (Long and Short Papers), pp. 3795–3805 (2019)
25. See, A., Liu, P.J., Manning, C.D.: Get to the point: summarization with pointer-generator networks. In: Proceedings of the 55th Annual Meeting of the Association for Computational Linguistics (Volume 1: Long Papers), pp. 1073–1083 (2017)
26. Wang, D., Ding, N., Li, P., Zheng, H.: CLINE: contrastive learning with semantic negative examples for natural language understanding. In: Proceedings of the 59th Annual Meeting of the Association for Computational Linguistics and the 11th International Joint Conference on Natural Language Processing (Volume 1: Long Papers), pp. 2332–2342 (2021)
27. Wang, Y., Zhao, J., Bao, J., Duan, C., Wu, Y., He, X.: LUNA: learning slot-turn alignment for dialogue state tracking. In: Proceedings of the 2022 Conference of the North American Chapter of the Association for Computational Linguistics: Human Language Technologies, pp. 3319–3328 (2022)
28. Wen, T.H., et al.: A network-based end-to-end trainable task-oriented dialogue system. In: Proceedings of the 15th Conference of the European Chapter of the Association for Computational Linguistics: Volume 1, Long Papers, pp. 438–449 (2017)
29. Wu, C.S., Madotto, A., Hosseini-Asl, E., Xiong, C., Socher, R., Fung, P.: Transferable multi-domain state generator for task-oriented dialogue systems. In: Proceedings of the 57th Annual Meeting of the Association for Computational Linguistics, pp. 808–819 (2019)
30. Xue, L., et al.: mT5: a massively multilingual pre-trained text-to-text transformer. In: Proceedings of the 2021 Conference of the North American Chapter of the Association for Computational Linguistics: Human Language Technologies, pp. 483–498 (2021)
31. Yuan, M., Zhang, M., Van Durme, B., Findlater, L., Boyd-Graber, J.: Interactive refinement of cross-lingual word embeddings. In: Proceedings of the 2020 Conference on Empirical Methods in Natural Language Processing (EMNLP), pp. 5984–5996 (2020)
32. Zeng, Y., Nie, J.Y.: Jointly optimizing state operation prediction and value generation for dialogue state tracking. arXiv preprint arXiv:2010.14061 (2020)
33. Zeng, Y., Nie, J.Y.: Multi-domain dialogue state tracking based on state graph. arXiv preprint arXiv:2010.11137 (2020)
34. Zhong, V., Xiong, C., Socher, R.: Global-locally self-attentive encoder for dialogue state tracking. In: Proceedings of the 56th Annual Meeting of the Association for Computational Linguistics (Volume 1: Long Papers), pp. 1458–1467 (2018)

Knowledge Graph and Information Extraction

Document Information Extraction via Global Tagging

Shaojie He[1,2], Tianshu Wang[2], Yaojie Lu[2], Hongyu Lin[2(✉)], Xianpei Han[2(✉)], Yingfei Sun[1], and Le Sun[2]

[1] University of Chinese Academy of Sciences, Beijing 101408, China
heshaojie2020@iscas.ac.cn, yfsun@ucas.ac.cn
[2] Chinese Information Processing Laboratory, Institute of Software, Chinese Academy of Sciences, Beijing 100190, China
{tianshu2020,luyaojie,hongyu,xianpei,sunle}@iscas.ac.cn

Abstract. Document Information Extraction (DIE) is a crucial task for extracting key information from visually-rich documents. The typical pipeline approach for this task involves Optical Character Recognition (OCR), serializer, Semantic Entity Recognition (SER), and Relation Extraction (RE) modules. However, this pipeline presents significant challenges in real-world scenarios due to issues such as unnatural text order and error propagation between different modules. To address these challenges, we propose a novel tagging-based method – Global TaggeR (GTR), which converts the original sequence labeling task into a token relation classification task. This approach globally links discontinuous semantic entities in complex layouts, and jointly extracts entities and relations from documents. In addition, we design a joint training loss and a joint decoding strategy for SER and RE tasks based on GTR. Our experiments on multiple datasets demonstrate that GTR not only mitigates the issue of text in the wrong order but also improves RE performance.

Keywords: Information extraction · Global tagger · Joint decoding

1 Introduction

Document Information Extraction (DIE), which is to extract key information from document with complex layouts, has become increasingly important in recent years [6,26]. It not only enables us to efficiently compress document data, but also facilitates the retrieval of important information from documents. A typical pipeline approach for the DIE task is depicted in Fig. 1(a) [5,7]. First, the document with complex layout is converted into text blocks using Optical Character Recognition (OCR) tools. Next, the serializer module organizes these text blocks into a more appropriate order. Finally, the well-ordered text blocks are input sequentially into the Semantic Entity Recognition (SER) and Relation Extraction (RE) modules to extract key-value pairs.

M. Sun et al. (Eds.): CCL 2023, LNAI 14232, pp. 145–158, 2023.
https://doi.org/10.1007/978-981-99-6207-5_9

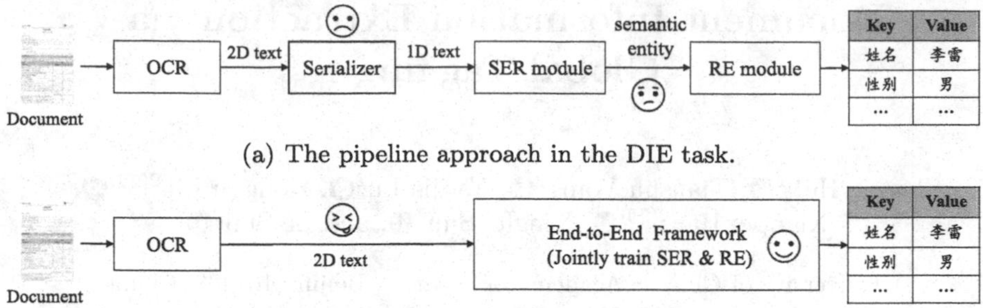

(a) The pipeline approach in the DIE task.

(b) The end-to-end approach in this paper.

Fig. 1. A comparison between (a) current pipeline approach and (b) our end-to-end approach.

However, the pipeline approach in Fig. 1(a) presents significant challenges in real-world scenarios. (1) Mainstream models for the DIE task, such as LayoutLM [23], LayoutLMv2 [22] and LayoutXLM [24], usually use sequence labeling in the Beginning-Inside-Outside (BIO) tagging schema, which assume that tokens belonging to the same semantic entity are grouped together after serialization. If the serializer module fails to order the text blocks correctly, the final performance can be severely impacted. A potential solution is to train a strong and robust serializer module, but this is difficult due to the labor-intensive labeling process under rich and diverse styles of documents; (2) In addition to the issue of text order, this pipeline also suffers from error propagation when using a SER module and a RE module. In research settings, the results of the SER and RE tasks are generally tested separately, with the ground truth of the SER results being used as default auxiliary information for the RE task. However, in real-world scenarios, the SER module in the pipeline cannot provide 100% accurate results, which ineluctably leads to error propagation on RE performance.

Researchers have explored alternative methods for modeling OCR results directly without serializer module to tackle the issue of text in the wrong order. Some have utilized graph convolution networks to model the relationships between tokens [11,20,25]. Others have converted the DIE task into a parsing problem, modeling tree structure for the document [8,15]. Besides, generative encoder-decoder frameworks are applied to avoid the weakness of the BIO tagging schema essentially [10]. While these methods can mitigate the problem of text in the wrong order, they still face challenges. For example, graph-based methods require a more delicate model design, and generative models are usually difficult to train and require a great amount of document data for pre-training.

To address above mentioned two problems, we propose a simple yet effective method named Global TaggeR (GTR). Our approach is inspired by [21] which converts the original sequence labeling task into a token relation classification task. For the SER task, we tag all token pairs and design a decoding strategy based on disjoint sets to decode the semantic entities. And we find GTR naturally resistant to wrong text order to a certain extent. For example, there is a document fragment"登记表姓名李雷性别男" and we tag the token pair {姓, 名} so that we know "姓名" is a semantic entity. Even if we shuffle this fragment to "登记表姓李性男名雷别", we still can know "姓名" is a semantic entity using the same tag {姓, 名}. In other words, GTR enables us to recognize discontinuous semantic entities, regardless of text in the wrong order. Additionally, for the RE task, we combine RE and SER tags for joint training and extend the decoding strategy for joint decoding. The pipeline of this study is depicted in Fig. 1(b). We remove the serializer module from the original pipeline to make it easier and propose an end-to-end extraction framework for jointly training the SER and RE tasks to prevent error propagation problem. The contributions of this work are summarized as follows:

- We propose an end-to-end extraction framework for the document information extraction, which simplifies the traditional pipeline approach and alleviates error propagation issues.
- In this end-to-end extraction framework, we propose the Global TaggeR (GTR) method, which contains a global tagging schema and a joint decoding strategy for the SER and RE tasks.
- Our experiments on multiple datasets demonstrate that the GTR proposed not only mitigates the issue of text in the wrong order but also facilitates the interaction of entity and relation information, resulting in improvement of RE performance.

2 Background

2.1 Task Definition

Given a document image I and its OCR results that containing a sequence of tokens $S = \{t_1, ..., t_n\}$ paired with corresponding bounding boxes $L = \{b_1, ..., b_n\}$, the goal of the DIE task is to extract a set of entities $E = \{e_1, ..., e_m\}$ in the document and their corresponding relations $R = \{(e_i, e_j)\}$. We usually divide the DIE task into two sub-tasks named SER and RE. For the SER task, we try to recognize all possible semantic entities in token sequence S and classify them with three entity types {[Header], [Question], [Answer]}. For the RE task, based on semantic entities that we have recognized, we match each two of them if they are question-answer pairs, or key-value pairs. The relations only have two types, paired or not.

2.2 LayoutXLM

We choose LayoutXLM [24] as our baseline model, which is a multilingual and multi-modal pre-trained language model designed with a single encoder architecture. The model first feeds token sequence S and bounding box sequence L, along with visual features extracted from document image I. Next, it adopts visual and text embedding, position embedding and layout embedding as the representation of tokens, and then employs multi-modal Transformer encoder layers to generate the representations of the given tokens $H = \{h_1, ..., h_n\}$. Finally, a simple classifier is connected to the encoder, enabling it to perform downstream SER and RE tasks.

2.3 BIO Tagging Schema

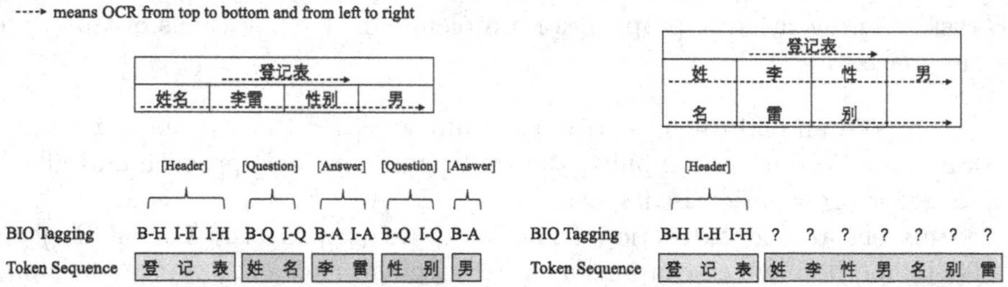

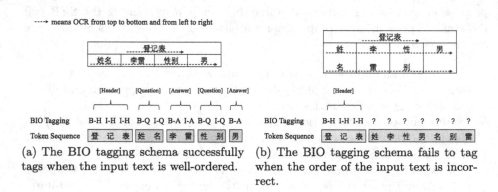

(a) The BIO tagging schema successfully tags when the input text is well-ordered.

(b) The BIO tagging schema fails to tag when the order of the input text is incorrect.

Fig. 2. The illustration of the BIO tagging schema.

The BIO tagging schema, which is a popular sequence labeling technique, is widely used for the SER task. In this schema, each token in the document is labeled with a prefix that indicates whether it is the beginning (B), inside (I), or outside (O) of an entity span. Figure 2(a) provides a simple illustration. However, layout-rich documents often result in OCR text in the wrong order. Given text in the wrong order, the BIO tagging schema cannot express span boundaries correctly, illustrated in Fig. 2(b). Therefore, it is necessary to find new approaches to tackle this issue.

3 Approach

In this section, we introduce our GTR approach in four parts. First, we propose the global tagging schema of the DIE task. Next, a token pair scoring layer added to baseline model is proposed. Then, we design a corresponding decoding strategy to decode entities and relations from the predicted tagging matrix. Finally, we introduce our training loss for jointly training SER and RE tasks.

3.1 Global Tagging Schema

For the DIE task, we use five tags {O, H, Q, A, P} to represent relations between token t_i and t_j. Table 1 shows the meanings of these five tags.

Table 1. The meanings of tags for the DIE task.

Tags	Meanings
H	Token t_i and t_j belong to the same entity span, and the entity type is [Header]
Q	Token t_i and t_j belong to the same entity span, and the entity type is [Question]
A	Token t_i and t_j belong to the same entity span, and the entity type is [Answer]
P	Token t_i and t_j belong to two paired entities, with the types of [Question] and [Answer]
O	No above four relations for token t_i and t_j

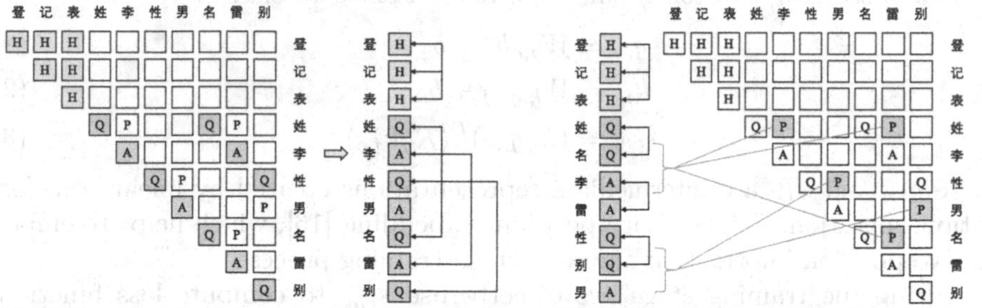

(a) **SER task. The left is the tagging matrix and the right is the corresponding semantic entities.**

(b) **RE task. The right is the tagging matrix and the left is the rearranged semantic entities.**

Fig. 3. The illustration of global tagging schema for jointly labeling (a) SER and (b) RE tasks. We only display the upper triangular of tagging matrix on account of its symmetry.

Figure 3(a) illustrates the global tagging schema tags entities that are difficult to tag using the BIO tagging schema in Fig. 2(b). Tokens in the same semantic entity are tagged with the same label pairwise. The labels are {H, Q, A}, representing the entity types {[Header], [Question], [Answer]}, respectively. For example, in Fig. 3(a), the token pair {姓, 名} = Q means that the tokens "姓" and "名" belong to the same entity span, and the entity type is [Question]. Similarly, {登, 记, 表} belongs to the [Header] entity, {性, 别} belongs to the [Question] entity, and {李, 雷}, {男} belong to the [Answer] entity.

Figure 3(b) illustrates the global tagging schema tags relations after tagging entities. For each [Question]-[Answer] (QA) relation in the document, tokens from the two associated entities, are tagged with the same label P pairwise. For example, given the premise that {姓, 名} belongs to [Question] entity and {李, 雷} belongs to [Answer] entity, the token pairs {姓, 李}, {姓, 雷}, {名, 雷} = P, indicating that {姓, 名} and {李, 雷} are paired QA relation. Similarly, {性, 别} and {男} are paired QA relation.

The global tagging schema offers two primary advantages in the DIE task. (1) First, it allows for the tagging of discontinuous semantic entity spans. Due to the diversity of document layouts, the token sequence produced by OCR tools is usually in an incorrect order. Even if the tokens in the same semantic entity span are discontinuous in the token sequence, they can still be tagged using this global tagging schema. (2) Second, it supports joint training of the SER and RE tasks. Using the global tagging schema, the SER task can be expanded to token-to-token relationship classification task. This schema unifies task format and enables unified modeling and joint training for the SER and RE tasks.

3.2 Token Pair Scoring

For the representations $H = \{h_1, ..., h_n\}$ generated from given token sequence S, we employ simple linear transformation and multiplication operation to obtain the global score $s_{ij|c}$ of token pair t_i and t_j classified to class c:

$$q_{i,c} = W_{q,c}h_i + b_{q,c} \tag{1}$$

$$k_{j,c} = W_{k,c}h_j + b_{k,c} \tag{2}$$

$$s_{ij|c} = (\mathcal{R}_i q_{i,c})^T (\mathcal{R}_j k_{j,c}) \tag{3}$$

where $q_{i,c}$ and $k_{j,c}$ are intermediate representations created by linear transformation operation. $\mathcal{R}$ is a rotary position embedding [16], which helps to embed relative position information and accelerate training process.

During the training stage, we directly use $s_{ij|c}$ to compute loss function. For the supervision signal of $s_{ij|c}$, we assign signal 1 to represent {H, Q, A, P} tags and signal -1 to represent the absence of any of the above four relations. Therefore, during the inference stage, we obtain the predicted tagging matrix by processing $s_{ij|c}$ with a threshold of 0, where values greater than 0 are regarded as tags.

3.3 Decoding Strategy

With the predicted tagging matrix, we design a decoding strategy to extract the semantic entities and relations, as shown in Algorithm 1. Following the proposed decoding strategy, we decode in two steps:

SER. Firstly, we recognize the diagonal tags, and use these tags to label the token sequence S. Then, we recognize the non-diagonal tags belonging to {H, Q, A}, and use these tags for merging tokens. Iterating through these tags, we use a disjoint set algorithm with additional judgement to merge semantic entity tokens. Therefore, we can extract the semantic entity set E.

RE. Using the semantic entity set E, we iterate through all possible [`Question`]-[`Answer`] entity pairs. If there exists any token pair t_k and t_l that t_k in an entity e_i with type [`Question`] and t_l in an entity e_j with type [`Answer`] and $T(t_k, t_l)$ is tagged with label P, we add (e_i, e_j) into relation set R. Finally, we can extract the semantic entity set E as well as the relation set R.

Algorithm 1. Decoding Strategy for DIE

Input: The predicted tagging matrix T. The predicted tag of token pair t_i and t_j is denoted as $T(t_i, t_j)$. The predicted tag of token pair t_i and t_i is abbreviated as $T(t_i)$. If all tokens in a set e share the same tag, abbreviated as $T(e)$.

Output: Entity set E and relation set R.

```
Initialize the entity set E and relation set R with ∅, and n ← len(S).
while i ≤ n do
    if T(t_i) ∈ {H, Q, A} then
        E ← E ∪ {t_i}
    end if
end while
while i ≤ n and j ≤ n do
    if i ≠ j and T(t_i, t_j) ∈ {H, Q, A} and T(t_i, t_j) = T(t_i) = T(t_j) then
        E ← Merge the set where t_i resides and the set where t_j resides in E.
    end if
end while
while e_i ∈ E and e_j ∈ E do
    if T(e_i) = Q and T(e_j) = A and any T(t_k, t_l) = P that t_k ∈ e_i and t_l ∈ e_j then
        R ← R ∪ {(e_i, e_j)}
    end if
end while
return the set E and the set R
```

3.4 Training Loss

For token pair t_i and t_j, we denote y_{ij} as the ground truth tag and $P_{ij}(\hat{y} = k)$ as the predicted probability for class k. A cross entropy loss is applied:

$$\mathcal{L} = -\sum_{i=1}^{n}\sum_{j=1}^{n}\sum_{k\in C}\mathbb{I}(y_{ij} = k)\log P_{ij}(\hat{y} = k), \quad P_{ij}(\hat{y} = k) = \frac{e^{s_{ij|k}}}{\sum\limits_{k'\in C} e^{s_{ij|k'}}} \tag{4}$$

where $\mathbb{I}$ is an indicator function and C is the label set {H, Q, A, P, O}. And $s_{ij|k}$ denotes the predicted score for token pair t_i and t_j classified to class k.

We attempt to train the baseline model using the above loss function but fail due to convergence issues. And the training results always output O tags. We suggest that our global tagging schema requires the prediction of a probability matrix of $n * n$, which results in very sparse supervised signals, facing a severe class imbalance problem, and making it challenging to train the model effectively. Inspired by [17], we improve $\log P_{ij}(\hat{y} = k)$ with a class imbalance likelihood:

$$\log P_{ij}(\hat{y} = k) = \log(1 + e^{-s_{ij|k}}) + \log(1 + \sum_{k'\in C, k'\neq k} e^{s_{ij|k'}}) \tag{5}$$

which turns loss into a pairwise comparison of target category scores and non-target category scores.

4 Experiments

4.1 Experimental Setup

Dataset. We use FUNSD [9] and XFUN [24] datasets to evaluate our proposed approach. (1) FUNSD is an English dataset for document understanding, comprising 199 annotated documents. The dataset is split into a training set of 149 documents and a testing set of 50 documents; (2) XFUN is a multilingual dataset for document understanding that comprises seven languages [Chinese (ZH), Japanese (JA), Spanish (ES), French (FR), Italian (IT), German (DE), Portuguese (PT)], totaling 1,393 annotated documents. Each language's data has separate training and testing sets, with 199 and 50 documents respectively.

Parameter Settings. For training, we follow the hyper-parameter settings of [24], setting the learning rate to 5e−5 and the warmup ratio to 0.1. The max length of input token sequence is set to 512, which means a split of chunk size 512 if the input token sequence is too long. For a fair comparison, we set the batch size to 64 and run the training for 2000 steps to ensure that the models have well converged.

Input Settings. Golden input and OCR input are two types of input text order for experiment input settings. (1) Golden input means that we concatenate the ground truth text blocks into a token sequence and feed it into the model, which implies that all semantic entity spans are continuous. (2) OCR input means that we concatenate all tokens following the recognition pattern of a common OCR from top to bottom and left to right before feeding them into the model. This implies that under complex layouts, the same semantic entity span may be discontinuous.

Evaluation Metrics. For evaluation, we use F1-score on two sub-tasks: (1) Semantic Entity Recognition (SER), where semantic entities are identified by tagging as either {[`Header`], [`Question`], [`Answer`]}. When the entity type and all entity tokens are correct, the entity is regarded as a correct entity. (2) Relation Extraction (RE), where paired relation of question and answer entities are identified. We use a strict evaluation metrics that only the paired two entities are exactly correct at the token-level, the relation is regarded as a correct relation.

Baseline Model. We use LayoutXLM$_{\text{BASE}}$ model as the baseline model. Its original RE results are tested based on the given ground truth semantic entities. To test the RE results in the pipeline for baseline model, we first reproduce the results of [24] and then re-test the RE results using the semantic entities generated by its SER module.

4.2 Result

We evaluate the baseline model with the BIO tagging and the global tagging on language-specific fine-tuning settings (training on X, and testing on X).

Table 2. Main result under Golden input settings. ♣: results reported in [24]. Best results are in **bold** comparing reproduced BIO tagging (abbreviated as BIO) with our global tagger (abbreviated as GTR). gtSER+RE denotes evaluating the RE results using ground truth SER results. And SER+RE denotes evaluating the RE results using SER results of the model.

	Model	FUNSD	ZH	JA	ES	FR	IT	DE	PT	Avg.
SER	BIO♣	0.7940	0.8924	0.7921	0.7550	0.7902	0.8082	0.8222	0.7903	0.8056
	BIO	0.8013	**0.8944**	0.7864	0.7426	0.7852	0.8073	0.7951	0.7848	0.7996
	GTR	**0.8079**	0.8818	**0.7972**	**0.7631**	**0.8067**	**0.8210**	**0.8032**	**0.8071**	**0.8110**
gtSER+RE	BIO♣	0.5483	0.7073	0.6963	0.6896	0.6353	0.6415	0.6551	0.5718	0.6432
	BIO	0.5560	0.7047	0.6519	0.7041	0.6664	0.6725	0.6485	0.5893	0.6492
SER+RE	BIO	0.4340	0.5965	0.5082	0.498	0.5064	0.4861	0.4258	0.3765	0.4789
	GTR	**0.5910**	**0.7739**	**0.6470**	**0.5363**	**0.6063**	**0.6594**	**0.5531**	**0.5247**	**0.6115**

Table 3. Main result under OCR input settings. Best results are in **bold** comparing reproduced BIO tagging (abbreviated as BIO) with our global tagger (abbreviated as GTR).

	Model	FUNSD	ZH	JA	ES	FR	IT	DE	PT	Avg.
SER	BIO	0.5735	0.3970	0.4017	0.6287	0.6916	0.7055	0.6823	0.6863	0.5958
	GTR	**0.7412**	**0.8444**	**0.7205**	**0.7165**	**0.7676**	**0.7772**	**0.7508**	**0.7811**	**0.7624**
SER+RE	BIO	0.2712	0.1441	0.1759	0.3665	0.4141	0.4206	0.3566	0.3086	0.3072
	GTR	**0.5828**	**0.6920**	**0.5427**	**0.5686**	**0.5712**	**0.5888**	**0.5933**	**0.5580**	**0.5872**

Table 2 presents the results under Golden input settings. We compare our global tagger approach with the reproduced baseline. The results show that our global tagger method outperforms the baseline model on average F1-score of the 8 languages for the SER task. Moreover, when combining the SER and RE tasks in an end-to-end extraction framework, the RE performance of average F1-score significantly surpassed that of the baseline model pipelined, and is even higher on two languages compared with the baseline model using ground truth semantic entity information.

Table 3 presents the result under OCR input settings. We directly use the baseline model trained under Golden input settings to predict the SER and RE results for evaluating the BIO tagging schema. We observe that the SER performance on average F1-score of the 8 languages for the baseline model is significantly impacted, making it difficult to perform the RE process based on its SER results. However, with joint training and decoding using our global tagger approach, we are able to alleviate this issue.

4.3 Analysis

Golden Input vs. OCR Input. The BIO tagging schema requires well-ordered input, while the global tagging schema accepts unordered input. Comparing the average F1-score of SER performance in Table 2 and Table 3, we observe a significant drop from 0.7996 to 0.5958 when changing Golden input settings into OCR input, indicating a great impact by the order of input tokens using the BIO tagging schema. On the other hand, under the global tagging schema, we find the model's average SER performance only drops from 0.8110 to 0.7624 between Golden input settings and OCR input settings, demonstrating that the global tagging schema can effectively alleviate suboptimal input token order issue.

Pipeline Framework vs. End-to-End Framework. The pipeline framework with the BIO tagging schema suffers from error propagation, while the end-to-end GTR method can greatly mitigate it. In Table 2, we observe a drop of average F1-score on the RE results from 0.6492 to 0.4789 when combining the SER and RE modules in the pipeline, demonstrating that pipeline framework can greatly impact performance. Particularly, when both SER and RE modules have poor performance under OCR input settings, we observe a terrible performance, which is only 0.3072 average F1-score on the RE task. In such case, joint training and decoding in GTR method can significantly alleviate error propagation issue with the average F1-score of 0.5872 rather than 0.3072 of 8 language datasets on the RE task.

Besides, in Table 2, the SER+RE results using GTR approach are even higher than the baseline RE results using ground truth semantic entities on English(FUNSD) and Chinese(ZH) language datasets, indicating that the end-to-end extraction framework is potential for facilitating the interaction of entity and relation information, resulting in better RE performance.

5 Related Work

In recent years, benefited from pre-training and fine-tuning paradigm, information extraction for documents has gained significant attention in both research and industry [1,12–14,18,19]. However, there are still numerous challenges in the pipeline when applied in real-world scenarios. Addressing the issue of text order in the pipeline, related works are organized into three perspectives.

5.1 Sequence-Based Perspective

Sequence-based models, such as LayoutLM [23] and LayoutLMv2 [22], aim to encode serialized token sequence from complex and diverse document, integrating layout, font, and other features. These models offer several advantages, such as simplicity, scalability, and suitability for Masked Language Modeling (MLM) pre-training. However, these models are constrained by the traditional BIO tagging mode and require a well-ordered token sequence as a basis.

5.2 Graph-Based Perspective

Graph-based models usually treat tokens as nodes in a graph and allow interactions between tokens explicitly to enhance their representations [11,20,25]. Even though these models leverage the graph structure to capture more complex relationships between entities, they still use the BIO paradigm for SER task. Alternatively, some works, like SPADE [8], take a different approach by converting DIE task into document parsing task. It models the document as a dependency tree to represent entities and relations.

Our work in this paper also lies in graph-based perspectives. Similar to the tack of SPADE that converting the DIE task to a different task, we view the DIE task as a token relation classification task. But unlike SPADE, we do not utilize a graph generator and graph decoder. Rather, we simply modify the tagging schema and do not change the encoding model.

5.3 End-to-End Perspective

End-to-End model typically combines the entire pipeline into one model. Dessurt [4], TRIE++ [3], for example, unify OCR, reordering, and extraction into a single model. Meanwhile, models like Donut [10], GMN [2], use a generative encoder-decoder architecture to unify OCR and generation. In contrast to extraction-based works, they directly generate the structured output, making it more flexible for varying output formats.

6 Conclusion

In this paper, we propose an end-to-end approach named global tagger to solve the document information extraction task. Experiments on the FUNSD and XFUN datasets demonstrate its efficacy in effectively mitigating the gap between token order in OCR input and golden input. Furthermore, our experimental results indicate that joint training and decoding of semantic entity recognition and relation extraction tasks in this end-to-end extraction framework can alleviate the negative impact of error propagation and improve the performance of the relation extraction results.

Acknowledgements. We sincerely thank the reviewers for their insightful comments and valuable suggestions. This research work is supported by the National Natural Science Foundation of China under Grants no. U1936207, 62122077 and 62106251.

References

1. Appalaraju, S., Jasani, B., Kota, B.U., Xie, Y., Manmatha, R.: DocFormer: end-to-end transformer for document understanding. In: 2021 IEEE/CVF International Conference on Computer Vision, ICCV 2021, Montreal, QC, Canada, 10–17 October 2021, pp. 973–983. IEEE (2021). https://doi.org/10.1109/ICCV48922.2021.00103
2. Cao, H., et al.: GMN: generative multi-modal network for practical document information extraction. In: Carpuat, M., de Marneffe, M., Ruíz, I.V.M. (eds.) Proceedings of the 2022 Conference of the North American Chapter of the Association for Computational Linguistics: Human Language Technologies, NAACL 2022, Seattle, WA, United States, 10–15 July 2022, pp. 3768–3778. Association for Computational Linguistics (2022). https://doi.org/10.18653/v1/2022.naacl-main.276
3. Cheng, Z., et al.: TRIE++: towards end-to-end information extraction from visually rich documents. CoRR (2022). https://doi.org/10.48550/arXiv.2207.06744
4. Davis, B.L., Morse, B.S., Price, B.L., Tensmeyer, C., Wigington, C., Morariu, V.I.: End-to-end document recognition and understanding with Dessurt. In: Karlinsky, L., Michaeli, T., Nishino, K. (eds.) Computer Vision - ECCV 2022 Workshops - Tel Aviv, Israel, 23–27 October 2022, Proceedings, Part IV. LNCS, vol. 13804, pp. 280–296. Springer, Cham (2022). https://doi.org/10.1007/978-3-031-25069-9_19
5. Denk, T.I., Reisswig, C.: BERTgrid: contextualized embedding for 2D document representation and understanding. In: Workshop on Document Intelligence at NeurIPS 2019 (2019). https://openreview.net/forum?id=H1gsGaq9US
6. Hong, T., Kim, D., Ji, M., Hwang, W., Nam, D., Park, S.: BROS: a pre-trained language model focusing on text and layout for better key information extraction from documents. Proc. AAAI Conf. Artif. Intell. **36**(10), 10767–10775 (2022). https://doi.org/10.1609/aaai.v36i10.21322, https://ojs.aaai.org/index.php/AAAI/article/view/21322
7. Hwang, W., Lee, H., Yim, J., Kim, G., Seo, M.: Cost-effective end-to-end information extraction for semi-structured document images. In: Moens, M., Huang, X., Specia, L., Yih, S.W. (eds.) Proceedings of the 2021 Conference on Empirical Methods in Natural Language Processing, EMNLP 2021, Virtual Event/Punta Cana, Dominican Republic, 7–11 November 2021, pp. 3375–3383. Association for Computational Linguistics (2021). https://doi.org/10.18653/v1/2021.emnlp-main.271
8. Hwang, W., Yim, J., Park, S., Yang, S., Seo, M.: Spatial dependency parsing for semi-structured document information extraction. In: Findings of the Association for Computational Linguistics: ACL-IJCNLP 2021, pp. 330–343. Association for Computational Linguistics, Online (2021). https://doi.org/10.18653/v1/2021.findings-acl.28, https://aclanthology.org/2021.findings-acl.28
9. Jaume, G., Kemal Ekenel, H., Thiran, J.P.: FUNSD: a dataset for form understanding in noisy scanned documents. In: 2019 International Conference on Document Analysis and Recognition Workshops (ICDARW), vol. 2, pp. 1–6 (2019). https://doi.org/10.1109/ICDARW.2019.10029
10. Kim, G., et al.: OCR-free document understanding transformer. In: Avidan, S., Brostow, G.J., Cissé, M., Farinella, G.M., Hassner, T. (eds.) Computer Vision - ECCV 2022–17th European Conference, Tel Aviv, Israel, 23–27 October 2022, Proceedings, Part XXVIII. LNCS, vol. 13688, pp. 498–517. Springer, Cham (2022). https://doi.org/10.1007/978-3-031-19815-1_29

11. Lee, C., et al.: FormNet: structural encoding beyond sequential modeling in form document information extraction. In: Muresan, S., Nakov, P., Villavicencio, A. (eds.) Proceedings of the 60th Annual Meeting of the Association for Computational Linguistics (vol. 1: Long Papers), ACL 2022, Dublin, Ireland, 22–27 May 2022, pp. 3735–3754. Association for Computational Linguistics (2022). https://doi.org/10.18653/v1/2022.acl-long.260
12. Li, C., et al.: StructuralLM: structural pre-training for form understanding. In: Zong, C., Xia, F., Li, W., Navigli, R. (eds.) Proceedings of the 59th Annual Meeting of the Association for Computational Linguistics and the 11th International Joint Conference on Natural Language Processing, ACL/IJCNLP 2021, (vol. 1: Long Papers), Virtual Event, 1–6 August 2021, pp. 6309–6318. Association for Computational Linguistics (2021). https://doi.org/10.18653/v1/2021.acl-long.493
13. Li, Q., et al.: Reinforcement learning-based dialogue guided event extraction to exploit argument relations. IEEE ACM Trans. Audio Speech Lang. Process. **30**, 520–533 (2022). https://doi.org/10.1109/TASLP.2021.3138670
14. Li, Y., et al.: Structext: structured text understanding with multi-modal transformers. In: Shen, H.T., et al. (eds.) MM 2021: ACM Multimedia Conference, Virtual Event, China, 20–24 October 2021, pp. 1912–1920. ACM (2021). https://doi.org/10.1145/3474085.3475345
15. Mathur, P., et al.: LayerDOC: layer-wise extraction of spatial hierarchical structure in visually-rich documents. In: IEEE/CVF Winter Conference on Applications of Computer Vision, WACV 2023, Waikoloa, HI, USA, 2–7 January 2023, pp. 3599–3609. IEEE (2023). https://doi.org/10.1109/WACV56688.2023.00360
16. Su, J., Lu, Y., Pan, S., Wen, B., Liu, Y.: RoFormer: enhanced transformer with rotary position embedding. CoRR abs/2104.09864 (2021). https://arxiv.org/abs/2104.09864
17. Su, J., et al.: Global pointer: novel efficient span-based approach for named entity recognition. CoRR abs/2208.03054 (2022). https://doi.org/10.48550/arXiv.2208.03054
18. Sun, K., Zhang, R., Mensah, S., Mao, Y., Liu, X.: Learning implicit and explicit multi-task interactions for information extraction. ACM Trans. Inf. Syst. **41**(2), 27:1–27:29 (2023). https://doi.org/10.1145/3533020
19. Wang, J., Jin, L., Ding, K.: LiLT: a simple yet effective language-independent layout transformer for structured document understanding. In: Muresan, S., Nakov, P., Villavicencio, A. (eds.) Proceedings of the 60th Annual Meeting of the Association for Computational Linguistics (vol. 1: Long Papers), ACL 2022, Dublin, Ireland, 22–27 May 2022, pp. 7747–7757. Association for Computational Linguistics (2022). https://doi.org/10.18653/v1/2022.acl-long.534
20. Wei, M., He, Y., Zhang, Q.: Robust layout-aware IE for visually rich documents with pre-trained language models. In: Huang, J.X., et al. (eds.) Proceedings of the 43rd International ACM SIGIR Conference on Research and Development in Information Retrieval, SIGIR 2020, Virtual Event, China, 25–30 July 2020, pp. 2367–2376. ACM (2020). https://doi.org/10.1145/3397271.3401442
21. Wu, Z., Ying, C., Zhao, F., Fan, Z., Dai, X., Xia, R.: Grid tagging scheme for aspect-oriented fine-grained opinion extraction. In: Findings of the Association for Computational Linguistics: EMNLP 2020, pp. 2576–2585. Association for Computational Linguistics, Online (2020). https://doi.org/10.18653/v1/2020.findings-emnlp.234, https://aclanthology.org/2020.findings-emnlp.234

22. Xu, Y., et al.: LayoutLMv2: multi-modal pre-training for visually-rich document understanding. In: Proceedings of the 59th Annual Meeting of the Association for Computational Linguistics and the 11th International Joint Conference on Natural Language Processing (vol. 1: Long Papers), pp. 2579–2591. Association for Computational Linguistics, Online (2021). https://doi.org/10.18653/v1/2021.acl-long.201, https://aclanthology.org/2021.acl-long.201
23. Xu, Y., Li, M., Cui, L., Huang, S., Wei, F., Zhou, M.: LayoutLM: pre-training of text and layout for document image understanding. In: Proceedings of the 26th ACM SIGKDD International Conference on Knowledge Discovery & Data Mining, KDD 2020, pp. 1192–1200. Association for Computing Machinery, New York, NY, USA (2020). https://doi.org/10.1145/3394486.3403172
24. Xu, Y., et al.: XFUND: a benchmark dataset for multilingual visually rich form understanding. In: Findings of the Association for Computational Linguistics: ACL 2022, pp. 3214–3224. Association for Computational Linguistics, Dublin, Ireland (2022). https://doi.org/10.18653/v1/2022.findings-acl.253, https://aclanthology.org/2022.findings-acl.253
25. Yu, W., Lu, N., Qi, X., Gong, P., Xiao, R.: PICK: processing key information extraction from documents using improved graph learning-convolutional networks. In: 25th International Conference on Pattern Recognition, ICPR 2020, Virtual Event/Milan, Italy, 10–15 January 2021, pp. 4363–4370. IEEE (2020). https://doi.org/10.1109/ICPR48806.2021.9412927
26. Zhang, Z., et al.: Layout-aware information extraction for document-grounded dialogue: dataset, method and demonstration. In: Magalhães, J., et al. (eds.) MM 2022: The 30th ACM International Conference on Multimedia, Lisboa, Portugal, 10–14 October 2022, pp. 7252–7260. ACM (2022). https://doi.org/10.1145/3503161.3548765

A Distantly-Supervised Relation Extraction Method Based on Selective Gate and Noise Correction

Zhuowei Chen[1], Yujia Tian[1], Lianxi Wang[1,2(✉)], and Shengyi Jiang[1,2]

[1] School of Information Science and Technology, Guangdong University of Foreign Studies, Guangzhou, China
{20211003051,20211003065}@gdufs.edu.cn, jiangshengyi@163.com
[2] Guangzhou Key Laboratory of Multilingual Intelligent Processing, Guangzhou, China
wanglianxi@gdufs.edu.cn

Abstract. Entity relation extraction, as a core task of information extraction, aims to predict the relation of entity pairs identified by text, and its research results are applied to various fields. To address the problem that current distantly supervised relation extraction (DSRE) methods based on large-scale corpus annotation generate a large amount of noisy data, a DSRE method that incorporates selective gate and noise correction framework is proposed. The selective gate is used to reasonably select the sentence features in the sentence bag, while the noise correction is used to correct the labels of small classes of samples that are misclassified into large classes during the model training process, to reduce the negative impact of noisy data on relation extraction. The results on the English datasets clearly demonstrate that our proposed method outperforms other baseline models. Moreover, the experimental results on the Chinese dataset indicate that our method surpasses other models, providing further evidence that our proposed method is both robust and effective.

Keywords: Entity relation extraction · Distant supervision · Selective gate · Noise correction

1 Introduction

Entity Relation Extraction (RE) is a crucial task in information extraction that aims to identify the relation between entity pairs in text. The findings of RE have practical applications in several fields, such as the construction of knowledge graphs (KG), semantic web annotation, and the development and optimization of question-and-answer systems and search engines, which have a significant impact on daily life. However, the task of RE is challenging due to the limited availability of annotated data. To address this challenge, distant supervision has been proposed, which automatically annotates data, significantly increasing the number of annotated samples.

M. Sun et al. (Eds.): CCL 2023, LNAI 14232, pp. 159–174, 2023.
https://doi.org/10.1007/978-981-99-6207-5_10

However, distant supervision suffers from a strong hypothesis, leading to a large number of noisy labels during data annotation. Training on a dataset with noisy labels can result in model overfitting to the noise, which adversely impacts the model's performance [4,9].

To mitigate these issues, this paper proposes a novel method for RE that incorporates selective gate and the end-to-end noise correction method. In our model, selective gate is utilized to rationally select sentence features in the sentence bag, while noise correction is used to correct the labels of small classes of samples that are misclassified into larger classes during model training. These techniques reduce the negative impact of noisy data on the distant DSRE model. Additionally, since common word embedding models, such as Word2Vec and Glove, produce static vectors that overlook contextual semantics and the flexible use of multiple-meaning words, this paper introduces a pre-trained language model (PLM) to encode and extract features from sentences. This approach provides richer sentence semantic features, effectively improving prediction accuracy and reducing training time. Experiment results demonstrate that this method significantly outperforms the baseline models, improving the DSRE model's performance.

The major contributions of this paper can be summarized as follows:

- We propose a DSRE method, named PLMG-Pencil, which combines PLM and selective gate and introduces an end-to-end noise correction training framework called pencil. Selective gate prevents the propagation of noisy representations and pencil corrects noise labels during the training process, reducing the impact of noise on the dataset and improving the performance of the DSRE model.
- We present a novel algorithm for DSRE that combines selective gate mechanism and pencil framework within a three-stage training process. This process involves training the backbone model, gradually correcting noisy labels, and subsequently fine-tuning our model using the corrected data. Empirical experiments demonstrate the robustness and effectiveness of our proposed method.
- Our experiments on three different Chinese and English datasets demonstrate that effective sentence-level feature construction methods and training methods, combined with noise correction, are crucial for improving the performance of models on DSRE tasks.

2 Related Work

2.1 Distantly Supervised Relation Extraction Models

Numerous RE models have been proposed, with deep learning-based models like convolutional neural networks (CNNs) being the current mainstream. CNNs can automatically extract features from sentences, making them a fundamental model for future research [24]. However, the maximum pooling operation used in this model ignores important structural and valid information about the sentence.

Socher [15] was the first to propose a recurrent neural network (RNN) to train relational extractors by encoding sentences. In addition, Zeng [23] proposed a piecewise convolutional neural network (PCNN) that uses maximum pooling processing based on CNN to effectively preserve the information features of long texts while also reducing the time complexity. Zhou [26] introduced an attention mechanism based on the long short-term memory network (LSTM) to form the classical BiLSTM-ATT model. The model can reasonably assign weights to features to obtain a better representation of the sentence. Riedel [13] proposed a multi-instance learning (MIL) framework with a basic annotation unit of a sentence bag containing a common entity pair, rather than a single individual sentence. For sentence bag level labeled data, the model can be made to implicitly focus on correctly labeled sentences through an attention mechanism, thus learning from noisy data to become a stable and robust model. Subsequently, Ye and Ling [21] proposed a DSRE method based on the intra- and inter-sentence bag, combining sentence-level and bag-level attention for noise correction. Alt [1] introduced a transformer-based PLM for DSRE. Chen [3] proposed a new contrastive instance learning method (CIL) to further improve the performance of DSRE models. Further, Li [7] introduces a hierarchical contrast framework (HiCLRE) on top of Chen's CIL method to enhance cross-layer semantic interaction and reduce the impact of noisy data. These methods are generally neural network driven and use neural network models that have strong generalization capabilities compared to traditional methods.

2.2 Noise Correction Methods

There are three categories of noise correction methods for DSRE: rule-based statistical methods, multi-instance learning-based methods, and adversarial and reinforcement learning-based methods. Multi-instance learning-based approaches have received the most attention from scholars, due to their effectiveness in correcting noise labels as demonstrated by Yao [20].

In deep neural networks, designing robust loss functions has also proven effective in coping with noise by making models robust during training. Several studies have examined the robustness of different loss functions such as mean square loss and cross-entropy loss. Zhang [25] combined the advantages of mean absolute loss and cross-entropy loss to obtain a better function. Li [8] proposed DivideMix framework that separates noisy samples using a Gaussian mixture model before training the model. Tanaka [16] proposed an optimization strategy while Jiang [6] introduced MentorNet technique for regularizing deep CNNs on test data with weakly supervised labels.

Moreover, Wu [18] and Shi [14] have investigated adversarial training based approaches where simulated noise is mixed with real samples during training in order to improve model's robustness against noisy datasets by distinguishing between real versus noisy samples. Although this type of approaches improves corpus quality up to some extent, it requires simultaneous training of two models which can lead to instability and difficulty when applied directly into production systems at scale.

3 Methodology

To mitigate the impact of noise on the DSRE model, this paper proposes a two-pronged approach, PLM-based selective gate pencil (PLMG-Pencil) method. As shown in Fig. 1, first, we encode the text using PLM and employ the selective gate mechanism to select sentence-level features that contribute to the bag-level feature. Second, we replace all labels with soft labels and train the model in the pencil framework. This framework uses soft labels that are updated during training and can be corrected for noisy data. This approach reduces the chances of noise being selected in the selective gate, even if it cannot be corrected in the pencil framework. These two methods complement each other, reducing the degree of noise interference and improving the model's RE performance. In this section, we will describe our approach from the backbone model architecture, noise correction framework, and the RE algorithm.

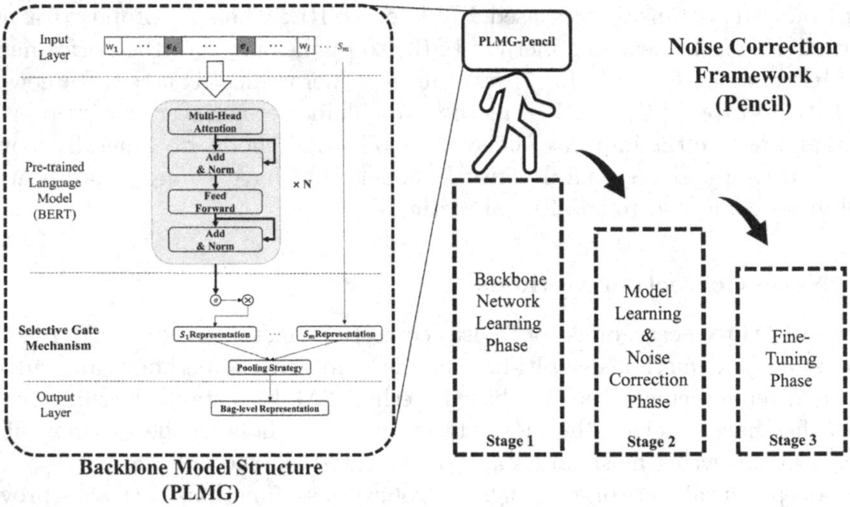

Fig. 1. Overview of PLMG-Pencil

3.1 Backbone Model

This paper proposes the PLM-based selective gate as the backbone model, inspired by the Entity-aware Self-attention Enhanced selective gate (SeG) framework proposed by Li [10]. The primary architecture of our model is presented in the backbone model structure part in Fig. 1, and it comprises two main components: (1) **PLM**, structured to encode sentence, entity, and location features for semantic enhancement. (2) **Selective gate**, which enhances the representation of bag-level features by assigning weights to different sentences in the bag. The selective gate mechanism reduces the impact of noise on the model by weighing the contribution of each sentence in the bag.

Input Embeddings. To convert a sentence into a sequence of tokens, we use the BERT tokenizer, which results in a token sequence $S = \{t_1, t_2, \ldots, e_1, \ldots, e_2, \ldots, t_L\}$, where t_n denotes tokens, e_1 and e_2 denote the head and tail entities, respectively, and L represents the maximum length of the input sentence. We add two special tokens, [CLS] and [SEP], to signify the beginning and end of the sentence, respectively.

However, the [CLS] token is not ideal for RE tasks as it only serves as a pooling token to represent the entire sentence. Therefore, to incorporate entity information into the input, we introduce four tokens: [unused1], [unused2], [unused3], and [unused4], which mark the start and end of each entity.

Selective Gate Enhanced Bag Representation. To obtain an effective bag representation, we introduce the selective gate mechanism, which dynamically calculates the weight of each sentence in the bag. We first represent each sentence using a PLM, such as BERT, which accepts structured sequences of tokens S that integrate entity information e_1 and e_2. The PLM's sentence encoder then sums the embeddings, including tokens, entities, and position, to generate context-aware sentence representations $H = \{h_{t_1}, h_{t_2}, \ldots, h_{e_1}, \ldots, h_{e_2}, \ldots, h_{t_L}\}$:

$$H = \text{PLM}(S) \tag{1}$$

where h_{t_n} denotes the hidden features of the token t_n and PLM represents a pre-trained language model, such as BERT, that serves as the sentence encoder. We use special tokens to encode sentences to generate structural representations of sentences for RE task, including [CLS] for sentence-level pooling, its hidden features denoted as $h_{[CLS]}$. [unused1] and [unused2] mark the start and end of the head entity, [unused3] and [unused4] for the tail entity.

$$h_{e_h} = \text{mean}(h_{t_{[unused1]}}, h_{t_{[unused2]}}) \tag{2}$$

$$h_{e_t} = \text{mean}(h_{t_{[unused3]}}, h_{t_{[unused4]}}) \tag{3}$$

Representations of two entities, h_{e_h} and h_{e_t}, are generated by Eq. (2) and Eq. (3). The hidden features of these special tokens are denoted as $h_{t_{[unused1]}}$, $h_{t_{[unused2]}}$, $h_{t_{[unused3]}}$ and $h_{t_{[unused4]}}$. The sentence representations are generated using the following formulas:

$$h_{S_i} = \sigma([h_{e_h} \mid\mid h_{e_t} \mid\mid h_{[CLS]}] \cdot W_S) + b_S \tag{4}$$

where $||$ represents the concatenation operation, σ is the activation function, W_S is a weight matrix, and b_S is the bias.

Bag Representation. The use of PLMs allows us to obtain sentence representations S_n, which can be stacked to form the initial bag representation $B = \{S_1, S_2, ..., S_n\}$. While selective attention modules are commonly used to aggregate sentence-level representations into bag-level representations, our proposed model leverages SeG's novel selective gate mechanism for this purpose.

Specifically, when dealing with noisy data, the selective attention mechanism may be inefficient or ineffective if there is only one sentence in the bag, or if that sentence is mislabeled. Given that approximately 80% of the RE benchmark datasets contain single-sentence bags with mislabeled instances, our selective gate mechanism offers a more effective solution by dynamically reducing the alignment of gating values with instances of mislabeling, thereby preventing the propagation of noisy representations.

To generate gate values for each S_j, we employ a two-layer feed-forward network with the following formula:

$$g_j = \sigma(W^{(g_1)}\sigma(W^{(g_2)}S_j + b^{(g_2)}) + b^{(g_1)}), \forall j = 1, ..., m \tag{5}$$

We have $W^{(g2)} \in R^{3d_c \times d_h}$ and $W^{(g1)} \in R^{d_h \times d_h}$, $\sigma(\cdot)$denotes the activation function and $g_i \in (0, 1)$, after that, values of the gates are calculated and the mean pooling aggregation is performed in the bag to generate bag-level representation thus the further relation classification can be performed. The formula of this process is as follows, and m denotes the size of the sentence bag.

$$Q = \frac{1}{m}\sum\nolimits_{j=1}^{m} S_j g_j \tag{6}$$

Classifier. We feed Q into a multi-layer perception (MLP) and apply the $|c|$-way softmax function to determine the relation between the head and tail entities, where $|c|$ represents the number of distinct relation classes. The formula for this process is as follows:

$$p = \text{Softmax}(\text{MLP}(Q)) \in R^{|c|} \tag{7}$$

Model Learning. To train the model, we minimize the negative log-likelihood loss plus an L2 regularization penalty, which is expressed by the following formula:

$$L_{NLL} = -\frac{1}{|D|}\sum_{k=1}^{|D|} \log p^k + \beta||\theta||_2^2 \tag{8}$$

where p^k represents the predicted distribution of the k-th example in the dataset D from Eq. (8). The term $\beta||\theta||_2^2$ is the L2 regularization penalty, where θ is the set of model parameters, and β controls the strength of the regularization.

By minimizing this loss function using an optimization algorithm such as stochastic gradient descent, the model learns to predict the correct relation between the head and tail entities.

3.2 Noise Correction Framework

In this section, we introduce pencil, a noise correction framework based on the end-to-end noise-labeled learning correction framework proposed by Yi and Wu

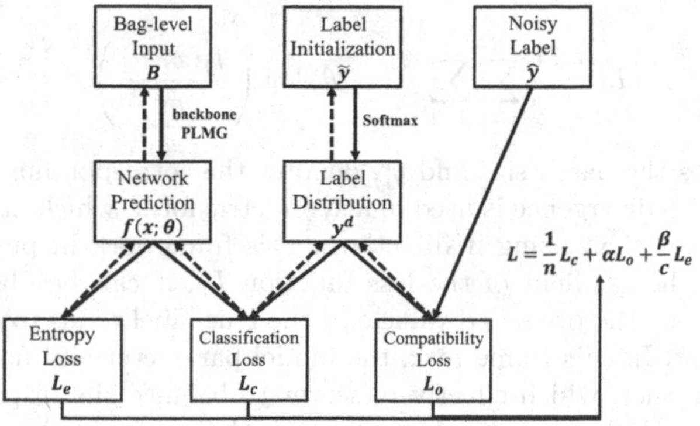

Fig. 2. Pencil Framework

[22]. The framework is illustrated in Fig. 2, with solid arrows representing forward computation and dashed arrows indicating backward propagation.

The pencil framework is designed to update both the network parameters and the data labels simultaneously using gradient descent and backpropagation. To accomplish this, the model generates a vector $\widetilde{y}$ to construct soft labels.

$$y^d = \text{Softmax}(\widetilde{y}) \tag{9}$$

With Equation (9), $\widetilde{y}$ can be updated by gradient descent and backpropagation. The following equation shows the initialized representation of the label with noise in the initial value.

$$\widetilde{y} = K\hat{y} \tag{10}$$

where $\hat{y}$ is the original label with noise, and K is a large constant which ensures y^d and $\hat{y}$ has the most similar distribution in Equation (9), i.e., $y^d \approx \hat{y}$.

An intricately devised loss function is employed to correct the noise labels during the model training procedure, with L_e and L_o as penalty terms and L_c as the classification loss. This loss function incorporates two hyperparameters, denoted as α and β, which can be flexibly adjusted to accommodate diverse datasets with varying proportions of noisy data. Specifically, increasing the value of α and reducing the value of β will yield a diminished degree of label correction. In a c-class classification problem, the loss function is presented as follows.

$$L = \frac{1}{c}L_c + \alpha L_o + \frac{\beta}{c}L_e \tag{11}$$

where c denotes the number of classes.

The classification loss, which works as the main loss of the model guiding the model to learn, is measured using the dual form of the KL divergence between the predicted distribution and the soft labels. The formula for the classification loss L_c is given by:

$$L_c = \frac{1}{n} \sum_{i=1}^{n} \sum_{j=1}^{c} f_j(x_j;\theta) \log \left(\frac{f_j(x_i;\theta)}{y_{ij}^d} \right) \tag{12}$$

where n denotes the batch size and y_{ij}^d denotes the corresponding soft label. In this equation, KL divergence is used in a symmetric form, which has been shown to perform better than using it directly in this framework in previous studies [18]. Based on the gradient of the loss function L_c, it can be observed that a larger gap between the predicted value and the true label tends to correspond to a larger gradient. In this framework, the model parameter and noise labels can be updated together, which effectively serves to balance the disparity between the prediction and the true label, facilitating the gradual correction of noisy labels.

To avoid falling into a local optimum, the model sets the entropy loss L_e, using the predicted values of the network and its calculation of the cross-entropy loss. The formula is as follows.

$$L_e = -\frac{1}{n} \sum_{i=1}^{n} \sum_{j=1}^{c} f_j(x_i;\theta) \log f_j(x_i;\theta) \tag{13}$$

The compatibility loss function L_o is formulated as follows, which uses noise labels and soft labels to calculate the cross-entropy loss so as to avoid large deviations between the corrected label and the original noise label.

$$L_o = -\frac{1}{n} \sum\nolimits_{i=1}^{n} \sum\nolimits_{j=1}^{c} \hat{y}_{ij} \log y_{ij}^d \tag{14}$$

3.3 PLMG-Pencil Relation Extraction Method

This paper presents a DSRE algorithm that utilizes selective gate and noise correction, as shown in Algorithm 1. The complete training process of the algorithm is described below.

- **Stage 1 - Backbone Network Learning Phase**: Initially, the PLMG-Pencil network is trained from scratch with a larger fixed learning rate. The noise in the data is not processed in this stage, and the loss calculation formula only utilizes the classification loss. The network parameters obtained at this stage serve as the initialized network parameters for the next training step.
- **Stage 2 - Model Learning and Noise Correction Phase**: In this stage, the network parameters and label distributions are updated together using the model, thus, noisy labels can be corrected. To avoid overfitting the label noise, the label distribution is corrected for the noise in the original labels. We obtain a vector of label distributions for each sentence bag at the end of this stage. Due to the dissimilarity of the learning rate used for soft labels update and the global model parameters update, a hyperparameter λ is set to adjust it.

Algorithm 1. PLMG-Pencil Distantly Supervised Relation Extraction Algorithm

Input: Dataset $D = x_i, \widetilde{y}_i(1 < i < n)$, epoch of stages T_1, T_2.

Stage 1:
Initialization: $t \leftarrow 1$.
while $t \leq T_1$ **do**
  Train and update the model parameters θ, while calculating the loss in equation (14) with $\alpha = 0$ and $\beta = 0$. Hold off on using $\widetilde{y}_i$;
  $t \leftarrow t + 1$;

Stage 2:
Initialization: $\widetilde{y}_i = K\hat{y}_i$.
while $T_1 \leq t \leq T_2$ **do**
  Train and update the model parameters θ and y_i^d;
  $t \leftarrow t + 1$;

Stage 3:
while $T_2 \leq t$ **do**
  Train and update the model parameters θ and y_i^d;
  Train and update the model parameters θ, while calculating the loss in equation (14) with $\alpha = 0$ and $\beta = 0$. Do not update sample labels.
  $t \leftarrow t + 1$;

Output: θ, noise-corrected labels.

- **Stage 3 - Final Fine-Tuning Phase**: The label distribution learned by the model in the previous stages are utilized to fine-tune the network in this stage. Sample labels in the training set are not updated, and the network parameters are updated using the classification loss as the loss function of the model. There are no additional adjustments to the learning rate, and the same decay rules are followed for general neural network training.

4 Experiments

4.1 Datasets

We evaluate our proposed model on three different datasets: the New York Times (NYT10) dataset and the GDS dataset in English, the SanWen dataset in Chinese. Datasets statistics are shown in Appendix A.

- NYT10 [13]: This dataset is widely used in models based on DSRE, which is annotated with 58 different relations and the NA relation account for over 80% of the total. It has 522K and 172K sentence sets in the training and test sets respectively.
- GDS [5]: This dataset is created from the Google RE corpus, which contains 5 relations. It has 18K and 5K instances in the training and test sets, respectively.

- SanWen [19]: This dataset contains 9 relations from 837 Chinese documents. It has 10K, 1.1K, and 1.3K sentences in the training set, test set, and validation set respectively.

4.2 Baselines

To validate the effectiveness of the RE model proposed in this paper, we compare it with mainstream RE methods on the three datasets mentioned above. The following baseline methods are used.
Mintz [12]: It concatenates various features of sentences to train a multi-class logistic regression classifier.
PCNN+ATT [11]: It uses selective attention to multiple instances to alleviate the problem of mislabelling.
RESIDE [17]: It exploits the information of entity type and relation alias to add a soft limitation for relation classification.
MTB-MIL [2]: It proposes a method for matching gaps and learning sentence representations through entity-linked text.
DISTRE [1]: It combines the selective attention with its PLM.
SeG [10]: It uses an entity-aware embedding-based self-attentive enhancement selective gate based on PCNN+ATT to rationally select sentence features within sentence bags to reduce the interference of noise.
CIL [3]: It proposes a comparative instance learning method in the MIL framework.
HiCLRE [7]: It incorporates global structural information and local fine-grained interactions to reduce sentence noise.

4.3 Parameter Settings

Table 1 presents the hyperparameter settings used in our experiments. The English datasets are trained on the bert-base-uncased model from the Huggingface platform, while the Chinese dataset uses the bert-base-chinese model. To effectively train our model, we use the parameter settings from Yi and Wu [22] as initialization settings for our experiments. The model's dropout rate, learning rate, α, β, batch size, and epoch settings are shown in the table.

Table 1. Parameter Settings. Epoch 1 and Epoch 2 mark the end of Stage 1 and Stage 2, respectively, and LR stands for the learning rate.

Params	Dropout	LR	α	β	BatchSize	Epoch 1	Epoch 2
Value	0.5	0.035	0.1	0.4	64	15	20

It is important to note that the optimal values for α and β may vary based on the level of noise in different datasets. Therefore, these values should be adjusted accordingly to improve the loss calculation and enhance the overall performance of the model.

4.4 Results

To evaluate the performance of our model in DSRE tasks, we use AUC and P@N values as evaluation metrics. AUC measures the area under the ROC curve, while P@N indicates the average accuracy of top N instances. Finally, P@M represents the average of these three P@N results.

Evaluation on English Dataset. Table 2 and Table 3 present a comparison of our proposed model with baseline models on dataset GDS and NYT10, respectively. Our model achieves promising results, as shown by the following observations: (1) Our proposed model shows competitive performance in terms of AUC values on both datasets. As shown in Table 2, on the GDS dataset, the AUC values of our model reach comparable levels with CIL and HiCLRE. Furthermore, as shown in Table 3, on the NYT10 dataset, our model outperforms CIL and DISTRE by 4.1% and 5.2% in AUC values respectively. (2) Our model demonstrates a clear advantage in terms of P@N values. On the NYT10 dataset, the P@100 value is 2.5% higher than CIL, which uses a contrast learning framework. The maximum difference in P@N values appears on the P@300 value, of which our method is 5.9% higher. In comparison to the DISTRE model, which also uses the PLM and MIL framework, our model outperforms it by 16%, 13.5%, and 12.7% on P@100, P@200, and P@300 values respectively.

We further conduct ablation experiments to highlight the benefits of the pencil framework. Specifically, we train our model using a conventional MIL training framework. When comparing the results of the PLMG model with the PLMG-Pencil model on the GDS dataset, we observe a 0.2% decrease in the AUC value and a 0.1% decrease in the P@1K value for the PLMG model. These findings provide compelling evidence for the effectiveness of the pencil framework and our proposed algorithm. On the dataset NYT10, the proposed model shows a significant improvement compared to the model without pencil framework. Precisely, we observe a 6%, 2.5% and 2% improvement in P@100, P@200 and P@300 values respectively.

Table 2. Model Performances on GDS. (†) marks the results are reported in the previous research.

Dataset	Models	AUC	P@500	P@1K	P@2K	P@M
GDS	Mintz† [12]	-	-	-	-	-
	PCNN-ATT† [11]	79.9	90.6	87.6	75.2	84.5
	MTB-MIL† [2]	88.5	94.8	92.2	87.0	91.3
	RESIDE† [1]	89.1	94.8	91.1	82.7	89.5
	REDSandT† [4]	86.1	95.6	92.6	84.6	91.0
	DISTRE† [1]	89.9	97.0	93.8	87.6	92.8
	CIL† [3]	90.8	**97.1**	94.0	87.8	93.0
	HiCLRE [7]	90.8	96.6	93.8	88.8	**93.1**
	PLMG-Pencil	**91.0**	95.4	**94.1**	88.8	92.8
	-without pencil (PLMG)	90.8	95.4	94.0	**89.0**	92.8

Table 3. Model Performances on NYT10. (†) marks the results are reported in the previous research.

Dataset	Models	AUC	P@100	P@200	P@300	P@M
NYT10	Mintz† [12]	10.7	52.3	50.2	45.0	49.2
	PCNN-ATT† [11]	34.1	73.0	68.0	67.3	69.4
	MTB-MIL† [2]	40.8	76.2	71.1	69.4	72.2
	RESIDE† [1]	41.5	81.8	75.4	74.3	77.2
	REDSandT† [4]	42.4	78.8	75.0	73.0	75.3
	DISTRE† [1]	42.2	68.0	67.0	65.3	66.8
	CIL† [3]	43.1	81.5	75.5	72.1	76.9
	HiCLRE [7]	45.3	82.0	78.5	74.0	78.2
	PLMG-Pencil	**47.0**	**84.0**	**80.5**	**78.0**	**80.8**
	-without pencil (PLMG)	47.0	78.0	78.0	76.0	77.3

Figure 3 shows the PR curves for our proposed model and the baseline model. Our model clearly outperforms the baselines, particularly compared to the DISTRE model, which also uses PLM and MIL. Based on the ablation experiments conducted on the NYT10 dataset, it can be observed that the PLMG-Pencil method demonstrates a notable superiority in terms of precision at N (P@N) values. These results suggest that the selective gate has a positive impact on constructing sentence bag features and improving model performance. Furthermore, the pencil framework effectively corrects for noisy samples during training, leading to improved performance.

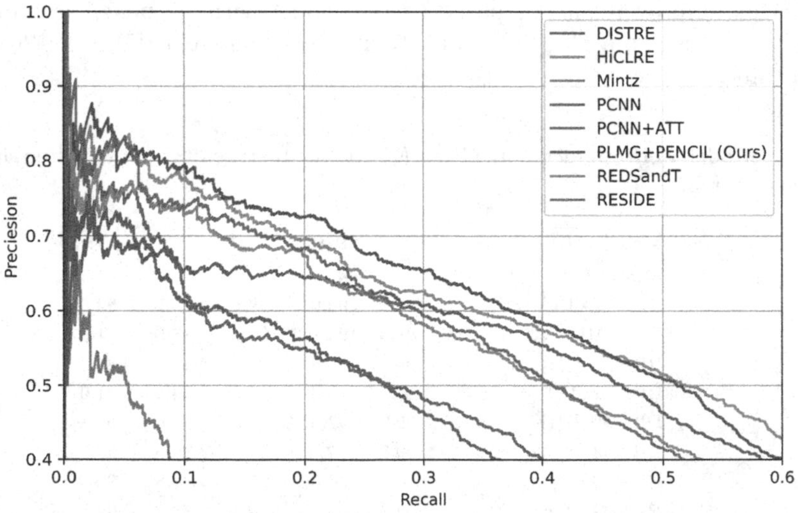

Fig. 3. PR-Curve on NYT10

Evaluation on Chinese Dataset. We conduct additional experiments on the SanWen dataset to further validate the effectiveness of the pencil framework and selective gate mechanism. Figure 4 presents the model performances on this dataset.

Our model exhibits superior performance compared to HiCLRE, which utilizes the contrast learning framework, with a notable increase of 4.4% in AUC values. Furthermore, when compared to the SeG model that employs the selective gate mechanism, our PLMG-Pencil model, which incorporates the pencil approach, demonstrates a significant enhancement in AUC values. The ablation experiment further validates the effectiveness and robustness of our method. These results highlights the positive influence of the PLM and noise correction framework on the RE task.

Based on the experimental results and the analysis of the dataset features described in Sect. 4.1, our model tends to perform better on datasets with more relations, such as NYT and SanWen. Compared with baselines, our model can achieve greater advantages on such datasets. In addition, the experimental results on the NYT10 dataset reveal that the pencil framework generates more significant performance enhancements compared to those obtained through experiments performed on the GDS dataset. The GDS dataset employs various methods to mitigate noise interferences and thus has higher quality annotations [5]. Moreover, the pencil framework is designed to conduct a noise correction process for optimizing model performance, thus, it tends to bring larger improvements on datasets with greater amounts of noisy data.

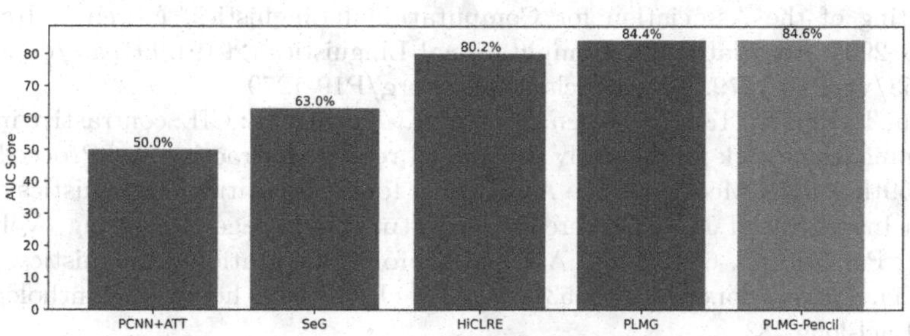

Fig. 4. AUC Values of Models on SanWen

5 Conclusion

In this paper, we propose the PLMG-Pencil method for DSRE. Our approach automatically learns the weights of different sentences in a sentence bag and selects the features that best represent the sentence bag through a gate mechanism. Additionally, we introduce a noise correction framework based on end-to-end probability with noise label learning for improved performance in RE. The experimental results clearly demonstrate that our proposed model outperforms baselines and achieves significant improvement in the RE task. Our approach shows great potential for practical application in the field of information extraction.

Acknowledgement. This work was supported by the National Social Science Fund of China (No. 22BTQ045).

A Datasets statistics

Table 4. Datasets statistics.

Dataset	#Relation	#Train	#Dev	#Test	Language
NYT	58	520K	-	172K	English
GDS	5	18K	-	5K	English
SanWen	9	10K	1.1K	1.3K	Chinese

References

1. Alt, C., Hübner, M., Hennig, L.: Fine-tuning pre-trained transformer language models to distantly supervised relation extraction. In: Proceedings of the 57th Annual Meeting of the Association for Computational Linguistics, Florence, Italy, pp. 1388–1398. Association for Computational Linguistics (2019). https://doi.org/10.18653/v1/P19-1134. https://aclanthology.org/P19-1134
2. Baldini Soares, L., FitzGerald, N., Ling, J., Kwiatkowski, T.: Matching the blanks: distributional similarity for relation learning. In: Proceedings of the 57th Annual Meeting of the Association for Computational Linguistics, Florence, Italy, pp. 2895–2905. Association for Computational Linguistics (2019). https://doi.org/10.18653/v1/P19-1279. https://aclanthology.org/P19-1279
3. Chen, T., Shi, H., Tang, S., Chen, Z., Wu, F., Zhuang, Y.: CIL: contrastive instance learning framework for distantly supervised relation extraction. In: Proceedings of the 59th Annual Meeting of the Association for Computational Linguistics and the 11th International Joint Conference on Natural Language Processing (Volume 1: Long Papers), pp. 6191–6200. Association for Computational Linguistics, Online (2021). https://doi.org/10.18653/v1/2021.acl-long.483. https://aclanthology.org/2021.acl-long.483
4. Christou, D., Tsoumakas, G.: Improving distantly-supervised relation extraction through BERT-based label and instance embeddings. IEEE Access **9**, 62574–62582 (2021)
5. Jat, S., Khandelwal, S., Talukdar, P.: Improving distantly supervised relation extraction using word and entity based attention. arXiv preprint arXiv:1804.06987 (2018)
6. Jiang, L., Zhou, Z., Leung, T., Li, L.J., Fei-Fei, L.: Mentornet: learning data-driven curriculum for very deep neural networks on corrupted labels. In: International Conference on Machine Learning, pp. 2304–2313. PMLR (2018)
7. Li, D., Zhang, T., Hu, N., Wang, C., He, X.: HiCLRE: a hierarchical contrastive learning framework for distantly supervised relation extraction. In: Findings of the Association for Computational Linguistics: ACL 2022, Dublin, Ireland, pp. 2567–2578. Association for Computational Linguistics (2022). https://doi.org/10.18653/v1/2022.findings-acl.202. https://aclanthology.org/2022.findings-acl.202

8. Li, J., Socher, R., Hoi, S.C.H.: Dividemix: learning with noisy labels as semi-supervised learning. arXiv abs/2002.07394 (2020)
9. Li, R., Yang, C., Li, T., Su, S.: MiDTD: a simple and effective distillation framework for distantly supervised relation extraction. ACM Trans. Inf. Syst. (TOIS) **40**(4), 1–32 (2022)
10. Li, Y., et al.: Self-attention enhanced selective gate with entity-aware embedding for distantly supervised relation extraction. In: Proceedings of the AAAI Conference on Artificial Intelligence, vol. 34, pp. 8269–8276 (2020)
11. Lin, Y., Shen, S., Liu, Z., Luan, H., Sun, M.: Neural relation extraction with selective attention over instances. In: Proceedings of the 54th Annual Meeting of the Association for Computational Linguistics (Volume 1: Long Papers), pp. 2124–2133 (2016)
12. Mintz, M., Bills, S., Snow, R., Jurafsky, D.: Distant supervision for relation extraction without labeled data. In: Proceedings of the Joint Conference of the 47th Annual Meeting of the ACL and the 4th International Joint Conference on Natural Language Processing of the AFNLP, pp. 1003–1011 (2009)
13. Riedel, S., Yao, L., McCallum, A.: Modeling relations and their mentions without labeled text. In: Balcázar, J.L., Bonchi, F., Gionis, A., Sebag, M. (eds.) ECML PKDD 2010. LNCS (LNAI), vol. 6323, pp. 148–163. Springer, Heidelberg (2010). https://doi.org/10.1007/978-3-642-15939-8_10
14. Shi, G., et al.: Genre separation network with adversarial training for cross-genre relation extraction. In: Proceedings of the 2018 Conference on Empirical Methods in Natural Language Processing, pp. 1018–1023 (2018)
15. Socher, R., Huval, B., Manning, C.D., Ng, A.Y.: Semantic compositionality through recursive matrix-vector spaces. In: Proceedings of the 2012 Joint Conference on Empirical Methods in Natural Language Processing and Computational Natural Language Learning, pp. 1201–1211 (2012)
16. Tanaka, D., Ikami, D., Yamasaki, T., Aizawa, K.: Joint optimization framework for learning with noisy labels. In: Proceedings of the IEEE Conference on Computer Vision and Pattern Recognition, pp. 5552–5560 (2018)
17. Vashishth, S., Joshi, R., Prayaga, S.S., Bhattacharyya, C., Talukdar, P.: RESIDE: improving distantly-supervised neural relation extraction using side information. In: Proceedings of the 2018 Conference on Empirical Methods in Natural Language Processing, Brussels, Belgium, pp. 1257–1266. Association for Computational Linguistics (2018). https://doi.org/10.18653/v1/D18-1157. https://aclanthology.org/D18-1157
18. Wu, Y., Bamman, D., Russell, S.: Adversarial training for relation extraction. In: Proceedings of the 2017 Conference on Empirical Methods in Natural Language Processing, pp. 1778–1783 (2017)
19. Xu, J., Wen, J., Sun, X., Su, Q.: A discourse-level named entity recognition and relation extraction dataset for Chinese literature text. arXiv preprint arXiv:1711.07010 (2017)
20. Yao, J., et al.: Deep learning from noisy image labels with quality embedding. IEEE Trans. Image Process. **28**(4), 1909–1922 (2018)
21. Ye, Z.X., Ling, Z.H.: Distant supervision relation extraction with intra-bag and inter-bag attentions. In: Proceedings of the 2019 Conference of the North American Chapter of the Association for Computational Linguistics: Human Language Technologies, Volume 1 (Long and Short Papers), Minneapolis, Minnesota, pp. 2810–2819. Association for Computational Linguistics (2019). https://doi.org/10.18653/v1/N19-1288. https://aclanthology.org/N19-1288

22. Yi, K., Wu, J.: Probabilistic end-to-end noise correction for learning with noisy labels. In: Proceedings of the IEEE/CVF Conference on Computer Vision and Pattern Recognition, pp. 7017–7025 (2019)
23. Zeng, D., Dai, Y., Li, F., Sherratt, R.S., Wang, J.: Adversarial learning for distant supervised relation extraction. Comput. Mater. Continua **55**(1), 121–136 (2018)
24. Zhang, Y., Wallace, B.: A sensitivity analysis of (and practitioners' guide to) convolutional neural networks for sentence classification. arXiv preprint arXiv:1510.03820 (2015)
25. Zhang, Z., Sabuncu, M.: Generalized cross entropy loss for training deep neural networks with noisy labels. In: Advances in Neural Information Processing Systems, vol. 31 (2018)
26. Zhou, P., et al.: Attention-based bidirectional long short-term memory networks for relation classification. In: Proceedings of the 54th Annual Meeting of the Association for Computational Linguistics (Volume 2: Short Papers), pp. 207–212 (2016)

Improving Cascade Decoding with Syntax-Aware Aggregator and Contrastive Learning for Event Extraction

Zeyu Sheng, Yuanyuan Liang, and Yunshi Lan(✉)

School of Data Science and Engineering, East China Normal University, Shanghai, China
{51205903051,leonyuany}@stu.ecnu.edu.cn, yslan@dase.ecnu.edu.cn

Abstract. Cascade decoding framework has shown superior performance on event extraction tasks. However, it treats a sentence as a sequence and neglects the potential benefits of the syntactic structure of sentences. In this paper, we improve cascade decoding with a novel module and a self-supervised task. Specifically, we propose a syntax-aware aggregator module to model the syntax of a sentence based on cascade decoding framework such that it captures event dependencies as well as syntactic information. Moreover, we design a type discrimination task to learn better syntactic representations of different event types, which could further boost the performance of event extraction. Experimental results on two widely used event extraction datasets demonstrate that our method could improve the original cascade decoding framework by up to 2.2 percentage points of F1 score and outperform a number of competitive baseline methods.

Keywords: Event Extraction · Cascade Decoding · Contrastive Learning

1 Introduction

As an important yet challenging task in natural language processing, event extraction has attracted much attention for decades [2,12,18,24,26,34,43,45]. This task aims at predicting event types, triggers and arguments from a given sentence. We display three examples in Fig. 1. Given an example sentence (a) "*In 2018, Chuangwei Tech acquired equity of Qianhong Electronics for 1.5 billion* ...", an event extraction system is able to recognize the trigger "*acquired*", that corresponds to the event type "*invest*", and the argument "*Chuangwei Tech*", that plays the subject role of "*sub*" in the event.

A great number of methods have been developed for event extraction. Early methods formulate the event extraction as a sequence labeling task, where each token is considered as a candidate for labeling. They perform trigger extraction and argument extraction with joint learning [17,25,27], which easily causes

M. Sun et al. (Eds.): CCL 2023, LNAI 14232, pp. 175–191, 2023.
https://doi.org/10.1007/978-981-99-6207-5_11

the label conflict issue. Considering the precedence relationship between the components in an event, pipeline methods are explored to perform trigger and argument extraction in separate stages [2,5,21,24]. But the error is accumulated along with the pipeline. Recently, a cascade decoding framework [32,37] is proposed to extract events with a cascade tagging strategy, which could not only handle the label conflict issue, but also avoid error propagation.

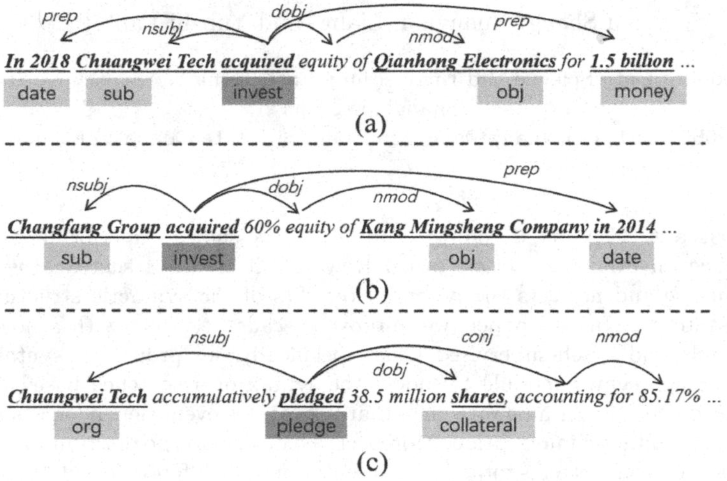

Fig. 1. Three examples of event extraction. We annotate the event types with blue boxes under the triggers, and label the argument roles with orange boxes under the arguments. (Color figure online)

In above methods, a sentence is treated as a sequence, and methods suffer from the low efficiency problem in capturing long-range dependency. We take sentence (a) in Fig. 1 as an example. The argument "*1.5 billion*" is far from the trigger "*acquired*" based on the sequential order while they are closely connected via the dependency arc. Therefore, it is necessary to take advantage of the syntactic structure to capture the relations between triggers and arguments. Some researches managed to include syntactic information of sentences in event extraction. Chen et al. [2] first employed dependency trees to conduct event extraction. Nguyen et al. [26] and Yan et al. [38] treated each dependency tree as a graph and adopted Graph Convolution Network (GCN) [11] to represent the sentence. More recent studies strengthened the graph representation via gate mechanism to filter out noisy syntactic information [13] or empowered the graph encoder with more advanced Transformer [1]. These methods could effectively solve the long-range dependency issue. However, they either follow the joint learning paradigm or pipeline paradigm thus still encounter the issue of label conflict or error propagation. In this paper, we develop our approach modeling syntactic information for event extraction based on cascade decoding framework. To achieve this, two main challenges should be addressed.

First, cascade decoding represents event types, triggers as well as arguments in the format of a triple. It sequentially predicts components in triples as subtasks and learns the implicit dependencies of the subtasks. It is not trivial to design a syntax encoder which is customized for the cascade decoders. In this paper, we propose a novel *Syntax-enhanced Aggregator* which could not only integrate the information from the precedent subtask with the current subtask but also model the syntactic structure of sentences. Moreover, this module could fuse the heterogeneous features together. In detail, our aggregator processes both subtask dependency and syntactic information via two channels. The final representation will be fused based on the alignment between tokens of a sentence and components in a dependency tree. Such aggregators are deployed in cascade decoders.

Second, existing methods involving syntactic structure rarely consider the interaction among event types. As examples (a) and (b) shown in Fig. 1, the sentences of the same event type usually have similar syntactic structure despite different involved entities. In contrast, the sentences of the different event types usually have different syntactic structure despite similar involved entities, as examples (a) and (c). We design *Contrastive Learning* of syntactic representation to capture the interactions between sentences. Specifically, we define a type discrimination task to distinguish whether two sentences belong to the same event type based on their syntactic representations. This is jointly trained with event extraction task.

We conduct experiments on two event extraction datasets, FewFC [46] and DuEE [20]. The experiments show that compared with original cascade framework, our method can clearly perform better on both datasets. Our method also outperforms competitive baseline methods that represent the state-of-the-art on event extraction tasks. To reveal the working mechanism of our method, we also conduct ablation study and visualization that shed light on where the improvement comes from.

We summarize the contributions of this paper as follows: (1) We propose a novel syntax-enhanced aggregator to model the syntactic structure of sentences, which is a good fit for the cascade decoding framework. This aggregator is able to model syntax and fuse with dependencies of events. (2) To further benefit from the syntax modeling, we design a type discrimination task to refine the syntactic representation via contrastive learning. (3) We empirically show the effectiveness of our method on two datasets. Our proposed method outperforms the baseline methods with remarkable margins based on F1 score of all measurement metrics.

2 Background

2.1 Problem Formulation

The task of event extraction aims at identifying event triggers with their types and event arguments with their roles. Specifically, a pre-defined event schema contains an event type set $\mathcal{C}$ and an argument role set $\mathcal{R}$. Given a sentence $x = \{w_1, w_2, ..., w_n\}$, the goal is to predict all events in gold set $\mathcal{E}_x$ of the sentence

x, where the components of $\mathcal{E}_x$ are in the format of triples (c, t, a_r). Here, $c \in \mathcal{C}$ is an event type, t is a trigger word in sentence x, and a_r is an argument word corresponding to the role $r \in \mathcal{R}$. A dataset $\mathcal{D}$ consists of a set of $(x, \mathcal{E}_x)$.

2.2 A Cascade Decoding Framework

To solve the task, we follow the existing cascade decoding approach, CasEE method [32], which is proposed to predict the events by maximizing the following joint likelihood:

$$\begin{aligned}&\prod_{(x,\mathcal{E}_x)\in\mathcal{D}} \Big[\prod_{(c,t,a_r)\in\mathcal{E}_x} P((c,t,a_r)|x)\Big] \\ =& \prod_{(x,\mathcal{E}_x)\in\mathcal{D}} \Big[\prod_{c\in\mathcal{C}} P(c|x) \prod_{t\in\mathcal{T}_x} P(t|x,c) \prod_{a_r\in\mathcal{A}_{x,r}} P(a_r|x,c,t)\Big], \end{aligned} \quad (1)$$

where $\mathcal{T}_x$ and $\mathcal{A}_{x,r}$ denote trigger and argument sets of x, respectively.

The joint likelihood explicates the dependencies among the type, trigger, and argument. The order of cascade decoding indicates that the framework first learns a *Type Decoder* $P(c|x)$ to identify the event types in the sentence. Then, it extracts the trigger words from the sentence via a *Trigger Decoder* $P(t|x, c)$ which corresponds to the detected type. After that, an *Argument Decoder* $P(a_r|x, c, t)$ is developed to extract role-specific arguments.

In the cascade decoding approach, the decoders are built upon a sharing BERT encoder:

$$\{\mathbf{h}_1, \mathbf{h}_2, ..., \mathbf{h}_n\} = \text{BERT}(x), \quad (2)$$

where $\mathbf{H} = \{\mathbf{h}_1, \mathbf{h}_2, ..., \mathbf{h}_n\}$ is the hidden representation of x for downstream decoding. Next, an attention layer followed by a simple feed-forward neural network is leveraged as the type decoder to predict the event type. We denote it as:

$$P(c|x) = \text{TypeDecoder}(\mathbf{H}). \quad (3)$$

After that, the predicted type embedding $\mathbf{c}$ is concatenated with each token representation. This will be further processed via a conditional layer normalization (CLN) [14] layer and a self-attention layer to form the hidden representation $\mathbf{H}^c$. A pointer network takes charge of predicting the position of start and end indexes based on $\mathbf{H}^c$. We denote the above trigger extraction procedure as follows:

$$\begin{aligned} \mathbf{H}^c &= \text{Aggregator}(\mathbf{H}, \mathbf{c}), \\ P(t|x, c) &= \text{Pointer}(\mathbf{H}^c). \end{aligned} \quad (4)$$

For argument decoder, the trigger information is concatenated with $\mathbf{H}^c$ and processed with a CLN to form the hidden representation $\mathbf{H}^{ct}$. Given $\mathbf{H}^{ct}$, the start and end indexes of role-specific arguments are then predicted as follows:

$$\mathbf{H}^{ct} = \text{Aggregator}(\mathbf{H}^{c}, \mathbf{t}),$$
$$P(a_r|x, c, t) = \text{Pointer}(\mathbf{H}^{ct}). \tag{5}$$

More details could be found in the original paper [32].

3 Our Approach

The cascade decoding framework that we described in Sect. 2.2 decodes different components of events in a cascading manner, the inputs of which are hidden representations of tokens featured with subtask dependencies. Our approach follows the framework, but we improve it by introducing a module to fuse the syntactic information over the decoding process and a self-supervised task to further refine the syntactic representation. Specifically, we propose *Syntax-enhanced Aggregators* to take place of the original aggregators. The proposed aggregator elaborately models the syntactic structure of the sentence and fuses syntax with the original hidden representation, as we will explain in Sect. 3.1. To

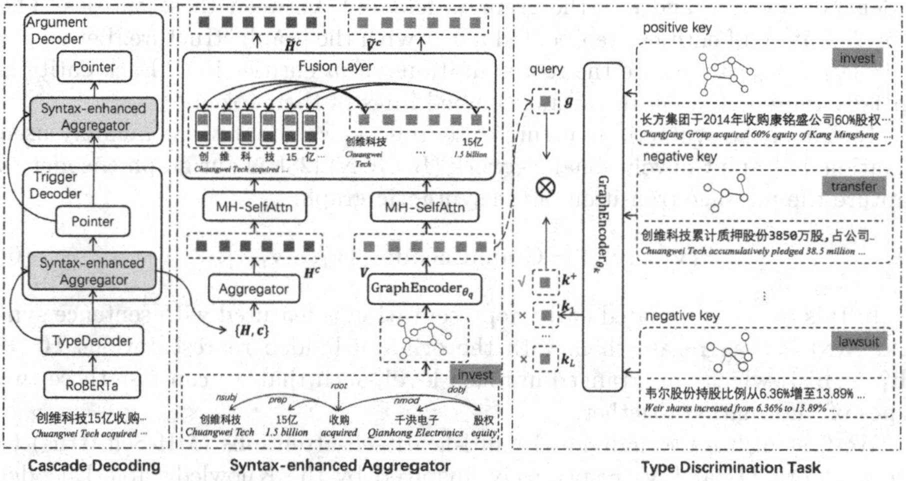

Fig. 2. The overall architecture of our approach. The network modules are annotated with solid boxes and data is annotated with imaginary boxes. The left part is the cascade decoding framework. We modify the original aggregators to syntax-enhanced aggregators. The middle part shows the details of proposed syntax-enhanced aggregator in trigger decoder, where dependency and syntactic information are carried via two channels and eventually fuse together in fusion layer. The right part shows the details of type discrimination task, where syntactic representations belonging to the same event type are learned to be closer. Please note the imaginary line from the aggregator to the discriminator is meant to show the input of the discriminator rather than forward pass of the architecture.

better capture the interactions among event types, we design a *Type Discrimination Task* to distinguish whether the representations belonging to the same type are syntactically close or not, which will be presented in Sect. 3.2. Eventually, event detection and type discrimination generate their training objectives and we join them together, as we will describe in Sect. 3.3. The overall architecture of our approach is displayed in Fig. 2.

3.1 Syntax-Enhanced Aggregator

Recall that we could prepare the hidden representations enriched with dependency information $\mathbf{H}^c$ and $\mathbf{H}^{ct}$ through the aggregators in trigger decoder and argument decoder, respectively. Now we describe, in our syntax-enhanced aggregator, how we obtain the syntactic representations and fuse these heterogeneous features to form new representations $\tilde{\mathbf{H}}^c$ and $\tilde{\mathbf{H}}^{ct}$. For simplicity, we take $\mathbf{H}^c$ in trigger decoder as the example. The similar procedure is conducted for $\mathbf{H}^{ct}$ in argument decoder.

We first extract the dependency tree of the sentence via existing parsing tools. To avoid one way message transition from the root to leaf nodes, we add reversed edges and distinguish them with different edge labels in the dependency tree. This results in a syntactic graph $\mathcal{G}(v, e)$, where v is the entity in a dependency tree and e is the grammatical link between these entities. The representation of entities are updated along with the graph structure. Let us use $\mathbf{V} = \{\mathbf{v}_1, ...\mathbf{v}_m\}$ to denote the representations of m entities in $\mathcal{G}$. Each entity is initially represented via the average embeddings of their tokens.

To model the syntactic structure of sentences, we adopt the commonly used Relational Graph Convolutional Network (R-GCN) [28] as our graph encoder to capture the message transition of the syntactic graph:

$$\{\mathbf{v}_1, ...\mathbf{v}_m\} = \text{GraphEncoder}(\{\mathbf{v}_1, ...\mathbf{v}_m)\}. \tag{6}$$

In this way, the updated entity representation is featured with sentence syntax. Next, we aggregate them with the original hidden representations $\mathbf{H}^c = \{\mathbf{h}_1^c, ..., \mathbf{h}_n^c\}$, which are arranged in token level, such that we can fuse these two types of information together.

We first utilize two individual multi-head self-attentions (MH-SelfAttns) to process both $\mathbf{H}^c$ and $\mathbf{V}$, respectively. Inspired by the Knowledgeable Encoder proposed in prior work [42], where the language representation is enhanced with knowledge graphs, we align an entity with its corresponding tokens or characters if it is formed by multiple tokens or characters. As shown in Fig. 2, the entity "创维科技 *(Chuangwei Tech)*" is aligned with "创", "维", "科" , and "技" . Thus there are explicit links between this entity and the four characters. We define the fusion layer as follows:

$$\mathbf{z}_j = \sigma(\mathbf{U}_1\mathbf{h}_j^c + \sum_{v_i \in \mathcal{A}lign(w_j)} \mathbf{W}_1\mathbf{v}_i + \mathbf{b}_1) \tag{7}$$

$$\tilde{\mathbf{h}}_j^c = \sigma(\mathbf{U}_2\mathbf{z}_j + \mathbf{b}_{21}) \tag{8}$$

$$\tilde{\mathbf{v}}_i^c = \sigma(\sum_{w_j \in Align(v_i)} \mathbf{W}_2\mathbf{z}_j + \mathbf{b}_{22}), \tag{9}$$

where σ is non-linear activation function GELU [7] and *Align* indicates the alignment between tokens and entities. The inputs are hidden representation $\mathbf{H}^c$ and entity representation $\mathbf{V}$. $\mathbf{U}$, $\mathbf{W}$ and $\mathbf{b}$ with subscripts are parameters to learn. $\mathbf{z}_j$ indicates fused hidden representation of j-th token. As a result, $\tilde{\mathbf{H}}^c = \{\tilde{\mathbf{h}}_1^c, \tilde{\mathbf{h}}_2^c, ..., \tilde{\mathbf{h}}_n^c\}$ is the token representation with fusion of syntax information. It will be leveraged as the input of pointer network in Eq. (4) for trigger extraction. $\tilde{\mathbf{V}}^c = \{\tilde{\mathbf{v}}_1^c, \tilde{\mathbf{v}}_2^c, ..., \tilde{\mathbf{v}}_m^c\}$ is the entity representation enriched with subtask dependencies. It will be utilized in downstream decoding.

When it comes to the argument decoder, $\tilde{\mathbf{V}}^c$ is used as the input entity representation to be continuously processed via the graph encoders and eventually fuse with the hidden representation $\mathbf{H}^{ct}$ to generate $\tilde{\mathbf{H}}^{ct}$. This will be fed into pointer network in Eq. (5) for argument extraction. Compared with the original aggregator, besides capturing dependency information, our syntax-enhanced aggregators encode syntactic structure and fuse both subtask dependencies and syntactic information to generate a more expressive representation for decoding.

3.2 Type Discrimination Task

Type discrimination task aims at predicting whether two sentences are syntactically close or not. The intuition behind is that sentences describing the same event type usually have similar syntactic structure. To this end, we adopt the idea of contrastive learning and push the syntactic representations of positive pairs closer than negative pairs. The syntactic representations learned from type discrimination task can further boost the performance of cascade decoding.

We conduct dependency parsing for all sentences and obtain a collection of syntactic graphs denoting as $\mathcal{U}$, each $\mathcal{G} \in \mathcal{U}$ deriving from a sentence is labeled with their event type. Then, we train the representations of a pair of syntactic graphs that share the same event type to be closer in the space. We adopt Momentum Contrast (MoCo) [6] for self-supervised representation learning, which formulates contrastive learning as a dictionary look-up task and is effective in maintaining a large-scale dynamic dictionary.

Specifically, given a syntactic graph $\mathcal{G}$ as a query, we represent it by the average of all entities encoded via the graph encoder of Eq. (6) and obtain $\mathbf{g} = \frac{1}{m}\sum_{i=1}^{m}\mathbf{v}_i$ to indicate the status of the syntactic graph. Meanwhile, we sample a set of syntactic graphs from $\mathcal{U}$ as keys of a dictionary and encode these key graphs via another graph encoder to obtain their representations. For clear presentation, we denote the query graph encoder and key graph encoder as $\text{GraphEncoder}_{\theta_q}$ and $\text{GraphEncoder}_{\theta_k}$, respectively. In the dictionary, the positive key (denoted as $\mathbf{k}^+$) is the only graph having the same type as the query. The others are negative keys $\{\mathbf{k}_1, \mathbf{k}_2, ..., \mathbf{k}_L\}$, as depicted in Fig. 2. We define the loss function of the type discrimination task as follows:

$$\mathcal{L}_{TD} = -\sum_{\mathcal{G}\in\mathcal{U}} log \frac{\exp(\mathbf{g}^{\intercal}\mathbf{k}^{+}/\tau)}{\sum_{i=0}^{L}\exp(\mathbf{g}^{\intercal}\mathbf{k}_i/\tau)}, \tag{10}$$

where τ is a temperature hyper-parameter. For each query, we construct one positive key and L negative keys.

Similar as MoCo, during training, the keys in the dictionary are progressively updated. For each new query graph $\mathcal{G}$, the old key graphs in the dictionary are removed and new key graphs are collected. Moreover, the parameters of the encoder of keys are driven by momentum update as follows:

$$\text{GraphEncoder}_{\theta_k} \leftarrow \gamma\text{GraphEncoder}_{\theta_k} + (1-\gamma)\text{GraphEncoder}_{\theta_q}, \tag{11}$$

where γ is the momentum coefficient. This results in a smooth evolution of $\text{GraphEncoder}_{\theta_k}$ as we can control the evolving progress.

3.3 Training Objective

During our training procedure, event extraction and type discrimination tasks are performed simultaneously. For each sampled data, a sentence and its corresponding syntactic graph are both collected for event extraction training. A dictionary of key graphs for a query graph is also prepared for contrastive learning.

The overall training objectives of our improved cascade decoding framework is shown as follows:

$$\mathcal{L} = \lambda\mathcal{L}_{EE} + (1-\lambda)\mathcal{L}_{TD}, \tag{12}$$

where $\mathcal{L}_{EE}$ is the negative logarithm of the joint likelihood of event extraction task in Eq. (1), and λ is a hyper-parameter. All the parameters except for $\text{GraphEncoder}_{\theta_k}$ are updated by back-propagation.

4 Experiments

In this section, we conduct experiments to evaluate the proposed method. We first introduce our experiment settings including datasets and evaluation metrics, comparable methods, and implementation details in Sect. 4.1, Sect. 4.2, and Sect. 4.3. Next, we discuss our main results in Sect. 4.4. We show further analysis in Sect. 4.5

4.1 Datasets and Evaluation Metrics

We conduct experiments on two commonly used event extraction datasets:

- **FewFC** [46][1] is a public Chinese dataset for event extraction in the financial domain. It contains 10 event types and 19 role types. There are 12,890 sentences in the dataset. Following previous setting [32], we split the dataset with the ratio 8 : 1 : 1 to form training, development, and test sets.
- **DuEE** [20][2] is a relatively large Chinese event extraction dataset, which contains 19,640 sentences in total. The data is collected by crowdsourcing and contains 65 event types associated with 121 role types in real-world scenarios. We follow its default split setting to construct the data sets.

We utilize the standard evaluation metrics [2,5] to evaluate performance of trigger detection and argument detection: (1) Trigger Identification (**TI**): If a predicted trigger word matches the gold word, this trigger is identified correctly. (2) Trigger Classification (**TC**): If a trigger is correctly identified and assigned to the correct type, it is correctly classified. (3) Argument Identification (**AI**): If an event type is correctly recognized and the predicted argument word matches the gold word, it is correctly identified. (4) Argument Classification (**AC**): If an argument is correctly identified and the predicted role matches the gold role type, it is correctly classified. We measure Precision, Recall and F1 score based on the above four metrics.

4.2 Comparable Methods

We choose a range of advanced approaches for event extraction as our baselines:

- **DMCNN** [2] is a pipeline with dynamic multi-pooling convolutional neural network and enriched encoded syntactic features. It is the early attempt adopting syntactic information into event extraction.
- **GCN-ED** [26] develops a GCN based on dependency trees to perform event detection, where each word is treated as a trigger candidate and joint learning is performed to label words with event types.
- **GatedGCN** [13] is GCN-based model for event detection which uses a gating mechanism to filter noisy information. It also follows a joint learning paradigm.
- **BERT+CRF** [5] is a sequence labeling model with advanced pre-trained language model BERT for encoding sentences and conditional random field (CRF) for tagging labels.
- **MQAEE** [15] is a pipeline method that formulates the extraction task as a multi-turn question answering without any syntactic information involved.
- **CasEE** [32] is the representative cascade decoding approach for event extraction, which simply treats a sentence as a sequence.

We either utilize official source codes or follow their descriptions to re-implement the baseline methods.

[1] https://github.com/TimeBurningFish/FewFC.
[2] http://ai.baidu.com/broad/download.

Table 1. Event extraction results on test set of FewFc dataset. P(%), R(%) and F1(%) denote percentages of precision, recall and F1 score, respectively. The methods annotated with "⋆" are those enriched with syntactic features.

Methods	TI			TC			AI			AC		
	P(%)	R(%)	F1(%)	P(%)	R(%)	F1(%)	P(%)	R(%)	F1(%)	P(%)	R(%)	F1(%)
DMCNN⋆	82.0	79.4	80.7	69.4	68.2	68.8	70.2	66.3	68.2	66.8	65.7	66.2
GCN-ED⋆	84.4	83.7	84.0	71.7	68.9	70.3	69.1	69.6	69.4	71.2	65.7	68.3
GatedGCN⋆	88.9	85.0	86.9	76.2	73.4	74.8	72.3	70.1	71.2	71.4	68.8	70.1
BERT-CRF	88.4	84.1	86.2	74.2	70.5	72.3	69.4	68.1	68.7	70.8	68.2	69.5
MQAEE	88.7	86.2	87.4	77.2	76.4	76.8	**72.7**	69.7	71.2	70.2	66.5	68.3
CasEE	89.1	87.8	88.4	77.8	78.6	78.2	71.6	73.2	72.4	71.2	72.4	71.8
Ours⋆	**90.1**	**88.9**	**89.5**	**78.1**	**79.4**	**78.7**	71.9	**77.0**	**74.4**	**71.5**	**75.7**	**73.5**

4.3 Implementation Details

For implementation, we use Chinese BERT Model [4] in Transformers library[3] as our basic textual encoder to convert words into vector representations. For other parameters, we randomly initialize them. To obtain syntactic graphs, we extract the syntactic dependency of sentences via StanfordNLP parsing tool[4] and convert dependency trees into graphs via DGL[5] library. In our syntax-enhanced aggregator, we use 8 heads for MH-SelfAttns layers and 2 stacked R-GCN layers to form a GraphEncoder. For hyper-parameters, we search via grid search through pre-defined spaces and decide the best configuration based on the best F1 score on the development set. The dimension of hidden representations in graph encoders or aggregators are all set to 768. We use an Adam optimizer [10] to train all trainable parameters. The initial learning rate is set to $1e-5$ for BERT parameters and $1e-4$ for the other parameters. A warmup proportion

Table 2. Event extraction results on test set of DuEE dataset. P(%), R(%) and F1(%) denote percentages of precision, recall and F1 score, respectively. The methods annotated with "⋆" are those enriched with syntactic features.

Methods	TI			TC			AI			AC		
	P(%)	R(%)	F1(%)	P(%)	R(%)	F1(%)	P(%)	R(%)	F1(%)	P(%)	R(%)	F1(%)
DMCNN⋆	78.4	80.2	79.3	79.4	76.3	77.8	69.2	67.4	68.3	67.2	65.6	66.4
GCN-ED⋆	82.4	76.2	79.2	81.6	76.2	78.8	71.3	69.5	70.4	70.9	64.5	67.5
GatedGCN⋆	**88.6**	83.0	85.7	82.4	80.5	81.4	**73.8**	71.6	72.7	**72.5**	68.4	70.4
BERT-CRF	87.2	77.6	82.1	80.4	77.4	78.8	70.6	68.1	69.3	70.5	66.7	68.5
MQAEE	87.9	82.1	84.9	80.9	79.4	80.1	73.2	71.7	72.4	71.0	69.7	70.3
CasEE	85.5	88.2	86.8	83.6	83.9	83.7	70.3	75.4	72.8	68.6	75.7	72.0
Ours⋆	87.7	**89.0**	**88.3**	**83.7**	**86.8**	**85.2**	72.8	**76.9**	**74.8**	71.2	**77.4**	**74.2**

[3] https://huggingface.co/.
[4] https://nlp.stanford.edu/software/lex-parser.shtml.
[5] https://www.dgl.ai/.

for learning rate is set to 10%. The training batch is set to 16 and the maximum training epoch is 30. The size of dictionary L is set to 1000 for contrastive learning. We set $\tau = 0.07$, $\lambda = 0.5$ and $\gamma = 0.8$. To avoid overfitting, we apply dropout layers in syntax-enhanced aggregators with a dropout ratio as 0.3.

4.4 Main Results

The performance of all methods on FewFC and DeEE datasets is displayed in Table 1 and Table 2, respectively. Based on the two tables, we have the following observations:

(1) For both datasets, our method surpasses all baseline methods with a remarkable margin and obtains new state-of-the-art results on F1 score of all measurement metrics. This shows that our method incorporating syntactic information with cascade decoding framework indeed brings the largest benefit for event extraction task. Compared with CasEE, our method shows gains on TI as well as AI measurement. This may because that leveraging syntactic relation of sentences captures long-range dependency and enables the model to retrieve more accurate trigger and arguments. Also, the gains on TC and AC may comes from contrastive learning, which helps the model label events by discriminating the different syntactic structure of event types.
(2) In the perspective of framework, compared with the joint learning and pipeline paradigms, cascade decoding could achieve better performance. CasEE outperforms BERT-CRF as well as MQAEE with marginal improvement on both datasets. As discussed in Sect. 1, cascade decoding framework could avoid label conflicts and error propagation effectively [32], which reveals the necessity of developing methods based on cascade decoding framework.
(3) For methods featured with syntactic information, different methods show different effects. Specifically, DMCNN and GCN-ED are methods involving syntactic information, their performance on both datasets are not ideal, this may because that these two methods are developed upon un-contextual word embeddings thus cannot fully capture the deep semantics of sentences.

Table 3. Results of ablation study on FewFC dataset. We display the percentages of F1 score on all measurement metrics. **SA** denotes Syntax-enhanced Aggregator.

	TI(%)	TC(%)	AI(%)	AC(%)
Our Model	**89.5**	**78.7**	**74.4**	**73.5**
w/o Contrastive learning	88.7	78.3	73.6	72.4
w/o Fusion Layer	89.0	78.4	73.6	72.8
w/o SA in Trigger Decoder	88.5	78.1	72.4	71.9
w/o SA in Argument Decoder	89.3	78.6	73.0	72.1

GatedGCN takes advantage of BERT encoder and encodes syntactic information via GCN model and it could outperform the BERT-CRF method. Our method is also built upon BERT encoder and featured with syntax-enhanced aggregator and type discrimination task, which is effective in solving the label conflict and modeling syntactic information of sentences.

4.5 Further Analysis

Ablation Study. To explore details of our proposed method, we show the result of ablation study in Table 3. As we can see, both syntax-enhanced aggregators and contrastive learning contribute to the entire system. After we omit the contrastive learning, the performance decreases. This indicates that capturing the syntactic structure of sentences is key for detecting the event types. Similarly, After we omit the fusion layer in syntax-enhanced aggregator and simply add the hidden representation of syntactic graph to $\mathbf{H}^c$, the performance drops. This indicates that the way to combine syntactic feature and subtask dependencies is critical. We remove the syntax-enhanced aggregators in trigger and argument decoders in turn. The performance decrease indicates that the proposed syntax-enhanced aggregators contribute to both trigger extraction and argument extraction.

Effect of L**.** In order to show the effect of L value in contrastive learning, we train our method on FewFC dataset with varying dictionary sizes and draw curves in Fig. 3(a). The figure shows that with the increase of L value in contrastive learning, the performance of trigger classification and argument classification increases. This is because seeing more interactions of different event types could help the model learn more distinct syntactic features.

Representation Visualization. In Fig. 3(b), we display the learned query representations in FewFC dataset by mapping them into two dimensional space via t-distributed stochastic neighbor embedding (t-SNE) [8]. The data points with different colors indicate query graphs of different categories of event types. As we can observe, the query representations of different event types without contrastive learning mix together and exhibit random distribution. In contrast, after including type discrimination task with contrative learning, the same event types clustered. This verifies that contrastive learning leads to a better syntactic representation for each sentence.

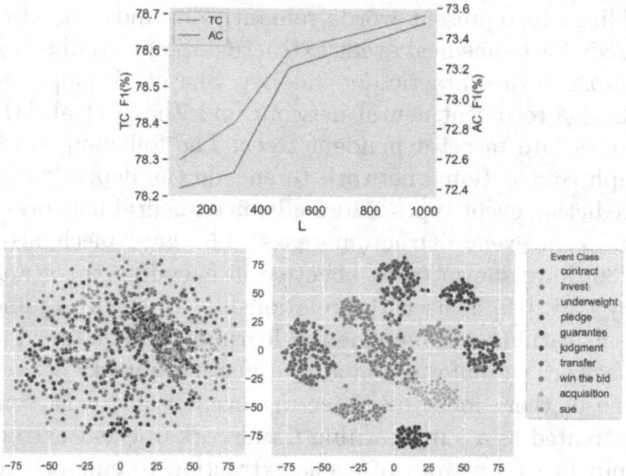

Fig. 3. (a) shows the performance change of TC and AC on FewFC with increasing L value in contrastive learning. (b) shows the t-SNE plots of representations of query graphs of FewFC without and with contrastive learning.

5 Related Work

5.1 Frameworks of Event Extraction

The frameworks of event extraction can be roughly categorized into three groups. Joint learning framework solves event extraction in a sequence labeling manner [9,17,22,25,27,29,31]. They treat each token as the candidate of a trigger or an argument and tag it with types. However, joint learning has the disadvantage of solving sentences where one token could have more than one event types. Pipeline framework performs trigger extraction and argument extraction in separate stages [3,5,15,21,24,33,40,45]. This framework could avoid the label conflict issue but it ignores the potential label dependencies in modeling and suffers from error propagation. The cascade decoding framework formulates triples to represent event types, triggers and arguments [32,37,39]. It jointly performs predictions for event triggers as well as arguments based on shared feature representations and learns the implicit dependencies of the triples. It could avoid label conflict and error propagation. Empirical results show it is an effective solution for event extraction. The cascade decoding framework is also effective in jointly extracting relations and entities from text [35,44].

5.2 Syntax Modeling for Event Extraction

There are a number of studies that incorporate the syntactic structure of sentences into event extraction tasks. The early work [2] collected syntactic features from the dependency tree and fed them into a dynamic multi-pooling convolutional neural network for extracting events. Li et al. [16] also utilized dependency-based embeddings to represent words semantically and syntactically and proposed a PMCNN for biomedical event extraction. Some studies tried to enhance the basic network with syntactic dependency, Sha et al. [30] proposed a novel dependency bridge recurrent neural network and Zhang et al. [41] transformed dependency trees into target-dependent trees. The follow-up studies [22,26,38] employed graph convolutional network to encode the dependency tree and utilized it for predicting event types. More advanced neural networks are leveraged to model syntax in event extraction tasks. The gate mechanism and Transformer [1,13,36] have shown to be effective in encoding the graph information of dependency tree. [19] utilized the relationships of event arguments based on a reinforcement learning and incremental learning. [23] designed a sequence-to-structure framework to uniformly models different subtasks of event extraction. However, some of them focus on detecting event types with syntax modeling which can be treated as a joint learning framework of event extraction, the others follow a pipeline framework of event extraction to enhance syntactic information. To fully make use of the cascade decoding framework, we propose our method based on the cascade decoding architecture, which captures the subtask dependencies and syntactic structure simultaneously.

6 Conclusions

In this paper, we improved cascade decoding with syntax-aware aggregator and contrastive learning for event extraction. We demonstrated the effectiveness of our proposed method on two datasets. The results showed that our method outperforms all baseline methods based on F1 score. Considering that many scenes have relatively high requirements for real-time performance, we will explore to optimize the computational complexity of the model and improving the universality of the model in the future.

Acknowledgements. This work was supported in part by ECNU Research Fund on Cultural Inheritance and Innovation (Grant No. 2022ECNU-WHCCYJ-31) and Shanghai Pujiang Talent Program (Project No. 22PJ1403000). We sincerely thank the anonymous reviewers for their valuable comments and feedback.

References

1. Ahmad, W.U., Peng, N., Chang, K.W.: Gate: graph attention transformer encoder for cross-lingual relation and event extraction. In: Proceedings of the AAAI Conference on Artificial Intelligence, pp. 12462–12470 (2021)
2. Chen, Y., Xu, L., Liu, K., Zeng, D., Zhao, J.: Event extraction via dynamic multi-pooling convolutional neural networks. In: Proceedings of the 53rd Annual Meeting of the Association for Computational Linguistics and the 7th International Joint Conference on Natural Language Processing (Volume 1: Long Papers), pp. 167–176 (2015)
3. Chen, Y., Chen, T., Ebner, S., White, A.S., Van Durme, B.: Reading the manual: event extraction as definition comprehension. In: Proceedings of the Fourth Workshop on Structured Prediction for NLP (2020)

4. Devlin, J., Chang, M.W., Lee, K., Toutanova, K.: BERT: pre-training of deep bidirectional transformers for language understanding. arXiv preprint arXiv:1810.04805 (2018)
5. Du, X., Cardie, C.: Event extraction by answering (almost) natural questions. In: Proceedings of the 2020 Conference on Empirical Methods in Natural Language Processing (EMNLP), pp. 671–683 (2020)
6. He, K., Fan, H., Wu, Y., Xie, S., Girshick, R.: Momentum contrast for unsupervised visual representation learning. In: 2020 IEEE/CVF Conference on Computer Vision and Pattern Recognition (CVPR), pp. 9726–9735 (2020)
7. Hendrycks, D., Gimpel, K.: Bridging nonlinearities and stochastic regularizers with gaussian error linear units. arXiv preprint arXiv:1606.08415 (2016)
8. Hinton, G.E., Roweis, S.: Stochastic neighbor embedding. In: Becker, S., Thrun, S., Obermayer, K. (eds.) Advances in Neural Information Processing Systems, vol. 15 (2002)
9. Huang, P., Zhao, X., Takanobu, R., Tan, Z., Xiao, W.: Joint event extraction with hierarchical policy network. In: Proceedings of the 28th International Conference on Computational Linguistics, pp. 2653–2664 (2020)
10. Kingma, D.P., Ba, J.: Adam: a method for stochastic optimization. In: ICLR (2015)
11. Kipf, T.N., Welling, M.: Semi-supervised classification with graph convolutional networks. In: International Conference on Learning Representations (ICLR) (2017)
12. Lai, V., Nguyen, M.V., Kaufman, H., Nguyen, T.H.: Event extraction from historical texts: a new dataset for black rebellions. In: Findings of the Association for Computational Linguistics: ACL-IJCNLP 2021, pp. 2390–2400 (2021)
13. Lai, V.D., Nguyen, T.N., Nguyen, T.H.: Event detection: gate diversity and syntactic importance scores for graph convolution neural networks. In: Proceedings of the 2020 Conference on Empirical Methods in Natural Language Processing (EMNLP), pp. 5405–5411 (2020)
14. Lee, D., Tian, Z., Xue, L., Zhang, N.L.: Enhancing content preservation in text style transfer using reverse attention and conditional layer normalization. In: Proceedings of the 59th Annual Meeting of the Association for Computational Linguistics and the 11th International Joint Conference on Natural Language Processing (Volume 1: Long Papers), pp. 93–102 (2021)
15. Li, F., et al.: Event extraction as multi-turn question answering. In: Findings of the Association for Computational Linguistics: EMNLP 2020, pp. 829–838 (2020)
16. Li, L., Liu, Y., Qin, M.: Extracting biomedical events with parallel multi-pooling convolutional neural networks. IEEE/ACM Trans. Comput. Biol. Bioinf. **17**(2), 599–607 (2018)
17. Li, Q., Ji, H., Huang, L.: Joint event extraction via structured prediction with global features. In: Proceedings of the 51st Annual Meeting of the Association for Computational Linguistics (Volume 1: Long Papers), pp. 73–82 (2013)
18. Li, Q., et al.: A survey on deep learning event extraction: approaches and applications. IEEE Trans. Neural Netw. Learn. Syst. (2022)
19. Li, Q., et al.: Reinforcement learning-based dialogue guided event extraction to exploit argument relations. IEEE/ACM Trans. Audio Speech Lang. Process. **30**, 520–533 (2021)
20. Li, X., et al.: DuEE: a large-scale dataset for Chinese event extraction in real-world scenarios. In: CCF International Conference on Natural Language Processing and Chinese Computing, pp. 534–545 (2020)
21. Liu, J., Chen, Y., Liu, K., Bi, W., Liu, X.: Event extraction as machine reading comprehension. In: Proceedings of the 2020 Conference on Empirical Methods in Natural Language Processing (EMNLP), pp. 1641–1651 (2020)

22. Liu, X., Luo, Z., Huang, H.: Jointly multiple events extraction via attention-based graph information aggregation. In: Proceedings of the 2018 Conference on Empirical Methods in Natural Language Processing, pp. 1247–1256 (2018)
23. Lu, Y., et al.: Text2event: controllable sequence-to-structure generation for end-to-end event extraction. arXiv preprint arXiv:2106.09232 (2021)
24. Ma, Y., et al.: Prompt for extraction? PAIE: prompting argument interaction for event argument extraction. In: Proceedings of the 60th Annual Meeting of the Association for Computational Linguistics (Volume 1: Long Papers) (2022)
25. Nguyen, T.H., Cho, K., Grishman, R.: Joint event extraction via recurrent neural networks. In: Proceedings of the 2016 Conference of the North American Chapter of the Association for Computational Linguistics: Human Language Technologies, pp. 300–309 (2016)
26. Nguyen, T.H., Grishman, R.: Graph convolutional networks with argument-aware pooling for event detection. In: Proceedings of the Thirty-Second AAAI Conference on Artificial Intelligence and Thirtieth Innovative Applications of Artificial Intelligence Conference and Eighth AAAI Symposium on Educational Advances in Artificial Intelligence, pp. 5900–5907 (2018)
27. Nguyen, T.M., Nguyen, T.H.: One for all: neural joint modeling of entities and events. In: Proceedings of the AAAI Conference on Artificial Intelligence, pp. 6851–6858 (2019)
28. Schlichtkrull, M., Kipf, T.N., Bloem, P., van den Berg, R., Titov, I., Welling, M.: Modeling relational data with graph convolutional networks. In: Gangemi, A., et al. (eds.) ESWC 2018. LNCS, vol. 10843, pp. 593–607. Springer, Cham (2018). https://doi.org/10.1007/978-3-319-93417-4_38
29. Sha, L., Qian, F., Chang, B., Sui, Z.: Jointly extracting event triggers and arguments by dependency-bridge RNN and tensor-based argument interaction. In: Proceedings of the Thirty-Second AAAI Conference on Artificial Intelligence and Thirtieth Innovative Applications of Artificial Intelligence Conference and Eighth AAAI Symposium on Educational Advances in Artificial Intelligence (2018)
30. Sha, L., Qian, F., Chang, B., Sui, Z.: Jointly extracting event triggers and arguments by dependency-bridge RNN and tensor-based argument interaction. In: Proceedings of the AAAI Conference on Artificial Intelligence, vol. 32 (2018)
31. Shen, S., Qi, G., Li, Z., Bi, S., Wang, L.: Hierarchical Chinese legal event extraction via pedal attention mechanism. In: Proceedings of the 28th International Conference on Computational Linguistics, pp. 100–113 (2020)
32. Sheng, J., et al.: CasEE: a joint learning framework with cascade decoding for overlapping event extraction. In: Findings of the Association for Computational Linguistics: ACL-IJCNLP 2021, pp. 164–174 (2021)
33. Wadden, D., Wennberg, U., Luan, Y., Hajishirzi, H.: Entity, relation, and event extraction with contextualized span representations. In: Proceedings of the 2019 Conference on Empirical Methods in Natural Language Processing and the 9th International Joint Conference on Natural Language Processing (EMNLP-IJCNLP), pp. 5784–5789 (2019)
34. Wang, Z., et al.: CLEVE: contrastive pre-training for event extraction. In: Proceedings of the 59th Annual Meeting of the Association for Computational Linguistics and the 11th International Joint Conference on Natural Language Processing (Volume 1: Long Papers), pp. 6283–6297 (2021)
35. Wei, Z., Su, J., Wang, Y., Tian, Y., Chang, Y.: A novel cascade binary tagging framework for relational triple extraction. In: Proceedings of the 58th Annual Meeting of the Association for Computational Linguistics, pp. 1476–1488 (2020)

36. Xie, J., Sun, H., Zhou, J., Qu, W., Dai, X.: Event detection as graph parsing. In: Findings of the Association for Computational Linguistics: ACL-IJCNLP 2021, pp. 1630–1640 (2021)
37. Xu, N., Xie, H., Zhao, D.: A novel joint framework for multiple Chinese events extraction. In: Proceedings of the 19th Chinese National Conference on Computational Linguistics, pp. 950–961 (2020)
38. Yan, H., Jin, X., Meng, X., Guo, J., Cheng, X.: Event detection with multi-order graph convolution and aggregated attention. In: Proceedings of the 2019 Conference on Empirical Methods in Natural Language Processing and the 9th International Joint Conference on Natural Language Processing (EMNLP-IJCNLP), pp. 5766–5770 (2019)
39. Yang, H., Sui, D., Chen, Y., Liu, K., Zhao, J., Wang, T.: Document-level event extraction via parallel prediction networks. In: Proceedings of the 59th Annual Meeting of the Association for Computational Linguistics and the 11th International Joint Conference on Natural Language Processing (Volume 1: Long Papers), pp. 6298–6308 (2021)
40. Yang, S., Feng, D., Qiao, L., Kan, Z., Li, D.: Exploring pre-trained language models for event extraction and generation. In: Proceedings of the 57th Annual Meeting of the Association for Computational Linguistics, pp. 5284–5294 (2019)
41. Zhang, W., Ding, X., Liu, T.: Learning target-dependent sentence representations for Chinese event detection. In: Zhang, S., Liu, T.-Y., Li, X., Guo, J., Li, C. (eds.) CCIR 2018. LNCS, vol. 11168, pp. 251–262. Springer, Cham (2018). https://doi.org/10.1007/978-3-030-01012-6_20
42. Zhang, Z., Han, X., Liu, Z., Jiang, X., Sun, M., Liu, Q.: ERNIE: enhanced language representation with informative entities. In: Proceedings of the 57th Annual Meeting of the Association for Computational Linguistics, pp. 1441–1451 (2019)
43. Zheng, S., Cao, W., Xu, W., Bian, J.: Doc2EDAG: an end-to-end document-level framework for Chinese financial event extraction. In: Proceedings of the 2019 Conference on Empirical Methods in Natural Language Processing and the 9th International Joint Conference on Natural Language Processing (EMNLP-IJCNLP), pp. 337–346 (2019)
44. Zheng, S., Wang, F., Bao, H., Hao, Y., Zhou, P., Xu, B.: Joint extraction of entities and relations based on a novel tagging scheme. In: Proceedings of the 55th Annual Meeting of the Association for Computational Linguistics (Volume 1: Long Papers), pp. 1227–1236 (2017)
45. Zhou, J., Zhang, Q., Chen, Q., Zhang, Q., He, L., Huang, X.: A multi-format transfer learning model for event argument extraction via variational information bottleneck. In: Proceedings of the 29th International Conference on Computational Linguistics (2022)
46. Zhou, Y., Chen, Y., Zhao, J., Wu, Y., Xu, J., Li, J.: What the role is vs. what plays the role: semi-supervised event argument extraction via dual question answering. In: Proceedings of the AAAI Conference on Artificial Intelligence, pp. 14638–14646 (2021)

TERL: Transformer Enhanced Reinforcement Learning for Relation Extraction

Yashen Wang[1,2], Tuo Shi[3], Xiaoye Ouyang[1], and Dayu Guo[4(✉)]

[1] National Engineering Laboratory for Risk Perception and Prevention (RPP), China Academy of Electronics and Information Technology, Beijing 100041, China
yswang.arthur@gmail.com

[2] Key Laboratory of Cognition and Intelligence Technology (CIT), Artificial Intelligence Institute of CETC, Beijing 100144, China

[3] Beijing Police College, Beijing 102202, China
shituo@bjpc.edu.cn

[4] CETC Academy of Electronics and Information Technology Group Co., Ltd., Beijing 100041, China
{ouyangxiaoye,guodayu1}@cetc.com.cn

Abstract. Relation Extraction (RE) task aims to discover the semantic relation that holds between two entities and contributes to many applications such as knowledge graph construction and completion. Reinforcement Learning (RL) has been widely used for RE task and achieved SOTA results, which are mainly designed with rewards to choose the optimal actions during the training procedure, to improve RE's performance, especially for low-resource conditions. Recent work has shown that offline or online RL can be flexibly formulated as a sequence understanding problem and solved via approaches similar to large-scale pre-training language modeling. To strengthen the ability for understanding the semantic signals interactions among the given text sequence, this paper leverages Transformer architecture for RL-based RE methods, and proposes a generic framework called **T**ransformer **E**nhanced **RL** (**TERL**) towards RE task. Unlike prior RL-based RE approaches that usually fit value functions or compute policy gradients, TERL only outputs the best actions by utilizing a masked Transformer. Experimental results show that the proposed TERL framework can improve many state-of-the-art RL-based RE methods.

Keywords: Relation Extraction · Reinforcement Learning · Transformer

1 Introduction

Relation Extraction (RE) aims to discover the binary semantic relation between two entities in a sequence of words. E.g., given a sentence "··· Carey will succeed Cathleen P. Black, who held the position for 15 years and will take on a new role as chairwoman of Hearst Magazines, the company said···" [37], and we aim to predict the relation type between two entities "Cathleen P. Black" and "chairwoman" and the result is "per:title".

Deep neural network (DNN) driven methods have gained decent performance when labeled data is available [7,12]. While Reinforcement Learning (RL) based RE methods

M. Sun et al. (Eds.): CCL 2023, LNAI 14232, pp. 192–206, 2023.
https://doi.org/10.1007/978-981-99-6207-5_12

gain a lot of attention recently and show encouraging effects [12,30,35], especially in low-resource and few-shot conditions. Since this kinds of work requires *fewer* labeled data or could expand limited labeled data by exploiting information on unlabeled data to iteratively improve the performance [12].

Recent works have shown Transformers [33] can model high-dimensional distributions of semantic concepts at scale, and several attempts have demonstrated the combination between transformers and RL architecture [22,23,39]. These works have shown that the Transformer's efficiency for modeling beneficial semantic interactions in the given sequence [1,44], which is very enlightening for RE task. Given the diversity of successful applications of such models [1], this paper seeks to investigate their application to sequential RE problems formalized as RL, because of the three main advantages of transformers: (i) Its ability to model long sequences has been demonstrated in many tasks; (ii) It could perform long-term *credit assignment* via self-attention strategy, contrary to Bellman backups [16] which slowly propagate rewards and are prone to distractor signals [13] in Q-learning, which could enable Transformer-based architecture to still work effectively in the presence of distracting rewards [1]; and (iii) It can model a wide distribution of behaviors, enabling better generalization [26]. Hence, inspired by [1,44], we try to view the RL-based RE as a conditional sequence understanding problem. Especially, we model the joint distribution of the sequence of states, actions and rewards, and discuss whether generative sequence understanding could can serve as a substitute for traditional RL algorithms in RE task. Overall, we propose **T**ransformer **E**nhanced **R**einforcement **L**earning (**TERL**), which abstracts RL paradigm as autoregressively sequence understanding and utilize Transformer architecture in BERT[1] to model text sequences with minimal modification to native transformer's architecture, and we investigate whether the sequence understanding paradigm can perform policy optimization by evaluating TERL on RL benchmarks in RE task. This enables us to leverage the scalability of the Transformer's architecture, as well as the related advancements in pre-training language modeling (such as the BERT's series).

Especially, following the backbone proposed in [1], we train Transformer architecture on collected experience with a sequence understanding objective for RE task, instead of training a policy through conventional RL algorithms [12,35]. This transformer is trained to predict next token in a sequence of rewards (forward-cumulative-rewards emphasized here), states, and actions. This paper shows that leveraging Transformers can open up another paradigm to solve RL-based RE problem. The main differences between this work and previous RL-based RE methods, can be concluded as follows: (i) RL is transformed into sequence understanding; (ii) We learn the natural projection from reward and state to action, instead of maximizing cumulative discount rewards or *only* modeling state and action in conventional behavior cloning paradigm [2]; (iii) Q/V-functions are *no* need to be learned, while we directly model it as a sequence problem, wherein as long as given the expected return, we can get the corresponding action; and (iv) Bellman backups or other temporal difference frameworks is *no* need; In RE tasks (even relation and entity joint extraction tasks) with our work, the expected target return is highly correlated with the actual observed return. Under certain conditions, the proposed TERL could successfully generate sequences that almost

[1] Other transformer architecture is also applicable.

completely match the required returns. In addition, we can prompt TERL with a higher return than the maximum event available in the dataset, indicating that our TERL can sometimes be extrapolated. Moreover, the proposed framework can also be used as a plug-in unit for any RL-based RE architecture, and be extended to relation and entity joint extraction task [46]. Experimental results show that the proposed TERL framework can improve many state-of-the-art RL-based RE methods.

2 Related Work

Relation Extraction (RE) aims to predict the binary relation between two entities in a sequence of words. Recent work leverages deep neural network (DNN) for learning the features among two entities from sentences, and then classify these features into pre-defined relation types [12]. These methods have achieved satisfactory performance when labeled data is sufficient [7,40], however, it's labor-intensive to obtain large amounts of manual annotations on corpus. Hence, few-shot (even zero-shot) RE methods gained a lot of attention recently, since these methods require *fewer* labeled data and could expand limited labeled information by exploiting information on unlabeled data to iteratively improve the performance. Wherein, Reinforcement Learning (RL) based methods have grown rapidly [35,41], which has been widely used in Nature Language Processing (NLP) [18,21,46]. These methods are all designed with rewards to force the correct actions to be chosen during the model's training procedure. For RE task, [24] proposes a RL strategy to generate the false-positive indicator, where it automatically recognizes false positives for each relation type without any supervised information. [18] addresses the RE task by capturing rich contextual dependencies based on the attention mechanism, and using distributional RL to generate optimal relation information representation. [12] proposes gradient imitation RL method to encourage pseudo label data to imitate the gradient descent direction on labeled data. For relation and entity joint extraction task, [30] proposes a hierarchical RL framework which decomposes the whole extraction process into a hierarchy of two-level RL policies for relation extraction and entity extraction, respectively. [41] applies policy gradient method to model future reward in a joint entity and relation extraction task. [35] jointly extracts entities and relations, and propose a novel bidirectional interaction RL model.

Recently, there exist many exciting works which formulate the Reinforcement Learning (RL) problem as a context-conditioned "sequence understanding" problem [1,44]. For *offline* RL settings, [1] trains a transformer [33] as a model-free context-conditioned policy, and [14] trains a transformer as both a policy and model and shows that beam search can be used to improve upon purely model-free performance. These works focus on exploring *fixed* datasets that transformers are traditionally trained with in NLP applications, which is similar to our focus. For *online* RL settings, [44] proposes a RL algorithm based on sequence understanding that blends offline pre-training with online fine-tuning in a unified framework. To best of our knowledge, this work is the *first* test to leverage Transformer for enhancing RL-based RE task.

3 Methodology

This section presents the proposed TERL for RE task, as summarized in Fig. 1.

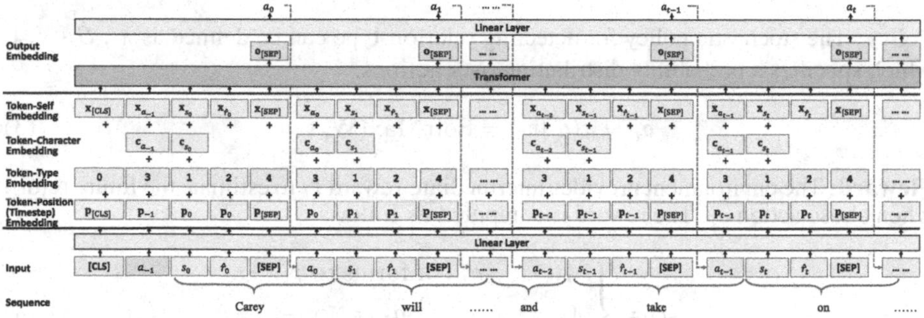

Fig. 1. The architecture of TERL for RE task.

3.1 Relation Extraction with RL

The RL policy π for Relation Extraction (RE), usually aims to detect the relations in the given word sequence $\tau_1 = \{w_0, w_1, w_2, \cdots, w_T\}$, which can be regarded as a conventional RL policy over actions. A Markov Decision Process (MDP) described by the tuple $(\mathcal{S}, \mathcal{A}, \mathcal{P}, \mathcal{R})$ [35], is usually used for learning procedure. Especially, the MDP tuple consists of states $s \in \mathcal{S}$, actions $a \in \mathcal{A}$, transition probability $P(s'|s,a)$ and rewards $r \in \mathcal{R}$. At timestep t, s_t, a_t, and $r_t = \mathcal{R}(s_t, a_t)$ denote the state, action, and reward, respectively. The goal in RL is to learn a desired policy which maximizes the expected reward $\mathbb{E}(\sum_{t=1}^{T} r_i)$ in MDP [1].

Action: The action a_t is selected from $\mathcal{A} = R \bigcup \texttt{None}$, wherein notation None indicates that *no* relation exists in the given context, and R is the pre-defined relation-type set.

State: The state $s_t \in \mathcal{S}$ of the relation extraction RL process at timestep t, can be represented by [31,35]: (i) the current hidden state vector $\mathbf{h}_t$, (ii) the relation-type vector $\mathbf{a}_{t-1}$ (the embedding of the latest action a_{t-1} that $a_{t-1} \neq \texttt{None}$, a learnable parameter), and (iii) the state from the last timestep $\mathbf{s}_{t-1}$, formally represented as follows:

$$\mathbf{s}_t = f(\mathbf{W}_{\mathcal{S}}[\mathbf{h}_t; \mathbf{a}_{t-1}; \mathbf{s}_{t-1}]) \tag{1}$$

where $f(\cdot)$ denotes a non-linear function implemented by MLP (Other encoder architecture is also applicable, which is not the focus of this paper). To obtain the current hidden state $\mathbf{h}_t$, sequence Bi-LSTM over the current input word embedding $\mathbf{x}_t$, character embedding $\mathbf{c}_t$, token-type embedding $\mathbf{v}_t$, and token-position embedding $\mathbf{p}_t$, can be used here, as follows:

$$
\begin{aligned}
\overrightarrow{\mathbf{h}_t} &= \overrightarrow{\texttt{LSTM}}(\overrightarrow{\mathbf{h}_{t-1}}, \mathbf{x}_t, \mathbf{c}_t, \mathbf{v}_t, \mathbf{p}_t) \\
\overleftarrow{\mathbf{h}_t} &= \overleftarrow{\texttt{LSTM}}(\overleftarrow{\mathbf{h}_{t+1}}, \mathbf{x}_t, \mathbf{c}_t, \mathbf{v}_t, \mathbf{p}_t) \\
\mathbf{h}_t &= [\overrightarrow{\mathbf{h}_t}; \overleftarrow{\mathbf{h}_t}]
\end{aligned} \tag{2}
$$

Policy: The stochastic policy for detecting relation-type can be defined as $\pi : \mathcal{S} \rightarrow \mathcal{A}$, which specifies a probability distribution over actions:

$$
a_t \sim \pi(a_t|s_t) = \text{SoftMax}(\mathbf{W}_\pi \mathbf{s}_t) \tag{3}
$$

Reward: The environment provides intermediate reward r_t to estimate the future return when chose action a_t. The reward is computed as follows:

$$
r_t = \begin{cases} \texttt{1}, & a_t \text{ conforms to } \tau_1, \\ \texttt{0}, & a_t = \texttt{None}, \\ \texttt{-1}, & a_t \text{ not conforms to } \tau_1. \end{cases} \tag{4}
$$

If a_t equals to None at certain timestep t, the agent transfers to a new relation extraction state at the next timestep $t+1$. Such a MDP procedure mentioned above continues until the *last* action about the *last* word w_T of current sequence is sampled. Finally, a final reward r_* is obtained to measure the RE's performance that the RL's policy π detects, which is obtained by the weighted harmonic mean of precision and recall in terms of the relations in given sentence sequence τ_1 [35]: $r_* = \frac{(1+\beta^2)\cdot Prec\cdot Rec}{\beta^2\cdot Prec+Rec}$. Wherein, notation $Prec$ and Rec indicate the precision value and recall value respectively, computed over the current sequence τ_1.

3.2 Transformer

For simplicity, we take BERT as an example. BERT [3] is the first bidirectional language model, which makes use of left and right word contexts simultaneously to predict word tokens. It is trained by optimizing Masked Language Model (MLM) objective etc. The architecture of conventional BERT is a multi-layer bidirectional transformer encoder [33], and the inputs are a sequence of tokens $\{x_1, x_2, \cdots, x_n\}$. The tokens go through several layers of *transformers*. At each layer, a new contextualized embedding is generated for each token by weighted-summing all other tokens' embeddings. The weights are decided by several attention matrices (*multi-head attention*). Note that: (i) tokens with *stronger* attentions are considered *more* related to the target word; (ii) *Different* attention matrices capture *different* types of token relations, such as exact match and synonyms.

The entire BERT model is pre-trained on large scale text corpora and learns linguistic patterns in language. It can be viewed as an interaction-based neural ranking model [6]. Given the widespread usage of BERT, we do not detail the architecture here. See [3] for more details about the conventional architecture of BERT and its variants for various applications.

3.3 Input Generation

Given sequence under RL's paradigm $\{s_0, r_0, a_0, s_1, r_1, a_1, \cdots, s_T, r_T, a_T\}$, the reward of a sequence at step t, is defined as the forward-cumulative-rewards from the current timestep, similar to [1]: $\hat{r}_t = \sum_{i=t}^{T} r_i$, without discount. Wherein, r_i denotes the reward from environment at timestep i. Because we want to generate actions based on *future* (forward direction) expected returns rather than *past* (backward direction) rewards. Hence the input sequence towards our Transformer, is defined as follows, which consists of states, actions and rewards:

$$\tau = \{a_{-1}, s_0, \hat{r}_0, a_0, s_1, \hat{r}_1, a_1, s_2, \hat{r}_2, a_2, \cdots, s_T, \hat{r}_T, a_T\} \tag{5}$$

It represents the whole sequence from the beginning to the end, but in the actual training process, we often only intercept K timesteps (i.e., context length) as input (details in Sect. 3.4). Wherein, K is a hyper-parameter with different values towards different tasks, and a_{-1} in Eq. (5) is a padding indicator.

3.4 Procedure

We feed the last K timesteps into TERL, for a total of $3 \times K$ tokens (one for each type: states, actions and rewards). As shown in Fig. 1, to obtain token embeddings: (i) for state and action, Eq. (1) and Eq. (2) are used to generate state embedding and action embedding, which consider word embeddings, character embeddings, type embeddings and position embeddings [35,46]; (ii) for forward-cumulative-rewards, we learn a linear-layer, which projects inputs to the embedding dimension, followed by layer-normalization [1,36].

Moreover, a token-position (respect to timestep) embedding, a token-type embedding for each token as well as a token-character embedding respect to action token or state token, is learned and added to each token, as one timestep corresponds to 4 types of tokens in our framework. Wherein, we define the token-type projection as: $\{[\text{CLS}], \textit{action}, \textit{state}, \textit{reward}, [\text{SEP}]\} \rightarrow \{0, 1, 2, 3, 4\}$. The tokens are then processed by a BERT [3] or GPT [25] model (as well as their variants), which predicts future (forward) action: $\{a_{t-1}, s_t, \hat{r}_t\} \rightarrow a_t$.

With efforts above, after executing the generated actions for the current state, we reduce the target return by the rewards we receive and repeat until the end of the episode. The output is action sequence $\{a_0, a_1, a_2, \cdots, a_T\}$, which is generated with a linear layer (on top of Fig. 1). Note that, the output can also includes sequence of states or rewards. For simplicity, we do not use them and leave for future discussion.

The details about training procedure and testing procedure, can be concluded as follows:

(i) In training procedure, we sample mini-batches of sequence length K (i.e., context length) from the training dataset, and mainly use the self-attention paradigm in Transformer. a_{-1} with zero-padding is added before the entire sequence. As shown in Fig. 1, predicting action at each timesetp a_t with cross-entropy loss, is used as the training objective.

(ii) At test time, we use the definition of Eq. (4) as the desired performance. At the beginning, given the desired performance (e.g., $\hat{r}_0 = 1$) as well as the initial state s_0, transformer generates action a_0. Let the agent perform actions a_0, the environment will give return r_0 and the next state s_0, and we can get $\hat{r}_1$. Then $\{a_0, s_1, \hat{r}_1\}$ can be added into the input sequence, and we can get a_1. The aforementioned testing procedure is *autoregressive*, because the output a_{t-1} in previous timestep will intuitively be the viewed as input in the following timestep: $\{a_{t-1}, s_t, \hat{r}_t\} \rightarrow a_t$.

4 Experiments

This paper constructs relation extraction task and relation and entity joint extraction task for evaluations.

4.1 Datasets and Metrics

For relation extraction (RE) task examination, we follow [12] to leverage two public RE datasets for conducting experiments on, including SemEval 2010 Task 8 (SemEval) [8], and TAC Relation Extraction Dataset (TACRED) [43]: (i) SemEval dataset is a standard benchmark dataset for testing RE models, which consists of training, validation and test set with 7,199, 800, 1,864 relation-mentions respectively, with totally 19 relations types (including `None`). (ii) TACRED dataset is a more large-scale crowd-sourced RE dataset, which is collected from all the prior TAC KBP relation schema. It consists of training, validation and test set with 75,049, 25,763, 18,659 relation-mentions respectively, with totally 42 relation types (including `None`).

We also test the extension of the proposed framework for relation and entity joint extraction task. For this task, we conduct experiments on two public datasets NYT [28] and WebNLG [4]: (i) NYT dataset is originally produced by a distant supervision method, which consists of 1.18M sentences with 24 predefined relation types; (ii) WebNLG dataset is created by Natural Language Generation (NLG) tasks and adapted by [42] for relational triple extraction task. It consists of 246 predefined relation types.

For both datasets, we follow the evaluation setting used in previous works. A triple (head entity, relation-type, tail entity) is regarded as *correct* if the relation-type (belongs to R) and the two corresponding entities (head entity and tail entity head entity) are all correct. Precision, Recall and F1-score are introduced here as metrics for all the compared models. For each dataset, we randomly chose 0.5% data from the training set for validation [35].

4.2 Baselines

For relation extraction task, the baselines include three categories:

(i) When comparing with supervised relation encoders with only labeled data, we choose **LSTM** [9], **PCNN** [40], **PRNN** [43], and **BERT** [3] as baselines.
(ii) When comparing with semi-supervised relation encoders with both labeled data and unlabeled (or pseudo labeled) data, we choose **Self-Training** [29], **Mean-Teacher** [32], **DualRE** [19], and **MetaSRE** [11] as baselines.

(iv) When comparing with the RL-based models, we choose **RDSRE** [24], **DAGCN** [18] and **GradLRE** [12] as baselines. **RDSRE** is a RL strategy to generate the false-positive indicator, where it automatically recognizes false positives for each relation type without any supervised information. **DAGCN** addresses the RE task by capturing rich contextual dependencies based on the attention mechanism, and using distributional RL to generate optimal relation information representation. **GradLRE** is gradient imitation RL method to encourage pseudo-label data to imitate the gradient descent direction on labeled data and bootstrap its optimization capability through trial and error. As our work can be viewed as a plug-in unit for this kind of RL-based model, the variant model with help of our work is named with suffix **"+TERL"**.

Our framework can be easily extended to relation and entity joint extraction method based on RL. For evaluating joint extraction task, the baselines include four categories:

(i) The traditional pipeline models are **FCM** [15] and **LINE** [5]. Wherein, **FCM** is a conventional and compositional joint model by combining hand-crafted features with learned word embedding for relation extraction task. **LINE** is a network embedding method which embeds very large information networks into low-dimensional vectors. Note that, following [35], both of them obtain the NER results by CoType [27], and then the results are fed into the two models to predict relations.

(ii) The joint learning baselines used here include feature-based methods (e.g., **DS-Joint** [38], **MultiR** [10] and **CoType** [27]), and neural-based methods (e.g., **SPTree** [17] and **CopyR** [42]). Wherein, **DS-Joint** is an incremental joint framework extracting entities and relations based on structured perceptron and beam-search. **MultiR** is a joint extracting approach for multi-instance learning with overlapping relation types. **CoType** extracts entities and relations by jointly embedding entity mentions, relation mentions, text features, and type labels into two meaningful representations. **SPTree** is a joint learning model that represents both word sequence and dependency tree structures using bidirectional sequential and tree-structured LSTM-RNNs. **CopyR** is a sequence-to-sequence learning framework with a copy mechanism for relation and entity jointly extracting.

(iii) The tagging mechanism based models include **Tagging-BiLSTM** [45] and **Tagging-Graph** [34]. Wherein, **Tagging-BiLSTM** utilizes a Bi-LSTM-based architecture to capture the context representation of the input sentences through and then uses an LSTM network to decode the tag sequences. **Tagging-Graph** converts the joint extraction task into a directed graph by designing a novel graph scheme.

(iv) RL-based joint extraction models include **HRL** [30], **JRL** [46], **Seq2SeqRL** [41] and **BIRL** [35]. Wherein, **HRL** presents a hierarchical RL framework decomposing the whole joint extraction process into a hierarchy of two-level RL policies for relation extraction and entity extraction, respectively. **JRL** consists of two components, including a joint network and a RL agent (which refines the training dataset for anti-noise). **Seq2SeqRL** applies RL strategy into a sequence-to-sequence model to take the extraction order into consideration. **BIRL** proposes a novel bidirectional interaction RL model for jointly extracting entities and relations with both inter-attention and intra-attention.

4.3 Experimental Settings

For a fair comparison, we build our **TERL** implementation for RE and joint extraction task with BERT [3], as BERT-based work has achieved the state-of-the-art performance in RE task. Besides, we adopt BERT as the base encoder for both our **TERL** and other RL-based baselines for a fair comparison. Although GPT is also tested, the experimental trend is consistent. All hyper-parameters are tuned on the validation set. The word vectors are initialized using Word2Vec vectors and are updated during training. DQN encoder [20] with an additional linear layer is introduced here for projecting to the embedding dimension. The main list of hyper-parameters is concluded as follows: Number of layers is 6; Number of attention heads is 8; Embedding dimensionality is 256; Batch size is 512; Context length $K = 30$; Max epochs is 5; Dropout is 0.1; Learning rate is 10^{-4}.

4.4 Performance Summary

F1 results with various labeled data on Relation Extraction (RE) task, are shown in Table 1. Average results over 20 runs are reported, and the best performance is bold-typed. As our work can be viewed as a plug-in unit for RL-based model, the variant model with help of our work is named with suffix "**+TERL**". RL-based methods outperforms all baseline models consistently. We could observe that **+TERL** improve all the RL-based methods. More specifically, compared with the previous SOTA model **GradLRE**, which defeats other models across various labeled data, **+TERL** is also

Table 1. Performance comparisons on Relation Extraction (RE) task (F1).

Model	SemEval			TACRED		
	5%↑	10%↑	30%↑	3%↑	10%↑	15%↑
LSTM [9]	0.226	0.329	0.639	0.287	0.468	0.494
PCNN [40]	0.418	0.513	0.637	0.400	0.504	0.525
PRNN [43]	0.553	0.626	0.690	0.391	0.522	0.546
BERT [3]	0.707	0.719	0.786	0.401	0.532	0.556
Self-Training [29]	0.713	0.743	0.817	0.421	0.542	0.565
Mean-Teacher [32]	0.701	0.734	0.806	0.443	0.531	0.538
DualRE [19]	0.744	0.771	0.829	0.431	0.560	0.580
MetaSRE [11]	0.783	0.801	0.848	0.462	0.570	0.589
RDSRE [24]	0.729	0.756	0.812	0.422	0.549	0.568
RDSRE+TERL(Ours)	0.787	0.801	0.853	0.435	0.560	0.574
DAGCN [18]	0.781	0.801	0.838	0.464	0.570	0.587
DAGCN+TERL(Ours)	0.804	0.817	0.846	0.478	0.582	0.593
GradLRE [12]	0.797	0.817	0.855	0.474	0.582	0.599
GradLRE+TERL(Ours)	**0.820**	**0.833**	**0.864**	**0.488**	**0.594**	**0.605**

more robust than all the baselines. Considering low-resource RE when labeled data is very scarce, e.g. 5% for SemEval and 3% for TACRED, the improvement from **+TERL** is significant: **+TERL** could achieve an average 3.15% F1 boost compared with **GradLRE**. Moreover, the improvement is still robust when more labeled data can be used (i.e., 30% for SemEval and 15% for TACRED), and the average F1 improvement is 1.15%. Especially, **RDSRE** fall behinds **DualRE** in most cases, while it outperforms **DualRE** when plugged with our **TERL** (i.e., **RDSRE+TERL**). This because the attention mechanism gives our **TERL** an excellent ability of long-term credit assignment, which can capture the effect of actions on rewards in a long sequence. We believe this phenomenon is meaningful and important for document-level RE task. Moreover, a key difference between our TERL and previous RL-based RE SOTA methods, can be concluded that this work dos *not* require policy regularization or conservatism to achieve optimal performance, which is consistent with the observation in [1] and [44]. Especially, our speculation is that an algorithm based on time difference learning paradigm learns an approximation function and improves the strategy by optimizing the value function.

Relation and entity joint extraction is a more challenging task, and the proposed Transformer enhanced RL framework can be easily extend to this task. The experimental results on NYT and WebNLG datasets are shown in Table 2. It can be concluded that,

Table 2. Performance comparisons on relation and entity joint extraction task (Precision, Recall, and F1).

Model	NYT			WebNLG		
	Precision↑	Recall↑	F1↑	Precision↑	Recall↑	F1↑
FCM [15]	0.561	0.118	0.193	0.472	0.072	0.124
LINE [5]	0.340	0.251	0.277	0.286	0.153	0.193
MultiR [10]	0.344	0.250	0.278	0.289	0.152	0.193
DS-Joint [38]	0.572	0.201	0.291	0.490	0.119	0.189
CoType [27]	0.521	0.196	0.278	0.423	0.175	0.241
SPTree [17]	0.492	0.557	0.496	0.414	0.339	0.357
CopyR [42]	0.569	0.452	0.483	0.479	0.275	0.338
Tagging-BiLSTM [45]	0.624	0.317	0.408	0.525	0.193	0.276
Tagging-Graph [34]	0.628	1.632	0.844	0.528	0.194	0.277
HRL [30]	0.714	0.586	0.616	0.601	0.357	0.432
HRL+TERL(Ours)	0.750	0.604	0.641	0.631	0.368	0.449
JRL [46]	0.691	0.549	0.612	0.581	0.334	0.410
JRL+TERL(Ours)	0.712	0.582	0.613	0.610	0.344	0.425
Seq2SeqRL [41]	0.779	0.672	0.690	0.633	0.599	0.587
Seq2SeqRL+TERL(Ours)	**0.802**	0.692	0.711	0.665	0.617	0.611
BIRL [35]	0.756	0.706	0.697	0.660	0.636	0.617
BIRL+TERL(Ours)	0.794	**0.727**	**0.725**	**0.693**	**0.655**	**0.643**

the proposed model consistently outperforms all previous SOTA models in most cases, especially RL-base methods. Especially, RL-based methods usually defeats encoder-decoder based methods. E.g., RL-based **HRL** and **JRL** significantly surpass **Tagging-BiLSTM** and **CopyR**. Compared with **HRL**, **JRL** and **BIRL**, the their **+TERL**'s variants improve the F1 score by 3.94%, 3.66% and 4.22% on WebNLG dataset, respectively. This phenomenon shows that, our **TERL**-based variant matches or exceeds the performance of SOTA model-free RL algorithms, even without using dynamic programming. Note that, the behavior of optimizing the learning function in previous work, may unfortunately exacerbate and exploit any inaccuracies in the approximation of the value function, leading to the failure of policy improvement. Due to the fact that the proposed TERL does *not* require explicit optimization with learning functions as the objective, it *avoids* the need for regularization or conservatism, to a certain degree. Moreover, when we represent the distribution of policies, just like sequence understanding, context allows the converter to identify which policies generate actions, thereby achieving better learning and improving training dynamics.

4.5 Analysis and Discussion

This section investigates whether our TERL variant can remain robust performance on metric of *imitation learning* (like **GradLRE** etc.,) on a *subset* of the dataset. Hence, we adopt baseline **GradLER** which is based on imitation learning, by following the experimental setting of Percentile Behavior Cloning strategy proposed by [1], wherein we run behavior cloning on *only* the top $X\%$ of timesteps in the corresponding dataset, following [1]. The Percentile Behavior Cloning variant of **GradLER** is denoted as %**GradLER** here in Table 3. The percentile $X\%$ interpolates between standard behavior cloning ($X = 100\%$) that trains on the complete dataset and only cloning the best observed sequence ($X \approx 0\%$), which in a manner trades off between better generalization by training on more data with training a specialized model that focuses on a subset of the dataset. Table 3 shows experimental results comparing %**GradLRE** to **+TERL**, when the value of X are chosen in $\{10\%, 30\%, 50\%, 100\%\}$. From the experimental results, we conclude that, lower X reduces the performances of **GradLRE**, however **+TERL** successfully exceeds the performance and pulls F1 metric back. Especially, when X is 30, with enhancement from our **TERL**, 30%**GradLRE+TERL** could even defeats 50%**GradLRE**, while 30%**GradLRE** lags behind 50%**GradLRE** obviously. Moreover, 50%**GradLRE+TERL** nearly matches the performance of 100%**GradLRE**. This phenomenon indicates that, the improvement of our **TERL** can be made to the specific subset, after training the distribution of the complete dataset.

Then, to evaluate the importance of accessing previous states, actions, and returns, we discuss the context length K. This is interesting because when using frame stacking, it is usually assumed that the previous state is sufficient for the RL algorithm. Figure 2 and Fig. 3 is evaluated on RE task (with TACRED dataset and 15% labeled data) and joint extraction task (with WebNLG dataset), respectively. TERL with different K is loaded into baselines **RDSRE**, **DAGCN** and **GradLRE**, as well as baselines **JRL**, **Seq2SeqRL** and **BIRL**. Experimental results show that performance of TERL is significantly worse when K is small (i.e., $K = 1$ or $K = 5$), indicating that past information

Table 3. Performance comparisons on Percentile Behavior Cloning (F1).

Model	TACRED		
	3%↑	10%↑	15%↑
10%**GradLRE**	0.190	0.233	0.240
10%**GradLRE+TERL**	0.342	0.416	0.424
30%**GradLRE**	0.356	0.437	0.449
30%**GradLRE+TERL**	**0.410**	**0.499**	**0.508**
50%**GradLRE**	0.379	0.466	0.479
50%**GradLRE+TERL**	0.464	0.564	0.575
100%**GradLRE**	0.474	0.582	0.599
100%**GradLRE+TERL**	0.488	0.594	0.605

(i.e., previous states s_t, actions a_t, and returns$\hat{r}_t$) is useful for RE task. Especially, when K becomes small, the performances have fallen off a cliff, even falling behind the original with side effect. Note that, the proposed framework still match the MDP properties when $K = 1$, while the results is worse, which demonstrates the sequence understanding is *highly* context dependent. When $K = 20$ and $K = 30$, **+TERL** defeats the corresponding original comparative baseline and the performances have changed little when K becomes larger. Besides, the context information (i.e., larger K) enables the transformer to figure out which actions are generated, which can lead to higher returns.

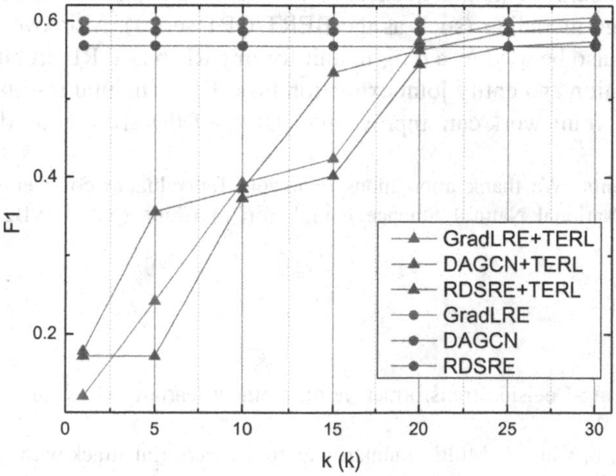

Fig. 2. Effect of context length K on RE task.

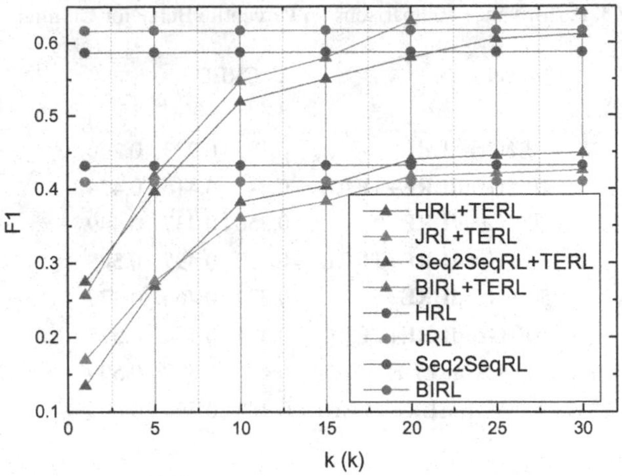

Fig. 3. Effect of context length K on joint extraction task.

5 Conclusion

In this work, we try to combine transformers and Reinforcement Learning (RL) based sequence relation extraction (RE), and extend Transformer paradigm to RL. We design a novel framework (TERL) that abstracts RL-based RE as a sequence understanding task, which could leverage the simplicity and scalability of the Transformer-based architecture for understanding textual sequence, as well as the advancements released by pre-training language modeling (such as the BERT/GPT series). Moreover, the proposed framework can also be used as a plug-in unit for any RL-based RE architecture, and be extended to relation and entity joint extraction task. Experimental results show that the proposed TERL framework can improve many state-of-the-art RL-based RE methods.

Acknowledgements. We thank anonymous reviewers for valuable comments. This work is funded by: the National Natural Science Foundation of China (No. U19B2026, 62106243, U22B2601).

References

1. Chen, L., et al.: Decision transformer: reinforcement learning via sequence modeling. In: NeurIPS (2021)
2. Chen, Y., Su, J., Wei, W.: Multi-granularity textual adversarial attack with behavior cloning. In: EMNLP (2021)
3. Devlin, J., Chang, M.W., Lee, K., Toutanova, K.: Bert: pre-training of deep bidirectional transformers for language understanding. In: NAACL-HLT (2019)
4. Gardent, C., Shimorina, A., Narayan, S., Perez-Beltrachini, L.: Creating training corpora for NLG micro-planners. In: ACL (2017)
5. Gormley, M.R., Yu, M., Dredze, M.: Improved relation extraction with feature-rich compositional embedding models. In: EMNLP (2015)

6. Guo, J., Fan, Y., Ai, Q., Croft, W.B.: A deep relevance matching model for ad-hoc retrieval. Proceedings of the 25th ACM International on Conference on Information and Knowledge Management (2016)
7. Guo, Z., Nan, G., Lu, W., Cohen, S.B.: Learning latent forests for medical relation extraction. In: IJCAI (2020)
8. Hendrickx, I., et al.: SemEval-2010 task 8: multi-way classification of semantic relations between pairs of nominals. In: *SEMEVAL (2010)
9. Hochreiter, S., Schmidhuber, J.: Long short-term memory. Neural Comput. **9**, 1735–1780 (1997)
10. Hoffmann, R., Zhang, C., Ling, X., Zettlemoyer, L., Weld, D.S.: Knowledge-based weak supervision for information extraction of overlapping relations. In: ACL (2011)
11. Hu, X., Ma, F., Liu, C., Zhang, C., Wen, L., Yu, P.S.: Semi-supervised relation extraction via incremental meta self-training. In: EMNLP (2021)
12. Hu, X., et al.: Gradient imitation reinforcement learning for low resource relation extraction. In: EMNLP (2021)
13. Hung, C.C., et al.: Optimizing agent behavior over long time scales by transporting value. Nat. Commun. **10**, 5223 (2019)
14. Janner, M., Li, Q., Levine, S.: Reinforcement learning as one big sequence modeling problem. arXiv abs/2106.02039 (2021)
15. Kim, Y.: Convolutional neural networks for sentence classification. In: EMNLP (2014)
16. Lee, K., Laskin, M., Srinivas, A., Abbeel, P.: Sunrise: a simple unified framework for ensemble learning in deep reinforcement learning. In: ICML (2021)
17. Li, Q., Ji, H.: Incremental joint extraction of entity mentions and relations. In: ACL (2014)
18. Li, Z., Sun, Y., Tang, S., Zhang, C., Ma, H.: Reinforcement learning with dual attention guided graph convolution for relation extraction. In: 2020 25th International Conference on Pattern Recognition (ICPR), pp. 946–953 (2021)
19. Lin, H., Yan, J., Qu, M., Ren, X.: Learning dual retrieval module for semi-supervised relation extraction. In: The World Wide Web Conference (2019)
20. Mnih, V., et al.: Human-level control through deep reinforcement learning. Nature **518**, 529–533 (2015)
21. Narasimhan, K., Yala, A., Barzilay, R.: Improving information extraction by acquiring external evidence with reinforcement learning. In: EMNLP (2016)
22. Parisotto, E., Salakhutdinov, R.: Efficient transformers in reinforcement learning using actor-learner distillation. arXiv abs/2104.01655 (2021)
23. Parisotto, E., et al.: Stabilizing transformers for reinforcement learning. In: ICML (2020)
24. Qin, P., Xu, W., Wang, W.Y.: Robust distant supervision relation extraction via deep reinforcement learning. In: ACL (2018)
25. Radford, A., Narasimhan, K.: Improving language understanding by generative pre-training (2018)
26. Ramesh, A., et al.: Zero-shot text-to-image generation. arXiv abs/2102.12092 (2021)
27. Ren, X., et al.: Cotype: joint extraction of typed entities and relations with knowledge bases. In: Proceedings of the 26th International Conference on World Wide Web (2017)
28. Riedel, S., Yao, L., McCallum, A.: Modeling relations and their mentions without labeled text. In: ECML/PKDD (2010)
29. Rosenberg, C., Hebert, M., Schneiderman, H.: Semi-supervised self-training of object detection models. In: 2005 Seventh IEEE Workshops on Applications of Computer Vision (WACV/MOTION 2005), vol. 1, pp. 29–36 (2005)
30. Takanobu, R., Zhang, T., Liu, J., Huang, M.: A hierarchical framework for relation extraction with reinforcement learning. In: AAAI (2018)
31. Takanobu, R., Zhang, T., Liu, J., Huang, M.: A hierarchical framework for relation extraction with reinforcement learning. arXiv abs/1811.03925 (2019)

32. Tarvainen, A., Valpola, H.: Mean teachers are better role models: weight-averaged consistency targets improve semi-supervised deep learning results. In: NIPS (2017)
33. Vaswani, A., et al.: Attention is all you need. arXiv abs/1706.03762 (2017)
34. Wang, S., Zhang, Y., Che, W., Liu, T.: Joint extraction of entities and relations based on a novel graph scheme. In: IJCAI (2018)
35. Wang, Y., Zhang, H.: BIRL: bidirectional-interaction reinforcement learning framework for joint relation and entity extraction. In: DASFAA (2021)
36. Xiong, R., et al.: On layer normalization in the transformer architecture. In: ICML (2020)
37. Xue, F., Sun, A., Zhang, H., Chng, E.S.: GDPNet: refining latent multi-view graph for relation extraction. arXiv abs/2012.06780 (2020)
38. Yu, X., Lam, W.: Jointly identifying entities and extracting relations in encyclopedia text via a graphical model approach. In: COLING (2010)
39. Zambaldi, V.F., et al.: Deep reinforcement learning with relational inductive biases. In: ICLR (2019)
40. Zeng, D., Liu, K., Chen, Y., Zhao, J.: Distant supervision for relation extraction via piecewise convolutional neural networks. In: EMNLP (2015)
41. Zeng, X., He, S., Zeng, D., Liu, K., Liu, S., Zhao, J.: Learning the extraction order of multiple relational facts in a sentence with reinforcement learning. In: EMNLP/IJCNLP (2019)
42. Zeng, X., Zeng, D., He, S., Liu, K., Zhao, J.: Extracting relational facts by an end-to-end neural model with copy mechanism. In: ACL (2018)
43. Zhang, Y., Zhong, V., Chen, D., Angeli, G., Manning, C.D.: Position-aware attention and supervised data improve slot filling. In: EMNLP (2017)
44. Zheng, Q., Zhang, A., Grover, A.: Online decision transformer. In: ICML (2022)
45. Zheng, S., Wang, F., Bao, H., Hao, Y., Zhou, P., Xu, B.: Joint extraction of entities and relations based on a novel tagging scheme. arXiv abs/1706.05075 (2017)
46. Zhou, X., Liu, L., Luo, X., Chen, H., Qing, L., He, X.: Joint entity and relation extraction based on reinforcement learning. IEEE Access **7**, 125688–125699 (2019)

P-MNER: Cross Modal Correction Fusion Network with Prompt Learning for Multimodal Named Entity Recognition

Zhuang Wang[1], Yijia Zhang[1(✉)], Kang An[1], Xiaoying Zhou[1], Mingyu Lu[2(✉)], and Hongfei Lin[3]

[1] College of Information Science and Technology, Dalian Maritime University, Dalian, China
{wang_1120211498,zhangyijia,1120221416_ankang,zhouxiaoying}@dlmu.edu.cn
[2] College of Artificial Intelligence, Dalian Maritime University, Dalian, China
lumingyu@dlmu.edu.cn
[3] College of Computer Science and Technology, Dalian University of Technology, Dalian, China
hflin@dlut.edu.cn

Abstract. Multimodal Named Entity Recognition (MNER) is a challenging task in social media due to the combination of text and image features. Previous MNER work has focused on predicting entity information after fusing visual and text features. However, pre-training language models have already acquired vast amounts of knowledge during their pre-training process. To leverage this knowledge, we propose a prompt network for MNER tasks (P-MNER). To minimize the noise generated by irrelevant areas in the image, we design a visual feature extraction model (FRR) based on FasterRCNN and ResNet, which uses fine-grained visual features to assist MNER tasks. Moreover, we introduce a text correction fusion module (TCFM) into the model to address visual bias during modal fusion. We employ the idea of a residual network to modify the fused features using the original text features. Our experiments on two benchmark datasets demonstrate that our proposed model outperforms existing MNER methods. P-MNER's ability to leverage pre-training knowledge from language models, incorporate fine-grained visual features, and correct for visual bias, makes it a promising approach for multimodal named entity recognition in social media posts.

Keywords: Prompt Learning · MNER · Faster RCNN · Multimodal fusion module

1 Introduction

With the rapid development of the Internet, social media platforms have experienced an exponential growth of content. These platforms offer a wealth of user-

This work is supported by the National Natural Science Foundation of China (No. 61976124).

M. Sun et al. (Eds.): CCL 2023, LNAI 14232, pp. 207–221, 2023.
https://doi.org/10.1007/978-981-99-6207-5_13

generated posts that provide valuable insights into the events, opinions, and preferences of both individuals and groups. Named Entity Recognition (NER) is a crucial task in which entities contained in textual data are detected and mapped to predefined entity types, such as location (LOC), person (PER), organization (ORG), and miscellaneous (MISC). Incorporating visual information from posts has been shown to significantly enhance the accuracy of entity prediction from social media content. For instance, as illustrated in Fig. 1, the sentence "Alban got Rikard a snowball in the snow" can be easily resolved by leveraging the visual cues in the accompanying image, allowing us to identify "Rikard" as an animal. However, relying solely on textual data to predict entities may lead to erroneous predictions, such as identifying "Rikard" as a name.

With the continuous evolution of deep learning models, several multi-modal Named Entity Recognition (NER) models have been proposed to enhance the prediction performance of entities by incorporating visual information. These models employ techniques such as cross-attention [17,20], adversarial learning [5, 6], and graph fusion [17,18]. However, previous methods fused text features with visual features and directly fed them into a neural network model for prediction. This approach overlooks the wealth of information embedded in the pre-training language model itself. To overcome this limitation, we propose the use of prompt learning [11] to process the fused features, followed by final training.

Fig. 1. An example for MNER with (A and B) the useful visual clues and the (C and D) useless visual clues.

The presence of irrelevant content in an image may negatively impact the performance of Named Entity Recognition (NER) models. As illustrated in Fig. 1, regions A and B in an image may aid in identifying entities in a sentence, while regions C and D may not contribute to model prediction. In previous Multi-modal NER (MNER) tasks, however, all visual regions were involved in cross-modal fusion. To address this issue, we propose a novel model(FRR), which utilizes visual objects in images for modal fusion. This approach effectively eliminates extraneous image features that are irrelevant to the corresponding text.

In this paper, we present a new Transformer-based [15] text correction fusion module (TCFM) to address the issue of cross-modal visual bias in the named entity recognition (NER) task. Inspired by the residual network, the TCFM continuously integrates the original text features with the fusion features to iteratively correct the fusion features. This approach effectively alleviates the problem of visual bias and enhances the performance of the NER task.

In order to showcase the effectiveness of our proposed approach, we conducted a comprehensive set of experiments on two publicly available datasets: Twitter-2015 and Twitter-2017. The obtained experimental results unequivocally demonstrate that our method outperforms the existing MNER algorithm in terms of performance.

The significant contributions of our work can be summarized as follows:

- We introduce a novel approach, the Prompt Network for Named Entity Recognition (P-MNER), which aims to leverage the abundant information present in pre-trained language models. To accommodate the specific requirements of our proposed prompt network, we further present a novel Text Correction Fusion Module (TCFM) that effectively minimizes the visual bias in the fusion process.
- To mitigate the impact of irrelevant visual regions on modal fusion, we propose a novel Feature Extraction Module (FRR) that leverages fine-grained visual objects for more precise feature extraction.
- Experimental results show that our proposed P-MNER network achieves SOTA performance on both datasets.

2 Related Work

Named Entity Recognition (NER) has emerged as a crucial component in a plethora of downstream natural language processing (NLP) applications, including but not limited to affective analysis [1], relationship extraction [7], and knowledge graph [3] construction. With the advent of neural network models, the use of Bi-LSTM [2] or Convolutional Neural Network (CNN) [21] as encoders, and Softmax [9], RNN [10], or Conditional Random Field (CRF) [23] as decoders has gained popularity in the NER community. For instance, Huang et al. [8] utilized BiLSTM and CRF as the encoder and decoder, respectively, for NER tasks. Similarly, Chiu and Nichols et al. [2] proposed a CNN-based encoder with CRF as the decoder to accomplish the final prediction.

Social media posts are characterized by their brevity and high levels of noise, which often lead to suboptimal performance of conventional NER methods when applied to such data. To address this challenge, several recent studies have proposed novel approaches for cross-modal fusion in the context of NER. For instance, Sun et al. [13,14] introduced a novel image-text fusion approach for NER tasks, while Zhang et al. [20] employed BiLSTM to combine visual and textual features in multimodal social posts. Similarly, Zheng et al. [22] proposed an adversarial learning approach to tackle the issue of semantic gap in multimodal NER tasks. Lu et al. [12] integrated an attention mechanism into the modal fusion process and introduced a visual gate to filter out noise in the image. Lastly, Yu et al. [19] designed a multimodal Transformer model for the MNER task and introduced an entity span module to facilitate the final prediction.

In order to utilize the vast amount of knowledge encoded in pre-trained language models, Wang et al. [16] proposed a prompt-based method, namely PromptMNER, which extracts visual features and subsequently fuses them with input text for enhanced performance.

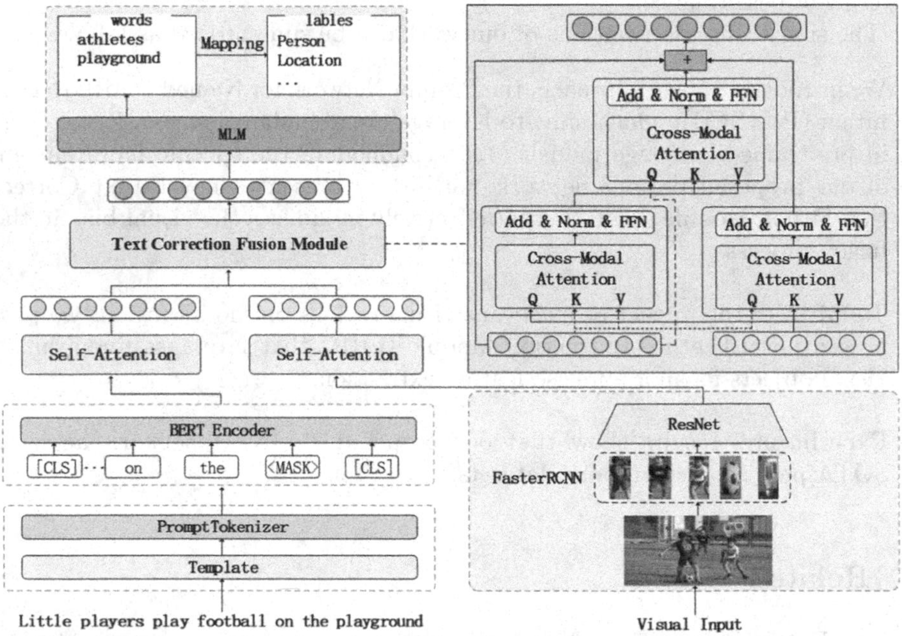

Fig. 2. An example for MNER with (A and B) the useful visual clues and the (C and D) useless visual clues.

Previous studies on named entity recognition (NER) in social media have yielded promising results. However, these methods have been unable to fully utilize the power of pre-training language models in capturing the contextual nuances of input text. This shortcoming has limited the overall effectiveness of NER in social media. To overcome this challenge, our paper proposes a novel prompt learning approach that directly leverages the knowledge embedded in pre-training language models to enrich input text and image features. By doing so, we are able to tap into the full potential of these models and achieve a higher level of accuracy in NER tasks. In essence, our approach represents a significant step forward in the field of NER for social media. It addresses a critical limitation of previous methods and provides a more effective way of leveraging pre-training language models. Our approach offers a promising new avenue for future research.

3 Methods

The objective of this study is to predict a tag sequence $L = (l_1, l_2, ..., l_n)$. given a sentence Y and an associated picture V as input. Here, belongs to a predefined set of tags for the BIO2 tagging pattern.

Figure 2 depicts the overall architecture of our proposed model, which comprises four modules: visual feature extraction, text feature extraction, modal fusion, and prompt learning. The visual feature extraction module takes the objects in the picture as input. In the text feature extraction module, we leverage BERT to extract features by processing the wrapped text. We also introduce a text correction fusion module to obtain more precise fusion features. In the prompt learning module, we utilize the Bert Masked Language Model for prompt learning.

3.1 Text Feature Extraction

In Fig. 2, the input sentence $Y = (y_1, y_2, ..., y_n)$ is demonstrated on the left. To structure the sentences, a wrapping class is utilized, which adheres to a predetermined template. For MNER direction, a prompt template is introduced: "<sentence>, the word of <entity> is <mask>." Within the template, <sentence> represents the sentence Y, <entity>∈y.

In order to effectively process complex information from input text and templates, a new Tokenizer has been introduced to tokenize the input sentences that are wrapped by the wrapper class. Following the pre-training models, special tokens are added to the tokenized sequences to form a sequence, denoted as $S = (s_0, s_1, ..., s_n + 1)$, where s_0 and $s_n + 1$ represent the two special tokens at the beginning and end of the final sequence. The tokenized sequences are then sent to the embedding layer where BERT embedding is utilized to convert each word into a vector form that includes token embedding, segment embeddings, and position embeddings.

$$x_i = e^t(s_i) + e^s(s_i) + e^p(s_i) \tag{1}$$

where $\{e^t, e^s, e^p\}$ denotes the embeddings lookup table.$X = (x_0, x_1, ...x_{n+1})$ is the word representation of S, where $x_i$is the sum of word, segment, and position embeddings for token y_i.

In various social media posts, the same word may have different meanings depending on the context. To address this challenge, we adopt BERT as the sentence encoder. The resulting embedding representation is fed into the BERT encoder, producing a signature of encodings $R = (r_0, r_1, ...r_{n+1})$.

The Self-Attention mechanism establishes direct links between any two words in a sentence through a calculation step, significantly reducing the distance between distance-dependent features and enabling their efficient use. Consequently, we feed the hidden representation output by BERT Encoder into Self-Attention to capture long-distance dependencies in a sentence.

$$T = softmax(\frac{[W_{q_t R}]^T [W_{k_t R}]}{\sqrt{d_t}})[W_{v_t R}]^T \quad (2)$$

where $\{W_{k_t}, W_{v_t}, W_{q_t}\}$ is parameter matrices for the key, value and query. The final text feature $T = (t_0, t_1, ...t_{n+1})$, where t_i is the generated contextualized representation for y_i.

3.2 Visual Feature Extraction

We utilize object-level visual features in the visual feature extraction module to aid named entity recognition, and introduce a novel method for feature extraction.

To begin with, we feed the image into the Faster RCNN [4] detection module to extract the visual object area. Specifically, we input the image into a feature extraction network that includes convolutional layers, pooling layers, and rectified linear unit (ReLU) layers to obtain feature maps of the image. Next, we pass the feature maps to the Region Proposal Networks (RPN) to train them to extract Region Proposal regions from the original maps. Then, we use RoI Pooling to normalize candidate recognition areas of different sizes and shapes into fixed-size target recognition areas. RoI Pooling collects proposals (coordinates of each box) generated by RPN and extracts them from feature maps. Finally, we process the resulting proposals with Fully Connected and Softmax to determine the probability that each proposal corresponds to a particular category.

Typically, only a small number of visual entities are needed to emphasize the entities in a sentence. To accomplish this, we choose the first m visual objects with a probability exceeding 0.95. Then, we crop the original picture based on these proposals to obtain the final visual object set, denoted as $I = \{I_1, I_2, ..., I_m\}$, where I_i represents the *i-th* visual object.

The residual network is among the most advanced CNN image recognition models, with the ability to extract meaningful features from input images. Thus, we feed the resulting visual objects into a pre-trained 152-layer ResNet and use the output of the last convolution layer as the visual characteristics of each object, denoted as $\widetilde{V} = \{\widetilde{V_1}, \widetilde{V_2}, ..., \widetilde{V_m}\}$, where $\widetilde{V_i} \in R^{1024}$ represents the features of the i-th object. We then employ Self-Attention to enable each visual block to fully comprehend the context of the visual features:

$$V = softmax(\frac{[W_{q_v} \widetilde{V}]^T [W_{k_v} \widetilde{V}]}{\sqrt{d_v}})[W_{v_v} \widetilde{V}]^T \quad (3)$$

where $\{W_{q_v}, W_{k_v}, W_{V_v}\}$ denote the weight matrices for the query, key and value. The final visual features are: $V = \{v_1, v_2, ..., v_m\}$, vi refer to the visual features processed by Self-Attention.

3.3 Text Correction Fusion Module

In the text feature extraction module, we have extracted text features through contextual comprehension. However, the short length of social media posts and the presence of irrelevant information make it challenging to accurately identify entities using text information alone. To address this issue, we utilize visual objects in pictures to guide text-based word representations for improved accuracy. Nevertheless, the challenge of visual bias in modal fusion remains. Therefore, we propose a text correction fusion module to generate the final fusion features.

As shown in the right of Fig. 2, we initially apply a k-head cross-modal attention mechanism. This involves using the visual features $V = \{v_1, v_2, ..., v_m\}$ as queries in the self-attention mechanism and utilizing the text features $T = \{t_0, t_1, ..., t_{n+1}\}$ as keys and values:

$$H_i(V,T) = softmax(\frac{[W_{q_i}V]^T[W_{k_i}T]}{\sqrt{d/k}})[W_{v_i}T]^T \tag{4}$$

$$M\_H(V,T) = W'[H_i(V,T), ..., H_k(V,T)]^T \tag{5}$$

where H_i refers to the *i-th* head of cross-modal attention, $\{W_{q_i}, W_{k_i}, W_{v_i}\}$ and W' denote the weight matrices for the query, key, value, and multi-head attention, respectively. By utilizing this cross-attention approach, we can derive feature representations based on the correlation between words and visual objects in the text. We then process the fused features through two normalization layers and a feed-forward neural network [15]:

$$\widetilde{P} = LN(V + M\_H(V,T)) \tag{6}$$

$$P = LN(\widetilde{P} + FFN(\widetilde{P})) \tag{7}$$

where FFN is the feed-forward network, LN is the layer normalization. Get the text features based on visual objects, denoting as $P = \{p_0, p_1, ..., p_{n+1}\}$. Similar to the description above, We use the text feature $T = \{t_0, t_1, ..., t_{n+1}\}$ as queries in our own attention and the visual feature $V = \{v_1, v_2, ..., v_m\}$ as keys and values. The result is a text-based visual object, denoting as $q = \{q_1, q_2, ..., q_m\}$.

During the process of acquiring visual object-based text features, the resulting features may exhibit bias towards the visual mode, as the queries used are primarily based on visual features. In order to alleviate such bias, we propose the use of a cross-modal layer for the refusion of text features. In this approach, the original text features are employed as queries, while the visual-based text fusion features are utilized as keys and values. The final cross-modal text representation is obtained as $C = \{c_0, c_1, ..., c_{n+1}\}$.

Previous studies have simply connected cross-modal visual features and cross-modal text features, which may lead to biased final fusion features. In this paper, we propose an alternative approach for the final stitching process by connecting initial text features to both cross-modal visual features and cross-modal text features. This method aims to mitigate bias and enhance the quality of the fusion features.

$$H = T + V + C \tag{8}$$

where T is the initial text features, V is the cross-modal visual features, and C is the cross-modal text features.

By incorporating the original text features in the final fusion process, it is effectively reduce visual bias. The resulting fusion feature is denoted as $H = \{h_0, h_1, ..., h_{n+1}\}$.

3.4 Prompt-Learning Module

In this module, we employ the Bert model as our Pre-trained Language Model (PLM). Our approach involves inputting the resulting fusion feature H into the PLM and leveraging the masked language model (MLM) to reconstruct sequences with <MASK>. The predicted part of the text is replaced with <MASK> during packaging to optimize the pre-training language model stimulation. Our method follows the pre-training language model training process for processing fusion features.

In PLM, our aim is to predict a probability distribution for the <MASK> section that aligns with the objectives of MLM. Here, we are only predicting that part of <MASK> belongs to a certain vocabulary. The ultimate goal is to predict <MASK> as predefined tags in a sentence. To accomplish this, we introduce a verbalizer class to process the output of the MLM model. This class constructs a mapping from original tags to words. When PLM predicts a probability distribution for a masked location in the vocabulary, the verbalizer maps the word to the original label. The output layer can be defined as:

$$c_i = plm(h_i) \tag{9}$$

$$d_i = ver(c_i) \tag{10}$$

where plm is masked language model (MLM), ver refers to the verbalizer. c_i is the probability distribution of predicted positions on the vocabulary, d_i is a label for prediction. Finally, the prediction tag distribution is $D = \{d_0, d_1, ..., d_{n+1}\}$.

During the training phase, we calculate the loss of verbalizer-mapped labels and real labels:

$$L = -\sum_{i=1}^{n} o_i log(d_i) \tag{11}$$

where o_i is the true tag for d_i.

4 Experiments

We tested the model on two common datasets. Furthermore, we compare our model with the single-mode NER model and the existing multimodal methods.

4.1 Experiment Settings

Datasets: During the model training and evaluation phase, we employed a publicly available dataset from Twitter, comprising four distinct entity types, namely PER, LOC, ORG, and MISC, with non-entity words marked as O. Following the same protocol established by Zhang et al. [20], the dataset was partitioned into training, development, and test sets. Table 1 provides an overview of the dataset, including the number of samples in each set and the count of each entity type.

Table 1. Statistics of Twitter datasets.

Entity Type	Train-15	Dev-15	Test-15	Train-17	Dev-17	Test-17
PER	2217	552	1816	2943	626	621
LOC	2091	552	1697	731	173	178
ORG	928	247	839	1674	375	395
MISC	940	225	726	701	150	157
Total	6176	1546	5078	6049	1324	1351
Tweets	4000	1000	3257	3373	723	723

Hyperparameter: Compared with other NER methods, our model is an experiment performed on a GUP. For visual object extraction, the first five objects with an accuracy above 0.95 are selected for feature extraction using a pre-trained 152-layer ResNet. The maximum sentence length is set to 128, and the batch size is 8. The input template has a maximum length of 20, while the encoded text length is set at 256. Cross-modal multi-head attention is applied to facilitate modal fusion, utilizing 12 attention heads. The learning rate and learning attenuation rate are set at 0.005 and 0.01, respectively. During the evaluation phase, standard precision, recall rate, and F1-score are employed as evaluation metrics. The model with the highest performance in the evaluation phase is selected, and its performance is reported on the test dataset.

4.2 Main Result

Table 2 presents the experimental results of our proposed model and the comparative approaches. During model evaluation, we calculated the precision (P), recall (R), and F1-score (F1) of our model.

In the upper section of Table 2, we initially conducted a series of experiments using a text-only model to extract features. Our findings revealed that employing BERT as the encoder for text feature extraction resulted in significantly superior results compared to other methods. We believe that the contextualized word representation and contextual understanding of the input text played a crucial role in enhancing the performance of the NER models. In order to achieve even deeper text representation, we leveraged BERT to extract hidden features of the text.

Table 2. Performance comparison on two TWITTER datasets. Specifically, B-L+CRF and C+B-L+CRF refers to Bi-LSTM+CRF and CNN+Bi-LSTM+CRF, respectively.

Models	TWITTER-2015			TWITTER-2017		
	P	R	F1	P	R	F1
B-L+CRF	68.14	61.09	64.42	79.42	73.42	76.31
C+B-L+CRF	66.24	68.09	67.15	80.00	78.76	79.31
T-NER	69.54	68.65	69.09	-	-	-
BERT-CRF	69.22	74.59	71.81	83.32	83.57	83.44
MNER-MA	72.33	63.51	67.63	-	-	-
AGBAN	74.13	72.39	73.25	-	-	-
UMT	71.67	75.23	73.41	85.28	85.34	85.31
UMGF	74.49	75.21	74.85	86.54	84.50	85.51
PromptMNER	78.03	79.17	78.60	89.93	90.10	90.27
Ours	79.18	79.55	79.43	90.11	91.23	91.31

Moreover, we took our analysis a step further and experimented with some representative multimodal NER models to compare their performance with single-mode NER models. As shown in Table 2, the results demonstrate that MNER-MA outperforms the single-mode NER models, indicating the effectiveness of combining visual information in NER tasks. However, we noticed that when BERT was utilized to replace the encoder in the model, the observed improvement was relatively modest. Therefore, it is evident that novel methods need to be developed and employed to address the current limitations in this area.

Prompt learning, a novel paradigm, has demonstrated strong potential in the field of NLP. Wang et al. [16] propose utilizing prompt learning to aid in the extraction of visual features. Specifically, they suggest employing the CLIP model as a prompt language model (PLM) to leverage the learned information from the pre-training stage for visual feature extraction. During training, both visual and text information are processed and fed into the PLM to obtain visual features based on prompts. Finally, the extracted visual and text features are fused together.

The results presented in Table 2 unequivocally demonstrate the superior performance of our proposed approach over existing single-mode approaches in the task of named entity recognition(NER). Our method outperforms the current state-of-the-art MNER method as well, owing to our incorporation of prompt learning, which allows us to extract rich information from the pre-trained language model. The primary reason for our success is the utilization of visual context, which enables us to make full use of the available information and improve the overall accuracy of the model. Our approach outperforms the promptMNER method as well. The incorporation of prompt learning in our model allows us to effectively fuse the visual and text features, thereby making the most of the pre-trained model's knowledge during the training process. As a result, we are able to achieve a better overall performance in the NER task. In summary, our proposed approach offers a significant improvement over existing single-mode approaches in the NER task. Our method outperforms both the current state-of-the-art MNER method and the promptMNER method. By incorporating visual context and prompt learning, we are able to effectively extract and utilize the rich information contained in the pre-trained language model, resulting in superior performance.

4.3 Ablation Result

To evaluate the effectiveness of each component in our proposed P-MNER model, we conduct ablation experiments. Our results, presented in Table 3, indicate that all components in the P-MNER model have contributed significantly to the final predicted results.

T+V is the baseline of our MNER task, with BERT utilized as the encoder for text feature extraction and ResNet employed as the encoder for visual data. The experimental results presented in Table 3 demonstrate that our proposed baseline model achieves a higher F1-score than all single-mode models, thereby validating the effectiveness of incorporating visual information into our model.

Table 3. The effect of each module in our model.

Models	TWITTER-2015			TWITTER-2017		
T+V	72.76	72.53	72.31	83.74	83.24	84.33
T+V+TCFM	74.38	74.12	73.35	85.16	84.35	85.41
T+FRR+TCFM	75.32	75.54	75.14	85.47	84.89	86.02
OURS	79.18	79.55	79.43	90.11	91.23	91.31

T+V+TCFM replaced the modal splicing part with TCFM. Table 3 shows a significant increase in F1-score of 1.22% and 1.08%, respectively, upon implementation of the proposed text correction fusion module, which validates our proposed modal fusion mechanism. Our TCFM module improved accuracy by 1.62% and 1.42% on the two datasets, due to its ability to continuously utilize text information to correct feature bias during mode fusion. This effectively addresses the problem of feature alignment and improves model performance.

T+FRR+TCFM uses a new visual feature extraction method (FRR). Table 3 illustrates that our proposed visual feature extraction module achieved F1-scores of 75.14% and 86.02% on the two datasets, respectively, surpassing other NER methods.

Our proposed model, OURS, is a comprehensive approach that employs prompt learning throughout the entire system. The effectiveness of prompt learning is demonstrated in Table 3, where F1-scores of 79.43% and 91.31% were achieved on two different datasets, respectively, surpassing the current state-of-the-art methods in MNER. The superiority of OURS can be attributed to its ability to deeply explore latent knowledge within pre-trained language models, thanks to the prompt learning technique. Moreover, we achieved a 0.83% and 1.04% improvement in F1-score compared to promptMNER, due to our use of prompt learning for feature fusion processing. Our method is more effective in extracting hidden knowledge from pre-trained language models.

4.4 Case Analysis

To further strengthen our argument regarding the effectiveness of our proposed method, we have conducted a comprehensive case study analysis. We present the results of this analysis in Fig. 3, where we compare the performance of three models for entity prediction: BERT-CRF, UMGF, and P-MNER.

BERT-CRF is a text-only NER model, while UMGF and P-MNER are MNER models that incorporate both visual and textual information. In the first case of our analysis, BERT-CRF failed to accurately predict the entity "Susie". We attribute this to the model's lack of attention to visual information. This highlights the importance of incorporating visual data to improve entity prediction accuracy.

In the second case, all three models correctly predicted the entities. However, this case also revealed that not all image information is semantically consistent with the accompanying text. Hence, the incorporation of visual data should be done thoughtfully and with a proper understanding of the context.

Finally, in the third case, both BERT-CRF and UMGF failed to accurately predict the entity types. In contrast, our P-MNER model leverages the pre-trained language model to effectively acquire knowledge and make accurate entity type predictions. Our model outperformed the other models by a considerable margin, thereby highlighting the superiority of our proposed method.

Visual Modaliy						
Textual Modality	**[Susie MISC]** is playing football in the **[park LOC]**		**[Sonam Kapoor PER]** to walk on red carpet at **[cannes film festival MISC]**		**[NFT ORG]** star **[patrick willis PER]** is thriving in retirement as a **[silicon valley LOC]** tech worker	
BERT-CRF	(Susie MISC) (park LOC)	× √	(Sonam Kapoor PER) (cannes film festival MISC)	√ √	(NFT ORG) (patrick willis PER) (silicon valley LOC)	× √ ×
UMGF	(Susie MISC) (park LOC)	√ √	(Sonam Kapoor PER) (cannes film festival MISC)	√ √	(NFT ORG) (patrick willis PER) (silicon valley LOC)	√ √ ×
P-MNER	(Susie MISC) (park LOC)	√ √	(Sonam Kapoor PER) (cannes film festival MISC)	√ √	(NFT ORG) (patrick willis PER) (silicon valley LOC)	√ √ √

Fig. 3. Three cases of the predictions by BERT-CRF, UMGF and OUR MODE.

In conclusion, the case study analysis provides strong evidence to support our claim that incorporating visual information enhances the accuracy of entity prediction. Additionally, our proposed P-MNER model outperforms the other models by leveraging the pre-trained language model to acquire knowledge and make accurate predictions.

5 Conclusion

In this paper, we have introduced the P-MNER architecture, which has been specifically designed to tackle named entity recognition (MNER) tasks. Our proposed architecture leverages the power of prompt learning to process modal fusion features, thereby enabling the model to fully exploit the wealth of knowledge that pre-trained language models have to offer during training. We also proposed a fine-grained visual object feature extraction module (FRR) to address the issue of noise caused by irrelevant visual areas. This module aids in the MNER task by extracting only the relevant visual information, thus improving the accuracy of the model. To further address the issue of visual bias across modes, we proposed a new text correction fusion module. This module aligns the fusion features with text features to reduce visual bias and improve the model's performance. Experimental results on benchmark datasets demonstrate that our P-MNER model outperforms state-of-the-art approaches. Our model's superior performance is attributed to its ability to effectively utilize pre-trained language models and its innovative feature extraction and fusion modules. Overall, our proposed P-MNER architecture offers a promising solution for named entity recognition tasks, and we believe that our approach can be extended to other natural language processing tasks to improve their performance.

References

1. Chen, C., Teng, Z., Wang, Z., Zhang, Y.: Discrete opinion tree induction for aspect-based sentiment analysis. In: Proceedings of the 60th Annual Meeting of the Association for Computational Linguistics (Volume 1: Long Papers), Dublin, Ireland, pp. 2051–2064. Association for Computational Linguistics, May 2022. https://doi.org/10.18653/v1/2022.acl-long.145. https://aclanthology.org/2022.acl-long.145
2. Chiu, J.P.C., Nichols, E.: Named entity recognition with bidirectional LSTM-CNNs. Computer Science (2015)
3. Cui, Z., Kapanipathi, P., Talamadupula, K., Gao, T., Ji, Q.: Type-augmented relation prediction in knowledge graphs. In: Proceedings of the AAAI Conference on Artificial Intelligence, vol. 35, pp. 7151–7159 (2021)
4. Ren, S., He, K., Girshick, R., Sun, J.: Faster R-CNN: towards real-time object detection with region proposal networks. In: Advances in Neural Information Processing Systems, vol. 28 (2015)
5. Frankle, J., Carbin, M.: The lottery ticket hypothesis: finding sparse, trainable neural networks. In: International Conference on Learning Representations (2019)
6. Goodfellow, I.J., Shlens, J., Szegedy, C.: Explaining and harnessing adversarial examples. arXiv preprint arXiv:1412.6572 (2014)

7. Gupta, N., Singh, S., Roth, D.: Entity linking via joint encoding of types, descriptions, and context. In: Proceedings of the 2017 Conference on Empirical Methods in Natural Language Processing, pp. 2681–2690 (2017)
8. Huang, Z., Xu, W., Yu, K.: Bidirectional LSTM-CRF models for sequence tagging. arXiv preprint arXiv:1508.01991 (2015)
9. Joulin, A., Cissé, M., Grangier, D., Jégou, H., et al.: Efficient softmax approximation for GPUs. In: International Conference on Machine Learning, pp. 1302–1310. PMLR (2017)
10. Liu, P., Qiu, X., Huang, X.: Recurrent neural network for text classification with multi-task learning. arXiv preprint arXiv:1605.05101 (2016)
11. Liu, P., Yuan, W., Fu, J., Jiang, Z., Hayashi, H., Neubig, G.: Pre-train, prompt, and predict: a systematic survey of prompting methods in natural language processing. ACM Comput. Surv. **55**(9), 1–35 (2023)
12. Lu, D., Neves, L., Carvalho, V., Zhang, N., Ji, H.: Visual attention model for name tagging in multimodal social media. In: Proceedings of the 56th Annual Meeting of the Association for Computational Linguistics (Volume 1: Long Papers), pp. 1990–1999 (2018)
13. Ritter, A., Clark, S., Etzioni, O., et al.: Named entity recognition in tweets: an experimental study. In: Proceedings of the 2011 Conference on Empirical Methods in Natural Language Processing, pp. 1524–1534 (2011)
14. Sun, L., Wang, J., Zhang, K., Su, Y., Weng, F.: RpBERT: a text-image relation propagation-based BERT model for multimodal NER. In: Proceedings of the AAAI Conference on Artificial Intelligence, vol. 35, pp. 13860–13868 (2021)
15. Vaswani, A., et al.: Attention is all you need. In: Advances in Neural Information Processing Systems, vol. 30 (2017)
16. Wang, X., et al.: PromptMNER: prompt-based entity-related visual clue extraction and integration for multimodal named entity recognition. In: Bhattacharya, A., et al. (eds.) Database Systems for Advanced Applications, DASFAA 2022. LNCS, vol. 13247. Springer, Cham (2022). https://doi.org/10.1007/978-3-031-00129-1_24
17. Wu, Z., Zheng, C., Cai, Y., Chen, J., Leung, H., Li, Q.: Multimodal representation with embedded visual guiding objects for named entity recognition in social media posts. In: Proceedings of the 28th ACM International Conference on Multimedia, pp. 1038–1046 (2020)
18. Xiao, Z., Wu, J., Chen, Q., Deng, C.: BERT4GCN: using BERT intermediate layers to augment GCN for aspect-based sentiment classification. arXiv preprint arXiv:2110.00171 (2021)
19. Yu, J., Jiang, J., Yang, L., Xia, R.: Improving multimodal named entity recognition via entity span detection with unified multimodal transformer. In: Proceedings of the 58th Annual Meeting of the Association for Computational Linguistics, Online, pp. 3342–3352. Association for Computational Linguistics (July 2020). https://doi.org/10.18653/v1/2020.acl-main.306. https://aclanthology.org/2020.acl-main.306
20. Zhang, Q., Fu, J., Liu, X., Huang, X.: Adaptive co-attention network for named entity recognition in tweets. In: Proceedings of the AAAI Conference on Artificial Intelligence, vol. 32 (2018)
21. Zhao, Z., et al.: Disease named entity recognition from biomedical literature using a novel convolutional neural network. BMC Med. Genomics **10**, 75–83 (2017)
22. Zheng, C., Wu, Z., Wang, T., Cai, Y., Li, Q.: Object-aware multimodal named entity recognition in social media posts with adversarial learning. IEEE Trans. Multimedia **23**, 2520–2532 (2020)

23. Zhuo, J., Cao, Y., Zhu, J., Zhang, B., Nie, Z.: Segment-level sequence modeling using gated recursive semi-Markov conditional random fields. In: Proceedings of the 54th Annual Meeting of the Association for Computational Linguistics (Volume 1: Long Papers), pp. 1413–1423 (2016)

Self Question-Answering: Aspect Sentiment Triplet Extraction via a Multi-MRC Framework Based on Rethink Mechanism

Fuyao Zhang[1], Yijia Zhang[1](✉), Mengyi Wang[1], Hong Yang[1], Mingyu Lu[1], and Liang Yang[2]

[1] Dalian Maritime University, Dalian, China
{zhangfuyao,zhangyijia,mengyiw,yanghong,lumingyu}@dlmu.edu.cn
[2] Dalian University of Technology, Dalian, China
liang@dlut.edu.cn

Abstract. The purpose of Aspect Sentiment Triplet Extraction (ASTE) is to extract a triplet, including the target or aspect, its associated sentiment, and related opinion terms that explain the underlying cause of the sentiment. Some recent studies fail to capture the strong interdependence between ATE and OTE, while others fail to effectively introduce the relationship between aspects and opinions into sentiment classification tasks. To solve these problems, we construct a multi-round machine reading comprehension framework based on a rethink mechanism to solve ASTE tasks efficiently. The rethink mechanism allows the framework to model complex relationships between entities, and exclusive classifiers and probability generation algorithms can reduce query conflicts and unilateral drops in probability. Besides, the multi-round structure can fuse explicit semantic information flow between aspect, opinion and sentiment. Extensive experiments show that the proposed model achieves the most advanced effect and can be effectively applied to ASTE tasks.

Keywords: ASTE · MRC · parameter sharing · joint learning

1 Introduction

Aspect-based Sentiment Analysis (ABSA) is a fine-grained task [25]. Its purpose is to detect the sentiments of different entities rather than infer the overall sentiment of sentences. As shown in Fig. 1, researchers proposed many subtasks of ABSA, such as Aspect Term Extraction (ATE) [9], Opinion Term Extraction (OTE) [26], Aspect-based Sentiment Classification (ABSC) [6], Aspect-oriented Opinion Extraction (AOE) [4], etc. Aspect terms refer to words or phrases that describe the attributes or characteristics of an entity. Opinion terms refer to words or phrases that express the corresponding attitudes of the aspect terms. ATE and OTE aim to extract aspects and opinions from sentences, respectively. For ABSC, given a sentence and an aspect within the sentence, it is possible to predict the sentiment (positive, neutral, or negative) associated with that

Supported by the Social and Science Foundation of Liaoning Province (No. L20BTQ008).

M. Sun et al. (Eds.): CCL 2023, LNAI 14232, pp. 222–236, 2023.
https://doi.org/10.1007/978-981-99-6207-5_14

aspect. In the sentence "The service is good, but the food is not so great", ATE extracts "service" and "food", and OTE extracts "good" and "not so great". ABSC predicts the sentiment polarity of "service" and "food" as positive and negative, respectively. However, these studies focus on individual tasks respectively while neglecting their interdependencies.

Recent studies have focused on joint tasks to explore the interactions among different tasks. Figure 1 provides examples of Aspect Term Extraction and Sentiment Co-classification (AESC) as well as Aspect-Opinion Pair Extraction(pair). However, these subtasks still cannot tell a complete story. Hence Aspect Sentiment Triplet Extraction (ASTE) was introduced. The purpose of ASTE is to extract aspect terms, related opinion terms, and sentiment polarities for each aspect simultaneously. ASTE has two advantages: first, opinions can enhance the expressiveness of the model, helping to determine the sentiment of the aspects better; second, the sentiment dependency between aspects and opinions can narrow the gap of sentiment decision-making, further improving the interpretability of the model.

Peng [11] proposed the first solution for ASTE, which jointly extracts aspect-sentiment pairs and opinions using two sequence taggers. Sentiment is attached to aspects through a unified tagging process, and then an exclusive classifier is used to pair the extracted aspect-sentiment pairs with opinions. While this method achieved significant results, there are also some issues. **Firstly**, the model has low computational efficiency because its framework involves two stages and requires training three independent models. **Secondly**, the model does not fully recognize the relationship between ATE and OTE, and does not effectively utilize the correspondence between aspect terms and opinion terms. **Thirdly**, the correspondence between aspect and opinion expressions can be very complex, involving various relationships such as one-to-many, many-to-one, overlapping, and nesting, which makes it difficult for the model to flexibly and accurately detect these relationships. Therefore, we take the solution to the above problems as our challenge.

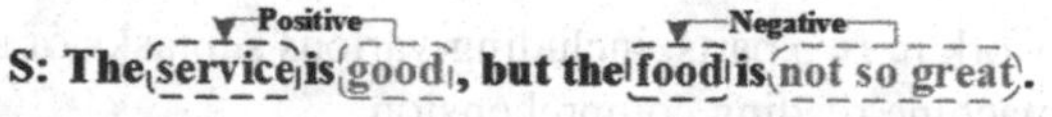
Positive
Negative
S: The service is good, but the food is not so great.

Substask	Input	Output
Aspect Term Extraction(ATE)	S	{service, food}
Opinion Term Extraction(OTE)	S	{good, not so great}
Aspect-based Sentiment Classification(ABSC)	S+service	Positive
	S+food	Negative
Aspect-oriented Opinion Extraction(AOE)	S+service	good
	S+food	not so great
Aspect Term and Sentiment Co-extraction(AESC)	S	{service, Positive}
	S	{food, Negative}
Aspect-Opinion Pair Extraction(Pair)	S	{service, good}
	S	{food, not so great}
Aspect Sentiment Triplet Extraction(ASTE)	S	{service, good, Positive}
	S	{food, not so great, Negative}

Fig. 1. Illustration of ABSA subtasks

To address the **first** problem mentioned above, inspired by [2], this paper proposes an improved multi-round MRC framework (R-MMRC) with a rethink mechanism to elegantly identify ASTE within a unified framework. To address the **second** problem, we decompose the ASTE into multiple rounds and introduce prior knowledge from the previous round to the current round, which effectively learns the associations between different subtasks. In the first round, we design static queries to extract the first entity of each aspect-opinion pair. In the second round, we design dynamic queries to identify the second entity of each aspect-opinion pair based on the previously extracted entity. In the third round, we design a dynamic sentiment query to predict the corresponding sentiment polarity based on the aspect-opinion pairs obtained in the previous round. In each step, the manually designed static and dynamic queries fully utilize the sentence's explicit semantic information to improve the extraction or classification performance. Based on these steps, we can flexibly capture complex relationships between entities, effectively mine the connection between ATE and OTE, and use these relationships to guide sentiment classification. To address the **third** issue, inspired by human two-stage reading behaviour [27], we introduce a rethink mechanism to validate candidate aspect-opinion pairs further, enhance the information flow between aspects and opinions, and improve overall performance. Our contributions are summarized as follows:

- We proposed an improved multi-round machine reading comprehension framework (R-MMRC) with a rethink mechanism to address the ASTE task effectively.
- The model introduced the rethink mechanism to enhance the information flow between aspects and opinions. The exclusive classifier was added to avoid interference and query conflicts between different Q&A steps. The probability generation algorithm was also introduced to improve the prediction performance further.
- The proposed model conducts extensive experiments on four public datasets, and experimental results show that our framework is very competitive.

2 Related Work

We present related work in two parts, including various subtasks of aspect-based sentiment analysis and machine reading comprehension.

2.1 Aspect-Based Sentiment Analysis

ATE. Locating and extracting terms that are pertinent for sentiment analysis and opinion mining is the task of ATE [17]. Recent studies use two ways to alleviate the noise from pseudo-labels generated by self-learning [15].
OTE. OTE is to extract opinion terms corresponding to aspect terms, hoping to find specific words or phrases that describe sentiment [3].
ABSC. The task's aim is to forecast sentiment polarity of specific aspects. The latest development of ABSC focuses on developing various types of deep learning models: CNN-based [7], memory-based methods [10], etc. Dependencies and graph structures have also been used effectively for sentiment classification problems [19,24].

AOE. Fan [4] first proposed this subtask, which aims to extract corresponding opinion terms for each provided aspect term. The difference between AOE and OTE is that the input of AOE contains aspect terms.
AESC. AESC aims to simultaneously extract aspect terms and sentiment. Recent work removes the boundaries of these two subtasks using a unified approach. Chen [3] proposes a relational awareness framework that allows subtasks to coordinate their work by stacking multitask learning and association propagation mechanisms.
Pair. The Pair task usually uses the pipeline method or directly uses the unified model. Gao [5] proposed a machine reading comprehension task based on question answering and span annotation.
ASTE. Peng [11] defined a triplet extraction task intending to extract all possible aspect terms, their corresponding opinion terms, and sentiment polarities. Xu [20] propose a span-based method to learn the interaction between target words and opinion words and propose a two-channel span pruning strategy.

2.2 Solving NLP Tasks by MRC

The purpose of machine reading comprehension (MRC) is to enable machines to answer questions from a specific context based on queries. Xu [20] proposed a post-training method for BERT. Yu [23] introduced role replacement into the reading comprehension model and solved the coupling problem in different aspects. To sum up, MRC is an effective and flexible framework for natural language processing tasks.

2.3 Aspect Sentiment Triplet Extraction

ASTE is the latest subtask in the field of ABSA. Xu [21] proposed a position-aware tagging scheme that efficiently captures interactions in triplets. However, they generally overlooked the relationship between words and language features. In a similar vein, Yan [22] converted the ASTE task into a generative formulation, but also tended to ignore the linguistic aspects of word features. Meanwhile, Chen [1] introduced an enhanced multi-channel GCN that incorporated various language features to enhance the model. However, they failed to consider the interaction between these different language features. In summary, there are still many issues waiting to be resolved in ASTE, and we will try our best to make breakthroughs in ASTE tasks.

3 Methodology

3.1 Model Framework

As shown in Fig. 2, to address the ASTE task, we propose a multi-round machine reading comprehension framework based on a rethink mechanism. Specifically, we design two modules: parameter sharing and joint learning. First, for the parameter sharing module, we design a bidirectional structure to extract aspect-opinion pairs, consisting of two querying rounds. The first round is static queries aimed at extracting all aspect or opinion sets based on the given query statements. The second round is dynamic queries, aimed at identifying the corresponding opinion or aspect sets based on the results of the static queries and generating aspect-opinion pairs. Then, the rethink mechanism is used to filter out invalid aspect-opinion pairs in the parameter sharing stage. For the joint learning module, the framework employs dynamic sentiment queries to predict the sentiment polarity of the filtered aspect-opinion pairs. During the probability generation stage, the model combines the answers from different queries and forms triplets.

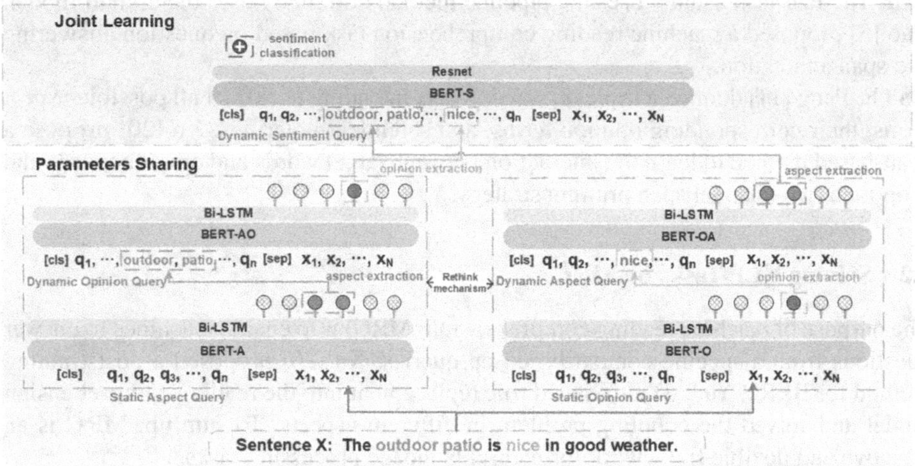

Fig. 2. Overview of R-MMRC framework

3.2 Query Template Construction

In R-MMRC, we build queries using a template-based method. Specifically, we designed static queries $Q^S = \{q_i^S\}_{i=1}^{|Q^S|}$ and dynamic queries $Q^D = \{q_i^D\}_{i=1}^{|Q^D|}$, where i represents the i-th token in the sentence. In particular, static queries do not carry any contextual information. Dynamic queries require the results of static queries as keywords to search for valid information in sentences. Static and dynamic queries are used to formalize the ASTE task as an MRC task:

Parameter Sharing

Static Aspect Query q_A^S: We design the query 'Find the aspect in the text?' to extract a set of aspects $A = \{a_i\}_{i=1}^{|A|}$ from a given review sentence X.

Dynamic Opinion Query q_O^D: We design the query 'Find the opinion of the aspect a_i?' to extract the relevant opinions $O_{ai} = \{o_{ai,j}\}_{j=1}^{|O_{ai}|}$ for each aspect a_i.

Static Opinion Query q_O^S: We design the query 'Find the opinion in the text?' to extract the collection of opinions $O = \{o_i\}_{i=1}^{|O|}$ from a given review sentence X.

Dynamic Aspect Query q_A^D: We design the query 'Find the aspect of the opinion o_i' to extract the corresponding aspects $A_{oi} = \{a_{oi,j}\}_{j=1}^{|A_{oi}|}$ for each opinion O_i.

Through the above queries, dynamic queries elegantly learn the conclusions of static queries and naturally integrates entity extraction and relationship detection. Although the entity results of these two queries are the same, the latter conveys the information of the former and searches for all entities described by the former, while the former does not carry any contextual information. Then, in the joint learning module, we classify the sentiment corresponding to the aspect-opinion pairs.

Joint Learning

Dynamic Sentiment Query $q^{D'}$: We build the query 'Find the sentiment of the aspect a_i and the opinion o_i?' to anticipate the sentiment polarity s_i of each aspect a_i.

Through the queries, we can fully consider the semantic relationship of aspect terms and corresponding opinion terms.

3.3 Input Representations

This section focuses on the triplet extraction task. Given a sentence $X = \{x_1, x_2, ..., x_N\}$ with max-length N as the input, and each query $q_i = \left\{q_1^i, q_2^i, ..., q_{|q_i|}^i\right\}$ with $|q_i|$ tokens. We use BERT as the model's encoder, and the encoding layer's role is to learn each token's context representation. First, we associate the query Q_i with the review sentence X and obtain the input $I = \left\{[CLS], q_1^i, q_2^i, ..., q_{|q_i|}^i, [SEP], x_1, x_2, ..., x_N\right\}$ after combination, where $[CLS]$ and $[SEP]$ are the start tag and the segment tag. Bert is used to encode an initial representation sequence $E = \left\{e_1, e_2, ..., e_{|q_i|+2+N}\right\}$, which is encoded as a hidden representation sequence $H_e = \left\{h_1, h_2, ..., h_{|q_i|+2+N}\right\}$ with stacked transformer blocks.

3.4 Query Answer Prediction

For the first two rounds of static and dynamic queries, the answer is to extract aspect terms or opinion terms from review sentence X. For instance, in Fig. 2, the aspect term "outdoor patio" should be extracted as the answer to the Static Aspect Query.

In the original BMRC [2], all queries shared a single classifier, which could lead to interference between different types of queries and cause query conflicts. Since there are four different queries in the parameter sharing part, we set an exclusive BERT classifier for each query, which can effectively avoid interference of query conflict and answering step. Classifiers are BERT-A, BERT-AO, BERT-O, and BERT-OA, respectively. The context representation generated by BERT is used for Bi-LSTM to generate sentence hidden state vectors. Since H_e already contains information about aspect or opinion, we obtain specific context representation by aggregating the hidden states of two directions: $H = \left[\overrightarrow{H_{e_f}}; \overleftrightarrow{H_{e_b}}\right]$, where $\overrightarrow{H_{e_f}}$ is the hidden state of the forward LSTM and $\overleftarrow{H_{e_b}}$ is of the backward LSTM. We adopted the strategy of [18] and employ two binary classifiers to predict the answer spans based on the hidden representation sequence H. We utilize two classifiers to predict the possibility that the token x_i is the start or end of the answer. Then, we obtain the logits and probabilities for start and end positions:

$$p_{x_i,q}^{\text{start}} = \text{softmax}\left(W_s h_{|q|+2+i}\right) \tag{1}$$

$$p_{x_i,q}^{end} = \text{softmax}\left(W_e h_{|q|+2+i}\right) \tag{2}$$

where $W_s \in R^{d\times 2}$ and $W_e \in R^{d\times 2}$ are model parameters, d represents the dimension of hidden representations, and $|q|$ stands for the query length.

For dynamic sentiment queries, we utilize the hidden representation of [CLS] to predict the answer. We add a three-class classifier in BERT, called "BERT-S" for short, to predict the sentiment of aspect-opinion pairs. In addition, we add two layers of ResNet network to protect the integrity of information and reduce the loss of information.

$$h = \sigma F\left(h_1, \{W_{ri}\}\right) + h_1 \tag{3}$$

$$p_{X,q}^{D'} = \operatorname{softmax}\left(W_c h\right) \tag{4}$$

where h_1 is the hidden representation of $[CLS]$, σ refers to ReLU activation function, $F()$ is the residual mapping of fitting, W_{ri} and $W_c = R^{d\times 3}$ is the model parameter.

3.5 Rethink Mechanism

During the inference process, we combine the answers from different queries into tuples. As shown in Fig. 2, the left-side static aspect query q_A^S first identifies all aspect items $A = \left\{a_1, a_2, \ldots, a_{|A|}\right\}$. For each aspect item a_i, the corresponding opinion expression set $O_i = \left\{o_{i,1}, o_{i,2}, \ldots, o_{i,|O_i|}\right\}$ is identified through the dynamic opinion query q_O^S, resulting in a set of aspect-opinion pairs $V_{AO} = \left[\left(a_i^k, o_{i,j}^k\right)\right]_{k=1}^{I}$, and ultimately obtaining the probability of each candidate pair $p\left(a_i, o_{i,j}\right) = p\left(a_i\right) p\left(o_{i,j} \mid a_i\right)$. Similarly, on the right side, the model first identifies all the opinion items and then queries all corresponding aspect items, and we finally obtain another set of aspect-opinion pairs $V_{OA} = \left[\left(a_{j,i}^k, o_j^k\right)\right]_{k=1}^{J}$, from which we obtain the probability of each candidate pair $p\left(a_{j,i}, o_j\right) = p\left(o_j\right) p\left(a_{j,i} \mid o_j\right)$.

However, the above approach may introduce incorrect aspect-opinion pairs. To better address this issue, we implement a rethink mechanism through a soft-selection strategy. If there exist identical candidate pairs in sets V_{AO} and V_{OA}, then the corresponding aspect-opinion pairs are added to the valid set V. If there are unmatched candidate pairs in V_{AO} and V_{OA}, it indicates that one side's output may be invalid. Therefore, in the soft selection strategy, we adjust the probabilities and introduce a probability threshold λ. If the probability $p(a, o)$ of a certain candidate pair in the difference set is greater than or equal to the probability threshold λ, then this candidate pair is added to the valid set V; otherwise, it is discarded. By using a rethink mechanism, invalid pairs can be better filtered out, reducing the interference of erroneous candidate pairs on the model.

3.6 Entity Pair Probability Generation

After filtering with the rethink mechanism, we obtained a set of valid aspect-opinion pairs, and the next step is to calculate the probability of each candidate pair. In BMRC, the probability of an entity is the product of the probabilities of its start and end positions, and the probability of a candidate pair is the product of the probabilities of the aspect item and opinion item. However, this can result in a product of high probabilities equaling a lower probability value, which does not well represent the model's prediction. As shown in the formula, we balance the probabilities of entities and candidate pairs by taking the square root, which keeps the probability within the range of two related probabilities. This approach can avoid unilateral decrease of probability and better meeting the expectation of the model.

$$p(e) = \sqrt{p(e_{\text{start}}) * p(e_{end})} \tag{5}$$

$$p(a,o) = \begin{cases} \sqrt{p(a) * p(o \mid a)} \cdots \text{ if } (a,o) \in V_{AO} \\ \sqrt{p(o) * p(a \mid o)} \cdots \text{ if } (a,o) \in V_{OA} \end{cases} \tag{6}$$

where e represents the aspect or opinion entity, $start$ and end represent the start and end positions of the entity, and $p(a,o)$ represents the probability of the final candidate pair.

Finally, we employ the dynamic sentiment query $q_i^{D'}$ to predict the various aspects of emotion a_i. We obtain the output of labeled triplets for input sentence X_i, denoted as $T_i = \{(a,o,s)\}$, where $s \in$(positive, neutral, negative) and (a,o,s) refers to (aspect term, opinion term, sentiment polarity).

3.7 Loss Function Construction

In order to learn triplet subtasks jointly and make them promote each other, we integrate loss functions from various queries. For static queries in different directions, we minimize the loss of cross-entropy:

$$L_S = -\sum_{i=1}^{|Q^S|}\sum_{j=1}^{|S|}\left[p_{x_j,q_i}^{start} \cdot \log \hat{p}_{x_j,q_i}^{start} + p_{x_j,q_i}^{end} \cdot \log \hat{p}_{x_j,q_i}^{end}\right] \tag{7}$$

where $p()$ represents the distribution of gold, $\hat{p}()$ indicates the predicted distribution.

Similarly, the loss of dynamic queries in different directions is as follows:

$$L_D = -\sum_{i=1}^{|Q^D|}\sum_{j=1}^{|D|}\left[p_{x_j,q_i}^{start} \cdot \log \hat{p}_{x_j,q_i}^{start} + p_{x_j,q_i}^{end} \cdot \log \hat{p}_{x_j,q_i}^{end}\right] \tag{8}$$

For dynamic sentiment classification queries, we minimize the cross-entropy loss function:

$$L_{D'} = -\sum_{i=1}^{|Q^{D'}|} p_{X,q_i}^{D'} \cdot \log \hat{p}_{X,q_i}^{D'} \tag{9}$$

Then, we integrate the aforementioned loss functions to generate the overall model's losses. In this paper, we used the method of AdamW [8] to optimize:

$$L(\theta) = L_S + L_D + L_{D'} \tag{10}$$

4 Experiments

4.1 Datasets

To verify the validity of our proposed approach, we conducted experiments on four benchmark datasets from the SemEval ABSA challenge [12–14] and listed the statistics for these datasets in Table 1.

Table 1. Statistics of 4 datasets. #S and #T denotes number of sentences and triples.

Datasets	Train		Dev		Test	
	#S	#T	#S	#T	#S	#T
14-Lap	920	1265	228	337	339	490
14-Res	1300	2145	323	524	496	862
15-Res	593	593	148	238	318	455
16-Res	842	1289	210	316	320	465

4.2 Subtasks and Baselines

To demonstrate the validity of the proposed model, we compared the R-MMRC with the following baseline.

- CMLA+ [11] modifies CMLA [23], the attention mechanism is used by CMLA to detect the relationship between words and to extract aspects and opinions jointly. CMLA+ incorporates MLP to further determine whether the triplet is accurate during the matching phase.
- Two-Stage [11] is a two-stage pipeline model for ASTE. The task of the first stage is to mark all aspects and opinions. The goal of the second stage is to match all aspects with the corresponding opinion expression.
- RACL+ is improved by RACL framework [3], which uses mechanisms for relationship propagation and multi-task learning to enable subtasks to cooperate in a stacked multi-layer network. Then researchers [2] construct the query "Matching aspect a_i and opinion expression o_j?" to detect relationships.
- JET [21] is a first end-to-end model with a novel position-aware tagging scheme that is capable of jointly extracting the triple.
- GTS-BERT [16] address the ASTE task in an end-to-end fashion with one unified grid tagging task.
- BMRC [2] transforms the ASTE task into a bi-directional MRC task and designs three types of queries to establish relationships between different subtasks.

4.3 Model Settings and Evaluation Metrics

We adopted a Bert [18] model for the encoding layer with 12 attention heads, 12 hidden layers, and 768 hidden sizes. The fine-tuning rate of BERT and the learning rate of the training classifier are set to 1e−5 and 1e−3, respectively. We use AdamW optimizer with a weight decay of 0.01 and a warm-up rate of 0.1. At the same time, we set the batch size to 8 and the dropout rate to 0.3. The F1-score is extracted according to the triplet state on the development set. The threshold λ manually adjusted to 0.8, and the step size is set to 0.1.

We use precision, recall, and f1-score as measurement indicators to measure performance, including aspect term and sentiment co-extraction, aspect-opinion pair extraction, and aspect sentiment triplet extraction, respectively. Only when the prediction of aspects, opinions, and sentiments is correct, the triplet's prediction is correct.

4.4 Main Results

Table 2 shows the comparison results for all approaches, from which we derive the following conclusions. The proposed model R-MMRC achieves competitive performance on all datasets, which demonstrates the efficacy of our model. Under the F1 metric, the R-MMRC model is superior to the pipeline method in all datasets. Our model's F1-score on AESC exceeded the baseline average by 2.09%, on Pair by 3.66%, and on ASTE by 2.67%, respectively. The result shows that our method extracts more practical features. We observe that the method based on MRC achieves more significant improvement than the pipeline method, because it establishes the correlation between these subtasks by jointly training multiple subtasks, and alleviates the error propagation problem. It is worth noting that our model also has a significant improvement in precision, which indicates that the model's prediction ability is more reliable than those baselines.

The Pair and ASTE of our model achieve the best performance on all datasets, but the scores of two datasets in AESC are inferior to RACL+. We think that the idea that RACL+ first jointly trains the underlying shared features, then independently trains the advanced private features, and finally exchanges subtask information clues through the relationship propagation mechanism is very effective. TS performs better than CMLA+, since it uses a unified tagging schema to resolve sentiment conflicts. It is noteworthy that the improvement of precision contributes the most to the increase in F1 score. We believe that the high precision score is due to the rethink mechanism filtering out some negative samples. Both JET and GTS-BERT used labeling schemes, but the latter yielded better results due to the use of more advanced grid labeling and the design of effective inference strategies. The sentiment classification task is more challenging than the previous extraction task because sentiment heavily relies on the extracted aspect-opinion pairs. However, with the help of dynamic sentiment queries constructed based on aspect-opinion information, compared to BMRC, an overall improvement has been achieved.

There is a certain performance gap between the baseline model and our proposed model, which confirms the rationality of the architecture we proposed. We believe that the design of static and dynamic queries can naturally integrate entity extraction and relation detection to enhance their dependency. The rethink mechanism validates each candidate aspect-opinion pair by modeling the information flow from aspect to opinion (or from opinion to aspect), effectively filtering out negative samples and improving the performance of the model. At the same time, the exclusive classifier we introduced, as well as the probability generation algorithm, further improve the performance of the model.

Table 2. Statistics of 4 datasets. #S and #T denotes number of sentences and triples.

	Models	14Lap			14Res			15Res			16Res		
		AESC	Pair	ASTE	AESC	Pair	ASTE	AESC	Pair	ASTE	AESC	Pair	ASTE
Precision	CMLA+	54.70	42.10	31.40	67.80	45.17	40.11	49.90	42.70	34.40	58.90	52.50	43.60
	TS	63.15	50.00	40.40	74.41	47.76	44.18	67.65	49.22	40.97	71.18	52.35	46.76
	RACL+	59.75	54.22	41.99	75.57	73.58	62.64	68.35	67.89	55.45	68.53	72.77	60.78
	JET	-	-	52.00	-	-	66.76	-	-	59.77	-	-	63.59
	GTS-BERT	-	66.41	57.52	-	76.23	70.92	-	66.40	59.29	-	71.70	68.58
	BMRC	**72.73**	74.11	**65.12**	77.74	76.91	71.32	72.41	**71.59**	63.71	**73.69**	76.08	67.74
	Ours	70.32	**74.60**	63.76	**78.95**	**78.36**	**72.69**	**72.95**	69.57	**63.96**	72.22	**78.04**	**68.64**
Recall	CMLA+	59.20	46.30	34.60	73.69	53.42	46.63	58.00	46.70	37.60	63.60	47.90	39.80
	TS	61.55	58.47	47.24	73.97	68.10	62.99	64.02	65.70	54.68	72.30	70.50	62.97
	RACL+	**68.90**	**66.94**	51.84	**82.23**	67.87	57.77	**70.72**	63.74	52.53	**78.52**	71.83	60.00
	JET	-	-	35.91	-	-	49.09	-	-	42.27	-	-	50.97
	GTS-BERT	-	64.95	51.92	-	74.84	69.49	-	68.71	58.07	-	**77.79**	66.60
	BMRC	62.59	61.92	54.41	75.10	75.59	70.09	62.63	65.89	58.63	72.69	76.99	**68.56**
	Ours	62.92	63.27	**54.69**	77.00	**78.54**	**72.85**	68.49	**70.33**	**62.64**	68.49	70.33	67.31
F1-score	CMLA+	56.90	44.10	32.90	70.62	48.95	43.12	53.60	44.60	35.90	61.20	50.00	41.60
	TS	62.34	53.85	43.50	74.19	56.10	51.89	65.79	56.23	46.79	71.73	60.04	53.62
	RACL+	64.00	59.90	46.39	**78.76**	70.61	60.11	69.51	65.46	53.95	**73.19**	72.29	60.39
	JET	-	-	42.48	-	-	56.58	-	-	49.52	-	-	56.59
	GTS-BERT	-	65.67	54.58	-	75.53	70.20	-	67.53	58.67	-	74.62	67.58
	BMRC	**67.27**	67.45	59.27	76.39	76.23	70.69	67.16	68.60	61.05	73.18	76.52	68.13
	Ours	66.41	**67.61**	**61.45**	77.96	**78.45**	**72.77**	**69.70**	**69.95**	**62.30**	72.41	**77.62**	**69.67**

4.5 Ablation Test

We conduct further ablation studies to analyze the impact of different components of R-MMRC. We present the results of ASTE in Table 3, where the first row shows the reproduced results of R-MMRC. The next three rows show the results after removing the rethink mechanism, exclusive classifier, and probability generation, respectively. The last row shows the final results after removing these three parts of the R-MMRC model.

The results show that each component improves the performance of the model, demonstrating their advantages and effectiveness. We remove the dynamic query in the parameter sharing stage of R-MMRC and keep only static queries and the dynamic sentiment query, which is referred to as "-dynamic query". Obviously, removing the dynamic query resulted in a significant drop in model performance. We analyze that after removing the dynamic query, the model could not capture the dependency relationships between entities and separated entity extraction from relation detection. The results indicate that the dynamic query in the parameter sharing stage is highly effective in capturing dependencies.

The advantage of the rethink mechanism is quite significant. Specifically, compared with R-MMRC, the rethink mechanism achieved F1-score improvements of 3.15%, 3.43%, 2.73%, and 2.35% on the four datasets, demonstrating the effectiveness of the rethink mechanism. The probability generation also has a certain improvement effect,

Table 3. Ablation study results (%). P represents precision, R represents recall, F1 represents Macro-F1 score.

Model	14Lap			14Res			15Res			16Res		
	P	R	F1	P	R	F1	P	R	F1	P	R	F1
R-MMRC	63.76	**54.69**	**61.45**	**72.69**	**72.85**	**72.77**	**63.96**	**62.64**	**62.30**	**68.64**	67.31	**69.67**
—rethink mechanism	**64.45**	53.21	58.30	71.76	65.42	68.34	60.21	59.26	59.57	67.61	65.02	67.32
—exclusive classifier	63.60	55.26	60.58	72.02	68.91	72.36	63.67	61.85	61.98	68.50	**68.39**	69.15
—probability generation	62.51	53.03	59.03	70.64	69.73	70.50	61.16	60.03	60.69	67.26	66.16	67.80
—dynamic query	60.12	50.41	53.27	65.32	67.63	61.16	55.71	56.63	54.05	62.74	60.56	60.13

which proves that our model better avoids unilateral decline of probability and is more consistent with the model's expectation. For the exclusive classifier, the model's F1 score improvement is relatively smaller compared to the previous two components. Moreover, we find that it has a significant downside of slowing down the model's runtime.

4.6 Case Study

We conduct a case study to illustrate the effectiveness and perform an error analysis in Table 4. We select three cases from datasets and compare our results with RACL+. The reason for choosing RACL+ is that its performance is second only to our R-MMRC model.

The first case has two aspect terms: "exterior patio" and "ambiance". RACL+ cannot extract the triplets corresponding to "ambiance". We speculate that the model only considers the relationship between sentence representations of subtasks, which weakens aspect terms in long and complicated sentences. Our proposed model considers all triplets in the sentence because it can guarantee that an aspect or an opinion can produce a pair, precisely like human reading behavior.

The second case is a long sentence with two triplets, and the corresponding sentiments are positive and neutral, respectively. Our R-MMRC correctly extracted aspect terms and opinion terms, and successfully predicted the corresponding polarity. However, RACL+ correctly extracts all aspect terms, but it misjudges the polarity of "seating". The reason is that RACL+ is good at making use of different semantic relationships between subtasks, so it may use irrelevant "rule" and "late" as keywords, and predict the sentiment of "seating" as "negative". On the contrary, R-MMRC can more accurately identify aspect terms and the corresponding opinion terms in complex sentences.

The third case is error analysis. Although the sentence is not long, both models predict the sentiment of "dinner" incorrectly. We analyze that "ok" is usually considered a positive opinion term, so the two models define "dinner" as positive. However, by carefully observing this sentence, we find that the seldom choices in "vegetarian options" are the reason why guests say "dinner" is just "okay" rather than "good". So, sentiment polarity should be "neutral" rather than "positive". We speculate that we are looking for the training loss of maximum likelihood cross entropy in the training set, which may be the reason for the wrong prediction in this case. More interestingly, RACL+

Table 4. Case study. Marker × indicates incorrect predictions. The table's abbreviations POS, NEU, and NEG represent positive, neutral, and negative sentiments, respectively.

Case	Ground Truth	RACL+	R-MMRC
The outdoor patio is really nice in good weather, but what ambience the indoors possesses is negated by the noise and the crowds.	(outdoor patio, nice, POS) (ambience, negated, NEG)	(outdoor patio, nice, POS)	(outdoor patio, nice, POS) (ambience, negated, NEG)
The food is pretty good, but after 2 or 3 bad experiences at the restaurant (consistently rude, late with RSVP'd seating).	(food, pretty good, POS) (seating, RSVP, NEU)	(food, pretty good, POS) (seating, rude, NEG) × (seating, late, NEG) ×	(food, pretty good, POS) (seating, RSVP, NEU)
Dinner is okay not many vegetarian options and the portions are small.	(Dinner, okay, NEU) (positions, small, NEG)	(Dinner, okay, POS) × (vegetarian options, not many, NEG) × (portions, small, NEG)	(Dinner, okay, POS) × (vegetarian options, not many, NEG) × (portions, small, NEG)

and our R-MMRC, as two excellent solutions, incorrectly consider (vegetarian options, not many, NEG) as a triplet. Therefore, we think that understanding sentence structure through logic and even causal reasoning may provide new ideas for the future research of sentiment analysis.

5 Conclusion

In this paper, we investigate ASTE task and propose an improved multi-round MRC framework with a rethink mechanism(R-MMRC). This framework sequentially extracts aspect-sentiment pairs and performs sentiment classification, which can handle complex correspondences between aspects, opinions, and sentiments. In each round, explicit semantic information can be effectively utilized. Additionally, the rethink mechanism models the bidirectional information flow to verify each candidate aspect-opinion pair, effectively utilizing the corresponding relationship between entities. Exclusive classifiers avoid interference between different queries, and probability generation algorithms further improve prediction performance. The experimental results demonstrate the effectiveness of the R-MMRC framework, further improving the overall performance of the system. More importantly, our model can serve as a general framework to address various tasks of ABSA. However, our model still suffers from the issue of high computational cost, and we hope to compress the model in the future to make it more lightweight.

Acknowledgements. This work is supported by a grant from the Social and Science Foundation of Liaoning Province (No. L20BTQ008).

References

1. Chen, H., Zhai, Z., Feng, F., Li, R., Wang, X.: Enhanced multi-channel graph convolutional network for aspect sentiment triplet extraction. In: Proceedings of the 60th Annual Meeting of the Association for Computational Linguistics (Volume 1: Long Papers), pp. 2974–2985 (2022)

2. Chen, S., Wang, Y., Liu, J., Wang, Y.: Bidirectional machine reading comprehension for aspect sentiment triplet extraction. In: Proceedings of the AAAI Conference on Artificial Intelligence, vol. 35, pp. 12666–12674 (2021)
3. Chen, Z., Qian, T.: Relation-aware collaborative learning for unified aspect-based sentiment analysis. In: Proceedings of the 58th Annual Meeting of the Association for Computational Linguistics, pp. 3685–3694 (2020)
4. Fan, Z., Wu, Z., Dai, X., Huang, S., Chen, J.: Target-oriented opinion words extraction with target-fused neural sequence labeling. In: Proceedings of the 2019 Conference of the North American Chapter of the Association for Computational Linguistics: Human Language Technologies, Volume 1 (Long and Short Papers), pp. 2509–2518 (2019)
5. Gao, L., Wang, Y., Liu, T., Wang, J., Zhang, L., Liao, J.: Question-driven span labeling model for aspect-opinion pair extraction. In: Proceedings of the AAAI Conference on Artificial Intelligence, vol. 35, pp. 12875–12883 (2021)
6. Hazarika, D., Poria, S., Vij, P., Krishnamurthy, G., Cambria, E., Zimmermann, R.: Modeling inter-aspect dependencies for aspect-based sentiment analysis. In: Proceedings of the 2018 Conference of the North American Chapter of the Association for Computational Linguistics: Human Language Technologies, Volume 2 (Short Papers), pp. 266–270 (2018)
7. Huang, B., Carley, K.M.: Parameterized convolutional neural networks for aspect level sentiment classification. arXiv preprint arXiv:1909.06276 (2019)
8. Loshchilov, I., Hutter, F.: Fixing weight decay regularization in Adam (2017)
9. Ma, D., Li, S., Wu, F., Xie, X., Wang, H.: Exploring sequence-to-sequence learning in aspect term extraction. In: Proceedings of the 57th Annual Meeting of the Association for Computational Linguistics, pp. 3538–3547 (2019)
10. Majumder, N., Poria, S., Gelbukh, A., Akhtar, M.S., Cambria, E., Ekbal, A.: IARM: inter-aspect relation modeling with memory networks in aspect-based sentiment analysis. In: Proceedings of the 2018 Conference on Empirical Methods in Natural Language Processing, pp. 3402–3411 (2018)
11. Peng, H., Xu, L., Bing, L., Huang, F., Lu, W., Si, L.: Knowing what, how and why: a near complete solution for aspect-based sentiment analysis. In: Proceedings of the AAAI Conference on Artificial Intelligence, vol. 34, pp. 8600–8607 (2020)
12. Pontiki, M., Galanis, D., Pavlopoulos, J., Papageorgiou, H., Manandhar, S.: SemEval-2014 Task 4: aspect based sentiment analysis. In: Proceedings of International Workshop on Semantic Evaluation (2014)
13. Pontiki, M., Galanis, D., Papageorgiou, H., Manandhar, S., Androutsopoulos, I.: SemEval-2015 Task 12: aspect based sentiment analysis. In: Proceedings of the 9th International Workshop on Semantic Evaluation (SemEval 2015), pp. 486–495 (2015)
14. Pontiki, M., et al.: SemEval-2016 Task 5: aspect based sentiment analysis. In: ProWorkshop on Semantic Evaluation (SemEval-2016), pp. 19–30. Association for Computational Linguistics (2016)
15. Wang, Q., Wen, Z., Zhao, Q., Yang, M., Xu, R.: Progressive self-training with discriminator for aspect term extraction. In: Proceedings of the 2021 Conference on Empirical Methods in Natural Language Processing, pp. 257–268 (2021)
16. Wu, Z., Ying, C., Zhao, F., Fan, Z., Dai, X., Xia, R.: Grid tagging scheme for aspect-oriented fine-grained opinion extraction. arXiv preprint arXiv:2010.04640 (2020)
17. Xu, H., Liu, B., Shu, L., Yu, P.S.: Double embeddings and CNN-based sequence labeling for aspect extraction. arXiv preprint arXiv:1805.04601 (2018)
18. Xu, H., Liu, B., Shu, L., Yu, P.S.: Bert post-training for review reading comprehension and aspect-based sentiment analysis. arXiv preprint arXiv:1904.02232 (2019)
19. Xu, L., Bing, L., Lu, W., Huang, F.: Aspect sentiment classification with aspect-specific opinion spans. In: Proceedings of the 2020 Conference on Empirical Methods in Natural Language Processing (EMNLP), pp. 3561–3567 (2020)

20. Xu, L., Chia, Y.K., Bing, L.: Learning span-level interactions for aspect sentiment triplet extraction. arXiv preprint arXiv:2107.12214 (2021)
21. Xu, L., Li, H., Lu, W., Bing, L.: Position-aware tagging for aspect sentiment triplet extraction. In: Conference on Empirical Methods in Natural Language Processing (2020)
22. Yan, H., Dai, J., Qiu, X., Zhang, Z., et al.: A unified generative framework for aspect-based sentiment analysis. arXiv preprint arXiv:2106.04300 (2021)
23. Yu, G., Li, J., Luo, L., Meng, Y., Ao, X., He, Q.: Self question-answering: aspect-based sentiment analysis by role flipped machine reading comprehension. In: Findings of the Association for Computational Linguistics, EMNLP 2021, pp. 1331–1342 (2021)
24. Zhang, M., Qian, T.: Convolution over hierarchical syntactic and lexical graphs for aspect level sentiment analysis. In: Proceedings of the 2020 Conference on Empirical Methods in Natural Language Processing (EMNLP), pp. 3540–3549 (2020)
25. Zhang, W., Li, X., Deng, Y., Bing, L., Lam, W.: A survey on aspect-based sentiment analysis: tasks, methods, and challenges. IEEE Trans. Knowl. Data Eng. (2022)
26. Zhao, H., Huang, L., Zhang, R., Lu, Q., Xue, H.: SpanMlt: a span-based multi-task learning framework for pair-wise aspect and opinion terms extraction. In: Proceedings of the 58th Annual Meeting of the Association for Computational Linguistics, pp. 3239–3248 (2020)
27. Zheng, Y., Mao, J., Liu, Y., Ye, Z., Zhang, M., Ma, S.: Human behavior inspired machine reading comprehension. In: Proceedings of the 42nd International ACM SIGIR Conference on Research and Development in Information Retrieval, pp. 425–434 (2019)

Enhancing Ontology Knowledge for Domain-Specific Joint Entity and Relation Extraction

Xiong Xiong[1,2], Chen Wang[1,2], Yunfei Liu[1,2], and Shengyang Li[1,2(✉)]

[1] Key Laboratory of Space Utilization, Technology and Engineering Center for Space Utilization, Chinese Academy of Sciences, Beijing, China
{xiongxiong20,wangchen21,liuyunfei,shyli}@csu.ac.cn
[2] University of Chinese Academy of Sciences, Beijing, China

Abstract. Pre-trained language models (PLMs) have been widely used in entity and relation extraction methods in recent years. However, due to the semantic gap between general-domain text used for pre-training and domain-specific text, these methods encounter semantic redundancy and domain semantics insufficiency when it comes to domain-specific tasks. To mitigate this issue, we propose a low-cost and effective knowledge-enhanced method to facilitate domain-specific semantics modeling in joint entity and relation extraction. Precisely, we use ontology and entity type descriptions as domain knowledge sources, which are encoded and incorporated into the downstream entity and relation extraction model to improve its understanding of domain-specific information. We construct a dataset called SSUIE-RE for Chinese entity and relation extraction in space science and utilization domain of China Manned Space Engineering, which contains a wealth of domain-specific knowledge. The experimental results on SSUIE-RE demonstrate the effectiveness of our method, achieving a 1.4% absolute improvement in relation F1 score over previous best approach.

Keywords: Joint Entity and Relation Extraction · Knowledge Enhancement · Transformer

1 Introduction

Extracting relational triples from plain text is a fundamental task in information extraction and it's an essential step in knowledge graph (KG) construction [14]. Traditional methods perform Named Entity Recognition (NER) and Relation Extraction (RE) in a pipelined manner, that is, first extract entities, and then perform relation classification on entity pairs [6,9,35]. However, since the entity model and relation model are modeled separately, pipelined methods suffer from the problem of error propagation. To address this issue, some joint methods have been proposed [13,21,25,26,30,33]. The task of joint entity and relation extraction aims to simultaneously conduct entity recognition and relation classification in an end-to-end manner.

In recent years, with the development of pre-trained language models (PLMs) such as BERT [8] and GPT [18], many entity and relation extraction methods have adopted

M. Sun et al. (Eds.): CCL 2023, LNAI 14232, pp. 237–252, 2023.
https://doi.org/10.1007/978-981-99-6207-5_15

the paradigm of pre-training and fine-tuning. They utilize PLMs to encode the contextual representations of input text and design various downstream models for task-specific fine-tuning. However, when employed for domain-specific entity and relation extraction, this paradigm suffers from problems of semantic redundancy and insufficiency of domain-specific semantics, particularly in highly specialized domains. On the one hand, PLMs are usually trained on general-domain corpora, which results in a significant amount of redundant semantic information that may not be relevant to specific domains and a lack of sufficient domain-specific semantic information. On the other hand, modeling domain-specific information in this paradigm depends primarily on the role of downstream model and domain-specific labeled data in the fine-tuning stage. However, due to the significantly smaller parameter size of downstream model compared to PLMs and the limited availability of domain-specific labeled data, the effectiveness of domain-specific semantic information modeling is constrained.

Consequently, some methods attempt to incorporate domain knowledge into entity and relation extraction models to enhance the their comprehension of domain-specific information. These methods can be broadly categorized into two groups according to how knowledge is introduced: pre-training domain-specific language models and integrating domain-specific knowledge graph information into models. Methods of domain-specific pre-training utilize large-scale domain corpora to facilitate continuous pre-training of existing general-domain language models [2, 12, 17] or, alternatively, to perform domain-specific pre-training from scratch [5, 10]. However, in certain specialized domains, there may be a dearth of enough domain-specific corpora to support domain-specific pre-training. Another category of methods involve integrating domain-specific knowledge graph information into models, where entity mentions in input text are linked to the corresponding entities in knowledge graph, and then the relevant information of the linked entities in the knowledge graph is incorporated into models [11, 19, 27, 32]. Some of these knowledge graph integration methods are designed simply for the task of relation extraction (RE) where the entities in the sentence are pre-specified, rather than the task of joint entity and relation extraction. In addition, a prerequisite for this kind of approaches is the availability of a well-constructed domain-specific knowledge graph, which is scarce and expensive for some highly specialized domains.

In this study, we explore how to incorporate domain knowledge for the task of joint entity and relation extraction in space science and utilization domain of China Manned Space Engineering. Due to the lack of sufficient domain-specific corpora to support the pre-training of large-scale language models and the absence of well-constructed domain-specific knowledge graphs, the aforementioned approaches cannot be directly used for domain knowledge enhancement. We propose an ontology-enhanced joint entity and relation extraction method (**OntoRE**) for space science and utilization domain. The predefined domain-specific ontology involves many highly specialized entity types that interconnected by different semantic relations, which frames the knowledge scope and defines the knowledge structure in this domain, so it is an appropriate source of domain knowledge. The ontology can be formalized as a graph structure containing nodes and edges, where nodes represent entity types and edges represent relation types. Furthermore, drawing inspiration from the manner in which humans comprehend specialized terminology, we add descriptions for each entity type in the ontology to enhance the semantic information of entity types. We serialize the ontology graph and then adopt an ontology encoder to learn the embeddings of ontology knowledge. The encoded ontology features are fused with input sentence features, and then the entity and relation extraction is carried out under the guidance of ontology knowledge. To evaluate our model, we construct a dataset called **SSUIE** (**S**pace **S**cience and **U**tilization **I**nformation **E**xtraction), which contains rich knowledge about space science and utilization in the aerospace field. This work exclusively pertains to the problem of entity and relation extraction, therefore our model was evaluated on the subset of SSUIE specifically designed for entity and relation extraction, namely **SSUIE-RE**.

The main contributions of this work are summarized below:

1. A dataset named SSUIE-RE is proposed for Chinese entity and relation extraction in space science and utilization domain of China Manned Space Engineering. The dataset is enriched with domain-specific knowledge, which contains 19 entity types and 36 relation types.
2. An ontology-enhanced method for domain-specific joint entity and relation extraction is proposed, which substantially enhances domain knowledge without the need of domain knowledge graphs or large-scale domain corpora. Experimental results show that our model outperforms previous state-of-the-art works in terms of relation F1 score.
3. The effect of domain ontology knowledge enhancement is carefully examined. Our supplementary experiments show that the ontology knowledge can improve the extraction of relations with varying degrees of domain specificity. Notably, the benefit of ontology knowledge augmentation is more evident for relations with higher domain specificity.

2 Related Work

Among the representative entity and relation extraction approaches in recent years, some focus on solving the problem of triple overlapping [16,23,24,29,31] and some focus on the problem of task interaction between NER and RE [22,25,26]. However, the challenge of effectively integrating domain knowledge into entity and relation extraction models to improve their applicability in specific fields, has not been solved well by previous works. We survey the representative works on topics that are most relevant to this research: *domain-specific pre-training* and *integrating knowledge graph information*.

Domain-Specific Pre-training. In order to enhance the domain-specific semantics in PLMs, this family of approaches uses domain corpora to either continue the pre-training of existing generic PLMs or pre-train domain-specific language models from scratch. FinBERT [2] is initialized with the standard BERT model [8] and then further pre-trained using financial text. BioBERT [12] and BlueBERT [17] are further pre-trained from BERT model using biomedical text. Alsentzer et al. [1] conduct continual pre-training on the basis of BioBERT, and PubMedBERT [10] is trained from scratch using purely biomedical text. Chalkidis et al. [5] have explored both strategies of further pre-training and pre-training from scratch and release a family of BERT models for the legal domain.

Integrating Knowledge Graph Information. This category of methods infuse knowledge into the entity and relation extraction models with the help of external knowledge graph. Lai et al. [11] adopt the biomedical knowledge base *Unified Medical Language System (UMLS)* [4] as the source of knowledge. For each entity, they extract its semantic type, sentence description and relational information from UMLS with an entity mapping tool MetaMap [3], and then integrate these information for joint entity and relation extraction from biomedical text. Roy and Pan [19] fuse UMLS knowledge into BERT model for clinical relation extraction and explore the effect of different fusion stage, knowledge type, knowledge form and knowledge fusion methods. Zhang et al. [32] integrate the knowledge from Wikidata[1] into a generative framework for relational fact extraction.

To the best of our knowledge, only a limited number of specialized domains can meet the conditions for applying the two aforementioned methods of enhancing domain knowledge, mainly including biomedical, financial, and legal fields. These fields are comparatively prevalent in human life, so there are more likely to be a considerable amount of domain corpora and data in these fields. However, in highly specialized fields like aerospace, both the large-scale domain-specific corpora and well-constructed domain-specific knowledge graph are scarce. Our proposed method only utilize the ontology and entity type descriptions to inject domain knowledge into entity and relation model without additional prerequisites.

3 Method

In this section, we introduce the architecture of OntoRE. As shown in Fig. 1, the model mainly includes four parts: knowledge source, knowledge serialization, knowledge encoding and knowledge fusion. In the following subsections, we provide a detailed description of each component.

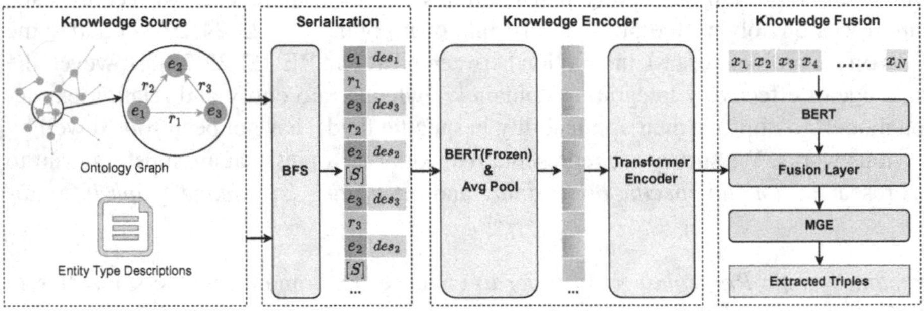

Fig. 1. The architecture of the proposed OntoRE framework. We formalize the ontology as a directed graph, where the nodes (blue) represent the predefined entity types and the edges (orange) represent the predefined relation types. The ontology graph is serialized through Breadth First Search (BFS) algorithm. The special marker "$[S]$" represents the end of each level of BFS. des_i denotes the descriptions of entity type e_i. MGE [25] is used as a baseline to verify the effect of our knowledge enhancement method. (Color figure online)

[1] https://www.wikidata.org.

3.1 Knowledge Source

In the process of human learning professional knowledge, a common practice is to first understand the meaning of each specialized term and then establish the interrelationships between them. Following this pattern, we leverage ontology and entity type descriptions as domain knowledge sources to augment the capacity of entity and relation extraction models to comprehend domain-specific information. Ontology defines the semantic associations among specialized entity types in the domain, while entity type descriptions provide further explanations for each type of specialized terms. For the space science and utilization domain, the ontology is predefined in SSUIE-RE dataset (see Sect. 4.1). We collect the official descriptions of domain-specific entity types from the *China Manned Space* official website[2]. Compared to large-scale pre-training corpora and domain-specific knowledge graphs, ontology and entity type descriptions are more accessible for highly specialized domains like space science and utilization.

3.2 Knowledge Serialization

The ontology is a graph structure, where nodes represent entity types and edges represent relation types. It can be formalized as a directed graph $G = (V, E)$, where $V = \{e_1, e_2, \ldots, e_M\}$ denotes the set of predefined entity types and M is the number of predefined entity types. E denotes a multiset of predefined relation types. Additionally, to enrich the semantic information of the entity type nodes in the graph, we append the corresponding entity type descriptions to each node:

$$V' = \{(e_1, des_1), (e_2, des_2), \ldots, (e_M, des_M)\}, \tag{1}$$

where des_m denotes the descriptions of entity type e_m. Then the resulting new graph with the added entity type descriptions can be represented as $G' = (V', E)$.

To facilitate the integration of ontology graph knowledge into entity and relation extraction models that are typically based on sequences, we serialize it using the Breadth First Search (BFS) algorithm while maintaining the structural and semantic properties of the original graph. The graph is represented as an adjacency list in BFS. Before performing the BFS traversal, we initially sort the nodes based on the frequency of their occurrence as entity types in the dataset. Subsequently, we sort the neighboring nodes and edges based on the sum of the node frequency and the edge frequency. This ensures that the nodes and edges with higher frequency in dataset will be traversed first. Then the sorted adjacency list of G is input into the BFS algorithm. During the BFS traversal, we insert a special marker "[*S*]" at the end of each layer of BFS traversal. Taking the nodes e_1, e_2, and e_3 shown in Fig. 1 as an example, the first special marker denotes the end of traversing the triple types with e_1 as the head entity, while the second special marker denotes the end of traversing the triple types with e_3 as the head entity, which conveys the structural information among the nodes in the graph. Formally, the BFS serialization process is summarized in Algorithm 1. Then we get an ontology sequence s^π of nodes and edges in the order visited by BFS with level markers:

$$s^\pi = \{s_1^\pi, s_2^\pi, \ldots, s_L^\pi\}, \tag{2}$$

where L represents the length of the ontology sequence obtained by BFS traversal.

[2] http://www.cmse.gov.cn.

Algorithm 1. BFS traversal with level markers

Input: A sorted adjacency list of ontology graph $G' = (V', E)$
Output: A list s^π of nodes and edges in the order visited by BFS, with level markers

```
s^π ← empty list
q ← empty queue
Enqueue the first node of G' into q
Mark all the nodes as unvisited
while q is not empty do
    size ← size of q
    for i ← 1 to size do
        v ← dequeue a node from q
        if v is visited then
            break
        end if
        Append v to s^π
        for each unvisited neighbor w of v do
            Enqueue w into q
            Append the edge (v, w) to s^π
            Append w to s^π
        end for
        Append a level marker "[S]" to s^π
        Mark v as visited    // The triple types with v as the head entity type have all been traversed
    end for
end while
return s^π
```

3.3 Knowledge Encoding

The elements in s^π consist of texts with varying lengths, which encompass relation type words, special markers, and texts formed by concatenating entity type words with their corresponding entity type description words. To get a preliminary semantic representations of these texts, we initialize the representation of each element in s^π with a frozen BERT encoder [8] and employ average pooling to unify the feature size. Then we can generate a representation h_k for each element in s^π as follows:

$$h_k = \text{AvgPool}(\text{BERT}_{\text{frozen}}(s_k^\pi)), k \in \{1, 2, \ldots, L\}, \tag{3}$$

where $h_k \in \mathbb{R}^d$ and d is the hidden size of BERT. AvgPool $(\cdot)$ denotes the operation of average pooling. The representations of the whole ontology sequence s^π is concatenated by h_k:

$$H_{s^\pi} = [h_1, h_2, \ldots, h_L], \tag{4}$$

where $H_{s^\pi} \in \mathbb{R}^{L \times d}$. The feature information in H_{s^π} are individually encoded from each element in s^π. To further capture the inherent information in the ontology sequence, we use a Transformer Encoder [20] to obtain the final ontology knowledge representations $H_{know} \in \mathbb{R}^{L \times d}$:

$$H_{know} = \text{TransformerEncoder}(H_{s^\pi}), \tag{5}$$

3.4 Knowledge Fusion

Given the encoded ontology knowledge representations H_{know}, it can be integrated into different downstream entity and relation extraction models for knowledge enhancement. We select the state-of-the-art methods that have performed best on publicly available benchmark datasets in recent years, and then we evaluate these algorithms on the SSUIE-RE dataset (evaluation results are shown in Table 1). We select the MGE model [25], which performs the best on SSUIE-RE, as our baseline for comparison, and infuse ontology knowledge into it to verify the effectiveness of ontology knowledge enhancement. MGE model uses BERT to encode the contextual information of input sentences, and designs a multi-gate encoder (MGE) based on gating mechanism to filter out undesired information and retain desired information, then performs decoding with table-filling module [15]. We infuse ontology knowledge at the position between the BERT layer and MGE layer, as shown in Fig. 1.

We have explored different fusion methods to integrate ontology knowledge representations with input sentence representations, including appending, concatenation and addition. Regarding the appending operation, we concatenate the ontology knowledge representations H_{know} with the input sentence representations along the sequence length dimension. We then apply a self-attention layer to model the guiding effect of ontology knowledge on the extraction of entities and relations from the sentence. The fused representations are calculated as follows:

$$H_{append} = \text{SA}\left([H_b; H_{know}]\right), \tag{6}$$

where SA $(\cdot)$ means the self-attention layer and H_b denotes the input sentence representations extracted by BERT. $[;]$ denotes the operation of appending, that is, concatenating along the sequence length dimension.

In the case of the concatenation and addition fusion methods, a linear transformation is initially employed to unify the feature dimensions. After this step, the input representations H_b and ontology knowledge representations H_{know} are concatenated along the hidden size dimension or added. The concatenation fusion method can be formalized as below:

$$H_{concat} = \text{Concat}\left(H_b, \text{Linear}(H_{know})\right), \tag{7}$$

where Concat $(\cdot)$ means the operation of concatenation along the hidden size dimension and Linear $(\cdot)$ denotes linear transformation. And the fusion method of addition can be formalized as below:

$$H_{add} = H_b + \text{Linear}(H_{know}). \tag{8}$$

Then the representations fused with ontology knowledge is input into the downstream MGE model to obtain the final results of entity and relation extraction.

4 Experiments

4.1 SSUIE-RE Dataset

To evaluate our method, we construct a SSUIE-RE dataset for entity and relation extraction in the space science and utilization domain, which contains rich domain expertise about space science and utilization in the aerospace field. The process of creating SSUIE-RE can be divided into two steps:

Corpora Collection and Preprocessing. The corpora is collected from published professional technical documents in the field, official websites related to China Manned Space Engineering, and Web pages returned by the Google search engine for in-domain professional terms. Before annotation, we preprocess the collected corpora using the following measures:

- We only select Chinese texts and discard texts that are in other languages.
- The invisible characters, spaces and tabs are removed, which are generally meaningless in Chinese.
- In order to eliminate excessively short sentences and incomplete sentences, we split the texts at the Chinese sentence-ending punctuation symbols (e.g., period, question mark, exclamation point), and only retain sentences with more than 10 characters.
- We deduplicate the segmented sentences.

Human Annotation. We invite annotators with related majors in aerospace field to annotate the processed corpora on the brat[3] platform. The brat platform is an online environment for collaborative text annotation. To ensure the annotation quality, pre-labeling is carried out prior to the formal labeling stage, which aims to ensure that all annotators reach a unified and accurate understanding of the labeling rules. During the annotation process, each sentence is annotated by at least two annotators. If there are inconsistent annotations, the annotation team will discuss the corresponding issue and reach a consensus.

Our final constructed dataset contains 19 entity types, 36 relation types, and 66 triple types. The dataset contains 6926 sentences, 58,771 labeled entities and 30,338 labeled relations. We randomly split the dataset into training (80%), development (10%) and test (10%) set.

4.2 Evaluation and Implementation Details

Following standard evaluation protocol, we use precision (Prec.), recall (Rec.), and micro F1 score (F1) to evaluate our model. The results of NER are considered as correct if the entity boundaries and entity types are both predicted correctly. The results of RE are considered correct if the relation types, entity boundaries and entity types are all predicted correctly.

We use the official implementation of the comparison models to evaluate them on the SSUIE-RE dataset. For fair comparison, we adopt *chinese-bert-wwm* [7] as the pre-trained language model for all the models. Our proposed OntoRE model is trained with Adam optimizer for 100 epochs, and the batch size and learning rate are set to be 4 and 2e−5 respectively. The max length of input sentence is set to 300 characters. All the models are trained with a single NVIDIA Titan RTX GPU. The models that achieves the best performance on the development set is selected, and its F1 score on the test set is reported.

[3] https://brat.nlplab.org/.

4.3 Comparison Models

To ensure a rigorous evaluation, we carefully select state-of-the-art algorithms that have demonstrated superior performance on publicly available benchmark datasets in recent years, and then evaluate their performance on the SSUIE-RE dataset. We compare our model with the following models: (1) **TPLinker** [23]: this method formulates the task of joint entity and relation extraction as a token pair linking problem, and introduces a handshaking tagging scheme that aligns the boundary tokens of entity pairs for each relation type. (2) **CasRel** [24]: it models the relations as functions that map subjects to objects rather than discrete labels of entity pairs, allowing for the simultaneous extraction of multiple triples from sentences without the issue of overlapping. (3) **PFN** [26]: this work utilizes a partition filter encoder to produce task-specific features, which enable effective modeling of inter-task interactions and improve the joint entity and relation extraction performance. (4) **PURE** [34]: this study constructs two distinct encoders for NER and RE, respectively, and conducts entity and relation extraction in a pipelined manner. (5) **PL-Marker** [28]: this work is similar to PURE except that it adopts a neighborhood-oriented packing strategy to better model the entity boundary information and a subject-oriented packing strategy to model the interrelation between the same-subject entity pairs. (6) **MGE** [25]: this work designs interaction gates to build bidirectional task interaction and task gates to ensure the specificity of task features, based on gating mechanism.

4.4 Main Result

Table 1 shows the comparison of our model OntoRE with other comparison models on SSUIE-RE dataset. As is shown, OntoRE achieves the best results in terms of relation F1 scores. Although PURE achieves the best performance on NER, its relation F1 score is relatively low due to the pipelined architecture which may encounter error accumulation issues. Similarly, PLMarker, which is also a pipelined method, achieves mediocre

Table 1. Overall results of different methods on SSUIE-RE Dataset. The results of all comparison models are implemented using official code. We use the same *chinese-bert-wwm* [7] pre-trained encoder for all these models. Results of PURE and PL-Marker are reported in single-sentence setting for fair comparison. Results of OntoRE are reported under the utilization of addition fusion method.

Model	NER			RE		
	Prec.(%)	Rec.(%)	F1(%)	Prec.(%)	Rec.(%)	F1(%)
TPLinker [23]	77.0	56.0	64.8	65.3	40.8	50.2
CasRel [24]	-	-	-	57.8	53.5	55.6
PFN [26]	74.9	75.8	75.4	57.8	62.0	59.8
PURE [34]	80.5	80.6	**80.6**	55.0	67.4	60.6
PL-Marker [28]	80.2	62.6	70.3	55.5	33.4	41.7
MGE [25]	75.8	76.3	76.0	60.0	64.2	62.0
OntoRE (Ours)	75.0	78.3	76.6	62.4	64.5	**63.4**

results on the SSUIE-RE dataset. Among other compared joint methods, MGE achieves the best relation extraction F1 score, and is therefore selected as the baseline model for ontology knowledge injection. As we can see in the table, OntoRE achieves an absolute entity F1 improvement of +0.6% and absolute relation F1 improvement of +1.4% compared to MGE, which indicates that the ontology knowledge injection can enhance the performance of entity and relation extraction in highly specialized domain. Further observation reveals that the models with the best performance on general domain datasets may not perform well in specific professional domains, which reflects the necessity of introducing domain knowledge for entity and relation extraction in specialized fields.

4.5 Effect of Domain Knowledge Enhancement

Although our proposed OntoRE achieves the best results on the SSUIE-RE dataset in terms of the overall relation F1 score, in this section, we take a deeper look and further investigate whether OntoRE's integration of domain knowledge essentially improves the model's ability to comprehend domain-specific information.

We observe that the SSUIE-RE dataset includes entity types with varying levels of specialization, ranging from highly specialized entity types (such as *Space Mission*, *Experimental Platform* and *Space Science Field*, etc.) to more general entity types (such as *Person*, *Location*, and *Organisation*, etc.). We refer to the former as in-domain entity types and the latter as general entity types. According to the degree of domain specificity, we categorize 15 out of the 19 entity types defined in the SSUIE-RE dataset as

Table 2. We divide entity types into in-domain and general entity types according to the degree of domain specificity.

Domain Specificity	Entity Types
In-domain (68%)	*Space Mission, Space Station Segment, Space Science Field, Prize, Experimental Platform, Experimental Platform Support System, Experimental System, Experimental System Module, Patent, Criterion, Experimental Project, Experimental Data, Academic Paper, Technical Report, Research Team*
General (32%)	*Organisation, Person, Time, Location*

Table 3. NER results of in-domain and general entity types on SSUIE-RE test set. In-domain entities account for 68% in the dataset, and general entities account for 32%.

Entity Type	Model	**NER**		
		Prec.(%)	Rec.(%)	F1(%)
In-domain (68%)	Baseline	73.4	73.0	73.2
	OntoRE	72.0	75.3	**73.6 (+0.4)**
General (32%)	Baseline	79.6	81.6	80.6
	OntoRE	79.8	83.0	**81.4 (+0.8)**

in-domain entity types, and the remaining 4 as general entity types, as shown in Table 2. Based on this categorization, in-domain entities account for 68% of the total entities in the SSUIE-RE dataset, while general entities account for 32%.

To more accurately evaluate OntoRE's ability to understand domain-specific information, we further differentiate the domain specificity of relation types. A triple type defined in the dataset is composed of a head entity type, a relation type, and a tail entity type in the form of (s, r, o). We assess the degree of domain specificity of a relation type by determining whether the head and tail entities it connects are classified as in-domain entity types, as listed in Table 2. Specifically, we consider a relation to be highly domain-specific when both the head and tail entity types are in-domain. If only one of the two entity types is in-domain and the other is general, the corresponding relation is considered to exhibit weaker domain specificity. Furthermore, relations with head and tail entity types are both general rather than in-domain entity types, are considered to exhibit the weakest domain specificity.

We compare our model with the baseline MGE on the performance of recognizing in-domain and general entities, respectively. And for relation extraction, we compare the performance of our model and baseline in extracting relation types with varying degrees of domain specificity. The experimental results are shown in Table 3 and Table 4.

As shown in Table 3, OntoRE outperforms the baseline in recognizing in-domain and general entity types, with a respective improvement of +0.4% and +0.8% in terms of entity F1 score. Table 4 demonstrates that OntoRE obtains an absolute relation F1 score improvement of +0.5%, +1.5% and 1.7% respectively, as the domain specificity of the relation types increases. The experimental results show that OntoRE improves the performance of extracting relation types with varying degrees of domain specificity, and the benefit of ontology knowledge augmentation is more evident for relations with higher domain specificity. This indicates that the incorporation of ontology knowledge appears to be an effective approach for enhancing the model's ability to understand domain-specialized information, while not weakening its understanding of general information.

4.6 Ablation Study

In this section, we conduct ablation study on the SSUIE-RE dataset to examine the effectiveness of our model, specifically with regard to three factors: knowledge source, knowledge fusion method, and the number of knowledge encoder layers.

Knowledge Source and Fusion Method. We put the two factors of knowledge source and knowledge fusion method together for experimental analysis. For the aspect of knowledge source, we remove the entity type descriptions (denoted as *Des* in Table 5) from the complete OntoRE framework to examine the role of entity type descriptions in knowledge enhancement. For knowledge fusion method, we examine the effects of three fusion methods: appending, concatenation and addition.

Table 5 presents a comparison of the experimental results for different combinations of these factors on the SSUIE-RE dataset. The experimental results show that, under the fusion methods of appending and concatenation, the incorporation of entity

Table 4. RE results of relation types with varying degrees of domain specificity on SSUIE-RE test set. IDE (In-Domain Entity) represents the number of in-domain entity types contained in a triple type according to ontology definition. The proportions of relations with IDE = 0, IDE = 1, and IDE = 2 in the SSUIE-RE dataset are 26%, 11%, and 63%, respectively.

Relation Type	Model	RE		
		Prec.(%)	Rec.(%)	F1(%)
IDE = 0 (26%)	Baseline	68.5	72.2	70.3
	OntoRE	69.7	71.8	**70.8 (+0.5)**
IDE = 1 (11%)	Baseline	55.5	42.7	48.2
	OntoRE	60.5	42.2	**49.7 (+1.5)**
IDE = 2 (63%)	Baseline	56.8	64.6	60.4
	OntoRE	59.3	65.3	**62.1 (+1.7)**

type descriptions improves NER F1 scores by 1.4% and 1.4% respectively. However, under the addition fusion method, there is a slight decrease in NER F1 score. This can be attributed to the need for compressing the dimension of the entity type description tensor to match the input sentence tensor before addition, leading to information loss. Across all three fusion methods, the inclusion of entity type descriptions consistently improve the relation F1 scores. Additionally, when using the same combination of knowledge sources, the performance of the appending and concatenation fusion methods is comparable, while the addition fusion method achieves the best relation F1 score. This suggests that the optimal approach is to employ ontology and entity type descriptions as knowledge sources and use the addition fusion method to integrate knowledge representations into the model.

Number of Knowledge Encoder Layers. In the knowledge encoding stage, we utilize Transformer encoder to encode the serialized ontology knowledge, as described in Sect. 3.3. We conduct ablation study to investigate whether stacking multiple layers of encoders could improve the model performance. Considering the parameter size of

Table 5. Ablation study on SSUIE-RE for knowledge source and knowledge fusion method. *Des* denotes entity type descriptions.

Knowledge Source	Fusion Method	NER			RE		
		Prec. (%)	Rec. (%)	F1 (%)	Prec. (%)	Rec. (%)	F1 (%)
Ontology	Append	71.3	77.9	74.5	61.0	62.2	61.6
Ontology	Concat.	72.9	78.3	75.5	61.3	64.4	62.8
Ontology	Add	74.2	79.4	76.7	62.2	64.4	63.3
Ontology + *Des*	Append	73.3	78.8	75.9	60.6	65.4	62.9
Ontology + *Des*	Concat.	75.7	78.0	76.9	63.0	63.0	63.0
Ontology + *Des*	Add	75.0	78.3	76.6	62.4	64.5	**63.4**

Transformer encoder, we only experiment with encoder layers up to three. As shown in Table 6, using two layers of Transformer encoders achieved the best performance (which we employed in our final model), and further stacking of encoders does not result in additional performance improvements.

Table 6. Ablation study on SSUIE-RE for the number of knowledge encoder layers.

Knowledge Encoder Layers	NER			RE		
	Prec.(%)	Rec.(%)	F1(%)	Prec.(%)	Rec.(%)	F1(%)
L = 1	70.6	80.8	75.3	58.4	64.9	61.5
L = 2	75.0	78.3	76.6	62.4	64.5	**63.4**
L = 3	75.0	77.7	76.4	61.1	62.0	61.5

5 Conclusion

In this work, we propose an ontology-enhanced method for joint entity and relation extraction in space science and utilization domain. Our model utilizes ontology and entity type descriptions as sources of domain knowledge, and incorporate them into downstream model to enhance model's comprehension of domain-specific information. We introduce a new dataset, SSUIE-RE, which contains rich domain-specialized knowledge. Experimental results on SSUIE-RE demonstrate that our approach outperforms previous state-of-the-art methods. Moreover, we conduct a detailed analysis of the extraction of entities and relations with different degrees of domain specificity and validate the effectiveness of ontology knowledge enhancement. Overall, our proposed method provides a promising direction for improving the performance of entity and relation extraction in specialized domains with limited resources. In the future, we would like to further explore how to generalize the ontology knowledge enhancement idea to other domain-specific information extraction tasks.

Acknowledgements. This work was supported by the National Defense Science and Technology Key Laboratory Fund Project of the Chinese Academy of Sciences: Space Science and Application of Big Data Knowledge Graph Construction and Intelligent Application Research and Manned Space Engineering Project: Research on Technology and Method of Engineering Big Data Knowledge Mining.

References

1. Alsentzer, E., et al.: Publicly available clinical BERT embeddings. In: Proceedings of the 2nd Clinical Natural Language Processing Workshop, Minneapolis, Minnesota, USA, June 2019, pp. 72–78. Association for Computational Linguistics (2019). https://doi.org/10.18653/v1/W19-1909. https://aclanthology.org/W19-1909
2. Araci, D.: FinBERT: financial sentiment analysis with pre-trained language models. arXiv preprint arXiv:1908.10063 (2019)

3. Aronson, A.R., Lang, F.M.: An overview of MetaMap: historical perspective and recent advances. J. Am. Med. Inform. Assoc. **17**(3), 229–236 (2010)
4. Bodenreider, O.: The unified medical language system (UMLS): integrating biomedical terminology. Nucleic Acids Res. **32**(suppl_1), D267–D270 (2004)
5. Chalkidis, I., Fergadiotis, M., Malakasiotis, P., Aletras, N., Androutsopoulos, I.: LEGAL-BERT: the Muppets straight out of law school. In: Findings of the Association for Computational Linguistics: EMNLP 2020, Online, November 2020, pp. 2898–2904. Association for Computational Linguistics (2020). https://doi.org/10.18653/v1/2020.findings-emnlp.261. https://aclanthology.org/2020.findings-emnlp.261
6. Chan, Y.S., Roth, D.: Exploiting syntactico-semantic structures for relation extraction. In: Proceedings of the 49th Annual Meeting of the Association for Computational Linguistics: Human Language Technologies, Portland, Oregon, USA, June 2011, pp. 551–560. Association for Computational Linguistics (2011). https://aclanthology.org/P11-1056
7. Cui, Y., Che, W., Liu, T., Qin, B., Yang, Z.: Pre-training with whole word masking for Chinese BERT. IEEE Trans. Audio Speech Lang. Process. (2021). https://doi.org/10.1109/TASLP.2021.3124365. https://ieeexplore.ieee.org/document/9599397
8. Devlin, J., Chang, M.W., Lee, K., Toutanova, K.: BERT: pre-training of deep bidirectional transformers for language understanding. In: Proceedings of the 2019 Conference of the North American Chapter of the Association for Computational Linguistics: Human Language Technologies, Volume 1 (Long and Short Papers), Minneapolis, Minnesota, June 2019, pp. 4171–4186. Association for Computational Linguistics (2019). https://doi.org/10.18653/v1/N19-1423. https://aclanthology.org/N19-1423
9. Gormley, M.R., Yu, M., Dredze, M.: Improved relation extraction with feature-rich compositional embedding models. In: Proceedings of the 2015 Conference on Empirical Methods in Natural Language Processing, Lisbon, Portugal, September 2015, pp. 1774–1784 (2015). Association for Computational Linguistics (2015). https://doi.org/10.18653/v1/D15-1205. https://aclanthology.org/D15-1205
10. Gu, Y., et al.: Domain-specific language model pretraining for biomedical natural language processing. ACM Trans. Comput. Healthc. (HEALTH) **3**(1), 1–23 (2021)
11. Lai, T., Ji, H., Zhai, C., Tran, Q.H.: Joint biomedical entity and relation extraction with knowledge-enhanced collective inference. In: Proceedings of the 59th Annual Meeting of the Association for Computational Linguistics and the 11th International Joint Conference on Natural Language Processing (Volume 1: Long Papers), Online, August 2021, pp. 6248–6260. Association for Computational Linguistics (2021). https://doi.org/10.18653/v1/2021.acl-long.488. https://aclanthology.org/2021.acl-long.488
12. Lee, J., et al.: BioBERT: a pre-trained biomedical language representation model for biomedical text mining. Bioinformatics **36**(4), 1234–1240 (2020)
13. Li, Q., Ji, H.: Incremental joint extraction of entity mentions and relations. In: Proceedings of the 52nd Annual Meeting of the Association for Computational Linguistics (Volume 1: Long Papers), Baltimore, Maryland, June 2014, pp. 402–412. Association for Computational Linguistics (2014). https://doi.org/10.3115/v1/P14-1038. https://aclanthology.org/P14-1038
14. Lin, Y., Liu, Z., Sun, M., Liu, Y., Zhu, X.: Learning entity and relation embeddings for knowledge graph completion. In: Twenty-Ninth AAAI Conference on Artificial Intelligence (2015)
15. Miwa, M., Sasaki, Y.: Modeling joint entity and relation extraction with table representation. In: Proceedings of the 2014 Conference on Empirical Methods in Natural Language Processing (EMNLP), Doha, Qatar, October 2014, pp. 1858–1869. Association for Computational Linguistics (2014). https://doi.org/10.3115/v1/D14-1200. https://aclanthology.org/D14-1200
16. Nayak, T., Ng, H.T.: Effective modeling of encoder-decoder architecture for joint entity and relation extraction. In: Proceedings of AAAI (2020)

17. Peng, Y., Yan, S., Lu, Z.: Transfer learning in biomedical natural language processing: an evaluation of BERT and ELMo on ten benchmarking datasets. In: Proceedings of the 18th BioNLP Workshop and Shared Task, Florence, Italy, August 2019, pp. 58–65. Association for Computational Linguistics (2019). https://doi.org/10.18653/v1/W19-5006. https://aclanthology.org/W19-5006
18. Radford, A., Narasimhan, K., Salimans, T., Sutskever, I., et al.: Improving language understanding by generative pre-training (2018)
19. Roy, A., Pan, S.: Incorporating medical knowledge in BERT for clinical relation extraction. In: Proceedings of the 2021 Conference on Empirical Methods in Natural Language Processing, Online and Punta Cana, Dominican Republic, November 2021, pp. 5357–5366. Association for Computational Linguistics (2021). https://doi.org/10.18653/v1/2021.emnlp-main.435. https://aclanthology.org/2021.emnlp-main.435
20. Vaswani, A., et al.: Attention is all you need. In: Advances in Neural Information Processing Systems, vol. 30 (2017)
21. Wang, J., Lu, W.: Two are better than one: joint entity and relation extraction with table-sequence encoders. In: Proceedings of the 2020 Conference on Empirical Methods in Natural Language Processing (EMNLP), Online, November 2020, pp. 1706–1721. Association for Computational Linguistics (2020). https://doi.org/10.18653/v1/2020.emnlp-main.133. https://aclanthology.org/2020.emnlp-main.133
22. Wang, S., Zhang, Y., Che, W., Liu, T.: Joint extraction of entities and relations based on a novel graph scheme. In: IJCAI, Yokohama, pp. 4461–4467 (2018)
23. Wang, Y., Yu, B., Zhang, Y., Liu, T., Zhu, H., Sun, L.: TPLinker: single-stage joint extraction of entities and relations through token pair linking. In: Proceedings of the 28th International Conference on Computational Linguistics, Barcelona, Spain (Online), December 2020, pp. 1572–1582. International Committee on Computational Linguistics (2020). https://doi.org/10.18653/v1/2020.coling-main.138. https://aclanthology.org/2020.coling-main.138
24. Wei, Z., Su, J., Wang, Y., Tian, Y., Chang, Y.: A novel cascade binary tagging framework for relational triple extraction. In: Proceedings of the 58th Annual Meeting of the Association for Computational Linguistics, Online, July 2020, pp. 1476–1488. Association for Computational Linguistics (2020). https://doi.org/10.18653/v1/2020.acl-main.136. https://aclanthology.org/2020.acl-main.136
25. Xiong, X., Yunfei, L., Anqi, L., Shuai, G., Shengyang, L.: A multi-gate encoder for joint entity and relation extraction. In: Proceedings of the 21st Chinese National Conference on Computational Linguistics, Nanchang, China, October 2022, pp. 848–860. Chinese Information Processing Society of China (2022). https://aclanthology.org/2022.ccl-1.75
26. Yan, Z., Zhang, C., Fu, J., Zhang, Q., Wei, Z.: A partition filter network for joint entity and relation extraction. In: Proceedings of the 2021 Conference on Empirical Methods in Natural Language Processing, Online and Punta Cana, Dominican Republic, November 2021, pp. 185–197. Association for Computational Linguistics (2021). https://doi.org/10.18653/v1/2021.emnlp-main.17. https://aclanthology.org/2021.emnlp-main.17
27. Yang, S., Zhang, Y., Niu, G., Zhao, Q., Pu, S.: Entity concept-enhanced few-shot relation extraction. In: Proceedings of the 59th Annual Meeting of the Association for Computational Linguistics and the 11th International Joint Conference on Natural Language Processing (Volume 2: Short Papers), Online, August 2021, pp. 987–991. Association for Computational Linguistics (2021). https://doi.org/10.18653/v1/2021.acl-short.124. https://aclanthology.org/2021.acl-short.124
28. Ye, D., Lin, Y., Li, P., Sun, M.: Packed levitated marker for entity and relation extraction. In: Proceedings of the 60th Annual Meeting of the Association for Computational Linguistics (Volume 1: Long Papers), Dublin, Ireland, May 2022, pp. 4904–4917. Association for Computational Linguistics (2022). https://doi.org/10.18653/v1/2022.acl-long.337. https://aclanthology.org/2022.acl-long.337

29. Yu, B., et al.: Joint extraction of entities and relations based on a novel decomposition strategy. In: Proceedings of ECAI (2020)
30. Yu, X., Lam, W.: Jointly identifying entities and extracting relations in encyclopedia text via a graphical model approach. In: Coling 2010: Posters, Beijing, China, August 2010, pp. 1399–1407. Coling 2010 Organizing Committee (2010). https://aclanthology.org/C10-2160
31. Zeng, X., Zeng, D., He, S., Liu, K., Zhao, J.: Extracting relational facts by an end-to-end neural model with copy mechanism. In: Proceedings of the 56th Annual Meeting of the Association for Computational Linguistics (Volume 1: Long Papers), Melbourne, Australia, July 2018, pp. 506–514. Association for Computational Linguistics (2018). https://doi.org/10.18653/v1/P18-1047. https://aclanthology.org/P18-1047
32. Zhang, S., Ng, P., Wang, Z., Xiang, B.: REKnow: enhanced knowledge for joint entity and relation extraction. In: NAACL 2022 Workshop on SUKI (2022). https://www.amazon.science/publications/reknow-enhanced-knowledge-for-joint-entity-and-relation-extraction
33. Zheng, S., Wang, F., Bao, H., Hao, Y., Zhou, P., Xu, B.: Joint extraction of entities and relations based on a novel tagging scheme. In: Proceedings of the 55th Annual Meeting of the Association for Computational Linguistics (Volume 1: Long Papers), Vancouver, Canada, July 2017, pp. 1227–1236. Association for Computational Linguistics (2017). https://doi.org/10.18653/v1/P17-1113. https://aclanthology.org/P17-1113
34. Zhong, Z., Chen, D.: A frustratingly easy approach for entity and relation extraction. In: Proceedings of the 2021 Conference of the North American Chapter of the Association for Computational Linguistics: Human Language Technologies, Online, June 2021, pp. 50–61. Association for Computational Linguistics (2021). https://doi.org/10.18653/v1/2021.naacl-main.5. https://aclanthology.org/2021.naacl-main.5
35. Zhou, G., Su, J., Zhang, J., Zhang, M.: Exploring various knowledge in relation extraction. In: Proceedings of the 43rd Annual Meeting of the Association for Computational Linguistics, Ann Arbor, Michigan, June 2005, ACL 2005, pp. 427–434. Association for Computational Linguistics (2005). https://doi.org/10.3115/1219840.1219893. https://aclanthology.org/P05-1053

Machine Translation and Multilingual Information Processing

FACT: A Dynamic Framework for Adaptive Context-Aware Translation

Linqing Chen(✉) and Weilei Wang

PatSnap Co., LTD., Suzhou, China
{chenlinqing,wangweilei}@patsnap.com

Abstract. Document-level neural machine translation (NMT) has garnered considerable attention since the emergence of various context-aware NMT models. However, these static NMT models are trained on fixed parallel datasets, thus lacking awareness of the target document during inference. In order to alleviate this limitation, we propose a dynamic adapter-translator framework for context-aware NMT, which adapts the trained NMT model to the input document prior to translation. Specifically, the document adapter reconstructs the scrambled portion of the original document from a deliberately corrupted version, thereby reducing the performance disparity between training and inference. To achieve this, we employ an adaptation process in both the training and inference stages. Our experimental results on document-level translation benchmarks demonstrate significant enhancements in translation performance, underscoring the necessity of dynamic adaptation for context-aware translation and the efficacy of our methodologies.

Keywords: Machine Translation · Context-aware Translation · Dynamic Translation

1 Introduction

Numerous recent studies have introduced a variety of context-aware models aiming to effectively harness document-level context either from the source side [1–6], target side [13,14,21], or both [15–19]. In the prevailing practice, a context-aware model remains fixed after training and is then employed for every testing document. Nonetheless, this approach presents a potential challenge, as the model is required to encapsulate all translation knowledge, particularly from diverse domains, within a predefined set of parameters. Accomplishing this task within the confines of reality poses a formidable undertaking.

The "one sentence one model" approach for sentence-level NMT, as proposed by [20], aims to familiarize the model with each sentence in the test dataset by fine-tuning the NMT model for every testing sentence. However, acquiring suitable fine-tuning sentences for a given testing sentence proves to be highly time-consuming, as they require meticulous extraction from the bilingual training data through similarity search. This presents a significant challenge when

M. Sun et al. (Eds.): CCL 2023, LNAI 14232, pp. 255–270, 2023.
https://doi.org/10.1007/978-981-99-6207-5_16

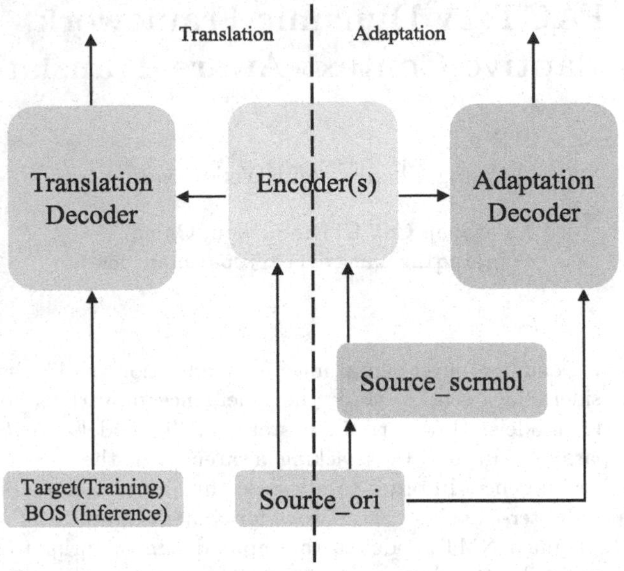

Fig. 1. The figure presented in this section depicts the adapter-translator architecture designed for context-aware neural machine translation. In this architecture, the encoder(s) are shared between the adapter denoted as ϕ and the translator denoted as ψ. It is important to note that the translator and adapter constitute two distinct stages within the same model, rather than being treated as separate models.

attempting to replicate their methodology by seeking similar documents from the bilingual document-level training data. Moreover, this approach assesses sentence similarity solely based on the Levenshtein distance, thereby disregarding the document-level context of these sentences extracted from distinct documents.

To address the potential challenge of employing a fixed, trained model for all testing documents, we propose the "one document one model" approach in this paper. This alternative approach aims to achieve the objective by introducing the *document adapter*. Unlike other methods, the adapter relies solely on the input document itself and does not require additional input forms. Its primary function is to reconstruct the original document from a deliberately corrupted version, thereby enabling the model to familiarize itself with the task of document-level translation. Notably, this approach differs from previous methods where the input and output are in different languages, as opposed to the same language. Following adaptation, this modified model is utilized to translate the document.

Both the adapter model and the NMT model employed in our study are context-aware and utilize shared encoder(s), while each having its dedicated decoder. In this paper, we present a training methodology that aims to adapt a pre-trained NMT model to a specific document through a process of alternating document reconstruction and document translation for each document batch. This approach is employed during both the training and inference stages. To

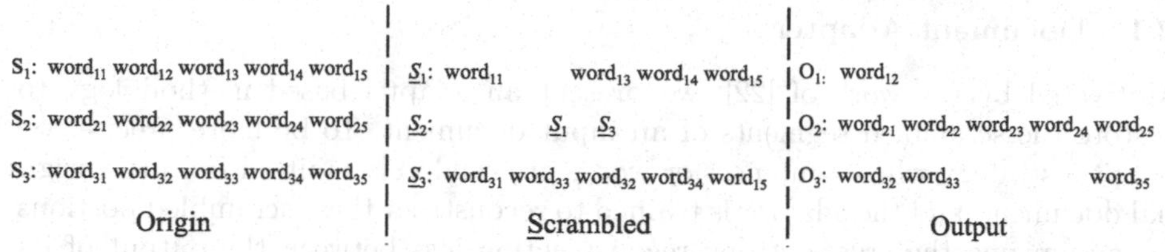

Fig. 2. Illustration of document reconstruction task.

evaluate the effectiveness of our proposed approach, we conducted experiments on three English-to-German document-level translation tasks. The results reveal significant enhancements in translation performance, providing strong evidence for the necessity of employing a one document one model approach and the efficacy of our proposed methodology.

Overall, we make the following contributions.

- We present an enhanced context-aware document-level auto-encoder task to facilitate dynamic adaptation of translation models.
- We propose an adapter-translator framework for context-aware NMT. To the best of our knowledge, this is the first study that investigates the one-document-one-model approach specifically for document-level NMT.

2 Adapter-Translator Architecture

The Adapter-Translator architecture entails an iterative procedure involving an adaptation process denoted as ϕ and a translation process denoted as ψ. Figure 1 presents a visual representation of the proposed architecture. The translator ψ, which is a context-aware NMT model, comprises context-aware encoder(s) and a decoder specific to translation.[1] The adapter shares the encoder(s) with the translator while possessing a decoder specifically designed for adaptation. Given a source document $\mathcal{X}$, the corpus processing script generates a deliberately corrupted version $\widehat{\mathcal{X}}$ of the document. This corrupted version is then utilized to optimize the adapter in order to reconstruct the scrambled segments of the original document $\mathcal{X}$. As the encoder(s) are shared between the adapter and the translator, the capability to capture context during document adaptation can also be harnessed during the document translation process. The translation component of this architecture resembles that of other document-level translation models. Due to its straightforward yet impactful architecture, the proposed method can be employed with diverse document-level translation models.

[1] It is worth noting that while not all context-aware NMT models possess an additional context encoder [23], the adapter-translator architecture can still be adapted to accommodate these models.

2.1 Document Adapter

Motivated by the work of [22], we present an adapter-based methodology to restore the scrambled segments of an input document. To be more precise, we adopt a strategy where sentences or words are randomly omitted from the original document, and the adapter is trained to reconstruct these scrambled portions by minimizing the cross-entropy reconstruction loss between the output of its decoder and the corresponding correct part of the original document.

Given a document $\mathcal{X} = (X_i)\,|_{i=1}^{N}$ consisting of N sentences, we apply token substitution, insertion, and deletion operations to each sentence X_i. Following the approach of BERT [37], we randomly select 15% of the tokens. However, unlike BERT, we do not replace these tokens with [MASK] tokens. Instead, the adapter is responsible for identifying the positions that require correct inputs. Furthermore, we do not preserve 10% of the selected tokens unchanged, as our method does not rely on the [MASK] token. In our experiments, we observed that compared to generating the entire original document, generating only the corrected scrambled part significantly reduced the computational time. Nevertheless, this modification did not significantly compromise the model's ability to capture context and become familiar with the document to be translated.

Figure 2 depicts an example involving 3 sentences in the original document. In this example, the first sentence undergoes a word deletion operation, while the third sentence experiences word scrambling and replacement operations. The scrambled preceding and succeeding sentences serve as context for the second sentence. The adapter produces the missing words in the first sentence, the corrected words in the third sentence, and the complete second sentence. While our document reconstruction task draws inspiration from the similar proposal in [37], there exist two significant distinctions. Firstly, instead of substituting selected words with `[MASK]` tokens, we introduce contextual document corruption by allowing token substitution, insertion, and deletion. Secondly, in contrast to BERT, our training objective simultaneously considers the utilization of both sentence-level and document-level context.

To summarize, we define the document adaptation task by employing the following two sub-tasks:

- Sentence-level: The adapter generates corrected words based on a deliberately scrambled version of the original sentence.
- Document-level: The adapter utilizes the concatenated context sentences to generate the original sentences.

2.2 Context-Aware Translator

The context-aware translation model in our framework is designed as a relatively independent model, which shares the encoder(s) with the adaptation model while having a dedicated decoder for translation. This design ensures the flexibility of the framework, allowing it to be easily integrated with different translation models by simply incorporating the adapter model's encoder.

Table 1. Performance on test sets. + Adapter indicates we use our proposed context-aware adapter to guidance the context-aware encoder. Significance test [25] shows that the improvement achieved by our approach is significant at 0.05 on almost all of the above models.

#	Model	TED		News		Europarl		Average	
		BLEU	Meteor	BLEU	Meteor	BLEU	Meteor	BLEU	Meteor
1	DocT [2]	24.00	44.69	23.08	42.40	29.32	46.72	25.47	44.60
2	+ Adapter	24.70	45.20	23.68	43.01	29.84	47.15	26.07	45.12
3	HAN [3]	24.58	45.48	25.03	44.02	28.60	46.09	26.07	45.20
4	+ Adapter	24.90	45.89	25.51	44.38	29.07	46.61	26.49	45.63
5	SAN [17]	24.42	45.26	24.84	44.17	29.75	47.22	26.34	45.55
6	+ Adapter	24.80	45.69	25.24	44.63	30.11	48.20	26.72	46.17
7	QCN [24]	25.19	46.09	22.37	41.88	29.82	47.86	25.79	45.28
8	+ Adapter	25.83	46.80	22.89	42.40	30.32	48.35	26.35	45.85
9	GCNMT [19]	25.81	46.33	25.32	44.35	29.80	47.77	26.98	46.15
10	+ Adapter	26.50	46.96	25.71	44.83	30.43	48.46	27.55	46.75
11	Transformer [8]	23.02	43.66	22.03	41.37	28.65	45.83	24.57	43.62

From a structural perspective, this approach facilitates the applicability of the framework to a wide range of translation models. However, in terms of translation performance, there are significant differences between the output of the adaptation phase and the translation phase. Sharing the decoder between these two phases may introduce bias towards shorter output text during translation, given the relatively short length of the corrected scrambled part produced in the adaptation phase. Furthermore, sharing the decoders may increase the vocabulary size of the translation model decoding end and the dimension of the vector, thereby increase the computational cost of training and inference. Additionally, changes in the decoder's vocabulary may alter the semantic space of the translation model, necessitating retraining even if a well-trained translation model is available.

As discussed earlier, the adapter model's decoder only generates the corrected part of the original document. Therefore, employing two different decoders does not significantly impact the time required during the translation inference phase.

2.3 Training and Inference

During the model training phase, the framework follows different procedures based on whether it is built upon a pre-trained translation model or trained from scratch. When using a pre-trained model, the parameters of the translator are frozen, and only the decoder part of the adapter is trained. In the case of training from scratch, parallel corpora are employed as input and output for the translator, while the source corpus and its scrambled versions are used as input and output for the adapter. Training is performed iteratively, alternating between the translation and reconstruction tasks.

Table 2. Performance on ZH-EN test sets with and without the context-aware adapter is presented in this Table. The "+Adapter" indicates that our proposed context-aware adapter was used to guide the context-aware encoder. Significance testing [25] demonstrates that the improvements achieved by our approach are statistically significant at the 0.05 level for almost all of the aforementioned models.

#	Model	MT06	MT02	MT03	MT04	MT05	MT08	All		
		BLEU	BLEU	BLEU	BLEU	BLEU	BLEU	BLEU	Meteor	d-BLEU
1	DocT [2]	37.08	43.40	43.83	41.51	41.79	32.47	40.35	27.45	42.91
2	+ Adapter	38.65	44.57	44.17	42.80	43.19	33.75	41.52	28.66	44.07
3	HAN [3]	37.20	42.96	44.53	41.89	42.31	32.57	40.83	28.00	43.28
4	+ Adapter	38.11	43.62	45.99	43.51	43.03	33.91	42.47	29.49	45.10
5	SAN [17]	37.40	43.28	44.82	41.99	42.60	32.46	41.01	28.19	43.54
6	+ Adapter	**39.62**	**45.37**	46.72	**43.91**	43.59	**34.48**	**42.93**	**30.01**	**45.38**
7	GCNMT [19]	38.39	44.33	46.43	42.92	43.60	33.41	41.51	28.73	44.08
8	+ Adapter	39.51	45.28	**47.26**	43.70	**44.56**	34.27	42.43	29.50	44.96
9	Transformer [8]	36.27	42.71	43.51	41.25	41.07	31.54	39.64	26.70	42.16

In the framework's inference phase, the decoders of both the translator and adapter are frozen for two primary reasons. Firstly, these decoders have undergone sufficient training during the training phase. Secondly, freezing them saves computational time during inference. Similarly, a certain percentage (P%) of the context-aware encoder parameters are also frozen for similar reasons. This not only reduces computational overhead but also facilitates multi-round learning by utilizing multiple scrambled versions of the same document, enabling the translation model to become familiar with the document to be translated. By freezing most of the encoder parameters and increasing the dropout rate, overfitting on a single document is mitigated, preventing potential performance degradation on other documents in the test set.

Specifically, the document restoration process consists of the following steps:

1. Expansion of $\mathcal{X}$: We expand the original document $\mathcal{X}$ by creating K copies, where K is the expansion ratio. Each copy is processed independently, forming instances for the document restoration task.
2. Freezing of Translator and Adapter Parameters: We freeze a portion of the parameters in both the translator and adapter. The dropout rate is set to 0.2, while P% (the percentage of frozen context-aware encoder parameters) is set to 99%.
3. Training the Context-Aware Model: We utilize the corrupted instances to train the context-aware model, which follows the adapter-translator architecture, with the aim of familiarizing it with the document. This involves updating part of the parameters in the context-aware encoder(s). During adaptation, the learning rate is set to 0.1.
4. Document Translation: We employ the adapted model to translate the original document $\mathcal{X}$. This entails utilizing the updated parameters in the context encoder and the sentence encoder to encode the source sentences, and employing the translator decoder to decode the target sentences.

3 Application to Various Document-Level NMT Model

To evaluate the effectiveness of our proposed framework in context-aware NMT, we select the following five representative NMT models:

- DocT [2]: This model considers two previous sentences as context. It employs a document-aware transformer that incorporates context representations into both the sentence encoder and decoder.
- HAN [3]: HAN leverages all previous source and target sentences as context and introduces a hierarchical attention network to capture structured and dynamic context. The context representations are then fed into the decoder.
- SAN [17]: SAN extends the context coverage to the entire document. It adopts sparse attention to selectively attend to relevant sentences and focuses on key words within those sentences.
- MCN [5]: MCN employs an encoder to generate local and global contexts from the entire document, enabling the model to understand inter-sentential dependencies and maximize the utilization of contextual information.
- GCNMT [19]: GCNMT comprises a global context encoder, a sentence encoder, and a sentence decoder. It incorporates two types of global context to enhance translation performance.

All of these models utilize a context encoder to encode global or local contexts, thereby improving document-level translation performance. To apply our proposed adapter-translator architecture to these models, we introduce an adapter decoder.

4 Experimentation

4.1 Settings

Datasets and Evaluation Metrics. We conduct experiments on English-to-German (EN→DE) translation tasks in three different domains: talks, news, and speeches. Additionally, we evaluate our proposed framework for the Chinese-to-English translation task.

- TED: This dataset is obtained from the IWSLT 2017 MT track [26]. We combine test2016 and test2017 as our test set, while the remaining data is used as the development set.
- News: This dataset is derived from the News Commentary v11 corpus. We use news-test2015 and news-test2016 as the development set and test set, respectively.
- Europarl: This dataset is extracted from the Europarl v7 corpus. We randomly split the corpus to obtain the training, development, and test sets.
- For ZH-EN: The training set consists of 41K documents with 780K sentence pairs.[2] We use the NIST MT 2006 dataset as the development set and the NIST

[2] It consists of LDC2002T01, LDC2004T07, LDC2005T06, LDC2005T10, LDC2009T02, LDC2009T15, LDC2010T03.

Table 3. Statistics of the training, development, and test sets of the three translation tasks.

Set	TED		News	
	#SubDoc	#Sent	#SubDoc	#Sent
Training	7,491	206,126	10,552	236,287
Dev	326	8,967	112	2,169
Test	87	2,271	184	2,999
Set	Europarl			
	#SubDoc	#Sent		
Training	132,721	1,666,904		
Dev	273	3,587		
Test	415	5,134		

Table 4. Averaged performance with respect to different data expansion ratio in infering stage.

K	BLEU	Meteor
0	26.98	46.15
1	27.33	46.50
5	27.55	46.75
10	27.41	46.50
15	27.13	46.32

MT 02, 03, 04, 05, and 08 datasets as the test sets. The Chinese sentences are segmented using Jieba, while the English sentences are tokenized and converted to lowercase using Moses scripts.

We obtained the three document-level translation datasets from [17].[3] For the source-side English sentences, we segmented them using the corresponding BPE model trained on the training data. Meanwhile, for the target-side German sentences, we used the BPE model with 25K operations trained on the corresponding target-side data. Table 3 provides a summary of the statistics for the three translation tasks. It should be noted that we divided long documents into sub-documents containing at most 30 sentences to enable efficient training.

Model Settings. For all translation models, we have set the hidden size to 512 and the filter size to 2048. The number of heads in the multi-head attention mechanism is 8, and the dropout rate is 0.1. During the training phase, we train the models for 100K steps using four A100 GPUs, with a batch size of 40960 tokens. We employ the Adam optimizer [27] with $\beta_1 = 0.9$, $\beta_2 = 0.98$, and a learning rate of 1, incorporating a warm-up step of 16K. As for the fine-tuning

[3] https://github.com/sameenmaruf/selective-attn/tree/master/data.

stage, we fine-tune the models for 40K steps on a single A100 GPU, with a batch size of 40960 tokens, a learning rate of 0.3, and a warm-up step of 4K. During the inference phase, we set the beam size to 5.

4.2 Experimental Results

We utilize two evaluation metrics, BLEU [28] and Meteor [29], to assess the quality of translation. The results, presented in Table 1, demonstrate that our proposed approach consistently achieves state-of-the-art performance, outperforming previous context-aware NMT models on average. We observe significant improvements across all datasets by adapting the NMT model to the characteristics of each input document. Of particular note is the comparison between models #9 and #10, where our approach demonstrates a notable improvement with a gain of +0.57 in BLEU and +0.60 in Meteor.

Table 2 showcases the performance results for Chinese-English translation. The table presents the BLEU scores for each sub-test set and the average Meteor score across all sets. The results demonstrate that our proposed adapter-translator framework consistently achieves state-of-the-art performance when compared to the original versions of previous context-aware NMT models. Moreover, we consistently observed improvements across all datasets by adapting the trained NMT model to fit each input document. For instance, comparing models #8 and #7, our approach achieves an improvement with a gain of +0.92 in BLEU, +0.77 in Meteor, and +0.88 in d-BLEU.

Effect of Hyper-Parameter K in Dynamic Translation. In the inference stage, the expansion ratio is an important hyperparameter for dynamic translation. A low ratio may restrict the effectiveness of adaptation in parameter optimization, whereas a high ratio may lead to overfitting of the model to the document restoration task. As indicated in Table 4, we observe that the optimal performance is attained with a ratio of 5 for the EN-DE translation task using the GCNMT model.

5 Analysis and Discussion

In this section, we employ the Chinese-to-English translation task as a representative to offer additional evidence for the efficacy of our proposed framework. In addition to reporting s-BLEU, we also present case-insensitive document-level BLEU (d-BLEU) scores.

5.1 Effect of Adapting Task

In a previous study (Li et al., 2020), it was suggested that context encoders not only utilize context to guide models but also encode noise. Therefore, the improvement in translation quality can sometimes be attributed to enhanced model robustness. The authors discovered that two context-aware models exhibited superior performance during inference even when the context input was replaced with noise. To ascertain whether our framework genuinely benefits from the document adaptation task, we compare the experimental results with and without an adapter in a Chinese-to-English translation task.

Table 5. Performance on ZH-EN test sets of effectiveness of adapting process.

Context	s-BLEU	d-BLEU	Meteor
HAN [3]	40.83	43.28	28.00
Fake adapting	39.35	42.00	26.29
Noisy adapting	40.80	43.55	28.33
ours	**42.47**	**45.10**	**29.49**

Table 6. Performance on ZH-EN test sets of sharing the sentence encoder, the context encoder, or both.

Share	s-BLEU	d-BLEU	Meteor
Sentence encoder	41.59	44.19	28.40
Context encoder	41.55	44.13	28.42
Both	**42.47**	**45.10**	**29.49**

We conducted an investigation on the impact of adapting a document prior to translation. We define **Fake adapting** as the process wherein nonsensical words are employed as the target output during the model's adaptation phase, and **Noisy adapting** as the process wherein the model employs shuffled noisy sentences as input and corrects portions of these sentences as output. The results in Table 5 demonstrate that our proposed framework achieves improvements of +3.12 and +1.67 compared to Fake adapting and Noisy adapting, respectively. Furthermore, a notable performance disparity is observed between the results of Fake adapting and Noisy adapting. The adapter that employs shuffled documents as input achieves a gain of +1.45 compared to Fake adapting, indicating that document adaptation indeed has a positive effect on the translation model.

5.2 Architecture of the Adapter

As elaborated in Sect. 2 on the **Adapter-Translator Architecture**, our proposed framework employs shared encoder(s) for both the adaptation process and translation process. It is worth noting that some previous context-aware models have utilized multiple encoders. To determine whether this architecture is the optimal choice for our research objectives, we investigated the impact of the adapter architecture on the translation model's performance.

In our framework, the encoder(s) are shared between the adapter and translator; however, the effectiveness of each encoder remains uncertain. To explore this, we conducted experiments and present the results in Table 6. The table demonstrates that sharing either the sentence encoder, the context decoder, or both leads to significant improvements in translation performance. These findings align with our intuition, and we observe that sharing both encoders yields the best performance, as indicated in the first row of the table. A possible explanation for these results is that sharing both encoders maximizes the preservation and exchange of information acquired during the reconstruction process in the adaptation phase, specifically concerning the test document.

Table 7. Performance of different document adapting task on ZH-EN translation task.

Task	s-BLEU	d-BLEU	Meteor
Translation	41.30	44.00	28.01
Masked sentences	41.98	44.60	28.33
Ours	**42.47**	**45.10**	**29.49**

Table 8. Evaluation on pronoun translations of ZH-EN.

Model	Pronoun
Transformer	68.68
GCNMT [19]	68.77
+ adapter	68.95
SAN [17]	69.37
+ adapter	**69.84**

5.3 Designing of Adapting Task

Masked sentence auto-encoding tasks have been extensively utilized in natural language processing and have consistently shown their effectiveness and generalizability in numerous previous studies. In Table 7, we present the performance of various document adaptation tasks on the Chinese-to-English translation task. Interestingly, we observe a decline in performance when using the translation process itself as a document adaptation task, which aligns with findings from prior research on double-translation. Similarly, the experiment employing the reconstruction of typical masked sentences as an adaptation task also exhibited a similar phenomenon. These findings indicate that our proposed approach effectively assists translation models in capturing valuable information from documents.

5.4 Pronoun Translation

To evaluate coreference and anaphora, we adopt the reference-based metric proposed by Werlen and Belis [38], following the methodology of Miculicich et al. [3] and Tan et al. [4]. This metric measures the accuracy of pronoun translation. Table 8 displays the performance results. We observe that our proposed approach significantly improves the translation of pronouns, indicating that pronoun translation benefits from leveraging global context. This finding is consistent with the results reported in related studies [3,4,38].

5.5 Adapting with Human Feedback

Adapting with human feedback has been widely employed in various natural language models, and its effectiveness and generalization have been demonstrated in numerous prior studies. We sought to investigate whether human feedback could enhance our translator-adapter framework.

Table 9. Performance of human feedback augmented adapting task on ZH-EN translation task.

Task	s-BLEU	d-BLEU	Meteor
Real feedback	42.64	45.37	29.60
Fake feedback	42.03	44.71	28.50
Ours	**42.47**	**45.10**	**29.49**

Table 9 presents the performance of the adapting task augmented with human feedback on the Chinese-to-English translation task. The term "**Fake feedback**" refers to using the adapter's outputs as simulated human feedback, while "**Real feedback**" denotes the process of reviewing and correcting the adapter's outputs, and using the corrected sequences as target sentences. From the results, we observe that using the adapter's output as simulated human feedback leads to a decrease in performance. Additionally, employing human-corrected sentences as feedback incurs a doubling of the adaptation task cost, but only yields marginal improvements in translation performance. One possible assumption is that significant positive impact on translation quality can be achieved only when a substantial amount of high-quality human feedback data is available. Therefore, we did not integrate this method into our adapter-translator framework.

5.6 The Impact of Frozen Encoder Parameters Proportion

We performed preliminary experiments to examine the optimal proportion of frozen encoder parameters during the inference phase of the translator. The results in Table 10 demonstrate that the translator's performance steadily improved as we increased the proportion of frozen encoder parameters, reaching its peak at 99%. However, when we further increased the proportion to 99.5%, the translator's performance started to decline. Consequently, in our experiments, we set the proportion of frozen encoder parameters to 99% during the inference phase of the translator.

6 Related Work

Local context has been extensively investigated in neural machine translation (NMT) models, including both RNN-based RNNSearch and Transformer-based models [7,8]. An early attempt in RNN-based NMT was the concatenation method proposed by [30]. Subsequently, the adoption of multiple encoders emerged as a promising direction in both RNNSearch and Transformer-based NMT models [2,24,31–35]. Cache/memory-based approaches [1,15,16] also fall under this category, as they utilize a cache to store word/translation information from previous sentences.

An alternative approach in document-level NMT treats the entire document as a unified translation unit and dynamically extracts pertinent global knowledge for each sentence within the document. This global context can be derived either from the source side [1,4,17,36] or the target side [21].

Table 10. The impact of frozen encoder parameters proportion.

K	BLEU	Meteor
97.0%	23.57	43.46
98.0%	26.69	45.83
99.0%	27.55	46.75
99.5%	27.50	46.68
99.7%	27.46	46.60

Moreover, several endeavors have been undertaken to enhance the performance of document-level translation through the utilization of monolingual document data. For instance, in order to improve translation coherence within a document, Voita et al. [39] propose DocRepair, which is trained on monolingual target language document corpora to address inconsistencies in sentence-level translations. Similarly, Yu et al. [14] train a document-level language model to re-evaluate sentence-level translations. In contrast, Dowmunt [40] harness monolingual source language document corpora to investigate multi-task training using the BERT-objective on the encoder.

7 Conclusion

To enhance the alignment between the trained context-aware NMT model and each input document, we present in this paper an adapter-translator framework, designed to facilitate the model's familiarity with a document prior to translation. Our modification to the NMT model involves incorporating an adapter encoder, which reconstructs the intentionally corrupted portions of the original document. Empirical findings from Chinese-to-English translation tasks and various English-to-German translation tasks demonstrate the considerable performance improvement achieved by our approach compared to several robust baseline models.

Limitations

Our experimental findings and analysis validate the effectiveness of the proposed adapter-translator framework in facilitating model familiarity with documents prior to translation, thereby yielding substantial enhancements across multiple evaluation benchmarks. However, it should be noted that the inclusion of the adapter module may introduce a certain degree of computational overhead to the framework's efficiency. Nevertheless, it is widely recognized that the time-consuming aspect of machine translation during the inference stage primarily stems from the serial decoding process of beam search. In contrast, our approach, as described in this paper, does not employ beam search during the adaptation stage; instead, it leverages parallel attention and mask mechanisms that align with the training stage. The main increase in computational time for this approach arises from the storage of checkpoints after the completion of parameter updates during the adaptation stage.

References

1. Maruf, S., Haffari, G.: Document context neural machine translation with memory networks. In: Proceedings of ACL, pp. 1275–1284 (2018)
2. Zhang, J., et al.: Improving the transformer translation model with document-level context. In: Proceedings of EMNLP, pp. 533–542 (2018)
3. Miculicich, L., Ram, D., Pappas, N., Henderson, J.: Document-level neural machine translation with hierarchical attention networks. In: Proceedings of EMNLP, pp. 2947–2954 (2018)
4. Tan, X., Zhang, L., Xiong, D., Zhou, G.: Hierarchical modeling of global context for document-level neural machine translation. In: Proceedings of EMNLP-IJCNLP, pp. 1576–1585 (2019)
5. Zheng, Z., Yue, X., Huang, S., Chen, J.: Towards making the most of context in neural machine translation. In: Proceedings of IJCAI, pp. 3983–3989 (2020)
6. Kang, X., Zha, Y., Zhang, J., Zong, C.: T: Dynamic context selection for document-level neural machine translation via reinforcement learning. In: Proceedings of EMNLP, pp. 2242–2254 (2020)
7. Bahdanau, D., Cho, K., Bengio, Y.: Neural machine translation by jointly learning to align and translate. In: Proceedings of ICLR (2018)
8. Vaswani, A., et al.: Attention is all you need. In: Proceedings of NIPS, pp. 5998–6008 (2017)
9. Sennrich, R., Haddow, B., Birch, A.: Neural machine translation of rare words with subword units. In: Proceedings of ACL, pp. 1715–1725 (2016)

10. Hassan, H., et al.: Achieving human parity on automatic Chinese to English news translation. In: Computing Research Repository (2018)
11. Liu, Y., et al.: RoBERTa: a robustly optimized BERT pretraining approach. In: Computing Research Repository (2019)
12. Yang, Z., et al.: XLNet: generalized autoregressive pretraining for language understanding. In: Proceedings of NeurIPS, pp. 5754–5764 (2019)
13. Sugiyama, A., Yoshinaga, N.: Context-aware decoder for neural machine translation using a target-side document-level language model. In: Proceedings of NAACL, pp. 5781–5791 (2021)
14. Yu, L., et al.: Better document-level machine translation with Bayes rule. In: Proceedings of Transactions of the Association for Computational Linguistics, pp. 346–360 (2020)
15. Kuang, S., Xiong, D., Luo, W., Zhou, G.: Modeling coherence for neural machine translation with dynamic and topic caches. In: Proceedings of COLING, pp. 596–606 (2018)
16. Tu, Z., Liu, Y., Shi, S., Zhang, T.: Learning to remember translation history with a continuous cache. In: Proceedings of Transactions of the Association for Computational Linguistics, pp. 407–420 (2018)
17. Maruf, S., Martins, A.F.T., Haffari, G.: Selective attention for context-aware neural machine translation. In: Proceedings of NAACL, pp. 3092–3102 (2019)
18. Chen, L., Li, J., Gong, Z.: Hierarchical global context augmented document-level neural machine translation. In: Proceedings of CCL, pp. 434–445 (2020)
19. Chen, L., Li, J., Gong, Z., Zhang, M., Zhou, G.: One type context is not enough: global context-aware neural machine translation. In: Proceedings of TALLIPL (2018)
20. Li, X., Zhang, J., Zong, C.: One sentence one model for neural machine translation. In: Proceedings of LREC, pp. 910–917 (2018)
21. Xiong, H., He, Z., Wu, H., Wang, H.: Modeling coherence for discourse neural machine translation. In: Proceedings of AAAI, pp. 7338–7345 (2019)
22. He, K., Chen, X., Xie, S., Li, Y., Dollár, P., Girshick, R.: Masked autoencoders are scalable vision learners. In: Proceedings of CVPR, pp. 16000–16009 (2022)
23. Ma, S., Zhang, D., Zhou, M.: A simple and effective unified encoder for document-level machine translation. In: Proceedings of ACL, pp. 3505–3511 (2020)
24. Yang, Z., Zhang, J., Meng, F., Gu, S., Feng, Y., Zhou, J.: Enhancing context modeling with a query-guided capsule network for document-level translation. In: Proceedings of EMNLP, pp. 1527–1537 (2020)
25. Koehn, P.: Statistical significance tests for machine translation evaluation. In: Proceedings of EMNLP, pp. 388–395 (2004)
26. Cettolo, M., Girardi, C., Federico, M.: WIT3: web inventory of transcribed and translated talks. In: Proceedings of EAMT, pp. 261–268 (2012)
27. Kingma, D.P., Ba, J.: Adam: a method for stochastic optimization. In: Proceedings of ICLR (2015)
28. Papineni, K., Roukos, S., Todd, W., Zhu, W.-J.: BLEU: a method for automatic evaluation of machine translation. In: Proceedings of ACL, pp. 311–318 (2002)
29. Lavie, A., Agarwal, A.: METEOR: an automatic metric for MT evaluation with high levels of correlation with human judgments. In: Proceedings of WMT, pp. 228–231 (2007)
30. Tiedemann, J., Scherrer, Y.: Neural machine translation with extended context. In: Proceedings of the Third Workshop on Discourse in Machine Translation, pp. 82–92 (2017)

31. Jean, S., Lauly, S., Firat, O., Cho, K.: Does neural machine translation benefit from larger context? In: Proceedings of Computing Research Repository (2017)
32. Wang, L., Tu, Z., Way, A., Liu, Q.: Exploiting cross-sentence context for neural machine translation. In: Proceedings of EMNLP, pp. 2826–2831 (2017)
33. Bawden, R., Sennrich, R., Birch, A., Haddow, B.: Evaluating discourse phenomena in neural machine translation. In: Proceedings of NAACL, pp. 1304–1313 (2018)
34. Voita, E., Serdyukov, P., Sennrich, R., Titov, I.: Context-aware neural machine translation learns anaphora resolution. In: Proceedings of ACL, pp. 1264–1274 (2018)
35. Voita, E., Sennrich, R., Titov, I.: When a good translation is wrong in context: context-aware machine translation improves on deixis, ellipsis, and lexical cohesion. In: Proceedings of ACL, pp. 1198–1212 (2019)
36. Mace, V., Servan, C.: Using whole document context in neural machine translation. In: Proceedings of IWSLT (2019)
37. Devlin, J., Chang, M.-W., Lee, K., Toutanova, K.: BERT: pre-training of Deep Bidirectional Transformers for Language Understanding. In: Proceedings of NAACL, pp. 4171–4186 (2019)
38. Werlen, L.M., Popescu-Belis, A.: Validation of an automatic metric for the accuracy of pronoun translation (APT). In: Proceedings of Workshop on Discourse in Machine Translation, pp. 17–25 (2017)
39. Voita, E., Sennrich, R., Titov, I.: Context-aware monolingual repair for neural machine translation. In: Proceedings of EMNLP, pp. 877–886 (2019)
40. Junczys-Dowmunt, M.: Microsoft translator at WMT 2019: towards large-scale document-level neural machine translation. In: Proceedings of WMT, pp. 225–233 (2019)

Language Resource and Evaluation

MCLS: A Large-Scale Multimodal Cross-Lingual Summarization Dataset

Xiaorui Shi(✉)

School of Information, Renmin University of China, Beijing, China
xiaorshi@gmail.com

Abstract. Multimodal summarization which aims to generate summaries with multimodal inputs, *e.g.*, text and visual features, has attracted much attention in the research community. However, previous studies only focus on monolingual multimodal summarization and neglect the non-native reader to understand the cross-lingual news in practical applications. It inspires us to present a new task, named Multimodal Cross-Lingual Summarization for news (MCLS), which generates cross-lingual summaries from multi-source information. To this end, we present a large-scale multimodal cross-lingual summarization dataset, which consists of 1.1 million article-summary pairs with 3.4 million images in 44 * 43 language pairs. To generate a summary in any language, we propose a unified framework that jointly trains the multimodal monolingual and cross-lingual summarization tasks, where a bi-directional knowledge distillation approach is designed to transfer knowledge between both tasks. Extensive experiments on many-to-many settings show the effectiveness of the proposed model.

Keywords: Multimodal Summarization · Cross-lingual Summarization · Knowledge Distillation

1 Introduction

The goal of multimodal summarization is to produce a summary with the help of multi-source inputs, *e.g.*, text and visual features. With the rapid growth of multimedia content on the Internet, this task has received increasing attention from the research communities and has shown its potential in recent years. It benefits users from better understanding and accessing verbose and obscure news, and thus can help people quickly master the core ideas of a multimodal article.

In the literature, many efforts have been devoted to the multimodal summarization fields, *e.g.*, SportsSum [57], MovieSum [13], MSMR [12], MMSS [28], MSS [27], How2 [51], MSMO [83], E-DailyMail [8], EC-product [26], MM-AVS [15], and MM-Sum [34]. All these datasets cover video summarization, movie summarization, meeting records summarization, sentence summarization, product summarization, and news summarization. With the predefined task, former state-of-the-art multimodal summarization models have achieved great

M. Sun et al. (Eds.): CCL 2023, LNAI 14232, pp. 273–288, 2023.
https://doi.org/10.1007/978-981-99-6207-5_17

Fig. 1. An example of our MM-CLS dataset. Inputs: an article and image sequence pair; Output: summaries in different language directions.

outcomes. For instance, [46] and [80] explore the hierarchy between the textual article and visual features, and integrate them into the MAS model. [39] design a multistage fusion network to model the fine-grained interactions between the two modalities. And [76] study multiple multimodal fusion methods to infuse the visual features into generative pre-trained language models, *e.g.*, BART [25]. Despite their efforts and effectiveness, existing methods are all conducted in monolingual scenarios. In practical applications, for non-native news viewers, they desire some native language summaries to better understand the contents of the news in other languages. To our knowledge, little research work has been devoted to multimodal cross-lingual summarization. One important season is the lack of a large-scale multimodal cross-lingual benchmark.

To assist those non-native readers, we propose a new task: Multimodal Cross-Lingual Summarization for news (MCLS). As shown in Fig. 1, the inputs consist of two parts: the image sequence and textual article in the source language (*e.g.*, English), and the summary outputs can be in any target language (*e.g.*, English, Chinese, Japanese, and French). Therefore, the MCLS seeks to generate summaries in any target language to reflect the salient new contents based on the image sequence and the article in the source language. To this end, based on CrossSum [5], we first construct a large-scale multimodal cross-lingual summarization dataset (MM-CLS) for news. The MM-CLS includes over 1.1 million article-summary pairs with 3.4 million images in 44 * 43 language pairs.

Based on the constructed MM-CLS, we benchmark the MCLS task by establishing multiple Transformer-based [59] systems adapted from the advanced representative multimodal monolingual models [76], based on mT5 [72]. Specifically, we incorporate multimodal features into the models for a suitable summarization in any language. Furthermore, to transfer the knowledge between monolingual summarization and cross-lingual summarization, we design a bidirectional knowledge distillation (BKD) method. Extensive experiments on many-to-many settings in terms of ROUGE scores [38], demonstrate the effectiveness of multimodal information fusion and the proposed BKD.

In summary, our main contributions are:

- We propose a new task: multimodal cross-lingual summarization for news named MCLS, to advance multimodal cross-lingual summarization research.
- We are the first that contributes the large-scale multimodal cross-lingual summarization dataset (MM-CLS), which contains 1.1 million article-summary pairs with 3.4 million images, in total 44 * 43 language pairs.
- We implement multiple Transformer-based baselines and provide benchmarks for the new task. Extensive experiments show that our model achieves state-of-the-art performance on the benchmark. We also conduct a comprehensive analysis and ablation study to offer more insights.

2 Related Work

2.1 Abstractive Text Summarization (ATS)

Given the input textual article, the goal of ATS is to generate a concise summary [19,67]. Thanks to the generative pre-trained language models [25], the ATS has achieved remarkable performance [17,41,47,50,68,69,71,77,79]. Different form them, this work mainly focuses on benchmarking multimodal cross-lingual summarization.

2.2 Multimodal Abstractive Summarization (MAS)

With the rapid growth of multimedia, many MAS datasets have been built such as SportsSum [57], MovieSum [13], MSMR [12], MMSS [28], MSS [27], How2 [40,51], MSMO [83], E-DailyMail [8], EC-product [26], MM-AVS [15], MM-Sum [34], and M^{3}Sum [32]. All these datasets, covering video summarization, movie summarization, meeting records summarization, sentence summarization, product summarization, and news summarization, aim to generate a summary based on multimodal inputs (text, vision, or audio). With the data resources extensively used, the MAS task has attracted much attention, where the existing work mainly focuses on how to effectively exploit the additional visual features, having achieved impressive performance in recent years [29,30,76,80,82,85,86]. The difference from ours lies in the cross-lingual summarization where we hope to generate a summary in any target language.

2.3 Cross-Lingual Summarization (CLS)

Cross-lingual summarization aims to generate a summary in a cross-lingual language, which has achieved significant progress [64,66]. Generally, besides some work of constructing datasets [5,23,48,52,58,75,84], existing methods mainly include: the pipeline methods [24,44,45,60,61,74,78], *i.e.*, translation and then summarization or summarization and then translation, mixed-lingual pre-training [70], knowledge distillation [43], contrastive learning [62], zero-shot approaches [2,10,11], and multi-task learning [3,4,6,7,37,55,87]. [65] concentrate on building a benchmark dataset for CLS on the dialogue field. We focus on offering additional visual features for multimodal cross-lingual summarization.

2.4 Multilingual Abstractive Summarization

It aims to train a model that can produce a summary in any language. Existing studies mainly pay attention to constructing the multilingual abstractive summarization dataset and there have been many datasets publicly available: MultiLing2015 [16], GlobalVoices [42], MultiSumm [7], MLSUM [52], MultiHumES [75], MassiveSumm [58], MLGSum [62], and XL-Sum [18]. Most of these datasets are automatically constructed from online websites due to high human cost, which involves at least two languages. Essentially, this line of work is still monolingual while we aim to generate summaries in a cross-lingual manner.

2.5 Knowledge Distillation (KD)

Knowledge distillation [20] is a method to train a model, called the student, by leveraging valuable information provided by soft targets output by another model, called the teacher. In particular, the framework initially trains a model on one designated task to extract useful features. Subsequently, given a dataset $D = \{(X_1, Y_1), (X_2, Y_2), \ldots (X_{|D|}, Y_{|D|})\}$, where $|D|$ is the size of the dataset, the teacher model will generate the output $\mathbf{H}_i^T = \{\mathbf{h}_1^T, \mathbf{h}_2^T, \ldots, \mathbf{h}_{L_T}^T\}$ for each input X_i. Dependent on the researchers' decision, the output might be hidden representations or final logits. As a consequence, to train the student model, the framework will use a KD loss that discriminates the output of the student model $\mathbf{H}_i^S = \{\mathbf{h}_1^S, \mathbf{h}_2^S, \ldots, \mathbf{h}_{L_S}^S\}$ given input X_i from the teacher output $\mathbf{H}_i^T$. Eventually, the KD loss for input X_i will possess the form as follows

$$\mathcal{L}_{\text{KD}} = dist(\mathbf{H}_i^T, \mathbf{H}_i^S), \tag{1}$$

where *dist* is a distance function to estimate the discrepancy of teacher and student outputs.

The explicated knowledge distillation framework has shown its effectiveness in many NLP tasks, such as question answering [1,21,73] and neural machine translation [31,54,56,63,81]. Nonetheless, its application for multimodal cross-lingual summarization has received little interest.

3 Method

3.1 Problem Formulation

Given an input article $\mathcal{X}_{L1}=\{x_k\}_{k=1}^{|\mathcal{X}_{L1}|}$ in the source language and the corresponding object sequence $\mathcal{O}=\{o_{ij}\}_{i=1,j=1}^{i\leq n,j\leq m}$, where x_k denotes the k-th token and o_{ij}

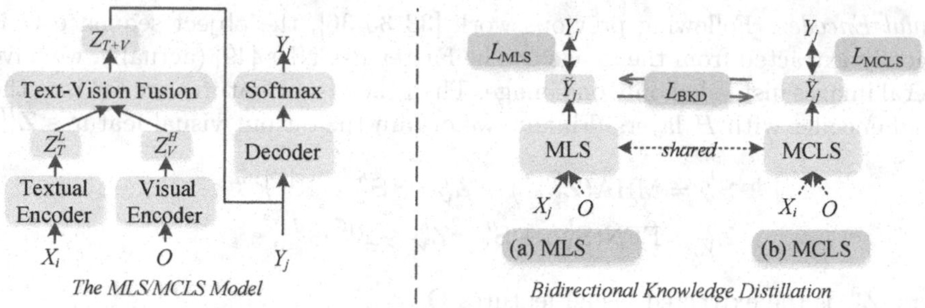

Fig. 2. The overview of our model architecture.

represents the detected j-th object of the i-th image (n, m is the number of images and detected objects in each image, respectively), the MCLS task is defined as:

$$p(\mathcal{Y}_{L2}|\mathcal{X}_{L1}, \mathcal{O}) = \prod_{t=1}^{|\mathcal{Y}_{L2}|} p(y_t|\mathcal{X}_{L1}, \mathcal{O}, y_{<t}),$$

where $y_{<t}$ indicates the previous tokens before the t-th time step of the summary $\mathcal{Y}_{L2}=\{y_t\}_{t=1}^{|\mathcal{Y}_{L2}|}$ in target language and $L_1 \neq L_2$.

3.2 The MCLS Model

[76] design a text-vision fusion method to inject the visual features into the generative pre-trained language models (*e.g.*, BART), which achieves state-of-the-art performance on MAS [34]. As shown in the left part of Fig. 2, the backbone of the MAS model is a variant of transformer [59] with four modules: textual encoder, visual encoder, text-vision fusion, and decoder.

Textual Encoder. The input text $\mathcal{X}_{L1}$ is firstly tokenized and mapped to a sequence of token embeddings $\mathbf{X}$. Then, the positional encodings $\mathbf{E}_{pe}$ are pointwisely added to $\mathbf{X}$ to keep the positional information [59]:

$$\mathbf{Z}_T^0 = \mathbf{X} + \mathbf{E}_{pe}, \ \{\mathbf{Z}_T^0, \mathbf{X}, \mathbf{E}_{pe}\} \in \mathbb{R}^{|\mathcal{X}_{L1}|\times d},$$

where d is the feature dimension. It forms the input features $\mathbf{Z}_T^0$ to the encoder, which consists of L stacked layers and each layer includes two sub-layers: 1) Multi-Head Attention (MHA) and 2) a position-wise Feed-Forward Network (FFN):

$$\mathbf{S}_T^l = \text{MHA}(\mathbf{Z}_T^{l-1}) + \mathbf{Z}_T^{l-1}, \ \mathbf{S}_T^l \in \mathbb{R}^{|\mathcal{X}_{L1}|\times d},$$
$$\mathbf{Z}_T^l = \text{FFN}(\mathbf{S}_T^l) + \mathbf{S}_T^l, \ \mathbf{Z}_T^l \in \mathbb{R}^{|\mathcal{X}_{L1}|\times d},$$

where $\mathbf{Z}_T^l$ is the state of the l-th encoder layer.

Visual Encoder. Following previous work [33,35,36], the object sequence $\mathcal{O}$ is typically extracted from the image by the Faster R-CNNs [49] (actually, we have several images instead of only one image. Then the visual features are fed into the visual encoder with H layers. Finally, we obtain the output visual features $\mathbf{Z}_V^H$:

$$\mathbf{S}_V^h = \text{MHA}(\mathbf{Z}_V^{h-1}) + \mathbf{Z}_V^{h-1}, \ \mathbf{S}_V^h \in \mathbb{R}^{|\mathcal{O}| \times d_v},$$
$$\mathbf{Z}_V^h = \text{FFN}(\mathbf{S}_V^h) + \mathbf{S}_V^h, \ \mathbf{Z}_V^h \in \mathbb{R}^{|\mathcal{O}| \times d_v},$$

where $\mathbf{Z}_V^0$ is the extracted visual features $\mathbf{O}$.

Text-Vision Fusion. The fusion method is vision-guided multi-head attention [76]. Firstly, the query $\mathbf{Q}$ is linearly projected from the textual features $\mathbf{Z}_T^L$, and the key $\mathbf{K}$ and value $\mathbf{V}$ are linearly projected from the visual features $\mathbf{Z}_V^H$. Secondly, a Cross-modal Multi-Head Attention (CMHA) is applied to get the text queried visual features $\mathbf{M}$. Then, a forget gate $\mathbf{G}$ is used to filter redundant and noisy information from the visual features. Finally, we obtain the vision-guided output $\mathbf{Z}_{T+V}$ by concatenating the textual features $\mathbf{Z}_T^L$ and the result of a point-wise multiplication $\mathbf{G} \otimes \mathbf{M}$, and then linearly project it to the original dimension d. Formally, the text-vision fusion process is:

$$\begin{aligned}
\mathbf{Q} &= \mathbf{Z}_T^L \mathbf{W}_q, \ \mathbf{Q} \in \mathbb{R}^{|\mathcal{X}_{L1}| \times d_c}, \\
\mathbf{K} &= \mathbf{Z}_V^H \mathbf{W}_k, \ \mathbf{V} = \mathbf{Z}_V^H \mathbf{W}_v, \ \mathbf{K}, \mathbf{V} \in \mathbb{R}^{|\mathcal{O}| \times d_c}, \\
\mathbf{M} &= \text{CMHA}(\mathbf{Q}, \mathbf{K}, \mathbf{V}), \ \mathbf{M} \in \mathbb{R}^{|\mathcal{X}_{L1}| \times d_c}, \\
\mathbf{G} &= \text{Sigmoid}(\text{Concat}(\mathbf{Z}_T^L, \mathbf{M})\mathbf{W}_g + \mathbf{b}_g), \\
\mathbf{Z}_{T+V} &= \text{Concat}(\mathbf{Z}_T^L, \mathbf{G} \otimes \mathbf{M})\mathbf{W}_z + \mathbf{b}_z,
\end{aligned}$$

where Concat is the concatenation operation and $\mathbf{W}_*$ and $\mathbf{b}_*$ are trainable weights.

Decoder. Similar to the encoder, but each of L decoder layers includes an additional Multi-Head Cross-Attention sub-layer (MHCA):

$$\begin{aligned}
\mathbf{S}_{dec}^l &= \text{MHA}(\mathbf{Z}_{dec}^{l-1}) + \mathbf{Z}_{dec}^{l-1}, \ \mathbf{S}_{dec}^{l-1} \in \mathbb{R}^{|\mathcal{Y}_{L2}| \times d}, \\
\mathbf{C}_{dec}^l &= \text{MHCA}(\mathbf{S}_{dec}^l, \mathbf{Z}_{T+V}) + \mathbf{S}_{dec}^l, \\
\mathbf{Z}_{dec}^l &= \text{FFN}(\mathbf{C}_{dec}^l) + \mathbf{C}_{dec}^l, \ \mathbf{C}_{dec}^l \in \mathbb{R}^{|\mathcal{Y}_{L2}| \times d},
\end{aligned} \tag{2}$$

where $\mathbf{Z}_{dec}^l \in \mathbb{R}^{|\mathcal{Y}_{L2}| \times d}$ denotes the state of the l-th decoder layer. Then, at each decoding time step t, the top-layer (L-th) decoder hidden state $\mathbf{Z}_{dec,t}^L$ is fed into the softmax layer to produce the probability distribution of the next target token as:

$$p(y_t | \mathcal{X}_{L1}, \mathcal{O}, y_{<t}) = \text{Softmax}(\mathbf{W}_o \mathbf{Z}_{dec,t}^L + \mathbf{b}_o),$$

where $\mathbf{W}_o$ and $\mathbf{b}_o$ are trainable weights.

3.3 Bidirectional Knowledge Distillation

Our framework is shown in the right part of Fig. 2, where we initiate the process by training the teacher model on the multimodal monolingual summarization task. In detail, given an input $X^{L_1} = \{x_1, x_2, \ldots, x_N\}$ and corresponding image features, the teacher model will aim to generate its monolingual summary $Y^{L_1} = \{y_1^{L_1}, y_2^{L_1}, \ldots, y_{M_1}^{L_1}\}$. Similar to previous multimodal monolingual summarization schemes, our model is trained with the cross-entropy loss:

$$\mathcal{L}_{\text{MLS}} = -\sum_{t=1}^{|\mathcal{Y}_{L1}|} \log(p(y_t^{L_1}|y_{<t}^{L_1}, \mathcal{X}^{L_1}, \mathcal{O})). \tag{3}$$

After finetuning the teacher model, we progress to train the student model, which also uses the Transformer architecture. Contrary to the teacher, the student model's task is to generate the cross-lingual output $Y^{L_2} = \{y_1^{L_2}, y_2^{L_2}, \ldots, y_{M_2}^{L_2}\}$ in language L_2, given the input document X^{L_1} in language L_1 and corresponding image features. We update the parameters of the student model by another cross-entropy loss:

$$\mathcal{L}_{\text{MCLS}} = -\sum_{t=1}^{|\mathcal{Y}_{L2}|} \log(p(y_t^{L_2}|y_{<t}^{L_2}, \mathcal{X}^{L_1}, \mathcal{O}). \tag{4}$$

To pull the cross-lingual and monolingual representations nearer, we implement a KD loss to penalize the large distance of two vector spaces. Specifically, let $\mathbf{H}^T = \{\mathbf{h}_1^T, \mathbf{h}_2^T, \ldots, \mathbf{h}_{L_T}^T\}$ denote the contextualized representations produced by the decoder of the teacher model, and $\mathbf{H}^S = \{\mathbf{h}_1^S, \mathbf{h}_2^S, \ldots, \mathbf{h}_{L_S}^S\}$ denote the representations from the decoder of the student model, our KD loss are defined as:

$$\mathcal{L}_{\text{KD}} = dist(\mathbf{H}^T, \mathbf{H}^S), \tag{5}$$

where *dist* is the distance function to evaluate the difference between two representations (*e.g.*, KL, and cosine similarity). Conversely, when the student model achieves better performance, we also distill its knowledge into the teacher model. Therefore, the knowledge between the teacher and student models can be transferred to each other and thus enhance both of them. The bidirectional knowledge distillation loss function can be defined as:

$$\mathcal{L}_{\text{BKD}} = dist(\mathbf{H}^T, \mathbf{H}^S) + dist(\mathbf{H}^S, \mathbf{H}^T). \tag{6}$$

3.4 Training and Inference

For training, the model can deal with inputs in multiple languages and predict the summary in the corresponding language. Specifically, for each language L_k in the set of K languages $Lang = \{L_1, l_2, ..., L_K\}$, the training objective is:

$$\mathcal{J} = \sum_{k=1}^{K} (\mathcal{L}_{\text{MLS}}^{L_k} + \mathcal{L}_{\text{MCLS}}^{L_k} + \alpha * \mathcal{L}_{\text{BKD}}). \tag{7}$$

During inference, the BKD is not involved and only the MLS or MCLS model is used to conduct summarization.

4 Experiments

4.1 MM-CLS Dataset

There is no large-scale multimodal cross-lingual benchmark dataset until now. We construct one as follows.

Data Source and Data Construction. Based on the CrossSum dataset [5], we construct our **M**ulti**M**odal **C**ross-**L**ingual **S**marization (MM-CLS) dataset. The original CrossSum dataset is automatically crawled from the BBC website[1]. However, the lacking of the associated image sequence in CrossSum, makes it impossible to directly conduct research on multimodal cross-lingual summarization. Therefore, we strictly follow the procedure of [5] to crawl the images for the corresponding textual summarization dataset given the article *URL*, where we maintain the article-summary pair if it contains images and keep the image order that appeared in the article.

Dataset Statistics and Splits. Table 1 shows that our MM-CLS covers 44 languages and totally includes 1,073,301 article-summary pairs with 3,381,456 images, where each article-summary pair contains about 3.15 images on average. According to the language directions, we select six languages and conduct experiments in the many-to-many setting. Due to space limit, here we show 6 * 5 language pairs in Table 1. In fact, we construct the MM-CLS dataset based on CrossSum [5] where 62% data of CrossSum are maintained. Therefore, our MM-CLS covers 44 * 43 language pairs and totally includes 1,073,301 article-summary pairs with 3,381,456 images, where each article-summary pair contains about 3.15 images on average. The average article and summary length for all languages is about 520 and 84, respectively.

Table 1. An example of 6 * 5 Language pairs covered by our MM-CLS dataset, and the number of images with the corresponding article-summary pair is 3 4. Here, we do not list them for simplicity.

Languages	English	French	Hindi	Chinese	Japanese	Russian
English	-	1,881	4,256	4,561	2,447	7,854
French	1,881	–	546	288	256	656
Hindi	4,256	546	–	1,234	5,23	4,256
Chinese	4,561	288	1,234	–	956	2,432
Japanese	2,447	256	523	956	–	1,253
Russian	7,854	656	4,256	2,432	1,253	–

[1] https://www.bbc.com/.

Table 2. Results on MM-CLS (ROUGE-1/ROUGE-2/ROUGE-L).

Src	Trg						
	Models	**English**	**French**	**Hindi**	**Chinese**	**Japanese**	**Russian**
English	mT5	35.80/13.45/27.99	31.29/11.17/22.28	33.22/11.72/26.20	29.49/15.24/23.85	30.62/15.02/23.94	24.47/8.22/19.88
	VG-mT5	36.08/13.84/28.23	31.67/11.56/22.77	33.47/11.98/26.58	29.88/15.76/24.34	30.99/15.54/24.61	24.85/8.77/20.44
	VG-mT5+BKD (Ours)	**36.85/14.51/29.44**	**32.55/12.45/23.67**	**34.67/13.48/27.89**	**30.49/17.13/25.67**	**31.86/16.74/25.87**	**25.88/9.88/21.58**
French	mT5	23.29/8.75/18.66	38.31/19.19/29.21	22.11/7.44/18.41	25.45/11.21/18.55	26.78/12.44/20.01	23.44/7.47/18.42
	VG-mT5	23.80/8.99/18.99	38.53/19.59/29.67	22.45/7.93/18.85	25.78/11.56/18.93	26.99/12.78/20.56	23.83/7.82/18.90
	VG-mT5+BKD (Ours)	**24.72/9.45/19.78**	**39.79/20.24/30.66**	**23.62/8.95/19.77**	**26.91/13.04/19.89**	**28.18/14.21/22.05**	**24.91/9.05/20.31**
Hindi	mT5	27.05/11.67/21.72	22.11/7.16/17.28	36.41/14.82/27.34	26.12/11.59/19.89	21.32/9.21/16.78	22.11/7.41/16.11
	VG-mT5	27.62/11.99/22.07	22.34/7.45/17.61	36.84/15.25/27.76	26.54/11.87/20.21	21.67/9.56/17.15	22.60/7.88/16.70
	VG-mT5+BKD (Ours)	**28.34/13.07/23.24**	**23.52/8.41/18.78**	**37.49/16.56/29.04**	**27.54/13.11/20.99**	**22.87/10.56/18.86**	**23.83/8.41/17.40**
Chinese	mT5	29.10/13.08/27.37	26.29/11.17/21.28	27.70/12.12/22.22	33.47/15.24/28.81	28.60/13.06/21.95	22.81/7.49/16.42
	VG-mT5	29.49/13.52/27.78	26.56/11.57/21.71	27.92/12.71/22.55	33.91/15.60/29.23	28.87/13.55/22.19	23.11/7.90/16.82
	VG-mT5+BKD (Ours)	**30.54/14.51/28.29**	**27.45/13.07/23.16**	**28.83/13.79/23.71**	**35.38/16.82/30.84**	**30.68/15.01/23.88**	**23.99/8.89/17.58**
Japanese	mT5	29.97/14.18/24.44	24.22/9.15/18.25	25.21/10.72/21.20	24.49/11.21/18.80	39.60/18.08/33.91	25.04/8.44/20.44
	VG-mT5	30.31/14.54/24.93	24.62/9.56/18.70	25.63/10.95/21.57	24.81/11.62/19.09	39.97/18.50/34.33	25.60/8.92/20.87
	VG-mT5+BKD (Ours)	**31.57/15.78/25.77**	**25.86/10.59/19.77**	**26.78/12.17/22.45**	**25.66/12.33/19.98**	**40.97/19.41/35.16**	**26.77/9.49/21.89**
Russian	mT5	29.47/9.86/22.82	25.28/10.17/20.26	28.01/11.28/26.51	27.49/13.24/20.85	27.62/12.02/20.94	29.32/11.32/23.72
	VG-mT5	29.89/10.05/23.18	25.67/10.51/20.60	28.60/11.57/26.97	27.91/13.65/21.28	27.98/12.55/21.46	29.66/11.70/24.12
	VG-mT5+BKD (Ours)	**30.56/11.18/24.13**	**26.76/11.45/21.85**	**29.45/12.88/27.59**	**28.88/14.41/22.87**	**28.88/14.01/22.91**	**30.93/12.88/24.87**

4.2 Implementation Details and Metrics

Data Pre-Processing. Following [5], we pre-process the textual data by truncating or padding them into sequences of 512 tokens for $\mathcal{X}$ and the outputs $\mathcal{Y}$ to 84 tokens after using the 250k wordpiece [72] vocabulary provided with the mT5 checkpoint. For the image sequence, we also truncate or pad the sequence length to 180 (*i.e.*, five images: $5 * 36$; $n = 5$, $m = 36$) (Table 2).

Hyper-Parameters. Following [5], we use the *base*[2] model of mT5 [72], in which $L = 12$ for both encoder and decoder. For the vision-related hyper-parameters mentioned in Sect. 3.2, we follow [76] for a fair comparison. Specifically, we use a 4-layer encoder (*i.e.*, $H = 4$) with 8 attention heads and a 2048 feed-forward dimension. For all models, the dropout is set to 0.1 and the label smoothing is set to 0.1. The d, d_c, and d_v are 768, 256, and 2048, respectively. During the training, following a similar training strategy [5,9], we sample each batch from a single language containing 256 samples and use a smoothing factor (0.5) so that batches of low-resource languages would be sampled at a higher rate, increasing their frequency during training. We set the training step to 35,000 steps on a distributed cluster of 8 NVIDIA Tesla V100 GPUs and trained for about 5 days. We use the Adafactor optimizer [53] with a linear warm-up of 5,000 steps and the "inverse square root" learning rate schedule.

For inference, we use beam search with beam size 4 and length penalty of $\gamma = 0.6$. When calculating the ROUGE scores, we use the multi-lingual rouge[3] toolkit following [18]. All experimental results reported in this paper are the average of three runs with different random seeds.

Metrics. Following [5], we use the standard ROUGE scores (R-1, R-2, and R-L) [38] with the statistical significance test [22] for a fair comparison.

[2] https://huggingface.co/google/mt5-base/tree/main.
[3] https://github.com/csebuetnlp/xl-sum/tree/master/multilingual_rouge_scoring.

4.3 Comparison Models

Text-Only MAS Systems

Table 3. Ablation results under different language directions (Avg. R-1/R-2/R-L results), where each loss is separately added on the baseline.

	Models	English→*	French→*	Hindi→*	Japanese→*	Russian→*	Chinese→*
0	Baseline (VG-mT5)	31.15/12.90/24.49	26.89/11.44/20.93	26.26/10.66/20.25	28.31/12.47/23.38	28.49/12.34/23.24	28.28/11.67/22.93
1	*w/* $\mathcal{L}_{\text{MLS}}^{L_k}$	31.62/13.41/24.92	27.45/11.86/21.45	26.69/11.06/20.77	28.87/12.88/23.81	28.66/12.58/23.66	28.51/11.99/23.35
2	*w/* $\mathcal{L}_{\text{BKD}}$	31.75/13.77/25.04	27.80/11.99/21.80	26.89/11.35/21.02	28.99/13.37/24.13	28.96/12.82/23.92	28.65/12.27/23.59
3	*w/* $\mathcal{L}_{\text{MLS}}^{L_k}$&$\mathcal{L}_{\text{BKD}}$	32.05/14.03/25.68	28.02/12.49/22.07	27.26/11.68/21.38	29.47/13.68/24.57	29.60/13.29/24.17	29.24/12.80/24.04

mT5: We choose the mT5 [72], a multilingual language model pre-trained on a large dataset of 101 languages, as the text-only baseline which is fine-tuned on our dataset.

Vision-Guided MAS Systems

VG-mT5: We implement the fusion method described in Fig. 3.2 to inject visual features into the mT5 model, which is a strong baseline.

VG-mT5+BKD (Ours): It is the proposed model where we design two summary-oriented vision modeling tasks to enhance the VG-mT5 model.

4.4 Main Results

Figure 2 presents the main results on many-to-many scenarios. Overall, our model obtains notably better results than the text-only "mT5" model and the vision-guided "VG-mT5" model no matter if it is the MLS or MCLS setting. Compared with the text-only model, the VG-mT5 model can substantially surpass it, showing that the vision plays a vital role and suggesting the value of our MM-Sum dataset. After adding the BKD approach, the model performance obtains further significant improvement, up to **1.35/0.92/1.42** ROUGE scores on average, showing the effectiveness of our proposed approach.

5 Analysis

5.1 Ablation Study

We conduct ablation studies to investigate how well the two auxiliary tasks work. The results are shown in Table 3. We have the following findings:

- The MLS task shows a positive impact on the model performance (row 1 vs. row 0), demonstrating that the knowledge of MLS can be transferred to MCLS, which is beneficial to the summary generation;
- The BKD substantially improves the MCLS model in terms of ROUGE scores (row 2 vs. row 0), suggesting that transferring knowledge into each other is helpful for summarization;
- The two loss functions exhibit notable cumulative benefits (row 3 vs. rows 0~2), showing that transferring the knowledge of MLS to the MCLS is effective;

5.2 Human Evaluation

To further evaluate the performances of mT5, VG-mT5 and our VG-mT5+BKD, we conduct human studies on 50 samples randomly selected from English and Chinese test sets. We invite three Chinese postgraduate students who highly proficient in English comprehension to compare the generated summaries under the multilingual training setting, and assess each summary from three independent perspectives: **fluency**, **conciseness** and **informativeness**. We ask them to assess each aspect with a score ranging from 1 (worst) to 5 (best). The average results are presented in Table 4.

Table 4 shows the human results on Chinese→English and English→Chinese. We find that our model outperforms all comparison models from all criteria in both languages, which further demonstrates the effectiveness and superiority of our model. The Fleiss' Kappa scores [14] of Flu., Conci and Info. are 0.72, 0.68 and 0.59, respectively, which indicates a substantial agreement among three evaluators.

Table 4. Human evaluation results.

Models	Chinese→English			English→Chinese		
	Fluency	Conciseness	Informativeness	Fluency	Conciseness	Informativeness
mT5	4.21	3.54	3.04	3.56	3.14	3.04
VG-mT5	4.44	3.68	3.26	3.82	3.36	3.22
VG-mT5+BKD (Ours)	**4.26**	**4.38**	**3.76**	**4.32**	**3.88**	**3.68**

6 Conclusion and Future Work

In this paper, we propose to benchmark the MCLS task and provide a large-scale MM-CLS dataset. We also propose a bidirectional knowledge distillation approach, which can explicitly enhance the knowledge transferring between VG-mT5 and MCLS, and thus improve the summary quality. Extensive experiments on multiple settings, show that our model significantly outperforms related baselines in terms of ROUGE scores. In the future, due to the difficulty of simultaneously learning cross-lingual alignment and cross-modal alignment, future work should focus on these directions.

Acknowledgements. The authors would like to thank the anonymous reviewers for their insightful comments and suggestions to improve this paper.

References

1. Arora, S., Khapra, M.M., Ramaswamy, H.G.: On knowledge distillation from complex networks for response prediction. In: NAACL, pp. 3813–3822 (2019)
2. Ayana, S., Chen, Y., Yang, C., Liu, Z.Y., Sun, M.: Zero-shot cross-lingual neural headline generation. IEEE/ACM TASLP **26**(12), 2319–2327 (2018)

3. Bai, Y., Gao, Y., Huang, H.: Cross-lingual abstractive summarization with limited parallel resources. In: ACL-IJCNLP, pp. 6910–6924 (2021). https://doi.org/10.18653/v1/2021.acl-long.538, https://aclanthology.org/2021.acl-long.538
4. Bai, Y., Huang, H., Fan, K., Gao, Y., Chi, Z., Chen, B.: Bridging the gap: cross-lingual summarization with compression rate. CoRR abs/2110.07936 (2021). https://arxiv.org/abs/2110.07936
5. Bhattacharjee, A., Hasan, T., Ahmad, W.U., Li, Y.F., Kang, Y.B., Shahriyar, R.: Crosssum: beyond English-centric cross-lingual abstractive text summarization for 1500+ language pairs (2022)
6. Cao, Y., Liu, H., Wan, X.: Jointly learning to align and summarize for neural cross-lingual summarization. In: ACL, pp. 6220–6231 (2020). https://doi.org/10.18653/v1/2020.acl-main.554, https://www.aclweb.org/anthology/2020.acl-main.554
7. Cao, Y., Wan, X., Yao, J., Yu, D.: Multisumm: towards a unified model for multi-lingual abstractive summarization. In: AAAI, vol. 34, pp. 11–18, April 2020. https://doi.org/10.1609/aaai.v34i01.5328, https://ojs.aaai.org/index.php/AAAI/article/view/5328
8. Chen, J., Zhuge, H.: Abstractive text-image summarization using multi-modal attentional hierarchical RNN. In: EMNLP, pp. 4046–4056 (2018). https://doi.org/10.18653/v1/D18-1438, https://aclanthology.org/D18-1438
9. Conneau, A., Lample, G.: Cross-lingual language model pretraining. In: NIPS (2019)
10. Dou, Z.Y., Kumar, S., Tsvetkov, Y.: A deep reinforced model for zero-shot cross-lingual summarization with bilingual semantic similarity rewards. In: NGT, pp. 60–68 (2020). https://doi.org/10.18653/v1/2020.ngt-1.7, https://www.aclweb.org/anthology/2020.ngt-1.7
11. Duan, X., Yin, M., Zhang, M., Chen, B., Luo, W.: Zero-shot cross-lingual abstractive sentence summarization through teaching generation and attention. In: ACL. pp. 3162–3172 (2019). https://doi.org/10.18653/v1/P19-1305, https://www.aclweb.org/anthology/P19-1305
12. Erol, B., Lee, D.S., Hull, J.: Multimodal summarization of meeting recordings. In: ICME, pp. III-25 (2003). https://doi.org/10.1109/ICME.2003.1221239
13. Evangelopoulos, G., et al.: Multimodal saliency and fusion for movie summarization based on aural, visual, and textual attention. IEEE Trans. Multimedia **15**(7), 1553–1568 (2013). https://doi.org/10.1109/TMM.2013.2267205
14. Fleiss, J.L., Cohen, J.: The equivalence of weighted kappa and the intraclass correlation coefficient as measures of reliability. Educ. Psychol. Meas. 613–619 (1973). https://doi.org/10.1177/001316447303300309
15. Fu, X., Wang, J., Yang, Z.: MM-AVS: a full-scale dataset for multi-modal summarization. In: NAACL, pp. 5922–5926 (2021). https://doi.org/10.18653/v1/2021.naacl-main.473, https://aclanthology.org/2021.naacl-main.473
16. Giannakopoulos, G., et al.: MultiLing 2015: multilingual summarization of single and multi-documents, on-line fora, and call-center conversations. In: SIGDIAL, pp. 270–274 (2015). https://doi.org/10.18653/v1/W15-4638, https://aclanthology.org/W15-4638
17. Goodwin, T., Savery, M., Demner-Fushman, D.: Flight of the PEGASUS? Comparing transformers on few-shot and zero-shot multi-document abstractive summarization. In: COLING, pp. 5640–5646 (2020). https://doi.org/10.18653/v1/2020.coling-main.494, https://aclanthology.org/2020.coling-main.494
18. Hasan, T., et al.: XL-sum: large-scale multilingual abstractive summarization for 44 languages. In: Findings of ACL-IJCNLP, pp. 4693–4703 (2021). https://doi.org/10.18653/v1/2021.findings-acl.413, https://aclanthology.org/2021.findings-acl.413

19. Hermann, K.M., et al.: Teaching machines to read and comprehend. In: NIPS, pp. 1693–1701 (2015)
20. Hinton, G., Vinyals, O., Dean, J.: Distilling the knowledge in a neural network. arXiv preprint arXiv:1503.02531 (2015)
21. Hu, M., et al.: Attention-guided answer distillation for machine reading comprehension. arXiv preprint arXiv:1808.07644 (2018)
22. Koehn, P.: Statistical significance tests for machine translation evaluation. In: EMNLP, pp. 388–395 (2004). https://www.aclweb.org/anthology/W04-3250
23. Ladhak, F., Durmus, E., Cardie, C., McKeown, K.: WikiLingua: a new benchmark dataset for cross-lingual abstractive summarization. In: Findings of EMNLP, pp. 4034–4048 (2020). https://doi.org/10.18653/v1/2020.findings-emnlp.360, https://www.aclweb.org/anthology/2020.findings-emnlp.360
24. Leuski, A., Lin, C.Y., Zhou, L., Germann, U., Och, F.J., Hovy, E.: Cross-lingual c*st*rd: English access to Hindi information. ACM TALIP **2**(3), 245–269 (2003). https://doi.org/10.1145/979872.979877
25. Lewis, M., et al.: BART: denoising sequence-to-sequence pre-training for natural language generation, translation, and comprehension. In: ACL, pp. 7871–7880 (2020). https://doi.org/10.18653/v1/2020.acl-main.703, https://aclanthology.org/2020.acl-main.703
26. Li, H., Yuan, P., Xu, S., Wu, Y., He, X., Zhou, B.: Aspect-aware multimodal summarization for Chinese e-commerce products. In: AAAI, vol. 34, pp. 8188–8195 (2020)
27. Li, H., Zhu, J., Liu, T., Zhang, J., Zong, C., et al.: Multi-modal sentence summarization with modality attention and image filtering. In: IJCAI, pp. 4152–4158 (2018)
28. Li, H., Zhu, J., Ma, C., Zhang, J., Zong, C.: Multi-modal summarization for asynchronous collection of text, image, audio and video. In: EMNLP, pp. 1092–1102 (2017). https://doi.org/10.18653/v1/D17-1114, https://aclanthology.org/D17-1114
29. Li, H., Zhu, J., Ma, C., Zhang, J., Zong, C.: Read, watch, listen, and summarize: multi-modal summarization for asynchronous text, image, audio and video. IEEE TKDE **31**(5), 996–1009 (2018)
30. Li, M., Chen, X., Gao, S., Chan, Z., Zhao, D., Yan, R.: VMSMO: learning to generate multimodal summary for video-based news articles. In: EMNLP, pp. 9360–9369 (2020). https://doi.org/10.18653/v1/2020.emnlp-main.752, https://aclanthology.org/2020.emnlp-main.752
31. Li, Y., Li, W.: Data distillation for text classification. arXiv preprint arXiv:2104.08448 (2021)
32. Liang, Y., Meng, F., Wang, J., Xu, J., Chen, Y., Zhou, J.: D2tv: dual knowledge distillation and target-oriented vision modeling for many-to-many multimodal summarization. arXiv preprint arXiv:2305.12767 (2023)
33. Liang, Y., Meng, F., Xu, J., Chen, Y., Zhou, J.: MSCTD: a multimodal sentiment chat translation dataset. In: ACL, pp. 2601–2613 (2022). https://doi.org/10.18653/v1/2022.acl-long.186, https://aclanthology.org/2022.acl-long.186
34. Liang, Y., Meng, F., Xu, J., Wang, J., Chen, Y., Zhou, J.: Summary-oriented vision modeling for multimodal abstractive summarization. arXiv preprint arXiv:2212.07672 (2022)
35. Liang, Y., Meng, F., Zhang, Y., Chen, Y., Xu, J., Zhou, J.: Infusing multi-source knowledge with heterogeneous graph neural network for emotional conversation generation. In: AAAI, pp. 13343–13352, May 2021. https://ojs.aaai.org/index.php/AAAI/article/view/17575

36. Liang, Y., Meng, F., Zhang, Y., Chen, Y., Xu, J., Zhou, J.: Emotional conversation generation with heterogeneous graph neural network. Artif. Intell. **308**, 103714 (2022). https://doi.org/10.1016/j.artint.2022.103714, https://www.sciencedirect.com/science/article/pii/S0004370222000546
37. Liang, Y., et al.: A variational hierarchical model for neural cross-lingual summarization. In: ACL, pp. 2088–2099 (2022). https://doi.org/10.18653/v1/2022.acl-long.148, https://aclanthology.org/2022.acl-long.148
38. Lin, C.Y.: ROUGE: a package for automatic evaluation of summaries. In: TSBO, pp. 74–81 (2004). https://aclanthology.org/W04-1013
39. Liu, N., Sun, X., Yu, H., Zhang, W., Xu, G.: Multistage fusion with forget gate for multimodal summarization in open-domain videos. In: EMNLP, pp. 1834–1845 (2020). https://doi.org/10.18653/v1/2020.emnlp-main.144, https://aclanthology.org/2020.emnlp-main.144
40. Liu, N., et al.: Assist non-native viewers: multimodal cross-lingual summarization for how2 videos. In: EMNLP, pp. 6959–6969 (2022). https://aclanthology.org/2022.emnlp-main.468
41. Liu, Y., Lapata, M.: Text summarization with pretrained encoders. In: EMNLP-IJCNLP, pp. 3730–3740 (2019). https://doi.org/10.18653/v1/D19-1387, https://aclanthology.org/D19-1387
42. Nguyen, K., Daumé III, H.: Global voices: crossing borders in automatic news summarization. In: NFS, pp. 90–97 (2019). https://doi.org/10.18653/v1/D19-5411, https://aclanthology.org/D19-5411
43. Nguyen, T., Tuan, L.A.: Improving neural cross-lingual summarization via employing optimal transport distance for knowledge distillation. CoRR abs/2112.03473 (2021). https://arxiv.org/abs/2112.03473
44. Orăsan, C., Chiorean, O.A.: Evaluation of a cross-lingual Romanian-English multi-document summariser. In: LREC (2008)
45. Ouyang, J., Song, B., McKeown, K.: A robust abstractive system for cross-lingual summarization. In: NAACL, pp. 2025–2031 (2019). https://doi.org/10.18653/v1/N19-1204, https://www.aclweb.org/anthology/N19-1204
46. Palaskar, S., Libovický, J., Gella, S., Metze, F.: Multimodal abstractive summarization for how2 videos. In: ACL, pp. 6587–6596 (2019). https://doi.org/10.18653/v1/P19-1659, https://aclanthology.org/P19-1659
47. Paulus, R., Xiong, C., Socher, R.: A deep reinforced model for abstractive summarization. In: ICLR (2018). https://openreview.net/forum?id=HkAClQgA-
48. Perez-Beltrachini, L., Lapata, M.: Models and datasets for cross-lingual summarisation. In: EMNLP, pp. 9408–9423 (2021). https://doi.org/10.18653/v1/2021.emnlp-main.742, https://aclanthology.org/2021.emnlp-main.742
49. Ren, S., He, K., Girshick, R., Sun, J.: Faster R-CNN: towards real-time object detection with region proposal networks. In: Cortes, C., Lawrence, N., Lee, D., Sugiyama, M., Garnett, R. (eds.) NIPS, vol. 28 (2015), https://proceedings.neurips.cc/paper/2015/file/14bfa6bb14875e45bba028a21ed38046-Paper.pdf
50. Rothe, S., Maynez, J., Narayan, S.: A thorough evaluation of task-specific pre-training for summarization. In: EMNLP, pp. 140–145 (2021). https://doi.org/10.18653/v1/2021.emnlp-main.12, https://aclanthology.org/2021.emnlp-main.12
51. Sanabria, R., et al.: How2: a large-scale dataset for multimodal language understanding. In: ViGIL (2018). http://arxiv.org/abs/1811.00347
52. Scialom, T., Dray, P.A., Lamprier, S., Piwowarski, B., Staiano, J.: MLSUM: the multilingual summarization corpus. In: EMNLP, pp. 8051–8067 (2020). https://doi.org/10.18653/v1/2020.emnlp-main.647, https://aclanthology.org/2020.emnlp-main.647

53. Shazeer, N., Stern, M.: Adafactor: adaptive learning rates with sublinear memory cost. In: Dy, J., Krause, A. (eds.) ICML, vol. 80, pp. 4596–4604 (2018). https://proceedings.mlr.press/v80/shazeer18a.html
54. Sun, H., Wang, R., Chen, K., Utiyama, M., Sumita, E., Zhao, T.: Knowledge distillation for multilingual unsupervised neural machine translation. arXiv preprint arXiv:2004.10171 (2020)
55. Takase, S., Okazaki, N.: Multi-task learning for cross-lingual abstractive summarization (2020)
56. Tan, X., Ren, Y., He, D., Qin, T., Zhao, Z., Liu, T.Y.: Multilingual neural machine translation with knowledge distillation. arXiv preprint arXiv:1902.10461 (2019)
57. Tjondronegoro, D., Tao, X., Sasongko, J., Lau, C.H.: Multi-modal summarization of key events and top players in sports tournament videos. In: IEEE WACV, pp. 471–478 (2011). https://doi.org/10.1109/WACV.2011.5711541
58. Varab, D., Schluter, N.: MassiveSumm: a very large-scale, very multilingual, news summarisation dataset. In: EMNLP, pp. 10150–10161 (2021). https://doi.org/10.18653/v1/2021.emnlp-main.797, https://aclanthology.org/2021.emnlp-main.797
59. Vaswani, A., et al.: Attention is all you need. In: NIPS, pp. 5998–6008 (2017). https://proceedings.neurips.cc/paper/2017/file/3f5ee243547dee91fbd053c1c4a845aa-Paper.pdf
60. Wan, X.: Using bilingual information for cross-language document summarization. In: ACL, pp. 1546–1555 (2011). https://www.aclweb.org/anthology/P11-1155
61. Wan, X., Li, H., Xiao, J.: Cross-language document summarization based on machine translation quality prediction. In: ACL, Uppsala, Sweden, pp. 917–926 (2010). https://www.aclweb.org/anthology/P10-1094
62. Wang, D., Chen, J., Zhou, H., Qiu, X., Li, L.: Contrastive aligned joint learning for multilingual summarization. In: Findings of ACL-IJCNLP, pp. 2739–2750 (2021). https://doi.org/10.18653/v1/2021.findings-acl.242, https://aclanthology.org/2021.findings-acl.242
63. Wang, F., Yan, J., Meng, F., Zhou, J.: Selective knowledge distillation for neural machine translation. arXiv preprint arXiv:2105.12967 (2021)
64. Wang, J., Liang, Y., Meng, F., Li, Z., Qu, J., Zhou, J.: Cross-lingual summarization via chatgpt. arXiv preprint arXiv:2302.14229 (2023)
65. Wang, J., et al.: Clidsum: a benchmark dataset for cross-lingual dialogue summarization. arXiv preprint arXiv:2202.05599 (2022)
66. Wang, J., et al.: Understanding translationese in cross-lingual summarization. arXiv preprint arXiv:2212.07220 (2022)
67. Wang, J., et al.: A survey on cross-lingual summarization. Trans. Assoc. Comput. Linguist. **10**, 1304–1323 (2022)
68. Wang, J., et al.: Towards unifying multi-lingual and cross-lingual summarization. arXiv preprint arXiv:2305.09220 (2023)
69. Xiao, W., Beltagy, I., Carenini, G., Cohan, A.: PRIMERA: pyramid-based masked sentence pre-training for multi-document summarization. In: ACL, pp. 5245–5263 (2022). https://doi.org/10.18653/v1/2022.acl-long.360, https://aclanthology.org/2022.acl-long.360
70. Xu, R., Zhu, C., Shi, Y., Zeng, M., Huang, X.: Mixed-lingual pre-training for cross-lingual summarization. In: AACL, Suzhou, China, pp. 536–541 (2020). https://www.aclweb.org/anthology/2020.aacl-main.53
71. Xu, S., Li, H., Yuan, P., Wu, Y., He, X., Zhou, B.: Self-attention guided copy mechanism for abstractive summarization. In: ACL, pp. 1355–1362 (2020). https://doi.org/10.18653/v1/2020.acl-main.125, https://aclanthology.org/2020.acl-main.125

72. Xue, L., et al.: mT5: A massively multilingual pre-trained text-to-text transformer. In: NAACL, pp. 483–498 (2021). https://doi.org/10.18653/v1/2021.naacl-main.41, https://aclanthology.org/2021.naacl-main.41
73. Yang, Z., Shou, L., Gong, M., Lin, W., Jiang, D.: Model compression with two-stage multi-teacher knowledge distillation for web question answering system. In: WSDM, pp. 690–698 (2020)
74. Yao, J.G., Wan, X., Xiao, J.: Phrase-based compressive cross-language summarization. In: EMNLP, pp. 118–127 (2015). https://doi.org/10.18653/v1/D15-1012, https://www.aclweb.org/anthology/D15-1012
75. Yela-Bello, J.P., Oglethorpe, E., Rekabsaz, N.: MultiHumES: multilingual humanitarian dataset for extractive summarization. In: EACL, pp. 1713–1717 (2021). https://doi.org/10.18653/v1/2021.eacl-main.146, https://aclanthology.org/2021.eacl-main.146
76. Yu, T., Dai, W., Liu, Z., Fung, P.: Vision guided generative pre-trained language models for multimodal abstractive summarization. In: EMNLP, pp. 3995–4007 (2021). https://doi.org/10.18653/v1/2021.emnlp-main.326, https://aclanthology.org/2021.emnlp-main.326
77. Yu, T., Liu, Z., Fung, P.: AdaptSum: towards low-resource domain adaptation for abstractive summarization. In: NAACL, pp. 5892–5904 (2021). https://doi.org/10.18653/v1/2021.naacl-main.471, https://aclanthology.org/2021.naacl-main.471
78. Zhang, J., Zhou, Y., Zong, C.: Abstractive cross-language summarization via translation model enhanced predicate argument structure fusing. IEEE/ACM TASLP **24**(10), 1842–1853 (2016). https://doi.org/10.1109/TASLP.2016.2586608
79. Zhang, J., Zhao, Y., Saleh, M., Liu, P.: PEGASUS: pre-training with extracted gap-sentences for abstractive summarization. In: ICML, 119, pp. 11328–11339 (2020). https://proceedings.mlr.press/v119/zhang20ae.html
80. Zhang, L., Zhang, X., Pan, J., Huang, F.: Hierarchical cross-modality semantic correlation learning model for multimodal summarization. arXiv preprint arXiv:2112.12072 (2021)
81. Zhang, S., et al.: Towards understanding and improving knowledge distillation for neural machine translation. arXiv preprint arXiv:2305.08096 (2023)
82. Zhang, Z., Meng, X., Wang, Y., Jiang, X., Liu, Q., Yang, Z.: Unims: a unified framework for multimodal summarization with knowledge distillation. arXiv preprint arXiv:2109.05812 (2021)
83. Zhu, J., Li, H., Liu, T., Zhou, Y., Zhang, J., Zong, C.: MSMO: multimodal summarization with multimodal output. In: EMNLP, pp. 4154–4164 (2018). https://doi.org/10.18653/v1/D18-1448, https://aclanthology.org/D18-1448
84. Zhu, J., et al.: NCLS: neural cross-lingual summarization. In: EMNLP-IJCNLP, Hong Kong, China, pp. 3054–3064 (2019). https://doi.org/10.18653/v1/D19-1302, https://www.aclweb.org/anthology/D19-1302
85. Zhu, J., Xiang, L., Zhou, Y., Zhang, J., Zong, C.: Graph-based multimodal ranking models for multimodal summarization. TALLIP **20**(4), 1–21 (2021)
86. Zhu, J., Zhou, Y., Zhang, J., Li, H., Zong, C., Li, C.: Multimodal summarization with guidance of multimodal reference. In: AAAI, vol. 34, pp. 9749–9756 (2020)
87. Zhu, J., Zhou, Y., Zhang, J., Zong, C.: Attend, translate and summarize: an efficient method for neural cross-lingual summarization. In: ACL, pp. 1309–1321 (2020). https://doi.org/10.18653/v1/2020.acl-main.121, https://www.aclweb.org/anthology/2020.acl-main.121

CHED: A Cross-Historical Dataset with a Logical Event Schema for Classical Chinese Event Detection

Congcong Wei[1,2], Zhenbing Feng[1,2], Shutan Huang[1,2], Wei Li[1,2], and Yanqiu Shao[1,2](✉)

[1] School of Information Science, Beijing Language and Culture University, Beijing, China
liweitj47@blcu.edu.cn, yqshao163@163.com
[2] Language Resources Monitoring and Research Center, Beijing, China

Abstract. Event detection (ED) is a crucial area of natural language processing that automates the extraction of specific event types from large-scale text, and studying historical ED in classical Chinese texts helps preserve and inherit historical and cultural heritage by extracting valuable information. However, classical Chinese language characteristics, such as ambiguous word classes and complex semantics, have posed challenges and led to a lack of datasets and limited research on event schema construction. In addition, large-scale datasets in English and modern Chinese are not directly applicable to historical ED in classical Chinese. To address these issues, we constructed a logical event schema for classical Chinese historical texts and annotated the resulting dataset, which is called classical Chinese Historical Event Dataset (CHED). The main challenges in our work on classical Chinese historical ED are accurately identifying and classifying events within cultural and linguistic contexts and addressing ambiguity resulting from multiple meanings of words in historical texts. Therefore, we have developed a set of annotation guidelines and provided annotators with an objective reference translation. The average Kappa coefficient after multiple cross-validation is 68.49%, indicating high quality and consistency. We conducted various tasks and comparative experiments on established baseline models for historical ED in classical Chinese. The results showed that BERT+CRF had the best performance on sequence labeling task, with an f1-score of 76.10%, indicating potential for further improvement (The CHED data is released on https://github.com/lcclab-blcu/CHED).

Keywords: Event detection · Classical Chinese · Dataset

1 Introduction

Event detection (ED) is a significant research area in natural language processing (NLP). The ED task mainly includes two steps. Firstly, recognizing and labeling

Z. Feng—Equal Contribution.

M. Sun et al. (Eds.): CCL 2023, LNAI 14232, pp. 289–305, 2023.
https://doi.org/10.1007/978-981-99-6207-5_18

triggers (words that best represent the occurrence of events) in the text, and secondly, determining the event types to which triggers belongs. For example, in the sentence "九月乙丑，太尉李修罢。" (*In September of Yi Chou, General Li Xiu was dismissed.*), the word "罢" (ba) means "dismiss". Therefore, the trigger in this sentence is "罢" (ba), and we label this sentence as a "职位-官位-免职" (*Position-Official_position–Dismiss_from_a_position*) event triggered by the word "罢" (ba).

Constructing high-quality datasets for specific domains is critical for ED tasks. Several high-quality ED datasets exist for English and Chinese, such as ACE 2005 [13], LEVEN [16], MAVEN [14], PoE [8] and DuEE [9]. However, classical Chinese lacks such datasets due to complex semantics and special era. Large-scale datasets in English and modern Chinese are not directly applicable to classical Chinese ED. The current research on ED in classical Chinese is limited by the lack of high-quality datasets that are specific, systematic, and scalable.

To address these crucial issues and enhance the accuracy and efficiency of classical Chinese ED, we have constructed the classical Chinese Historical Event Dataset (CHED). This dataset has the potential to serve as a benchmark for developing and evaluating ED algorithms for classical Chinese historical texts. The hierarchical and logical event schema of the CHED can be extended and adapted to other NLP domains, making it a valuable resource not only for NLP researchers but also for scholars in other humanities fields. Moreover, CHED offers a unique historical perspective for exploring ancient societies, enhancing our comprehension of their cultures and interconnections. It also supports the digital humanities research and helps preserve cultural heritage through the study of classical Chinese texts.

During the construction of our dataset, we encountered three primary challenges: **1)** developing an event schema that could encompass the majority of events described in classical Chinese literature; **2)** accurately identifying and classifying events within cultural and linguistic contexts while accounting for the ambiguity resulting from multiple meanings of words in historical texts; **3)** ensuring consistent annotation results, which was essential throughout the entire dataset construction process.

To address these challenges, we proposed several approaches. One such approach involved subjecting the processed data and preliminary event schema to trial annotation and expert review. Through several revisions and validations, we constructed a hierarchical and logical event schema with fine granularity, consisting of 9 major event categories and 67 subcategories that cover significant events in ancient Chinese history. The 9 major categories of events include ***Life***, ***Position***, ***Communication***, ***Movement***, ***Ritual***, ***Military***, ***Law***, ***Economy***, and ***Nature***. The complete event schema has been placed in the Appendix A, as shown in Figs. 11 and 12. In addition, we have annotated a total of 8,122 valid sentences.

To ensure further accuracy, our annotators possessed extensive knowledge of classical Chinese and actively sought expert opinions while constructing the dataset. Multiple cross-validation were also conducted, yielding an average

Kappa coefficient of **68.49%**, which denotes a high level of consistency and quality. Additionally, we conducted various tasks and comparative experiments on established baseline models for historical ED in classical Chinese. The outcomes indicated that BERT+CRF exhibited the highest performance on sequence labeling task, achieving an f1-score of **76.10%**.

We conclude three main contributions as follows: **1)** We constructed the CHED, which provides a rich cross-historical data foundation for classical Chinese ED, making it a valuable resource for scholars and researchers. The dataset contains 8,122 valid sentences; **2)** We proposed a hierarchical and logical event schema, which has a fine-grained structure that can be adapted more effectively to other NLP domains; **3)** We excavated a unique and profound historical perspective from the CHED, promoting the advancement of digital humanities research.

2 Related Work

In the realm of event detection (ED) tasks in deep learning, sparse and imbalanced training data, complex text, and semantic ambiguity still pose problems, highlighting the importance of dataset construction and feature extraction through text refinement processing.

A high-quality dataset is essential for ED tasks. It should be large enough to support various learning algorithms, has high accuracy and consistency in labeled data, and contains diverse event types. Several high-quality annotated ED datasets have been constructed, including the widely used English dataset ACE 2005 [13], the legal ED dataset LEVEN [16], the large-scale cross-domain ED dataset MAVEN [14], the electrical power ED dataset PoE [8] and the Chinese event dataset DuEE [9] based on real-world scenarios. While many studies have summarized the primary methods of Chinese ED based on literature, classical Chinese field ED faces challenges due to differences in context and expression of historical texts.

There have been studies using deep learning methods to investigate historical ED in classical Chinese texts [6], such as researching the war events in the ZuoZhuan (左传). For example, the RoBERTa-CRF model was established [15], and pattern matching and CRF models were used to extract events from the ZuoZhuan (左传) [17]. Additionally, mixed techniques using information extraction have been applied to classical Chinese texts, including entity recognition and event extraction, with the extracted information being visualized using electronic charts [10]. Furthermore, studies have been conducted on extracting historical events and event elements from Shiji (史记) and ZuoZhuan (左传) [2]. However, these studies have only produced coarse-grained event type constructions, mostly focused on a single text and based on relatively small dataset sizes.

3 Event Schema Construction

The construction of event types in a given context should fulfill the criteria of comprehensive coverage, precise granularity, and high accuracy. To achieve

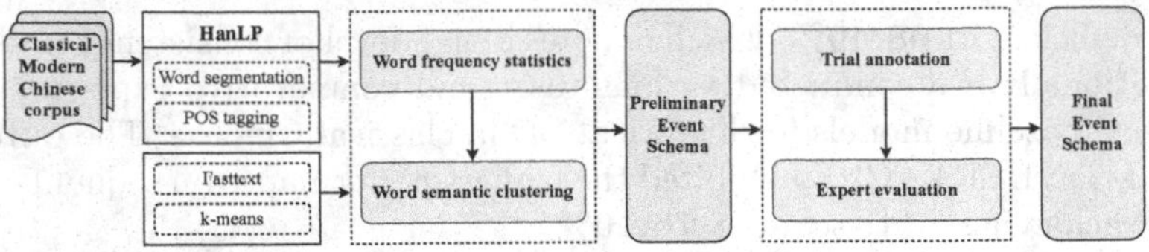

Fig. 1. This is the complete process for constructing the event schema. The preliminary construction was based on word frequency statistics and semantic clustering of the translations corpus, and it was finalized through trial annotation and expert evaluation.

these goals, we mainly carried out work in four aspects, as shown in Fig. 1: **1) Word frequency statistics**; **2) Word semantic clustering**; **3) Trial annotation**; **4) Expert evaluation**. Eventually, we constructed an event schema that includes 9 major categories and 67 subcategories. Figure 2 depicts the structure of one of the major categories, ***Position***.

We assume that the words with higher frequency in the text reflect the main content and central theme of the text, which is closely related to the event types. Therefore, it is necessary to conduct comprehensive word frequency statistics on the text to ensure the coverage of event types. We selected the translated works of the Twenty-Four Histories from NiuTrans[1]and used HanLP[2] for basic word segmentation and part-of-speech tagging on the corpus, and conducted word frequency statistics based on the results. After removing stop words and irrelevant part-of-speech tags, we analyzed the word frequency statistics results of nouns, verbs, and gerunds. We discovered that certain high-frequency words, such as "进攻" (attack), could serve as event types for historical events in classical Chinese.

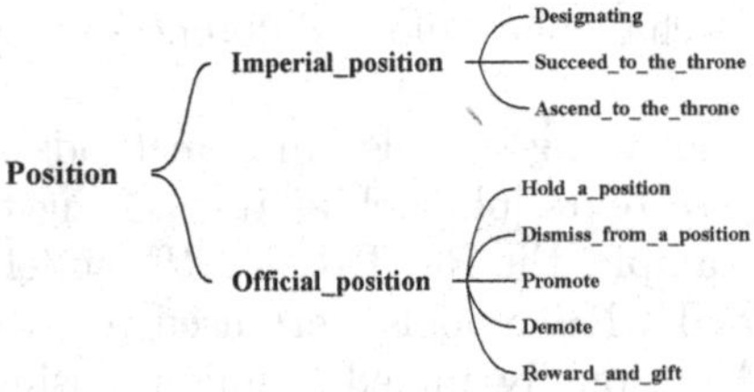

Fig. 2. ***Position*** is one of the 9 major event categories in the CHED event schema, and this diagram shows the complete hierarchical structure of ***Position***.

Semantic clustering analysis was further conducted on words to automatically classify similar semantic words, aiming to provide more refined classification references for the construction of classical Chinese event types. We used Fasttext[3]

[1] https://github.com/NiuTrans/Classical-Modern.
[2] https://github.com//hankcs/pyhanlp.
[3] https://github.com/facebookresearch/fastText.

to generate vector representations for each word and the k-means clustering algorithm to cluster words with high semantic similarity. Based on the analysis, and inspired by the ACE [13], MEVEN [14], LEVEN [16] and other datasets, we preliminarily summarized the classical Chinese historical event types, including 15 major categories and 73 subcategories.

To evaluate the actual event coverage in real-world texts, we randomly selected 15 volumes from the Benji (本纪) and Liezhuan (列传) sections of each book in the Corpus of the Twenty-Four Histories provided by the Hancheng website[4], which included a total of 8,304 sentences,for trial annotation. Finally, we obtained 2,913 annotated sentences and 4,047 event labels. Based on the trial annotation results and the actual situation during the annotation process,we modified and merged some event types.

In addition, to ensure the accuracy of classical Chinese historical event types and avoid personal subjective bias, we invited experts and students with linguistic and computer science backgrounds to evaluate our event types. After these efforts, we constructed the final event schema for CHED.

4 Annotation Process

We used Fig. 3 to illustrate our process.

4.1 Document Selection

In order to ensure the completeness and high quality of the corpus, we chose the published book *The Twenty-Four Histories (12 volumes of annotated editions with comparison of classical Chinese and modern Chinese)* published by Xianzhuang Shuju (线装书局) as our main source of annotated corpus.

There are three main reasons for choosing published books: **1) High-quality corpus**: the corpus in published books has been carefully selected and strictly reviewed multiple times; **2) Reduced workload**: the standardized typesetting of books eliminates the need for additional data prepossessing; **3) Provide reference translations**: the books provide high-quality aligned classical Chinese and modern Chinese corpus, facilitating reference for annotation personnel.

We mainly focused our annotations on the Benji (本纪) and Liezhuan (列传) (the main body of the histories), selecting 2–3 complete volumes at random from each of the Twenty-Four Histories to ensure complete historical figure records. In total, we selected 61 volumes, comprising 61 historical figures, 13,159 sentences, and 236,842 characters. Our main objective is to identify and label triggers in classical Chinese texts, and determine the event categories to which these triggers belong.

[4] https://guoxue.httpcn.com/zt/24shi/.

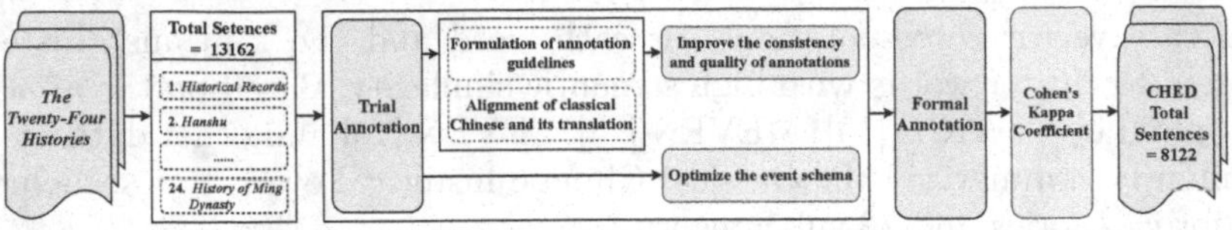

Fig. 3. The entire annotation process from raw corpus to dataset is presented, including two main stages, as well as the measures taken to ensure the quality of annotation.

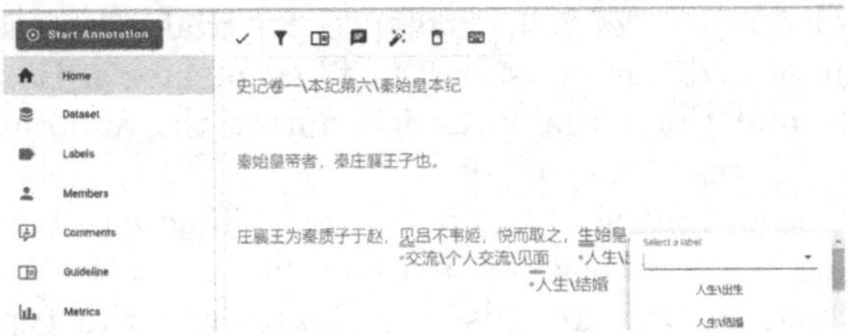

Fig. 4. The Doccano annotation interface contains three events in this example, with triggers "见" (jian), "取" (qu), and "生" (sheng). We can select the corresponding event type below each trigger for annotation.

4.2 Annotation Stage

The annotation process mainly consisted of two stages: **1) Trial annotation** was to preliminary test and refine the types of historical events in classical Chinese, as well as to unify the annotation discrepancies between the two annotators. This was helpful for improving the consistency and accuracy of the formal annotation stage; **2) Formal annotation**: the two annotators were assigned different tasks. Annotator 1 was responsible for annotating the first 12 books of the Twenty-Four Histories, while annotator 2 for the latter 12 books. Specifically, as shown in the Fig. 4, we created a sequence annotation project on the Doccanno platform[5] and split the documents into units of sentences delimited by periods for ease of annotation.

4.3 Annotation Quality

In this section, we introduce our three main measures taken to ensure the accuracy and consistency of the annotated corpus.

Annotation Guidelines. To ensure dataset quality and improve manual annotation consistency, rules and standards have been established for selecting triggers.

Contextual and Semantic Priority. We should focus on the semantics of the translation and its original context because the problem of polysemy is particularly prominent in classical Chinese, and the process of annotation is prone

[5] https://github.com/doccano.

to errors in understanding. In example (1) and (2), "胜之" (sheng zhi) and "败之" (bai zhi) have different usages, but both semantically denote victory. We annotated both of them as "Military-Ceasefire-Vanquish" based on the semantic meaning of the translated text.

(1) 军事-停战-战胜：四月，友宁引兵西，至兴平，及李茂贞战于武功，大败之。

(*Military-Ceasefire-Vanquish: In April, Youning led his army westward to Xingping and fought against Li Maozhen in Wugong, where he achieved a resounding victory.*)

(2) 军事-停战-战胜：与晋战河阳，胜之。

(*Military-Ceasefire-Vanquish: In the battle against Jin at Heyang, they emerged victorious.*)

Simplest Trigger. It's best to use simple triggers that are easy to understand and annotate, as this reduces the time and cost of annotation, minimizes subjective differences among annotators, simplifies subsequent processing and analysis, and ultimately improves the accuracy and reliability of the annotated data. For example (3), we only label the noun "水" (flood), while "大" (massive) is not labeled.

(3) 自然-灾害-水灾：秋七月乙酉，三郡大水。

(*Nature-Disaster-Flood/Drought: In the second month of autumn, there was a severe flood in three counties.*)

Event Property. It is difficult to immediately determine event attributes such as tense and polarity in classical Chinese because crucial information is often omitted. We have adopted LEVEN's event annotation guidelines [16] and annotate any events that are mentioned. In example (4), even if the attack has not yet taken place, we still annotate it.

(4) 军事-攻击-征伐：引兵欲攻燕，屯中山。

(*Military-Attack-Conquest: The army is preparing to attack Yan kingdom and stationed at Zhongshan.*)

Incorporation of Ancient Cultural Knowledge. Classical Chinese contains a wealth of historical and cultural background knowledge that must be taken into consideration when constructing event schema and annotating them. For example, Classical Chinese has specific vocabulary expressions for the change of official positions, such as "去" (qu) and "罢" (ba), which means "dismiss".

Alignment of Classical Chinese and Its Translation. It was necessary to provide annotators with an objective reference translation standard during the annotation process to ensure consistency, given the difficulty of understanding the semantics of classical Chinese. Our aligned classical Chinese and modern Chinese data mainly came from the *Twenty-Four Histories (12 volumes of annotated editions with comparison of classical Chinese and modern Chinese)* published by Xianzhuang Shuju (线装书局).

Cohen's Kappa Coefficient. To verify the consistency of the annotations and ensure the validity and reliability of the dataset, we conducted cross-validation using Cohen's Kappa coefficient. Specifically, the labeled sentences were divided into two datasets, A and B, with annotator 1 and annotator 2 each annotating a portion of the sentences. A random sample of 10% of the sentences was taken from each dataset, and the annotators swapped datasets to annotate the sampled sentences.

Regarding the calculation standard for Cohen's kappa coefficient, we considered the annotation to be consistent if both annotators labeled the same event labels for the same sentence, and considered it to be inconsistent if they labeled different event labels. After conducting 4 rounds of cross-validation, the average kappa coefficient was **68.49%**, indicating a relatively high level of consistency between the two annotators and a high level of reliability for the annotation results. Inconsistent annotations often stem from ambiguity resulting from multiple meanings of words in historical texts. Such as example (5), the character "屯" may have been incorrectly labeled as the trigger for the "Military-Garrisoning" event. However, it is actually a noun that means "military camp". Therefore, the sentence should be annotated with "还" as the trigger word for the "Movement-Arrive" event type.

(5) 坚还屯。 (*Sun Jian returned to the military camp.*)

*Annotator 1: *Military-Garrisoning*: 坚还屯。
Annotator 2: *Movement-Arrival*: 坚还屯。

5 Data Analysis

In this section, we mainly introduce the scale and distribution of the dataset, as well as the phenomenon of data sparsity that has been observed, and provide possible explanations for it.

5.1 Data Size

The dataset consists of 61 volumes and 61 historical figures from the Twenty-Four Histories, comprising a total of 13,159 sentences and 236,842 characters. Among them, there are 8,122 sentences with event labels, totaling 145,973 characters, and a total of 14,154 labels.

The scale of the dataset we finally constructed is moderate due to the difficulty and high cost of cross-historical annotation. However, it contains rich information on classical Chinese history texts from different dynasties and historical figures, and has certain representativeness. It can be used in the future to train and evaluate algorithms and models for classical Chinese historical event detection.

5.2 Data Distribution

An imbalanced distribution of event types is indicated by Fig. 5 in the CHED dataset. The major event types-including *Military*, *Communication*, *Movement* and *Position*, account for the vast majority of the dataset. Among the event subtypes depicted in Fig. 6, including *Arrive*, *Hold_a_position*, *Conquest*, *Dispatch* and others, the proportions are higher. This imbalance may result in insufficient recognition of minority events by models, posing a challenge for future classical Chinese ED tasks.

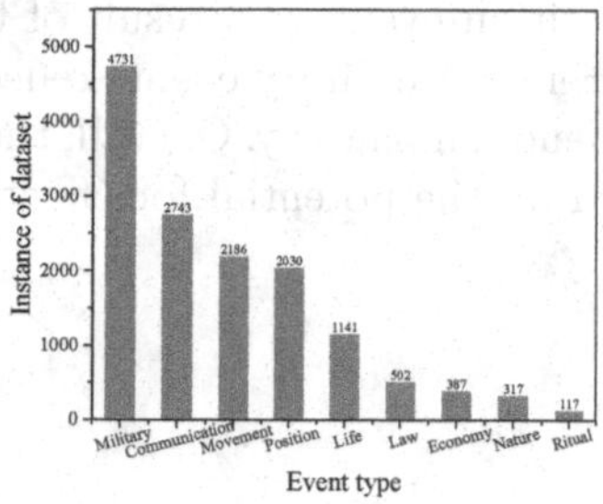

Fig. 5. Distribution of event types in CHED.

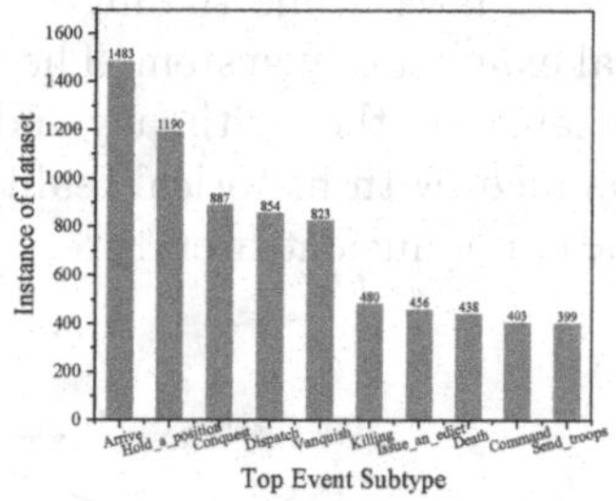

Fig. 6. Top event sub-types in CHED.

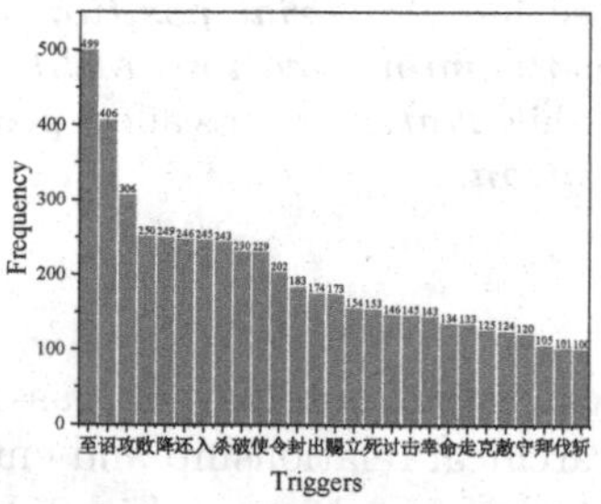

Fig. 7. The triggers that appear with a frequency greater than 100 in the sentences of the CHED.

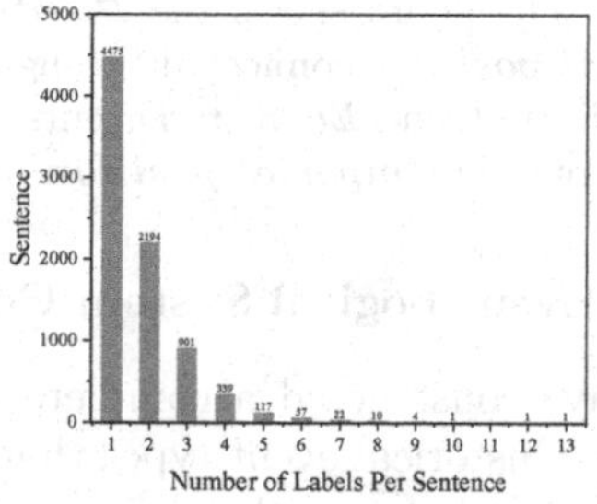

Fig. 8. The number of event labels that appear per sentence in the CHED.

Following our previous annotation standards, Figure 7 displays the triggers that appear at a frequency greater than 100 in the sentences, which primarily consist of monosyllabic words. The frequency distribution of triggers corresponds to the proportion of event types. For instance, "至" (zhi) corresponds to the *Arrival* event. This indicates that identifying high-frequency triggers in a sentence to predict the corresponding event type is a vital aspect in classical Chinese historical ED.

Displaying the number of event labels that appear in a single sentence, Fig. 8 reveals that a single sentence typically contains one or multiple event types, with 1–3 event types being the most common. This poses a challenge for accurately detecting multiple event types in classical Chinese.

Several possible explanations for the imbalanced distribution observed in the CHED dataset have been identified based on historical facts from ancient China. The frequency of certain events in historical texts reveals significant aspects of ancient Chinese political, social, and cultural life. The emphasis on posthumous honor is shown by the disparity in the frequency of birth and death events. The prevalence of imperial edict events indicates a society governed by men rather than laws, while the high proportion of position events is a result of the imperial examination system. The frequent occurrence of military events reflects the challenges to the legitimacy and orthodoxy of feudal monarchy. Overall, these findings align with historical reality and demonstrate the potential for effective digitization of ancient literature.

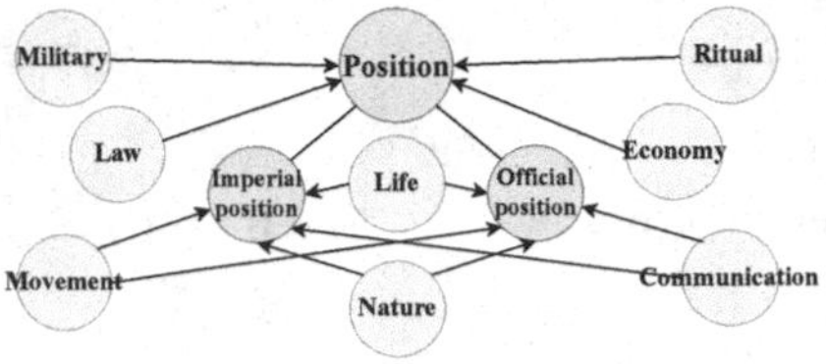

Fig. 9. The figure shows the ***Position*** event divided into ***Imperial position*** and ***Official position*** connected through ***Movement*** and ***Communication***. ***Military***, ***Law***, ***Ritual***, and ***Economy*** events serve ***Position*** while ***Nature*** events affect people represented by ***Imperial position*** and ***Official position***.

5.3 Event Logical System Construction

We have constructed a complete and logically consistent ontology of classical Chinese historical event types that exhibit a hierarchical relationship and entail connections between the major categories of event types, as shown in Fig. 9. It is our belief that the central theme of records in Twenty-Four Histories continues to revolve around political power struggles and the pursuit of authority. Therefore, we focus on the ***Position*** events as the core, which are further divided into ***imperial position*** and ***official position***, reflecting the two major relationships between emperors and officials in ancient China.

The transition of political power is generally reflected in ***Military*** events, which seize power through warfare and maintain power through ***Law*** events, supported by the ***Economy*** events that are centered around the taxation system. In order to strengthen the legitimacy of their political power, emperors often hold ***Ritual*** events, including the worship of heavenly deities to emphasize the divine right of emperors, the worship of ancestral spirits to emphasize the continuity of their bloodline-based inheritance system centered around the eldest son, and the worship of sages (e.g. Confucius) to provide a source of legitimate political ideology for their regimes.

In a political system that centers around imperial power, there exists a relationship between emperors and officials, where ***Movement*** and ***Communication*** events are utilized to facilitate the transmission of political orders and the implementation or abolition of measures from top to bottom. The ***Life*** events mainly refer to the lives of the emperor and the officials, which are the main records of figures in the Benji (本纪), Liezhuan (列传) and Shijia (世家) sections of the Twenty-Four Histories.

Table 1. The detailed statistics of subsets of CHED

Dataset	Sentences	Event_labels	Characters
Training	5,685	9,979	102,636
Validation	1,218	2,056	21,618
Test	1,219	2,119	21,719
Total	8,122	14,154	145,973

At the same time, the records of ***Nature*** events in the Twenty-Four Histories mainly focus on how natural events affected the behavior of the emperor and the officials. For example, in Volume One of Song Shi (宋史), in the Benji (本纪) of Taizu (太祖), the sentence following contains *famine* event, which affected the emperor's subsequent actions, namely, ordering the opening of granaries to provide relief for the people due to the occurrence of famine in eight provinces.

(6) 辛亥, 澶, 滑, 卫, 魏, 晋, 绛, 蒲, 孟八州饥, 命发廪振之。

(In Xinhai year, there was a famine in eight provinces, including Chanzhou, Huazhou, Weizhou, Jinzhou, Jingzhou, Puqizhou, and Mengzhou. The emperor commanded the opening of granaries to provide relief for the people.)

6 Experiments

6.1 Setting

We randomly shuffled the dataset and divided it into training set, validation set, and test set in a ratio of 0.7:0.15:0.15. The sizes of each part of the dataset are shown in the Table 1.

Regarding the hyper parameters of the model, including BERT, BiLSTM, IDCNN, CRF, we set the seed number of the random number generator to 123 to ensure the reproducibility and stability of the model. We set the maximum input sequence length to 150 to ensure model performance. The train batch size is set to 32, and the eval batch size is set to 12 for training and validation batches, respectively. Due to the specificity of the corpus and the imbalance of the labels, we set the number of training epochs to 30, the learning rate to 3e-05, dropout to 0.3, and adam epsilon to 1e−08 to prevent the model from over-fitting.

Inspired by Leven [16], we used two perspectives of micro and macro for the evaluation metrics of the model, including precision, recall, and f1-score. This was because we noticed the imbalance of the labels for classical Chinese event types. The micro perspective focuses on categories with a large number of samples, considering the frequency of each category's occurrence in the samples. The macro perspective treats each category equally, enabling us to evaluate the model from multiple aspects.

Table 2. The experimental results by modeling ED as a sequence labeling task on the CHED.

Model	Micro			Macro		
	Precision	Recall	F1-score	Precision	Recall	F1-score
BERT	74.58	77.11	75.82	**67.95**	65.05	65.19
BERT+CRF	**75.15**	77.06	**76.10**	67.69	65.22	64.98
BiLSTM	70.40	64.98	67.58	58.40	51.36	53.15
BiLSTM+CRF	70.24	66.73	68.44	60.77	52.91	54.76
IDCNN	71.70	60.97	65.90	57.98	44.40	49.05
IDCNN+CRF	71.04	63.66	67.15	55.50	46.88	49.44
BERT+BiLSTM+CRF	72.93	**77.68**	75.23	66.17	**66.64**	**65.23**

6.2 Baseline

We approached the ED task by dividing it into two tasks: **1) Sequence labeling task**: We labeled the event type corresponding to the triggers to detect events in a sentence, using BERT, BiLSTM, IDCNN, and CRF as baseline models. BERT from chinese-bert-wwm-ext [3] was used as the input vector representation for BiLSTM and IDCNN models, and the project code was based on tianshan1994[6] [12]; **2) Multi-class classification task**: We utilized BERT [3] and T5 [11] with human-crafted prompts to predict the upcoming sentence given the known context, and transformed the multi-label classification problem into a binary classification problem to detect events in a sentence. We designed a prompt template: (***["placeholder":"text_a"] Does the sentence contain ["placeholder":"text_b"]? [MASK]***), and "text_a" represents the sentence text and "text_b" represents the event type. The project code was based on Openprompt [4][7].

The baseline models used in each task were: BERT [3] and T5 [11] are pre-trained language models that have demonstrated state-of-the-art performance on a range of NLP tasks. BiLSTM is a widely used sequence modeling method that captures bidirectional context [5]. IDCNN is a convolutional neural network that

[6] https://github.com/taishan1994/pytorch_bert_bilstm_crf_ner.

[7] https://github.com/thunlp/OpenPrompt.

uses different dilation kernel sizes to capture contextual information at different ranges [1]. CRF is a commonly used sequence labeling model that improves labeling accuracy by considering the dependencies between labels [7]. Prompt is a novel technique for zero-shot learning tasks that allows the model to perform new tasks without any training examples by adding special prompts [4] (Tables 2 and 3).

6.3 Result and Analysis

In the sequence labeling task, overall, the micro-average results outperformed the macro-average results, due to the imbalanced distribution of event labels where some labels had fewer instances in the dataset, resulting in insufficient learning by the model. The results showed that the BERT+CRF model performed the best, while the performance of the BiLSTM and IDCNN models was inferior, respectively. Additionally, the BERT+BiLSTM+CRF model had the highest macro-average f1-score while the IDCNN model had the lowest macro-average f1-score.

Table 3. The experimental results by modeling ED as a multi-class classification task on the CHED.

Model	Micro			Macro		
	Precision	Recall	F1-score	Precision	Recall	F1-score
BERT+Prompt	87.36	87.36	87.36	86.88	74.26	76.27
T5+Prompt	87.93	87.93	87.93	83.39	74.70	75.69

These results indicate that the BERT+CRF model is better suited for this task than other models, as it can capture richer contextual information and the use of CRF can address label dependencies and enhance algorithm performance. However, in the historical ED task in classical Chinese texts, triggers are often monosyllabic, and label dependencies may not be as strong, hence the influence of the CRF model may not be as significant.

In multi-class classification tasks, the difference between the results of micro-average and macro-average is not significant compared to sequence labeling tasks. This may be because Prompt is more suitable for handling datasets with few samples, and it provides additional information to the pre-trained language model through manually designed prompts, enabling the model to better utilize existing knowledge for classification tasks. Moreover, the Prompt method performed well. Unlike sequence labeling tasks, multi-class classification tasks focus more on the classification of historical events in classical Chinese texts, and therefore, the BERT/T5 + Prompt model may have an advantage in classification.

There may be several reasons for such results: **1) Model structure**: The superior performance of BERT in historical ED tasks in classical Chinese texts

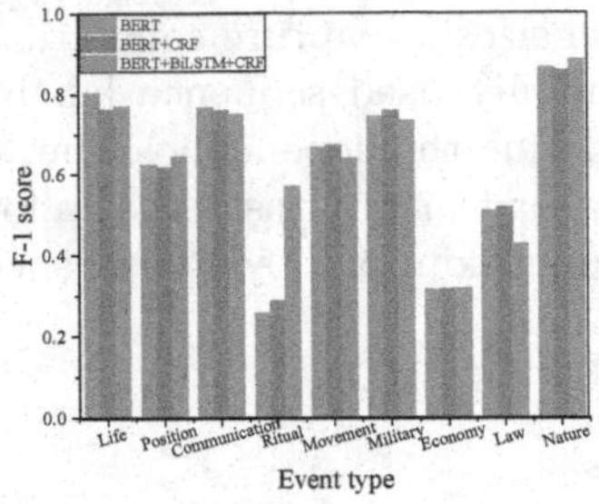

Fig. 10. The comparison results of f1-scores for different models across different event types in CHED.

may be attributed to its pre-trained Transformer-based architecture that effectively captures contextual information, compared to traditional neural network models like BiLSTM and IDCNN that may be affected by sequence length limitations and gradient vanishing. However, combining BERT with BiLSTM and CRF in the BERT+BiLSTM+CRF model did not yield the expected performance level, possibly due to increased noise or conflicts resulting from the introduction of more complexity and parameters. **2) Annotation errors**: Despite our efforts to ensure the quality and consistency of the annotations, the complexity of the context and cultural context of classical Chinese, as well as the ambiguity of word meanings, may lead to some annotation errors in the dataset, especially when the annotator's knowledge level is limited. These errors may have an impact on the performance of the models. **3) Sparse samples**: As shown in the Fig. 10, the f1-scores of different event types on different models are displayed. We can see that the performance of the Ritual, Economy, and Law events is poorer compared to other events, and the number of samples for these three event types in the dataset is also the smallest. With an imbalanced distribution, the presence of some noise or mislabeling may lead to poor recognition ability of the model for certain event types and stronger recognition ability for other types.

Overall, the BERT+CRF model performed the best in the task of historical ED in classical Chinese texts. The Prompt method also performed well. However, there is still significant room for improvement and challenges in future research.

7 Conclusion and Future Work

In conclusion, we have constructed a hierarchical and logical schema for classical Chinese events and used it to create the CHED based on the Twenty-four Histories corpus. The CHED can effectively facilitate the advancement of digital humanities research by providing a unique and profound historical perspective. Despite encountering various challenges during the construction of the dataset, we ensured the consistency and quality of the annotations. We assessed the effectiveness and quality of the dataset by testing it against several baselines and calculating kappa scores, and we obtained satisfactory results. Nevertheless, there is scope for further enhancement, and our future work will concentrate on expanding and optimizing the dataset to meet a wider range of application needs. Our dataset is a valuable resource not only for natural language processing but also for classical literature and cultural studies. Furthermore, it makes a significant contribution to the field of event detection in classical Chinese, and we anticipate that it will inspire further research and exploration.

Acknowledgements. This research project is supported by the National Natural Science Foundation of China (61872402), Science Foundation of Beijing Language and Culture University (supported by "the Fundamental Research Funds for the Central Universities") (18ZDJ03).

A Event Schema of the CHED

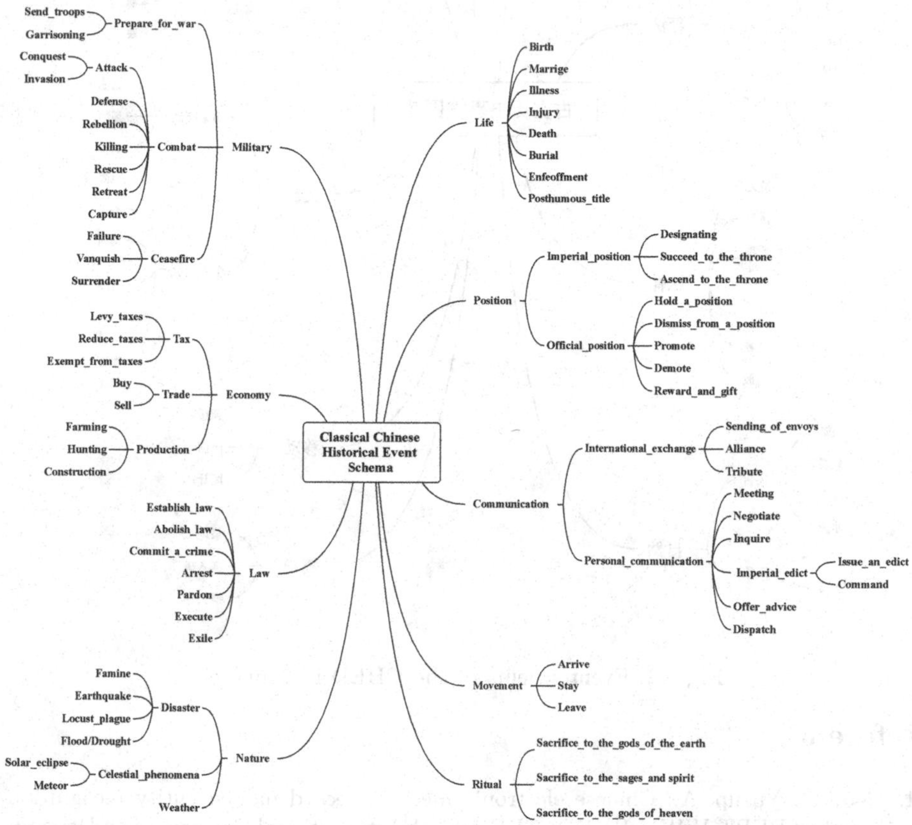

Fig. 11. Event schema of the CHED in English

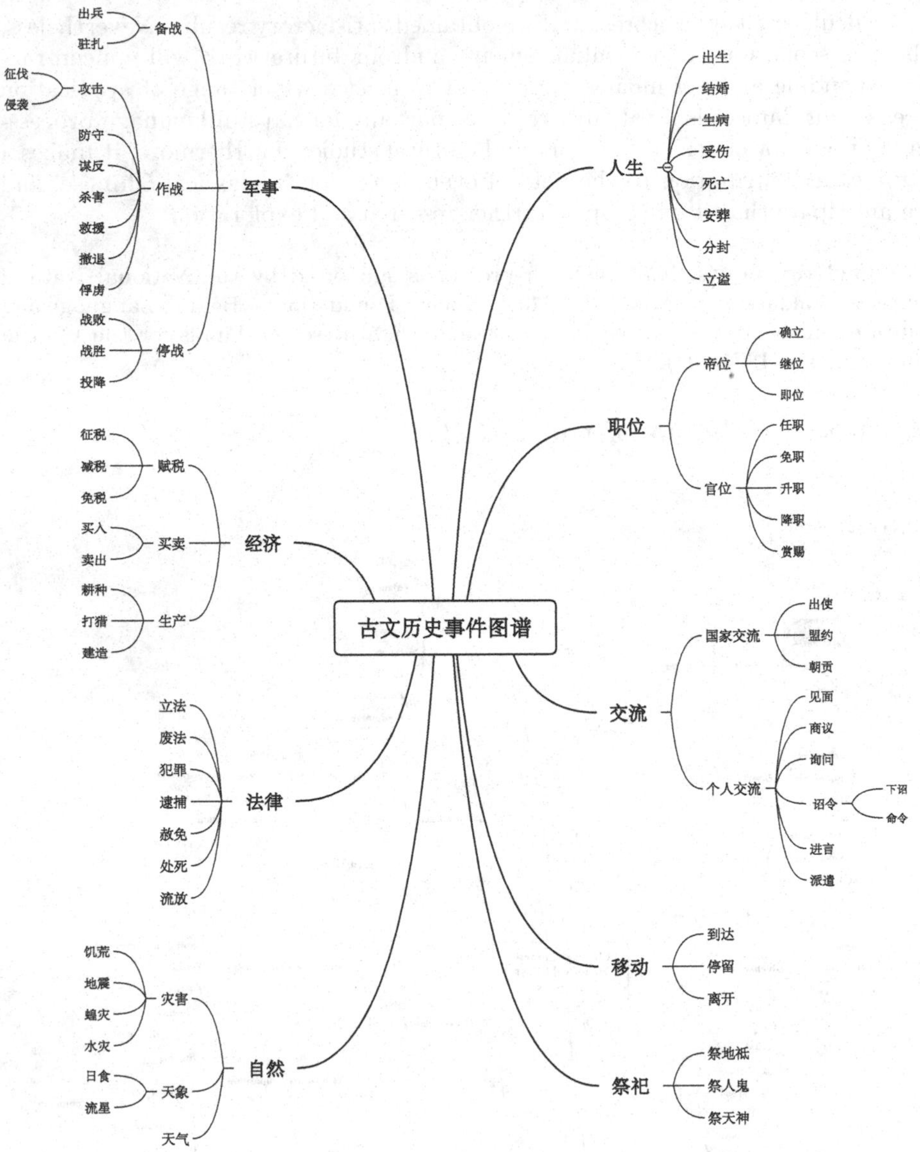

Fig. 12. Event schema of the CHED in Chinese

References

1. Cao, Y., Yusup, A.: Chinese electronic medical record named entity recognition based on BERT-WWM-IDCNN-CRF. In: 9th International Conference on Dependable Systems and Their Applications, DSA 2022, Wulumuqi, China, 4–5 August 2022. pp. 582–589. IEEE (2022). https://doi.org/10.1109/DSA56465.2022.00084
2. Dang, J.: Research on Knowledge Extraction Method of Chinese Classics Based on Deep Learning. Master's thesis, North University of China (2021)

3. Devlin, J., Chang, M., Lee, K., Toutanova, K.: BERT: pre-training of deep bidirectional transformers for language understanding. In: Burstein, J., Doran, C., Solorio, T. (eds.) Proceedings of the 2019 Conference of the North American Chapter of the Association for Computational Linguistics: Human Language Technologies, NAACL-HLT 2019, Minneapolis, MN, USA, 2–7 June 2019, Volume 1 (Long and Short Papers), pp. 4171–4186. Association for Computational Linguistics (2019). https://doi.org/10.18653/v1/n19-1423
4. Ding, N., et al.: Openprompt: an open-source framework for prompt-learning. In: Basile, V., Kozareva, Z., Stajner, S. (eds.) Proceedings of the 60th Annual Meeting of the Association for Computational Linguistics, ACL 2022 - System Demonstrations, Dublin, Ireland, 22–27 May 2022, pp. 105–113. Association for Computational Linguistics (2022). https://doi.org/10.18653/v1/2022.acl-demo.10
5. Hochreiter, S., Schmidhuber, J.: Long short-term memory. Neural Comput. **9**(8), 1735–1780 (1997). https://doi.org/10.1162/neco.1997.9.8.1735
6. Ji, J., Chen, J., N.L.J.S.: Effect analysis of Chinese event extraction method based on literatures. J. Mod. Inf. **35**(12)(3–10) (2015)
7. Lafferty, J.D., McCallum, A., Pereira, F.C.N.: Conditional random fields: probabilistic models for segmenting and labeling sequence data. In: Brodley, C.E., Danyluk, A.P. (eds.) Proceedings of the Eighteenth International Conference on Machine Learning (ICML 2001), Williams College, Williamstown, MA, USA, 28 June–1 July 2001, pp. 282–289. Morgan Kaufmann (2001)
8. Li, Q., et al.: Type information utilized event detection via multi-channel GNNs in electrical power systems. CoRR abs/2211.08168 (2022). https://doi.org/10.48550/arXiv.2211.08168
9. Li, X., et al.: DuEE: a large-scale dataset for Chinese event extraction in real-world scenarios. In: Zhu, X., Zhang, M., Hong, Yu., He, R. (eds.) NLPCC 2020. LNCS (LNAI), vol. 12431, pp. 534–545. Springer, Cham (2020). https://doi.org/10.1007/978-3-030-60457-8_44
10. Li, Z.: The study on the extraction of war events in Zuo Zhuan based on mixed approaches. Master's thesis, Nanjing Agricultural University (2019)
11. Raffel, C., et al.: Exploring the limits of transfer learning with a unified text-to-text transformer. CoRR abs/1910.10683 (2019). http://arxiv.org/abs/1910.10683
12. Shi, X., Chen, Y., Huang, X.: Key problems in conversion from simplified to traditional Chinese characters. In: International Conference on Asian Language Processing (2011)
13. Walker, C., Strassel, S., Medero, J., Maeda, K.: ACE 2005 multilingual training corpus. Linguist. Data Consort. Philadelphia **57**, 45 (2006)
14. Wang, X., et al.: MAVEN: a massive general domain event detection dataset. In: Webber, B., Cohn, T., He, Y., Liu, Y. (eds.) Proceedings of the 2020 Conference on Empirical Methods in Natural Language Processing, EMNLP 2020, Online, 16–20 November 2020, pp. 1652–1671. Association for Computational Linguistics (2020). https://doi.org/10.18653/v1/2020.emnlp-main.129
15. Xuehan Yu, L.H.J.X.: Extracting events from ancient books based on RoBERTa-CRF. Data Anal. Knowl. Discov. **5**(26–35) (2021)
16. Yao, F., et al.: LEVEN: a large-scale Chinese legal event detection dataset. In: Muresan, S., Nakov, P., Villavicencio, A. (eds.) Findings of the Association for Computational Linguistics: ACL 2022, Dublin, Ireland, 22–27 May 2022, pp. 183–201. Association for Computational Linguistics (2022). https://doi.org/10.18653/v1/2022.findings-acl.17
17. Zhongbao Liu, J.D.Z.Z.: Research on automatic extraction of historical events and construction of event graph based on historical records. Libr. Inf. Serv. **64**(116–124) (2020). https://doi.org/10.13266/j.issn.0252-3116.2020.11.013

Training NLI Models Through Universal Adversarial Attack

Jieyu Lin, Wei Liu, Jiajie Zou, and Nai Ding(✉)

Key Laboratory for Biomedical Engineering of Ministry of Education, College of Biomedical Engineering and Instrument Sciences, Zhejiang University, Hangzhou, China
{jieyu_lin,liuweizju,jiajiezou,ding_nai}@zju.edu.cn

Abstract. Pre-trained language models are sensitive to adversarial attacks, and recent works have demonstrated universal adversarial attacks that can apply input-agnostic perturbations to mislead models. Here, we demonstrate that universal adversarial attacks can also be used to harden NLP models. Based on NLI task, we propose a simple universal adversarial attack that can mislead models to produce the same output for all premises by replacing the original hypothesis with an irrelevant string of words. To defend against this attack, we propose Training with UNiversal Adversarial Samples (TUNAS), which iteratively generates universal adversarial samples and utilizes them for fine-tuning. The method is tested on two datasets, i.e., MNLI and SNLI. It is demonstrated that, TUNAS can reduce the mean success rate of the universal adversarial attack from above 79% to below 5%, while maintaining similar performance on the original datasets. Furthermore, TUNAS models are also more robust to the attack targeting at individual samples: When search for hypotheses that are best entailed by a premise, the hypotheses found by TUNAS models are more compatible with the premise than those found by baseline models. In sum, we use universal adversarial attack to yield more robust models.

1 Introduction

Pre-trained models have achieved impressive performance among natural language processing (NLP) tasks, including natural language inference (NLI) and machine reading comprehension (MRC) [8,12]. Nevertheless, these models are vulnerable under adversarial attacks [1]. For most adversarial attack methods, the adversarial samples are input-specific, i.e., the adversarial perturbation is targeted at a specific input. More recently, however, studies have also shown the existence of universal adversarial attacks, which are input-agnostic [1,20]. Multiple methods have been proposed to find universal adversarial samples. One method is to append an input-agnostic string of words to any input to convert the input into an adversarial sample. For example, Wallace et al. [20] use gradient-based search to find strings that, when concatenated to any input, could result in specific model output. For instance, for models trained on SNLI, prepending

M. Sun et al. (Eds.): CCL 2023, LNAI 14232, pp. 306–324, 2023.
https://doi.org/10.1007/978-981-99-6207-5_19

"nobody" to the hypothesis could cause >99% of the samples to be judged as being contradictory to the premise, even when all the tested hypotheses are in fact entailed by the premises. Another method is to randomly sample a large number of sentences and screen for universal adversarial samples. For example, Lin et al. [11] use such a method to find sentences that a model always judges as the correct answer to multiple-choice MRC questions.

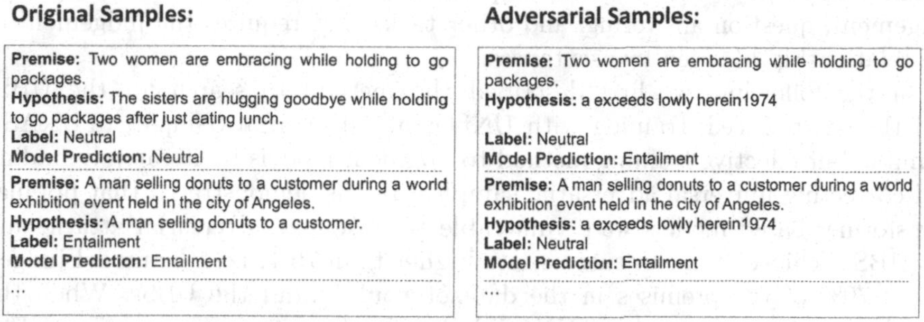

Original Samples:
Premise: Two women are embracing while holding to go packages.
Hypothesis: The sisters are hugging goodbye while holding to go packages after just eating lunch.
Label: Neutral
Model Prediction: Neutral
Premise: A man selling donuts to a customer during a world exhibition event held in the city of Angeles.
Hypothesis: A man selling donuts to a customer.
Label: Entailment
Model Prediction: Entailment
...
Adversarial Samples:
Premise: Two women are embracing while holding to go packages.
Hypothesis: a exceeds lowly herein1974
Label: Neutral
Model Prediction: Entailment
Premise: A man selling donuts to a customer during a world exhibition event held in the city of Angeles.
Hypothesis: a exceeds lowly herein1974
Label: Neutral
Model Prediction: Entailment
...

Fig. 1. Examples of the NLI task and universal adversarial attack method adopted in this work. The model originally output the correct answers. Nonetheless, when UBS, i.e., "a exceeds lowly herein1974", is presented as the hypothesis, the model is fooled to give out entailment prediction, even though they are actually irrelevant.

The mainstream method to increase the robustness of models against adversarial attacks is adversarial training [7, 13, 24]. In this process, adversarial samples are generated and injected into the training batch. Adversarial training generally focuses on input-specific attacks, which involve small perturbations and targeting at individual samples. Therefore, models fine-tuned with these methods still fail in universal adversarial attacks [17]. Besides, unlike input-specific attacks, universal attacks use single perturbation to cause the model fail in lots of samples, making it more effective to generate adversarial samples. Recently, in the domain of vision, some studies have also proposed to use universal adversarial samples for adversarial training [17, 23], which is proved to be helpful for improving the robustness of the models. Nonetheless, in the domain of NLP, efficient training with universal adversarial samples appears to be more challenging. Generally, universal adversarial attacks for NLP models are achieved by appending an input-agnostic adversarial sequence to the input. Training with such adversarial samples can easily lead to a degenerated solution of ignoring the appended adversarial sequence [9].

To avoid such degenerated solutions, we propose a new universal adversarial attack method, where the adversarial samples are created by directly replacing specific components of the input with adversarial sequence. This work is based on NLI, a task requires models to judge whether a premise can entail a hypothesis. Specifically, instead of appending an adversarial sequence to the hypothesis, we create adversarial samples by replacing the original hypothesis with a string of words, referred to as the Universal Biased Strings (UBSs), as shown in Fig. 1. Here, UBSs are the strings wrongly judged as being entailed by a large number of premises by the model. For an effective UBS, the model judges that it is entailed by any premise. We automatically generate UBSs, and present them as hypothesis sentence to fool the models. The advantage of using UBSs for attack is that they are guaranteed to be irrelevant to individual premises, since no string can be entailed by all premises. Notably, although this work is based on the NLI task, it can be easily adapted to describe, e.g., sentence similarity judgement, question answering, and other tasks that requires the judgement of the relationship between two sentences.

In the following, we first described the method to search for the UBSs and then introduced Training with UNiversal Adversarial Samples (TUNAS), a simple but effective training method to augment models by iteratively finding and correcting universal adversarial samples. It was demonstrated that popular transformer-based models were vulnerable to universal adversarial attack, and the UBSs achieved a mean success rate higher than 79%, i.e., the model judged that >79% of the premises in the dataset could entail the UBSs. When the models were fine-tuned using TUNAS, however, the mean success rate of UBSs dropped to <5%. Furthermore, when searching for strings that could be best entailed by a particular premise, the strings found by a model fine-tuned with TUNAS were more reasonable compared with that found by a baseline model.

2 Method

2.1 Task and Models

Our work was based on two standard NLI datasets, i.e., SNLI [2] and MNLI [21]. In these datasets, each sample contained a pair of sentences, one being the premise and the other being the hypothesis, and a label indicating the relation between the premise and hypothesis, i.e., entailment, contradiction, or neutral. We tested three mainstream pre-trained transformer models, i.e., BERT [5], RoBERTa [12], and DeBERTa-v3 [8], and considered both the base version and large version of the models. The pre-trained models were provided by Huggingface [22] and were fine-tuned based on SNLI or MNLI, respectively. During fine-tuning, the inputs were formatted as [CLS, premise, SEP, hypothesis, SEP]. At the output, the final embedding of the CLS token, denoted as C, was run through a linear layer to obtain three logits for each label, i.e., logits $= WC + b$. The label with the highest logit was selected as the model prediction. The models were trained based on the cross-entropy loss between the golden label and the model prediction. The fine-tuning parameters and model performance were shown in Appendix A.

Algorithm 1. UBS Generation (Gradient-based search)

Input: input premises, P; vocabulary, V; target model, f; embedding layer, E; loss function, $Loss$;
Parameter: search times, T; UBS length, L; iterations, N; candidates number, K; return UBSs number, M;
Output: M UBSs

```
result ← ∅
for i ← 1 to T do                                  ▷ Repeat search procedure for T times
    result ← result + SearchingBiasedStringsStep(...)
end for
return result
function SEARCHINGBIASEDSTRINGSSTEP
    UBS ← s_{0:L}, s ∈ hypothesis set                ▷ Initialize current UBS
    memory ← ∅
    for iteration ← 1 to N do                      ▷ Select candidates for each token in UBS
        V_cand ← top-k_{w∈V}(−E(w)^⊤ · ∇_UBS Loss(f(P, UBS), entailment), K)
        for i ← 0 to L do                          ▷ for each token position
            for t ∈ V_cand^(i) do                   ▷ for each candidate
                UBS' ← UBS_{0:i} ⊕ t ⊕ UBS_{i+1:L}    ▷ Generate potential UBSs
                memory[UBS'] ← −Loss(f(P, UBS'), entailment)    ▷ Evaluate potential UBSs
            end for
            UBS ← argmax_{s∈memory} memory[s]       ▷ Update current UBS
        end for
    end for
    return top-k_{s∈memory}(memory[s], M)
end function
```

2.2 UBS Generation

We used two methods, i.e., gradient-based search and dataset-based sampling, to search for the UBSs. Operationally, all strings returned by the search algorithms were referred to as UBSs. The effectiveness of a UBS was quantified by its success rate $A\%$, i.e., the target model judged that the UBS was entailed by $A\%$ of the premises in a premise set. To balance the process time and the effectiveness, for each UBS, the success rate was calculated based on 256 premises randomly sampled from the dataset being analyzed.

Gradient-Based Search. The UBSs were generated using a variant of the gradient-based search method proposed by Wallace et al. [20]. The length of the UBS, i.e., L, was fixed, and an L-word UBS was initialized by randomly selecting a hypothesis from hypothesis set, which contained all hypotheses in the dataset being analyzed. The UBS was updated for N iterations to maximize the success rate. The tokens in the current UBS were iteratively replaced to create potential UBSs with higher success rate (Eq. 1), and the top M UBSs with the highest success rate were returned (see Algorithm 1).

Algorithm 2. UBS Generation (Dataset-based Sampling)

Input: input premises, P; target model, f; loss function, $Loss$;
Parameter: hypothesis set, H; return UBSs number, M;
Output: M Magnet UBSs

1: $result \leftarrow \emptyset$
2: **for** $h \in H$ **do**
3: $result[h] \leftarrow -Loss(f(P, h), entailment)$ ▷ Evaluate each hypothesis string
4: **end for**
5: **return** $\underset{s \in result}{top\text{-}k}\ (result[s], M)$

In the iteration procedure, we calculated the first-order Taylor approximation of the change in loss to entailment label caused by replacing each token in the UBS [6,20]. A candidate set $V_{cand} \in \mathbb{R}^{L \times K}$ was identified (Eq. 1), where the top K tokens estimated to cause the greatest decrease to loss for each position were collected. For each token at the position i ($i \in [1, L]$) of the current UBS, potential UBSs were generated by replacing the token with the candidates (Eq. 2). The potential UBS with the highest success rate was retained as the current UBS.

$$V_{cand} = \underset{w \in V}{top\text{-}k}(-E(w)^{\intercal} \cdot \nabla_{UBS} Loss(\cdot), K) \tag{1}$$

$$potential\ UBSs = \{UBS_{0:i} \oplus t \oplus UBS_{i+1:L} | t \in V_{cand}^{(i)}\} \tag{2}$$

where $E(w)$ was the input embedding of token w. $Loss(\cdot)$ was the cross-entropy loss, and $\nabla_{UBS} Loss(\cdot)$ was the average gradient of the loss to entailment label over a batch. $\oplus$ denoted token concatenation. The search procedure was repeated T times with different initialization strings to ensure the diversity of the UBSs. The hyperparameters were set as following: $T = 10$, $M = 50$, $N = 20$, and $K = 20$ (full hyperparameters for UBS attack and TUNAS were listed in Appendix B). Therefore, for each model, a total of 500 (10 × 50) UBSs were generated.

Dataset-Based Sampling. We also utilized the hypotheses extracted from the validation split of each dataset to find effective UBSs [11]. Three hundred of hypotheses with the highest success rate were referred to as the magnet UBSs. Details of the algorithm were shown in Algorithm 2.

Table 1. The accuracies for models on the validation split.

Dataset	BERT base		BERT large	
	Baseline	TUNAS	Baseline	TUNAS
SNLI	0.8962	0.8920	0.9186	0.9191
MNLI	0.8404	0.8360	0.8625	0.8661

Algorithm 3. TUNAS

Input: input batches, X={{(premise, hypothesis, label), ...}, ...}; total training step, N_{step};
Parameter: added adversarial samples ratio, R; UBSs update times, N_{update};

1: **procedure** COLLECT UBSs
2: Using Gradient-based search to collect UBS set $UBSs$
3: $UBSs \leftarrow FILTER(UBSs)$, s.t., the success rate of $UBSs$ is above 0.33
4: **end procedure**
5: $step_{update} \leftarrow$ LINSPACE(0, N_{step}, N_{update}) ▷ Initialize steps for collecting UBSs
6: $step_{augment} \leftarrow$ RANDOM_CHOICE(range(0, N_{step}), R) ▷ Initialize steps for data augment
7: **for** $step \leftarrow$ 1 to N_{step} **do**
8: **if** $step$ in $step_{update}$ **then**
9: Collect UBSs
10: **end if**
11: get current training batch {(premise, hypothesis, label), ...} from X
12: TRAIN({(premise, hypothesis, label), ...}) ▷ Train model with the genuine samples
13: **if** $step$ in $step_{augment}$ **then** ▷ Train model with the adversarial samples
14: **if** $UBSs$ is not empty **then**
15: TRAIN({(premise, UBS, *neutral*), ...}), $UBS \in UBSs$
16: **end if**
17: **end if**
18: Update learning rate and other settings
19: **end for**

2.3 Training with Universal Adversarial Samples

For the baseline fine-tuning procedure, the model was initialized with the pre-trained parameters, and then fine-tuned based on the downstream NLI task. Here, we proposed an augmented fine-tuning procedure, i.e., Training with UNiversal Adversarial Samples (TUNAS), to generate models that are more robust to UBS attack. TUNAS differed from the baseline fine-tuning procedure in the following way (lines 8–10 and 13–17 in Algorithm 3): On the one hand, we uniformly selected N_{update} steps from the entire training procedure N_{step} steps, and collected the UBSs found in these steps for augmented training. We utilized the gradient-based search to generate the UBSs that were between 5 and 7 words. On the other hand, we randomly selected R% of the N_{step} steps, where the same amounts of adversarial samples as the original samples were added to the training batch. The inferential relation between the UBSs and any premise was labeled as neutral. The hyperparameters were set as following: $N_{update} = 40$, $R\% = 0.3$.

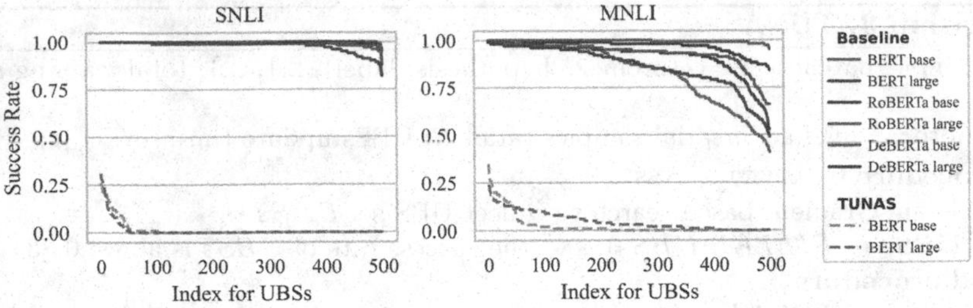

Fig. 2. Success rate of the top 500 UBSs.

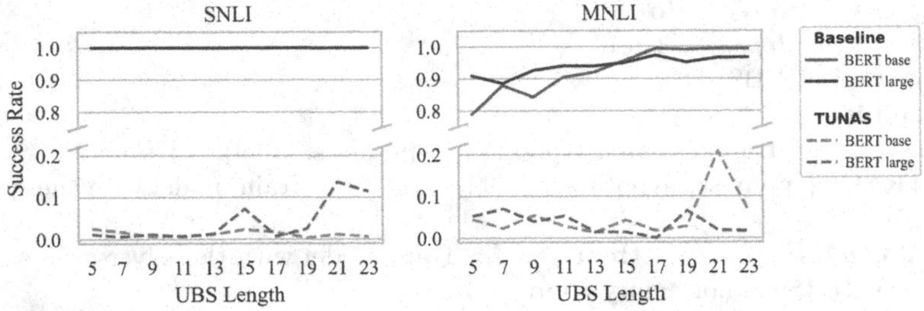

Fig. 3. Mean success rate of UBSs with different lengths.

3 Experiments

3.1 UBS Attack on Baseline Models

We tested whether models fine-tuned using the baseline procedure were sensitive to the UBS attack. The UBSs were generated using gradient-based search and the UBS length was set to 5. Over 75% of the UBSs achieved a success rate above 70%, and the mean success rate averaged across all the 500 UBSs returned by the gradient-based search was above 79% for all models (Fig. 2). The UBSs were mostly ungrammatical nonsense word strings. For instance, "a exceeds lowly herein1974" was an UBS that achieved a success rate of 100% for RoBERTa-large fine-tuned on SNLI. In other words, the models judged that all premises in the validation split of the dataset entailed this string. More examples were shown in Appendix C.

3.2 UBS Attack on TUNAS Models

Next, we asked whether TUNAS could improve the robustness of models. We fine-tuned BERT-base and BERT-large using TUNAS. The performance on MNLI/SNLI were comparable for models fine-tuned using the baseline procedure and TUNAS (Table 1). Nevertheless, for over 80% of the UBSs returned by the gradient-based search, the success rate was below 10%, and the mean success rate was below 5% (Fig. 2). These results suggested that TUNAS could

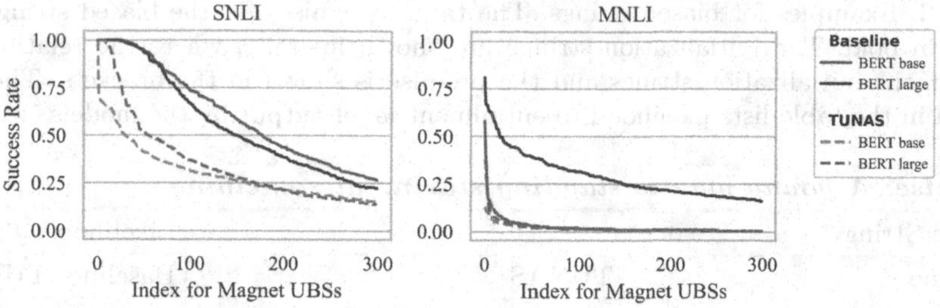

Fig. 4. Success rate of the top 300 magnet UBSs.

significantly improve the robustness of models to UBS attack, while maintaining the same task performance.

3.3 Generalization of Robustness Against UBSs

The current TUNAS procedure only considered 5-word, 6-word, and 7-word UBSs. Here, we further evaluated whether the model fine-tuned using these UBSs were also robust to UBSs of other lengths. We varied the length of the UBS from 5 to 23, in steps of 2, and found that models fine-tuned using TUNAS were more robust to UBSs of all tested lengths (Fig. 3). Furthermore, the UBSs generated by the gradient-based search were generally ungrammatical word strings (Appendix C), it was possible that TUNAS only instructed the models to output "neutral" for ungrammatical word strings. To rule out this possibility, we further tested the models on the magnet UBSs, which were grammatical meaningful sentences. On SNLI, TUNAS decreased the success rate of magnet UBSs by 31% and 21% on average, for BERT-base and BERT-large (Fig. 4). On MNLI, magnet UBSs were only effective at attacking BERT-large and TUNAS decreased the success rate of magnet UBSs by 27% on average.

4 Biased Strings for Individual Premises

TUNAS could effectively increase the robustness to the UBS attack. The UBS attack, however, were particularly strong attacks that utilized a single word string to attack all possible premises. Next, we evaluated whether TUNAS could also increase the robustness to attacks targeting at individual premises. Here, the BERT base model fine-tuned on SNLI was used as an example. The other TUNAS models showed similar results, which were shown in Appendix D.

4.1 Biased Strings Generation

We applied the same gradient-based search to find word strings that were best entailed by single premise. Specifically, the algorithm was the same as Algorithm 1, except that the input premise set P was replaced by a particular premise. Here,

Table 2. Examples for biased strings. The target premises for the biased strings are shown in bold. The initialization strings are shown in italic, where the relationship between the initialization strings and the premise is shown in the brackets. The last column in the table lists likelihood to entailment label output by the models.

Premise: A young man is standing staring at something			
Biased String		Likelihood	
Baseline	TUNAS	Baseline	TUNAS
(Premise Itself) *A young man is standing staring at something*		96.98	98.31
a human person was standing. at thisceded	A human human is standing staring at something	99.51	98.92
(Neutral) *A young man is looking intently at a young woman*		0.92	0.47
Humans existuffed or movementifiable concerningoir young persons	Elustient is seen peers at a young something	99.27	93.20
(Contradiction) *A young man is asleep*		0.01	0.03
near males Humansestive remotely present	foss staringthating	99.25	86.12
(Entailment) *A young man has his eyes open*		96.61	96.64
sts human individual has bodily eyes encounteredrricular	an young man has his eyes open	99.38	97.22
Premise: A black dog and a goose swim in the water			
Biased String		Likelihood	
Baseline	TUNAS	Baseline	TUNAS
(Premise Itself) *A black dog and a goose swim in the water*		96.99	97.14
A human beings and a freshwateristed in thebol	A black animal or a human swim in the water	99.35	98.51
(Neutral) *The goose has something in its mouth*		63.87	82.43
humansnial possessing something wet or bodily	An dog with one of dark color	99.33	98.19
(Contradiction) *The animals are not in the water*		2.95	3.90
Human animals comprisedroats bodyddling water	Human animals are together in the water	99.37	98.28
(Entailment) *There are two animals in the water*		98.57	98.41
There comprises animal objectsluk In human	There are animals mammals in the water	99.42	98.88

the strings returned were referred to as biased strings. We randomly selected 100 premises from the SNLI validation split for this analysis. Since the gradient-based search was sensitive to the initial condition, we tested 4 initialization strings for

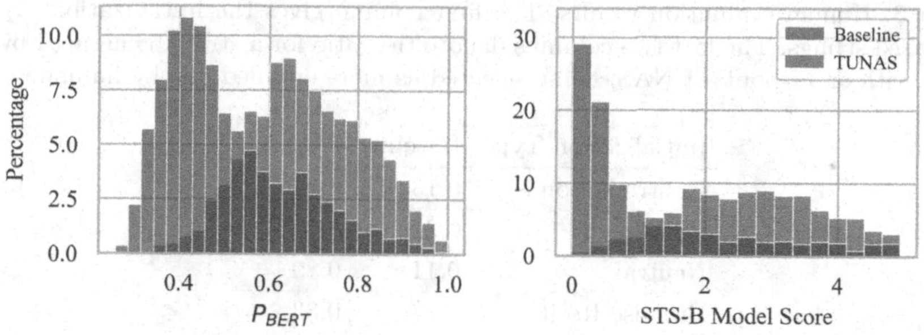

Fig. 5. Histograms of BERTScore Precision and STS-B model score for sentence pairs, where the hypotheses were generated by the model with or without TUNAS based on the given premise.

each premise: One string was the premise itself, the other 3 strings were the 3 hypotheses associated with the premise in the dataset, which were separately labeled as entailment, neutral, and contradiction. For each initialization string, the search returned 30 biased strings. The search was separately applied to the baseline model and models fine-tuned using TUNAS.

4.2 Relatedness Between Biased Strings and Premises

Examples of the biased strings were shown in Table 2. In general, the biased strings generated based on the TUNAS models were more readable and more related to the premise, compared to the biased strings generated based on the baseline model.

We further quantified the relatedness between the premises and the biased strings based on human judgement and model-based metrics. For human judgement, we recruited subjects to judge which of the two biased strings (generated by the baseline model or the TUNAS model) were more related to the premise. Automatic model-based metrics were also carried out to evaluate the relatedness between the premise and the biased strings, i.e., BERTScore [25] and STS-B model score [4]. BERTScore was a sentence-level metric to compare the semantic similarity between two sentences, which ranged from 0 to 1. Likewise, STS-B was a regression task of predicting the semantic similarity score of two sentences, which ranged from 0 to 5. We used the base version of BERT fine-tuned with STS-B task to score for the sentence pairs.

Human Judgement. Two hundred samples were randomly selected, and each sample contained a premise and 2 hypotheses that were separately generated by the baseline and TUNAS models using the same initialization string. For each sample, 10 subjects judged which hypothesis was more related to the premise. Subjects could choose that they could not judge which hypothesis was more related. Such responses (22% of all collected responses) were excluded from final

Table 3. Human evaluation results. The first column gives the initialization type of the biased strings. The last two columns denote the ratio for a string, generated by the model with or without TUNAS, being selected as more entailed one by human.

Initialization Type	Baseline	TUNAS
Contradiction	0.16	0.84
Entailment	0.21	0.79
Neutral	0.11	0.89
Premise Itself	0.17	0.83

analysis. Results showed that 84% of the biased strings generated by TUNAS model were judged as being more related to the premise (Table 3).

Model-Based Metrics. We reported BERTScore Precision and the STS-B model score (Fig. 5). Results showed that the biased strings generated by models fine-tuned using TUNAS achieved a higher similarity score on average (P_{BERT} = 0.69 and STS-B model score = 2.72), compared to the baseline model (P_{BERT} = 0.50 and STS-B model score = 1.11), indicating that the models fine-tuned with TUNAS could generate biased strings with more similar semantics to the premises.

5 Related Work and Discussion

Adversarial Attack. Generally, the adversarial attacks are input-specific, which generate specialized perturbations for each input. Jia and Liang [9] attack the reading comprehension models by adding a distractor sentence to the input paragraph. Song et al. [18] use natural attacks to cause semantic collisions, i.e., irrelevant sentence pairs are judged to be similar by the NLP models. In these methods, an extra evaluation should be used to verify the golden labels of the adversarial samples. In this paper, we avoid human evaluation by generating UBSs, which are inherent to be neutral with most of the premises.

Universal adversarial attacks are input-agnostic. Wallace et al. [20] and Behjati et al. [1] oncurrently propose to perform gradient-based search strategies to generate input-agnostic sequences, referred to as triggers, that can cause a model to output a specific prediction when concatenated to any input. Song et al. [19] extend it to generate natural triggers. Parekh et al. [15] propose a data-free attack method. Most of the previous works construct the attack based on appending strategy, and aim at generating and analyzing universal adversarial triggers. In this work, we propose to use UBSs directly for attack, and aim at augmenting the models through universal adversarial samples. Here, we do not use append strategy to avoid models from learning to ignore attack positions during augmentation.

Adversarial Training. Adversarial training is one of the most successful approaches for defending against adversarial attacks [7,13], where adversarial samples are used for training to improve the robustness of models. Universal adversarial training has proven to be beneficial in the domain of computer vision [14,17], and malware classification [3]. Lin et al. [11] augment the training procedure for multi-choice models using magnet options: The options irrelevant to the questions are still prone to be selected as the answer by the models. Our work is more extensive as we utilize a searching method for generating UBSs automatically, which is more effective in digging out the biases of the models.

In this work, we use ungrammatical UBSs for adversarial training. Although the ungrammatical UBSs are unlikely to appear in real-world scenarios, they have potential to reveal the biases learned by the models. Meanwhile, they can serve as a cheap method to augment the models. Results suggest that the model augmented by ungrammatical UBSs also perform better in defending grammatical UBSs attack. Moreover, this work is based on NLI task, but the UBSs generation and application can be extended to many NLP tasks. For example, in multiple-choice task, e.g., RACE [10], the model can be fooled to choose a certain biased option as the answer. In span extraction tasks, e.g., SQuAD [16], the model can be fooled to always output a certain biased span. In these cases, it is still feasible to generate universal adversarial examples and use them for adversarial training.

6 Conclusion

Universal adversarial attacks are effective in revealing the shallow heuristics learned by the models [20]. Here, we propose TUNAS, which utilizes universal adversarial samples to harden the models. A simple yet effective universal adversarial attack method is designed by replacing the hypotheses with UBSs, which can achieve above 79% success rate among 2 NLI tasks. The UBSs are generated automatically by gradient-based method. In TUNAS, the universal adversarial samples are generated and used to train the models. The models fine-tuned using TUNAS show robustness against UBS attack, while maintaining comparable task performance. Moreover, when searching biased strings for individual premises, models fine-tuned using TUNAS could generate strings better entailed by the premise.

Acknowledgements. This work was partly supported by the STI2030-Major Project, grant number: 2021ZD0204105. We would like to thank the anonymous reviewers for their valuable comments on this work.

Appendix A Hyperparameters for Fine-Tuning

Table 4. Hyperparameters for fine-tuning on SNLI and MNLI.

MNLI/SNLI	BERT		RoBERTa		DeBERTa	
Version	base	large	base	large	base	large
Learning rate	2e−5/3e−5	2e−5/3e−5	2e−5/2e−5	6e−6/6e−6	2e−5/2e−5	6e−6/5e−6
Train epochs	3/2	3/2	3/3	2/2	3/2	2/2
Batch size	32/32	32/32	32/32	64/64	64/64	32/32
Weight decay	0.01/0.1	0.01/0.1	0.1/0.01	0.0/0.0	0.0/0.0	0.0/0.0

Table 5. The fine-tuned models' performance on the validation splits.

Model/Accuracy	Dataset		
	SNLI	MNLI	
		matched	mismatched
BERT base	0.8962	0.8404	0.8393
BERT large	0.9186	0.8625	0.8651
RoBERTa base	0.9103	0.8784	0.8762
RoBERTa large	0.9265	0.9034	0.9013
DeBERTa base	0.9330	0.9024	0.9070
DeBERTa large	0.9392	0.912	0.9105

The parameters we used in the process of fine-tuning the pre-trained models were shown in Table 4 [5,8,12]. Model performance after fine-tuning was shown in Table 5.

Appendix B Hyperparameters for UBS Attack and TUNAS

The hyperparameters used for UBS attack and TUNAS were shown in Table 6. The usage for hyperparameters were described in Algorithm 1 and Algorithm 3. Here, the filter threshold for loss referred to the filtering condition for UBSs used in TUNAS. The potential UBSs with task loss on entailment label above the filter threshold would be filtered.

Table 6. Hyperparameters for UBS attack and TUNAS.

Hyperparameters	TUNAS		UBS attack	Single Test
	SNLI	MNLI		
UBS length, L	5–7/5	5/5	5–23(step = 2)	Initialization string length
Split for evaluation	test	test matched	dev	Single premise
hypothesis set	Randomly selected hypothesis and magnet hypotheses	Randomly selected hypothesis	Randomly selected hypotheses	none
Iterations, N	20	20	20	40
Candidates number, K	20	20	20	30
Return UBSs number, M	50	50	50	30
Batch size	256	256	256	1
Search times, T	10	10	10	1
Added adversarial samples ratio, R	0.3	0.3	–	–
UBSs update times, N_{update}	40	40	–	–
Filter threshold for loss	1	1	–	–

Appendix C Examples for UBSs

We selected several UBSs with high success rate obtained from 256-sample evaluation, and re-evaluated them on the full validation splits. The UBSs as well as their success rate were reported in Table 7. The UBSs were all meaningless token sequences.

Table 7. Success rate of the UBSs on models that are fine-tuned with or without TUNAS. For each model, the UBSs with the highest success rate are selected, and are evaluated on the test splits. The fine-tuning dataset used for the model are shown in the brackets. For MNLI, success rate show on both matched and mismatched sets, in the format of "matched set result/mismatched set result".

Model	SNLI		MNLI	
	UBS	Success rate	UBS	Success rate
Baseline				
BERT base	individuals physically something geographicallymered	1.0000	Across Miraentry crosses aspect	0.9937/0.9865
BERT large	of lungs Ad bearing a	1.0000	bakeryple encounters words referring	0.9937/0.9898
RoBERTa base	sufficientAbility humanoid circumstanceUSE	1.0000	votationInsert word something	0.9975/0.9971
RoBERTa large	a exceeds lowly herein1974	1.0000	Supportedpired upholding utilizingSupported	0.9960/0.9957
DeBERTa base	footed humans mobilised locomotionAthletic	1.0000	representative Ostensiblysomething instantiated a	0.9687/0.9699
DeBERTa large	corporeal individuals Emotionally humPub	0.9987	antly viewer usage Audience utilization	0.9922/0.9939
TUNAS				
BERT base	human person played outside	0.3236	We can cross concerns	0.2808/0.3343
BERT large	The man ps up	0.2717	Something receives recognizable involvement	0.2729/0.3862

Appendix D Model-Based Metrics on Biased Strings

Here was the result for other TUNAS models equal to the test in Sect. 4 on model-based metrics, as shown in Fig. 6. The results were similar to BERT base model on SNLI. The biased strings generated by models fine-tuned using TUNAS achieved a higher similarity scores in both of the metrics.

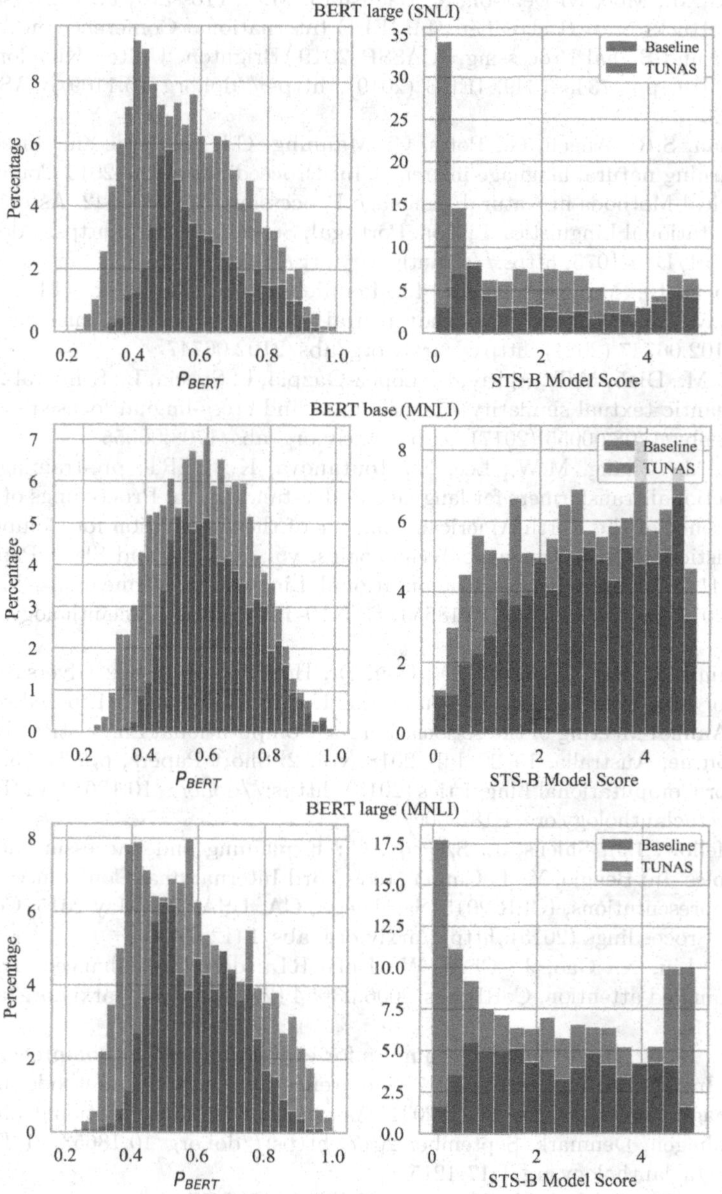

Fig. 6. Histograms of semantic similarity evaluated by BERTScore or STS-B model score. Biased strings were generated based on baseline models or models fine-tuned with TUNAS.

References

1. Behjati, M., Moosavi-Dezfooli, S., Baghshah, M.S., Frossard, P.: Universal adversarial attacks on text classifiers. In: IEEE International Conference on Acoustics, Speech and Signal Processing, ICASSP 2019, Brighton, United Kingdom, 12–17 May 2019, pp. 7345–7349. IEEE (2019). https://doi.org/10.1109/ICASSP.2019.8682430
2. Bowman, S.R., Angeli, G., Potts, C., Manning, C.D.: A large annotated corpus for learning natural language inference. In: Proceedings of the 2015 Conference on Empirical Methods in Natural Language Processing, pp. 632–642. Association for Computational Linguistics, Lisbon, Portugal, September 2015. https://doi.org/10.18653/v1/D15-1075, https://aclanthology.org/D15-1075
3. Castro, R.L., Muñoz-González, L., Pendlebury, F., Rodosek, G.D., Pierazzi, F., Cavallaro, L.: Universal adversarial perturbations for malware. CoRR abs/2102.06747 (2021). https://arxiv.org/abs/2102.06747
4. Cer, D.M., Diab, M.T., Agirre, E., Lopez-Gazpio, I., Specia, L.: SemEval-2017 task 1: semantic textual similarity - multilingual and cross-lingual focused evaluation. CoRR abs/1708.00055 (2017). http://arxiv.org/abs/1708.00055
5. Devlin, J., Chang, M.W., Lee, K., Toutanova, K.: BERT: pre-training of deep bidirectional transformers for language understanding. In: Proceedings of the 2019 Conference of the North American Chapter of the Association for Computational Linguistics: Human Language Technologies, vol. 1 (Long and Short Papers), pp. 4171–4186. Association for Computational Linguistics, Minneapolis, Minnesota, June 2019. https://doi.org/10.18653/v1/N19-1423, https://aclanthology.org/N19-1423
6. Ebrahimi, J., Rao, A., Lowd, D., Dou, D.: HotFlip: white-box adversarial examples for text classification. In: Gurevych, I., Miyao, Y. (eds.) Proceedings of the 56th Annual Meeting of the Association for Computational Linguistics, ACL 2018, Melbourne, Australia, 15–20 July 2018, vol. 2: Short Papers, pp. 31–36. Association for Computational Linguistics (2018). https://doi.org/10.18653/v1/P18-2006, https://aclanthology.org/P18-2006/
7. Goodfellow, I.J., Shlens, J., Szegedy, C.: Explaining and harnessing adversarial examples. In: Bengio, Y., LeCun, Y. (eds.) 3rd International Conference on Learning Representations, ICLR 2015, San Diego, CA, USA, 7–9 May 2015, Conference Track Proceedings (2015). http://arxiv.org/abs/1412.6572
8. He, P., Liu, X., Gao, J., Chen, W.: DeBERTa: decoding-enhanced BERT with disentangled attention. CoRR abs/2006.03654 (2020). https://arxiv.org/abs/2006.03654
9. Jia, R., Liang, P.: Adversarial examples for evaluating reading comprehension systems. In: Proceedings of the 2017 Conference on Empirical Methods in Natural Language Processing, pp. 2021–2031. Association for Computational Linguistics, Copenhagen, Denmark, September 2017. https://doi.org/10.18653/v1/D17-1215, https://aclanthology.org/D17-1215
10. Lai, G., Xie, Q., Liu, H., Yang, Y., Hovy, E.: RACE: large-scale reading comprehension dataset from examinations. In: Proceedings of the 2017 Conference on Empirical Methods in Natural Language Processing, pp. 785–794. Association for Computational Linguistics, Copenhagen, Denmark, September 2017. https://doi.org/10.18653/v1/D17-1082, https://aclanthology.org/D17-1082

11. Lin, J., Zou, J., Ding, N.: Using adversarial attacks to reveal the statistical bias in machine reading comprehension models. In: Proceedings of the 59th Annual Meeting of the Association for Computational Linguistics and the 11th International Joint Conference on Natural Language Processing (vol. 2: Short Papers), pp. 333–342. Association for Computational Linguistics, Online, August 2021. https://doi.org/10.18653/v1/2021.acl-short.43, https://aclanthology.org/2021.acl-short.43
12. Liu, Y., et al.: RoBERTa: a robustly optimized BERT pretraining approach. CoRR abs/1907.11692 (2019). http://arxiv.org/abs/1907.11692
13. Madry, A., Makelov, A., Schmidt, L., Tsipras, D., Vladu, A.: Towards deep learning models resistant to adversarial attacks. In: 6th International Conference on Learning Representations, ICLR 2018, Vancouver, BC, Canada, 30 April–3 May 2018, Conference Track Proceedings. OpenReview.net (2018). https://openreview.net/forum?id=rJzIBfZAb
14. Mummadi, C.K., Brox, T., Metzen, J.H.: Defending against universal perturbations with shared adversarial training. In: 2019 IEEE/CVF International Conference on Computer Vision, ICCV 2019, Seoul, Korea (South), 27 October–2 November 2019, pp. 4927–4936. IEEE (2019). https://doi.org/10.1109/ICCV.2019.00503
15. Parekh, S., Singla, Y.K., Singh, S., Chen, C., Krishnamurthy, B., Shah, R.R.: Minimal: mining models for data free universal adversarial triggers. CoRR abs/2109.12406 (2021). https://arxiv.org/abs/2109.12406
16. Rajpurkar, P., Zhang, J., Lopyrev, K., Liang, P.: Squad: 100, 000+ questions for machine comprehension of text. In: Su, J., Carreras, X., Duh, K. (eds.) Proceedings of the 2016 Conference on Empirical Methods in Natural Language Processing, EMNLP 2016, Austin, Texas, USA, 1–4 November 2016, pp. 2383–2392. The Association for Computational Linguistics (2016). https://doi.org/10.18653/v1/d16-1264
17. Shafahi, A., Najibi, M., Xu, Z., Dickerson, J.P., Davis, L.S., Goldstein, T.: Universal adversarial training. In: The Thirty-Fourth AAAI Conference on Artificial Intelligence, AAAI 2020, The Thirty-Second Innovative Applications of Artificial Intelligence Conference, IAAI 2020, The Tenth AAAI Symposium on Educational Advances in Artificial Intelligence, EAAI 2020, New York, NY, USA, 7–12 February 2020, pp. 5636–5643. AAAI Press (2020). https://ojs.aaai.org/index.php/AAAI/article/view/6017
18. Song, C., Rush, A.M., Shmatikov, V.: Adversarial semantic collisions. In: Webber, B., Cohn, T., He, Y., Liu, Y. (eds.) Proceedings of the 2020 Conference on Empirical Methods in Natural Language Processing, EMNLP 2020, Online, 16–20 November 2020, pp. 4198–4210. Association for Computational Linguistics (2020). https://doi.org/10.18653/v1/2020.emnlp-main.344
19. Song, L., Yu, X., Peng, H.T., Narasimhan, K.: Universal adversarial attacks with natural triggers for text classification. In: Proceedings of the 2021 Conference of the North American Chapter of the Association for Computational Linguistics: Human Language Technologies, pp. 3724–3733. Association for Computational Linguistics, Online, June 2021. https://doi.org/10.18653/v1/2021.naacl-main.291, https://aclanthology.org/2021.naacl-main.291
20. Wallace, E., Feng, S., Kandpal, N., Gardner, M., Singh, S.: Universal adversarial triggers for attacking and analyzing NLP. In: Proceedings of the 2019 Conference on Empirical Methods in Natural Language Processing and the 9th International Joint Conference on Natural Language Processing (EMNLP-IJCNLP), pp. 2153–2162. Association for Computational Linguistics, Hong Kong, China, November 2019. https://doi.org/10.18653/v1/D19-1221, https://aclanthology.org/D19-1221

21. Williams, A., Nangia, N., Bowman, S.: A broad-coverage challenge corpus for sentence understanding through inference. In: Proceedings of the 2018 Conference of the North American Chapter of the Association for Computational Linguistics: Human Language Technologies, vol. 1 (Long Papers), pp. 1112–1122. Association for Computational Linguistics, New Orleans, Louisiana, June 2018. https://doi.org/10.18653/v1/N18-1101, https://aclanthology.org/N18-1101
22. Wolf, T., et al.: Transformers: state-of-the-art natural language processing. In: Proceedings of the 2020 Conference on Empirical Methods in Natural Language Processing: System Demonstrations, pp. 38–45. Association for Computational Linguistics, Online, October 2020. https://doi.org/10.18653/v1/2020.emnlp-demos.6, https://aclanthology.org/2020.emnlp-demos.6
23. Wong, E., Rice, L., Kolter, J.Z.: Fast is better than free: revisiting adversarial training. In: 8th International Conference on Learning Representations, ICLR 2020, Addis Ababa, Ethiopia, 16–20 April 2020. OpenReview.net (2020). https://openreview.net/forum?id=BJx040EFvH
24. Zhang, D., Zhang, T., Lu, Y., Zhu, Z., Dong, B.: You only propagate once: accelerating adversarial training via maximal principle. In: Wallach, H.M., Larochelle, H., Beygelzimer, A., d'Alché-Buc, F., Fox, E.B., Garnett, R. (eds.) Advances in Neural Information Processing Systems, vol. 32, Annual Conference on Neural Information Processing Systems 2019, NeurIPS 2019 (December), pp. 8–14, 2019, Vancouver, BC, Canada, pp. 227–238 (2019). https://proceedings.neurips.cc/paper/2019/hash/812b4ba287f5ee0bc9d43bbf5bbe87fb-Abstract.html
25. Zhang, T., Kishore, V., Wu, F., Weinberger, K.Q., Artzi, Y.: BERTScore: evaluating text generation with BERT. In: 8th International Conference on Learning Representations, ICLR 2020, Addis Ababa, Ethiopia, 26–30 April 2020. OpenReview.net (2020). https://openreview.net/forum?id=SkeHuCVFDr

Pre-trained Language Models

Revisiting k-NN for Fine-Tuning Pre-trained Language Models

Lei Li, Jing Chen, Botzhong Tian, and Ningyu Zhang(✉)

Zhejiang University & AZFT Joint Lab for Knowledge Engine, Hangzhou, China
{leili21,chenjing_1984,tbozhong,zhangningyu}@zju.edu.cn

Abstract. Pre-trained Language Models (PLMs), as parametric-based *eager learners*, have become the de-facto choice for current paradigms of Natural Language Processing (NLP). In contrast, k-Nearest-Neighbor (k-NN) classifiers, as the *lazy learning* paradigm, tend to mitigate over-fitting and isolated noise. In this paper, we revisit k-NN classifiers for augmenting the PLMs-based classifiers. From the methodological level, we propose to adopt k-NN with textual representations of PLMs in two steps: (1) Utilize k-NN as prior knowledge to calibrate the training process. (2) Linearly interpolate the probability distribution predicted by k-NN with that of the PLMs' classifier. At the heart of our approach is the implementation of k-NN-calibrated training, which treats predicted results as indicators for easy versus hard examples during the training process. From the perspective of the diversity of application scenarios, we conduct extensive experiments on fine-tuning, prompt-tuning paradigms and zero-shot, few-shot and fully-supervised settings, respectively, across eight diverse end-tasks. We hope our exploration will encourage the community to revisit the power of classical methods for efficient NLP (Code and datasets are available in https://github.com/zjunlp/Revisit-KNN).

1 Introduction

Pre-trained Language Models (PLMs) (Radford et al., 2018, Devlin et al., 2019, Raffel et al., 2020) have shown superior performance across a wide range of language-related downstream tasks (Kowsari et al., 2019, Nan et al., 2020). Afterward, the conventional paradigm *fine-tuning*, which extends extra task-specific classifiers on the top of PLMs, has been proposed to apply PLMs for downstream tasks. Recently, a new paradigm called prompt-tuning, which originated from GPT-3 (Brown et al., 2020), has been introduced and has shown better results for PLMs on few-shot and zero-shot tasks. Fine-tuning has proved to be effective on supervised tasks and is widely used as the standard method for natural language processing (NLP). Despite the effectiveness of adapting PLMs, parametric-based *eager learners* (Friedman, 2017), like PLMs with neural networks, require estimating the model parameters with an intensive learning stage. Besides, Training a large PLM model can require significant computing resources and energy, which have negative environmental consequences. As a result, there

M. Sun et al. (Eds.): CCL 2023, LNAI 14232, pp. 327–338, 2023.
https://doi.org/10.1007/978-981-99-6207-5_20

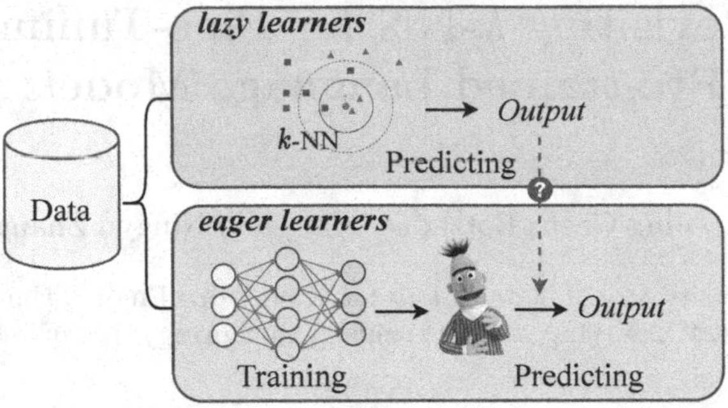

Fig. 1. Revisiting how does a lazy learner (k-NN) help the eager learner (PLM).

has been a growing interest in developing more efficient and sustainable methods for training and deploying PLMs (Fig. 1).

A stark contrast to PLMs is the k-NN classifier: a simplest machine learning algorithm that does not have a training phase but simply predicts labels based on the nearest training examples instead. NLP researchers (Khandelwal et al., 2020, He et al., 2021) have found that k-NN enable excellent unconditional language modeling (Khandelwal et al., 2020, He et al., 2021) during test phrase. According the definition in (Friedman, 2017), k-NN is actually a *lazy learner* that can avoid over-fitting of parameters (Boiman et al., 2008) and effectively smooths out the impact of isolated noisy training data (Orhan, 2018). Though k-NN has the above advantages, previous works only leverage k-NN for testing, and there is no systematic examination of the full utilization of k-NN for PLMs.

To this end, we have conducted a comprehensive and in-depth empirical study of the k-NN classifier for natural language understanding (NLU). Our approach involves leveraging the predictive results of a k-NN classifier and augmenting conventional parametric PLM classifiers in two steps: (1) We explore the role of k-NN as prior knowledge for calibrating training by using k-NN results as an indicator of easy vs. hard examples in the training set; (2) During inference, we linearly interpolate probability distributions with the PLM's predicted distributions to make the final prediction; (3) We conduct extensive experiments with fine-tuning in fully-supervised, few-shot and zero-shot settings, aiming to reveal the different scenarios where k-NN is applicable. We hope this work can open up new avenues for improving NLU of PLMs via k-NN and inspire future research to reconsider the role of "old-school"methods.

2 Related Work

k-NN in the Era of PLMs. The k-Nearest Neighbor (kNN) classifier is a classic non-parametric algorithm that predicts based on representation similarities. While kNN has lost some visibility compared to current deep learning approaches in recent years, it has not fallen off the radar completely. In fact, kNN has been used to enhance pre-trained language models (PLMs) in various tasks, such as unconditional language modeling (Khandelwal et al., 2020, He et al., 2021), machine translation (Khandelwal et al., 2021, Gu et al., 2018), and question answering (Kassner and Schütze, 2020). Most recently, (Alon et al., 2022, Meng et al., 2021) further respectively propose automaton-augmented and GNN-augmented retrieval to alleviate the computationally costly datastore search for language modeling. However, previous researchers (He et al., 2021, Khandelwal et al., 2021, Kassner and Schütze, 2020, Li et al., 2021, Meng et al., 2021, Alon et al., 2022, Zhang et al., 2022) mainly focus on generative tasks or adopt simple interpolation strategies to combine k-NN PLMs only at test time. (Shi et al., 2022) propose to leverage k-NN for zero-shot inference.

Revisiting k-NN for PLMs. Unlike them, we focus on empirically demonstrating that incorporating k-NN improves PLMs across a wide range of NLP tasks in fine-tuning and prompt-tuning paradigms on various settings, including the fully-supervised, few-shot and zero-shot settings. Note that our work is the first to comprehensively explore k-NN during both the training and inference process further for fruitful pairings: in addition to the approaches mentioned above, we propose to regard the distribution predicted by k-NN as the prior knowledge for calibrating training, so that the PLM will attend more to the examples misclassified by k-NN.

3 Methodology

The overall framework is presented in Fig. 2. We regard the PLM as the feature extractor that transforms the input textual sequence x into an instance representation $\mathbf{x}$ with dimensions D. We revisit k-NN in Sect. 3.1 and then introduce our method to integrate k-NN with tuning paradigms in Sect. 3.2.

3.1 Nearest Neighbors Revisited

Given the training set of n labeled sentences $\{x_1, \dots, x_n\}$ and a set of target labels $\{y_1, \dots, y_n\}$, $y \in [1, C]$, the k-NN classifier can be illustrated in the next three parts:

Feature Representations. For k-NN, we firstly have to collect the corresponding set of features $\mathcal{D} = \{\mathbf{x}_1, \dots, \mathbf{x}_n\}$ from the training set. Concretely, we assign $\mathbf{x}$ with the embedding of the `[CLS]` token of the last layer of the PLM for the fine-tuning procedure. More specifically, we define the feature representations as follows:

$$\mathbf{x} = \mathbf{h}_{\texttt{[CLS]}}, \tag{1}$$

The feature representation $\mathbf{q}$ of a query example x_q also follows the above equation.

Retrieve k Neighbors. Following the commonly practiced in k-NN (Friedman, 2017, Wang et al., 2019), we pre-process both $\mathbf{q}$ and features in the training set

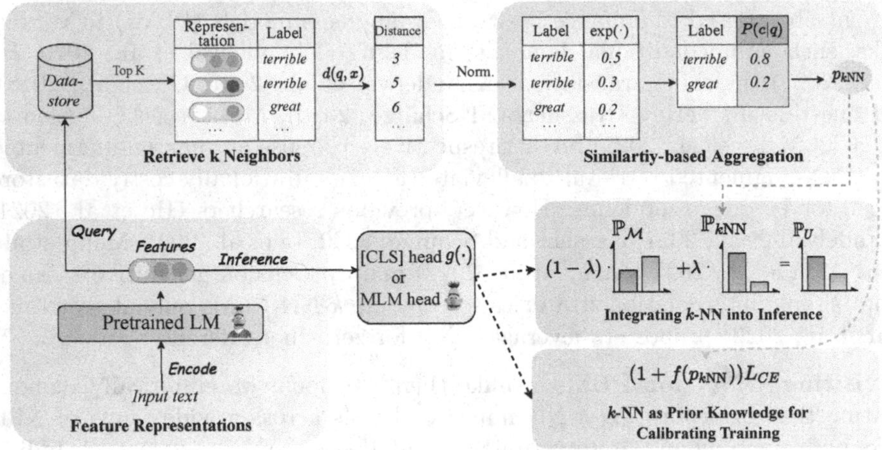

Fig. 2. Overview of incorporating k-NN for PLMs

$\mathcal{D}$ with $l2$-normalization. We then compute the similarity between the query $\mathbf{q}$ and each example in $\mathcal{D}$ with Euclidean distance as : $d(\mathbf{q}, \mathbf{x})$, $\forall \mathbf{x} \in \mathcal{D}$, where $d(\cdot, \cdot)$ is the Euclidean distance calculation function. According to the similarity, we select the top-k representations from $\mathcal{D}$, which are the closest in the distance to $\mathbf{q}$ in the embedding space.

Similarity-Based Aggregation. Let $\mathcal{N}$ donate the set of retrieved top-k neighbors, and $\mathcal{N}_y$ be the subset of $\mathcal{N}$ where the whole examples have the same class y. Then the k-NN algorithm converts the top-k neighbors to $\mathbf{q}$ and the corresponding targets into a distribution over $\mathcal{C}$ labels. The probability distribution of $\mathbf{q}$ being predicted as c is:

$$p_{k\text{NN}}(c|\mathbf{q}) = \frac{\sum_{\mathbf{x} \in \mathcal{N}_y} \exp\left(-d(\mathbf{q}, \mathbf{x})/\tau\right)}{\sum_{y \in C} \sum_{\mathbf{x} \in \mathcal{N}_y} \exp\left(-d(\mathbf{q}, \mathbf{x})/\tau\right)}, \tag{2}$$

where τ is the hyper-parameter of temperature.

3.2 Comprehensive Exploiting of k-NN

In this section, we propose to comprehensively leverage the k-NN, the representative of *lazy learning*, to augment the PLM-based classifier.

Role of k-NN as Prior Knowledge for Calibrating Training. As k-NN can easily make predictions for each query instance encountered without any training, it is intuitive to regard its predictions as priors to guide the network in focusing on hard examples during the training process of language models. We distinguish between easy and hard examples based on the results of k-NN. Given the probability distribution $p_{k\text{NN}}$ of $\mathbf{q}$ being predicted as true label y, we propose to adjust the relative loss for the correctly-classified or misclassified instances identified by k-NN, in order to reweight the cross-entropy loss $\mathcal{L}_{CE}$. Specifically, we define the calibrated training loss $\mathcal{L}_J$ as:

$$\mathcal{L}_U = (1 + f(p_{k\text{NN}}))\,\mathcal{L}_{CE}, \tag{3}$$

where $f(p_{k\text{NN}})$ donates the modulating factor[1] for calibration. We are inspired by Focal-loss (Lin et al., 2018) to employ the modulating factor, while our focus is on exploring the application of k-NN in the fine-tuning of PLMs.

Integrating k-NN into Inference. Let $\mathbb{P}_{\mathcal{M}}$ denote the class distribution predicted by the PLM, and $\mathbb{P}_{k\text{NN}}$ be the class distribution predicted by a k-NN classifier. Then, the $\mathbb{P}_{\mathcal{M}}$ is reformulates by interpolating the non-parametric k nearest neighbor distribution $P_{k\text{NN}}$ using parameter λ (Khandelwal et al., 2020) to calculate the final probability $\mathbb{P}_U$ of the label as:

$$\mathbb{P}_U = \lambda \mathbb{P}_{k\text{NN}} + (1 - \lambda)\mathbb{P}_{\mathcal{M}}, \tag{4}$$

where $\lambda \in [0, 1]$ is an adjustable hyper-parameter.

4 Experiments

Table 1. Detailed dataset statistics.

Dataset	Type	# Class	Test Size
SST-5	sentiment	5	2,210
TREC	question cls	5	500
MNLI	NLI	3	9,815
QNLI	NLI	2	5,463
BoolQ	QA	2	3,245
CB	NLI	3	250
SemEval	relation extraction	19	2,717
TACREV	relation extraction	42	15,509

4.1 Datasets

We choose a variety of NLP tasks to evaluate our proposed methods, including sentiment analysis task (SST-5 (Socher et al., 2013)), question classification task (TREC (Voorhees and Tice, 2000)), NLI tasks (MNLI (Williams et al., 2018) and QNLI (Rajpurkar et al., 2016)), sentence-pair classification task (BoolQ (Clark et al., 2019) and CB (De Marneffe et al., 2019)), and information extraction tasks (SemEval (Hendrickx et al., 2010) and TACREV (Alt et al., 2020)). We also list a detailed introduction of datasets in Table 1.

[1] We specify the $f(p_{k\text{NN}}) = (1 - p_{k\text{NN}})^{\gamma}$, and other factors are also alternative.

4.2 Experimental Settings

Compared Baseline Methods. We adopt RoBERTa$_{\text{large}}$ (Liu et al., 2019) as the underline PLM and conduct comprehensive experiments to integrate k-NN into PLMs. We choose the baseline approaches and the variant of our proposed method as follows: (1) **k-NN:** the method described in Sect. 3.1, which performs classification directly through nearest neighbor retrieval of instance features without relying on any pre-trained language models (PLMs). (2) **FT:** which denotes vanilla fine-tuning with PLMs. (3) **FT_Scratch:** which denotes vanilla PLMs in zero-shot setting. (4) **PT:** which denotes prompt-tuning with PLMs, similar to (Gao et al., 2021). (5) **UNION-INF:** a variant of our method, which simply linear interpolate k-NN and paradigms of PLMs during the test time. (6) **UNION-ALL:** the completeness of our approach, which involves applying k-NN as prior knowledge for calibrating training and also integrating k-NN into inference.

Table 2. Results on eight NLP tasks across the fully-supervised, few-shot (16-shot) and zero-shot settings. For the 16-shot setting, we provide the mean and standard deviation across three different random seeds. Scores that are marked with an underline signify the best results among all methods.

Shot	Method	SST-5	TREC	MNLI	QNLI	BoolQ	CB	SemEval	TACREV	AVG
		Acc.	F1.	Acc.	Acc.	Acc.	F1.	F1.	F1.	Score.
Full	**k-NN**	35.8	80.0	41.5	57.2	61.4	42.3	2.5	5.3	40.8
	FT	59.2	97.8	83.9	89.1	81.7	89.5	89.4	72.5	82.9
	UNION-INF	59.5	98.0	84.0	89.2	82.9	89.6	89.2	67.8	82.5
	UNION-ALL	$\underline{60.9}$	$\underline{98.2}$	$\underline{84.2}$	$\underline{90.8}$	$\underline{83.4}$	$\underline{90.5}$	$\underline{89.6}$	$\underline{73.1}$	$\underline{83.8}$
16	**k-NN**	$25.6_{2.4}$	$46.1_{5.0}$	$33.7_{0.3}$	$51.6_{1.3}$	$50.4_{2.6}$	$40.8_{4.9}$	$0.5_{0.4}$	$0.9_{0.3}$	31.1
	FT	$43.3_{0.7}$	$86.6_{4.7}$	$44.4_{4.5}$	$55.3_{3.7}$	$56.0_{4.2}$	$68.3_{4.7}$	$64.1_{2.3}$	$25.6_{0.3}$	55.5
	UNION-INF	$43.0_{1.2}$	$86.7_{4.5}$	$44.5_{4.5}$	$55.4_{3.4}$	$55.4_{4.3}$	$65.6_{4.7}$	$65.1_{2.1}$	$30.5_{1.7}$	55.8
	UNION-ALL	$\underline{43.7_{0.5}}$	$\underline{90.0_{3.9}}$	$\underline{51.7_{1.8}}$	$\underline{58.1_{2.7}}$	$\underline{57.6_{2.7}}$	$\underline{69.8_{4.5}}$	$\underline{67.2_{3.3}}$	$\underline{32.1_{3.1}}$	$\underline{58.9}$
0	**FT_Scratch**	23.8	22.6	31.6	49.5	37.8	21.5	8.2	0.1	24.4
	PT	36.7	38.2	50.9	50.8	62.2	39.7	10.9	1.1	36.3
	UNION-INF	$\underline{51.6}$	$\underline{82.4}$	$\underline{67.5}$	$\underline{67.4}$	$\underline{62.9}$	$\underline{56.9}$	$\underline{11.8}$	$\underline{3.2}$	$\underline{50.5}$
	UNION-ALL	35.1	38.0	53.7	50.4	62.4	50.3	11.3	1.4	37.8

Settings. We test the above methods in full-supervised, few-shot and zero-shot experiments, we assign different settings, respectively: (1) **Full-supervised setting:** We use full trainsets to train the PLMs and as neighbors to retrieve. (2) **Few-shot setting:** We follow LM-BFF (Gao et al., 2021) to conduct 16-shot experiment and test the average performance with a fixed set of seeds $\mathcal{S}_{\text{seed}}$, across three different sampled $\mathcal{D}_{\text{train}}$ for each task. In this setting, we use the few-shot training set as k-NN neighbors to retrieve. (3) **Zero-shot setting:** We directly evaluate the vanilla FT and UNION-INF on the test set **without training**. As for UNION-ALL, we take the prompt tuning (Gao et al., 2021) to tag the pseudo labels on **unlabeled** trainsets and apply untrained k-NN in the training and inference.

4.3 Hyper-parameter Settings

We report the hyper-parameters in Table 3. For the GLUE and SuperGLUE datasets, we follow LM-BFF[2] to construct templates and verbalizer for prompt-tuning. While for RE datastes, we follow KnowPrompt (Chen et al., 2021) to construct templates and verbalizer. We utilize Pytorch to conduct experiments with 1 Nvidia 3090 GPUs. We used the AdamW optimizer for all optimizations, with a linear warmup of the learning rate followed by a linear decay over the remainder of the training. The hyper-parameter settings used in our experiments are listed below.

Table 3. Hyper-parameter settings.

Hyper-parameter	Value
maximum sequence length	{128, 256}
max training step	1000
evaluation step	100
learning rate	{1e−5, 2e−5, 5e−5}
batch size	8
gradient accumulation step	{2, 4, 8}
adam epsilon	1e−8
k	{16, 32, 128}
λ	{0.1 : .1 : 0.9}
τ	{0.01, 0.1, 1, 10}

4.4 Main Results

k-NN Features Result in Performance Gains. We compare the specific results with baseline models and provide comprehensive insights of k-NN on different paradigms and different settings. The results as shown in Table 1. Leverage k-NN features results in performance gains in both few-shot and fully-supervised settings. In the zero-shot setting, PT-based methods outperform FT-based and k-NN features further enhance the performance of PT-based methods, which demonstrates that it is flexible and general to integrate k-NN for PLMs.

Calibrating Training vs. Incorporating into Inference. It is necessary to study the different application scenarios of incorporating k-NN during the

[2] https://github.com/princeton-nlp/LM-BFF.

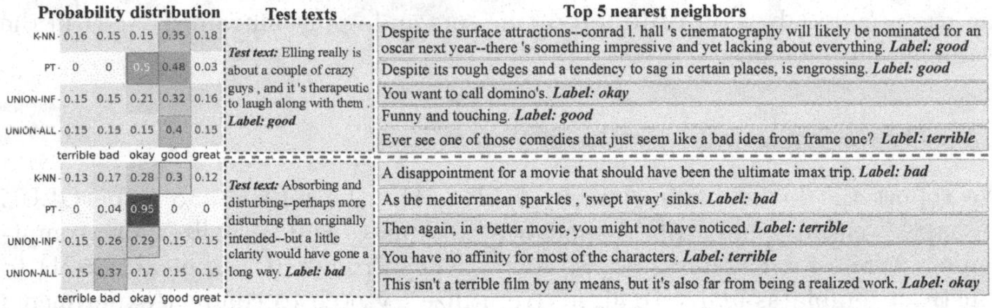

Fig. 3. Case analysis to show how k-NN benefits the prediction of PLMs. We illustrate the test texts, the predicted probability distribution, and the top-5 nearest neighbors from the 16-shot training set of the SST-5 dataset.

training and testing phases. From Table 2, we observe the following: (1) Leveraging k-NN during the test phrase is especially helpful for the zero-shot setting. While **Union-all** performs worse due to the noise brought from the pseudo-labels on unsupervised data. (2) **Union-inf** is not doing as well in the fully-supervised and few-shot setting. In contrast, **Union-all** outperforms **Union-inf** in these settings, especially in the few-shot setting. These findings reveal to us the applicable scenarios of incorporating k-NN and inspire further studies to utilize k-NN classifier more practically for efficient NLP.

4.5 Analysis

Q1: How Does the Lazy Learner Benefit Eager Learner? To further understand how does the *lazy learner* (k-NN) benefit the *eager learner* (PLM), we manually check cases in which k-NN, PT, Union-inf and Union-all produce different results. As shown in the example of the upper row of Fig. 3, k-NN and Union-all predict correctly when PT fails. This result is because Union-all produces a more confident probability for the correct class via calibrating the attention on the easy vs. hard examples identified by the k-NN classifier. Note that the bottom row shows that Union-all predicts correctly even when k-NN predicts wrongly, possibly due to the robustness of k-NN calibration.

Q2: Does the Similarity Metric Matter? In the above experiments, we mainly utilize negative $L2$ distance to measure the similarity between the query $\mathbf{q}$ and the instance representation of the data store. It is intuitive to estimate the impact of different similarity metrics, such as cosine similarity. Thus, we present the performance of Union-all using both metrics with the same hyperparameters as below.

We can find that Union-all with cosine distance achieves nearly the same performance as those trained with $L2$, revealing that our Union-all is robust to the similarity metric.

Q3: How Does the Modulating Factor $f(p_{k\mathrm{NN}})$ works? Since we adopt focal loss (Focal) as the modulating factor for main experiments, we further

Similarity Metric	$L2$	cos
16-shot SST-5 (%)	**43.7**	42.8
16-shot TREC (%)	**90.0**	89.4
16-shot QNLI (%)	**58.1**	57.2

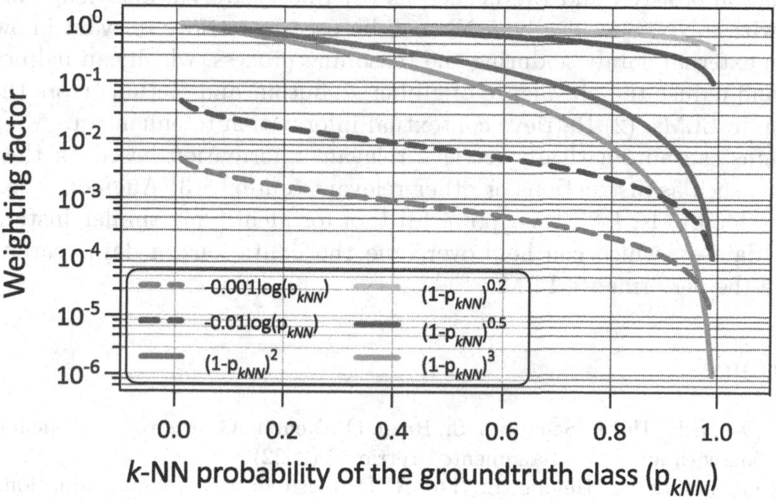

Fig. 4. Comparison between the modulating factors NLL and Focal.

explore other functions as modulating factors, such as negative log-likelihood (NLL). As shown in Fig. 4, we visualize two modulating factors with different settings of α and γ, where α donates a scalar that represent the proportion of the term of NLL, and γ is the exponential coefficient for Focal. We can find that NLL and Focal produce large weights for the misclassified examples, demonstrating the diversity of modulating factor selection.

5 Limitations

We only explore leveraging the training data for k-NN search, while various external domain data are also suitable for k-nearest neighbor retrieval. Moreover, incorporating k-NN also faces the following limitations: (1) the requirement of a large memory for retrieval; (2) hyper-parameters (such as λ and α) used for retrieval have an impact on the performance of model training; (3) if the number of nearest neighbors k is too large, it will also affect the efficiency.

6 Conclusion and Future Work

In this paper, we propose a novel method to enhance PLM-based classifiers using k-NN. Specifically, we introduce a calibration process and linear interpolation of inference phrases to effectively integrate k-NN into the training pipeline. To evaluate the effectiveness of our approach, we conduct a comprehensive and in-depth analysis of the role of k-NN in various NLU tasks and tuning paradigms. Our results demonstrate that the integration of k-NN is flexible and can significantly enhance the performance of large models. Future work should explore the combination of k-NN and LLMs such as (1) Inject external knowledge into the LLMs with k-NN. Specifically, k-NN can be used to retrieve relevant knowledge from an external database during the reasoning process, which can help correct errors and reduce the prevalence of gibberish output and factual errors that are common in LLMs. (2) Retrieve contextual information to enhance LLMs. k-NN algorithms can automatically retrieve relevant information based on the input sentence, such as instructions or other relevant context. (3) Augment the training data for LLMs. k-NN is a powerful tool for identifying similar instances in a large dataset, which can help overcome the limitations of data scarcity and improve the performance LLMs.

References

Alon, U., Xu, F.F., He, J., Sengupta, S., Roth, D., Neubig, G.: Neuro-symbolic language modeling with automaton-augmented retrieval (2022)

Alt, C., Gabryszak, A., Hennig, L.: TACRED revisited: a thorough evaluation of the TACRED relation extraction task. In: Proceedings of ACL 2020 (2020)

Boiman, O., Shechtman, E., Irani, M.: In defense of nearest-neighbor based image classification. pp. 1–8. IEEE (2008)

Brown, T.B., et al.: Language models are few-shot learners. In: Proceedings of NeurIPS 2020 (2020)

Chen, X., et al.: Knowprompt: knowledge-aware prompt-tuning with synergistic optimization for relation extraction. CoRR, abs/2104.07650 (2021)

Clark, C., Lee, K., Chang, M.-W., Kwiatkowski, T., Collins, M., Toutanova, K.: BoolQ: exploring the surprising difficulty of natural yes/no questions. In: Proceedings of NAACL-HLT (2019)

De Marneffe, M.-C., Simons, M., Tonhauser, J.: The commitmentbank: investigating projection in naturally occurring discourse. In: Proceedings of Sinn und Bedeutung (2019)

Devlin, J., Chang, M.-W., Lee, K., Toutanova, K.: BERT: pre-training of deep bidirectional transformers for language understanding. In: Burstein, J., Doran, C., Solorio, T. (eds.) Proceedings of the 2019 Conference of the North American Chapter of the Association for Computational Linguistics: Human Language Technologies, NAACL-HLT 2019, Minneapolis, MN, USA, 2–7 June 2019, Volume 1 (Long and Short Papers), pp. 4171–4186. Association for Computational Linguistics (2019)

Friedman, J.H.: The Elements of Statistical Learning: Data Mining, Inference, and Prediction. Springer, New York (2017). https://doi.org/10.1007/978-0-387-84858-7

Gao, T., Fisch, A., Chen, D.: Making pre-trained language models better few-shot learners. In: Proceedings of ACL (2021)

Gu, J., Wang, Y., Cho, K., Li, V.O.K.: Search engine guided neural machine translation. In: McIlraith, S.A., Weinberger, K.Q. (eds.) Proceedings of the Thirty-Second AAAI Conference on Artificial Intelligence, (AAAI-18), the 30th innovative Applications of Artificial Intelligence (IAAI-18), and the 8th AAAI Symposium on Educational

Advances in Artificial Intelligence (EAAI-18), New Orleans, Louisiana, USA, 2–7 February 2018, pp. 5133–5140. AAAI Press (2018)

He, J., Neubig, G., Berg-Kirkpatrick, T.: Efficient nearest neighbor language models. In: Proceedings of EMNLP (2021)

Hendrickx, I., et al.: SemEval-2010 task 8: multi-way classification of semantic relations between pairs of nominals. In: Proceedings of SemEval, pp. 33–38 (2010)

Kassner, N., Schütze, H.: BERT-KNN: adding a KNN search component to pretrained language models for better QA. In: Findings of EMNLP (2020)

Khandelwal, U., Levy, O., Jurafsky, D., Zettlemoyer, L., Lewis, M.: Generalization through memorization: Nearest neighbor language models. In: 8th International Conference on Learning Representations, ICLR 2020, Addis Ababa, Ethiopia, 26–30 April 2020. OpenReview.net (2020)

Khandelwal, U., Fan, A., Jurafsky, D., Zettlemoyer, L., Lewis, M.: Nearest neighbor machine translation. In: 9th International Conference on Learning Representations, ICLR 2021, Virtual Event, Austria, 3–7 May 2021. OpenReview.net (2021)

Kowsari, K., Meimandi, K.J., Heidarysafa, M., Mendu, S., Barnes, L., Brown, D.: Text classification algorithms: a survey. Information **10**(4), 150 (2019)

Li, L., Song, D., Ma, R., Qiu, X., Huang, X.: KNN-BERT: fine-tuning pre-trained models with KNN classifier. CoRR, abs/2110.02523 (2021)

Lin, T.-Y., Goyal, P., Girshick, R., He, K., Dollár, P.: Focal loss for dense object detection (2018)

Liu, Y., et al.: RoBERTa: a robustly optimized BERT pretraining approach. CoRR, abs/1907.11692 (2019)

Meng, Y., et al.: GNN-LM: language modeling based on global contexts via GNN. CoRR, abs/2110.08743 (2021)

Nan, G., Guo, Z., Sekulić, I., Lu, W.: Reasoning with latent structure refinement for document-level relation extraction. In: Proceedings of ACL (2020)

Orhan, E.: A simple cache model for image recognition, **31**, 10107–10116 (2018)

Radford, A., Narasimhan, K., Salimans, T., Sutskever, I.: Improving language understanding by generative pre-training. OpenAI (2018)

Raffel, C., et al.: Exploring the limits of transfer learning with a unified text-to-text transformer. J. Mach. Learn. Res. **21**, 140:1–140:67 (2020)

Rajpurkar, P., Zhang, J., Lopyrev, K., Liang, P.: Squad: 100, 000+ questions for machine comprehension of text. In: Su, J., Carreras, X., Duh, K. (eds.) Proceedings of the 2016 Conference on Empirical Methods in Natural Language Processing, EMNLP 2016, Austin, Texas, USA, 1–4 November 2016, pp. 2383–2392. The Association for Computational Linguistics (2016)

Shi, W., Michael, J., Gururangan, S., Zettlemoyer, L.: Nearest neighbor zero-shot inference. CoRR, abs/2205.13792 (2022)

Socher, R., et al.: Recursive deep models for semantic compositionality over a sentiment treebank. In: Proceedings of the 2013 Conference on Empirical Methods in Natural Language Processing, EMNLP 2013, 18–21 October 2013, Grand Hyatt Seattle, Seattle, Washington, USA, A meeting of SIGDAT, a Special Interest Group of the ACL, pp. 1631–1642. ACL (2013)

Voorhees, E.M., Tice, D.M. Building a question answering test collection. In: the 23rd Annual International ACM SIGIR Conference on Research and Development in Information Retrieval (2000)

Wang, Y., Chao, W.-L., Weinberger, K.Q., van der Maaten, L.: Simpleshot: revisiting nearest-neighbor classification for few-shot learning. arXiv preprint arXiv:1911.04623 (2019)

Williams, A., Nangia, N., Bowman, S.R.: A broad-coverage challenge corpus for sentence understanding through inference. In: Walker, M.A., Ji, H., Stent, A. (eds.) Proceedings of the 2018 Conference of the North American Chapter of the Association for Computational Linguistics: Human Language Technologies, NAACL-HLT 2018, New Orleans, Louisiana, USA, 1–6 June 2018, Volume 1 (Long Papers), pp. 1112–1122. Association for Computational Linguistics (2018)
Zhang, N., et al.: Reasoning through memorization: nearest neighbor knowledge graph embeddings. CoRR, abs/2201.05575 (2022)

Adder Encoder for Pre-trained Language Model

Jianbang Ding[1(✉)], Suiyun Zhang[1], and Linlin Li[2]

[1] Huawei Technologies Co., Ltd., Shenzhen, China
{dingjianbang1,zhangsuiyun}@huawei.com
[2] Huawei Noah's Ark Lab, Montreal, Canada
lynn.lilinlin@huawei.com

Abstract. BERT, a pre-trained language model entirely based on attention, has proven to be highly performant for natural language understanding tasks. However, pre-trained language models (PLMs) are often computationally expensive and can hardly be implemented with limited resources. To reduce energy burden, we introduce adder operations into the Transformer encoder and propose a novel AdderBERT with powerful representation capability. Then, we adopt mapping-based distillation to further improve its energy efficiency with an assured performance. Empirical results demonstrate that AddderBERT$_6$ achieves highly competitive performance against that of its teacher BERT$_{\text{BASE}}$ on the GLUE benchmark while obtaining a 4.9x reduction in energy consumption.

Keywords: PLMs · Distillation · AdderBERT

1 Introduction

The last five years have seen great success achieved by large-scale pre-trained language models, such as BERT [8], ELECTRA [6], and GPT3 [3]. By modeling long-distance dependencies based on self-attention, they can learn powerful language representations from the unlabeled corpus.

While these models lead to significant improvement on many downstream tasks (e.g., the GLUE benchmark [25]), the growing computation costs have impaired their deployment, especially on limited-resource devices such as mobile phones, AR glasses, and smartwatch. Since attending to all tokens yields a complexity of $O(n^2)$ with respect to sequence length, prior works aim to investigate efficient Transformers with lower complexity. [15] replaces dot-product attention with one using locality-sensitive hashing. [26] decomposes the original attention into multiple smaller ones by linear projections. However, they can only solve the problem partway, for the consumption except self-attention has not been changed in the encoder.

Various attempts also focus on model compression techniques, including quantization [11], weights pruning [12], and knowledge distillation (KD) [19]. As one of the most popular methods, KD aims to transfer knowledge from a large teacher network to a small student network, employed by DistilBERT [20], BERT-PKD [23], TinyBERT [14], and FastBERT [17]. Beyond these methods, [5] proposed Adder Neural Network (AdderNet), which replaced massive multiplications with cheaper additions to reduce

M. Sun et al. (Eds.): CCL 2023, LNAI 14232, pp. 339–347, 2023.
https://doi.org/10.1007/978-981-99-6207-5_21

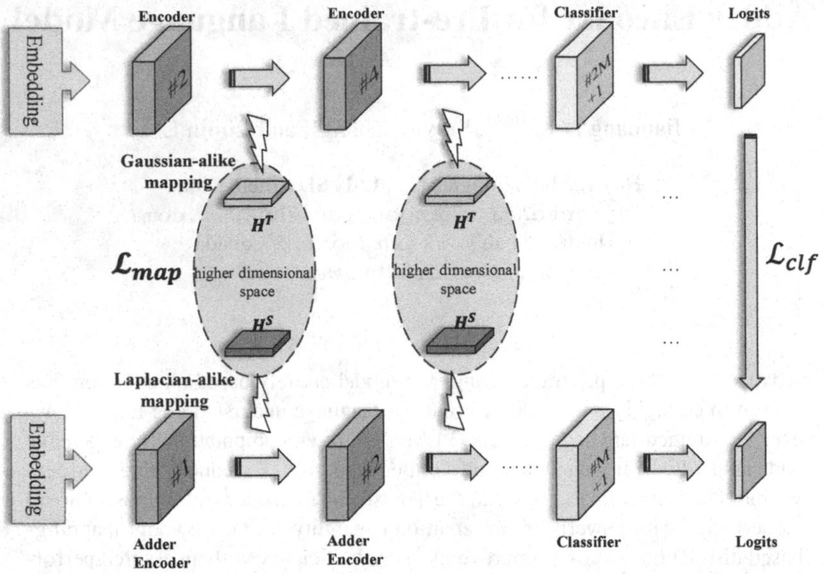

Fig. 1. Depiction of AdderBERT learning. AdderBERT implements the encoder block with cheaper adder operations, and it has a unique mapping-based distillation. $\mathbf{H}^S$ and $\mathbf{H}^T$ are the hidden states of the student and teacher networks, respectively. M denotes the number of adder encoders.

computation costs, and achieved better performance on the ImageNet dataset compared to CNNs. Then researchers attempt to build efficient deep-learning models based on AdderNet for computer vision tasks [21,29]. Inspired by this, it is an interesting idea to investigate the feasibility of replacing multiplications with additions in pre-trained language models like BERT.

In this paper, we first present AdderBERT, a pre-trained model consisting of several adder encoders, in which key modules including multi-head attention and feed-forward network are implemented with cheaper adder operations. As shown in Fig. 1, it also has a unique mapping-based distillation that could make it to be more energy-efficient with an assured performance. Finally, we conduct full experiments on the GLUE benchmark. Empirical results demonstrate that our method can achieve comparable performance with the baselines in much lower energy consumption.

The contributions are summarized as follows:

- We propose AdderBERT, which introduces adder operations into the mechanism of self-attention and feed-forward network.
- We adopt a novel mapping-based distillation to encourage that linguistic knowledge can be adequately transferred from the teacher network to AdderBERT.
- Experimental results show that AddderBERT_6 can achieve highly competitive performance against that of its teacher $\text{BERT}_{\text{BASE}}$ on the GLUE benchmark while obtaining a 4.9x reduction in energy consumption.

2 Preliminary

In this section, we revisit the related works including AdderNet and knowledge distillation. We are motivated by them to design AdderBERT.

2.1 Adder Neural Networks (AdderNet)

Denote the input feature as $\mathbf{X} \in \mathbb{R}^{h \times w \times c_{in}}$, in which h and w are the height and width of the feature map, respectively. Consider a filter $\mathbf{W} \in \mathbb{R}^{d \times d \times c_{in} \times c_{out}}$ in an arbitrary layer of AdderNet, where d is the kernel size, c_{in} and c_{out} are the number of input channels and output channels, respectively. The original adder operation is defined as:

$$\mathbf{Y}(m, n, v) = -\sum_{i=1}^{d} \sum_{j=1}^{d} \sum_{u=1}^{c_{in}} |\mathbf{X}(m+i, n+j, u) - \mathbf{W}(i, j, u, v)|, \quad (1)$$

where $|\cdot|$ is the absolute value function. m and n are the spatial locations of features. v denotes the index of output channels. Given that Eq. 1 has been proven to be used to replace the traditional convolution operation, it is an interesting idea to transport this success of CNNs to PTMs.

2.2 Knowledge Distillation (KD)

As one of the most popular compression techniques, KD was used to help a small student network S mimic the behavior of a large teacher network T for better performance. Given f^T and f^S represent the mapping functions of teacher and student networks, respectively. The student network can be optimized with the following objective function:

$$\mathcal{L}_{\text{KD}} = \sum_{x \in \Omega} \mathcal{L}(f^S(x), f^T(x)), \quad (2)$$

where $L(\cdot)$ is an arbitrary loss function, x is the input sequence and Ω denotes the training dataset, $f^S(x)$ and $f^T(x)$ are the outputs of student network and teacher network, respectively. Based on Eq. 2, we adopt a unique kernel-based distillation to encourage that linguistic knowledge can be adequately transferred from the teacher network to the student AdderBERT.

3 Method

This section describes our proposed AdderBERT as well as its training method. Concisely, AdderBERT implements the encoder block with cheaper adder operations, and it takes advantage of mapping-based distillation to be better in performance and efficient in energy.

3.1 Adder Encoder

Given that linear transformation is equivalent to 1×1 convolution with fixed input size in mathematical, in this paper, the adder operation can be redefined as:

$$\mathbf{Y}(l, v) = -\sum_{u=1}^{d_{embd}} |\mathbf{X}(l, u) - \mathbf{W}(u, v)| = \mathbf{X} \oplus \mathbf{W}, \tag{3}$$

where l is the sequence length, d_{embd} is the dimension of embedding, and $\oplus$ denotes the adder operation between matrices.

Following the original Transformer [24], We first consider creating output queries $\mathbf{Q} \in \mathbb{R}^{l \times d_q}$, keys $\mathbf{K} \in \mathbb{R}^{l \times d_k}$, and values $\mathbf{V} \in \mathbb{R}^{l \times d_v}$ by weight matrices $\mathbf{W}_Q \in \mathbb{R}^{d_{embd} \times d_q}$, $\mathbf{W}_K \in \mathbb{R}^{d_{embd} \times d_k}$, $\mathbf{W}_V \in \mathbb{R}^{d_{embd} \times d_v}$ in the projection layer of a single-head self-attention. d_q, d_k, d_v is the dimension of queries, keys, and values, respectively. We employ Eq. 3 to measure the ℓ_1-distance between embedding and the weight matrices as:

$$\mathbf{Q} = \mathcal{LN}(\mathbf{X} \oplus \mathbf{W}_Q), \quad \mathbf{K} = \mathcal{LN}(\mathbf{X} \oplus \mathbf{W}_K), \quad \mathbf{V} = \mathcal{LN}(\mathbf{X} \oplus \mathbf{W}_V), \tag{4}$$

where $\mathbf{X} \in \mathbb{R}^{l \times d_{embd}}$ is the input embedding and $\mathcal{LN}(\cdot)$ denotes layer normalization [1]. [5] first indicated that the output values of the adder operation should be followed by batch normalization. We also apply layer normalization to stabilize the hidden state dynamics for better learning. Similarly, Eq. 3 can be easily modified for a batch matrix-matrix product to realize self-attention:

$$\text{Attention}(\mathbf{Q}, \mathbf{K}, \mathbf{V}) = \text{softmax}(\frac{\mathbf{Q} \oplus \mathbf{K}^T}{\sqrt{d_k}}) \oplus \mathbf{V}, \tag{5}$$

where softmax$(\cdot)$ is the normalized exponential function and d_k is used for scaling. The attention matrix is calculated from the similarity of $\mathbf{Q}$ and $\mathbf{K}$ by adder operation and acts as the weighted sum factor to $\mathbf{V}$ to get the final output. Multi-head self-attention concatenated different heads from different representing subspaces as follows:

$$\text{MHA}(\mathbf{Q}, \mathbf{K}, \mathbf{V}) = \mathcal{LN}(\text{Concat}(\text{head}_1, ..., \text{head}_n) \oplus \mathbf{W}_O), \tag{6}$$

where head$_i$ is the i-th attention head obtained by Eq. 5 and n is the number of heads. Then we use $\mathbf{W}^O$ to realize an adder projection for dimensional transformation followed by layer normalization. Finally, the feed-forward network can also be reformulated as:

$$\text{FFN}(X) = \mathcal{LN}(\text{ReLU}(\mathbf{X} \oplus \mathbf{W}_1) \oplus \mathbf{W}_2). \tag{7}$$

The new FFN consists of two adder linear transformations, one ReLU activation, and one layer normalization.

3.2 Mapping-Based Distillation

Since the basic calculation paradigm of AdderBERT is completely different from that of the original BERT, we adopt a novel mapping-based distillation to adequately transport linguistic knowledge from Teacher BERT to student AdderBERT.

Specifically, we distill the output of each encoder block, and the objective function is as follows:

$$\mathcal{L}_{map} = \text{MSE}(\mathbf{H}^S, \mathbf{H}^T), \tag{8}$$

where $\mathbf{H}^S$ and $\mathbf{H}^T$ are the hidden states of the student and teacher networks, respectively. MSE(·) denotes the mean square error loss function. As discussed in AdderNet [5], the weight distribution in a well-trained ANN is Laplacian distribution rather than Gaussian distribution. Thus we attempt to map the inputs and weights to a higher dimensional space to minimize the distribution gap between $\mathbf{H}^S$ and $\mathbf{H}^T$.

Given $\{\mathbf{X}^S, \mathbf{W}_1^S, \mathbf{W}_2^S\}$, $\{\mathbf{X}^T, \mathbf{W}_1^T, \mathbf{W}_2^T\}$ are the inputs and weights of the FFN of the student and teacher network, respectively. During the distillation process, we transform the hidden states by feature mapping as follows:

$$\begin{aligned} \mathbf{H}^S &= k_1 < \mathbf{X}^S, \mathbf{W}_1^S, \mathbf{W}_2^S >= e^{-\frac{\mathbf{x}^S \oplus \mathbf{w}_1^S \oplus \mathbf{w}_2^S}{\sigma_s}}, \\ \mathbf{H}^T &= k_2 < \mathbf{X}^T, \mathbf{W}_1^T, \mathbf{W}_2^T >= e^{-\frac{\mathbf{x}^T \mathbf{w}_1^T \mathbf{w}_2^T}{2\sigma_t^2}}, \end{aligned} \tag{9}$$

where σ_s and σ_t are two learnable smoothing factors. $k_1 < \cdot >$ is a designed Laplacian-alike kernel that takes the adder operation of two matrices, while $k_2 < \cdot >$ is a Gaussian-alike kernel. After applying Eq. 9, the inputs and weights are mapped into a higher dimensional space, thus we can calculate the hidden states by the new smoothing representation.

We also use the cross-entropy loss for classifier distillation $\mathcal{L}_{clf}$ as in previous work [13]. Then the final loss function is defined as:

$$\mathcal{L}_{model} = \alpha \mathcal{L}_{map} + \mathcal{L}_{clf} = \sum_{x \in \Omega} \left(\sum_{m=1}^{M} \alpha \mathcal{L}_{map}^{m}(x) + \mathcal{L}_{clf}(x) \right), \tag{10}$$

where M is the number of encoder blocks of AdderBERT, and m denotes the m-th block. α is the hyper-parameter for seeking the balance between $\mathcal{L}_{map}$ and $\mathcal{L}_{clf}$.

4 Experiment

In this section, we verify the effectiveness of AdderBERT on three tasks with different model settings.

4.1 Datasets

We evaluate our method on the General Language Understanding Evaluation (GLUE) benchmark [25]. For Sentiment classification, we test on CoLA [27], SST-2 [22]. For similarity matching, we conduct on QQP[1], MRPC [10], and STS-B [4]. For language inference, we use MNLI [28], QNLI [18], WNLI [16] and RTE [2].

4.2 AdderBERT Settings

For a fair comparison, We build AdderBERT$_{12}$ with the same configuration as the original BERT$_{\text{BASE}}$ (the number of layers is 12, the hidden size is 768, the feed-forward size is 3072, the number of heads is 12). BERT$_{\text{BASE}}$ uses pre-trained parameters released by Google, and we train AdderBERT$_{12}$ from scratch with the same pre-training settings. We fine-tune them both using the AdaMod [9] optimizer for better performance, the learning rate is set to 2e−5, and the batch size is set to 32. We then select the model with the best accuracy in 3 epochs.

We also use the fine-tuned BERT$_{\text{BASE}}$ as the teacher model and use 6 and 3 layers of AdderBERT as the student models (i.e. AdderBERT$_6$ and AdderBERT$_3$). The student models learn from every 2 and 4 layers of the teacher model, respectively. We increase the learning rate to 5e−5 and distill them for 5 epochs. All the experiments are conducted on NVIDIA Tesla-V100 GPUs.

Given that hyperparameters can exert a great impact on the ultimate result, we report the full details about how to find them. We follow the grid search method until the best-performing parameters are at one of the middle points in the grid. For fine-tuning, we tune over hyperparameters to work well across all tasks about batch size: $\{8, 16, 32, 64\}$, the initial learning rate of AdaMod: $\{2e-5, 3e-5, 5e-5, e-4\}$, and the number of epochs: $\{2, 3, 4, 5\}$.

4.3 Baselines

We compare AdderBERT against two strong baselines as follows:

- **BERT** The 12-layer BERT$_{\text{BASE}}$ model, which was pre-trained on Wiki corpus and released by Google [8].
- **DistilBERT** The most famous distillation version of BERT with 6 layers, which was released by Huggingface [20]. In addition, we use the same method to distill the DistilBERT with 3 layers.

4.4 Experiments on GLUE

We submitted our model predictions to the official GLUE evaluation server to get results on the test data, as reported in Table 1. Note that values in both models are 32-bit floating numbers and the energy consumptions for a 32-bit multiplication and addition are $3.7pJ$ and $0.9pJ$, respectively [7]. The original BERT$_{\text{BASE}}$ achieves a 79.7 score on average with 11.27B multiplications and 11.27B additions, and AdderBERT$_{12}$ achieves a 79.0 score with 0.31B multiplications and 22.23B additions. By replacing massive multiplications with additions, our proposed model obtains about a 2.5x reduction in energy

[1] https://data.quora.com/First-Quora-Dataset-Release-Question-Pairs.

Table 1. Results from the GLUE test server. The best results for each group are in-bold. All models are learned in a single-task manner. The energy consumption is calculated from the number of multiplications and additions, respectively. Nothing that T denotes the teacher model, and all the 3-layers and 6-layer models are distilled from it while AdderBERT$_{12}$ is undistilled.

Model	# Mul.	# Add.	Energy (pJ)	MNLI-(m/mm)	QQP	QNLI	SST-2	CoLA	STS-B	MRPC	RTE	Avg
BERT$_{BASE}$ (T)	11.27B	11.27B	51.8B	83.8/83.1	71.0	90.7	93.9	52.5	85.5	89.1	68.1	**79.7**
AdderBERT$_{12}$	0.31B	22.23B	**21.1B**	84.3/83.4	70.4	90.9	92.5	50.7	83.7	89.0	65.9	79.0
DistilBERT$_6$	5.64B	5.64B	25.9B	82.1/81.3	69.9	88.9	92.4	47.4	76.2	88.1	56.3	75.8
AdderBERT$_6$	0.16B	11.12B	**10.6B**	84.9/83.1	71.3	91.2	93.8	51.3	83.2	87.9	69.5	**79.6**
DistilBERT$_3$	2.82B	2.82B	13.0B	73.4/72.9	66.0	81.3	85.6	27.5	75.1	80.2	61.0	69.2
AdderBERT$_3$	0.08B	5.56B	**5.3B**	80.7/80.9	68.6	88.0	90.7	45.9	79.3	87.2	65.2	**76.3**

consumption from 51.8BpJ to 21.1BpJ at the cost of a little performance loss (0.7 drops relative to BERT$_{\text{BASE}}$ on the average score). This demonstrates that AdderBERT performs a powerful representation capacity like BERT even with few multiplications.

We then evaluate the distillation versions of our model against the strong KD baselines, respectively. For 6 layers, DistilBERT$_6$ achieves a 75.8 score on average with 5.64B multiplications and 5.64B additions while AdderBERT-6 achieves a higher 79.6 score with 0.16B multiplications and 11.12B additions. With mapping-based distillation, our proposed model AdderBERT-6 significantly outperforms DistilBERT$_6$ by a margin of 3.8 on average and obtains a 2.5x reduction in energy consumption as well. Compared to BERT$_{\text{BASE}}$, AdderBERT$_6$ is in much lower energy consumption (4.9x reduction) while maintaining competitive performance (79.7 vs 79.6). This indicates that our proposed KD method can adequately transport linguistic knowledge from the teacher model to the student model. For 3 layers, AdderBERT$_3$ is consistently better than DistilBERT$_3$ (a large improvement of 8.1 on average), especially on the challenging CoLA dataset, and it only consumes less than one-tenth of the energy of the teacher model. In conclusion, empirical results validate our motivation that AdderBERT combines the advantage of both BERT and AdderNet, that is, it could obtain comparable results with the teacher model but substantially reduce the energy burden.

4.5 Ablation Study

We further investigate the effectiveness of different distillation objectives on AdderBERT learning. The baselines include without mapping-based distillation (w/o map) or classification distillation (w/o clf), respectively.

The results are summarized in Table 2. We can find the performance without mapping-based distillation drops significantly from 76.9 to 71.8, which demonstrates that our proposed method plays the most important role of the two objectives. The reason for the significant drop lies in the distribution gap between H^S and H^T. Linguistic knowledge is hard to transport across completely different representations.

Table 2. Ablation studies of different distillation objectives in the AdderBERT learning. The results are validated on the dev set.

Model	MNLI-m	MNLI-mm	MRPC	CoLA	Avg
$AdderBERT_6$	84.3	83.4	89.0	50.7	76.9
w/o map	80.5	77.8	84.3	44.6	71.8
w/o clf	82.0	79.3	88.6	46.9	74.2

5 Conclusion

In this paper, we propose an energy-efficient version of BERT, called AdderBERT. Specifically, AdderBERT consists of several adder encoders implemented by cheap addition operations but has a powerful representation capacity. It adopts a unique mapping-based distillation method to narrow the gap in feature distribution between the teacher and student model. Empirical results on the GLUE benchmark demonstrate that our method can achieve highly competitive performance to the teacher $BERT_{BASE}$ while reducing energy consumption significantly.

References

1. Ba, L.J., Kiros, J.R., Hinton, G.E.: Layer normalization. CoRR abs/1607.06450 (2016)
2. Bentivogli, L., Magnini, B., Dagan, I., Dang, H.T., Giampiccolo, D.: The fifth PASCAL recognizing textual entailment challenge. In: TAC. NIST (2009)
3. Brown, T.B., et al.: Language models are few-shot learners. In: NeurIPS (2020)
4. Cer, D.M., Diab, M.T., Agirre, E., Lopez-Gazpio, I., Specia, L.: SemEval-2017 task 1: semantic textual similarity multilingual and cross lingual focused evaluation. In: SemEval@ACL, pp. 1–14. Association for Computational Linguistics (2017)
5. Chen, H., et al.: AdderNet: do we really need multiplications in deep learning? In: CVPR, pp. 1465–1474. Computer Vision Foundation/IEEE (2020)
6. Clark, K., Luong, M., Le, Q.V., Manning, C.D.: ELECTRA: pre-training text encoders as discriminators rather than generators. In: ICLR. OpenReview.net (2020)
7. Dally, B.: High-performance hardware for machine learning (2015)
8. Devlin, J., Chang, M., Lee, K., Toutanova, K.: BERT: pre-training of deep bidirectional transformers for language understanding. In: NAACL-HLT (1), pp. 4171–4186. Association for Computational Linguistics (2019)
9. Ding, J., Ren, X., Luo, R., Sun, X.: An adaptive and momental bound method for stochastic learning. CoRR abs/1910.12249 (2019)
10. Dolan, W.B., Brockett, C.: Automatically constructing a corpus of sentential paraphrases. In: IWP@IJCNLP. Asian Federation of Natural Language Processing (2005)
11. Gong, Y., Liu, L., Yang, M., Bourdev, L.D.: Compressing deep convolutional networks using vector quantization. CoRR abs/1412.6115 (2014)
12. Han, S., Pool, J., Tran, J., Dally, W.J.: Learning both weights and connections for efficient neural network. In: NIPS, pp. 1135–1143 (2015)
13. Hinton, G.E., Vinyals, O., Dean, J.: Distilling the knowledge in a neural network. CoRR abs/1503.02531 (2015)

14. Jiao, X., et al.: TinyBERT: distilling BERT for natural language understanding. In: EMNLP (Findings). Findings of ACL, EMNLP 2020, pp. 4163–4174. Association for Computational Linguistics (2020)
15. Kitaev, N., Kaiser, L., Levskaya, A.: Reformer: the efficient transformer. In: ICLR. OpenReview.net (2020)
16. Levesque, H.J., Davis, E., Morgenstern, L.: The Winograd schema challenge. In: KR. AAAI Press (2012)
17. Liu, W., Zhou, P., Wang, Z., Zhao, Z., Deng, H., Ju, Q.: FastBERT: a self-distilling BERT with adaptive inference time. In: ACL, pp. 6035–6044. Association for Computational Linguistics (2020)
18. Rajpurkar, P., Zhang, J., Lopyrev, K., Liang, P.: Squad: 100, 000+ questions for machine comprehension of text. In: EMNLP, pp. 2383–2392. The Association for Computational Linguistics (2016)
19. Romero, A., Ballas, N., Kahou, S.E., Chassang, A., Gatta, C., Bengio, Y.: FitNets: hints for thin deep nets. In: ICLR (Poster) (2015)
20. Sanh, V., Debut, L., Chaumond, J., Wolf, T.: DistilBERT, a distilled version of BERT: smaller, faster, cheaper and lighter. CoRR abs/1910.01108 (2019)
21. Shu, H., Wang, J., Chen, H., Li, L., Yang, Y., Wang, Y.: Adder attention for vision transformer. In: NeurIPS, pp. 19899–19909 (2021)
22. Socher, R., et al.: Recursive deep models for semantic compositionality over a sentiment treebank. In: EMNLP, pp. 1631–1642. ACL (2013)
23. Sun, S., Cheng, Y., Gan, Z., Liu, J.: Patient knowledge distillation for BERT model compression. In: EMNLP/IJCNLP (1), pp. 4322–4331. Association for Computational Linguistics (2019)
24. Vaswani, A., et al.: Attention is all you need. In: NIPS, pp. 5998–6008 (2017)
25. Wang, A., Singh, A., Michael, J., Hill, F., Levy, O., Bowman, S.R.: GLUE: a multi-task benchmark and analysis platform for natural language understanding. In: ICLR (Poster). OpenReview.net (2019)
26. Wang, S., Li, B.Z., Khabsa, M., Fang, H., Ma, H.: Linformer: self-attention with linear complexity. CoRR abs/2006.04768 (2020)
27. Warstadt, A., Singh, A., Bowman, S.R.: Neural network acceptability judgments. Trans. Assoc. Comput. Linguist. **7**, 625–641 (2019)
28. Williams, A., Nangia, N., Bowman, S.R.: A broad-coverage challenge corpus for sentence understanding through inference. In: NAACL-HLT, pp. 1112–1122. Association for Computational Linguistics (2018)
29. Xu, Y., Xu, C., Chen, X., Zhang, W., Xu, C., Wang, Y.: Kernel based progressive distillation for adder neural networks. In: NeurIPS (2020)

Exploring Accurate and Generic Simile Knowledge from Pre-trained Language Models

Shuhan Zhou[1], Longxuan Ma[2], and Yanqiu Shao[1(✉)]

[1] School of Information Science, Beijing Language and Culture University, Beijing, China
yqshao163@163.com

[2] Research Center for Social Computing and Information Retrieval, Faculty of Computing, Harbin Institute of Technology, Harbin, China
lxma@ir.hit.edu.com

Abstract. A simile is an important linguistic phenomenon in daily communication and an important task in natural language processing (NLP). In recent years, pre-trained language models (PLMs) have achieved great success in NLP since they learn generic knowledge from a large corpus. However, PLMs still have hallucination problems that they could generate unrealistic or context-unrelated information. In this paper, we aim to explore more accurate simile knowledge from PLMs. To this end, we first fine-tune a single model to perform three main simile tasks (recognition, interpretation, and generation). In this way, the model gains a better understanding of the simile knowledge. However, this understanding may be limited by the distribution of the training data. To explore more generic simile knowledge from PLMs, we further add semantic dependency features in three tasks. The semantic dependency feature serves as a global signal and helps the model learn simile knowledge that can be applied to unseen domains. We test with seen and unseen domains after training. Automatic evaluations demonstrate that our method helps the PLMs to explore more accurate and generic simile knowledge for downstream tasks. Our method of exploring more accurate knowledge is not only useful for simile study but also useful for other NLP tasks leveraging knowledge from PLMs. Our code and data will be released on GitHub.

Keywords: NLP · Pre-trained language model · Simile knowledge

1 Introduction

A simile is a figure of speech that compares two things from different categories (called the tenor and the vehicle) via shared properties [17]. A tenor and a vehicle are usually connected with comparator words such as "like" or "as". For example, the sentence "The girl is as pretty as an angel." is a simile where the tenor is "The girl", the vehicle is "an angel", the comparator is "as ... as" and the shared

M. Sun et al. (Eds.): CCL 2023, LNAI 14232, pp. 348–363, 2023.
https://doi.org/10.1007/978-981-99-6207-5_22

property is "pretty". Simile plays an important role in human language to make utterances more vivid, interesting, and graspable [26], comprehending similes is essential to appreciate the inner connection between different concepts and is useful for other natural language processing (NLP) tasks [8,20].

In recent years, pre-trained language models (PLMs) have achieved great success in NLP since they learn generic knowledge from a large corpus and could serve as a knowledge base [5,18]. Considerable attention has been paid to exploring simile knowledge from PLMs to solve downstream simile tasks, such as recognition, interpretation, and generation [4,8]. However, PLMs are known to suffer from hallucination problems [7,12,19], they could generate unrealistic or unfaithful information about the provided source content, which will impact their performance on downstream tasks. For example, when completing the blank in a simile sentence "Are you feeling ill? You are as __ as a ghost.", a PLM may generate "creepy" instead of the expected shared property "pale".

In this paper, we study how to explore more accurate and generic simile knowledge from PLMs. Specifically, we first train PLMs with three main simile tasks (recognition, interpretation, and generation). In this way, the PLMs can learn the shared semantic feature among different tasks and gain a better understanding of the simile knowledge. However, this understanding may be limited by the distribution of the training data. The performance of the model will drop when applied to unseen domains. To explore more generic simile knowledge, we further add semantic dependency features in the fine-tuning process. The semantic dependency feature serves as a global signal, helps the model learn simile knowledge shared among similar syntax structures, and enhances the model's performance on unseen domains. During tests, we conduct experiments on both seen and unseen test sets to verify the effectiveness of our method. To sum up, our contributions are:

- We propose a novel method to explore more accurate and generic simile knowledge from PLMs.
- We test our model with both seen and unseen test sets. Experimental results demonstrate the effectiveness of our method and we give a detailed analysis of the results.
- Our code and data (including a new manually annotated simile data set) will be released on GitHub[1].

2 Related Work

In this section, we will introduce previous work related to this paper.

2.1 Simile and Metaphor

Metaphor is often used in human language to make speech more vivid and easy to understand [15]. [2] categorized metaphor into Noun phrases, Adjectives,

[1] https://github.com/realZsh/simile-tasks.

Table 1. Different metaphor categories. For similes, we use underline font to show **tenors** and use italic font to show *vehicles*.

Metaphor Category	Example	Is a simile?
Noun phrase	The judge is like *an angel.*	Yes
Adjective	The boy has a warm heart.	No
Verbal	He kills the seeds of peace.	No
Adverb-Verb	The child speaks France fluidly.	No
Verbal phrase	Raising little cats is like *taking care of children.*	Yes
Sentence	The man walks into the crowd like *a fish swims into the ocean.*	Yes

Verbs, and Multi-word. [10] defined metaphor as Nominal, Verbal (Subject-Verb-Object), Adjective-Noun, and Adverb-Verb. Table 1 shows examples of these categories. The Noun phrase metaphor is usually defined as a simile [4,8,10]. In this paper, we not only study the Noun phrase metaphor. Meanwhile, to test whether the trained model performs well on unseen domains, we construct a new test set. In this new test set, the tenor and vehicle can be verbal phrases/sentences that perform a similar role to Noun phrases. The examples of verbal phrases and sentences as simile components are shown in Table 1.

2.2 Tasks in Simile

The current simile study usually focus on recognition [1,11], interpretation [24], and generation [10]. The recognition task [10,14,22,25] is judging whether a triplet or a sentence contains a simile. The interpretation [11] assigns an appropriate interpretation to a simile expression [2] or infers the shared properties of the tenor and the vehicle [4,8,20]. The generation task generates a simile sentence [3,10,23,26] or the vehicle [4,20]. In this paper, we follow previous work and study the simile recognition/interpretation/generation (SR/SI/SG) tasks. Since there are not enough simile data that can be used for all three simile tasks. We construct the data we need based on existing SI data.

2.3 Exploring Simile Knowledge in PLMs

Previous simile work usually exploited the simile knowledge from PLMs for resolving downstream tasks. [20] fine-tune BERT [5] for simile recognition and simile component (tenor, shared property, and vehicle) extraction. [3] fine-tune BART [9] on the literal-simile pairs to generate novel similes given a literal sentence. [8] design a simile property probing task to let the PLMs infer the shared properties of similes for the interpretation task. [4] propose an Adjective-Noun mask Training method to explore simile knowledge from BERT for simile interpretation and generation tasks. [10] fine-tune a GPT-2 [18] model for simile generation. In this paper, we also study how to explore simile knowledge from PLMs. However, different from previous work, we investigate how to leverage three simile tasks to explore more generic simile knowledge from PLMs.

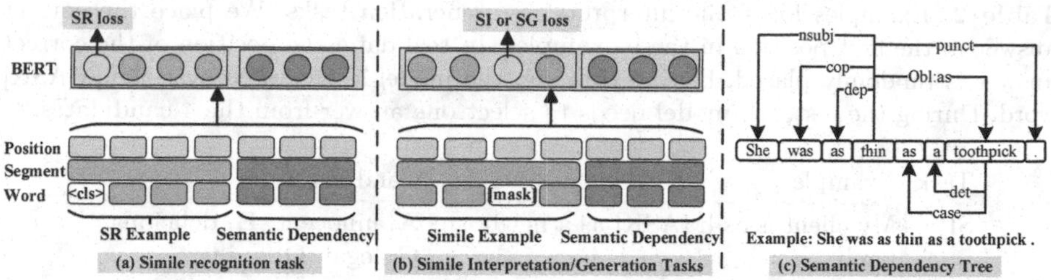

Fig. 1. Demonstration of the training method and semantic dependency.

3 Our Proposed Method

In this section, we formalize the simile recognition/simile interpretation/simile generation (SR/SI/SG) tasks and introduce our method in detail. For a fair comparison with previous work [4,8], we use BERT-base [5] as the backbone of our model. Figure 1 shows the model structure of SR/SI/SG tasks.

3.1 Training of Simile Recognition (SR) Task

We follow previous work [10,11] and define SR as a binary classification task. The SR model needs to distinguish whether an input sequence contains a simile. The input to the SR model is a sequence and the output is a binary label: True for simile and False for literal. The only common feature between simile data and literal data is that they both contains the comparator words [11]. For example, the sentence "the boy runs like a deer." is a simile, but the sentence "the girl looks like her mother." is literal.

Following the original BERT paper, we use the first output position (a special token <cls>) to calculate the classification score, such as (a) part in Fig. 1. We denote the corresponding output vector of <cls> as E_{cls}. Then the final score $\mathcal{S}$ of the input sequence is calculated as follows:

$$\mathcal{S} = \sigma(W_2 \cdot \mu(W_1 \cdot E_{cls} + b_1) + b_2), \tag{1}$$

where $W_{1,2}$ and $b_{1,2}$ are training parameters; σ/μ is the sigmoid/tanh function, respectively. The example with $\mathcal{S} \geq 0.5$ is classified as a simile, otherwise literal. The training loss is cross-entropy between predicted labels y_i and ground-truth label $\bar{y}_i$:

$$\mathcal{L}_{SR} = -\frac{1}{N}\sum_{i=1}^{N}(\bar{y}_i log P(y_i)) \tag{2}$$

where N is the number of training examples. After this fine-tuning, we can test the model on the SR test sets. We input an example and verify whether the SR model gives a correct classification for it.

Table 2. Examples for simile interpretation/generation tasks. We place the correct answer in the first position in these examples. In real data, the position of the correct answer is randomly placed. During training, the model learns to recover the [MASK] word. During the test, the model needs to select one answer from the 4 candidates.

Task	Example	Candidates
SI	My client is as [MASK] as a newborn lamb.	**A**. innocent. **B**. delicious. **C**. legal. **D**. guilty.
SG	The participant swims like a [MASK].	**A**. dolphin. **B**. plait. **C**. depiction. **D**. pod.

3.2 Training of Simile Interpretation (SI) and Simile Generation (SG) Tasks

Following the previous simile interpretation (SI) and simile generation (SG) work [8,20], we define the training of SI and SG as a masked language model task where the BERT learns to recover the masked words, such as (b) part in Fig. 1. Two examples are shown in Table 2. In SI, the masked word is the shared property. In SG, the masked word is the vehicle.

During the test, we also follow the previous work [8,20] and define SI/SG as a multi-choice task which chooses an answer from 4 candidates. Given an input simile sentence or dialogue with a masked shared property/vehicle, the SI/SG model needs to select the correct property/vehicle from the candidates, respectively. We use the masked-word-prediction heads of BERT to compute the probability for each candidate. The candidate with the highest probability will be chosen as the final choice.

3.3 Training with Semantic Dependency Features

Through the training process with SR/SI/SG, the PLM learns to use simile knowledge for three different simile tasks. However, the distribution of the training data may restrict the model's performance when applied to unseen domains. To this end, we enhance the PLM with global semantic dependency information, which can help the model learn simile knowledge across different syntax structures. This more generic simile knowledge can help the model's performance on unseen domains.

We adopt the semantic dependency tool[2] to get the semantic dependency tree of each input sequence. One example is shown in (c) part of Fig. 1. The dependency tree for "She was as thin as a toothpick." is a list of tuples: "[('ROOT', '.', 'thin'), ('nsubj', 'thin', 'She'), ('cop', 'thin', 'was'), ('dep', 'thin', 'as'), ('case', 'toothpick', 'as'), ('det', 'toothpick', 'a'), ('obl', 'thin', 'toothpick'), ('punct', 'thin', '.')]". The word "thin" is the root of this tree and please refer to [13] for the definition of each semantic dependency relation.

---

[2] https://stanfordnlp.github.io/CoreNLP.

Table 3. Statistics of datasets.

Dataset	Train/Dev/Test	Words/Example	Data Format
MSP-original (for SI)	4,510/-/1,633	12.2	sentence
MSP-modified for SG	4,510/-/1,633	12.3	sentence
MSP-modified for SR	7,216/902/902	12.3	sentence
New test set	-/-/957	30.6	three-turn dialogue

For the SR task, we can directly use the semantic dependency results. However, in SI or SG task, key simile component such as the vehicle "toothpick" of the above example is masked. We change the example to "She was as thin as a UNK.", where UNK represents the [MASK] vehicle. Then the output semantic dependency tree changes to "[('ROOT', '.', 'thin'), ('nsubj', 'thin', 'She'), ('cop', 'thin', 'was'), ('dep', 'thin', 'as'), ('case', 'UNK', 'as'), ('det', 'UNK', 'a'), ('obl', 'thin', 'UNK'), ('punct', 'thin', '.')]". In this way, the model is aware of the semantic dependency tree of the input sentence but does not see the masked word.

The final input to BERT is the concatenation of the semantic dependency tree and the original sentence. We use different segment embedding to distinguish the data example and its semantic dependency information, such as the (a)/(b) part of Fig. 1.

After training, we test with two different settings, one is the MSP test set, and the other is an unseen test set that is newly constructed by us. Next, we will introduce the data sets.

4 Experimental Setup

4.1 Datasets

We use simile data sets with "as ... as" comparator since the shared property naturally exists in the comparator, which is suitable for our experiments since we want conduct all SR/SI/SG tasks with this data. This kind of simile data can be used for all three simile tasks. The data statistics are shown in Table 3 and we introduce the data details next.

MSP Dataset (for SI Task). Since we could not find enough data for all three simile tasks, we construct the required data based on a recently released simile benchmark. The multi-choice simile probe (MSP) data [8] is originally proposed for SI task. It has a total of 5,410 training examples and 1,633 test examples. All examples in MSP are simile sentences with comparator "as ... as". Each example in the MSP test set has three distractors for the shared property. During training, the model learns to recover the masked property in MSP training data. During the test, the model needs to choose the correct answer from 4 candidates in the MSP test set.

Table 4. Relations in ConceptNet we used to find distractors. "<->" means Symmetric relation for A and B. "->" means Asymmetric relation that A entails B.

Relation:	*Definition*
RelatedTo:	*The most general relation. There is some positive relationship between A and B, but ConceptNet can't determine what that relationship is based on the data. Symmetric. exercise <-> fit*
IsA:	*A is a subtype or a specific instance of B; every A is a B. This can include specific instances; the distinction between subtypes and instances is often blurry in language. This is the hyponym relation in WordNet. car -> vehicle; Mexico -> Country*
Causes:	*A and B are events, and it is typical for A to cause B. run -> tired*
Desires:	*A is a conscious entity that typically wants B. Many assertions of this type use the appropriate language's word for "person" as A. person -> respect*
DistinctFrom:	*A and B are distinct member of a set; something that is A is not B. Symmetric. red <-> blue; June <-> May*
SymbolOf:	*A symbolically represents B. blue -> cold*
MannerOf:	*A is a specific way to do B. Similar to "IsA", but for verbs. auction -> sale*
LocatedNear:	*A and B are typically found near each other. Symmetric. computer <-> table*
CausesDesire:	*A makes someone want B. hungry -> eat food*
MadeOf:	*A is made of B. porcelain -> ceramic*

MSP-Modified Data (for SG Task). To perform the SG task, we introduce a modified version of MSP. During training, we mask the vehicle and train the model to recover it. During the test, we provide 4 vehicle candidates for the multi-choice task. Besides the real vehicle, the other 3 distractors are constructed with ConceptNet [21]. The ConceptNet is a knowledge graph that connects words and phrases of natural language with labeled relations [21]. We show 10 relations of ConceptNet in Table 4. They are used to find the related concepts to the vehicle as the distractors. For the example "She was as thin as a toothpick.", the vehicle is the word "toothpick". We find that "toothpick" is usually located near to (LocatedNear) "food" and can be made of (MadeOf) "plastic" or "wooden". So the three distractors can be "food, plastic, wooden". When we find more than three distractors with the relations in Table 4, we randomly choose 3 of them as the final distractors. Notice that there are a few cases we could not find enough distractors, we manually construct distractors for these cases.

MSP-Modified Data (for SR Task). Similarly to the SG task, we introduce another modified version of MSP for the SR task. Since the SR task needs both simile examples and literal examples [10,11], we use certain relations in ConceptNet to obtain the literal data we need. For example, we replace the tenor "his muscle" in the simile example "his muscle is as hard as a rock" with the phrase "a stone", the Synonym concept of "a rock", then we get a literal sentence "a stone is as hard as a rock". This is different from replacing "his muscle" with a random word such as "air". Because the sentence "air is as hard as a rock" does not have a practical meaning. If we use "air is as hard as a rock" as a literal sample to train an SR model. The model may classify this sample as literal by identifying that it is against common sense. Instead, when we use the literal sentence "a stone is as hard as a rock", the SR model needs to use simile knowledge to judge whether this example is a simile. The knowledge is that simile only exists when comparing things from different categories. "stone" and "rock" are in the same category so this sentence is literal. Besides the Synonym relation, we can also use other relations of the vehicle including DistinctFrom/IsA/RelatedTo/SimilarTo in ConceptNet to find a concept to replace the tenor. When we find more than one distractor, we randomly choose one of them as the literal sentence. By this method, we not only obtain the required training literal data but also has more difficult literal data. Because the syntax structure of the literal data is the same as the original simile example but the semantic information is different. These literal examples will help the model to learn more accurate simile knowledge. Finally, we obtain 9020 examples. We randomly split this data into train/dev/test (8:1:1) to train our model. During training, the model learn to give a higher/lower score for the simile/literal data. During the test, the model assigns a score for the input. In both training and testing, an example with a score ≥ 0.5 will be set as simile, <0.5 will be set as literal.

A New Test Data (for SR/SI/SG Task). After the above data set construction, we now have the training/testing MSP sets for SR/SI/SG tasks. We denote the MSP test sets as a seen set because the training and testing data are in a similar domain and similar range of length. To test whether our method can help to explore more generic simile knowledge, we provide unseen test sets for SR/SI/SG tasks.

The new test data is collected from Reddit-dialogue corpus [6] which has ~15 million English dialogues. The dialogues are comments from the Reddit forum and each dialogue has three turns. We extract 1,000 dialogue examples from the Reddit dataset with three rules. First, the dialogue length is around 30 tokens so it is informative and not too long. Second, the last turn must contain a comparator "as ... as" with an adjective word in the comparator. Third, we use the semantic dependency tool to ensure that the tenor and vehicle are in the response. Then we manually annotate whether they are similes or literal. For the simile sentences, we further check whether the tenor and vehicle labeled by the semantic dependency tool are correct. Notice that we do not make any change to the data. Therefore, for dialogue examples that tenor or vehicle is missing, we withdraw this example even it contains a simile. We make sure that all simile components are in the example so that we can use it for all simile tasks. We finally have 486 simile examples and 471 literal examples, total 957 examples. When testing on SI/SG, we construct the distractors using the same method as we construct MSP-modified data. For the examples in this new test set that we could not find enough vehicle distractors, we randomly choose the vehicles from other dialogues as the distractors.

The new test set is different from the training data (MSP) in the following respects: 1) the data format is dialogue and the length is much longer than data in MSP; 2) the tenor and vehicle in dialogue can be verbal phrase or sentence, which is different from the noun phrase in MSP. We use the new test set to verify whether our method can perform well on a different simile distribution compared to MSP.

4.2 Baselines

We introduce the baselines we used in this section.

Baselines for SR. BERT-base is fine-tuned on the MSP modified SR training set. The checkpoint for test is selected based on the performance on the corresponding dev set.

Baselines for SI/SG. The first baseline is a BERT-base model without fine-tuning with the data sets in this paper. It takes the input with key simile component masked and predicts the masked words. The second baseline is BERT-ANT [4] which is trained with masked word prediction with a number of metaphor data. It is based on a BERT-large-uncased model and can solve the SI and SG tasks in a unified framework of simile triple completion. For example, when giving tenor = fireman and vehicle = bull, BERT-ANT can generate a list of words including the shared property like "strong" or "brave". When performing our SI/SG tasks, we match the candidates of each example with the output list of BERT-ANT. An example is counted correct if the ground truth answer is listed before the other three distractors. The BERT-Probe baseline is from [8] that fine-tuned BERT with MSP-original data for simile interpretation task. To compare both SI and SG tasks with this baseline, we further fine-tuned the BERT-Probe model with MSP-modified SG training data and report its results on the MSP-modified SG test data.

Our Models. Besides the fully fine-tuned model, we also provide several settings for our model. (- SR training) means we remove the simile recognition data in the unified training process. Similarly, (- SI training) and (- SG training) means we remove the SI and SG data in training, respectively. (- Semantic Dependency) means we do not use syntax features. These settings can reflect the contribution of the removing part.

4.3 Evaluation Metrics

Following previous work [11], we use macro Precision/Recall/F1 and Accuracy to measure the simile recognition results. Following previous work on simile interpretation and generation [4], we use Hit@1 to measure the multi-choice accuracy.

Table 5. Simile recognition results. The BERT-base (fine-tuned with MSP-modified SR train set) is the base model to do the significant test for our models (* means statistically significant with $p < 0.01$).

Model	Precision	Recall	F1	Accuracy
MSP-modified SR Test set				
BERT-base	0.7127	0.6981	0.6939	0.6996
Ours	**0.7904***	**0.7905***	**0.7905***	**0.7905***
(- SR training)	0.5000*	0.5000*	0.3768*	0.5000*
(- SI training)	0.7712*	0.7725*	0.7718*	0.7717*
(- SG training)	0.7774*	0.7801*	0.7781*	0.7779*
(- Semantic Dependency)	0.7822*	0.7805*	0.7836*	0.7821*
Our Proposed Test set				
BERT-base	0.4949	0.4963	0.4559	0.4922
Ours	**0.5419***	**0.5393***	**0.5332***	**0.5413***
(- SR training)	0.4927	0.4968	0.4179	0.5026
(- SI training)	0.5030*	0.5020*	0.4532*	0.4974*
(- SG training)	0.5152*	0.5136*	0.4985*	0.5110*
(- Semantic Dependency)	0.5325*	0.5284*	0.5114*	0.5256*

4.4 Implementation Details

Our model is implemented by PyTorch [16]. The implementations of the pre-trained models in this paper are all based on the public Pytorch implementation (https://github.com/huggingface/transformers). During the training, the maximum input length is set to 512. We use a single Tesla v100s GPU with 32 gb memory for experiments. The batch size is all set to 24. The model is optimized using the Adam optimizer with a learning rate of 5e−6. The learning rate is scheduled by a warm-up and linear decay. A dropout rate of 0.1 is applied for all linear transformation layers. The gradient clipping threshold is set as 10.0. Early stopping on the corresponding validation data is adopted as a regularization strategy. The training epochs are ~3. For SI/SG testing on the new unseen set, if the masked position is a single word, we select the answer with the highest probability of the masked position; if there are multiple masked words, we encode the predicted words and the candidates into dense vectors with a sentence-transformer (https://www.huggingface.co/sentence_transformers/all-MiniLM-L6-v2). Then we compute the cosine similarity between the predicted words and each of the candidates. The candidate with the highest similarity is chosen as the answer.

5 Results and Analysis

In this section, we introduce the experimental results and provide our analysis of the results.

5.1 Simile Recognition

Table 5 shows the simile recognition results. The experiments are conducted on the MSP-modified SR test set and our new unseen test set.

Comparing with Baseline. The BERT-base model is fine-tuned with the MSP-modified SR train set and is tested with two test sets. One is the MSP-modified SR test set and the other is our new test set. We can see that on both test sets, our model performs better than the baselines. On the MSP-modified SR test set, our model surpasses BERT-base by around 7.8% on accuracy. On our proposed test set, our model outperforms BERT-base by around 4.9% on accuracy. On Macro Precision/Recall/F1, our model also outperforms the BERT-base model. The results show that our method not only can help PLM to use a more accurate simile knowledge but also perform better on a more difficult unseen test set. The results on the new test set are much lower than the MSP-modified SR test set, which indicates the new test set is much harder. Although our method helps the PLM to obtain a better performance on this new test set, there is still a lot of room to improve.

Ablation Study on SR. We also report the ablation study in Table 5. We can see that on both the MSP test set and the new test set, removing the key component of our model will cause declines. On the MSP test set, (- SR training) is exactly 50% because the model does not understand the SR task without the SR training. On the new test set, similar results are observed. The results are also around 50% and are not statistically significant.

On both test sets, (- SI training) performs worse than (- SG training). The results indicate that the SI fine-tuning task (recovering the masked property) is more useful than the SG fine-tuning task (recovering the masked vehicle) for the model to learn SR knowledge. It is because the shared property usually serves as the root of the semantic dependency tree. As shown in the (c) part of Fig. 1, the shared property connects most words in a simile sentence and the vehicle only connects a few words. When training with SI, the model learns more semantic relations between words than training with SG, so that the model can better leverage this semantic dependency knowledge for the SR task.

(- Semantic Dependency) causes more declines on the new test set (from 0.9–2.2% on all metrics) than on the MSP test set (from 0.7–1.0% on all metrics). It means the semantic dependency information helps the PLM to learn a more generic simile knowledge. This generic simile knowledge brings more gains in an unseen domain.

To sum up, experimental results on SR verify that 1) our method can explore more accurate and generic simile knowledge; 2) each fine-tuning task and the semantic dependency signal contributes to the performance.

Table 6. Simile interpretation and generation results (Hit@1) on MSD-En. The BERT-Probe is the base model to do the significant test for other models (* means statistically significant with $p < 0.01$).

Model	Interpretation	Generation
MSP-original SI Test set and MSP-modified SG Test set		
BERT-base (without fine-tuning)	0.7436	0.8155
BERT-Probe [8]	0.8015	0.8667
BERT-ANT [4]	0.8020	0.8675
Ours	**0.8101***	**0.8986***
(- SR training)	0.8006*	0.8819*
(- SI training)	0.7273*	0.8608*
(- SG training)	0.7832*	0.8113*
(- Semantic Dependency)	0.8089*	0.8799*
Our proposed Test set (the simile data)		
BERT-base (without fine-tuning)	0.5905	0.4510
BERT-Probe [8]	0.6454	0.5031
BERT-ANT [4]	0.5921	0.5094
Ours	**0.6142***	**0.5232***
(- SR training)	0.6084*	0.5189*
(- SI training)	0.5801*	0.4976*
(- SG training)	0.6025*	0.4888*
(- Semantic Dependency)	0.6031*	0.5022*

5.2 Simile Interpretation and Generation

Table 6 shows the simile interpretation and simile generation results. The SI task uses the MSP-original SI test set and our new test set. The SG task uses the MSP-modified SG test set and our new test set.

Comparing with Baselines. The first baseline is the BERT-base model without any fine-tuning. We can see that BERT-Probe performs better than BERT-base on both SI/SG tasks. The results are reasonable since BERT-Probe benefits from the fine-tuning of MSP-original/MSP-modified data on SI/SG tasks, respectively.

Different from the above two baselines, BERT-ANT is based on BERT-large and trained with a large corpus through Adjective-Noun mask Training. Benefiting from both a larger parameter size and the training process, BERT-ANT outperforms the BERT-Probe on both SI/SG tasks.

On the other hand, our model surpasses the strong BERT-ANT on both SI/SG even though our model uses BERT-base as the backbone. The results again verify that our method can enhance PLM with more accurate and generic simile knowledge.

The results on the new test set are still lower than the MSP test sets. One notable result is that the gap between results on the SG task is much larger than the gap on the SI task. The results show that the MSP-modified SG test set is easier than the MSP-original SI test set. The Hit@1 results are 89.86% and 81.01%, respectively. This may also be one of the reasons why SI training contributes more than SG training in Table 5. We can try constructing more difficult SG training data to improve the learning efficiency of our model.

Ablation Study on SI/SG. We also report the ablation study in Table 6. We can see that on both MSP test sets and the new test set, removing the training component of our model will cause declines.

On the MSP-original SI test set, (- SI training) causes ~8.3% declines. On the new test set, (- SI training) only has ~2.4% declines. The results are reasonable since the unseen test set is not as sensitive to the training data as the seen test set. A similar trend can be observed with the SG task. On the MSP-modified SG test set, (-SG training) causes ~8.7% declines. On the new test set, (- SG training) only entails ~3.4% declines.

On all test sets, (- SR training) only causes a little decline, which indicates that the SR fine-tuning contributes little to SI/SG tasks. This is different from the experimental results in Table 5, where SI/SG training contribute more to the SR task. How to leverage SR training to improve the SI/SG tasks requires further study.

Similar to the SR experiments, (- Semantic Dependency) causes more declines on the new test set (~1.1% on SI and ~2.1% on SG) than on MSP test sets (~0.1% on SI and ~1.9% on SG). The results mean the semantic dependency information helps more on an unseen set than the seen set, which is consistent with the results of the SR task.

To sum up, experimental results on SI/SG again verify that 1) our method can explore more accurate and generic simile knowledge; 2) each fine-tuning task and the semantic dependency signal have positive effects on the performance.

6 Conclusion

We propose a novel method to explore more accurate and generic simile knowledge from PLMs. We fine-tune PLM with three simile tasks (recognition, interpretation, and generation) to explore local simile knowledge between key simile components (tenor, shared property, vehicle). Then we use the semantic dependency feature for global simile knowledge among different examples. This global simile knowledge can help our model perform well across domains. Experiments with seen and unseen test sets verify the effectiveness of our method. Our exploring method may be useful for other NLP tasks that leverage knowledge from PLMs. Since our method does not need an expensive pre-training process, it may also be useful for leveraging more large-scaled PLMs. Future works include but are not limited to **1)** testing our method on other knowledge-intensive tasks; **2)** verifying whether our method can be transferred to auto-regressive-based PLMs.

Acknowledgements. This research project is supported by the National Natural Science Foundation of China (61872402), Science Foundation of Beijing Language and Culture University (supported by "the Fundamental Research Funds for the Central Universities") (18ZDJ03).

References

1. Birke, J., Sarkar, A.: A clustering approach for nearly unsupervised recognition of nonliteral language. In: McCarthy, D., Wintner, S. (eds.) EACL 2006, 11st Conference of the European Chapter of the Association for Computational Linguistics, Proceedings of the Conference, 3–7 April 2006, Trento, Italy. The Association for Computer Linguistics (2006). https://aclanthology.org/E06-1042/
2. Bizzoni, Y., Lappin, S.: Predicting human metaphor paraphrase judgments with deep neural networks. In: Klebanov, B.B., Shutova, E., Lichtenstein, P., Muresan, S., Leong, C.W. (eds.) Proceedings of the Workshop on Figurative Language Processing, Fig-Lang@NAACL-HLT 2018, New Orleans, Louisiana, 6 June 2018, pp. 45–55. Association for Computational Linguistics (2018). https://doi.org/10.18653/v1/W18-0906
3. Chakrabarty, T., Muresan, S., Peng, N.: Generating similes effortlessly like a pro: a style transfer approach for simile generation. In: Webber, B., Cohn, T., He, Y., Liu, Y. (eds.) Proceedings of the 2020 Conference on Empirical Methods in Natural Language Processing, EMNLP 2020, Online, 16–20 November 2020, pp. 6455–6469. Association for Computational Linguistics (2020). https://doi.org/10.18653/v1/2020.emnlp-main.524
4. Chen, W., et al.: Probing simile knowledge from pre-trained language models. In: Muresan, S., Nakov, P., Villavicencio, A. (eds.) Proceedings of the 60th Annual Meeting of the Association for Computational Linguistics (vol. 1: Long Papers), ACL 2022, Dublin, Ireland, 22–27 May 2022, pp. 5875–5887. Association for Computational Linguistics (2022). https://doi.org/10.18653/v1/2022.acl-long.404
5. Devlin, J., Chang, M., Lee, K., Toutanova, K.: BERT: pre-training of deep bidirectional transformers for language understanding. In: Burstein, J., Doran, C., Solorio, T. (eds.) Proceedings of the 2019 Conference of the North American Chapter of the Association for Computational Linguistics: Human Language Technologies, NAACL-HLT 2019, Minneapolis, MN, USA, 2–7 June 2019, vol. 1 (Long and Short Papers), pp. 4171–4186. Association for Computational Linguistics (2019)
6. Dziri, N., Kamalloo, E., Mathewson, K.W., Zaïane, O.R.: Augmenting neural response generation with context-aware topical attention. CoRR abs/1811.01063 (2018). http://arxiv.org/abs/1811.01063
7. Dziri, N., Milton, S., Yu, M., Zaïane, O.R., Reddy, S.: On the origin of hallucinations in conversational models: is it the datasets or the models? In: Carpuat, M., de Marneffe, M., Ruíz, I.V.M. (eds.) Proceedings of the 2022 Conference of the North American Chapter of the Association for Computational Linguistics: Human Language Technologies, NAACL 2022, Seattle, WA, United States, 10–15 July 2022, pp. 5271–5285. Association for Computational Linguistics (2022). https://doi.org/10.18653/v1/2022.naacl-main.387
8. He, Q., Cheng, S., Li, Z., Xie, R., Xiao, Y.: Can pre-trained language models interpret similes as smart as human? In: Muresan, S., Nakov, P., Villavicencio, A. (eds.) Proceedings of the 60th Annual Meeting of the Association for Computational Linguistics (vol. 1: Long Papers), ACL 2022, Dublin, Ireland, 22–27 May 2022, pp. 7875–7887. Association for Computational Linguistics (2022). https://doi.org/10.18653/v1/2022.acl-long.543

9. Lewis, M., et al.: BART: denoising sequence-to-sequence pre-training for natural language generation, translation, and comprehension. In: Jurafsky, D., Chai, J., Schluter, N., Tetreault, J.R. (eds.) Proceedings of the 58th Annual Meeting of the Association for Computational Linguistics, ACL 2020, Online, 5–10 July 2020, pp. 7871–7880. Association for Computational Linguistics (2020). https://www.aclweb.org/anthology/2020.acl-main.703/
10. Li, Y., Lin, C., Guerin, F.: CM-GEN: a neural framework for Chinese metaphor generation with explicit context modelling. In: Calzolari, N., et al. (eds.) Proceedings of the 29th International Conference on Computational Linguistics, COLING 2022, Gyeongju, Republic of Korea, 12–17 October 2022, pp. 6468–6479. International Committee on Computational Linguistics (2022). https://aclanthology.org/2022.coling-1.563
11. Liu, L., Hu, X., Song, W., Fu, R., Liu, T., Hu, G.: Neural multitask learning for simile recognition. In: Riloff, E., Chiang, D., Hockenmaier, J., Tsujii, J. (eds.) Proceedings of the 2018 Conference on Empirical Methods in Natural Language Processing, Brussels, Belgium, 31 October–4 November 2018, pp. 1543–1553. Association for Computational Linguistics (2018). https://doi.org/10.18653/v1/d18-1183
12. Liu, T., et al.: A token-level reference-free hallucination detection benchmark for free-form text generation. In: Muresan, S., Nakov, P., Villavicencio, A. (eds.) Proceedings of the 60th Annual Meeting of the Association for Computational Linguistics (vol. 1: Long Papers), ACL 2022, Dublin, Ireland, 22–27 May 2022, pp. 6723–6737. Association for Computational Linguistics (2022). https://doi.org/10.18653/v1/2022.acl-long.464
13. Manning, C.D., Surdeanu, M., Bauer, J., Finkel, J.R., Bethard, S., McClosky, D.: The Stanford CoreNLP natural language processing toolkit. In: Proceedings of the 52nd Annual Meeting of the Association for Computational Linguistics, ACL 2014, 22–27 June 2014, Baltimore, MD, USA, System Demonstrations, pp. 55–60. The Association for Computer Linguistics (2014). https://doi.org/10.3115/v1/p14-5010
14. Mohler, M., Brunson, M., Rink, B., Tomlinson, M.T.: Introducing the LCC metaphor datasets. In: Calzolari, N., et al. (eds.) Proceedings of the Tenth International Conference on Language Resources and Evaluation LREC 2016, Portorož, Slovenia, 23–28 May 2016. European Language Resources Association (ELRA) (2016). http://www.lrec-conf.org/proceedings/lrec2016/summaries/1156.html
15. Niculae, V., Danescu-Niculescu-Mizil, C.: Brighter than gold: figurative language in user generated comparisons. In: Moschitti, A., Pang, B., Daelemans, W. (eds.) Proceedings of the 2014 Conference on Empirical Methods in Natural Language Processing, EMNLP 2014, 25–29 October 2014, Doha, Qatar, A Meeting of SIGDAT, a Special Interest Group of the ACL, pp. 2008–2018. ACL (2014). https://doi.org/10.3115/v1/d14-1215
16. Paszke, A., et al.: PyTorch: an imperative style, high-performance deep learning library. In: Wallach, H.M., Larochelle, H., Beygelzimer, A., d'Alché-Buc, F., Fox, E.B., Garnett, R. (eds.) Advances in Neural Information Processing Systems: Annual Conference on Neural Information Processing Systems 2019, NeurIPS 2019 (December), vol. 32, pp. 8–14, 2019, Vancouver, BC, Canada, pp. 8024–8035 (2019). https://proceedings.neurips.cc/paper/2019/hash/bdbca288fee7f92f2bfa9f7012727740-Abstract.html
17. Paul, A.M.: Figurative language. In: Philosophy and Rhetoric, pp. 225–248 (1970)
18. Radford, A., Wu, J., Child, R., Luan, D., Amodei, D., Sutskever, I.: Language models are unsupervised multitask learners. OpenAI Blog **1**(8), 9 (2019)

19. Shuster, K., Poff, S., Chen, M., Kiela, D., Weston, J.: Retrieval augmentation reduces hallucination in conversation. In: Moens, M., Huang, X., Specia, L., Yih, S.W. (eds.) Findings of the Association for Computational Linguistics: EMNLP 2021, Virtual Event/Punta Cana, Dominican Republic, 16–20 November 2021, pp. 3784–3803. Association for Computational Linguistics (2021). https://doi.org/10.18653/v1/2021.findings-emnlp.320
20. Song, W., Guo, J., Fu, R., Liu, T., Liu, L.: A knowledge graph embedding approach for metaphor processing. IEEE ACM Trans. Audio Speech Lang. Process. **29**, 406–420 (2021). https://doi.org/10.1109/TASLP.2020.3040507
21. Speer, R., Chin, J., Havasi, C.: ConceptNet 5.5: an open multilingual graph of general knowledge. In: Singh, S., Markovitch, S. (eds.) Proceedings of the Thirty-First AAAI Conference on Artificial Intelligence, 4–9 February 2017, San Francisco, California, USA, pp. 4444–4451. AAAI Press (2017). http://aaai.org/ocs/index.php/AAAI/AAAI17/paper/view/14972
22. Steen, G.: A Method for Linguistic Metaphor Identification: From MIP to MIPVU, vol. 14. John Benjamins Publishing, Amsterdam (2010)
23. Stowe, K., Beck, N., Gurevych, I.: Exploring metaphoric paraphrase generation. In: Bisazza, A., Abend, O. (eds.) Proceedings of the 25th Conference on Computational Natural Language Learning, CoNLL 2021, Online, 10–11 November 2021, pp. 323–336. Association for Computational Linguistics (2021). https://doi.org/10.18653/v1/2021.conll-1.26
24. Su, C., Tian, J., Chen, Y.: Latent semantic similarity based interpretation of Chinese metaphors. Eng. Appl. Artif. Intell. **48**, 188–203 (2016). https://doi.org/10.1016/j.engappai.2015.10.014
25. Tsvetkov, Y., Boytsov, L., Gershman, A., Nyberg, E., Dyer, C.: Metaphor detection with cross-lingual model transfer. In: Proceedings of the 52nd Annual Meeting of the Association for Computational Linguistics, ACL 2014, 22–27 June 2014, Baltimore, MD, USA, vol. 1: Long Papers, pp. 248–258. The Association for Computer Linguistics (2014). https://doi.org/10.3115/v1/p14-1024
26. Zhang, J., et al.: Writing polishment with simile: Task, dataset and A neural approach. In: Thirty-Fifth AAAI Conference on Artificial Intelligence, AAAI 2021, Thirty-Third Conference on Innovative Applications of Artificial Intelligence, IAAI 2021, The Eleventh Symposium on Educational Advances in Artificial Intelligence, EAAI 2021, Virtual Event, 2–9 February 2021, pp. 14383–14392. AAAI Press (2021). https://ojs.aaai.org/index.php/AAAI/article/view/17691

Social Computing and Sentiment Analysis

Learnable Conjunction Enhanced Model for Chinese Sentiment Analysis

Bingfei Zhao, Hongying Zan(✉), Jiajia Wang, and Yingjie Han

Zhengzhou University, Zhengzhou, China
{iehyzan,ieyjhan}@zzu.edu.cn

Abstract. Sentiment analysis is a crucial text classification task that aims to extract, process, and analyze opinions, sentiments, and subjectivity within texts. In current research on Chinese text, sentence and aspect-based sentiment analysis is mainly tackled through well-designed models. However, despite the importance of word order and function words as essential means of semantic expression in Chinese, they are often underutilized. This paper presents a new Chinese sentiment analysis method that utilizes a Learnable Conjunctions Enhanced Model (LCEM). The LCEM adjusts the general structure of the pre-trained language model and incorporates conjunctions location information into the model's fine-tuning process. Additionally, we discuss a variant structure of residual connections to construct a residual structure that can learn critical information in the text and optimize it during training. We perform experiments on the public datasets and demonstrate that our approach enhances performance on both sentence and aspect-based sentiment analysis datasets compared to the baseline pre-trained language models. These results confirm the effectiveness of our proposed method.

Keywords: Sentiment Analysis · Conjunction Enhanced · Residual Structure

1 Introduction

Sentiment analysis is a crucial area of research within the field of natural language processing. Before the advent of Transformer [33], Recurrent Neural Networks (RNNs) were the primary method used to model sequences in language modeling tasks [12,13,21,31]. RNN, along with its variants LSTM (Long-Short Term Memory) and GRU (Gated Recurrent Unit), are powerful models for processing sequences of varying lengths and addressing long-term dependencies. However, the sequential nature of RNNs makes parallelization difficult. Transformer introduces the attention mechanism to encode the context information, which can well capture the internal correlation and ease the problem of long-term dependencies. This allows for greater parallelization and improved performance on certain tasks.

Nevertheless, since self-attention discards sequential operations when processing sequences, the position information in the sequence cannot be fully utilized. In languages such as Chinese, word order plays a crucial role in conveying grammatical meaning[1], making it important to consider the sequential nature of the language when

[1] Higher Education Press.

M. Sun et al. (Eds.): CCL 2023, LNAI 14232, pp. 367–381, 2023.
https://doi.org/10.1007/978-981-99-6207-5_23

developing natural language processing models. Word order refers to the sequence of words in a phrase or sentence, while Chinese word order is relatively fixed, and the change of word order can make the phrase or sentence express different meanings. “Speak well/说好话” , “easy to speak with/好说话” , and “easier said/话好说” are three Chinese phrases that demonstrate the importance of word order in conveying meaning. Although these phrases share similar characters, their meanings differ greatly depending on how those characters are arranged. “Speak well/说好话” means to speak positively or say good things about someone or something, while “easy to speak with/好说话” describes someone who is easy to communicate with. Lastly, “easier said/话好说” implies that something may sound simple or easy to do but can be more difficult in practice. It’s essential to consider both the context and word order when interpreting or translating Chinese phrases. In addition, function words in Chinese play an important role in constructing the grammatical structure of a sentence and reflecting specific grammatical relationships. They are a crucial grammatical tool necessary for expressing meaning[2]. Among them, conjunctions connect grammatical units at different levels, and their positions in sentences are significantly different [17], which can be used as an essential aspect of studying syntactic distribution.

Therefore, in this paper, we propose LCEM, a learnable conjunctions augmentation model for Chinese sentiment analysis. By adjusting the structure of the pre-trained language model, LCEM introduces the conjunction position information into the fine-tuning process. The paper also explores variants of residual structure and constructs an enhanced model capable of learning critical information during training and optimization of the residual structure.

The main contributions of this paper can be summarized as follows:

- LCEM is a generic structure that can be easily integrated into a pre-trained language model based on Transformer using an adaptive update optimized network of learnable parameter factors.
- By incorporating the relative position of conjunctions in each layer of the pre-trained language model, LCEM enhances multi-head self-attention and effectively considers the sentiment range of sentences connected by conjunctions.
- Additionally, LCEM combines a learnable residual structure to better balance the network and optimize semantic representation more efficiently.
- LCEM is evaluated on benchmark datasets for sentence and aspect-based sentiment analysis. Experiments show that LCEM consistently achieves state-of-the-art performance across all test datasets.

2 Related Work

2.1 Chinese Sentiment Analysis

Early Chinese sentiment analysis methods [19,27,43] primarily relied on sentiment lexicons, such as HowNet sentiment word dictionary and National Taiwan University Sentiment Dictionary (NTUSD), and classified sentiment polarity based on dictionaries and

[2] The Commercial Press.

rules. However, these methods are limited by the quality and coverage of lexicons. The sentiment analysis in a specific field needs to construct a specific dictionary, which is time-consuming and laborious. When traditional machine learning algorithms are used in sentiment classification, different features enable different classifiers to obtain higher accuracy than dictionary methods [6,36,38]. However, traditional machine learning methods rely on the quality of the annotated corpus and cannot fully use contextual semantic information.

With the rapid development of deep learning, neural network and attention mechanism have been widely concerned and applied in Chinese sentiment analysis [2,23]. Transformer with self-attention mechanism, which employs an encoder-decoder framework to better address long-term dependencies and allows for more robust scalability of parallel computations, is widely used in natural language processing. Based on the Transformer architecture, a series of landmark pre-trained language models have emerged, showing a strong ability to learn generic Chinese representations. Li [14] fully extracted context information using improved attention to encode relative position between words based on ELMo [24]. Xie [35] used BERT to encode the set of sentiment words extracted from texts and used attention to obtain sentiment information. However, in the above studies, although the pre-trained language model has powerful modeling ability, it neglects the application of syntactic structure or semantic information in sentiment analysis and fails to use sentiment features effectively.

2.2 Relative Position Feature

In order to leverage the sequential information contained within input text, Transformers incorporate position embeddings into the original input embedding. This process is calculated as follows:

$$\begin{aligned} PE_{(pos,2i)} &= sin(pos/10000^{(2i/d_{model})}) \\ PE_{(pos,2i+1)} &= cos(pos/10000^{(2i/d_{model})}) \end{aligned} \tag{1}$$

where pos represents position, i represents the number of dimensions, d_{model} is the input and output vector dimensions. The sines and cosines enable the model to learn the relative position and easily extend to longer sequences.

The BERT-based pre-trained language model adopts the encoder structure in Transformer and selects absolute position embedding to better adapt to downstream tasks. In the input layer, word embedding is combined with position embedding to ensure that identical words at different positions can learn representations that are appropriate for their respective contexts. Li [14] improved attention by encoding relative positions between words. Shaw [26] used relative encoding as an additional value in the self-attention to capture information about the relative position differences between input elements. According to different task characteristics, different position embeddings contain different meanings. For instance, in the named entity recognition task, entity term is often introduced by designing different position features [11,22,37]. In the causality extraction task, position features can reflect the position of connectives and the distance between causal events and connectives [42].

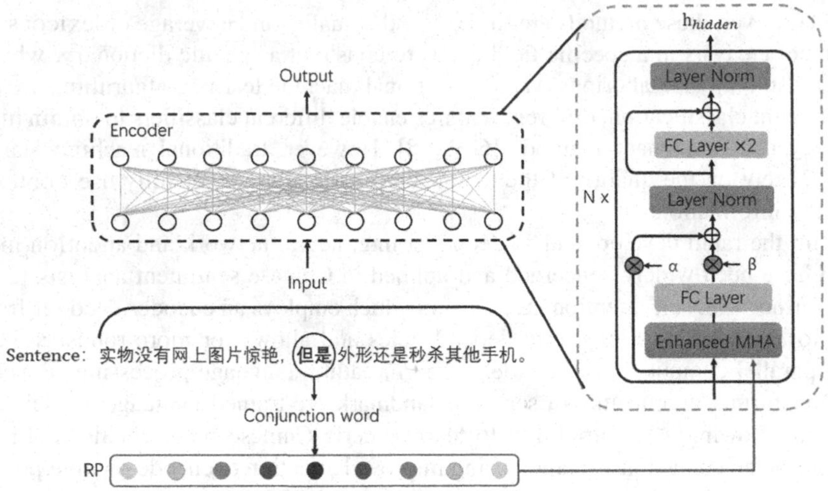

Fig. 1. Overview of LCEM

2.3 Residual Structure

Neural networks have a strong representation ability and can optimize and update the network structure through the back propagation algorithm. However, during backpropagation, gradients may either vanish or increase exponentially, resulting in ineffective updates to the underlying parameters, or gradient explosion. Furthermore, deeper networks are susceptible to degradation problems. He [5] verified that adding more layers to a network model with a certain depth will lead to higher training errors.

Recently, residual learning has been widely used in natural language processing and computer vision as a technique for optimization of deep neural network to alleviate gradient vanishing or explosion problems [5, 15, 16, 28]. Since each sub-module of the Transformer encoder contains residual structures with layer normalization, BERT-based pre-trained variants can also make full use of residual connections to optimize the network.

This paper introduces the learnable residual structure based on enhanced self-attention by the position features of conjunctions. By assigning learnable parameters to each branch, the residual structure can be adjusted adaptively, and performance can be improved through simple model adjustment.

3 Methodology

3.1 Overview

LCEM is based on the basic architecture of the pre-trained language model. The overall structure of LCEM is described in Fig. 1. LCEM uses the conjunction relative position enhanced multi-head attention to replace the multi-head attention module in each layer of the pre-trained language model. By combining the relative position feature with the attention mechanism, the model can learn global semantic information while still paying close attention to important local ranges. In addition, the residual structure of the pre-trained language model is improved to a more flexible structure to optimize the network and enable better internal information sharing. The learnable factors can adaptively control the residual structure, better integrating the semantic information learned by the relative position feature and further optimizing by assigning different importance to each residual branch.

3.2 Conjunction Relative Position Enhanced Multi-head Attention

LCEM uses the relative position feature to enhance attention to learn the interaction between input text and the conjunctions representation. Conjunctions of transition, progression, selection, and coordinate are selected in the Chinese Function Word Usage Knowledge Base (CFKB) [10,39,41], and the distance $d(d \geq 0)$ between each character in a sentence and the first character of the conjunction is calculated. We map the relative position of conjunctions into the interval of $(0, 1)$ to obtain the relative position feature RP, and the calculation is as follows:

$$RP = 1 - Sigmoid(d) = 1 - \frac{1}{1 + e^{-d}} \tag{2}$$

If there is no conjunctions in the sentences, the *d* in the formula is the distance between each word in the sentences and the beginning of the sentences.

Then, as shown in Fig. 2, RP increases the attention to the context near conjunctions. At the same time, the learnable parameter ω is introduced to reduce the noise caused by introducing the relative position feature to the original input representation H. The attention after adding the relative position feature is as follows:

$$\begin{aligned} Attetnion(Q, K, V) &= Softmax(\frac{QK^T}{\sqrt{d_K}} + \omega RP)V \\ where \quad Q &= HW^Q, K = HW^K, V = HW^V \end{aligned} \tag{3}$$

3.3 Learnable Residual Structure

Some studies [15,16] divided the problems existing in residual connection into two types: the balance problem of each residual branch and the optimization problem. Liu [15] analyzed existing works and summarized the general residual structure as follows:

$$\mathcal{Y} = \alpha x + \beta \mathcal{F} + \gamma LN(x + \mathcal{F}) \tag{4}$$

where x is the input branch, i.e., the skip connection, $\mathcal{F}$ is the residual branch, LN is layer normalization, $\mathcal{Y}$ is the output of the residual block, and α, β, γ are the weight factors. The residual block can be adjusted and optimized adaptively by adjusting values for α, β, and γ. Liu [16] proposed formula 5 to summarize the residual connection with normalization. Normalization $\mathcal{G}$ was placed outside the sum of input x and nonlinear transformation $\mathcal{F}(x, W)$, and λ was used to enhance the input branch.

$$\mathcal{Y} = \mathcal{G}(\lambda x + \mathcal{F}(x, W)) \tag{5}$$

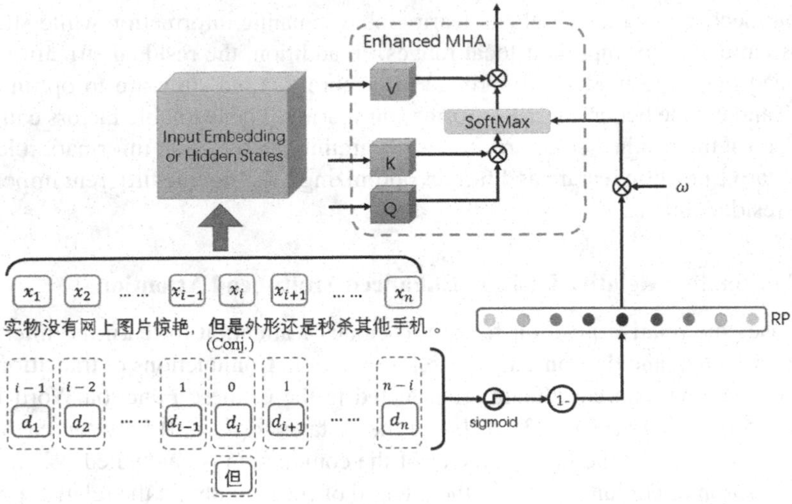

Fig. 2. Details of Conjunction Relative Position Enhanced Multi-Head Attention

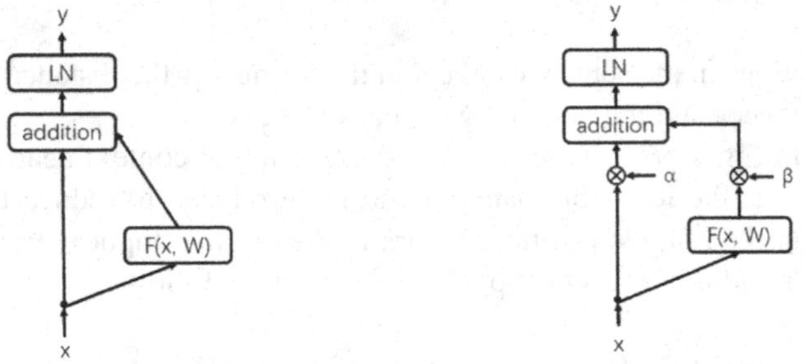

(a) Transformer (b) Learnable Residual Structure in LCEM

Fig. 3. Residual Structure in Transformer and LCEM

Drawing inspiration from the residual structure present in every layer of the Transformer (Fig. 3 (a)), layer normalization plays a crucial role in the model's overall performance. It can help the optimization of nonlinear transformation to a certain extent. And, in combination with the idea of adjusting each branch of residual in the neural network by the weight factor mentioned above, the residual structure is summarized as follows:

$$\mathcal{Y} = LN(\alpha x + \beta \mathcal{F}) \tag{6}$$

As shown in Fig. 3 (b), the residual structure in Transformer can be regarded as a particular case $\mathcal{Y} = LN(x + \mathcal{F})$ when $\alpha = \beta = 1$. In Transformer, the residual branch $\mathcal{F}$ can be either multi-headed attention or feedforward networks. In this paper, we focus on the residual structure of multi-head attention. We propose to replace the residual branch with conjunctions relative position enhanced attention. Meanwhile, α and β are set as learnable parameters so that the model can self-learn appropriate scaling factors.

Table 1. Statistical data of each category in the datasets.

Datasets	COAE2013		NLPCC2014		SemEval16_CAM		SemEval16_PHO	
	Train	Test	Train	Test	Train	Test	Train	Test
Positive	753	305	5000	1250	809	344	758	310
Negative	876	239	5000	1250	450	137	575	219

The proportion of input branch x and residual branch $\mathcal{F}$ in the network is constantly modified to achieve optimization.

The semantic representation obtained by the enhanced attention will further learn the appropriate proportion in the propagation under the adjustment of scaling factor β, reducing the noise caused by the introduction of the relative position feature. Scaling factors α and β jointly determine the different distribution of x and $\mathcal{F}$. The layer normalization is used to make the distribution of each layer in the network relatively consistent to avoid gradient vanishing or explosion caused by the change of learnable parameters. Through multi-layer structure with learnable conjunctions enhanced attention, the final output is obtained by a linear classifier.

4 Experimental Settings

4.1 Datasets

In this paper, we study two granular subtasks in Chinese sentiment analysis. Statistical data of the above datasets are shown in Table 1.

For Chinese sentence-level sentiment analysis, COAE2013 and NLPCC2014 are selected. COAE2013 is a dataset of annotated data from The Fifth Chinese Opinion Analysis Evaluation, consisting of 1004 positive reviews and 834 negative reviews. The dataset was divided into train set and test set according to the ratio of 9:1. NLPCC2014 is from the 3rd CCF Conference on Natural Language Processing & Chinese Computing, including reviews of books, DVDs, electronic products, and other domains. The train set consisted of 5,000 positive and 5,000 negative texts, and the test set consisted of 2,500 texts.

For the Chinese aspect-based sentiment analysis task, this paper selects SemEval2016 [25]. Task 5 of SemEval2016 provides a Chinese dataset of electronic product aspect-based reviews in two specific domains, including phone and camera, including 400 samples, a total of about 4100 sentences.

4.2 Baselines

We evaluate LCEM with typical sentiment analysis and text classification models as baselines for sentence-level sentiment analysis, including BiLSTM [41], BiLSTM+Att [40], TextCNN [9], DPCNN [8], and pre-trained language models like EBiSAN [14], BERT, BERT_wwm [3], RoBERTa [18], ERNIE [30]. For aspect-based sentiment analysis, we compare our solution to several models that can be applied to Chinese text, including MemNet [32], ATAE-LSTM [34], IAN [20], Ram [1], AOA [7], MGAN [4], Tnet [12], and QA-B [29] and NLI-B [29], and also BERT and ERNIE.

The word vector pre-trained by the Sogou News corpus is selected as the initial embedding in the general baselines. The batch size is 128, the learning rate is 1E−5, and 30 epochs are trained by Adam optimization. Based on the pre-trained model, the baselines all follow the default 12 hidden layers with a size of 768, the batch size is 20, and the learning rate is 5E−5. Adam is used to optimize the cross-entropy loss function and fine-tunes the parameters.

5 Experimental Results

5.1 Results on Sentence-Level Sentiment Analysis

Table 2 shows the results of comparative experiments on the sentence-level datasets. Compared with the pre-trained model ERNIE and neural network models based on RNN and CNN, such as TextCNN and DPCNN, the results indicate that the fine-tuned pre-trained language model performs better on the datasets than the neural network models based on RNN and CNN, highlighting the huge advantage of pre-trained language models in sentiment analysis tasks. Additionally, compared to other pre-trained models, ERNIE performs better on two sentiment analysis datasets. By using relative positional encoding of conjunctions and learnable residual structures based on ERNIE, LCEM further optimized the model and improved its performance, demonstrating the effectiveness of the proposed method in this paper.

Table 2. Results on sentence-level sentiment analysis datasets.

Datasets	COAE2013		NLPCC2014	
	Acc(%)	F1(%)	Acc(%)	F1(%)
BiLSTM	85.74	85.39	60.48	60.48
BiLSTM+Att	86.91	86.76	69.60	69.56
TextCNN	89.65	89.46	69.04	68.85
DPCNN	87.30	87.07	62.48	58.88
EBi-SAN	–	–	79.08	78.48
BERT	93.57	93.53	79.61	79.61
BERT_wwm	94.88	94.83	80.21	80.20
RoBERTa	94.99	95.01	79.57	79.56
ERNIE	95.77	95.74	80.89	80.88
LCEM	**96.69**	**96.68**	**81.08**	**81.08**

5.2 Results on Aspect-Based Sentiment Analysis

Experimental results are shown in Table 3 compared with aspect-based sentiment analysis baselines. Under the accuracy and F1, LCEM outperforms all baselines in SemEval16_CAM and SemEval16_PHO. The accuracy of LCEM on the

Table 3. Results on aspect-based sentiment analysis datasets.

Datasets		SemEval16_CAM		SemEval16_PHO	
		Acc(%)	F1(%)	Acc(%)	F1(%)
ATAE-LSTM		87.11	82.79	79.02	78.78
MemNet		88.57	85.33	77.88	76.77
IAN		88.77	85.97	79.40	78.91
Ram		85.65	82.66	77.69	76.81
Tnet		87.32	83.47	79.77	79.14
AOA		88.36	85.52	79.58	79.21
MGAN		85.45	82.65	79.96	79.38
BERT		87.94	85.57	83.74	83.22
ERNIE		93.14	91.45	90.17	89.84
ERNIE-SPC		92.52	90.65	90.36	90.07
ERNIE-based	QA-B	92.41	92.41	89.23	89.22
	NLI-B	91.48	91.48	88.94	88.94
LCEM		**94.39**	**93.13**	**91.12**	**90.79**

Table 4. Results of ablation experiment

Datasets	COAE2013		NLPCC2014		SemEval16_CAM		SemEval16_PHO	
	Acc(%)	F1(%)	Acc(%)	F1(%)	Acc(%)	F1(%)	Acc(%)	F1(%)
Baseline(ERNIE)	95.77	95.74	80.89	80.88	93.14	91.45	90.17	89.84
$+RP$	95.96	95.94	80.76	80.75	92.93	91.77	89.60	89.17
$+\omega RP$	95.96	95.93	80.92	80.91	92.93	91.32	90.74	90.42
$+LRS$	96.51	96.49	80.40	80.40	92.31	90.74	90.17	89.83
$+RP\&LRS$	95.96	95.93	80.96	80.95	93.35	**93.35**	90.55	90.27
$+\omega RP\&LRS$(LCEM)	**96.69**	**96.68**	**81.08**	**81.08**	**94.39**	93.13	**91.12**	**90.79**

SemEval16_CAM is 1.25% higher than that of ERNIE, and the F1 value is 0.72% higher than that of QA-B. Compared with IAN, MGCN, and other non-pre-trained language models, the fine-tuned results of the pre-trained model have great advantages. On the one hand, the pre-trained model has been trained on large text corpus and has learned rich language representation capabilities, which enables the pre-trained model to better understand the semantics and context of the text, which is very helpful for sentiment analysis tasks. On the other hand, pre-trained models can achieve better results on small datasets, while recurrent neural networks require large amounts of manually annotated training data, and the size of the training data will limit the performance of the model.

5.3 Ablation Study

Table 4 shows the results of LCEM ablation experiments on four datasets.

In which, $+RP$ and $+\omega RP$ respectively represent adding relative position encoding (RP) and weighted relative position encoding (Weighted RP) only in the self-attention module on top of the baseline model. Comparing $+RP$ and $+\omega RP$ with baseline ERNIE, we can see that $+\omega RP$ is better than $+RP$, improves performance on both sentence-level datasets and SemEval16_PHO. But on SemEval16_CAM, neither $+RP$ nor $+\omega RP$ can achieve effective performance enhancement, which may be because the relative position feature is added to each layer of the pre-trained language model. The output of each layer will serve as input to the next layer and participate in the residual structure. As the network depth increases, each addition of the relative position feature will introduce some noise into the original representation. Although the weighted relative position feature($+\omega RP$) introduces parameters that can learn relative positional shifts with the network structure, its effect varies on different datasets.

$+LRS$ represents only the learnable residual structure added to ERNIE. The comparison results also show that $+LRS$ has a slight improvement, indicating that the structure of the pre-trained language model, especially the residual structure, has the advantages of efficiency, stability, and universality.

Accuracy and macro-F1 of $+RP\&LRS$ are better than $+RP$, $+\omega RP$, and $+LRS$ in both datasets. This suggests that scaling within the residual structure can effectively adjust the enhanced multi-head attention as a branch of residual connection. In addition, the output of the previous layer serves as the skip connection branch of the residual structure of the next layer, and residual scaling can adjust the input branch and the residual branch adaptively. At the same time, it shows that enhanced attention by relative location features can capture both content and distance information, and learn richer context representation under the role of location information.

The proposed model LCEM($+\omega RP\&LRS$) achieves the highest accuracy and F1 in both sentence-level datasets. In the two datasets of SemEval16, the F1 improved by 1.68% and 0.95%, respectively, compared with baseline model ERNIE, and achieved the highest accuracy in both datasets. Compared with $+RP\&LRS$, the accuracy is significantly improved, indicating that weighted relative position encoding can achieve more effective optimization. The learnable weights during network training also reduce the noise effects introduced by relative position encoding, better capture the balance within the network and maximizing the gain of residual scaling.

5.4 Case Study

For further analysis of the model, the LCEM and ERNIE models are analyzed in this paper, as shown in Table 5.

For the adversative conjunction "但是" , it serves as a transitional element between two sentences or clauses. It indicates a contrast or contradiction between the information presented before and after it. In the given context, the emotional tone of the sentence preceding the transition is predominantly negative. However, the emotional tone of the sentence following the use of "但是" changes from negative to positive. Therefore, the emotional label of the first sentence in Table 5 is 1, signifying a shift from negative to positive emotion.

On the other hand, the coordinating conjunction "而且" is used to connect two sentences or clauses to express a progression or addition of information. While the emo-

Table 5. Case studies of LCEM and ERNIE models

Type of conjunction	Conjunction	Example	Model	Label
转折	但是	拿到的时候还觉得像盗版，但确实是正版的，很完整，非常不错	ERNIE	0
			LCEM	1
递进	而且	是真正的职场小说，感觉更像《圈子圈套》，而且厚厚的一大本，很值。	ERNIE	0
			LCEM	1

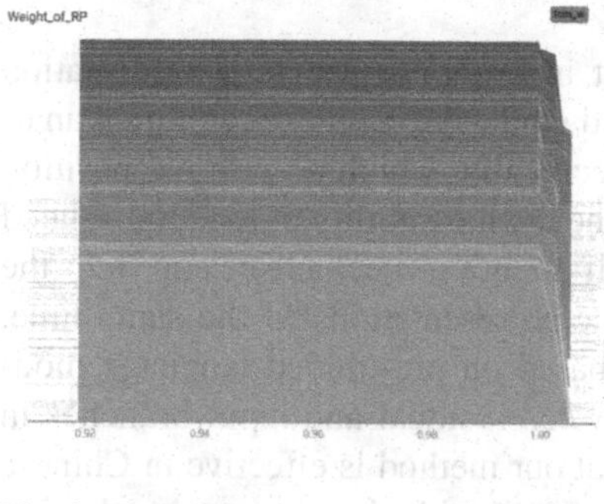

Fig. 4. The parameter ω of RP over time.

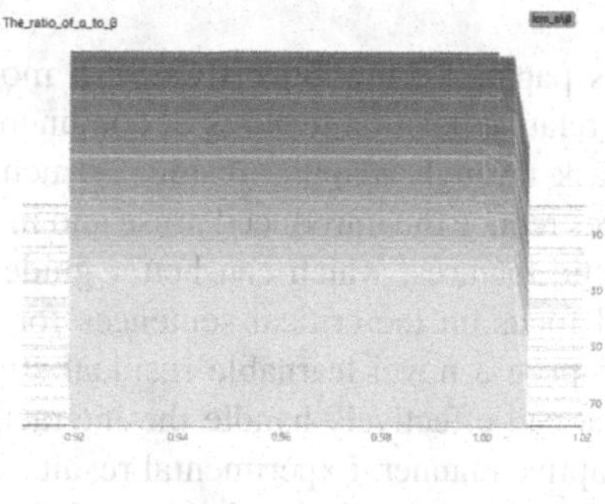

Fig. 5. The ratio of α to β over time.

tional information in the sentence before the conjunction may not be overtly expressed, it is more fully conveyed in the sentence that follows the use of "而且." Consequently, the emotional label of the second sentence in Table 5 is 1, indicating the enhanced expression of emotional content instead of label 0. When compared to ERNIE, LCEM, which incorporates conjunctive information, provides more accurate predictions of emotional labels.

6 Learnable Parameters Analysis

Figures 4 and 5 show the changes of relative position parameter ω and α to β ratio over time. The X-axis represents the range of parameter values, while the Y-axis on the right represents the number of training steps. Each slice in the figure is a single histogram, representing the distribution of parameters in a training step. The number of training steps is gradually increased from back to front.

According to Fig. 4, the learnable parameter ω of the relative position feature RP is more evenly distributed in $[0.919, 0.999]$, indicating that the relative position feature occupies a vital proportion of attention. Moreover, combined with the ablation experiment results in Sect. 5.4, relative location feature enhanced attention can capture both content and distance information and learn a richer context representation under the effect of location information.

Figure 5 shows that the ratio of α to β is evenly distributed in $[0.919, 1.01]$. In most cases, the proportion of input branches is smaller than that of residual branches. In each Transformer encoder, the proportion of representations from the previous layer is smaller than that of expressions enhanced by the relative position of the conjunctions. It demonstrates the significance of the semantic representation obtained through enhanced attention in the network. Moreover, input branches also play an important role in network. Through layer-by-layer propagation, the semantic representation acquired by each layer can be preserved in the lower layers and will participate in the attention mechanism to further extract abstract semantics. The learnable parameters greatly help the information transfer and optimization of network structure.

7 Conclusion

In this paper, we introduce LCEM, a model that incorporates semantic information using relative position features of conjunctions, and guides the Chinese sentiment analysis task through adaptive residual structure. Specifically, weighted relative position features reduce the introduced noise and improve the learning ability of location-related syntactic features, which can better guide the self-attention mechanism and help the model focus on the critical sentences for semantic representation. At the same time, we propose a novel learnable residual structure based on pre-trained language models that can effectively handle the interaction between residual and input branches in an adaptive manner. Experimental results show that our method is effective in Chinese sentiment analysis, where relative position and adaptive residual structure complement each other. The relative position information helps the model to focus on crucial information for sentiment analysis, while the residual structure in each layer balances the learned knowledge within the network structure.

Acknowledgements. This research is supported by the key research and development and promotion project of Henan Provincial Department of Science and Technology in 2023: Research on Automatic Question Answering System in Science and Technology Management Based on Knowledge Graph (232102211041) and the National Social Science Foundation project: Research on Knowledge Base and Application of Modern Chinese Function Word Usage for Natural Language Processing (14BYY096). The author would like to thank the anonymous reviewers for their valuable comments and suggestions on the improvement of this paper.

References

1. Chen, P., Sun, Z., Bing, L., Yang, W.: Recurrent attention network on memory for aspect sentiment analysis. In: Proceedings of the 2017 Conference on Empirical Methods in Natural Language Processing, pp. 452–461 (2017)
2. Cheng, Y., Ye, Z., Wang, M., Zhang, Q., Zhang, G.: Chinese text sentiment orientation analysis based on convolution neural network and hierarchical attention network. J. Chin. Inf. Process. **33**(01), 133–142 (2019)
3. Cui, Y., Che, W., Liu, T., Qin, B., Yang, Z.: Pre-training with whole word masking for Chinese BERT. IEEE/ACM Trans. Audio Speech Lang. Process. **29**, 3504–3514 (2021). https://doi.org/10.1109/TASLP.2021.3124365
4. Fan, F., Feng, Y., Zhao, D.: Multi-grained attention network for aspect-level sentiment classification. In: Proceedings of the 2018 Conference on Empirical Methods in Natural Language Processing, pp. 3433–3442 (2018)
5. He, K., Zhang, X., Ren, S., Sun, J.: Deep residual learning for image recognition. In: Proceedings of the IEEE Conference on Computer Vision and Pattern Recognition, pp. 770–778 (2016)

6. He, Y., Zhao, S., He, L.: Micro-text emotional tendentious classification based on combination of emotion knowledge and machine-learning algorithm. J. Intell **37**(5), 189–194 (2018)
7. Huang, B., Ou, Y., Carley, K.M.: Aspect level sentiment classification with attention-over-attention neural networks. In: Thomson, R., Dancy, C., Hyder, A., Bisgin, H. (eds.) SBP-BRiMS 2018. LNCS, vol. 10899, pp. 197–206. Springer, Cham (2018). https://doi.org/10.1007/978-3-319-93372-6_22
8. Johnson, R., Zhang, T.: Deep pyramid convolutional neural networks for text categorization. In: Proceedings of the 55th Annual Meeting of the Association for Computational Linguistics (vol. 1: Long Papers), pp. 562–570 (2017)
9. Kim, Y.: Convolutional neural networks for sentence classification. In: Proceedings of the 2014 Conference on Empirical Methods in Natural Language Processing (EMNLP), pp. 1746–1751. Association for Computational Linguistics, Doha, Qatar, October 2014. https://doi.org/10.3115/v1/D14-1181, https://aclanthology.org/D14-1181
10. Kunli, Z., Hongying, Z., Yumei, C., Yingjie, H., Dan, Z.: Construction and application of the Chinese function word usage knowledge base (2013)
11. Li, X., Yan, H., Qiu, X., Huang, X.: FLAT: Chinese NER using flat-lattice transformer. In: Proceedings of the 58th Annual Meeting of the Association for Computational Linguistics, pp. 6836–6842. Association for Computational Linguistics, Online, July 2020. https://doi.org/10.18653/v1/2020.acl-main.611, https://aclanthology.org/2020.acl-main.611
12. Li, X., Bing, L., Lam, W., Shi, B.: Transformation networks for target-oriented sentiment classification. In: Proceedings of the 56th Annual Meeting of the Association for Computational Linguistics (vol. 1: Long Papers), pp. 946–956. Association for Computational Linguistics, Melbourne, Australia, July 2018. https://doi.org/10.18653/v1/P18-1087, https://aclanthology.org/P18-1087
13. Li, X., Bing, L., Li, P., Lam, W.: A unified model for opinion target extraction and target sentiment prediction. In: Proceedings of the AAAI Conference on Artificial Intelligence, vol. 33, pp. 6714–6721 (2019)
14. Li, Z., Chen, L., Zhang, S.: Chinese text sentiment analysis based on ELMo and Bi-SAN. Appl. Res. Comput. **38**(8), 2301–2307 (2021)
15. Liu, F., Gao, M., Liu, Y., Lei, K.: Self-adaptive scaling approach for learnable residual structure. In: Proceedings of the 23rd Conference on Computational Natural Language Learning (CoNLL), pp. 862–870 (2019)
16. Liu, F., Ren, X., Zhang, Z., Sun, X., Zou, Y.: Rethinking skip connection with layer normalization in transformers and ResNets. arXiv preprint arXiv:2105.07205 (2021)
17. Liu, Q.: Study of conjunctive scope and its "special category" in modern Chinese. J. Jiangsu Normal Univ. Philos. Soc. Sci. Ed. **42**, 85–90 (2016). https://doi.org/10.16095/j.cnki.cn32-1833/c.2016.01.014
18. Liu, Y., et al.: RoBERTa: a robustly optimized BERT pretraining approach. arXiv preprint arXiv:1907.11692 (2019)
19. Liu, Y., Ju, S., Wu, S., Su, C.: Classification of Chinese texts sentiment based on semantic and conjunction. J. Sichuan Univ. Nat. Sci. Ed. **52**, 57–62 (2015)
20. Ma, D., Li, S., Zhang, X., Wang, H.: Interactive attention networks for aspect-level sentiment classification. AAAI Press (2017)
21. Majumder, N., Bhardwaj, R., Poria, S., Gelbukh, A., Hussain, A.: Improving aspect-level sentiment analysis with aspect extraction. Neural Comput. Appl. **34**(11), 8333–8343 (2022). https://doi.org/10.1007/s00521-020-05287-7
22. Mengge, X., Yu, B., Liu, T., Zhang, Y., Meng, E., Wang, B.: Porous lattice transformer encoder for Chinese NER. In: Proceedings of the 28th International Conference on Computational Linguistics, pp. 3831–3841. International Committee on Computational Linguistics, Barcelona, Spain (Online), December 2020. https://doi.org/10.18653/v1/2020.coling-main.340, https://aclanthology.org/2020.coling-main.340

23. Peng, H., Ma, Y., Li, Y., Cambria, E.: Learning multi-grained aspect target sequence for Chinese sentiment analysis. Knowl.-Based Syst. **148**, 167–176 (2018)
24. Peters, M.E., et al.: Deep contextualized word representations. In: Proceedings of the 2018 Conference of the North American Chapter of the Association for Computational Linguistics: Human Language Technologies, vol. 1 (Long Papers), pp. 2227–2237. Association for Computational Linguistics, New Orleans, Louisiana, June 2018. https://doi.org/10.18653/v1/N18-1202, https://aclanthology.org/N18-1202
25. Pontiki, M., et al.: SemEval-2016 task 5: aspect based sentiment analysis. In: Proceedings of the 10th International Workshop on Semantic Evaluation (SemEval-2016), pp. 19–30. Association for Computational Linguistics, San Diego, California, June 2016. https://doi.org/10.18653/v1/S16-1002, https://aclanthology.org/S16-1002
26. Shaw, P., Uszkoreit, J., Vaswani, A.: Self-attention with relative position representations. In: Proceedings of the 2018 Conference of the North American Chapter of the Association for Computational Linguistics: Human Language Technologies, vol. 2 (Short Papers), pp. 464–468. Association for Computational Linguistics, New Orleans, Louisiana, June 2018. https://doi.org/10.18653/v1/N18-2074, https://aclanthology.org/N18-2074
27. Wei, S., Fu, Y.: Microblog short text mining considering context: a method of sentiment analysis. Comput. Sci. **48**(6A), 158 (2021). https://doi.org/10.11896/jsjkx.210200089, https://www.jsjkx.com/EN/abstract/article_19978.shtml
28. Srivastava, R.K., Greff, K., Schmidhuber, J.: Highway networks. arXiv preprint arXiv:1505.00387 (2015)
29. Sun, C., Huang, L., Qiu, X.: Utilizing BERT for aspect-based sentiment analysis via constructing auxiliary sentence. In: Proceedings of the 2019 Conference of the North American Chapter of the Association for Computational Linguistics: Human Language Technologies, vol. 1 (Long and Short Papers), pp. 380–385. Association for Computational Linguistics, Minneapolis, Minnesota, June 2019. https://doi.org/10.18653/v1/N19-1035, https://aclanthology.org/N19-1035
30. Sun, Y., et al.: ERNIE: enhanced representation through knowledge integration. arXiv preprint arXiv:1904.09223 (2019)
31. Tang, D., Qin, B., Feng, X., Liu, T.: Effective LSTMs for target-dependent sentiment classification. In: Proceedings of COLING 2016, the 26th International Conference on Computational Linguistics: Technical Papers, pp. 3298–3307. The COLING 2016 Organizing Committee, Osaka, Japan, December 2016. https://aclanthology.org/C16-1311
32. Tang, D., Qin, B., Liu, T.: Aspect level sentiment classification with deep memory network. In: Proceedings of the 2016 Conference on Empirical Methods in Natural Language Processing, pp. 214–224. Association for Computational Linguistics, Austin, Texas, November 2016. https://doi.org/10.18653/v1/D16-1021, https://aclanthology.org/D16-1021
33. Vaswani, A., et al.: Attention is all you need. In: Advances in Neural Information Processing Systems, vol. 30 (2017)
34. Wang, Y., Huang, M., Zhu, X., Zhao, L.: Attention-based LSTM for aspect-level sentiment classification. In: Proceedings of the 2016 Conference on Empirical Methods in Natural Language Processing, pp. 606–615 (2016)
35. Xie, R., Li, Y.: Text sentiment classification model based on BERT and dual channel attention. J. Data Acquisit. Process. **35**(4), 642–652 (2020)
36. Xu, J., Ding, Y.X., Wang, X.L.: Sentiment classification for Chinese news using machine learning methods. J. Chin. Inf. Process. **21**(6), 95–100 (2007)
37. Yan, H., Deng, B., Li, X., Qiu, X.: TENER: adapting transformer encoder for named entity recognition. arXiv preprint arXiv:1911.04474 (2019)
38. Yang, J., Lin, S.: Emotion analysis on text words and sentences based on SVM. Jisuanji Yingyong yu Ruanjian **28**(9), 225–228 (2011)

39. Zan, H., Zhang, K., Zhu, X., Yu, S.: Research on the Chinese function word usage knowledge base. Int. J. Asian Lang. Process. **21**(4), 185–198 (2011)
40. Zhang, D., Wang, D.: Relation classification via recurrent neural network. arXiv preprint arXiv:1508.01006 (2015)
41. Zhang, K., Zan, H., Chai, Y., Han, Y., Zhao, D.: Survey of the Chinese function word usage knowledge base. J. Chin. Inf. Process. **29**(3), 1–8 (2015)
42. Zhao, S., Liu, T., Zhao, S., Chen, Y., Nie, J.Y.: Event causality extraction based on connectives analysis. Neurocomputing **173**, 1943–1950 (2016)
43. Zhu, Y.L., Min, J., Zhou, Y.Q., Huang, X.J., Wu, L.D.: Semantic orientation computing based on HowNet. J. Chin. Inf. Process. **20**(1), 14–20 (2006)

Enhancing Implicit Sentiment Learning via the Incorporation of Part-of-Speech for Aspect-Based Sentiment Analysis

Junlang Wang, Xia Li(✉), Junyi He, Yongqiang Zheng, and Junteng Ma

School of Information Science and Technology, Guangdong University of Foreign Studies, Guangzhou, China
{junlangwang,xiali}@gdufs.edu.cn

Abstract. Implicit sentiment modeling in aspect-based sentiment analysis is a challenging problem due to complex expressions and the lack of opinion words in sentences. Recent efforts focusing on implicit sentiment in ABSA mostly leverage the dependency between aspects and pretrain on extra annotated corpora. We argue that linguistic knowledge can be incorporated into the model to better learn implicit sentiment knowledge. In this paper, we propose a PLM-based, linguistically enhanced framework by incorporating Part-of-Speech (POS) for aspect-based sentiment analysis. Specifically, we design an input template for PLMs that focuses on both aspect-related contextualized features and POS-based linguistic features. By aligning with the representations of the tokens and their POS sequences, the introduced knowledge is expected to guide the model in learning implicit sentiment by capturing sentiment-related information. Moreover, we also design an aspect-specific self-supervised contrastive learning strategy to optimize aspect-based contextualized representation construction and assist PLMs in concentrating on target aspects. Experimental results on public benchmarks show that our model can achieve competitive and state-of-the-art performance without introducing extra annotated corpora.

Keywords: Aspect-based Sentiment Analysis · Implicit Sentiment · Part-of-Speech Alignment

1 Introduction

Aspect-based Sentiment Analysis (ABSA) aims to identify the sentiment polarities towards specific aspects in sentences. For example, in the sentence "*The dessert is incredible but the service is terrible,*" the sentiment polarities towards the aspects "*dessert*" and "*service*" are *positive* and *negative* respectively.

Previous work on aspect-based sentiment analysis has focused on explicit sentiment expression for specific aspect terms. It means that the sentiment polarities towards the aspects can be explicitly revealed by opinion words. e.g., the sentence "*The dessert is incredible*" contains the opinion word "*incredible*" which carries the positive sentiment towards the corresponding aspect "*dessert*". Many studies have been proposed and achieved promising results towards this task, such as attention mechanism-based

M. Sun et al. (Eds.): CCL 2023, LNAI 14232, pp. 382–399, 2023.
https://doi.org/10.1007/978-981-99-6207-5_24

Table 1. Several examples of reviews with implicit sentiment expressions about laptops and restaurants where aspects are marked in bold. The "**Polarity**" column indicates the sentiment polarities of aspects.

Domain	Example	Polarity
Restaurant	(1) The **waiters** even forget their high-tipping regulars	negative
	(2) They're a bit more expensive than typical, but then again, so is their **food**.	positive
Laptop	(3) My **voice recording** sounds like interplanetary transmissions in Star Wars	negative
	(4) Can you buy any laptop that matches the **quality** of a MacBook?	positive

methods [15,29,50,60], graph neural network-based methods [26,47,61,64], and pre-trained language model-based methods [3,6,36,41].

However, due to the diversity and flexibility of natural language, sentences containing implicit sentiment expressions are common in human speech. For implicit sentiment, we refer to the recognition of subjective textual units where no polarity markers, opinion words or obvious descriptions are present but people are still able to state whether the text portion under analysis expresses the sentiment [38]. As shown in Table 1, the four sentences can clearly express the sentiment without any opinion words. Taking the second sentence as an example, no opinion words can be found to determine the sentiment polarities towards the aspects "*food*", but people can still recognize that its polarity is negative. Additionally, we find that some complex expressions, such as factual statements and rhetorical techniques, are often used to express implicit sentiment, which always contains complex semantics. For example, sentence (1) and sentence (4) in Table 1 are factual statement and rhetorical question respectively. These complex expressions and the absence of opinion words make it more challenging to detect the implicit sentiment of sentences in the ABSA task.

Few previous studies have paid more attention to the implicit sentiment in ABSA. Among them, Yang et al. [57] propose a local sentiment aggregation paradigm for learning the implicit sentiments in a local sentiment aggregation window. Li et al. [24] adopt supervised contrastive pre-training on large-scale sentiment annotated corpora to capture both implicit and explicit sentiment orientation towards aspects in reviews. Their results demonstrate promising performance. However, we argue that the complex implicit expressions can be handled with the help of linguistic knowledge. Motivated by the applications of Parts of Speech (POS) in ABSA [12,36] and opinion mining [8], we suppose that POS-based linguistic knowledge has the potential to enhance implicit sentiment learning in ABSA. Intuitively, specific POS categories imply the orientation of sentiment polarity. As shown in Fig. 1, although the sentence lacks opinion words, the verbs also carry rich sentiment information [5,32]. The verb "*runs*" states the fact about "*virus scan*" without more related descriptions of this aspect. However, "*flickers*" shows the problem of the aspect "*display screen*". The polarities of the sentiments towards them should be neutral and negative, respectively. Such heuristics motivate us to incorporate POS-based linguistic knowledge into ABSA models for enhancing implicit sentiment prediction.

review:	My	computer	**runs**	a	*virus*	*scan*	but	the	*display*	*screen*	**flickers**
POS:	PRON	NOUN	**VERB**	DET	NOUN	NOUN	CONJ	DET	NOUN	NOUN	**VERB**

Fig. 1. Review example with its corresponding POS sequence, marked with Universal POS tags [34]. The aspect terms and the verbs are marked in italics and bold.

Inspired by the exploitation of natural language prompts [21,30] and linguistic knowledge in ABSA [19,36], we propose a PLM-based, linguistically enhanced framework for aspect-based sentiment analysis that incorporates Part-of-Speech. We first design a template with POS sequences as PLMs' input. With the multi-head self-attention mechanism, PLMs based on the transformer architecture are able to pay attention to the POS tags and their context information [45], thereby acquiring potential sentiment knowledge from POS sequences. Considering that the POS sequences are essentially the ordered permutations of the POS tags corresponding to the input sequences and not independent natural language sentences, we leverage token-POS alignment to minimize the semantic impact of POS sequences. In addition, motivated by the applications of contrastive learning to optimize the sentence embeddings derived from BERT [11,16,56], an aspect-specific self-supervised contrastive learning strategy is proposed to enhance the construction of contextualized representations, which would focus on aspect-related words in context and the target aspects when handling reviews with multiple aspects. We carry out the experiments on the SemEval 2014 [37] and Twitter [9] benchmark datasets. The experimental results demonstrate the efficacy of our proposed framework.

The main contributions of this work are as follows:

- We analyze the feasibility of incorporating Part-of-Speech to assist PLMs in modeling implicit sentiment and design an input template for PLMs to focus on both aspect-related contextualized features and POS-based linguistic features.
- We propose the token-POS alignment to reduce the influence of POS sequences on semantics. Additionally, the proposed aspect-specific self-supervised contrastive learning can optimize aspect-based contextualized representations construction and help PLMs concentrate on target aspects.
- Experimental results show the effectiveness of our method, which boosts PLMs to achieve competitive and state-of-the-art performance in ABSA with fewer additional parameters.

2 Related Work

In this section, we will briefly review the studies on aspect-based sentiment analysis from three perspectives: methods based on attention mechanisms, graph neural networks (GNNs), and pre-trained language models (PLMs). Then we will introduce implicit sentiment study.

ABSA Methods Based on Attention Mechanism. The majority of early attention mechanism-based methods construct the relationship between context and aspects to tackle the ABSA task. Wang et al. [48] and Ma et al. [29] equip neural networks with attention mechanisms, promoting the model's ability to identify related information about aspects from input reviews. Li et al. [23] propose a framework that combines contextual features with word representations. Except for concentrating on the relationship between context and aspects. Zhang et al. [61] exploit syntactic features from dependency and mark each word in reviews by proximity values.

ABSA Methods Based on GNNs. ABSA has demonstrated excellent performance in extracting syntactic features from graph structure since the development of graph neural networks. Sun et al. [43] and Zhao et al. [63] use the Graph Convolutional Network (GCN) with the dependency graph to model the dependencies of input sentences. Wang et al. [47] leverage distances between words in the dependency tree and syntactic tags simultaneously to extract syntactic features by the Graph Attention Network (GAT). Xu et al. [54] propose to divide sentences into structural scopes according to the results of constituency parsing, which improve the performance of GCN in ABSA.

ABSA Methods Based on PLMs. The emergence of pre-trained language models in recent years has given ABSA methods a new trend. On the one hand, in order to reduce the gap between pre-training and fine-tuning, numerous works propose sentiment-aware pre-training tasks [10, 17, 58] based on capturing sentiment semantics and incorporating external knowledge [1]. On the other hand, recent efforts to help PLMs overcome the disadvantages of aspect-aware sentiment perception are flourishing. Cao et al. [3] remove the sentiment bias of aspect terms and proposes a model trained with differential sentiment loss that is based on the model of Song et al. [41]. Ma et al. [30] design three aspect-specific input transformations for BERT and RoBERTa that enable the enhancement of aspect-specific context modeling. Moreover, other PLM-based methods solve the ABSA task from the perspective of machine reading comprehension [53] and natural language generation [55].

For handling implicit sentiment in ABSA, Li et al. [24] propose supervised contrastive pre-training that facilitates BERT in learning sentiment knowledge from large-scale sentiment-annotated corpora. The representation of implicit sentiment expressions is aligned with those of explicit sentiment expressions with the same sentiment polarities through supervised contrastive learning. Yang and Li [57] build the local sentiment aggregation to model sentiment dependency, which promotes the model's ability to learn implicit sentiment by capturing sentiment information from adjacent aspects. A differentially weighted strategy is also proposed for controlling adjacent aspects that contribute different sentiment information. While these approaches improve the learning and modeling of implicit sentiment in ABSA, external large-scale annotated corpora for encoding adjacent aspects are required. In view of the limitations of these approaches, we propose to leverage POS-based linguistic knowledge to assist PLMs in learning and modeling implicit sentiment in ABSA.

3 Our Method

3.1 Overall Architecture

As mentioned above, in this paper, we propose a PLM-based linguistically enhanced framework for Aspect-based Sentiment Analysis. Our framework consists of three components: aspect-aware token-POS concatenation, token-POS alignment, and aspect-

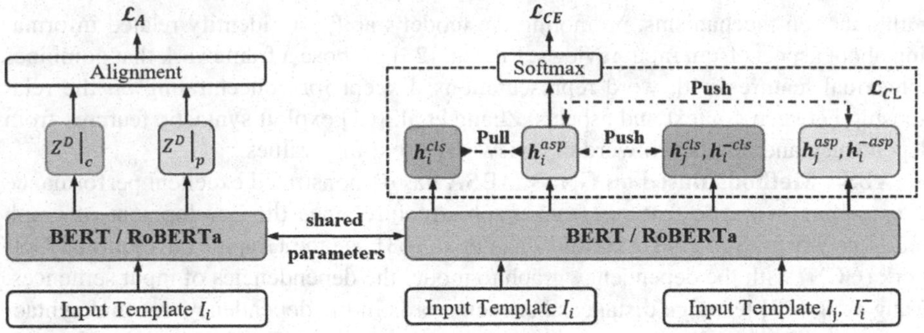

Fig. 2. Overall architecture of our proposed framework. In a mini-batch, the input template I_i is derived from the i-th input sentence. I_j, I_i^- represent templates with the other sentence in the mini-batch and the disordered i-th input sentence. $Z^D|_c$ and $Z^D|p$ denote the representations of the input sentences subset and POS sequences subset. $\mathbf{h}_i^{cls}$, $\mathbf{h}_i^{asp}$, $\mathbf{h}_j^{cls}$, $\mathbf{h}_j^{asp}$, $\mathbf{h}_i^{-cls}$ and $\mathbf{h}_i^{-asp}$ are the representations from I_i, I_j and I_i^-, which are elaborated in Sect. 3.4.

specific self-supervised contrastive learning. It is expected that POS-based linguistic knowledge will facilitate PLM's learning of implicit sentiment in ABSA. And self-supervised contrastive learning is applied to optimize the representation construction of the target aspect. Our method is shown in Fig. 2.

Generally, an input sentence contains one or more aspect terms that correspond to multiple sentiments. In this paper, we focus on the sentiment analysis of a specific aspect. Given a sentence $\mathbf{x} = \{w_1, \ldots, w_t, a_1, \ldots, a_m, w_{t+1}, \ldots, w_n\}$ where w_i indicates the ith word and $asp = \{a_1, \ldots, a_m\}$ denotes the target aspect in $\mathbf{x}$, an input template of our proposed framework I is composed of $\mathbf{x}$ and asp. We will elaborate on the detail of input template I in Sect. 3.2. The goal of ABSA is to predict the sentiment polarity towards asp according to the sentence $\mathbf{x}$.

3.2 Aspect-Aware Token-POS Concatenation

Motivated by natural language prompt [2], we treat the POS sequence as a type of prompt with linguistic knowledge and change the input schema of the PLM. In a mini-batch, for each input sentence $\mathbf{x}_i$, we utilize spaCy[1] to perform Part-of-Speech tagging on it and combine POS tags into the POS sequence $pos_i = \{p_1, p_2, \ldots, p_n\}$ according to the order of $\mathbf{x}_i$. Instead of concatenating $\mathbf{x}_i$ and pos_i as the input template I_i directly, we additionally append the target aspect term asp_i to I_i following Song et al. [41], which allows the PLM to capture dependencies between the context and the target aspect:

$$I_i = [CLS] + \mathbf{x}_i + [SEP] + pos_i + [SEP] + asp_i + [SEP] \tag{1}$$

Special tokens "[CLS]" and "[SEP]" of BERT should be "⟨s⟩" and "⟨/s⟩" in RoBERTa. After encoding I_i by BERT or RoBERTa, the pooled representation of asp_i is denoted

[1] https://spacy.io/.

as $\mathbf{h}_i^{asp} \in \mathbb{R}^{d \times l}$ $(l \geq m)$. Here d is the hidden size of the PLM and l is the length of the tokenized aspect by WordPiece [52] or Byte Pair Encoding [39].

3.3 Token-POS Alignment

Unlike the discrete templates used in previous research, the POS sequence pos_i is not an independent natural language sentence but the ordered permutation of the POS tags corresponding to the given sentence $\mathbf{x}_i$. To reduce the effects of POS sequences on semantics and promote the interaction of POS sequences and input sentences, we design a token-POS alignment strategy referring to word patch alignment [18]. As illustrated in Fig. 2, in this method, the outputs of the PLM corresponding to the input sentences subset and POS sequences subset in each mini-batch are represented as $Z^D|_c$ and $Z^D|_p$ respectively. After the encoding, $Z^D|_c \in \mathbb{R}^{\mathcal{B} \times k \times d}$ and $Z^D|_p \in \mathbb{R}^{\mathcal{B} \times h \times d}$ can be treated as two different probability distributions, where $\mathcal{B}$ is the mini-batch size, h, k are the lengths of the tokenized input sentence and POS sequence, d is the hidden size. Thus, we convert the alignment into computing the statistical distance between $Z^D|_c$ and $Z^D|_p$, and the alignment score is optimized according to Optimal Transport theory [35]. Following such theory, we utilize Wasserstein distance [44] to measure the statistical distance between $Z^D|_c$ and $Z^D|_p$:

$$W_p(Z^D|_c, Z^D|_p) := \mathbb{L}_{M^p}(Z^D|_c, Z^D|_p)^{\frac{1}{p}} \tag{2}$$

where p denotes the p-dimensional Wasserstein distance, $\mathbb{L}_{M^p}$ represents computing Wasserstein distance by Sinkhorn-Knopp algorithm [20] with the constraint of cost matrix $M \in \mathbb{R}^{d \times d}$, and the metric of Sinkhorn-Knopp algorithm is set to the cosine similarity considering the hidden size d of the PLM. Consequently, for $Z^D|_c$ and $Z^D|_p$ within a mini-batch B, the token-POS alignment loss can be defined as:

$$\mathcal{L}_A = \sum_{Z^D|_c, Z^D|_p \in B} W_p(Z^D|_c, Z^D|_p) \tag{3}$$

3.4 Aspect-Specific Self-supervised Contrastive Learning

Inspired by the applications of contrastive learning in ABSA [24,25], we propose to utilize self-supervised contrastive learning to enhance the representation construction of target aspects. According to the aim of contrastive learning [13], one of the keys is constructing the proper positive instances. Following the previous research in ABSA, both the embedding of the "[CLS]" token [25,62] and the aspect features [6,30] can be used as the final representation for sentiment polarity classification. Hence, those two representations from the same instance can be treated as positives and others from different in-batch instances are taken as negatives. We denote $\mathbf{h}_i^{asp} = f_\theta^{asp}(\mathbf{x}_i)$ where $f_\theta(\cdot)$ represents the encoder. And the embedding of the "[CLS]" token from the same instance is represented as $\mathbf{h}_i^{cls} = f_\theta^{cls}(\mathbf{x}_i)$. Moreover, in order to further leverage the training data and improve the ability of the model to identify the aspect-related context, we construct hard negatives by disordering the input sentence as

$\mathbf{x}_i^{dis} = \{w_{t+1}, \ldots, w_n, a_1, \ldots, a_m, w_1, \ldots, w_t\}$. Thus, the input template filled with the disordered input sentence I_i^- is defined as:

$$I_i^- = [CLS] + \mathbf{x}_i^{dis} + [SEP] + pos_i^{dis} + [SEP] + asp_i + [SEP] \tag{4}$$

where pos_i^{dis} is the POS sequence derived from $\mathbf{x}_i^{dis}$. The embedding of the "[CLS]" token and the pooled hidden vector of the aspect term from $\mathbf{x}_i^{dis}$ can be denoted as $\mathbf{h}_i^{-cls} = f_\theta^{cls}(\mathbf{x}_i^{dis})$ and $\mathbf{h}_i^{-asp} = f_\theta^{asp}(\mathbf{x}_i^{dis})$ respectively. Therefore, the aspect-specific self-supervised contrastive loss is defined as ($\mathcal{B}$ is the mini-batch size):

$$\mathcal{L}_{CL} = -\log \frac{e^{sim(\mathbf{h}_i^{asp}, \mathbf{h}_i^{cls})/\tau}}{\sum_{j=1}^{\mathcal{B}}(e^{sim(\mathbf{h}_i^{asp}, \mathbf{h}_j^{cls})/\tau} + e^{sim(\mathbf{h}_i^{asp}, \mathbf{h}_j^{-cls})/\tau} + e^{sim(\mathbf{h}_i^{asp}, \mathbf{h}_j^{-asp})/\tau})} \tag{5}$$

where τ is a temperature hyperparameter and $sim(\mathbf{h}_1, \mathbf{h}_2)$ is the function that computes the cosine similarity between $\mathbf{h}_1$ and $\mathbf{h}_2$.

3.5 Joint Training

Except for applying the two losses mentioned above to optimize the training of our proposed framework, we also use the cross-entropy loss $\mathcal{L}_{CE}$ as the fine-tuning object of the PLM for sentiment polarity prediction:

$$\mathcal{L}_{CE} = -\sum_{i=1}^{\mathcal{B}}\sum_{j=1}^{N} y_i^j \log \hat{y}_i^j + \lambda||\theta||^2 \tag{6}$$

where N is the number of labels, $\mathcal{B}$ is the mini-batch size, λ and θ represent the L_2 regularization and the parameter of the model. As shown in previous studies [31], Dropout [42] may induce inconsistency between the training and inference stages of the model. We argue that such inconsistency will be severe when introducing POS sequences into the input sentences. In order to regularize Dropout, we use the bidirectional Kullback-Leibler (KL) divergence loss $\mathcal{L}_{KL}$ based on R-Drop [51] in our models. The overall loss function $\mathcal{L}$ for joint training is:

$$\mathcal{L} = \mathcal{L}_{CE} + \lambda_1\mathcal{L}_A + \lambda_2\mathcal{L}_{CL} + \alpha\mathcal{L}_{KL} \tag{7}$$

where λ_1 and λ_2 are trainable parameters as the weights of token-POS alignment loss and aspect-specific self-supervised contrastive loss. The coefficient α is a hyperparameter.

4 Experiments

4.1 Datasets

We conduct experiments using three publicly available benchmark datasets. They are Restaurant and Laptop from SemEval 2014 Task 4 [37] and Twitter [9]. The statistics of the three datasets are shown in Table 2. Due to the lack of development sets, 10% of items from the training sets are randomly selected and treated as development sets. Following previous research, we remove examples with conflicting sentiment polarities.

Table 2. Statistics on three benchmark datasets of ABSA.

Dataset	Positive		Neutral		Negative		Total	
	Train	Test	Train	Test	Train	Test	Train	Test
Restaurant	2164	728	637	196	807	196	3608	1120
Laptop	994	341	464	169	870	128	2328	638
Twitter	1561	173	3127	346	1560	173	6248	692

4.2 Implement Details

We fine-tune the BERT-base-uncase [7] and RoBERTa-base [27] models pre-trained by HuggingFace Transformers [49] and implemented by PyTorch [33]. The learning rate is set as 2×10^{-5} and the batch size is 32. We adopt Dropout strategy and the drop probability is adjusted as 0.1. The model is trained with AdamW [28] optimizer and the L_2 regularization parameter λ is 10^{-5}. The temperature hyperparameter τ of aspect-specific self-supervised contrastive learning is 0.1. The coefficient α is set as 0.3. Following the work of Chen et al. [4], we utilize the 2-dimensional Wasserstein distance for token-POS alignment. Since not all of the Universal POS tags exist in the vocabularies of BERT and RoBERTa, we map the tags to their complete names before encoding them to overcome the problem of out-of-vocabulary. We perform our proposed models three runs with different seeds and report their average performance.

4.3 Compared Models

In order to demonstrate the effectiveness of our proposed method which can benefit various PLMs in ABSA, we compare the proposed models with several state-of-the-art baselines and models focusing on implicit sentiment in ABSA from the perspectives of BERT-based models and RoBERTa-based models:

- **BERT**, **RoBERTa** denote the vanilla BERT and RoBERTa proposed by Devlin et al. [7] and Liu et al. [27] respectively. We fine-tune them by ABSA datasets and keep their default settings.
- **BERT-SPC** [41] transforms the input reviews into sentence-aspect pairs and takes the "[CLS]" token for sentiment polarity classification.
- **LCF-BERT** [59] utilizes the local context focus mechanism to model the relation between global context and local context.
- **BERTAsp** and **BERTAsp+SCAPT** [24] are fine-tuned BERT for ABSA. The latter is pre-trained on large-scale annotated corpora by supervised contrastive learning before fine-tuning.
- **ASGCN-RoBERTa**, **RGAT-RoBERTa** are implemented by Dai et al. [6]. They are based on ASGCN [60] and RGAT [47] respectively and RoBERTa is applied including its induced tree and embeddings.
- **LSA$_P$-RoBERTa** [57] aggregates local sentiments by BERT-SPC [41] and models implicit sentiment by exploiting adjacent aspects' sentiment information.

- **BERT+AM** and **RoBERTa+AM** [30] uses the tokens "$\langle$asp$\rangle$" and "$\langle$/asp$\rangle$" to mark boundaries of aspects, which promotes PLMs to construct aspect-specific contextualized features.

4.4 Overall Results and Analysis

The experimental results of the aforementioned compared models and ours are shown in Table 3. Specifically, the accuracy and Macro-F1 score are utilized to evaluate the performance of models. According to the results, we have the following observations:

1) Incorporating linguistic knowledge improves the performance of ABSA models. Compared to the vanilla BERT and RoBERTa, on the one hand, incorporating syntactic knowledge by graph neural networks such as GCN and GAT promotes PLMs to capture the related information about the aspects, which is directly represented as the improvement of ASGCN-RoBERTa and RGAT-RoBERTa. On the other hand, leveraging Part-of-Speech to assist PLMs in modeling implicit sentiment benefits the ABSA task. By incorporating Part-of-Speech and aspect-specific self-supervised contrastive learning, both BERT and RoBERTa improve significantly on three ABSA benchmarks, achieving approximate 2.7%/1.6%/2.4% and 1.6%/1.7%/2.0% performance gains in accuracy as well as 3.6%/2.6%/3.7% and 2.5%/2.3%/2.2% in Macro-F1 score on Laptop/Restaurant/Twitter benchmarks respectively.

2) Without introducing numerous additional parameters and extra corpora, our model can perform similarly to state-of-the-art models and even outperform them. The proposed model IPOS-RoBERTa has a similar number of parameters (125.2M) to the vanilla RoBERTa-base model (125M). The difference between them lies in the layer for sentiment polarity classification. However, IPOS-RoBERTa can achieve state-of-the-art performance on Laptop and Twitter benchmarks, demonstrating the effectiveness of our method. Unlike LSA$_P$-RoBERTa and BERTAsp+SCAPT, our method optimizes the fine-tuning of RoBERT to learn implicit sentiment rather than introducing additional parameters for encoding adjacent aspects and extra corpora for pre-training. Specifically, the parameters of the compared models mentioned above are 138.2M and 133.3M respectively[2], indicating millions of parameters are added compared to our proposed model. However, on the test set of the Laptop benchmark, the Macro-F1 score of **IPOS-RoBERTa** is 80.91%, which is 1.76% higher than **BERTAsp+SCAPT** (Macro-F1=79.15%) and 0.44% higher than **LSA$_P$-RoBERTa** (Macro-F1=80.47%). Though the results of RoBERT-based models on Twitter are not shown in [57], the accuracy and Macro-F1 score of **IPOS-RoBERTa** are 0.55% and 0.73% higher than **LSA$_P$-DeBERTa** (Accuracy=76.91%, Macro-F1=75.90%), which is based on a progressive PLM called DeBERTa [14].

Though the difficulty of improving RoBERTa-based models in ABSA is indicated by Dai et al. [6], these results prove that POS-based linguistic knowledge and aspect-specific self-supervised contrastive learning are actually beneficial for enhancing the performance of fine-tuned RoBERTa in this task.

---

[2] The statistics of parameters are derived from open-source repositories released by Yang and Li [57] and Li et al. [24].

Table 3. Overall results (%) in three benchmark datasets where the "IPOS-BERT" and "IPOS-RoBERTa" are the proposed models that indicate combining BERT and RoBERTa with our method. The experimental results of the models we reproduced are marked by "*". For a fair comparison, we mark BERTAsp+SCAPT by "†" and additionally list it in the category "SCAPT" because of its in-domain pre-training and underline its state-of-the-art performance. The best results within other models are highlighted in bold according to different categories.

Category	Model	Laptop		Restaurant		Twitter	
		Accuracy	Macro-F1	Accuracy	Macro-F1	Accuracy	Macro-F1
BERT	BERT [7]*	77.90	73.37	84.20	76.76	73.70	70.86
	BERT-SPC [41]	78.99	75.03	84.46	76.98	74.13	72.73
	LCF-BERT [59]*	80.09	76.42	85.65	78.68	74.32	73.32
	BERTAsp [24]	78.53	74.07	85.80	78.95	-	-
	BERT+AM [30]	76.33	71.93	84.71	78.07	-	-
	IPOS-BERT (Ours)	**80.56**	**76.99**	**85.83**	**79.41**	**76.11**	**74.52**
RoBERTa	RoBERTa [27]*	81.97	78.38	87.23	81.00	75.43	74.47
	ASGCN-RoBERTa [6]	83.33	80.32	86.87	80.59	76.10	75.07
	RGAT-RoBERTa [6]	83.33	79.95	87.52	81.29	75.81	74.91
	LSAP-RoBERTa [57]	83.39	80.47	88.04	82.96	-	-
	RoBERTa+AM [30]	82.07	78.50	86.41	79.58	-	-
	IPOS-RoBERTa (Ours)	**83.54**	**80.91**	**88.93**	**83.30**	**77.46**	**76.63**
SCAPT	BERTAsp+SCAPT [24]†	82.76	79.15	<u>89.11</u>	<u>83.79</u>	-	-

4.5 Effectiveness on Implicit Sentiment Learning

Besides conducting extensive experiments on three benchmarks mentioned above, we also report the results of the experiment on Implicit Sentiment Expression (ISE) slices of Laptop and Restaurant that are derived from the work of Li et al. [24]. As shown in Table 4, on both two ISE slices, our proposed models IPOS-BERT and IPOS-RoBERTa outperform compared models based on the same PLMs with them. Though predicting sentiment polarities conveyed by implicit sentiment expressions is challenging, IPOS-RoBERTa's accuracy on ISE slices is higher than that of vanilla RoBERTa by large margins, which indicates the obvious improvement of 5.71% and 2.62%. And the other improvement (6.46% and 1.12%) of Accuracy-ISE can be observed by the comparison of IPOS-BERT and BERT-SPC on the ISE slices of Laptop and Restaurant respectively. Such progresses demonstrates the effectiveness of incorporating POS-based linguistic knowledge for learning implicit sentiment in ABSA.

Table 4. Model performance (%) on the Laptop and Restaurant benchmarks and their Implicit Sentiment Expression slices (ISE). The "Accuracy-ISE" column denotes the performance of models on ISE, which is measured by accuracy.

Models	Laptop-test		Restaurant-test	
	Accuracy	Accuracy-ISE	Accuracy	Accuracy-ISE
BERT-SPC [41]	78.99	69.54	84.46	65.54
IPOS-BERT (Ours)	**80.56**	**76.00**	**85.83**	**66.66**
RoBERTa [27]	81.97	78.86	87.23	68.54
IPOS-RoBERTa (Ours)	**83.54**	**84.57**	**88.93**	**71.16**

Table 5. Ablation studies of different components and temperatures on the Laptop benchmark (%). "w/o $\mathcal{L}_A$, $\mathcal{L}_{CL}$, $\mathcal{L}_{KL}$" indicates the models without token-POS alignment, aspect-specific self-supervised contrastive learning and R-Drop respectively. In the ablation study of temperatures (τ), we compare the original setting ($\tau = 0.1$) with three variants.

(a) Different components			(b) Different temperatures		
Model Variant	Laptop		Model Variant	Laptop	
	Accuracy	Macro-F1		Accuracy	Macro-F1
IPOS-RoBERTa	83.54	80.91	IPOS-RoBERTa	83.54	80.91
w/o $\mathcal{L}_A$	81.97	78.80	$\tau = 0.01$	81.03	77.77
w/o $\mathcal{L}_{CL}$	82.29	78.85	$\tau = 0.05$	83.23	80.65
w/o $\mathcal{L}_{KL}$	82.60	79.25	$\tau = 0.5$	83.07	79.37

5 Discussion

5.1 Ablation Study

Considering that each component of the proposed framework plays a different role as well as the temperatures contribute variously, extensive ablation experiments are conducted on Laptop benchmark and results are shown in Table 5. We find that removing the token-POS alignment degrades the proposed model drastically and even leads to the suboptimal performance of the proposed model, which is similar to that of the vanilla RoBERTa. We suppose that the POS sequences imported from the external parser affect contextual semantics without the token-POS alignment (Similar visual examples are shown in the rows of "RoBERTa (with POS)" in Fig. 3). Thus, though keeping the aspect-specific self-supervised contrastive learning and R-Drop, their effects are obscure while importing POS sequences directly. Such degradation indicates the importance of incorporating Part-of-Speech knowledge properly.

Table 6. A case study in the domain of laptops. For each case example, the original review and its POS sequence are shown. The model marked by "*" denotes BERTAsp+SCAPT proposed by Li et al. [24] and the aspect terms are underlined. We use "Pos, Neu, Neg" to indicate three sentiment polarities ("Positive, Neutral, Negative"). The correct predictions are associated with the symbol "✓" and the wrong predictions are marked with "×".

Example and POS Sequence	RoBERTa	BERTAsp*	Ours
However, I can refute that <u>OSX</u> is FAST	Pos	Pos	Neg
ADV PRON AUX VERB SCONJ PROPN AUX ADJ	(×)	(×)	(✓)
<u>Fan</u> only comes on when you are <u>playing a game</u>	Neg, Neu	Neu, Neu	Neu, Neu
NOUN ADV VERB ADP SCONJ PRON AUX VERB DET NOUN	(×), (✓)	(✓), (✓)	(✓), (✓)
It has so much more <u>speed</u> and the <u>screen</u> is very sharp	Pos, Pos	Pos, Neg	Pos, Pos
PRON VERB ADV ADV ADJ NOUN CCONJ DET NOUN AUX ADV ADJ	(✓), (✓)	(✓), (×)	(✓), (✓)
I did swap out the <u>hard drive</u> for a <u>Samsung 830 SSD</u> which I highly recommend	Neu, Neu	Neu, Neu	Neu, Pos
PRON AUX VERB ADP DET NOUN ADP DET PROPN PRON PRON ADV VERB	(✓), (×)	(✓), (×)	(✓), (✓)

Another noticeable performance degradation is caused by the absence of aspect-specific self-supervised contrastive learning since it promotes the model to concentrate on target aspects. Similarly, our model benefits from R-Drop [51] due to the regularization of the predictions.

Moreover, in order to investigate the influence of different temperatures, we set the temperature $\tau \in \{0.01, 0.05, 0.1, 0.5\}$ and keep other settings of our model. Compared to the carefully tuned temperature ($\tau = 0.1$), the other lead to different degrees of impact. It is worth noting that an extremely small temperature ($\tau = 0.01$) causes an obvious drop in the performance, which makes the model focus much on hard negatives [46]. However, a high temperature is also inappropriate. Specifically, both the accuracy and the Macro F1 score of the proposed model trained with a high temperature ($\tau = 0.5$) are lower than those of the model with a carefully tuned temperature by large margins.

5.2 Case Study

To verify the effectiveness of our method, we select several cases in the laptop domain that contain implicit sentiment expressions, as shown in Table 6. According to these cases, the capabilities of modeling implicit sentiment and capturing syntactic features are demanded. Hence, BERTAsp+SCAPT [24] and RoBERTa [27] are chosen as strong compared models for the case study. Following the comparison results, both BERTAsp+SCAPT and RoBERTa fail to correctly predict all the case examples. For example, RoBERTa wrongly comprehends the semantics of the second review and predicts the sentiment polarity towards "**fan**" as negative, which is represented by implicit sentiment expression. Additionally, for the aspect "**screen**" in the third case, BERTAsp+SCAPT mistakes the opinion "sharp" and incorrectly infers the corresponding polarity as negative. However, when given some complicated cases carrying multiple aspects and intricate implicit sentiment, both of them improperly capture the aspect-related contextualized features such as the aspects "**OSX**" and "**Samsung 830 SSD**" in the first and the last cases.

Owing to the POS-based linguistic knowledge, the proposed IPOS-RoBERTa model can precisely predict all aforementioned cases. We suppose that POS sequences encourage the model to learn implicit sentiment and distinguish sentiment expressions about different aspects, as suggested by the good performance of our proposed model. For the first case, the adjective "FAST" is related to the aspect "**OSX**" from the view of syntax but it implies the contrary sentiment polarity due to the verb "refute", which helps to perceive the implicit sentiment. Moreover, when inferring multiple aspects "**hard drive**" and "**Samsung 830 SSD**" in the same sentence, IPOS-RoBERTa can distinguish the related information about them and predict the correct sentiment polarity towards "**Samsung 830 SSD**".

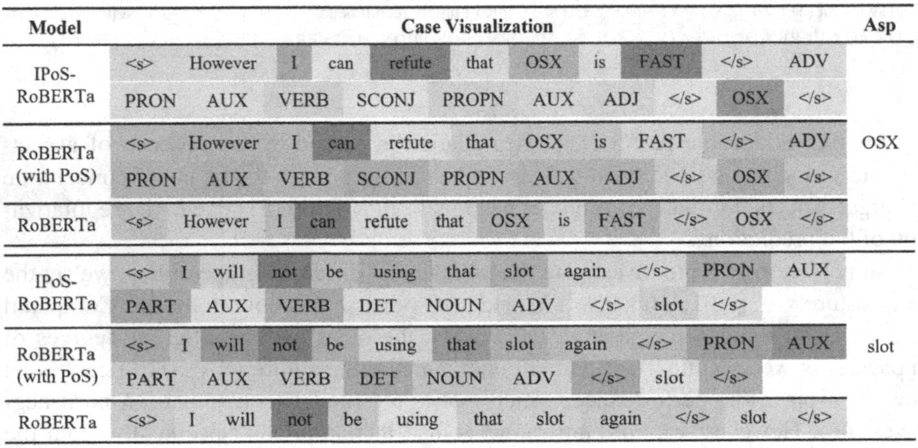
Model
Case Visualization
Asp
IPoS-RoBERTa
<s> However I can refute that OSX is FAST </s> ADV PRON AUX VERB SCONJ PROPN AUX ADJ </s> OSX </s>
RoBERTa (with PoS)
<s> However I can refute that OSX is FAST </s> ADV PRON AUX VERB SCONJ PROPN AUX ADJ </s> OSX </s>
RoBERTa
<s> However I can refute that OSX is FAST </s> OSX </s>
OSX
IPoS-RoBERTa
<s> I will not be using that slot again </s> PRON AUX PART AUX VERB DET NOUN ADV </s> slot </s>
RoBERTa (with PoS)
<s> I will not be using that slot again </s> PRON AUX PART AUX VERB DET NOUN ADV </s> slot </s>
RoBERTa
<s> I will not be using that slot again </s> slot </s>
slot

Fig. 3. Visualization of two selected cases. Both two target aspects are expressed by implicit sentiment. The gradient saliency maps [40] for the embedding of input tokens are shown, including words and POS tags. For each token, the darker color denotes the higher gradient saliency score. The "**Asp**" column indicates the aspect terms.

5.3 Visualization

Since it seems that the effect of appending POS tags to the input tokens is intricate, we visualize the gradient saliency scores of the embedding of input templates for two selected cases, which can be employed for model interpretation [22]. As shown in Fig. 3, we compare our model with two backbones and keep the setting that appends the aspect terms to the input sequences for all of them. However, "RoBERTa (with POS)" denotes only employing aspect-aware token-POS concatenation to RoBERTa but ignoring the token-POS alignment and "RoBERTa" indicates the vanilla RoBERTa model.

In the first case, the words "refute" and "FAST" are assigned different saliency scores among the three models, signifying these words differently contributing to the predictions. Compared to another two models, we suppose that our model pays more attention to such important words in comprehending the semantics. Furthermore, due to the token-POS alignment, our model can distinguish the importance of different POS tags instead of treating them equally. Similarly, though the three selected models focus on the word "not", the neglect of the verb "using" leads to incorrect predictions of sentiment polarity towards the aspect "slot". In contrast, our model can precisely capture essential words and their POS for prediction, demonstrating the effect of aspect-aware token-POS concatenation and token-POS alignment.

6 Conclusion

In this paper, we propose a PLM-based linguistically enhanced framework for aspect-based sentiment analysis based on the analysis of the feasibility of incorporating Part-of-Speech into the ABSA task. Using POS-based linguistic knowledge, our method optimizes the PLMs' fine-tuning for implicit sentiment capturing. Aspect-specific self-supervised contrastive learning allows the model to concentrate on target aspects when handling sentences containing multiple aspect terms. Extensive experiments show that our proposed model can achieve competitive and state-of-the-art performance relative to baseline models without introducing extra corpora. Although the introduction of POS as linguistic knowledge can effectively improve the enhancement of implicit sentiment detection in ABSA, there are still limitations. If there are difficulties in deriving precise POS sequences in low-resource settings, the POS-based solution might not provide sufficient information. Further research can investigate approaches for integrating various linguistic knowledge into models for learning implicit sentiment without external sources.

Acknowledgements. This work is supported by National Natural Science Foundation of China (No. 61976062).

References

1. Baccianella, S., Esuli, A., Sebastiani, F., et al.: Sentiwordnet 3.0: an enhanced lexical resource for sentiment analysis and opinion mining. In: Lrec, vol. 10, pp. 2200–2204 (2010)
2. Brown, T., Mann, B., Ryder, N., Subbiah, M., Kaplan, J.D., Dhariwal, P., Neelakantan, A., Shyam, P., Sastry, G., Askell, A., et al.: Language models are few-shot learners. Adv. Neural. Inf. Process. Syst. **33**, 1877–1901 (2020)
3. Cao, J., Liu, R., Peng, H., Jiang, L., Bai, X.: Aspect is not you need: No-aspect differential sentiment framework for aspect-based sentiment analysis. In: Proceedings of the 2022 Conference of the North American Chapter of the Association for Computational Linguistics: Human Language Technologies, pp. 1599–1609. Association for Computational Linguistics, Seattle, United States, July 2022. https://doi.org/10.18653/v1/2022.naacl-main.115. https://aclanthology.org/2022.naacl-main.115
4. Chen, Y.-C., et al.: UNITER: UNiversal image-TExt representation learning. In: Vedaldi, A., Bischof, H., Brox, T., Frahm, J.-M. (eds.) ECCV 2020. LNCS, vol. 12375, pp. 104–120. Springer, Cham (2020). https://doi.org/10.1007/978-3-030-58577-8_7
5. Chesley, P., Vincent, B., Xu, L., Srihari, R.K.: Using verbs and adjectives to automatically classify blog sentiment. Training **580**(263), 233 (2006)

6. Dai, J., Yan, H., Sun, T., Liu, P., Qiu, X.: Does syntax matter? a strong baseline for aspect-based sentiment analysis with RoBERTa. In: Proceedings of the 2021 Conference of the North American Chapter of the Association for Computational Linguistics: Human Language Technologies, pp. 1816–1829. Association for Computational Linguistics, Online, June 2021. https://doi.org/10.18653/v1/2021.naacl-main.146. https://aclanthology.org/2021.naacl-main.146
7. Devlin, J., Chang, M.W., Lee, K., Toutanova, K.: BERT: Pre-training of deep bidirectional transformers for language understanding. In: Proceedings of the 2019 Conference of the North American Chapter of the Association for Computational Linguistics: Human Language Technologies, Volume 1 (Long and Short Papers), pp. 4171–4186. Association for Computational Linguistics, Minneapolis, Minnesota (Jun 2019). https://doi.org/10.18653/v1/N19-1423,https://aclanthology.org/N19-1423
8. Dey, L., Haque, S.K.M.: Opinion mining from noisy text data. In: Proceedings of the Second Workshop on Analytics for Noisy Unstructured Text Data, AND 2008, pp. 83–90. Association for Computing Machinery, New York (2008). https://doi.org/10.1145/1390749.1390763. https://doi.org/10.1145/1390749.1390763
9. Dong, L., Wei, F., Tan, C., Tang, D., Zhou, M., Xu, K.: Adaptive recursive neural network for target-dependent Twitter sentiment classification. In: Proceedings of the 52nd Annual Meeting of the Association for Computational Linguistics (Volume 2: Short Papers), pp. 49–54. Association for Computational Linguistics, Baltimore, June 2014. https://doi.org/10.3115/v1/P14-2009,https://aclanthology.org/P14-2009
10. Fan, S., et al.: Sentiment-aware word and sentence level pre-training for sentiment analysis. In: Proceedings of the 2022 Conference on Empirical Methods in Natural Language Processing, pp. 4984–4994. Association for Computational Linguistics, Abu Dhabi, December 2022. https://aclanthology.org/2022.emnlp-main.332
11. Gao, T., Yao, X., Chen, D.: SimCSE: simple contrastive learning of sentence embeddings. In: Proceedings of the 2021 Conference on Empirical Methods in Natural Language Processing, pp. 6894–6910. Association for Computational Linguistics, Online and Punta Cana, Dominican Republic, November 2021. https://doi.org/10.18653/v1/2021.emnlp-main.552. https://aclanthology.org/2021.emnlp-main.552
12. Gong, C., Yu, J., Xia, R.: Unified feature and instance based domain adaptation for aspect-based sentiment analysis. In: Proceedings of the 2020 Conference on Empirical Methods in Natural Language Processing (EMNLP), pp. 7035–7045 (2020)
13. Hadsell, R., Chopra, S., LeCun, Y.: Dimensionality reduction by learning an invariant mapping. In: 2006 IEEE Computer Society Conference on Computer Vision and Pattern Recognition (CVPR 2006), vol. 2, pp. 1735–1742. IEEE (2006)
14. He, P., Gao, J., Chen, W.: Debertav 3: Improving deberta using electra-style pre-training with gradient-disentangled embedding sharing. arXiv preprint arXiv:2111.09543 (2021)
15. Huang, B., Ou, Y., Carley, K.M.: Aspect level sentiment classification with attention-over-attention neural networks. In: Thomson, R., Dancy, C., Hyder, A., Bisgin, H. (eds.) SBP-BRiMS 2018. LNCS, vol. 10899, pp. 197–206. Springer, Cham (2018). https://doi.org/10.1007/978-3-319-93372-6_22
16. Jiang, T., et al.: PromptBERT: improving BERT sentence embeddings with prompts. In: Proceedings of the 2022 Conference on Empirical Methods in Natural Language Processing, pp. 8826–8837. Association for Computational Linguistics, Abu Dhabi, December 2022. https://aclanthology.org/2022.emnlp-main.603
17. Ke, P., Ji, H., Liu, S., Zhu, X., Huang, M.: Sentilare: sentiment-aware language representation learning with linguistic knowledge. In: Proceedings of the 2020 Conference on Empirical Methods in Natural Language Processing (EMNLP), pp. 6975–6988 (2020)

18. Kim, W., Son, B., Kim, I.: Vilt: vision-and-language transformer without convolution or region supervision. In: International Conference on Machine Learning, pp. 5583–5594. PMLR (2021)
19. Kiritchenko, S., Zhu, X., Cherry, C., Mohammad, S.: Nrc-canada-2014: detecting aspects and sentiment in customer reviews. In: Proceedings of the 8th International Workshop on Semantic Evaluation (SemEval 2014), pp. 437–442 (2014)
20. Knight, P.A.: The sinkhorn-knopp algorithm: convergence and applications. SIAM J. Matrix Anal. Appl. **30**(1), 261–275 (2008)
21. Li, C., et al.: Sentiprompt: sentiment knowledge enhanced prompt-tuning for aspect-based sentiment analysis. arXiv preprint arXiv:2109.08306 (2021)
22. Li, J., Chen, X., Hovy, E., Jurafsky, D.: Visualizing and understanding neural models in NLP. In: Proceedings of the 2016 Conference of the North American Chapter of the Association for Computational Linguistics: Human Language Technologies, pp. 681–691. Association for Computational Linguistics, San Diego, California, June 2016. https://doi.org/10.18653/v1/N16-1082. https://aclanthology.org/N16-1082
23. Li, X., Bing, L., Lam, W., Shi, B.: Transformation networks for target-oriented sentiment classification. arXiv preprint arXiv:1805.01086 (2018)
24. Li, Z., Zou, Y., Zhang, C., Zhang, Q., Wei, Z.: Learning implicit sentiment in aspect-based sentiment analysis with supervised contrastive pre-training. In: Proceedings of the 2021 Conference on Empirical Methods in Natural Language Processing, pp. 246–256. Association for Computational Linguistics, Online and Punta Cana, Dominican Republic, November 2021. https://doi.org/10.18653/v1/2021.emnlp-main.22. https://aclanthology.org/2021.emnlp-main.22
25. Liang, B., et al.: Enhancing aspect-based sentiment analysis with supervised contrastive learning. In: Proceedings of the 30th ACM International Conference on Information & Knowledge Management, pp. 3242–3247 (2021)
26. Liang, B., Su, H., Gui, L., Cambria, E., Xu, R.: Aspect-based sentiment analysis via affective knowledge enhanced graph convolutional networks. Knowl.-Based Syst. **235**, 107643 (2022)
27. Liu, Y., et al.: Roberta: a robustly optimized bert pretraining approach. arXiv preprint arXiv:1907.11692 (2019)
28. Loshchilov, I., Hutter, F.: Decoupled weight decay regularization. arXiv preprint arXiv:1711.05101 (2017)
29. Ma, D., Li, S., Zhang, X., Wang, H.: Interactive attention networks for aspect-level sentiment classification. arXiv preprint arXiv:1709.00893 (2017)
30. Ma, F., Zhang, C., Zhang, B., Song, D.: Aspect-specific context modeling for aspect-based sentiment analysis. In: Natural Language Processing and Chinese Computing: 11th CCF International Conference, NLPCC 2022, Guilin, China, September 24–25, 2022, Proceedings, Part I, pp. 513–526 (2022)
31. Ma, X., Gao, Y., Hu, Z., Yu, Y., Deng, Y., Hovy, E.: Dropout with expectation-linear regularization. arXiv preprint arXiv:1609.08017 (2016)
32. Nicholls, C., Song, F.: Improving sentiment analysis with part-of-speech weighting. In: 2009 International Conference on Machine Learning and Cybernetics, vol. 3, pp. 1592–1597. IEEE (2009)
33. Paszke, A., et al.: Pytorch: an imperative style, high-performance deep learning library. In: Wallach, H., Larochelle, H., Beygelzimer, A., d'Alché-Buc, F., Fox, E., Garnett, R. (eds.) Advances in Neural Information Processing Systems, vol. 32. Curran Associates, Inc. (2019). https://proceedings.neurips.cc/paper_files/paper/2019/file/bdbca288fee7f92f2bfa9f7012727740-Paper.pdf

34. Petrov, S., Das, D., McDonald, R.: A universal part-of-speech tagset. In: Proceedings of the Eighth International Conference on Language Resources and Evaluation (LREC'12). pp. 2089–2096. European Language Resources Association (ELRA), Istanbul, Turkey, May 2012. https://www.lrec-conf.org/proceedings/lrec2012/pdf/274_Paper.pdf
35. Peyré, G., Cuturi, M., et al.: Computational optimal transport: with applications to data science. Found. Trends Mach. Learn. **11**(5–6), 355–607 (2019)
36. Phan, M.H., Ogunbona, P.O.: Modelling context and syntactical features for aspect-based sentiment analysis. In: Proceedings of the 58th Annual Meeting of the Association for Computational Linguistics, pp. 3211–3220. Association for Computational Linguistics, Online, July 2020. https://doi.org/10.18653/v1/2020.acl-main.293. https://aclanthology.org/2020.acl-main.293
37. Pontiki, M., Galanis, D., Pavlopoulos, J., Papageorgiou, H., Androutsopoulos, I., Manandhar, S.: SemEval-2014 task 4: aspect based sentiment analysis. In: Proceedings of the 8th International Workshop on Semantic Evaluation (SemEval 2014), pp. 27–35. Association for Computational Linguistics, Dublin, August 2014. https://doi.org/10.3115/v1/S14-2004. https://aclanthology.org/S14-2004
38. Russo, I., Caselli, T., Strapparava, C.: Semeval-2015 task 9: clipeval implicit polarity of events. In: Proceedings of the 9th International Workshop on Semantic Evaluation (SemEval 2015), pp. 443–450 (2015)
39. Sennrich, R., Haddow, B., Birch, A.: Neural machine translation of rare words with subword units. In: Proceedings of the 54th Annual Meeting of the Association for Computational Linguistics (Volume 1: Long Papers), pp. 1715–1725 (2016)
40. Simonyan, K., Vedaldi, A., Zisserman, A.: Deep inside convolutional networks: visualising image classification models and saliency maps. In: Proceedings of the International Conference on Learning Representations (ICLR). ICLR (2014)
41. Song, Y., Wang, J., Jiang, T., Liu, Z., Rao, Y.: Attentional encoder network for targeted sentiment classification. arXiv preprint arXiv:1902.09314 (2019)
42. Srivastava, N., Hinton, G., Krizhevsky, A., Sutskever, I., Salakhutdinov, R.: Dropout: a simple way to prevent neural networks from overfitting. J. Mach. Learn. Res. **15**(1), 1929–1958 (2014)
43. Sun, K., Zhang, R., Mensah, S., Mao, Y., Liu, X.: Aspect-level sentiment analysis via convolution over dependency tree. In: Proceedings of the 2019 Conference on Empirical Methods in Natural Language Processing and the 9th International Joint Conference on Natural Language Processing (EMNLP-IJCNLP), pp. 5679–5688 (2019)
44. Vaserstein, L.N.: Markov processes over denumerable products of spaces, describing large systems of automata. Problemy Peredachi Informatsii **5**(3), 64–72 (1969)
45. Vaswani, A., et al.: Attention is all you need. Advances in neural information processing systems 30 (2017)
46. Wang, F., Liu, H.: Understanding the behaviour of contrastive loss. In: Proceedings of the IEEE/CVF Conference on Computer Vision and Pattern Recognition, pp. 2495–2504 (2021)
47. Wang, K., Shen, W., Yang, Y., Quan, X., Wang, R.: Relational graph attention network for aspect-based sentiment analysis. In: Proceedings of the 58th Annual Meeting of the Association for Computational Linguistics, pp. 3229–3238 (2020)
48. Wang, Y., Huang, M., Zhu, X., Zhao, L.: Attention-based LSTM for aspect-level sentiment classification. In: Proceedings of the 2016 Conference on Empirical Methods in Natural Language Processing, pp. 606–615 (2016)
49. Wolf, T., et al.: Transformers: state-of-the-art natural language processing. In: Proceedings of the 2020 Conference on Empirical Methods in Natural Language Processing: System Demonstrations, pp. 38–45. Association for Computational Linguistics, Online, October 2020. https://www.aclweb.org/anthology/2020.emnlp-demos.6

50. Wu, H., Zhang, Z., Shi, S., Wu, Q., Song, H.: Phrase dependency relational graph attention network for aspect-based sentiment analysis. Knowl.-Based Syst. **236**, 107736 (2022)
51. Wu, L., et al.: R-drop: Regularized dropout for neural networks. Adv. Neural. Inf. Process. Syst. **34**, 10890–10905 (2021)
52. Wu, Y., et al.: Google's neural machine translation system: Bridging the gap between human and machine translation. arXiv preprint arXiv:1609.08144 (2016)
53. Xu, H., Liu, B., Shu, L., Yu, P.: Bert post-training for review reading comprehension and aspect-based sentiment analysis. In: Proceedings of the 2019 Conference of the North American Chapter of the Association for Computational Linguistics: Human Language Technologies, vol. 1 (2019)
54. Xu, L., Pang, X., Wu, J., Cai, M., Peng, J.: Learn from structural scope: improving aspect-level sentiment analysis with hybrid graph convolutional networks. Neurocomputing **518**, 373–383 (2023)
55. Yan, H., Dai, J., Ji, T., Qiu, X., Zhang, Z.: A unified generative framework for aspect-based sentiment analysis. In: Proceedings of the 59th Annual Meeting of the Association for Computational Linguistics and the 11th International Joint Conference on Natural Language Processing (Volume 1: Long Papers), pp. 2416–2429 (2021)
56. Yan, Y., Li, R., Wang, S., Zhang, F., Wu, W., Xu, W.: Consert: a contrastive framework for self-supervised sentence representation transfer. In: Proceedings of the 59th Annual Meeting of the Association for Computational Linguistics and the 11th International Joint Conference on Natural Language Processing (Volume 1: Long Papers), pp. 5065–5075 (2021)
57. Yang, H., Li, K.: Improving implicit sentiment learning via local sentiment aggregation. arXiv e-prints pp. arXiv-2110 (2021)
58. Yin, D., Meng, T., Chang, K.W.: Sentibert: a transferable transformer-based architecture for compositional sentiment semantics. arXiv preprint arXiv:2005.04114 (2020)
59. Zeng, B., Yang, H., Xu, R., Zhou, W., Han, X.: LCF: a local context focus mechanism for aspect-based sentiment classification. Appl. Sci. **9**(16), 3389 (2019)
60. Zhang, C., Li, Q., Song, D.: Aspect-based sentiment classification with aspect-specific graph convolutional networks. In: Proceedings of the 2019 Conference on Empirical Methods in Natural Language Processing and the 9th International Joint Conference on Natural Language Processing (EMNLP-IJCNLP), pp. 4568–4578 (2019)
61. Zhang, C., Li, Q., Song, D.: Syntax-aware aspect-level sentiment classification with proximity-weighted convolution network. In: Proceedings of the 42nd International ACM SIGIR Conference on Research and Development in Information Retrieval, pp. 1145–1148 (2019)
62. Zhang, K., et al.: Incorporating dynamic semantics into pre-trained language model for aspect-based sentiment analysis. In: Findings of the Association for Computational Linguistics: ACL 2022, pp. 3599–3610. Association for Computational Linguistics, Dublin, May 2022. https://doi.org/10.18653/v1/2022.findings-acl.285. https://aclanthology.org/2022.findings-acl.285
63. Zhao, P., Hou, L., Wu, O.: Modeling sentiment dependencies with graph convolutional networks for aspect-level sentiment classification. Knowl.-Based Syst. **193**, 105443 (2020)
64. Zheng, Y., Li, X., Nie, J.Y.: Store, share and transfer: learning and updating sentiment knowledge for aspect-based sentiment analysis. Inf. Sci. **635**, 151–168 (2023). https://doi.org/10.1016/j.ins.2023.03.102. https://www.sciencedirect.com/science/article/pii/S0020025523004279

Improving Affective Event Classification with Multi-perspective Knowledge Injection

Wenjia Yi, Yanyan Zhao(✉), Jianhua Yuan, Weixiang Zhao, and Bing Qin

Harbin Institute of Technology, Harbin 150001, China
{wjyi,yyzhao,jhyuan,wxzhao,qinb}@ir.hit.edu.cn

Abstract. In recent years, many researchers have recognized the importance of associating events with sentiments. Previous approaches focus on generalizing events and extracting sentimental information from a large-scale corpus. However, since context is absent and sentiment is often implicit in the event, these methods are limited in comprehending the semantics of the event and capturing effective sentimental clues. In this work, we propose a novel Multi-perspective Knowledge-injected Interaction Network (MKIN) to fully understand the event and accurately predict its sentiment by injecting multi-perspective knowledge. Specifically, we leverage contexts to provide sufficient semantic information and perform context modeling to capture the semantic relationships between events and contexts. Moreover, we also introduce human emotional feedback and sentiment-related concepts to provide explicit sentimental clues from the perspective of human emotional state and word meaning, filling the reasoning gap in the sentiment prediction process. Experimental results on the gold standard dataset show that our model achieves better performance over the baseline models.

Keywords: Affective Event Classification · Sentiment Analysis · Knowledge Injection

1 Introduction

Affective Event Classification (AEC) aims at predicting the sentiment polarity of the given event. We consider events that have positive effects on people who experience them as positive events. For instance, typically positive events include *having a new crush*, *going to the bonfire*, *seeing a rainbow*. On the contrary, events that have negative effects on people who experience them are treated as negative events, such as *breaking a marriage*, *going to the funeral*, *hearing a loud noise*. Since events often trigger sentiments and sentiments are often implicit, recognizing affective events is of great values to various natural language processing applications, covering dialogue systems [22], question-answering systems [15], implicit sentiment analysis [31] and opinion mining [28].

The challenges of AEC lie in the limited context and the implicit sentiment of the event. To be specific, we often rely on the context to analyze sentiments, but

M. Sun et al. (Eds.): CCL 2023, LNAI 14232, pp. 400–416, 2023.
https://doi.org/10.1007/978-981-99-6207-5_25

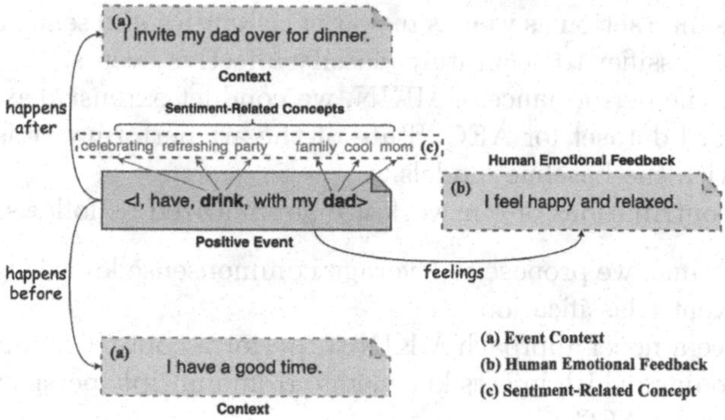

Fig. 1. An example of an affective event for identifying the sentiment with the help of event contexts, human emotional feedback and sentiment-related concepts.

there is no rich context to understand the event. Besides, traditional sentiment analysis methods rely on the occurrence of explicit sentiment words, but there are few explicit sentimental clues in the event. Many previous approaches have been devoted to cope with the challenges by extracting sentimental information from a large-scale corpus [5,19,32]. However, such attempts are not effective enough to understand the event and capture sentimental clues due to weak context modeling and insufficient sentimental information.

We believe that this task would benefit from multi-perspective knowledge injection. Specifically, context can provide additional semantic information to understand the event, and human emotional feedback as well as sentiment-related concepts can provide explicit sentimental information from two perspectives to fill the reasoning gap. Figure 1 shows an example of an affective event, demonstrating the significance of contexts, human emotional feedback and sentiment-related concepts in understanding events and detecting implied sentiments. On the one hand, the given event ("⟨I, have, drink, with my dad⟩") could be thoroughly understood by supplying contexts ("I invite my dad over for dinner.", "I have a good time."). On the other hand, from people's positive emotional feedback towards the event ("happy", "relaxed"), we could know that the event would typically have a positive effect on them. Moreover, the meaning of "drink" and "dad" in the event are enriched by sentiment-related concepts ("celebrating", "party", "cool", etc.). Thus, the implicit sentiment of the event could be identified more easily via enhanced emotions and enriched concepts.

In this paper, to cope with the aforementioned challenges, we propose a novel Multi-perspective Knowledge-injected Interaction Network (MKIN) to thoroughly comprehend the event and precisely infer its sentiment. Specifically, we utilize a pre-trained generative commonsense reasoning model to create event contexts and human emotional feedback of the event. Meanwhile, a commonsense knowledge base and an emotion dictionary are adopted to retrieve sentiment-related concepts. Then, we devise a Multi-Source Text Encoding Module to encode these events and knowledge. To better integrate contextual information and sentimental clues, we construct a Semantic and Sentimental Fusion Module, which performs interaction as well as fusion of semantics and sentiments. Finally, we introduce a classifier to accurately classify affective events.

To evaluate the performance of MKIN, we conduct extensive experiments on the gold standard dataset for AEC. State-of-the-art performance is achieved by us compared with the baseline models.

The main contributions of our work are summarized as follows:

- For the first time, we propose to leverage commonsense knowledge to improve Affective Event Classification.
- We introduce a novel approach MKIN to perform context modeling and sentiment reasoning, which injects knowledge from multiple perspectives to meet the challenges of AEC.
- Extensive experimental results on the benchmark dataset demonstrate the superiority of MKIN. Our source code will be publicly available.

2 Related Work

Relevant work mainly includes two directions, one is affective event classification, and the other is incorporating external knowledge in sentiment analysis tasks.

2.1 Affective Event Classification

Prior work has focused on producing lexical resources of verbs or event phrases with corresponding sentiment polarity values. Goyal et al. (2010) [6] created a new type of lexicon for narrative text comprehension, consisting of patient polarity verbs that impart positive or negative states on their patients. Vu et al. (2014) [26] created a manually-constructed dictionary of emotion-provoking events, then used seed expansion and clustering to automatically acquire and aggregate events from web data. Li et al. (2014) [9] extracted major life events from Twitter by clustering tweets corresponding to speech act words, such as "congratulations" or "condolences". Ding and Riloff (2016) [4] first defined stereotypical affective events as triples ⟨Agent, Verb, Object⟩ that are independent of context, and used a semi-supervised label propagation algorithm to discover affective events from Blogs.

More recently, many researches on affective event classification exert much effort to extract sentimental information from a large-scale corpus. Ding and Riloff (2018) [5] expanded affective events as tuples ⟨Agent, Predicate, Theme, Prepositional Phrase⟩, and introduced a weakly supervised semantic consistency model for inducing a large collection of affective events from a personal story corpus. Saito et al. (2019) [19] proposed to exploit discourse relations to propagate sentiment polarity from seed predicates. They extracted events that co-occur with seeds in a Japanese web corpus, and used discourse relations as constraints in the model learning process. Zhuang et al. (2020) [32] first utilized the pre-trained model and presented a discourse-enhanced self-training method, which combines the classifier's predictions with information from local discourse contexts, and iteratively improves the classifier with unlabeled data. Another line of related work is Event-related Sentiment Analysis, which explicitly models events to improves sentiment analysis because events often trigger sentiments in sentences. Zhou et al. (2021) [31] proposed a hierarchical tensor-based composition mechanism for event-centered text representation and develop a multi-task learning framework to improve sentiment analysis with event type classification.

However, existing methods only induce affective events based on semantic relations or discourse relations, or purely focus on sentimental information from local discourse contexts. Unlike the previous work, we consider multiple perspectives of knowledge, covering event contexts, human emotional feedback and sentiment-related concepts.

2.2 Sentiment Analysis with Knowledge

In recent years, there is a growing number of researches on incorporating external knowledge in various sentiment analysis tasks. Turcan et al. (2021) [24] explored the use of commonsense knowledge via adapted knowledge models to understand implicitly expressed emotions and the reasons of those emotions for Emotion Cause Extraction. Sabour et al. (2021) [18] leveraged commonsense knowledge to obtain more information about the user's situation and feelings to further enhance the empathy expression in the generated responses for Empathetic Response Generation. Zhao et al. (2022) [29] utilized commonsense knowledge to provide causal clues to guide the process of causal utterance traceback for Emotion Recognition in Conversations. Peng et al. (2022) [16] employed commonsense knowledge to obtain the psychological intention of the help-seeker to generate the supportive responses for Emotional Support Conversation. Xu et al. (2022) [27] used a knowledge graph to supplement a large amount of knowledge and common sense omitted in implicit emotional sentences for Implicit Sentiment Analysis.

There are also many studies on integrating external knowledge in other natural language processing tasks, but less studies on Affective Event Classification. To the best of our knowledge, this is the first attempt to introduce external knowledge into Affective Event Classification task.

3 Methodology

The problem of the AEC task could be formulated as follows. Given an event tuple $\langle$ Agent: $agent = \{w_1, w_2, \cdots, w_{n_{agent}}\}$, Predicate: $pred = \{w_1, w_2, \cdots, w_{n_{pred}}\}$, Theme: $theme = \{w_1, w_2, \cdots, w_{n_{theme}}\}$, Prepositional Phrase: $prep = \{w_1, w_2, \cdots, w_{n_{prep}}\}$ $\rangle$ with the corresponding sentiment category, the goal of this task is to predict the sentiment distribution over three sentiment polarities.

The overall architecture of our proposed model MKIN is shown in Fig. 2, which consists of four modules: Knowledge Acquisition Module, Multi-Source Text Encoding Module, Semantic and Sentimental Fusion Module, Sentiment Classification Module. Each one of the four modules will be elaborated in the rest of this section.

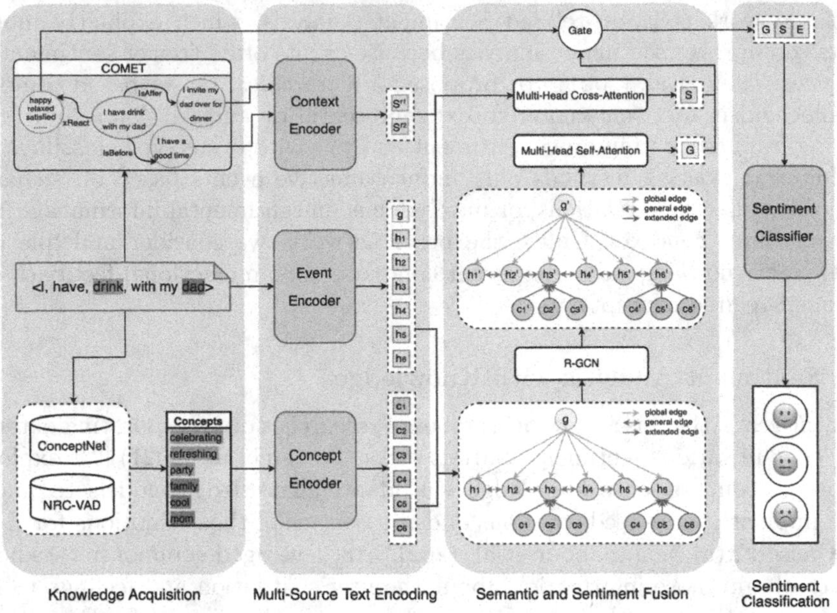

Fig. 2. The overall architecture of our proposed model.

3.1 Knowledge Acquisition Module

Event Context Acquisition. Since retrieving context from corpus is expensive and noisy, we turn to the commonsense knowledge base to provide the context for the given event. In this work, we employ ATOMIC-2020 [7] as our commonsense knowledge base, which is a commonsense knowledge graph of general-purpose everyday inferential knowledge covering social, physical, and event-centered aspects.

To be more specific, we explore two event-centered categories of commonsense knowledge from ATOMIC-2020, called *isAfter* and *isBefore*. These two relations provide reasoning about event scripts or sequences, respectively introducing events that can precede or follow an event. Therefore, we use *isAfter* and *isBefore* to introduce two events that happened before and happened after the given event, respectively. The two introduced events could form the context of a given event, and the three events can be treated as a narrative event chain. Then the given event could be fully understood via context awareness.

In order to acquire contexts for given events, we adopt a generative model COMET [2] which is a pre-trained GPT-2 model [17] finetuned on ATOMIC [20]. More precisely, we use a BART-based [8] variation of COMET, which is trained on ATOMIC-2020. This model can generate accurate and representative knowledge for new, unseen events. It is suitable and necessary for AEC task, because affective event has a broad scope and many events may not exist in the static ATOMIC-2020 dataset. An event is given to form the input format

$(e, r, [GEN])$, where e is the sequence that comprise an event tuple. For instance, ⟨I, have, drink, with my dad⟩ is converted into the sequence "I have drink with my dad". And r is the relations we select, including *isAfter* and *isBefore*. Then we use COMET to generate five commonsense inferences for each relation r.

Human Emotional Feedback Acquisition. In this work, ATOMIC-2020 is also utilized to acquire human emotional feedback. We explore one type of social-interaction commonsense knowledge called *xReact*, which manifests the emotional states of the participants in a given event. The introduced emotion reactions could fill the reasoning gap between events and sentiments. We acquire human emotional feedback in the same way that we acquire event contexts. As the commonsense inferences for *xReact* are usually emotion words (e.g., happy, sad, angry, etc.) rather than events or sentences, we simply adopt the hidden state representation from the last encoder layer of COMET as the human emotional feedback representation.

Sentiment-Related Concept Acquisition. Following [10], we use a commonsense knowledge base ConceptNet [23] combined with an emotion lexicon NRC_VAD [14] to obtain sentiment-related concepts.

ConceptNet is a large-scale multilingual semantic graph proposed to describe general human knowledge, allowing natural language applications to better understand the meanings behind the words. We introduce the tuple *(head concept, relation, tail concept, confidence score)* to represent the assertions in ConceptNet graph and their associated confidence scores, and denote the tuple as $\tau = (h, r, t, c)$. For instance, one such tuple from Conceptnet is *(birthday, RelatedTo, happy, 4.16)*. Let W be a collection of words in a given event tuple. For each non-stopword $h \in W$, we retrieve a set of tuples $T_i = \left\{\tau_i^j = \left(h_i, r_i^j, t_i^j, c_i^j\right)\right\}$ containing its immediate neighbors from ConceptNet, where i, j are indices of non-stopwords and the retrieved tuples.

To refine the retrieved concepts, we first remove tuples where concepts t_i^j are stopwords or not in our vocabulary. We further filter tuples where confidence scores c_i^j are smaller than 1 to reduce annotation noises. As many of the tuples are still useless for our AEC task, we select 10 relevant relations from 38 relations in ConceptNet as [11] did, they analyzed the effects of various relations on implicit sentiment analysis in detail. And then we remove the tuples where relations r_i^j belong to other relations.

To highlight sentimental information, we adopt NRC_VAD to measure sentimental intensity of the external concepts. NRC_VAD is a lexicon with valence, arousal, and dominance (VAD) scores. The interpretations of three dimensions are presented in Table 1. Such as the VAD score vector $[V_a, A_r, D_o]$ of word "happy" is $[1.000, 0.735, 0.772]$. Following [30], sentimental intensity value of a concept x is computed as:

$$\eta(x) = min\text{-}max\left(\left\|V_a(x) - \frac{1}{2}, \frac{A_r(x)}{2}\right\|_2\right) \tag{1}$$

where *min-max*() denotes min-max normalization, $\|.\|_k$ denotes L_k norm, $V_a(x)$ and $A_r(x)$ denote the valence and arousal scores in VAD vector of concept x, respectively. For concept x not in NRC_VAD, $\eta(x)$ will be set to 0. We rank the tuples according to the sentimental intensity values $\eta(t_i^j)$ of concepts t_i^j. Based on the order of tuples, we reserve at most three external concepts with adequate sentimental intensity values (i.e., $\eta(t_i^j) \geq 0.6$) for each word h.

Table 1. Interpretations of NRC_VAD dimensions

Dimensions	Values	Interpretations
Valence	[0,1]	Negative - Positive
Arousal	[0,1]	Calm - Excited
Dominance	[0,1]	Submissive - Dominant

3.2 Multi-source Text Encoding Module

Multi-source text encoder considers text from three sources, including raw event, event context and external concepts. The event encoder, context encoder and concept encoder are the same encoder, which employ widely-used pre-trained model BERT [3].

Firstly, the events are encoded. For each event $e = \{w_1, w_2, \cdots, w_n\}$, we concatenate two special tokens $[CLS]$ and $[SEP]$ to the beginning and end of the event. Then the sequence $\{[CLS], w_1, w_2, \cdots, w_n, [SEP]\}$ is fed to the encoder, leading to a series of hidden states:

$$h_i = \text{BERT}(\,[CLS], w_1, w_2, \cdots, w_n, [SEP]\,) \tag{2}$$

where $h_i \in \mathbb{R}^{d_m}$ is the i-th token in the input sequence, d_m is the dimension of hidden states in BERT. And the vectorized representation of an event is H. It is worth noting that we specifically denote $[CLS]$ token as g.

Secondly, the contexts are encoded. For both *isAfter* and *isBefore*, we concatenate the five generated commonsense inferences to get a context sequence CS^r:

$$CS^r = cs_1^r \oplus cs_2^r \cdots \oplus cs_5^r \tag{3}$$

where $\oplus$ is the concatenation operation, r is the relation we select from ATOMIC-2020. Then we pass each context sequence in the same input format as $\{[CLS], CS_r, [SEP]\}$, to derive a series of hidden states from the last layer:

$$s_j^r = \text{BERT}(\,[CLS], CS_r, [SEP]\,) \tag{4}$$

where $s_j^r \in \mathbb{R}^{d_m}$ is the j-th token in the input sequence. And the vectorized representation of a context sequence is S^r.

Thirdly, the concepts are encoded. For each concept x, we perform mean-pooling operation from the last hidden layer to obtain its representation $c \in \mathbb{R}^{d_m}$:

$$c = \text{Mean-pooling}(\,\text{BERT}(\,[CLS], x, [SEP]\,)\,) \tag{5}$$

3.3 Semantic and Sentimental Fusion Module

As contexts and sentimental clues have been collected, Semantic and Sentimental Fusion Module is devised to perform interaction as well as fusion of contextual and sentimental information.

Semantic Interaction. In order to highlight the more important semantic features from the contexts, we utilize multi-head cross-attention mechanism [25] to achieve the interaction of contexts and the event. Then for each context sequence CS^r, a context-aware representation $S^{r\prime}$ is learned:

$$S^{r\prime} = \text{MH}(f(H), f(S^r), f(S^r)) \tag{6}$$

where f is a linear transformation, each vector is transformed to the dimension of d_h with f, and

$$\text{MH}(Q, K, V) = \text{Concat}(head_1, \cdots, head_h)W^O \tag{7}$$

$$head_i = \text{Att}(QW_i^Q, KW_i^K, VW_i^V) \tag{8}$$

$$\text{Att}(Q, K, V) = \text{Softmax}(\frac{QK^T}{\sqrt{d_k}})V \tag{9}$$

where Q, K, and V are sets of queries, keys and values, respectively, the projections are parameter matrices $W^O \in \mathbb{R}^{md_v \times d_h}$, $W_i^Q \in \mathbb{R}^{d_h \times d_k}$, $W_i^K \in \mathbb{R}^{d_h \times d_k}$, $W_i^V \in \mathbb{R}^{d_h \times d_v}$, and $d_k = d_v = d_h/h$. The final context representation S is obtained by:

$$S = \bigoplus_{r \in \{isAfter, isBefore\}} \text{Max-pooling}(S^{r\prime}) \tag{10}$$

then S is transformed to the dimension of d_h with a linear projection.

Sentimental Interaction. We construct a graph network for modeling the event and relevant concepts. Specifically, each event token and concept are represented as vertices in the graph, including the $[CLS]$ token as a global vertex for aggregating information. Furthermore, three relation types of edges are applied to connect the vertices: (1) *global edge*, a directed edge which connects global node to each event node; (2) *general edge*, an undirected edge between two successive event nodes; (3) *extended edge*, a directed edge which connects a concept node to the corresponding event node.

Let $\mathcal{G} = (\mathcal{V}, \mathcal{E}, \mathcal{R})$ denotes our graph, where $\mathcal{V}$, $\mathcal{E}$, and $\mathcal{R}$ are sets of vertices, edges and relation types, respectively. We initialize each vertex with the corresponding encoded feature vector, and denote vertex features as $V = \{v_1, v_2, \cdots, v_N\} = \{g, h_1, \cdots, h_n, c_1, \cdots, c_m\}$.

We feed the initial vertex features into a graph encoder to propagate semantic and sentimental information. Considering different relation types of edges, we adopt relational graph convolutional networks [21] to update vertex representations. The convolutional computation for a vertex at the $(l+1)$-th layer which takes the representation $v_i^{(l)}$ at the l-th layer as input is defined as:

$$v_i^{(l+1)} = \mathrm{ReLU}\left(\sum_{r\in\mathcal{R}}\sum_{v\in\mathbb{N}_i^r}\frac{1}{|\mathbb{N}_i^r|}W_r^{(l)}v_i^{(l)}\right) \tag{11}$$

where ReLU [1] is an activation function, $\mathbb{N}_i^r$ is the set of neighbor vertices under relation type r, and $W_r^{(l)}$ are relation-specific learnable parameters at the l-th layer.

To selectively attend to the more important sentimental features within the enriched event representation, we pass the updated vertex features to a multi-head self-attention layer, then a sentiment-enhanced representation V' is learned:

$$V' = \mathrm{MH}(V^{(L)}, V^{(L)}, V^{(L)}) \tag{12}$$

where $V^{(L)} = \left\{v_1^{(L)}, v_2^{(L)}, \cdots, v_N^{(L)}\right\} = \{g', h'_1, \cdots, h'_n, c'_1, \cdots, c'_m\}$ are the outputs of the graph encoder. We take the global vertex feature as the final event representation G, and G is transformed to the dimension of d_h with a linear projection.

Feature Fusion. We first transform the human emotional feedback representation E to the dimension of d_h via a linear transformation. Inspired by [12], we fuse the three representations with a gated manner, including context representation S, event representation G, and human emotional feedback representation E. The gate is formulated as:

$$G_S = \mathrm{ReLU}(\mathrm{FC}([G, S, G-S, G\odot S])) \tag{13}$$

$$G_E = \mathrm{ReLU}(\mathrm{FC}([G, E, G-E, G\odot E])) \tag{14}$$

$$p = \mathrm{Sigmoid}(\mathrm{FC}[G_S, G_E]) \tag{15}$$

where FC is a fully-connected layer and [., .] means concatenation. Then the three features are fused as:

$$F = G + p\odot S + (1-p)\odot E \tag{16}$$

3.4 Sentiment Classification Module

Finally, taking the above fused representation as input, a sentiment classifier is applied to predict the sentiment of the event:

$$\hat{y} = \mathrm{Softmax}(\mathrm{MLP}(F)) \tag{17}$$

where MLP is a multi-layer perception.

Cross entropy loss is adopted to train the model, the loss function is defined as:

$$\mathcal{L} = -\frac{1}{T}\sum_{i=1}^{T}\sum_{j=1}^{C} y_i^j \cdot log(\hat{y_i}^j) \tag{18}$$

where T and C denote the number of training examples and the number of sentiment categories, respectively, and y_i^j represents the ground-truth label.

4 Experiments

In this section we present the dataset, evaluation metrics, baseline models, model variants, and other experimental settings.

4.1 Dataset and Evaluation Metrics

We conduct experiments on the gold standard dataset for AEC. It is collected from Twitter Dataset with sentiment category labels annotated by [32], and the sentiment categories belong to negative, neutral and positive. Statistics of the dataset are shown in Table 2.

Following [32], we report the precision, recall and F1 score for each of the three categories, and weighted average results for each metric.

Table 2. Dataset statistics

Category	Number
Negative Event	348
Neutral Event	717
Positive Event	435

4.2 Baselines and Comparison Models

We compare our proposed model with the following method:

BERT-Base/Large [3]: BERT is a widely-used pre-trained language model with excellent performance in various natural language processing tasks. We adopt the base version and the large version of BERT as the basis for our classifier and perform fine-tuning during the training process.

RoBERTa-Base/Large [13]: RoBERTa has the same model architecture as BERT but with a robustly optimized pre-training scheme allowing it to generalize better to downstream tasks. Similarly, we adopt the base version and the large version of RoBERTa for experiments.

DEST [32]: DEST is a discourse-enhanced self-training model which is the state-of-the-art model for AEC. It introduces BERT-base model for classification and combines the classifier's predictions with information from local discourse contexts to iteratively assign high-quality labels to new training instances.

4.3 Implementation Details

Following [32], we performed 10-fold cross-validation over the dataset, where each of the 10 runs used 8 folds of the data for training, 1 fold of the data for validation and tuning, and 1 fold of the data for testing.

Base version of BERT is adopted as the encoder, and the dimension of hidden states d_m in the encoder is 768. For all representations in the rest of our model, the dimension d_h is set to 300. For the multi-head cross-attention layer and the multi-head self-attention layer, the number of attention head is 5 and 12, respectively. For sentiment classification, the dimensions of MLP are set to [300, 100, 3] and the dropout rate is set to 0.1. We train our model with AdamW optimizer in a learning rate of 1e−5 and a linear warmup rate of 0.1. And the batch size is set to 8. We implemented all models in PyTorch with a single Tesla V100 GPU. Reported results are medians over 5 times of 10-fold cross-validation with the same 5 distinct random seeds.

5 Results and Analysis

In this section we present model evaluation results, ablation study, and case study.

5.1 Overall Results

As depicted in Table 3, our proposed model achieves state-of-the-art results. Benefiting from the effective context modeling with event contexts and accurate sentiment reasoning with human emotional feedback and sentiment-related concepts, MKIN achieves the best results on each metrics and the highest F1 score in each category compared with the state-of-the-art model DEST and other baselines.

Table 3. Performance of all models. The best results among all models are highlighted in **bold**.

Model	NEG			NEU			POS			P	R	F1
	P	R	F1	P	R	F1	P	R	F1			
BERT-base (110M)	71.6	77.4	74.1	76.5	78.1	77.1	76.8	69.9	73	75.8	75.3	75.3
BERT-large (340M)	72.5	75.5	73.5	76.7	78.6	77.5	77.6	72	74.3	76.4	75.7	75.7
RoBERTa-base (125M)	73.4	74.9	73.6	78	79.6	78.7	78.3	74.5	76	77.3	76.9	76.8
RoBERTa-large (355M)	74.4	75.3	74.5	77.7	82.3	79.8	78.9	71.7	74.8	77.7	77.3	77.2
DEST (110M)	78.9	**77.6**	78	78	83.7	80.6	**80.2**	71.5	75	79.2	78.6	78.5
MKIN (ours) (110M)	**83.7**	75.9	**79.1**	**80.1**	**84.3**	**82**	80	**78.8**	**79.1**	**81.3**	**80.7**	**80.6**

For the state-of-the-art model DEST, we reproduce the performance in the same setting as the original model. Although DEST utilizes a large number of coreferent sentiment expressions to provide explicit sentiment clues, it is unreliable because coreferent sentiment expressions are quite noisy due to imperfect coreference and issues like sarcasm, which leads to low-quality pseudo labels, even if an additional event classifier is introduced. Instead of retrieving information from corpus, we turn to the commonsense knowledge base for context information and explicit sentiment clues. MKIN improves precision of negative events from 78.9 to 83.7 and improves recall of positive events from 71.5 to 78.8. The substantial gain demonstrates the effectiveness of injecting multi-perspective knowledge to improve affective event classification, and shows the strong ability of our Semantic and Sentimental Fusion Module in extracting important features for enriching the event representation.

For other baselines models, they are not comparable with our proposed model MKIN. It suggests that the event representations extracted by pre-trained language models are not sufficient for classification, and only slight improvements are gained when a larger model is adopted. Besides, two instructive conclusions can be derived. On the one hand, it is of great significance to perform context modeling and capture semantic relationships between events and contexts, which lead to the thorough understanding of the events. On the other hand, explicit sentiment clues provided by human emotional feedback and sentiment-related concepts can fill the reasoning gap between events and sentiments.

5.2 Ablation Study

To gain better insight into the performance of our proposed model MKIN, we conduct an ablation study to verify the contributions of its main components.

Results in Table 4 show that each component is beneficial to the final performance. First, when the Event Context component is removed, the semantic features of the context are not integrated in the final representation of the event. The performance of the model degrades to a certain extent, which proves that context modeling is crucial to AEC. Since there is very limited information in the event, the model needs additional semantic information from the context for better event representation learning. Second, when removing the Human Emotional Feedback component, human's feelings are not taken into account. The dropped results demonstrate that human emotional feedback are powerful sentimental signals. Third, when the Sentiment-Related Concept component is removed, external concepts are not introduced to expand the original word meaning. The performance of the model decreased even more, which suggests that sentiment-related concepts have a considerable impact on sentiment classification. Introducing external sentimental commonsense knowledge and enriching the meaning of words in events can help the model detect implicit sentiments. Besides, the use of R-GCN enables more accurate capturing of interactive information, while the gate can better fuse complementary information.

5.3 Case Study

We provide several cases from the Twitter dataset to analyze the influence brought by event contexts, human emotional feedback and sentiment-related concepts. As illustrated in Table 5, the injected knowledge provide interpretable results for the prediction of our model. For events that do not contain sentiment

Table 4. Results of ablation study on model components.

Model	P	R	F1
MKIN	**81.3**	**80.7**	**80.6**
w/o Event Context	79.9	79.3	79.2
w/o Human Emotional Feedback	79.7	79	78.9
w/o Sentiment-Related Concept	79.4	78.8	78.8
w/o R-GCN	79.8	78.9	78.8
w/o Gate	79.7	79.1	79.1

words, such as those listed in Table 5, baseline models tend to classify them as neutral, whereas our model gives the correct predictions. From the cases, it can be observed that the three perspectives of knowledge injection play different roles in sentiment prediction. In most cases, intuitively, context information is of relatively little help in the reasoning process, because the model often does not get direct sentiment-related information from context. However, context information helps the model understand the event, which enriches the original event semantics. Moreover, compared with the other two kinds of information, human emotional feedback brings stronger sentimental signals. Especially when external concepts do not provide obvious sentimental clues, human emotional feedback plays a greater role. Finally, with the help of sentiment-related concepts, the model gains more profound insight into the meaning of words in the event. Since the sentiment of an event is often derived from its predicate and entities, important sentimental clues can be obtained from the extended concepts. Then the implied sentiment can be inferred more easily and more accurately.

Table 5. Cases that our model makes the correct predictions.

Event & Label	Event Context	Emotional Feedback	Sentiment-Related Concept
⟨I, go, -, on date⟩ Positive	I meet a girl. I have a great time.	happy, excited, romantic	go → energy, travel, journey date → lover, engagement
⟨I, have been, -, at hospital⟩ Negative	I was in a car accident. I was released from hospital.	worried, sick, scared	hospital → death, disease, injury
⟨I, save, much money, -⟩ Positive	I work hard at my job. I buy a new car.	happy, satisfied, proud	save → rescue, protect money → rich, reward, earnings
⟨-, separate, child, from family⟩ Negative	Parents go to jail. Mother cries.	sad, unhappy, scared	separate → divorce, abduction child → cute, naughty, noisy family → fellowship, mother
⟨I, have, free weekend, -⟩ Positive	I work all week. I go to the beach to relax.	relaxed, happy, excited	free → fun, gift, independent
⟨I, hear, loud noise, -⟩ Negative	I am walking down the street. I call the police.	scared, alarmed, alert	loud → strong, nightclub, vulgar noise → explosion, bang, trouble

6 Conclusion and Future Work

In this paper, we propose a novel Multi-perspective Knowledge-injected Interaction Network (MKIN) for affective event classification. MKIN models various aspects of information by considering contexts, human emotional feedback, and sentiment-related concepts, to fully comprehend the event as well as accurately predict its sentiment. To be more specific, in order to complement the semantic information of the event, we leverage context information and perform context modeling to capture the semantic association between the event and the context. To enhance the sentimental information of the event, we take advantage of human emotional feedback to provide sentimental clues from the perspective of people's emotional state. In addition, external sentiment-related concepts are introduced to enrich the word-level representations. Both emotional state information and concept information fill the reasoning gap between events and sentiments. Experiment results show that knowledge injection from all perspectives improve the model performance, and our model achieves 2.1% performance improvement over the state-of-the-art model on the gold standard dataset.

For future work, to apply the model in a variety of natural language processing applications, we would like to explore event-centered sentiment analysis. Affective event classification can be employed as an additional subtask to improve sentiment analysis.

Acknowledgements. We thank the anonymous reviewers for their insightful comments and suggestions. This work was supported by the National Key RD Program of China via grant 2021YFF0901602 and the National Natural Science Foundation of China (NSFC) via grant 62176078.

References

1. Agarap, A.F.: Deep learning using rectified linear units (relu). CoRR abs/1803.08375 (2018). http://arxiv.org/abs/1803.08375
2. Bosselut, A., Rashkin, H., Sap, M., Malaviya, C., Celikyilmaz, A., Choi, Y.: COMET: commonsense transformers for automatic knowledge graph construction. In: Proceedings of the 57th Annual Meeting of the Association for Computational Linguistics, pp. 4762–4779. Association for Computational Linguistics, Florence, July 2019. https://doi.org/10.18653/v1/P19-1470. https://aclanthology.org/P19-1470
3. Devlin, J., Chang, M.W., Lee, K., Toutanova, K.: BERT: pre-training of deep bidirectional transformers for language understanding. In: Proceedings of the 2019 Conference of the North American Chapter of the Association for Computational Linguistics: Human Language Technologies, Volume 1 (Long and Short Papers). pp. 4171–4186. Association for Computational Linguistics, Minneapolis, June 2019. https://doi.org/10.18653/v1/N19-1423, https://aclanthology.org/N19-1423
4. Ding, H., Riloff, E.: Acquiring knowledge of affective events from blogs using label propagation. In: Thirtieth AAAI Conference on Artificial Intelligence (2016)
5. Ding, H., Riloff, E.: Weakly supervised induction of affective events by optimizing semantic consistency. In: Proceedings of the AAAI Conference on Artificial Intelligence 32(1), April 2018. https://doi.org/10.1609/aaai.v32i1.12061. https://ojs.aaai.org/index.php/AAAI/article/view/12061

6. Goyal, A., Riloff, E., Daumé III, H.: Automatically producing plot unit representations for narrative text. In: Proceedings of the 2010 Conference on Empirical Methods in Natural Language Processing, pp. 77–86. Association for Computational Linguistics, Cambridge, October 2010. https://aclanthology.org/D10-1008
7. Hwang, J.D., et al.: (comet-) atomic 2020: on symbolic and neural commonsense knowledge graphs. In: Thirty-Fifth AAAI Conference on Artificial Intelligence, AAAI 2021, Thirty-Third Conference on Innovative Applications of Artificial Intelligence, IAAI 2021, The Eleventh Symposium on Educational Advances in Artificial Intelligence, EAAI 2021, Virtual Event, 2–9 February, 2021, pp. 6384–6392. AAAI Press (2021). https://ojs.aaai.org/index.php/AAAI/article/view/16792
8. Lewis, M., et al.: BART: denoising sequence-to-sequence pre-training for natural language generation, translation, and comprehension. In: Proceedings of the 58th Annual Meeting of the Association for Computational Linguistics, pp. 7871–7880. Association for Computational Linguistics, Online, July 2020. https://doi.org/10.18653/v1/2020.acl-main.703. https://aclanthology.org/2020.acl-main.703
9. Li, J., Ritter, A., Cardie, C., Hovy, E.: Major life event extraction from Twitter based on congratulations/condolences speech acts. In: Proceedings of the 2014 Conference on Empirical Methods in Natural Language Processing (EMNLP), pp. 1997–2007. Association for Computational Linguistics, Doha, Qatar, October 2014. https://doi.org/10.3115/v1/D14-1214. https://aclanthology.org/D14-1214
10. Li, Q., Li, P., Ren, Z., Ren, P., Chen, Z.: Knowledge bridging for empathetic dialogue generation. In: Thirty-Sixth AAAI Conference on Artificial Intelligence, AAAI 2022, Thirty-Fourth Conference on Innovative Applications of Artificial Intelligence, IAAI 2022, The Twelveth Symposium on Educational Advances in Artificial Intelligence, EAAI 2022 Virtual Event, 22 February–1 March 2022, pp. 10993–11001. AAAI Press (2022), https://ojs.aaai.org/index.php/AAAI/article/view/21347
11. Liao, J., Wang, M., Chen, X., Wang, S., Zhang, K.: Dynamic commonsense knowledge fused method for Chinese implicit sentiment analysis. Inf. Process. Manag. **59**(3), 102934 (2022). https://doi.org/10.1016/j.ipm.2022.102934
12. Liu, L., Zhang, Z., Zhao, H., Zhou, X., Zhou, X.: Filling the gap of utterance-aware and speaker-aware representation for multi-turn dialogue. In: Thirty-Fifth AAAI Conference on Artificial Intelligence, AAAI 2021, Thirty-Third Conference on Innovative Applications of Artificial Intelligence, IAAI 2021, The Eleventh Symposium on Educational Advances in Artificial Intelligence, EAAI 2021, Virtual Event, 2–9 February, 2021, pp. 13406–13414. AAAI Press (2021). https://ojs.aaai.org/index.php/AAAI/article/view/17582
13. Liu, Y., et al.: Roberta: a robustly optimized BERT pretraining approach. CoRR abs/1907.11692 (2019). http://arxiv.org/abs/1907.11692
14. Mohammad, S.: Obtaining reliable human ratings of valence, arousal, and dominance for 20,000 English words. In: Proceedings of the 56th Annual Meeting of the Association for Computational Linguistics (Volume 1: Long Papers), pp. 174–184. Association for Computational Linguistics, Melbourne, July 2018. https://doi.org/10.18653/v1/P18-1017. https://aclanthology.org/P18-1017
15. Oh, J.H., et al.: Why question answering using sentiment analysis and word classes. In: Proceedings of the 2012 Joint Conference on Empirical Methods in Natural Language Processing and Computational Natural Language Learning, pp. 368–378. Association for Computational Linguistics, Jeju Island, Korea, July 2012. https://aclanthology.org/D12-1034

16. Peng, W., Hu, Y., Xing, L., Xie, Y., Sun, Y., Li, Y.: Control globally, understand locally: A global-to-local hierarchical graph network for emotional support conversation. In: Raedt, L.D. (ed.) Proceedings of the Thirty-First International Joint Conference on Artificial Intelligence, IJCAI-22, pp. 4324–4330. International Joint Conferences on Artificial Intelligence Organization, July 2022. https://doi.org/10.24963/ijcai.2022/600. https://doi.org/10.24963/ijcai.2022/600 main Track
17. Radford, A., Narasimhan, K., Salimans, T., Sutskever, I., et al.: Improving language understanding by generative pre-training (2018). https://s3-us-west-2.amazonaws.com/openai-assets/research-covers/language-unsupervised/language_understanding_paper.pdf
18. Sabour, S., Zheng, C., Huang, M.: Cem: Commonsense-aware empathetic response generation. In: AAAI Conference on Artificial Intelligence (2021)
19. Saito, J., Murawaki, Y., Kurohashi, S.: Minimally supervised learning of affective events using discourse relations. In: Proceedings of the 2019 Conference on Empirical Methods in Natural Language Processing and the 9th International Joint Conference on Natural Language Processing (EMNLP-IJCNLP), pp. 5758–5765. Association for Computational Linguistics, Hong Kong, November 2019. https://doi.org/10.18653/v1/D19-1581. https://aclanthology.org/D19-1581
20. Sap, M., et al.: Atomic: an atlas of machine commonsense for if-then reasoning. In: Proceedings of the AAAI Conference on Artificial Intelligence, vol. 33, pp. 3027–3035 (2019). https://doi.org/10.1609/aaai.v33i01.33013027. https://doi.org/10.1609/aaai.v33i01.33013027
21. Schlichtkrull, M., Kipf, T.N., Bloem, P., van den Berg, R., Titov, I., Welling, M.: Modeling relational data with graph convolutional networks. In: Gangemi, A., et al. (eds.) ESWC 2018. LNCS, vol. 10843, pp. 593–607. Springer, Cham (2018). https://doi.org/10.1007/978-3-319-93417-4_38
22. Shi, W., Yu, Z.: Sentiment adaptive end-to-end dialog systems. In: Proceedings of the 56th Annual Meeting of the Association for Computational Linguistics (Volume 1: Long Papers), pp. 1509–1519. Association for Computational Linguistics, Melbourne, July 2018. https://doi.org/10.18653/v1/P18-1140. https://aclanthology.org/P18-1140
23. Speer, R., Chin, J., Havasi, C.: Conceptnet 5.5: an open multilingual graph of general knowledge. In: Proceedings of the Thirty-First AAAI Conference on Artificial Intelligence, 4–9 February, 2017, San Francisco, California, USA, pp. 4444–4451. AAAI Press (2017). http://aaai.org/ocs/index.php/AAAI/AAAI17/paper/view/14972
24. Turcan, E., Wang, S., Anubhai, R., Bhattacharjee, K., Al-Onaizan, Y., Muresan, S.: Multi-task learning and adapted knowledge models for emotion-cause extraction. In: Findings of the Association for Computational Linguistics: ACL-IJCNLP 2021, pp. 3975–3989. Association for Computational Linguistics, August 2021. https://doi.org/10.18653/v1/2021.findings-acl.348. https://aclanthology.org/2021.findings-acl.348
25. Vaswani, A., et al.: Attention is all you need. In: Advances in Neural Information Processing Systems 30: Annual Conference on Neural Information Processing Systems 2017(December), pp. 4–9, 2017. Long Beach, CA, USA, pp. 5998–6008 (2017). https://proceedings.neurips.cc/paper/2017/hash/3f5ee243547dee91fbd053c1c4a845aa-Abstract.html

26. Vu, H.T., Neubig, G., Sakti, S., Toda, T., Nakamura, S.: Acquiring a dictionary of emotion-provoking events. In: Proceedings of the 14th Conference of the European Chapter of the Association for Computational Linguistics, volume 2: Short Papers, pp. 128–132. Association for Computational Linguistics, Gothenburg, April 2014. https://doi.org/10.3115/v1/E14-4025. https://aclanthology.org/E14-4025
27. Xu, M., Wang, D., Feng, S., Yang, Z., Zhang, Y.: KC-ISA: an implicit sentiment analysis model combining knowledge enhancement and context features. In: Proceedings of the 29th International Conference on Computational Linguistics, pp. 6906–6915. International Committee on Computational Linguistics, Gyeongju, Republic of Korea, October 2022. https://aclanthology.org/2022.coling-1.601
28. Xu, R., et al.: ECO v1: towards event-centric opinion mining. In: Findings of the Association for Computational Linguistics: ACL 2022, pp. 2743–2753. Association for Computational Linguistics, Dublin, Ireland, May 2022. https://doi.org/10.18653/v1/2022.findings-acl.216. https://aclanthology.org/2022.findings-acl.216
29. Zhao, W., Zhao, Y., Lu, X.: Cauain: Causal aware interaction network for emotion recognition in conversations. In: Raedt, L.D. (ed.) Proceedings of the Thirty-First International Joint Conference on Artificial Intelligence, IJCAI-22, pp. 4524–4530. International Joint Conferences on Artificial Intelligence Organization, June 2022. https://doi.org/10.24963/ijcai.2022/628. https://doi.org/10.24963/ijcai.2022/628. main Track
30. Zhong, P., Wang, D., Miao, C.: Knowledge-enriched transformer for emotion detection in textual conversations. In: Proceedings of the 2019 Conference on Empirical Methods in Natural Language Processing and the 9th International Joint Conference on Natural Language Processing (EMNLP-IJCNLP), pp. 165–176. Association for Computational Linguistics, Hong Kong, November 2019. https://doi.org/10.18653/v1/D19-1016. https://aclanthology.org/D19-1016
31. Zhou, D., Wang, J., Zhang, L., He, Y.: Implicit sentiment analysis with event-centered text representation. In: Proceedings of the 2021 Conference on Empirical Methods in Natural Language Processing, pp. 6884–6893. Association for Computational Linguistics, Online and Punta Cana, Dominican Republic, November 2021. https://doi.org/10.18653/v1/2021.emnlp-main.551. https://aclanthology.org/2021.emnlp-main.551
32. Zhuang, Y., Jiang, T., Riloff, E.: Affective event classification with discourse-enhanced self-training. In: Proceedings of the 2020 Conference on Empirical Methods in Natural Language Processing (EMNLP), pp. 5608–5617. Association for Computational Linguistics, November 2020. https://doi.org/10.18653/v1/2020.emnlp-main.452. https://aclanthology.org/2020.emnlp-main.452

NLP Applications

Adversarial Network with External Knowledge for Zero-Shot Stance Detection

Chunling Wang[1], Yijia Zhang[1(✉)], Xingyu Yu[1], Guantong Liu[2], Fei Chen[1], and Hongfei Lin[3]

[1] College of Information Science and Technology, Dalian Maritime University, Dalian, China
{wangchunling,zhangyijia,1120211509,chenf}@dlmu.edu.cn

[2] College of Artificial Intelligence, Dalian Maritime University, Dalian, China
lgt@dlmu.edu.cn

[3] College of Computer Science and Technology, Dalian University of Technology, Dalian, China
hflin@dlut.edu.cn

Abstract. Zero-shot stance detection intends to detect previously unseen targets' stances in the testing phase. However, achieving this goal can be difficult, as it requires minimizing the domain transfer between different targets, and improving the model's inference and generalization abilities. To address this challenge, we propose an adversarial network with external knowledge (ANEK) model. Specifically, we adopt adversarial learning based on pre-trained models to learn transferable knowledge from the source targets, thereby enabling the model to generalize well to unseen targets. Additionally, we incorporate sentiment information and common sense knowledge into the contextual representation to further enhance the model's understanding. Experimental results on several datasets reveal that our method achieves excellent performance, demonstrating its validity and feasibility.

Keywords: Zero-shot stance detection · Adversarial learning · External knowledge · Contrastive learning

1 Introduction

Stance detection [3,12,19] is a significant task in NLP, focusing on identifying the stance (e.g., against, favor, or neutral) conveyed in the text towards a given target. It can be efficiently applied to social opinion analysis [14], rumor detection [13], and other research fields by mining text opinions.

Traditional intra-target stance detection [19] has limited applications since it requires training and testing under the same target and depends heavily on labeled data to achieve excellent performance. With the frequent and vast updates of topics on social platforms, manually labeling new targets becomes expensive and time-consuming, making it impractical to create a labeled dataset with all potential targets [22]. Therefore, the study of zero-shot stance detection [1] for unseen targets is essential and promising.

M. Sun et al. (Eds.): CCL 2023, LNAI 14232, pp. 419–433, 2023.
https://doi.org/10.1007/978-981-99-6207-5_26

Table 1. Examples of zero-shot stance detection.

Text	Target	Gold Label
I do not understand why the **Republicans** don't dismiss him.	Donald Trump	Against
@HillaryClinton **bad** wife, **bad** role model for women, **bad** lawyer, **bad** First Lady, **bad** Senator, **horrible** Secretary of State.	Hillary Clinton	Against

To tackle the zero-shot stance detection task, existing works generally incorporate external knowledge [18] as support for inference or introduce attention mechanisms [1] to capture the relationships between targets, which do not explicitly model of the transferable knowledge between source and destination targets. Some methods solely focus on employing adversarial training [2,24] to learn a target-invariant representation of the text content, disregarding the possibility that the model may encounter challenges in correctly predicting sentences that contain implicit viewpoints or require more profound understanding.

For example 1 in Table 1, the document does not explicitly mention the target "Donald Trump". If the model is unaware that Donald Trump is affiliated with the Republican Party, it is easy to misclassify the stance as neutral. Therefore, by incorporating common sense knowledge into adversarial networks and supplementing the target-related concept representations in the knowledge base, we can help the model more efficiently understand the text content, thus improving its generalization. In addition, we find a certain correlation between sentiment information and stance detection [15]. For example 2 in Table 1, when a document contains some negative words, it generally implies an Against stance. Stance detection will perform better if some sentiment knowledge can be acquired concurrently.

Motivated, on the one hand, based on the knowledge transfer ability of pre-trained models, we jointly embed the text and target into BERT and sentiment-aware BERT (noted as SentiBERT), and employ a cross-attention module to integrate the sentiment information extracted by SentiBERT with the contextual representations, resulting in semantic feature representations of the text. Meanwhile, we impose supervised contrastive learning [16] to make the model learn to distinguish stance category features in the potential distribution space. We separate the target-specific and target-invariant representations using a feature separator, then feed the target-invariant representation into the target discriminator for adversarial training, which enables the model to learn robust and transferable representations that can generalize well across different targets. On the other hand, we extract document-specific subgraphs from ConceptNet, and obtain concept representations of the common sense graph by using a graph autoencoder trained on the ConceptNet subgraph, which is fused into the text representation to enhance the model's performance. Our contributions are as follows:

(1) Our proposed ANEK model utilizes semantic information, sentiment information and common sense knowledge for zero-shot stance detection, especially adding sentiment information to assist stance detection and implicit background knowledge to enhance the model's comprehension.
(2) We employ adversarial training to learn target-invariant information to transfer knowledge effectively. Stance contrastive learning is used to enhance the inference of the model.
(3) We experimentally demonstrate that ANEK obtains competitive results on three datasets, and the extension to target stance detection is also effective.

2 Related Work

2.1 Stance Detection

Stance detection is the study of determining a text's viewpoint on a prescriptive target. [12]. Previous studies have primarily focused on scenarios where the training and testing sets share the same target, known as intra-target stance detection [3,19]. However, when new topics emerge, there is insufficient labeled data. Some studies explore cross-target stance detection [17,23,25], which trains a model on one target and tests it on another related target. Xu et al. [25] presented a self-attentive model to extract shared features between targets. Wei et al. [23] further exploited the hidden topics between targets as transferred knowledge. In contrast, zero-shot stance detection does not rely on any assumption of target correlation and is a more general study that can handle irregular target emergence.

Allaway et al. [1] developed a dataset containing multiple targets and presented a topic-grouping attention model to capture implicit relationships between them. Liu et al. [18] utilized the structural and semantic information of the common sense knowledge graph to enhance the model's inference. Allaway et al. [2] regarded each target as a domain and modeled the task as a domain adaptation problem, which successfully learnd the target-invariant representation. Liang et al. [16] designed an agent task that distinguished stance expression categories and implemented hierarchical contrastive learning. These works are considered incomplete as they overlook the impact of external knowledge containing sentiment information on the model. Whereas, we not only learn transferable target-invariant knowledge, but also take into account the introduction of multiple knowledge to enhance semantic information, further improving the model's predictive ability. To the best of our knowledge, we are the first to systematically introduce external knowledge into adversarial networks and achieve good results.

2.2 Adversarial Domain Adaptation

Domain adaptation mainly aims to minimize domain differences, ensure available knowledge transfer, and increase the model's generalization ability. Adversarial loss methods, inspired by the generative adversarial network (GAN) [8], have been commonly applied to domain adaptation. Ganin et al. [5] proposed a domain adversarial neural network (DANN), which utilized a gradient reversal layer to obfuscate the domain discriminator and enable the feature extractor to capture domain-invariant knowledge. Tzeng et al. [21] presented an adversarial discriminative domain adaptation (ADDA) model, which involved a discriminative method, GAN loss, and unshared weights to decrease the domain disparity. Therefore domain adaptation is an effective solution for the zero-shot stance detection task.

2.3 External Knowledge

Neural networks enhanced with external knowledge have been used for various NLP tasks, like dialogue generation, sentiment classification, and stance detection. Ghosal et al. [6] employed a domain adversary framework to handle cross-domain sentiment analysis and further improved the performance by injecting common sense knowledge using ConceptNet. Zhu et al. [27] incorporated target background knowledge from Wikipedia into the stance detection model. In addition, sentiment information is useful external knowledge for stance detection tasks. Li et al. [15] designed a sentiment classification task as an auxiliary task and built sentiment and stance vocabularies to guide attention mechanisms. Hardalov et al. [9] adopted a pre-trained sentiment model to generate sentiment annotations for text, which improved cross-lingual stance detection performance. Based on the above work, we simultaneously consider introducing common sense and sentiment knowledge to aid stance detection.

3 Method

The structure of our ANEK model is displayed in Fig. 1, which mainly contains two parts. (1) Knowledge graph training: we train a graph autoencoder using ConceptNet relation subgraphs. (2) Stance detection: we obtain context and sentiment information with pre-trained models, use contrastive learning to improve representation quality, separate features and perform adversarial learning, and finally incorporate the extracted common sense knowledge graph features to implement stance detection.

3.1 Task Description

Suppose we are given an annotated dataset $D_s = \{x_s^i, t_s^i, y_s^i\}_{i=1}^{N_s}$ from source targets and an unlabeled dataset $D_d = \{x_d^i, t_d^i\}_{i=1}^{N_d}$ from a destination target (unknown target), where x is a document, t and y are its corresponding target and stance label, respectively, and N is the number of examples. The purpose of zero-shot stance detection is to train the model using labeled data from multiple source targets to predict the stance labels of the unknown target examples.

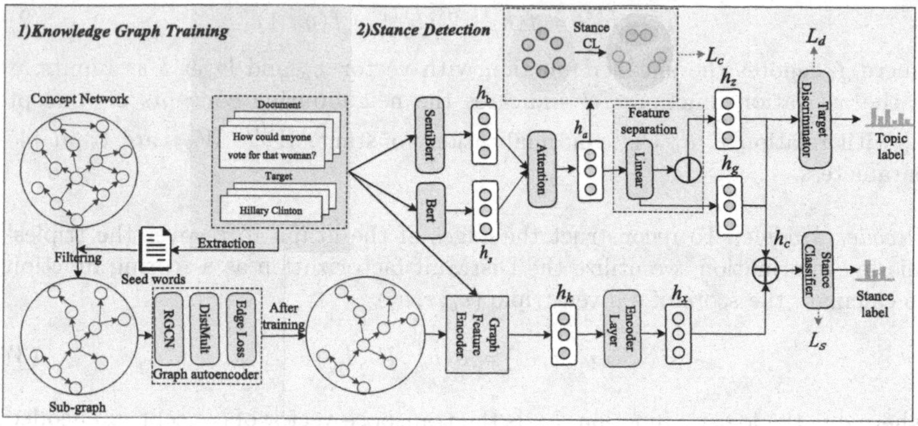

Fig. 1. Overview of the ANEK model.

3.2 Knowledge Graph Training

Common Sense Subgraph Generation. ConceptNet is a common sense knowledge base denoted as a directed graph $G = (V, E, R)$, where concepts $v_p \in V$, edges $(v_p, r, v_q) \in E$, and $r \in R$ is the relation type of the edge between v_p and v_q. Given that ConceptNet contains tens of millions of triplet relations like (cake, IsA, dessert), we use it to construct our knowledge subgraph. To be specific, we extract unique nouns, adverbs, and adjectives from the datasets of all targets as seed words. We then extract all triples that are one edge distance away from these seed concepts to obtain a subgraph $G' = \left(V', E', R'\right)$.

Graph Autoencoder Pre-training. To integrate common sense knowledge into our model, we obtain the concept representations in the subgraph G' by training a graph autoencoder composed of a RGCN encoder and a DistMult decoder [20]. We feed the incomplete set of edges $\hat{E}'$ from E' into the autoencoder. We then assigns scores to the potential edges (v_p, r, v_q) to ascertain the possibility of these edges being in E'.

Encoder Module. To obtain enriched feature representations of the target-related concepts, we utilize two stacked RGCN encoders to compose our encoder module. RGCN can create a rich stance aggregated representation for each concept by combining related concepts in the process of neighborhood-based convolutional feature transformation. Specifically, we randomly initialize the hidden vector g_p of concept v_p and then transform it into the stance aggregated hidden vector h_p by a two-step graph convolution.

$$f(x_p, l) = \sigma(\sum_{r \in R} \sum_{q \in N_p^r} \frac{1}{a_{p,r}} W_r^{(l)} x_q + W_0^{(l)} x_p) \tag{1}$$

$$h_p = h_p^{(2)} = f(h_p^{(1)}, 2); h_p^{(1)} = f(g_p, 1) \tag{2}$$

where f denotes the encoder function with vector x_p and layer l as inputs, σ is the activation function, N_p^r indicates the neighbouring concepts of concept v_p with relation r, $a_{p,r}$ is a normalization constant, $W_r^{(l)}$, $W_0^{(l)}$ are trainable parameters.

Decoder Module. To reconstruct the edges of the graph to recover the triples' missing information, we utilize the DistMult factorization as a scoring function to calculate the score of a given triple (v_p, r, v_q).

$$s(v_p, r, v_q) = \sigma(h_p^T, R_r, h_q) \tag{3}$$

where σ is the logistic function, h_p^T is the transpose vector of concept v_p encoded by RGCN.

Training. We use negative sampling to train our graph autoencoder model [6]. Specifically, for the triples in $\hat{E}'$ (i.e., positive samples), we generate the same amount of negative examples by destroying the concepts or relation of links at random, resulting in the complete sample set Z. Our training goal is to perform binary classification between positive/negative triples with optimization using a cross-entropy loss function.

$$L_{G'} = -\frac{1}{2|\hat{E}'|} \sum_{(v_p, r, v_q, y) \in Z} (y \log s(v_p, r, v_q) + (1-y) \log(1 - s(v_p, r, v_q))) \tag{4}$$

where y is an indication that is set to 0 for negative triples and 1 for positive triples.

3.3 Stance Detection Training

Commonsense Feature Encoding. After training the graph autoencoder, we utilize it to generate common sense graph features for a specific target t and document x. Specifically, we extract all seed words in the document and denote them as the set K. Then the subgraph $G_K^{'}$ is extracted from $G^{'}$, where triples consist of concepts in K or around radius 1 of any concept in K. Next, we feed $G_K^{'}$ to the pre-trained RGCN encoder module and make a forward pass to get the feature representations. We calculate the average of the representations h_p for all concepts p of document x as its common sense graph features h_k. Finally, we input h_k to an encoder layer to obtain its hidden representation h_x.

$$h_x = W_x h_k + b_x \tag{5}$$

where W_x and b_x are trainable parameters.

Encoding with Sentiment Information. Considering that the stance of a text is influenced by sentiment information, we learn the sentiment knowledge of the text to increase prediction accuracy. Following Zhou et al. [26], we exploit a perceptual sentiment language model (SentiBERT) to extract sentiment knowledge. We input the given document x and target t into the pretrained SentiBERT model in the form of "$[CLS]x[SEP]t[SEP]$" to obtain a hidden vector h_s with sentiment information.

$$h_s = SentiBERT([CLS]x[SEP]t[SEP]) \tag{6}$$

Moreover, to take advantage of the contextual information, we also adopt a pretrained BERT [11] model to jointly embed document x and target t to obtain a hidden vector h_b of each example.

$$h_b = BERT([CLS]x[SEP]t[SEP]) \tag{7}$$

Then h_b and h_s are concatenated, and the information of both is fused by the cross-attention module. Cross-attention can effectively capture the interdependencies between text and sentiment, facilitating the integration of knowledge and resulting in the generation of more accurate and meaningful features. The final output h_a is the hidden state of the $[CLS]$ token.

$$h_a = CrossAttention([h_b, h_s])[CLS] \tag{8}$$

Stance Contrastive Learning. Supervised contrastive learning can bring examples of identical categories closer together and push examples of distinct categories apart, thus learning a superior semantic representation space. To improve the generalization of the stance representation, based on the stance label information of the examples, we perform contrastive learning on their hidden vectors h_a [16]. Specifically, given the hidden vectors $H = \{h_m\}_{m=1}^{N_b}$ of a batch of examples, for a specific anchor $h_m \in H$, if $h_n \in H$ and h_m have the same stance label, i.e., $y_n = y_m$, then h_n is considered to be a positive example of h_m, while other examples $h_o \in H$ are considered to be negative examples. The final contrastive loss is calculated over all positive pairs, including (h_m, h_n) and (h_n, h_m) in a batch:

$$L_c = \frac{1}{N_B} \sum_{h_m \in H} l(h_m) \tag{9}$$

$$l(h_m) = -\log \frac{\sum_{n=1}^{N_b} \mathbf{1}_{[n \neq m]} \mathbf{1}_{[y_m = y_n]} \exp(sim(\mathbf{h}_m, \mathbf{h}_n)/\tau)}{\sum_{o=1}^{N_b} \mathbf{1}_{o \neq m} \exp(sim(\mathbf{h}_m, \mathbf{h}_o)/\tau)} \tag{10}$$

$$sim(\mathbf{s}, \mathbf{t}) = \frac{\mathbf{s}^T \mathbf{t}}{||\mathbf{s}||||\mathbf{t}||} \tag{11}$$

where $1_{[m=n]} \in (0,1)$ is an indicator function that evaluates to 1 iff $m = n$. $sim\,(\mathbf{s}, \mathbf{t})$ represents the cosine similarity of vectors $\mathbf{s}$ and $\mathbf{t}$. τ denotes a temperature parameter.

Target Discriminator. The contextual representations generated by Bert and the fused sentiment information contain both target-specific and target-invariant information. Learning and exploiting transferable target knowledge is effective in enhancing the model's generalization to new targets. We separate and differentiate target-specific and target-invariant features by a simple linear transformation, which can decrease the transfer challenge with no removal of stance cues. We first extract target-specific features using a linear transformation layer [24]:

$$h_g = W_g h_a + b_g \tag{12}$$

where W_g and b_g are trainable parameters. By subtracting target-specific features from h_a, the target-invariant features h_z can be obtained:

$$h_z = h_a - h_g \tag{13}$$

To further make the feature representation h_z target invariant and facilitate automatic adaptation of the model among different targets, we utilize a target discriminator to identify the target that the h_z comes from. If the discriminator cannot accurately predict the target label of h_z, we consider h_z has target-invariance. Our target discriminator is a linear network with softmax, which is trained with a cross-entropy loss function.

$$\hat{y_d} = Softmax(W_d h_z + b_d) \tag{14}$$

$$L_d = \sum_{x \in D_s} CrossEntropy(y_d, \hat{y_d}) \tag{15}$$

where W_d and b_d are the trainable parameters of the target discriminator, $\hat{y_d}$ and y_d are the predicted and true target labels. Specifically, h_z attempts to confound the target discriminator and increase the target classification loss L_d in order to learn the target-invariant features. Meanwhile, the discriminator itself struggles to decrease L_d. So we adopt the gradient reversal layer (GRL) technique, inspired by [5], to achieve this adversarial effect by placing the GRL before the target discriminator. The essence of adversarial training is the minimum-maximum game:

$$\underset{\theta_Z}{min}\ \underset{\theta_D}{max}\ -\lambda \log f_D(h_z) \tag{16}$$

where θ_Z are the parameters of all network layers that generate h_z, including fine-tuned Bert, graph encoder, W_g and b_g, etc., θ_D is the discriminator parameters, and f_D is the discriminator function.

Stance Classifier. Since stances are essentially dependent on targets, target-specific information for each target is also indispensable. We concatenate the common sense knowledge graph features h_x, the target-invariant features h_z and the target-specific features h_g to obtain h_c, as the input for the stance classifier with softmax normalization. We minimize the stance classification loss using cross-entropy loss.

$$h_c = h_x \oplus h_z \oplus h_g \tag{17}$$

$$\hat{y} = Softmax(W_c h_c + b_c) \tag{18}$$

$$L_s = \sum_{x \in D_s} CrossEntropy(y, \hat{y}) \tag{19}$$

where W_c and b_c are the trainable parameters of the stance classifier, $\hat{y}$ and y are the predicted stance probability and ground-truth distribution.

The training goal of our proposed model is to minimize the overall loss, defined as follows:

$$L = L_s + \alpha L_c + \beta L_d \tag{20}$$

where α and β are hyperparameters.

4 Experiments

4.1 Datasets

We conduct experiments on three publicly available datasets. 1)**SEM16** [19] is a Twitter dataset that contains six targets for stance detection, including the Legalization of Abortion (LA), Feminist Movement (FM), Hillary Clinton (HC), Donald Trump (DT), Atheism (A), and Climate Change is a Real Concern (CC). 2)**WT-WT** [4] is a stance detection dataset in the financial domain. The dataset contains four targets, including ANTM_CI (AC), AET_HUM (AH), CVS_AET(CA), and CI_ESRX (CE). 3)**COVID-19** [7] is a dataset related to COVID-19 health tasks, which includes four targets: Anthony S. Fauci, M.D. (AF), Wearing a Face Mask (WA), Keeping Schools Closed (SC), and Stay at Home (SH). Each text in the three datasets contains a stance (favor, against, neutral) for a specific target.

Following [16], we utilize the data from one target as the test set and the remaining targets as the training set. Moreover, we report the F1_avg (the Macro-averaged F1 of against and favor) as evaluation metrics.

Table 2 represents the statistics for the three datasets, listing all targets under each dataset and the number of samples labeled "favor, against, neutral, unlabeled" (where WT-WT and COVID-19 have no unlabeled samples) for each target.

4.2 Experimental Implementation

We employ the pretrained SentiBERT and BERT models as the encoder, whose maximum sequence length is 85. Adam [11] is used to optimize the model. In the graph autoencoder training stage, the graph batch size is 10000, the learning rate

Table 2. Statistics of the SEM16, WT-WT and COVID-19 datasets

Dataset	Target	Favor	Against	Neutral	Unlabeled
SEM16	DT	148	299	260	2,194
	HC	163	565	256	1,898
	FM	268	511	170	1,951
	LA	167	544	222	1,899
	A	124	464	145	1,900
	CC	135	26	203	1,900
WT-WT	CA	2,469	518	5,520	-
	CE	773	253	947	-
	AC	970	1,969	3,098	-
	AH	1,038	1,106	2,804	-
COVID-19	WA	515	220	172	-
	SC	430	102	85	-
	AF	384	266	307	-
	SH	151	201	396	-

is 0.01, the dropout rate is 0.25, and we apply gradient clipping to 1.0. In the stance detection training stage, the batch size is 8, the learning rate is 1.5e-5, the dropout rate is 0.1, we train up to 50 epochs, the patience is 5, the temperature parameter for contrastive loss is 0.07. We use different seeds to train our model and record the best results.

4.3 Baselines

We compare the ANEK with several strong baselines, including **BiCond** [3]: bidirectional conditional encoding model, **CrossNet** [25]: BiCond with topic-specific attention, **TOAD** [2]: BiCond with adversarial learning, **BERT** [10]: pretrained language model, **BERT-GCN** [18]: BERT with GCN for node information aggregation, **TGA Net** [1]: Bert with topic-group attention, **TPDG** [17]: GCN-based model for designing target-adaptive pragmatic dependency graphs, **PT-HCL** [16]: hierarchical contrastive learning model.

4.4 Main Results

We implemented comparison experiments on three datasets and show the F1_avg results (Percentage System) in Table 3. Our proposed ANEK model presents superior performance compared to the baseline models on most target datasets. Specifically, BiCond and CrossNet perform the worst overall, as they do not consider the target invisibility to learn transferable information. Although TOAD also adopts an adversarial strategy to learn target-invariant information, its use of BiLSTM encoding is prone to poor performance in case of an unbalanced target distribution. It can be observed that it performs even less efficiently than Bert on multiple targets. As a strong baseline in NLP, BERT has good generalization because it learns rich semantic information in a large corpus, despite

Table 3. Experimental results on three datasets. Bold indicates the best score for each test target.

Model	SEM16						WT-WT				COVID-19			
	DT	HC	FM	LA	A	CC	CA	CE	AC	AH	WA	SC	AF	SH
BiCond	30.5	32.7	40.6	34.4	31.0	15.0	56.5	52.5	64.9	63.0	30.1	33.9	26.7	19.3
CrossNet	35.6	38.3	41.7	38.5	39.7	22.8	59.1	54.5	65.1	62.3	38.2	40.0	41.3	40.4
TOAD	49.5	51.2	54.1	46.2	46.1	30.9	55.3	57.7	58.6	61.7	37.9	47.3	40.1	42.0
BERT	40.1	49.6	41.9	44.8	55.2	37.3	56.0	60.5	67.1	67.3	44.3	45.1	47.5	39.7
BERT-GCN	42.3	50.0	44.3	44.2	53.6	35.5	67.8	64.1	70.7	69.2	-	-	-	-
TPDG	47.3	50.9	53.6	46.5	48.7	32.3	66.8	65.6	74.2	73.1	48.4	**51.6**	46.0	37.3
TGA Net	40.7	49.3	46.6	45.2	52.7	36.6	65.7	63.5	69.9	68.7	-	-	-	-
PT-HCL	50.1	54.5	54.6	**50.9**	**56.5**	38.9	**73.1**	69.2	**76.7**	76.3	**58.8**	44.7	41.7	**53.3**
ANEK	**50.3**	**54.7**	**55.0**	49.0	54.1	**39.2**	71.4	**69.8**	74.8	**76.3**	52.9	49.8	**48.6**	50.3

ignoring transferable information between targets. However, when it is applied to target transfer, it causes performance degradation due to its tendency to fit the source data. Our model explores adversarial learning based on pre-trained models, which can learn enhanced target-invariant features and improve the model's transferability.

Table 3 shows that relying solely on the introduction of common sense knowledge to help the model understand is not enough for Bert-GCN, and our model also accounts for learning sentiment information to enhance the discriminative capability of the model. We can find that ANEK slightly outperforms the PT-HCL method with hierarchical contrastive learning. Although PT-HCL obtains excellent generalization by identifying the invariant stance expressions from specific syntactic levels, it requires pre-processing the data to generate pseudo-labels, which increases the complexity of the model. Moreover, the noise brought by pseudo-labels may affect the prediction results. In contrast, our model has stronger generality and interpretability.

Table 4. Experimental results of the ablation study

Model	SEM16						WT-WT				COVID-19			
	DT	HC	FM	LA	A	CC	CA	CE	AC	AH	WA	SC	AF	SH
ANEK	**50.3**	**54.7**	**55.0**	**49.0**	**54.1**	**39.2**	**71.4**	**69.8**	**74.8**	**76.3**	**52.9**	**49.8**	**48.6**	**50.3**
w/o LC	49.2	52.8	52.9	47.8	53.2	38.0	69.2	66.5	73.2	75.2	51.3	48.2	48.1	49.2
w/o SK	48.7	51.8	53.4	47.2	52.0	37.8	68.1	67.5	71.3	74.0	51.0	49.3	47.2	48.0
w/o CK	48.0	52.4	53.0	46.8	51.1	36.5	67.6	66.8	72.0	73.8	49.7	48.7	46.5	47.9
w/o TD	47.8	51.2	52.3	46.5	52.9	37.8	69.0	68.8	72.6	73.3	50.4	47.9	47.8	47.2

4.5 Ablation Study

We further designed several variants of ANEK for ablation experiments to analyze the effects of different components on the model, where "w/o CL", "w/o

SK", "w/o CK", "w/o TD" denote the removal of contrastive learning, sentiment information, common sense knowledge and adversarial learning, respectively.

We report the F1_avg scores (Percentage System) of the ablation study in Table 4. The experimental results indicate that removing stance contrastive learning ("w/o CL") significantly decreases the model's performance, which suggests that we perform stance contrastive learning on the text representation assists the encoder in learning better category representations from samples, leading to better generalization. The removal of sentiment information ("w/o SK") reduces model performance, implying that the model may learn the potential relationship between stance and sentiment and make judgments with the help of sentiment knowledge. Removing common sense knowledge ("w/o CK") leads to poor performance in stance detection, indicating that introducing common sense knowledge can indeed help the model understand text information and improve its reasoning ability. "w/o TD" indicates that the removal of the target discriminator becomes less effective on multiple targets, demonstrating the success of adversarial learning applied to zero-shot scenarios, generalizing to unseen targets by encouraging the encoder to generate target-invariant representations.

4.6 Generalizability Analysis

We further performed experiments on the SEM16 dataset for cross-target stance detection and report the F1_avg results (Percentage System) in Table 5. The cross-target stance detection task is treated as a particular zero-shot setting, as we need to train using data from a source target related to the test target. Table 5 illustrates that our ANEK model achieves better performance. We can also find that the cross-target setting outperforms the zero-shot setting, which indicates that knowing the relationship between targets in advance can learn more reliable target-invariant representations to generalize to unseen targets, illustrating the challenges of zero-shot stance detection. Additionally, enhancing the understanding and generalization of the model by introducing external knowledge is also effective.

Table 5. Experimental results of cross-target stance detection. "FM→LA" indicates training on FM, testing on LA, etc.

Model	SEM16			
	FM→LA	LA→FM	HC→DT	DT→HC
BiCond	45.0	41.6	29.7	35.8
CrossNet	45.4	43.3	43.1	36.2
BERT	47.9	33.9	43.6	36.5
TPDG	58.3	54.1	50.4	52.9
PT-HCL	**59.3**	54.6	53.7	55.3
ANEK	58.5	**54.8**	**54.3**	**56.4**

4.7 Case Study

To qualitatively analyze our model, we conduct a case study and error analysis. We select four cases from the test data of SEM16 and compare our results to the predictions of BERT and TOAD. Table 6 reports these results. In the first case, our model and TOAD with adversarial learning output the correct labels, while the output of BERT is wrong. We believe that because the training data contains the target "Hillary Clinton", the model learns the election relationship between the two targets and transfers the knowledge, and semantically focuses more on the stance-related words rather than the target words, with a robust target generalization. In the second case, only our method makes the correct prediction, demonstrating that depending only on contextual information is insufficient. Adding sentiment information strengthens the model's comprehension of texts with a sarcastic sentiment. In the third case, our method still correctly predicts the outcome. Although no words about Trump appear in the text, we speculate that the model learns the hidden connection between "Republican" and "Donald Trump" and understands the implied meaning of the text, further confirming the validity of common sense knowledge.

Table 6. Four cases of the predictions by BERT, TOAD and ANEK.

Text	Target	Gold Label	BERT	TOAD	ANEK
Your have to wonder if Hillary will attempt to replace #ObamaCare with #HillaryCare.	Donald Trump	Against	Neutral	Against	Against
Donald trump is way better than ANY candidate out there. Because he's real, not a lobbyist backed puppet.	Donald Trump	Against	Favor	Favor	Against
I do not understand why the Republicans don't dismiss him.	Donald Trump	Against	Neutral	Neutral	Against
......and some, I assume, are good people.	Donald Trump	Against	Favor	Favor	Favor

In the fourth case, all models output incorrect results. We suspect that this is because the text is too brief, resulting in less valid information being learned, and the background knowledge is too complex, which reveals that we can explore data augmentation methods in the future to improve the performance of zero-shot stance detection by expanding the data.

5 Conclusion

This paper proposes an adversarial network with external knowledge (ANEK) to handle the zero-shot stance detection task. The model applies adversarial learning based on pre-trained models to ensure knowledge transferability, and introduces common sense knowledge and sentiment information to enhance the model's deep understanding and assist stance detection. In addition, stance contrastive learning is used to improve the model's generalization. The experimental results on three benchmark datasets indicate that our method performs competitively on some unseen targets. In future work, we will design a data enhancement method to alleviate the data scarcity problem in zero-shot settings and improve performance.

Acknowledgements. This work is supported by a grant from the Social and Science Foundation of Liaoning Province (No. L20BTQ008)

References

1. Allaway, E., Mckeown, K.: Zero-shot stance detection: a dataset and model using generalized topic representations. In: Proceedings of the 2020 Conference on Empirical Methods in Natural Language Processing (EMNLP). pp. 8913–8931 (2020)
2. Allaway, E., Srikanth, M., Mckeown, K.: Adversarial learning for zero-shot stance detection on social media. In: Proceedings of the 2021 Conference of the North American Chapter of the Association for Computational Linguistics: Human Language Technologies. pp. 4756–4767 (2021)
3. Augenstein, I., Rocktäschel, T., Vlachos, A., Bontcheva, K.: Stance detection with bidirectional conditional encoding. In: Proceedings of the 2016 Conference on Empirical Methods in Natural Language Processing. pp. 876–885 (2016)
4. Conforti, C., Berndt, J., Pilehvar, M.T., Giannitsarou, C., Toxvaerd, F., Collier, N.: Will-they-won't-they: a very large dataset for stance detection on twitter. In: Proceedings of the 58th Annual Meeting of the Association for Computational Linguistics. pp. 1715–1724 (2020)
5. Ganin, Y., et al.: Domain-adversarial training of neural networks. J. Mach. Learn. Res. **17**(1), 2030–2096 (2016)
6. Ghosal, D., Hazarika, D., Roy, A., Majumder, N., Mihalcea, R., Poria, S.: Kingdom: knowledge-guided domain adaptation for sentiment analysis. In: Proceedings of the 58th Annual Meeting of the Association for Computational Linguistics. pp. 3198–3210 (2020)
7. Glandt, K., Khanal, S., Li, Y., Caragea, D., Caragea, C.: Stance detection in COVID-19 tweets. In: Proceedings of the 59th Annual Meeting of the Association for Computational Linguistics and the 11th International Joint Conference on Natural Language Processing vol. 1: Long Papers. pp. 1596–1611 (2021)
8. Goodfellow, I.J., et al.: Generative adversarial networks (2014). arXiv preprint arXiv:1406.2661 (2014)
9. Hardalov, M., Arora, A., Nakov, P., Augenstein, I.: Few-shot cross-lingual stance detection with sentiment-based pre-training. In: Proceedings of the AAAI Conference on Artificial Intelligence. vol. 36, pp. 10729–10737 (2022)
10. Kenton, J.D.M.W.C., Toutanova, L.K.: Bert: pre-training of deep bidirectional transformers for language understanding. In: Proceedings of NAACL-HLT. pp. 4171–4186 (2019)
11. Kingma, D.P., Ba, J.: Adam: A method for stochastic optimization. arXiv preprint arXiv:1412.6980 (2014)
12. Küçük, D., Can, F.: Stance detection: a survey. ACM Comput. Surv. (CSUR) **53**(1), 1–37 (2020)

13. Kumar, S., Carley, K.M.: Tree LSTMs with convolution units to predict stance and rumor veracity in social media conversations. In: Proceedings of the 57th Annual meeting of the Association for Computational Linguistics. pp. 5047–5058 (2019)
14. Lai, M., Cignarella, A.T., Farías, D.I.H., Bosco, C., Patti, V., Rosso, P.: Multilingual stance detection in social media political debates. Comput. Speech Lang. **63**, 101075 (2020)
15. Li, Y., Caragea, C.: Multi-task stance detection with sentiment and stance lexicons. In: Proceedings of the 2019 Conference on Empirical Methods in Natural Language Processing and the 9th International Joint Conference on Natural Language Processing (EMNLP-IJCNLP). pp. 6299–6305 (2019)
16. Liang, B., Chen, Z., Gui, L., He, Y., Yang, M., Xu, R.: Zero-shot stance detection via contrastive learning. In: Proceedings of the ACM Web Conference 2022. pp. 2738–2747 (2022)
17. Liang, B., et al.: Target-adaptive graph for cross-target stance detection. In: Proceedings of the Web Conference 2021. pp. 3453–3464 (2021)
18. Liu, R., Lin, Z., Tan, Y., Wang, W.: Enhancing zero-shot and few-shot stance detection with commonsense knowledge graph. In: Findings of the Association for Computational Linguistics: ACL-IJCNLP 2021. pp. 3152–3157 (2021)
19. Mohammad, S., Kiritchenko, S., Sobhani, P., Zhu, X., Cherry, C.: Semeval-2016 task 6: detecting stance in tweets. In: Proceedings of the 10th international workshop on semantic evaluation (SemEval-2016). pp. 31–41 (2016)
20. Schlichtkrull, M., Kipf, T.N., Bloem, P., van den Berg, R., Titov, I., Welling, M.: Modeling Relational Data with Graph Convolutional Networks. In: Gangemi, A., et al. (eds.) ESWC 2018. LNCS, vol. 10843, pp. 593–607. Springer, Cham (2018). https://doi.org/10.1007/978-3-319-93417-4_38
21. Tzeng, E., Hoffman, J., Saenko, K., Darrell, T.: Adversarial discriminative domain adaptation. In: Proceedings of the IEEE Conference on Computer Vision and Pattern Recognition. pp. 7167–7176 (2017)
22. Wang, Z., Wang, Q., Lv, C., Cao, X., Fu, G.: Unseen target stance detection with adversarial domain generalization. In: 2020 International Joint Conference on Neural Networks (IJCNN). pp. 1–8. IEEE (2020)
23. Wei, P., Mao, W.: Modeling transferable topics for cross-target stance detection. In: Proceedings of the 42nd International ACM SIGIR Conference on Research and Development in Information Retrieval. pp. 1173–1176 (2019)
24. Xie, F., Zhang, Z., Zhao, X., Zou, J., Zhou, B., Tan, Y.: Adversarial learning-based stance classifier for COVID-19-related health policies. arXiv preprint arXiv:2209.04631 (2022)
25. Xu, C., Paris, C., Nepal, S., Sparks, R.: Cross-target stance classification with self-attention networks. In: Proceedings of the 56th Annual Meeting of the Association for Computational Linguistics (Volume 2: Short Papers). pp. 778–783 (2018)
26. Zhou, J., Tian, J., Wang, R., Wu, Y., Xiao, W., He, L.: Sentix: a sentiment-aware pre-trained model for cross-domain sentiment analysis. In: Proceedings of the 28th International Conference on Computational Linguistics. pp. 568–579 (2020)
27. Zhu, Q., Liang, B., Sun, J., Du, J., Zhou, L., Xu, R.: Enhancing zero-shot stance detection via targeted background knowledge. In: Proceedings of the 45th International ACM SIGIR Conference on Research and Development in Information Retrieval. pp. 2070–2075 (2022)

Case Retrieval for Legal Judgment Prediction in Legal Artificial Intelligence

Han Zhang[1] and Zhicheng Dou[2(✉)]

[1] School of Information, Renmin University of China, Beijing, China
zhanghanjl@ruc.edu.cn

[2] Gaoling School of Artificial Intelligence, Renmin University of China, Beijing, China
dou@ruc.edu.cn

Abstract. Legal judgment prediction (LJP), which consists of subtasks including relevant law article prediction, charge prediction, and penalty term prediction, is a basic task in legal artificial intelligence. In recent years, many deep learning methods have been proposed for this task. Most of them improve their performance by integrating law articles and the fact description of a legal case. However, they rarely consider that the judges usually look up historical cases to help make the final judgment in real practice. To simulate this scenario, in this paper, we propose a new framework for LJP, which explicitly incorporates retrieved historical cases in the process of LJP. Specifically, we select some cases from the training dataset. Then, we retrieve the most similar Top-k historical cases of the given case and use the vector representation of these Top-k historical cases to help predict the judgment results. We experiment with two widely used legal datasets, and the results show that our model outperforms several state-of-the-art baseline models.

Keywords: Legal Judgment Prediction · Case Retrieval · Historical Case

1 Introduction

Recently, it has become a trend to use artificial intelligence to help judicial personnel. Legal judgment prediction (LJP) is a typical legal artificial intelligence task. As shown in Table 1, given a legal case with a fact description, the LJP task can predict the judgment result of the case. The predicted result consists of three parts: relevant law article, charge and term of penalty. LJP can not only give the judgment results efficiently for reference for judicial personnel but also provide legal suggestions for ordinary people when there is a legal dispute [20,27–29] in daily life.

Currently, various methods have been proposed to help improve the performance of the LJP task. Some methods [24,28] consider using the order information among the three subtasks of LJP in reality to enhance the ability to represent the fact description. Further, some methods [4,13,26] consider a fine-grained division of the fact description to improve the fact representation. Additionally,

M. Sun et al. (Eds.): CCL 2023, LNAI 14232, pp. 434–448, 2023.
https://doi.org/10.1007/978-981-99-6207-5_27

Table 1. An example of the legal judgment prediction task.

Fact Description On XX, XXX, the procuratorate accused the defendant Yang XX of taking gasoline out of his motorcycle fuel tank after quarrelling with his girlfriend Tang XX, putting it into a beer bottle, and pouring gasoline through the crack of the door into room X of the rental room opposite the XX Internet cafe in the XX community where Tang XX is located, and using a lighter to ignite the gasoline. The fire spread to the room along with the gasoline and was extinguished by Tang XX and other people in the room. On the morning of that day, the public security police arrested the defendant Yang XX ...
Relevant Law Article *Article #114* [Crime of Arson] Whoever commits arson, breaches a dike, causes an explosion, spreads toxic, radioactive, infectious disease pathogens and other substances or endangers public security by other dangerous methods, but has not caused serious consequences, shall be sentenced to **fixed-term imprisonment of not less than three years but not more than ten years.**
Charge: Crime of Arson
Term of Penalty: **A fixed-term imprisonment of thirty-six months**

some methods [8,12,20,23] consider the important role of law articles in reality and introduce them to improve the performance. These efforts have effectively improved the performance of the LJP task. However, the existing methods are affected by the fact that the law articles are too concise and still have limitations in modelling the judgment process.

On the one hand, the law articles are very concise and lack specific details and some law articles have similar provisions and so easy to be confused. As shown in Fig. 1, *Article #114* and *Article #115* both stipulate the same charge *Crime of Arson* and the provisions in the two law articles are very short. In order to distinguish them, the judge usually re-finds and analyzes historical cases because the fact description information of historical cases usually contains more detailed information than the law articles.

On the other hand, most of the previous methods predict the judgment results mainly based on the fact description of a single case, however, they overlook the practical scenario that judges usually look up typical historical cases for reference before making a judgment. As we all know, historical cases are very important for making a judgment, whether in the Case Law system or the Statutory Law system.[1] In the Case Law system, judges mainly refer to historical cases to make a judgment. In the Statutory Law system, before making a judgment the judges

[1] The details of the Case Law and Statutory Law system can be found in https://en.wikipedia.org/wiki/Case_law and https://en.wikipedia.org/wiki/Statutory_law.

Article #114: Charge 1-5
Whoever commits arson, breaches a dike, causes explosion, spreads toxic, ..., endangers public security by dangerous means, ..., or endangers public security by other dangerous means, but **has not caused serious consequences**, shall be sentenced to fixed-term imprisonment of not less than three years but not more than 10 years.

Article #115: Charge 1-5
Whoever commits arson, breaches a dike, causes explosion, spreads toxic, radioactive, infectious disease pathogens and other substances or uses other dangerous methods to **cause serious injury or death to people or heavy losses to public or private property** shall be sentenced to fixed-term imprisonment of not less than 10 years, life imprisonment or death.
Charge 6 ...

Charge 1: Crime of Arson
Charge 2: Crime of Breaking Dikes
Charge 3: Crime of Causing Explosions
Charge 4: Crime of Throwing Dangerous Substances
Charge 5: Crime of Endangering Public Security by Dangerous Means

Fig. 1. Article #114 and Article #115 both stipulate the same charges (Charge 1–5). There is little difference between the specific provisions of Article #114 and Article #115 on the Crime of Arson.

should not only look up the law articles but also look up typical historical cases. Obviously, historical cases are indispensable references for judges in their work.

To solve the above challenges, we propose a framework for legal judgment prediction based on a historical case retrieval module to simulate the actual legal scenario of looking up historical cases before making a judgment.

First, we consider that the number of cases looked up by judges in actual work is usually limited and select a part of cases from the training dataset as historical cases.

Second, in order to avoid the impact of highly unbalanced class distribution of the dataset on the model performance [8,27], we consider selecting the same number of historical cases for each category.

Third, we retrieve the most similar Top-k historical cases of the current legal case and concatenate the vector representation of these Top-k cases and the fact description of the current case to predict the judgment results. Finally, we train our model with a cross-entropy loss function. We call our model **CR4LJP**, which stands for **C**ase **R**etrieval framework for **L**egal **J**udgment **P**rediction.

Our contributions are three-fold:

(1) We take into account that judges usually look up historical cases before making a judgment after investigating the human justice system.
(2) We propose a case retrieval framework for the legal judgment prediction task to use historical cases to help predict the judgment results.
(3) Experimental results on two real large-scale legal datasets show that our model outperforms the state-of-the-art models and verify the effectiveness of our framework. This study shows that case retrieval is effective in improving the legal judgment prediction task.

2 Related Work

2.1 Legal Judgment Prediction

The earliest legal judgment prediction (LJP) methods [5,10,16,17,19] mainly use mathematical and statistical tools. These methods are based on artificial features or rules, so they are difficult to extend. In recent years, some researchers have proposed a lot of models [3,24,28,29] based on deep learning to predict judgment results. Specifically, some research works [24,28] consider that the legal judgment prediction task is composed of three subtasks, and there are dependencies among them which are useful information. Some research works [4, 13,26] consider that the fact description is usually long, and the fact description can be better represented by dividing or extracting the fine-grained information. Some research works [8,12,20,23] consider the important role of law articles in reality and then try to use the information of law articles. These previous works improve the performance of LJP, but they fail to take into account that historical cases are also important information.

2.2 Retrieval Methods

For deep learning models, even the pre-trained models, such as Bert [2], can not remember all samples. Therefore, it is worth considering using a retrieval model to obtain additional information. Generally, retrieval models can be divided into two types: sparse representation based on bag-of-word (BOW) [1] and dense vector representation based on neural networks [9,31]. The retrieval models based on sparse representation have been applied in machine translation [6] and open domain question answering [1,11,21]. The retrieval models based on dense vector representation [9,31] have attracted more attention from researchers in recent years. This method can achieve better recall performance than the sparse retrieval model on various Natural Language Processing (NLP) tasks, such as personalized search [14,31] and domain question answering [7,9,25]. Considering that judges usually only need some typical cases and the good performance of dense vector representation, we use the dense vector representation retrieval method.

3 Problem Definition

Before introducing our model, we first introduce some concepts and definitions of legal judgment prediction.

A **legal case** in our paper consists of a fact description and three judgment results, which are made by human judges. The **fact description** is a text that describes the criminal facts of a suspect. As shown in Fig. 2, our model uses f to represent it. The three **judgment results** are the relevant law article, charge and term of penalty and we use y_1, y_2 and y_3 to represent them respectively. Then a legal case can be represented as:

$$\text{Case} = (f, y_1, y_2, y_3), \tag{1}$$

where f, y_1, y_2, y_3 are defined above.

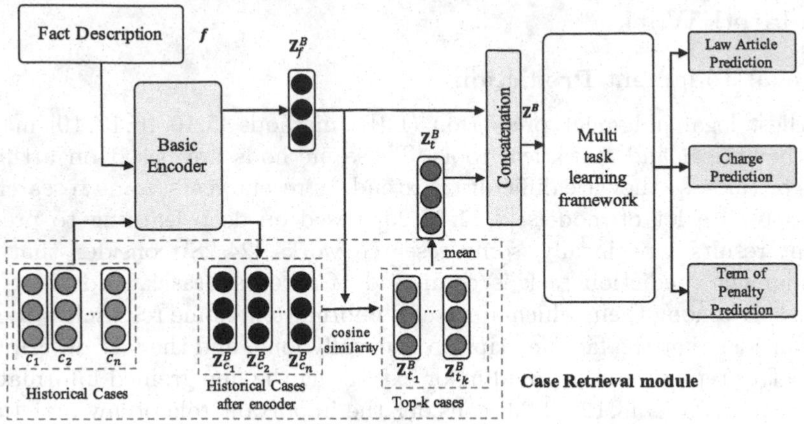

Fig. 2. The framework of our model. The main module of our framework is the Basic Encoder and the Case Retrieval module.

Referring to previous studies [12,23,28], we adopt a multi-task learning framework to solve the LJP task. Our goal is to train a model $F(\cdot)$ which can be used to predict a case f_t in the test dataset with a given training dataset D, namely:

$$F(f_t) = (\hat{y}_1, \hat{y}_2, \hat{y}_3), \quad (2)$$

where $\hat{y}_1$, $\hat{y}_2$ and $\hat{y}_3$ are the predicted judgment results. Consistent with the existing works [23,28], we only consider the legal cases with one relevant law article and one charge label.

4 Model Framework

In a practical situation, judges usually look up some typical historical cases for reference. To simulate this situation, we propose a framework (CR4LJP) with a historical case retrieval module.

4.1 Overview

Our model framework is shown in Fig. 2. In general, our model is a multi-task learning framework, which jointly solves three legal judgment prediction subtasks, with the case retrieval module we proposed. The main modules and training process of our model framework are as follows:

(1) The fact description f is converted into vector representation Z_f^B through the basic encoder.
(2) All selected historical cases are transformed into vector representations by the basic encoder. We select the Top-k cases which are most similar to the vector Z_f^B from these cases according to the cosine similarity. Then, we get the mean vector Z_t^B of these Top-k cases as auxiliary information.

(3) The representation vector Z_f^B and the mean vector Z_t^B of these Top-k cases are concatenated to solve the three legal judgment prediction subtasks.
(4) Our model is optimized by the losses of three subtasks. In the test phase, we also use the historical case vectors as auxiliary information to predict the judgment results.

4.2 Basic Encoder

As shown in Fig. 2, our model framework uses the same encoder for the current case and historical cases. Considering the consistency with the previous models [23,26,28] and the operation efficiency, we adopt the recurrent neural network (RNN) based encoder. Although we use RNN based encoder, our framework can flexibly select the neural network. Other neural networks, such as the current neural network (CNN) and pre-trained language models (PLMs), can also be used as encoders.

Specifically, the fact description of a legal case with m words is represented as:

$$f = (w_1, \cdots, w_m), \tag{3}$$

where w_i is a word in the fact description. Then we convert it to a word embedding sequence $\mathbf{f}$ though looking up a pre-trained word embedding table $\mathbf{E}$:

$$\mathbf{f} = [\mathbf{e}_1, \mathbf{e}_2, \cdots, \mathbf{e}_m], \mathbf{e}_i \in \mathbf{E}, \tag{4}$$

where $\mathbf{f} \in \mathbf{R}^{m \times d_e}$, and $\mathbf{e}_i \in \mathbf{R}^{d_e}$ is the embedding vector of the i-th word w_i. Then we use Bi-GRU neural network to encode the fact description.

$$\mathbf{Z}_\mathbf{f}^\mathbf{B} = \text{Bi-GRU}(\mathbf{f}), \tag{5}$$

where $\mathbf{Z}_\mathbf{f}^\mathbf{B} = (h_1, \cdots, h_l) \in \mathbf{R}^{l \times d_h}$, d_h is the length of the hidden layer of Bi-GRU encoder.

After introducing RNN based encoder, we introduce an alternative neural network Bert [2] as the encoder. First, the fact description $\mathbf{f}$ is set as the input of Bert after an embedding layer. After the multi-layer self-attention encoder, the output of "[CLS]" token of Bert is set as the vector representation of the fact description. It can also be represented as:

$$\mathbf{Z}_f^{\text{Bert}} = \text{BERT}(f)_{[\text{CLS}]}, \tag{6}$$

where "[CLS]" is one of the tokens output by the Bert model.

4.3 Case Retrieval Module

In the actual judgment process, judges usually look up some typical historical cases as references. So we design a case retrieval module to simulate the scenario.

As the performance of the dense representation retrieval method is usually better, we choose the dense representation retrieval method for our retrieval module.

Case Selection. In reality, the number of historical cases is huge and judges usually only look up some cases as references. For the efficiency of the model, we consider only selecting part of the cases instead of all the cases in the training dataset as historical cases to be retrieved. It should be noted that some law articles stipulate the same charges as shown in Fig. 1. And considering the unbalanced distribution of categories, we select the same number of cases for each charge under each law article.

Case Retrieval. In order to realize the historical case retrieval module, we first represent all historical cases $(c_1, c_2, \cdots, c_n)$ as word embedding sequences through Formula 4, and then represent them as n encoded vectors $(\mathbf{Z}^B_{c_1}, \cdots, \mathbf{Z}^B_{c_n})$ through Formula 5. Then we calculate the similarity scores of these n historical cases and the fact vector representation $\mathbf{Z}^B_f$ of the current case according to cosine similarity. Finally, we select the **Top-k** most similar cases as the reference cases by ranking the similarity scores, and then we calculate the mean vector of these Top-k cases:

$$\mathbf{Z}^B_t = \text{Mean}(\mathbf{Z}^B_{t_1}, \cdots, \mathbf{Z}^B_{t_k}). \tag{7}$$

The final mean vector $\mathbf{Z}^B_t$ of these **k** historical cases is the output of the case retrieval module.

4.4 Prediction and Optimization

Before predicting the judgment results for calculating the losses of three legal judgment prediction subtasks, we concatenate the vector representation of the current case and the historical cases as follows:

$$\mathbf{Z}^B = [\mathbf{Z}^B_f; \mathbf{Z}^B_t], \tag{8}$$

and then we use a multi-layer perceptron layer to predict the results as follows:

$$y_i = \text{MLP}_i(\mathbf{Z}^B), \tag{9}$$

where i represent the i-th subtask of legal judgment prediction.

Total Loss. The legal judgment prediction task includes three subtasks (relevant law article prediction, charge prediction and term of penalty prediction). We use the cross-entropy loss to calculate the loss of each subtask and train our model. The total loss is calculated as follows:

$$\mathcal{L}_{\text{LJP}} = -\sum_{i=1}^{3} \alpha_i \sum_{j=1}^{|N_j|} y_{i,j} \log(\hat{y}_{\text{i,j}}), \tag{10}$$

where $|N_{ij}|$ represent the number of labels of subtask i, and α_i is the weight of subtask i which is hyper parameter.

Table 2. The statistics of the CAIL2018 dataset [22] used in this paper.

Dataset	CAIL-small dataset	CAIL-big dataset
Number of the Training Cases	106,750	1,648,600
Number of the Test Cases	25,652	200,449
Number of Law Articles Referenced	94	115
Number of Distinct Charges	109	129
Number of Distinct Term of Penalty	11	11

5 Experiments

5.1 Datasets and Preprocessing

Following existing works, we experiment with the Chinese AI and Law challenge (CAIL2018) dataset [22]. The dataset consists of a large of legal cases published by the Supreme People's Court of China. There are two sub-datasets, CAIL-small and CAIL-big, in this dataset. Every case has a fact description, together with the judgment results given by human judges. We show the statistics of the dataset in Table 2.

In addition, to be consistent with the baseline methods [23,26,30], we focus on the simple legal cases and remove the legal cases with multiple article/charge labels. We then remove the low-frequency law articles and charges which have less than 100 cases. Finally, we remove the legal cases with missing or error law article labels. We experiment with the left legal cases which are supposed to be high-quality legal cases.

5.2 Baselines

In order to verify the effectiveness of our model, we select several representative legal judgment prediction models as the baselines.

(1) **FLA** [12] first considers the important role of law articles in the actual legal judgment process and uses the attention module to introduce the law article information.
(2) **Attribute-Att** [8] considers distinguishing the confusing charges is hard by introducing brief and concise law articles, and then designs ten common artificial attributes for charges.
(3) **TOPJUDGE** [28] first takes into account the sequence dependency of the three subtasks of LJP in the actual scenario. This model designs a topological multi-task learning framework to use the dependency information.
(4) **MPBFN-WCA** [24] takes into account that the judge needs to check again whether the relevant law articles, charges and term of penalty are suitable.
(5) **LADAN** [23] considers distinguishing the confusing law articles and design a graph distillation operator to learn the differences among law articles.

(6) **Neurjudge** [26] takes into account the circumstances in the actual scenario and use the intermediate results to separate the fact description vector representation. It is one of the state-of-the-art models.
(7) **CR4LJP** is our method.

Table 3. Results with GRU-based encoder on the CAIL-small dataset. The best results are in bold.

Method	Law Articles				Charges				Term of Penalty			
	Acc.	MP	MR	F1	Acc.	MP	MR	F1	Acc.	MP	MR	F1
FLA	0.8853	0.8463	0.8067	0.8188	0.8732	0.8414	0.8134	0.8119	0.3566	0.3279	0.3176	0.3104
Attribute-Att	0.8910	0.8490	0.8357	0.8396	0.8896	0.8587	0.8343	0.8450	0.3686	0.3355	0.3288	0.3246
TOPJUDGE	0.8940	0.8578	0.8348	0.8430	0.8819	0.8513	0.8331	0.8379	0.3668	0.3296	0.3494	0.3275
MPBFN-WCA	0.8944	0.8600	0.8434	0.8478	0.8820	0.8537	0.8393	0.8425	0.3677	0.3417	0.3346	0.3357
LADAN	0.9016	0.8711	0.8556	0.8604	0.8871	0.8588	0.8451	0.8464	0.3718	0.3496	0.3488	0.3383
Neurjudge	0.9112	0.8853	0.8661	0.8720	0.8913	0.8663	0.8486	0.8512	**0.4064**	**0.3780**	**0.3641**	**0.3656**
CR4LJP	**0.9137**	**0.8868**	**0.8785**	**0.8791**	**0.8932**	**0.8675**	**0.8570**	**0.8596**	0.3802	0.3714	0.3398	0.3431

Table 4. Results with GRU-based encoder on the CAIL-big dataset. The best results are in bold.

Method	Law Articles				Charges				Term of Penalty			
	Acc.	MP	MR	F1	Acc.	MP	MR	F1	Acc.	MP	MR	F1
FLA	0.9436	0.8471	0.7870	0.8091	0.9383	0.8390	0.7765	0.7993	0.5338	0.4223	0.4033	0.4097
Attribute-Att	0.9512	0.8787	0.7849	0.8137	0.9469	0.8759	0.7821	0.8148	0.5503	0.4552	0.3941	0.4126
TOPJUDGE	0.9502	0.8648	0.8021	0.8246	0.9461	0.8643	0.7943	0.8201	0.5574	0.4583	0.4040	0.4206
MPBFN-WCA	0.9507	0.8733	0.8054	0.8291	0.9457	0.8656	0.7957	0.8189	0.5583	0.4429	0.4110	0.4221
LADAN	0.9530	0.8719	0.8141	0.8345	0.9427	0.8607	0.8070	0.8263	0.5799	0.4833	0.4334	0.4413
Neurjudge	0.9568	0.8841	0.8307	0.8497	0.9505	0.8707	0.8197	0.8356	**0.5805**	0.4851	**0.4611**	**0.4638**
CR4LJP	**0.9594**	**0.8850**	**0.8449**	**0.8576**	**0.9524**	**0.8800**	**0.8235**	**0.8436**	0.5801	**0.4864**	0.4537	0.4560

5.3 Experiment Setting

For the GRU-based encoder, we first use the tool THULAC [18] to do word segmentation for the fact description and pre-train the word embedding with the dimension of 200 using word2vec [15]. The maximum text length of the fact description is set to 400 for all the models. The hidden size is set to 150 for all the models. The learning rate is set to 1e−3. For the Bert-based encoder, the learning rate is set to 1e−5. Our model is trained on one V100 GPU (2 V100 GPUs for Bert-based encoder) for 20 epochs and the batch size is 128. We set the hyperparameter α_i to 1 for three subtasks and we use the AdamW optimizer to train our model. For the case retrieval module, we select the same number of 20 cases for each charge under each law article and set the k of Top-k as 5. We use Accuracy (Acc.), Macro Precision (MP), Macro Recall (MR), and Macro F1 (F1) to measure all models following the previous works.

5.4 Overall Results

The overall results on the two datasets are shown in Table 3 and Table 4. Compared with the best baseline model Neurjudge, our model CR4LJP increases F1 scores of the law article and charge prediction subtasks by 0.81% and 0.98% respectively on the CAIL-small dataset and increases F1 scores of these two subtasks by 0.93% and 0.96% respectively on the CAIL-big dataset. This proves the effectiveness of our model. It should be noted that our model still underperforms Neurjudge in the term of penalty prediction task on both datasets. Neurjudge simulates the actual judicial process and makes fine-grained division of the case description which is based on human knowledge and proved very effective for the term of penalty prediction.

Table 5. Results with Bert-based encoder on CAIL-small dataset.

Method	Law Articles				Charges				Term of Penalty			
	Acc.	MP	MR	F1	Acc.	MP	MR	F1	Acc.	MP	MR	F1
Bert	0.9238	0.8987	0.8822	0.8859	0.9139	0.8897	0.8759	0.8792	0.4083	0.3837	0.3486	0.3425
Bert-Crime	0.9235	0.8948	0.8875	0.8872	0.9145	0.8898	0.8844	0.8838	0.4100	0.4013	0.3409	0.3441
Neurjudge+Bert	0.9314	0.9112	0.9041	0.9064	0.9230	0.9065	0.8994	0.9010	**0.4126**	**0.3977**	**0.3594**	**0.3670**
CR4LJP+Bert	**0.9343**	**0.9140**	**0.9043**	**0.9070**	**0.9245**	**0.9067**	**0.9007**	**0.9022**	0.4072	0.3857	0.3447	0.3501

Compared with the results of other baseline models, we further draw the following conclusions:

(1) TOPJUDGE and MPBFN-WCA both make use of the relationship among the three subtasks to improve the fact representation of a single case. Our model is able to outperform these two models, showing that retrieving historical cases help LJP get a better representation of the fact and finally improves the performance of judgment prediction.
(2) The performance of FLA is worse than those of other neural network models because it directly introduces the Top-k law articles, but the law articles are short and confusing, which may bring some noise. To solve the confusing law article problem, Attribute-Att designs ten artificial attributes and LADAN designs a graph distillation operator to improve the representation of introduced law articles. The better results of our model CR4LJP show that historical case information is more helpful to improve the performance of the legal judgment prediction task than law article information.

5.5 Results with Bert Based Encoder

The pre-trained language models, such as Bert [2], have achieved the best results on many NLP tasks. These models can be used as encoders in our framework, which usually leads to better results. In order to show the flexibility of our model, we compare our model based on the Bert encoder with other methods.

- **Bert** only uses the fact description as the input, and it uses the output of "[CLS]" token as the representation of the case. We fine-tune it on the CAIL dataset for the LJP subtasks.

- **Bert-Crime** [30] pre-trains Bert on a larger legal dataset. The process of fine-tuning is the same as **Bert**.
- **Neurjudge+Bert** is the Bert-based Neurjudge model, which replaces the GRU encoder with Bert.
- **CR4LJP+Bert** is our Bert-based model.

Due to the limitation of computing resources and the huge amount of parameters of Bert, we only experiment with the CAIL-small dataset. Specifically, on the CAIL-small dataset, the time required for one epoch of training CR4LJP+Bert is about 36 times that of GRU based model (41400 s vs 1140 s). Experimental results are shown in Table 5. We find that CR4LJP+Bert achieves better results than the original GRU-based encoder. This shows the flexibility and effectiveness of CR4LJP.

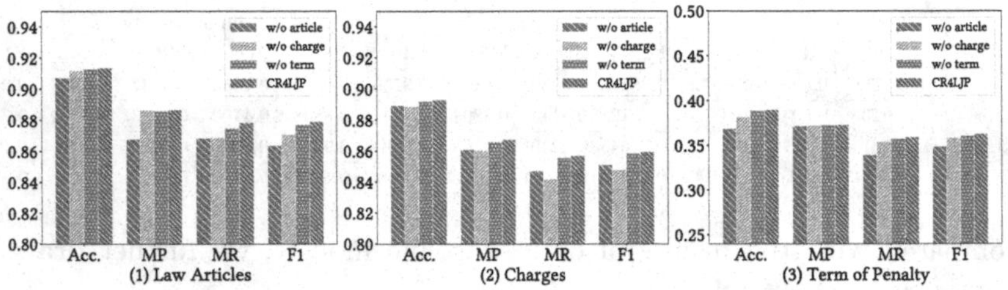

Fig. 3. Ablation study on the CAIL-small dataset. We remove the Top-k historical cases' mean vector from each subtask to study the impact of the case retrieval module.

Compared with other Bert-based baseline models, we find that:

(1) Our model (CR4LJP+Bert) is better than Bert and Bert-Crime, indicating that additional case information can indeed improve the performance of the legal judgment prediction task.
(2) Our model is superior to Neurjudge+Bert, which proves once again the effectiveness of our case retrieval framework.

5.6 Ablation Study

We perform an ablation study to verify the effectiveness of the case retrieval module for the three subtasks. Specifically, we remove the Top-k historical cases' mean vector from each subtask to study the impact of the case retrieval module. The corresponding models are expressed as **w/o article**, **w/o charge**, and **w/o term**. The ablation study results on the CAIL-small dataset are shown in Fig. 3. We find:

(1) Removing the case retrieval module will degrade the performance of the three subtasks. This shows that the case retrieval module is effective.

(2) Removing the case retrieval module has the least impact on the term of penalty prediction subtask, which is in line with our expectations. In reality, the term of penalty prediction needs to be discussed and determined in more detail.
(3) In general, removing the case retrieval module from the law article prediction subtask has the most impact on the legal judgment prediction task. The underlying reason is that the law article prediction subtask provides the basis for the other two tasks in reality, so it plays the most important role in the LJP task.

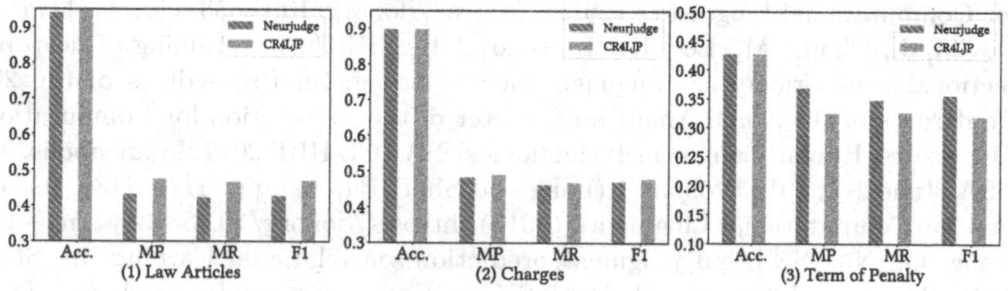

Fig. 4. Case study on confusing charges.

5.7 Confusing Case Study

As shown in Fig. 1, Article #114 and Article #115 stipulate some similar charges. It is difficult to distinguish these cases with similar charge labels for neural network models. To illustrate the impact of the models in identifying easily confusing cases, we choose the cases related to Article #114 and Article #115 in the CAIL-small test set as a tiny dataset and test the baseline model Neurjudge and our model CR4LJP on the dataset.

From the experimental results in Fig. 4, it can be seen that our model CR4LJP has better performance on the law article and charge prediction subtasks than Neurjudge, which shows that the case retrieval framework we proposed can effectively improve the ability to distinguish confusing cases.

6 Conclusion

In this paper, we first consider that judges usually look up some typical historical cases before making a judgment. We design a historical case retrieval model framework to simulate this scenario. For the current case, we retrieve the Top-k similar historical cases and get vector representation of these cases using the basic encoder, then we concatenate the mean vector of them to the fact description vector to predict the judgment results. Experimental results show that our method is effective.

Acknowledgements. We thank all the reviewers for their insightful comments. The work was partially done at the Engineering Research Center of Next-Generation Intelligent Search and Recommendation, Ministry of Education, and Beijing Key Laboratory of Big Data Management and Analysis Methods.

References

1. Chen, D., Fisch, A., Weston, J., Bordes, A.: Reading Wikipedia to answer open-domain questions. In: Barzilay, R., Kan, M. (eds.) Proceedings of the 55th Annual Meeting of the Association for Computational Linguistics, ACL 2017, Vancouver, Canada, July 30 - August 4, Volume 1: Long Papers. pp. 1870–1879. Association for Computational Linguistics (2017). https://doi.org/10.18653/v1/P17-1171
2. Devlin, J., Chang, M., Lee, K., Toutanova, K.: BERT: pre-training of deep bidirectional transformers for language understanding. In: Proceedings of the 2019 Conference of the North American Chapter of the Association for Computational Linguistics: Human Language Technologies, NAACL-HLT 2019, Minneapolis, MN, USA, June 2–7, 2019, Volume 1 (Long and Short Papers), pp. 4171–4186. Association for Computational Linguistics (2019). https://doi.org/10.18653/v1/n19-1423
3. Dong, Q., Niu, S.: Legal judgment prediction via relational learning. In: SIGIR 2021: The 44th International ACM SIGIR Conference on Research and Development in Information Retrieval, Virtual Event, Canada, July 11–15, 2021, pp. 983–992. ACM (2021). https://doi.org/10.1145/3404835.3462931
4. Feng, Y., Li, C., Ng, V.: Legal judgment prediction via event extraction with constraints. In: Proceedings of the 60th Annual Meeting of the Association for Computational Linguistics (Volume 1: Long Papers), Dublin, Ireland, May 2022, pp. 648–664. Association for Computational Linguistics (2022). https://doi.org/10.18653/v1/2022.acl-long.48, https://aclanthology.org/2022.acl-long.48
5. Gardner, A.V.D.L.: An artificial intelligence approach to legal reasoning. Ph.D. thesis, Stanford University (1984)
6. Gu, J., Wang, Y., Cho, K., Li, V.O.K.: Search engine guided neural machine translation. In: McIlraith, S.A., Weinberger, K.Q. (eds.) Proceedings of the Thirty-Second AAAI Conference on Artificial Intelligence, (AAAI-18), the 30th Innovative Applications of Artificial Intelligence (IAAI-18), and the 8th AAAI Symposium on Educational Advances in Artificial Intelligence (EAAI-18), New Orleans, Louisiana, USA, February 2–7, 2018, pp. 5133–5140. AAAI Press (2018), https://www.aaai.org/ocs/index.php/AAAI/AAAI18/paper/view/17282
7. Guu, K., Lee, K., Tung, Z., Pasupat, P., Chang, M.: REALM: retrieval-augmented language model pre-training. CoRR abs/2002.08909 (2020). https://arxiv.org/abs/2002.08909
8. Hu, Z., Li, X., Tu, C., Liu, Z., Sun, M.: Few-shot charge prediction with discriminative legal attributes. In: Proceedings of the 27th International Conference on Computational Linguistics, COLING 2018, Santa Fe, New Mexico, USA, 20–26 August 2018, pp. 487–498. Association for Computational Linguistics (2018). https://aclanthology.org/C18-1041/
9. Karpukhin, V., et al.: Dense passage retrieval for open-domain question answering. In: Webber, B., Cohn, T., He, Y., Liu, Y. (eds.) Proceedings of the 2020 Conference on Empirical Methods in Natural Language Processing, EMNLP 2020, Online, 16–20 November 2020, pp. 6769–6781. Association for Computational Linguistics (2020). https://doi.org/10.18653/v1/2020.emnlp-main.550

10. Kort, F.: Predicting supreme court decisions mathematically: a quantitative analysis of the "right to counsel" cases. Am. Pol. Sci. Rev. **51**(1), 1–12 (1957)
11. Lin, Y., Ji, H., Liu, Z., Sun, M.: Denoising distantly supervised open-domain question answering. In: Gurevych, I., Miyao, Y. (eds.) Proceedings of the 56th Annual Meeting of the Association for Computational Linguistics, ACL 2018, Melbourne, Australia, 15–20 July 2018, Volume 1: Long Papers, pp. 1736–1745. Association for Computational Linguistics (2018). https://doi.org/10.18653/v1/P18-1161, https://aclanthology.org/P18-1161/
12. Luo, B., Feng, Y., Xu, J., Zhang, X., Zhao, D.: Learning to predict charges for criminal cases with legal basis. In: Proceedings of the 2017 Conference on Empirical Methods in Natural Language Processing, EMNLP 2017, Copenhagen, Denmark, 9–11 September 2017, pp. 2727–2736. Association for Computational Linguistics (2017). https://doi.org/10.18653/v1/d17-1289
13. Ma, L., et al.: Legal judgment prediction with multi-stage case representation learning in the real court setting. In: SIGIR 2021: The 44th International ACM SIGIR Conference on Research and Development in Information Retrieval, Virtual Event, Canada, 11–15 July 2021, pp. 993–1002. ACM (2021). https://doi.org/10.1145/3404835.3462945
14. Ma, Z., Dou, Z., Bian, G., Wen, J.: PSTIE: time information enhanced personalized search. In: d'Aquin, M., Dietze, S., Hauff, C., Curry, E., Cudré-Mauroux, P. (eds.) CIKM 2020: The 29th ACM International Conference on Information and Knowledge Management, Virtual Event, Ireland, October 19–23, 2020, pp. 1075–1084. ACM (2020). https://doi.org/10.1145/3340531.3411877
15. Mikolov, T., Sutskever, I., Chen, K., Corrado, G.S., Dean, J.: Distributed representations of words and phrases and their compositionality. In: Advances in Neural Information Processing Systems 26: 27th Annual Conference on Neural Information Processing Systems 2013. Proceedings of a Meeting held, 5–8 December 2013, Lake Tahoe, Nevada, United States, pp. 3111–3119 (2013). https://proceedings.neurips.cc/paper/2013/hash/9aa42b31882ec039965f3c4923ce901b-Abstract.html
16. Nagel, S.S.: Applying correlation analysis to case prediction. Tex. L. Rev. **42**, 1006 (1963)
17. Segal, J.A.: Predicting supreme court cases probabilistically: the search and seizure cases, 1962–1981. Am. Polit. Sci. Rev. **78**(4), 891–900 (1984)
18. Sun, M., Chen, X., Zhang, K., Guo, Z., Liu, Z.: Thulac: an efficient lexical analyzer for Chinese (2016)
19. Ulmer, S.S.: Quantitative analysis of judicial processes: some practical and theoretical applications. Law Contemp. Probl. **28**(1), 164–184 (1963)
20. Wang, P., Fan, Y., Niu, S., Yang, Z., Zhang, Y., Guo, J.: Hierarchical matching network for crime classification. In: Proceedings of the 42nd International ACM SIGIR Conference on Research and Development in Information Retrieval, SIGIR 2019, Paris, France, 21–25 July 2019, pp. 325–334. ACM (2019). https://doi.org/10.1145/3331184.3331223, https://doi.org/10.1145/3331184.3331223
21. Wang, S., et al.: R^3: Reinforced ranker-reader for open-domain question answering. In: McIlraith, S.A., Weinberger, K.Q. (eds.) Proceedings of the Thirty-Second AAAI Conference on Artificial Intelligence, (AAAI-18), the 30th Innovative Applications of Artificial Intelligence (IAAI-18), and the 8th AAAI Symposium on Educational Advances in Artificial Intelligence (EAAI-18), New Orleans, Louisiana, USA, 2–7 February 2018, pp. 5981–5988. AAAI Press (2018). https://www.aaai.org/ocs/index.php/AAAI/AAAI18/paper/view/16712
22. Xiao, C., et al.: CAIL2018: a large-scale legal dataset for judgment prediction. CoRR abs/1807.02478 (2018). http://arxiv.org/abs/1807.02478

23. Xu, N., Wang, P., Chen, L., Pan, L., Wang, X., Zhao, J.: Distinguish confusing law articles for legal judgment prediction. In: Proceedings of the 58th Annual Meeting of the Association for Computational Linguistics, ACL 2020, Online, 5–10 July 2020, pp. 3086–3095. Association for Computational Linguistics (2020). https://doi.org/10.18653/v1/2020.acl-main.280
24. Yang, W., Jia, W., Zhou, X., Luo, Y.: Legal judgment prediction via multi-perspective bi-feedback network. In: Proceedings of the Twenty-Eighth International Joint Conference on Artificial Intelligence, IJCAI 2019, Macao, China, 10–16 August 2019, pp. 4085–4091. ijcai.org (2019). https://doi.org/10.24963/ijcai.2019/567
25. Yu, D., et al.: Kg-fid: infusing knowledge graph in fusion-in-decoder for open-domain question answering. In: Muresan, S., Nakov, P., Villavicencio, A. (eds.) Proceedings of the 60th Annual Meeting of the Association for Computational Linguistics (Volume 1: Long Papers), ACL 2022, Dublin, Ireland, 22–27 May 2022, pp. 4961–4974. Association for Computational Linguistics (2022). https://aclanthology.org/2022.acl-long.340
26. Yue, L., et al.: Neurjudge: a circumstance-aware neural framework for legal judgment prediction. In: SIGIR 2021: The 44th International ACM SIGIR Conference on Research and Development in Information Retrieval, Virtual Event, Canada, 11–15 July 2021, pp. 973–982. ACM (2021). https://doi.org/10.1145/3404835.3462826
27. Zhang, H., Dou, Z., Zhu, Y., Wen, J.: Few-shot charge prediction with multi-grained features and mutual information. In: Li, S., et al. (eds.) CCL 2021. LNCS (LNAI), vol. 12869, pp. 387–403. Springer, Cham (2021). https://doi.org/10.1007/978-3-030-84186-7_26
28. Zhong, H., Guo, Z., Tu, C., Xiao, C., Liu, Z., Sun, M.: Legal judgment prediction via topological learning. In: Proceedings of the 2018 Conference on Empirical Methods in Natural Language Processing, Brussels, Belgium, 31 October *– 4 November 2018, pp. 3540–3549. Association for Computational Linguistics (2018). https://doi.org/10.18653/v1/d18-1390
29. Zhong, H., Xiao, C., Tu, C., Zhang, T., Liu, Z., Sun, M.: How does NLP benefit legal system: a summary of legal artificial intelligence. In: Jurafsky, D., Chai, J., Schluter, N., Tetreault, J.R. (eds.) Proceedings of the 58th Annual Meeting of the Association for Computational Linguistics, ACL 2020, Online, 5–10 July 2020, pp. 5218–5230. Association for Computational Linguistics (2020). https://doi.org/10.18653/v1/2020.acl-main.466, https://doi.org/10.18653/v1/2020.acl-main.466
30. Zhong, H., Zhang, Z., Liu, Z., Sun, M.: Open Chinese language pre-trained model zoo. Technical report (2019). https://github.com/thunlp/openclap
31. Zhou, Y., Dou, Z., Wen, J.: Encoding history with context-aware representation learning for personalized search. In: Huang, J., et al. (eds.) Proceedings of the 43rd International ACM SIGIR Conference on Research and Development in Information Retrieval, SIGIR 2020, Virtual Event, China, 25–30 July 2020, pp. 1111–1120. ACM (2020). https://doi.org/10.1145/3397271.3401175

SentBench: Comprehensive Evaluation of Self-Supervised Sentence Representation with Benchmark Construction

Xiaoming Liu[1,3], Hongyu Lin[1(✉)], Xianpei Han[1,2(✉)], and Le Sun[1,2]

[1] Chinese Information Processing Laboratory, Beijing, China
{xiaoming2021,hongyu,xianpei,sunle}@iscas.ac.cn
[2] State Key Laboratory of Computer Science, Institute of Software, Chinese Academy of Sciences, Beijing, China
[3] University of Chinese Academy of Sciences, Beijing, China

Abstract. Self-supervised learning has been widely used to learn effective sentence representations. Previous evaluation of sentence representations mainly focuses on the limited combination of tasks and paradigms while failing to evaluate their effectiveness in a wider range of application scenarios. Such divergences prevent us from understanding the limitations of current sentence representations, as well as the connections between learning approaches and downstream applications. In this paper, we propose SentBench, a new comprehensive benchmark to evaluate sentence representations. SentBench covers 12 kinds of tasks and evaluates sentence representations with three types of different downstream application paradigms. Based on SentBench, we re-evaluate several frequently used self-supervised sentence representation learning approaches. Experiments show that SentBench can effectively evaluate sentence representations from multiple perspectives, and the performance on SentBench leads to some novel findings which enlighten future researches.

Keywords: Self-supervised learning · Sentence Representation · Benchmark

1 Introduction

Self-supervised representation learning is considered an important reason for breakthroughs in NLP [12,22,28,29]. And learning effective sentence representations has long been a fundamental challenge. [7,9,18]. In recent years, various self-supervised sentence representation learning approaches leverage different self-constrained signals, e.g., sentence pairs in the same narratives [12], sentence order [19], or sentence permutation [20], to learn representations by training models to distinguish positive instances from negatives.

M. Sun et al. (Eds.): CCL 2023, LNAI 14232, pp. 449–463, 2023.
https://doi.org/10.1007/978-981-99-6207-5_28

Even though current self-supervised sentence representation approaches have reached significant progress on some datasets like Semantic Textual Similarity (STS) [14,15], benchmarks for evaluation lag far behind the development of methods [34]. Currently, sentence representations are evaluated in limited tasks and specific paradigms. For example, the most commonly used SentEval benchmark [8] mainly focuses on single sentence classification and semantic similarity tasks. Unfortunately, prior literature shows that performance on STS cannot reflect the effectiveness of sentence representations on a wider range of tasks [30,34,41]. And available evaluation toolkits assess the same downstream task with a singular paradigm, limiting our perception of methods in different application scenarios. Moreover, current self-supervised sentence representation learning approaches are coupled with multiple factors, including diverse contrastive signals, training losses, and model architectures. Consequently, evaluating whether, where, and how a learning method will benefit the downstream tasks is difficult.

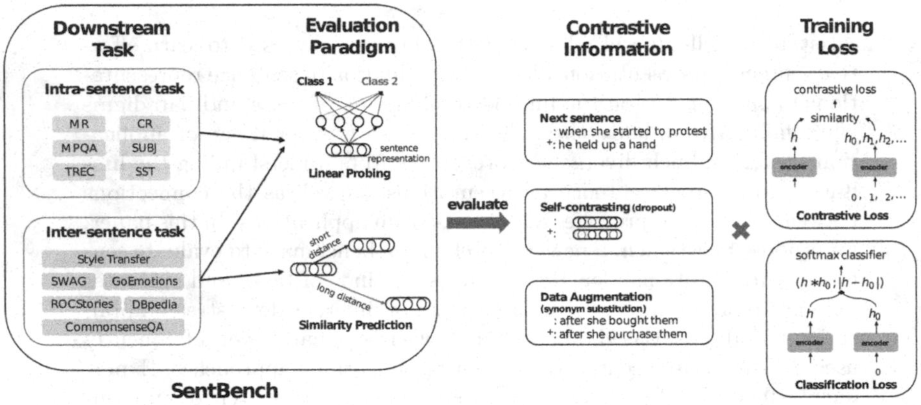

Fig. 1. The framework of the paper (SentBench and decoupling analysis scheme).

In this paper, we propose SentBench, a new benchmark to comprehensively evaluate sentence representations with various downstream tasks and evaluation paradigms. As shown in Fig. 1, SentBench contains 12 kinds of NLP tasks, including sentiment classification, question answering, story cloze, etc., and three evaluation paradigms, including single sentence classification, sentence pair classification and sentence pair contrasting [42]. The classification paradigm trains a simple additional classifier to assess information within representations for single sentence tasks or identify the connection between two candidate representations for pair-wise tasks. Besides, contrasting paradigm is similar to common retrieval or ranking scenario. Finally, SentBench constructs 18 datasets, which cover diverse tasks and common applications of sentence representations.

Based on SentBench, we re-evaluate several widely used self-supervised sentence representation learning approaches. We decouple previous approaches from two perspectives to identify critical factors: contrasting knowledge applied to construct positive instances and training losses used to optimize models. Specifically, we concentrate on three contrasting knowledge, including next sentence prediction [12], self-contrasting [14,38] and data augmentation [13,40], as well as two widespread training losses, including contrastive loss and classification loss. By thoroughly comparing different approaches on SentBench, we find that the advantages of the state-of-the-art methods can not be exhibited consistently to a broader range of downstream tasks and evaluation paradigms. Furthermore, the applied training loss leads to more significant impacts than contrasting knowledge. These findings shed some light on future research on sentence representation learning.

2 Benchmark Construction

2.1 Tasks

SentBench covers 12 downstream tasks for evaluating sentence representations, divided into single sentence and sentence pair tasks. In the following, we will briefly describe tasks in SentBench.

Single sentence tasks aim to classify sentence representations into corresponding categories. Because the previous SentEval [1] benchmark has covered extensive single sentence classification tasks, SentBench inherits all of them, including sentiment analysis (MR, SST) [27,31], Opinion Polarity (MPQA, SUBJ) [26,36], Question type (TREC) [33], product reviews (CR) [16].

Sentence pair tasks aim to identify sentence pairs with specific connections. We investigate six tasks covering various fields of downstream applications of NLP (Table 1):

Table 1. The statistics of sentence pair tasks.

Dataset	Classification			Contrasting
	Train size	Valid Size	Test Size	
SWAG	56,131	18,711	18,711	20,006
DBpedia	89,965	27,988	27,989	69,971
GoEmotions	54,535	18,178	18,179	4,590
ROCStories	2,513	-	629	1,571
StyleTransfer	24,986	8,328	8,330	2,500
CommonsenseQA	13,154	4,384	4,386	1,221

- **DBpedia** [40], which identifies whether a pair of sentences come from the same category;
- **Style Transfer** (ST) [17], which distinguishes whether modern English and Shakespearean English expresses same content;

[1] https://github.com/facebookresearch/SentEval.

- **GoEmotions** (GoEmo) [11], which recognizes whether a sentence pair expresses similar fine-grained emotion;
- **ROCStories** (ROC) [23], which predicts whether a given sentence is the proper ending to a four-sentence story;
- **CommonsenseQA** (CQA) [32], which determines if candidate answers match a commonsense question;
- **SWAG** [39], which predicts correct answer for a question about grounded situations.

2.2 Evaluation Paradigm

We design three evaluation paradigms in SentBench:

- **single sentence classification** directly leverage sentence representations as features with a simple classifier to assess how much desirable information is contained in representations;
- **sentence pair classification** trains a simple classifier that determines whether there is a specific connection between candidate sentences, that is mapping a pair of sentence representation $(\mathbf{x_1}, \mathbf{x_2})$ into corresponding label;
- **sentence pair contrasting** distinguishes a sentence from candidates that are more likely to share a specific relationship with the given sentence, i.e., given a target sentence x and two candidates (x^+, x^-), sentence pair contrasting selects more suitable candidate based on the similarity between x, x^+, and x^-.

Note that the classification paradigm requires data to train additional classifier parameters, while sentence pair contrasting depends on the similarity between sentence pairs by directly calculating certain distance metrics (e.g., cosine similarity) without additional training instances. Therefore, we provide training and development sets for classification tasks.

3 Experiment Setup

Based on SentBench, we re-evaluate several most frequently used self-supervised sentence representation methods. Since contrasting knowledge and training losses are usually coupled, it is challenging to directly identify critical factors for successful sentence representations from previous works. To this end, this paper explores different combinations of contrasting knowledge and training losses to investigate the effects of distinct factors.

Contrasting Knowledge. We exploit three popular contrasting knowledge sources:

- **narrative contrasting**, which predicts whether a hypothesis sentence belongs to the same narrative with a premise, is also known as next sentence prediction (NSP);

- **self-contrasting**, which disturbs sentence representations at feature-level, tries to distinguish representations stemming from the same instance. SimCSE [14] is one of the most popular methods, which creates contrasting pairs via random dropout from neural networks;
- **data augmentation**, which modifies the original instances via some rule-based modification, and tries to distinguish original instances from others.

In this paper, we apply NSP [12], two-times Dropout (Dropout) [14], and synonym substitution (DA) [37] as each knowledge sources, respectively.

Training Loss. Contrastive loss and classification loss are the most popular loss functions in self-supervised sentence representation learning. Given an instance **x**, **contrastive loss** (CTR) [25] aims to distinguish positive instance representation $\mathbf{x}^+$ from a batch of negatives:

$$\mathcal{L}_{CTR}(\theta) = -\log \frac{e^{sim(\mathbf{x},\mathbf{x}^+)/\tau}}{\sum_{\mathbf{x}_i \in batch} e^{sim(\mathbf{x},\mathbf{x}_i)/\tau}}$$

where τ is a temperature hyperparameter and *sim* is a similarity function (e.g., cosine similarity).

classification loss (CLS) classifies sentence pairs representation into corresponding semantic labels:

$$\mathcal{L}_{CLS}(\theta) = -\log P(y = 1|\mathbf{x} * \mathbf{x}^+) - \sum_{\mathbf{x}^- \in batch} \log P(y = 0|\mathbf{x} * \mathbf{x}^-)$$

where $*$ is the concatenation of representations.

Implementation Details. We implement the above-mentioned approaches based on $\text{BERT}_{\textsf{base}}$ (uncased) [19] and $\text{RoBERTa}_{\textsf{base}}$ [21]. To compare the benefit of different approaches, we also implement two token-aggregation approaches without further learning as baselines, which regard average representations of all tokens or the [CLS][2] representation of the last layer of models as sentence representation.

In this paper, we use BookCorpus [43] to construct the next sentence samples. [12] concatenate two sentences with [SEP] and feed the [CLS] representation into the classifier. A slight difference from the above approach is that we first obtain the [CLS] representations of two sentences separately and then concatenate them to learn the next sentence prediction. For self-supervised sentence representation learning with different combinations of loss functions and contrasting knowledge, we train models for one epoch on 10^6 sentences from BookCorpus and set batch size to 64. The temperature τ of contrastive loss is set to 0.05, and max sequence length is set to 32. Cosine similarity is the default distance metric and similarity function. All experiments are run in NVIDIA TITAN RTX GPUs. Following

[2] We discard the MLP layer over [CLS] for evaluation.

[14,37], the best checkpoint on the development set of STS is saved for evaluation. We use NLPAUG[3] for synonym substitution and take other sentences in the same mini-batch as negatives.

4 Empirical Findings

Table 2, 3 and 4 show the experiment results on three evaluation paradigms in SentBench, respectively. From these empirical results, we obtain the following findings.

Table 2. Accuracies on single sentence classification tasks and corner markers represent the performance rank. CTR: contrastive loss; CLS: classification loss.

Model	MR	CR	MPQA	SUBJ	SST	TREC	AVG
BERT-AVG	**82.24**^{1}	87.39^{1}	**88.71**^{2}	95.45^{3}	84.62^{4}	**91.80**^{1}	88.37^{2}
BERT-[CLS]	81.83^{2}	**87.39**^{1}	88.21^{6}	**95.48**^{2}	**86.91**^{1}	91.33^{2}	**88.53**^{1}
Dropout (CTR)	80.43^{4}	85.09^{5}	88.43^{4}	94.64^{6}	84.66^{3}	**90.67**^{3}	87.32^{4}
Dropout (CLS)	67.73^{8}	70.09^{8}	85.50^{7}	87.93^{8}	75.36^{8}	79.33^{8}	77.66^{8}
NSP (CTR)	**81.13**^{3}	**87.18**^{3}	88.34^{5}	**95.53**^{1}	**85.05**^{2}	89.67^{5}	**87.82**^{3}
NSP (CLS)	78.92^{6}	85.59^{4}	88.54^{3}	95.10^{4}	83.42^{6}	89.87^{4}	86.91^{6}
DA (CTR)	80.16^{5}	84.64^{6}	**89.33**^{1}	94.72^{5}	83.98^{5}	89.67^{5}	87.08^{5}
DA (CLS)	73.89^{7}	77.25^{7}	80.10^{8}	90.74^{7}	77.46^{7}	84.73^{7}	80.70^{7}
RoBERTa-AVG	**83.43**^{3}	**88.58**^{2}	**86.75**^{5}	**95.22**^{2}	**87.26**^{3}	**91.93**^{1}	**88.80**^{2}
RoBERTa-[CLS]	81.27^{4}	86.01^{5}	84.18^{6}	94.15^{4}	86.66^{4}	83.00^{6}	85.88^{6}
Dropout (CTR)	80.18^{5}	85.43^{6}	87.55^{2}	93.22^{6}	85.35^{5}	87.80^{5}	86.59^{5}
Dropout (CLS)	60.58^{7}	63.84^{8}	77.82^{7}	81.10^{7}	70.45^{7}	66.60^{7}	70.07^{7}
NSP (CTR)	**85.90**^{1}	**90.60**^{1}	**88.96**^{1}	**95.39**^{1}	**91.12**^{1}	**91.33**^{2}	**90.55**^{1}
NSP (CLS)	83.62^{2}	88.51^{3}	87.51^{3}	94.72^{3}	87.75^{2}	89.67^{3}	88.63^{3}
DA (CTR)	80.03^{6}	86.78^{4}	87.12^{4}	93.23^{5}	84.47^{6}	89.13^{4}	86.79^{4}
DA (CLS)	56.02^{8}	63.97^{7}	74.10^{8}	77.59^{8}	61.25^{8}	65.60^{8}	66.42^{8}

Finding 1. **Training loss is a more critical factor than contrasting knowledge.** We find that the selection of training loss has more significant impacts than the selection of contrasting knowledge, and contrastive loss significantly outperforms classification loss across all contrasting knowledge, models, and evaluation paradigms. Note that previously NSP is commonly coupled with classification loss and therefore achieves little performance superiority [21]. However,

[3] https://github.com/makcedward/nlpaug.

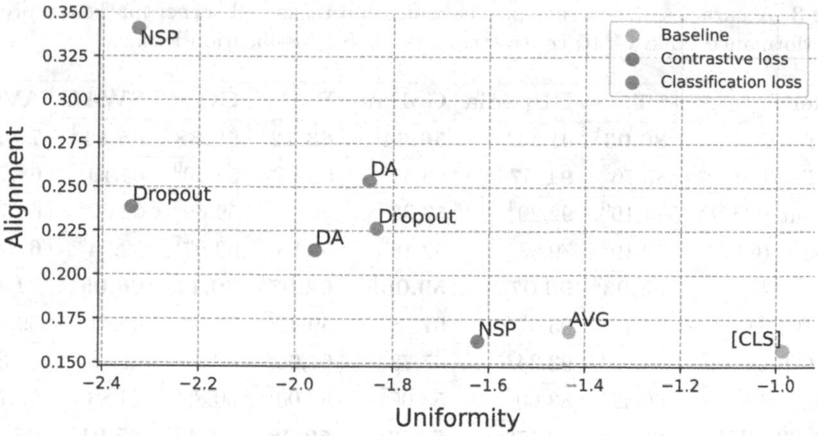

Fig. 2. Alignment and uniformity plot of models based on BERT. For both alignment and uniformity, lower numbers are better.

from our experiments, NSP trained with contrastive loss can bring significant performance improvements. To further investigate how contrasting knowledge and training loss influence sentence representations, we calculate the alignment and uniformity, two quantified quality evaluation metrics for sentence representations [35]. As shown in Fig. 2, we can see that different contrasting information is essentially a trade-off between alignment and uniformity. And contrastive loss outperforms classification loss with better alignment and uniformity, which reveals the underlying reason for the superior performances.

Finding 2. **Narrative contrasting provides more useful information for a wide range of single sentence and sentence pair tasks.** Experiments show that the NSP with contrastive loss achieves satisfactory performance in almost all settings. Besides, we can see that performance improvement on RoBERTa is more significant than that of BERT. This may be because the [CLS] representation of BERT has been pretrained with NSP signals and therefore already contain such kind of knowledge. Furthermore, we find that self-contrasting strategies, which are reported to achieve superior performance on STS benchmarks [2–6], do not perform well in SentBench. We believe that this is because, as previous findings have shown [34], STS tasks have a weak correlation with downstream tasks. Therefore, evaluations on STS benchmarks are not universal, revealing the necessity of building SentBench.

Finding 3. **Self-supervised contrastive sentence representation learning leads to more significant improvements on sentence pair contrasting tasks.** We can see that for BERT-AVG and RoBERTa-AVG, there are 6.2% and 12% of average performance improvements of all methods with contrastive loss, which is significantly higher than that on the other two tasks. We speculate that contrastive loss is more appropriate for similarity-based evaluation,

Table 3. Accuracies on sentence pair classification tasks and corner markers represent the performance rank. CTR: contrastive loss; CLS: classification loss.

Model	ST	DBpedia	GoEmo	ROC	CQA	SWAG	AVG
BERT-AVG	**86.03**^{1}	91.35^{6}	**56.64**^{5}	**63.12**^{2}	**58.38**^{3}	**65.81**^{2}	**70.22**^{2}
BERT-[CLS]	85.76^{3}	**91.57**^{5}	56.51^{6}	60.15^{4}	54.30^{6}	64.19^{3}	68.75^{6}
Dropout (CTR)	84.19^{6}	92.29^{4}	57.33^{3}	56.60^{6}	59.69^{2}	62.52^{5}	68.77^{5}
Dropout (CLS)	79.19^{8}	79.83^{8}	52.18^{8}	53.58^{8}	50.97^{7}	52.94^{8}	61.45^{8}
NSP (CTR)	**85.93**^{2}	**96.07**^{1}	**59.06**^{1}	**64.07**^{1}	**60.11**^{1}	**66.05**^{1}	**71.88**^{1}
NSP (CLS)	84.40^{5}	95.67^{2}	57.18^{4}	59.41^{5}	55.88^{5}	63.41^{4}	69.33^{4}
DA (CTR)	84.92^{4}	93.34^{3}	57.78^{2}	61.05^{3}	57.83^{4}	61.08^{6}	69.33^{3}
DA (CLS)	80.42^{7}	83.60^{7}	53.06^{7}	54.00^{7}	50.82^{8}	54.83^{7}	62.79^{7}
RoBERTa-AVG	**83.41**^{3}	89.17^{6}	**54.90**^{5}	**59.46**^{4}	**54.43**^{5}	**65.91**^{1}	**67.88**^{4}
RoBERTa-[CLS]	81.60^{5}	**89.78**^{5}	53.76^{6}	55.12^{6}	50.47^{7}	64.22^{2}	65.83^{6}
Dropoput (CTR)	82.09^{4}	92.74^{4}	55.38^{4}	55.75^{5}	56.72^{2}	60.46^{5}	67.19^{5}
Dropout (CLS)	75.16^{7}	69.62^{7}	50.72^{7}	53.15^{8}	49.93^{8}	51.76^{7}	58.39^{7}
NSP (CTR)	**84.83**^{1}	**96.49**^{1}	**58.95**^{1}	**66.93**^{1}	**60.41**^{1}	**63.85**^{3}	**71.91**^{1}
NSP (CLS)	83.46^{2}	95.74^{2}	56.70^{3}	63.01^{2}	55.82^{4}	61.54^{4}	69.38^{2}
DA (CTR)	81.47^{6}	94.69^{3}	57.88^{2}	59.62^{3}	55.83^{3}	59.15^{6}	68.11^{3}
DA (CLS)	74.12^{8}	66.97^{8}	50.16^{8}	53.21^{7}	50.52^{6}	51.30^{8}	57.71^{8}

which substantially improves the consistency between sentence representation distribution and downstream applications. Furthermore, single sentence and sentence pair classification tasks introduce an additional trainable classifier, which may weaken the effectiveness of self-supervised pretraining. Consequently, self-supervised contrastive sentence representation is more suitable for similarity-based scenarios without additional supervised signals, which is also consistent with recent advances of these methods on previous STS benchmarks [14].

5 Related Works

SentEval vs SentBench SentEval and SentBench are both benchmarks that evaluate the quality of sentence representations in natural language processing tasks. SentEval consists of a set of 17 downstream tasks and 10 probe tasks, including sentiment analysis, natural language inference, paraphrase detection, and text similarity. However, the tasks and methods in SentEval have fallen behind in recent years due to the rapid development of models and methods.

SentBench builds on SentEval, expanding the sentence-pair tasks to include six new datasets such as commonsense QA, story generation, and fine-grained sentiment analysis. Previous studies have shown that the performance of text semantic similarity tasks cannot reflect the effectiveness of sentence representations in more downstream tasks [30, 34, 41]. Unlike SentEval, SentBench replaces

Table 4. Accuracies on sentence pair contrasting tasks and corner markers represent the performance rank.

Model	ST	DBpedia	GoEmo	ROC	CQA	SWAG	AVG
BERT-AVG	63.88^{8}	**85.89**^{5}	**57.02**^{4}	58.75^{4}	**52.99**^{5}	**56.50**^{5}	**62.50**^{5}
BERT-[CLS]	**65.52**^{6}	74.72^{6}	53.09^{6}	**59.90**^{3}	52.09^{6}	54.19^{6}	59.92^{6}
Dropout (CTR)	73.16^{2}	91.43^{4}	57.56^{2}	60.53^{2}	**67.49**^{1}	62.01^{2}	68.70^{2}
Dropout (CLS)	73.16^{2}	66.53^{7}	52.96^{7}	52.45^{8}	51.68^{7}	51.30^{7}	58.01^{7}
NSP (CTR)	71.84^{4}	**94.68**^{1}	**57.82**^{1}	**62.70**^{1}	65.85^{3}	**63.24**^{1}	**69.35**^{1}
NSP (CLS)	64.72^{7}	94.62^{2}	56.27^{5}	56.02^{6}	61.51^{4}	57.48^{4}	65.10^{4}
DA (CTR)	**75.52**^{1}	91.76^{3}	57.47^{3}	57.73^{5}	66.83^{2}	59.64^{3}	68.16^{3}
DA (CLS)	71.48^{5}	64.02^{8}	52.14^{8}	52.51^{7}	49.80^{8}	50.86^{8}	56.80^{8}
RoBERTa-AVG	61.20^{8}	67.91^{6}	50.11^{8}	52.13^{8}	55.61^{6}	51.32^{6}	56.38^{7}
RoBERTa-[CLS]	**73.96**^{3}	**86.20**^{5}	**51.90**^{5}	**58.82**^{5}	**56.35**^{5}	**60.32**^{3}	**64.59**^{5}
Dropout (CTR)	**75.68**^{1}	90.76^{4}	55.88^{3}	60.09^{3}	64.86^{2}	61.98^{2}	68.21^{2}
Dropout (CLS)	70.60^{6}	63.38^{7}	51.35^{6}	56.72^{6}	52.25^{7}	49.94^{7}	57.37^{6}
NSP (CTR)	69.64^{7}	**96.78**^{1}	**58.26**^{1}	**64.74**^{1}	**65.44**^{1}	**62.96**^{1}	**69.64**^{1}
NSP (CLS)	70.80^{4}	95.17^{2}	55.53^{4}	63.91^{2}	61.43^{4}	59.77^{4}	67.77^{3}
DA (CTR)	74.76^{2}	94.17^{3}	57.71^{2}	59.01^{4}	61.92^{3}	57.00^{5}	67.43^{4}
DA (CLS)	70.72^{5}	59.48^{8}	50.13^{7}	52.32^{7}	46.85^{8}	49.75^{8}	54.87^{8}

text similarity tasks with contrasting tasks, which can more objectively reflect the actual application performance of sentence representations. Additionally, SentBench adds different evaluation paradigms to enrich the evaluation forms of the data, which can provide different understanding perspectives for the same downstream task.

GLUE vs SentBench The General Language Understanding Evaluation (GLUE) benchmark is a collection of nine natural language processing tasks designed to assess the performance of language models in various natural language understanding tasks, including sentiment analysis, question answering, and natural language inference. Unlike SentBench, which aims to evaluate sentence representation models and methods, GLUE is designed to evaluate and analyze natural language understanding systems. Although both benchmarks contain sentence representation-related applications, the differences in their design goals result in differences in datasets and usage methods. While SentBench focuses on the generalization and universality of sentence representations, GLUE tests the overall ability of the model. Additionally, the datasets used in GLUE and SentBench are complementary, as SentBench does not currently collect data relevant to natural language inference tasks. Thus, SentBench could look to GLUE's relevant content for future expansion.

Probing Researchers have not only focused on building more efficient evaluation benchmarks but also used various probing tasks to uncover the underlying principles of sentence representation, such as identifying syntactic and semantic information, as well as subtle perturbations. These evaluation tasks offer insights into which factors are challenging for sentence representation and which can better distinguish different models, driving the development of sentence representation. In their attempt to analyze sentence representation, [1] designed three evaluation tasks that focused only on surface information, such as sentence length, sentence content, and word order, and experimented with popular methods. However, these evaluation tasks failed to reflect the syntactic, semantic, and other knowledge of sentence representation. To address this limitation, [10] designed and collected 10 probing tasks that were divided into categories of surface, syntactic, and semantic information, revealing differences and connections between different methods. Furthermore, [42] proposed a triplet evaluation framework that generated triplet sentences to explore how syntactic structure or semantic changes in a given sentence affected inter-sentence similarity. This approach not only evaluated the performance of different sentence representation methods in capturing different semantic attributes but also avoided bias from human annotation data, providing a better understanding of these methods. Our work is similar to the previously mentioned research in that we aim to investigate the underlying mechanisms of sentence representation learning through thorough more comprehensive evaluation and decoupling analysis.

6 Conclusion

In this paper, we propose a new universal sentence evaluation benchmark SentBench, which introduces more downstream tasks and evaluation paradigms. Furthermore, we decouple and analyze the effects of contrasting knowledge and training losses on sentence representations. Empirical findings show that training losses play a more critical role in self-supervised sentence representation learning and help us better understand and design sentence representation learning algorithms.

7 Limitations

Currently, SentBench mainly covers English datasets, and therefore can not evaluate whether self-supervised representation learning methods have some language-specific properties. Besides, due to the limitation of time, we mainly experiment with BERT and RoBERTa without evaluating more self-supervised sentence representations methods, such as Sentence-T5 [24]. Finally, we mainly focus on the performance of models on SentBench without discussing more details of the training process, which is also an important aspect of self-supervised sentence representations.

Acknowledgements. We sincerely thank the reviewers for their insightful comments and valuable suggestions. This research work is supported by the National Natural Science Foundation of China under Grants no. U1936207, 62122077 and 62106251.

References

1. Adi, Y., Kermany, E., Belinkov, Y., Lavi, O., Goldberg, Y.: Fine-grained analysis of sentence embeddings using auxiliary prediction tasks. arXiv preprint arXiv:1608.04207 (2016)
2. Agirre, E., et al.: SemEval-2015 task 2: Semantic textual similarity, English, Spanish and pilot on interpretability. In: Proceedings of the 9th International Workshop on Semantic Evaluation (SemEval 2015). pp. 252–263. Association for Computational Linguistics, Denver, Colorado (2015). https://doi.org/10.18653/v1/S15-2045
3. Agirre, E., et al.: SemEval-2014 task 10: multilingual semantic textual similarity. In: Proceedings of the 8th International Workshop on Semantic Evaluation (SemEval 2014). pp. 81–91. Association for Computational Linguistics, Dublin, Ireland (2014). https://doi.org/10.3115/v1/S14-2010
4. Agirre, E., et al.: SemEval-2016 task 1: Semantic textual similarity, monolingual and cross-lingual evaluation. In: Proceedings of the 10th International Workshop on Semantic Evaluation (SemEval-2016). pp. 497–511. Association for Computational Linguistics, San Diego, California (2016). https://doi.org/10.18653/v1/S16-1081
5. Agirre, E., Cer, D., Diab, M., Gonzalez-Agirre, A.: SemEval-2012 task 6: a pilot on semantic textual similarity. In: SEM 2012: The First Joint Conference on Lexical and Computational Semantics – Volume 1: Proceedings of the main conference and the shared task, and Volume 2: Proceedings of the Sixth International Workshop on Semantic Evaluation (2012). pp. 385–393. Association for Computational Linguistics, Montréal, Canada (2012), https://aclanthology.org/S12-1051
6. Agirre, E., Cer, D., Diab, M., Gonzalez-Agirre, A., Guo, W.: SEM 2013 shared task: semantic textual similarity. In: Second Joint Conference on Lexical and Computational Semantics (*SEM), Volume 1: Proceedings of the Main Conference and the Shared Task: Semantic Textual Similarity. pp. 32–43. Association for Computational Linguistics, Atlanta, Georgia, USA (2013), https://aclanthology.org/S13-1004
7. Cer, D., et al.: Universal sentence encoder for English. In: Proceedings of the 2018 Conference on Empirical Methods in Natural Language Processing: System Demonstrations. pp. 169–174. Association for Computational Linguistics, Brussels, Belgium (2018). https://doi.org/10.18653/v1/D18-2029
8. Conneau, A., Kiela, D.: SentEval: an evaluation toolkit for universal sentence representations. In: Proceedings of the Eleventh International Conference on Language Resources and Evaluation (LREC 2018). European Language Resources Association (ELRA), Miyazaki, Japan (2018), https://aclanthology.org/L18-1269
9. Conneau, A., Kiela, D., Schwenk, H., Barrault, L., Bordes, A.: Supervised learning of universal sentence representations from natural language inference data. In: Proceedings of the 2017 Conference on Empirical Methods in Natural Language Processing. pp. 670–680. Association for Computational Linguistics, Copenhagen, Denmark (2017). https://doi.org/10.18653/v1/D17-1070

10. Conneau, A., Kruszewski, G., Lample, G., Barrault, L., Baroni, M.: What you can cram into a single vector: probing sentence embeddings for linguistic properties. In: Proceedings of the 56th Annual Meeting of the Association for Computational Linguistics (Volume 1: Long Papers). pp. 2126–2136. Association for Computational Linguistics, Melbourne, Australia (2018). https://doi.org/10.18653/v1/P18-1198
11. Demszky, D., Movshovitz-Attias, D., Ko, J., Cowen, A., Nemade, G., Ravi, S.: GoEmotions: A dataset of fine-grained emotions. In: Proceedings of the 58th Annual Meeting of the Association for Computational Linguistics. pp. 4040–4054. Association for Computational Linguistics, Online (2020). https://doi.org/10.18653/v1/2020.acl-main.372
12. Devlin, J., Chang, M.W., Lee, K., Toutanova, K.: BERT: pre-training of deep bidirectional transformers for language understanding. In: Proceedings of the 2019 Conference of the North American Chapter of the Association for Computational Linguistics: Human Language Technologies, Volume 1 (Long and Short Papers). pp. 4171–4186. Association for Computational Linguistics, Minneapolis, Minnesota (2019). https://doi.org/10.18653/v1/N19-1423
13. Feng, S.Y., et al.: A survey of data augmentation approaches for NLP. In: Findings of the Association for Computational Linguistics: ACL-IJCNLP 2021. pp. 968–988. Association for Computational Linguistics, Online (2021). https://doi.org/10.18653/v1/2021.findings-acl.84
14. Gao, T., Yao, X., Chen, D.: SimCSE: Simple contrastive learning of sentence embeddings. In: Proceedings of the 2021 Conference on Empirical Methods in Natural Language Processing. pp. 6894–6910. Association for Computational Linguistics, Online and Punta Cana, Dominican Republic (2021). https://doi.org/10.18653/v1/2021.emnlp-main.552
15. Ho, C.H., Nvasconcelos, N.: Contrastive learning with adversarial examples. In: Larochelle, H., Ranzato, M., Hadsell, R., Balcan, M., Lin, H. (eds.) Advances in Neural Information Processing Systems. vol. 33, pp. 17081–17093. Curran Associates, Inc. (2020), https://proceedings.neurips.cc/paper/2020/file/c68c9c8258ea7d85472dd6fd0015f047-Paper.pdf
16. Hu, M., Liu, B.: Mining and summarizing customer reviews. In: Proceedings of the Tenth ACM SIGKDD International Conference on Knowledge Discovery and Data Mining. p. 168–177. KDD '04, Association for Computing Machinery, New York, NY, USA (2004). https://doi.org/10.1145/1014052.1014073
17. Jhamtani, H., Gangal, V., Hovy, E., Nyberg, E.: Shakespearizing modern language using copy-enriched sequence to sequence models. In: Proceedings of the Workshop on Stylistic Variation. pp. 10–19. Association for Computational Linguistics, Copenhagen, Denmark (Sep 2017). https://doi.org/10.18653/v1/W17-4902
18. Kiros, R., Zhu, Y., Salakhutdinov, R.R., Zemel, R., Urtasun, R., Torralba, A., Fidler, S.: Skip-thought vectors. In: Cortes, C., Lawrence, N., Lee, D., Sugiyama, M., Garnett, R. (eds.) Advances in Neural Information Processing Systems. vol. 28. Curran Associates, Inc. (2015), https://proceedings.neurips.cc/paper/2015/file/f442d33fa06832082290ad8544a8da27-Paper.pdf
19. Lan, Z., Chen, M., Goodman, S., Gimpel, K., Sharma, P., Soricut, R.: Albert: A lite bert for self-supervised learning of language representations. arXiv preprint arXiv:1909.11942 (2019)

20. Lewis, M., et al.: BART: denoising sequence-to-sequence pre-training for natural language generation, translation, and comprehension. In: Proceedings of the 58th Annual Meeting of the Association for Computational Linguistics. pp. 7871–7880. Association for Computational Linguistics, Online (2020). https://doi.org/10.18653/v1/2020.acl-main.703
21. Liu, Y., et al.: Roberta: A robustly optimized Bert pretraining approach. arXiv preprint arXiv:1907.11692 (2019)
22. Mikolov, T., Chen, K., Corrado, G., Dean, J.: Efficient estimation of word representations in vector space. In: Bengio, Y., LeCun, Y. (eds.) 1st International Conference on Learning Representations, ICLR 2013, Scottsdale, Arizona, USA, May 2-4, 2013, Workshop Track Proceedings (2013), http://arxiv.org/abs/1301.3781
23. Mostafazadeh, N., et al.: A corpus and cloze evaluation for deeper understanding of commonsense stories. In: Proceedings of the 2016 Conference of the North American Chapter of the Association for Computational Linguistics: Human Language Technologies. pp. 839–849. Association for Computational Linguistics, San Diego, California (2016). https://doi.org/10.18653/v1/N16-1098
24. Ni, J., et al.: Sentence-t5: scalable sentence encoders from pre-trained text-to-text models. In: Findings of the Association for Computational Linguistics: ACL 2022. pp. 1864–1874. Association for Computational Linguistics, Dublin, Ireland (2022), https://aclanthology.org/2022.findings-acl.146
25. Van den Oord, A., Li, Y., Vinyals, O.: Representation learning with contrastive predictive coding. arXiv preprint arXiv:1807.03748 (2018)
26. Pang, B., Lee, L.: A sentimental education: Sentiment analysis using subjectivity summarization based on minimum cuts. In: Proceedings of the 42nd Annual Meeting of the Association for Computational Linguistics (ACL-04). pp. 271–278. Barcelona, Spain (2004). https://doi.org/10.3115/1218955.1218990
27. Pang, B., Lee, L.: Seeing stars: exploiting class relationships for sentiment categorization with respect to rating scales. In: Proceedings of the 43rd Annual Meeting of the Association for Computational Linguistics (ACL'05). pp. 115–124. Association for Computational Linguistics, Ann Arbor, Michigan (2005). https://doi.org/10.3115/1219840.1219855
28. Pennington, J., Socher, R., Manning, C.D.: Glove: global vectors for word representation. In: Proceedings of the 2014 Conference on Empirical Methods in Natural Language Processing (EMNLP). pp. 1532–1543 (2014)
29. Peters, M.E., et al.: Deep contextualized word representations. In: Proceedings of the 2018 Conference of the North American Chapter of the Association for Computational Linguistics: Human Language Technologies, Volume 1 (Long Papers). pp. 2227–2237. Association for Computational Linguistics, New Orleans, Louisiana (2018). https://doi.org/10.18653/v1/N18-1202
30. Reimers, N., Beyer, P., Gurevych, I.: Task-oriented intrinsic evaluation of semantic textual similarity. In: Proceedings of COLING 2016, the 26th International Conference on Computational Linguistics: Technical Papers. pp. 87–96. The COLING 2016 Organizing Committee, Osaka, Japan (2016), https://aclanthology.org/C16-1009
31. Socher, R., et al.: Recursive deep models for semantic compositionality over a sentiment treebank. In: Proceedings of the 2013 Conference on Empirical Methods in Natural Language Processing. pp. 1631–1642. Association for Computational Linguistics, Seattle, Washington, USA (2013), https://aclanthology.org/D13-1170

32. Talmor, A., Herzig, J., Lourie, N., Berant, J.: CommonsenseQA: a question answering challenge targeting commonsense knowledge. In: Proceedings of the 2019 Conference of the North American Chapter of the Association for Computational Linguistics: Human Language Technologies, Volume 1 (Long and Short Papers). pp. 4149–4158. Association for Computational Linguistics, Minneapolis, Minnesota (2019). https://doi.org/10.18653/v1/N19-1421
33. Voorhees, E.M., Tice, D.M.: Building a question answering test collection. In: Proceedings of the 23rd Annual International ACM SIGIR Conference on Research and Development in Information Retrieval. pp. 200–207 (2000)
34. Wang, B., Kuo, C.C.J., Li, H.: Just rank: rethinking evaluation with word and sentence similarities. In: Proceedings of the 60th Annual Meeting of the Association for Computational Linguistics (Volume 1: Long Papers). pp. 6060–6077. Association for Computational Linguistics, Dublin, Ireland (May 2022). https://doi.org/10.18653/v1/2022.acl-long.419
35. Wang, T., Isola, P.: Understanding contrastive representation learning through alignment and uniformity on the hypersphere. In: Proceedings of the 37th International Conference on Machine Learning, ICML 2020, 13–18 July 2020, Virtual Event. Proceedings of Machine Learning Research, vol. 119, pp. 9929–9939. PMLR (2020), http://proceedings.mlr.press/v119/wang20k.html
36. Wiebe, J., Wilson, T., Cardie, C.: Annotating expressions of opinions and emotions in language. Lang. Resour. Eval. **39**(2), 165–210 (2005)
37. Wu, Z., Wang, S., Gu, J., Khabsa, M., Sun, F., Ma, H.: Clear: contrastive learning for sentence representation. arXiv preprint arXiv:2012.15466 (2020)
38. Yan, Y., Li, R., Wang, S., Zhang, F., Wu, W., Xu, W.: ConSERT: a contrastive framework for self-supervised sentence representation transfer. In: Proceedings of the 59th Annual Meeting of the Association for Computational Linguistics and the 11th International Joint Conference on Natural Language Processing (Volume 1: Long Papers). pp. 5065–5075. Association for Computational Linguistics, Online (Aug 2021). https://doi.org/10.18653/v1/2021.acl-long.393
39. Zellers, R., Bisk, Y., Schwartz, R., Choi, Y.: SWAG: a large-scale adversarial dataset for grounded commonsense inference. In: Proceedings of the 2018 Conference on Empirical Methods in Natural Language Processing. pp. 93–104. Association for Computational Linguistics, Brussels, Belgium (2018). https://doi.org/10.18653/v1/D18-1009
40. Zhang, X., Zhao, J., LeCun, Y.: Character-level convolutional networks for text classification. In: Proceedings of the 28th International Conference on Neural Information Processing Systems - Volume 1. p. 649–657. NIPS'15, MIT Press, Cambridge, MA, USA (2015)
41. Zhelezniak, V., Savkov, A., Shen, A., Hammerla, N.: Correlation coefficients and semantic textual similarity. In: Proceedings of the 2019 Conference of the North American Chapter of the Association for Computational Linguistics: Human Language Technologies, Volume 1 (Long and Short Papers). pp. 951–962. Association for Computational Linguistics, Minneapolis, Minnesota (2019). https://doi.org/10.18653/v1/N19-1100

42. Zhu, X., Li, T., de Melo, G.: Exploring semantic properties of sentence embeddings. In: Proceedings of the 56th Annual Meeting of the Association for Computational Linguistics (Volume 2: Short Papers). pp. 632–637. Association for Computational Linguistics, Melbourne, Australia (2018). https://doi.org/10.18653/v1/P18-2100
43. Zhu, Y., Kiros, R., Zemel, R., Salakhutdinov, R., Urtasun, R., Torralba, A., Fidler, S.: Aligning books and movies: towards story-like visual explanations by watching movies and reading books. In: Proceedings of the IEEE International Conference on Computer Vision (ICCV) (2015)

Author Index

M. Sun et al. (Eds.): CCL 2023, LNAI 14232, pp. 465–466, 2023.
https://doi.org/10.1007/978-981-99-6207-5

Printed in the United States
by Baker & Taylor Publisher Services

Printed in the United States
by Baker & Taylor Publisher Services